A Collaborative Approach to Transition Planning for Students With Disabilities

A Collaborative Approach to Transition Planning for Students With Disabilities

JoAnn M. Rae, EdD
St. Joseph's University
Philadelphia, Pennsylvania

SLACK Incorporated
6900 Grove Road
Thorofare, NJ 08086 USA
856-848-1000   Fax: 856-848-6091
www.Healio.com/books
ISBN: 978-1-63091-498-1
© 2020 by SLACK Incorporated

Senior Vice President: Stephanie Arasim Portnoy
Vice President, Editorial: Jennifer Kilpatrick
Acquisitions Editor: Tony Schiavo
Managing Editor: Allegra Tiver
Creative Director: Thomas Cavallaro
Cover Artist: Katherine Christie
Project Editor: Erin O'Reilly

A Collaborative Approach to Transition Planning for Students With Disabilities includes ancillary materials. To access those for faculty use, please visit http://www.efacultylounge.com. To access those for student use, please visit http://www.healio.com/books/transitionplanning.

Dr. JoAnn M. Rae has no financial or proprietary interest in the materials presented herein.

Library of Congress Control Number:2019945484

Printed in the United States of America.
Last digit is print number: 10   9   8   7   6   5   4   3   2   1

DEDICATION

This book is dedicated in memory of Dr. Cathleen Spinelli. Her commitment to children and youth with disabilities inspired me and those who knew her.

Dr. Spinelli encouraged me to write this book to reach special educators and school communities. She understood well the challenges students in special education face as they transition to adulthood. Dr. Spinelli also recognized the needs of special educators as they work with students during this crucial period.

She felt a book was needed to provide practical guidance to special educators involved in transition planning. When Dr. Spinelli believed something important needed to be done, she was quite convincing. So, inspired, I began to write.

Dr. Spinelli worked to make a difference in the lives of students with disabilities. I hope that her giving spirit lives on in this book, as I remember her mentorship, kindness, intelligence, and commitment to the field of special education.

CONTENTS

ACKNOWLEDGMENTS

I want to thank the following people for their support and for sharing their thoughts and concerns about themselves and their children throughout my career:

To my students, who shared their hopes and dreams with me while I was their teacher, I am grateful to have known each of you. So many of you changed who I was as a person through listening to you and learning about how your lives with a disability affected you. I hope this book helps students not unlike yourselves to reach their goals.

To the parents of children and youth with disabilities, your ongoing advocacy has been instrumental in increasing educational opportunities for children. Hopefully, this book can increase the engagement of families and school communities as you work together for positive outcomes for children as they transition to young adulthood.

To my parents and my son for their ongoing support and encouragement, and especially to Barbara Montague-Graham for her inspirational faith in me.

To Dr. Christina Ager for her ongoing support and mentorship throughout my doctoral studies at Arcadia University (Glenside, Pennsylvania).

I also want to thank the St. Joseph's University Graduate School Department of Education for their continued support of scholarly pursuits and accomplishments for all members of the educational community, especially within the Department of Special Education.

Again, I say thank you.

JoAnn M. Rae, EdD

ABOUT THE AUTHOR

JoAnn M. Rae, EdD started her career as an educator when she earned a bachelor of science degree in special education and elementary education at West Chester University in West Chester, Pennsylvania. Later, Dr. Rae earned a master's degree with distinction in educational administration, and she became certified as a general education principal and special education supervisor. As a master's student, she was nominated to Who's Who Among Students in American Universities and Colleges in recognition of merit and accomplishment. Throughout 18 years of direct teaching experience, Dr. Rae worked with students throughout the transition planning process. As a transition planning specialist using legislative guidelines and research-based practices, she worked with students, their families, and school districts using a collaborative approach to transition planning.

Dr. Rae earned a doctorate with distinction in education, specializing in special education. Her studies and dissertation reported on effective practices that have the potential to lead to positive post-school outcomes for students with disabilities.

As she earned her doctorate, Dr. Rae was a special education administrator for 7 years, prior to moving to university teaching. In the special education supervisor role, she monitored transition plans and the implementation of transition strategies through the work of the special educators in her department. In this role, Dr. Rae worked with school district officials, families, and community agencies to facilitate smooth transitions to post-school life.

Currently, Dr. Rae teaches graduate school courses in the Department of Special Education at St. Joseph's University, Graduate Division, in Philadelphia, Pennsylvania. She also teaches courses on the administration of special education programs. Dr. Rae's work reflects her expertise in collaborating within school communities to develop effective transition plans grounded in research-based practices. Dr. Rae's education and practical experience working directly with students, their families, school personnel, and district administrators makes her uniquely qualified to write this text.

PREFACE

This text was written to provide current information on the legislation and implementation of transition planning to aspiring teachers in teaching preparation courses, students and teachers seeking to learn about transition planning, currently practicing transition planning specialists, special education teams, and new and aspiring special and general education school administrators. It addresses the goals of transition planning and describes methods of implementing plans to instruct students and families about transition. It also provides examples of situations in case reports to inform new educators in special education and currently practicing educators about creating an organized documentation system of collaboration, instruction, services, and supports during the transition planning process. In addition, the text provides a systematic approach to collaborating with students, families, special education teams, administrators, school boards, and community agencies to increase opportunities and develop more effective transition plans. Therefore, the content of this text serves as an essential resource to those educators and community agencies.

JoAnn M. Rae, EdD

INTRODUCTION

Congratulations! You are about to embark on a learning experience based on the author's expertise and direct experience as a transition planning specialist. This text describes the process of how special educators can guide students with disabilities through the tumultuous adolescent period. It promotes using the best practices that are most likely to increase positive post-school outcomes for students with disabilities.

Special educators will learn to give explicit instruction to students during transition in areas such as participating in the Individualized Education Plan (IEP) meeting; developing goals for transition; and collaborating with the transition planning specialist, the IEP team, and families.

Transition planning specialists and special education teams benefit from learning about the framework of transition with examples of what the process of transition planning looks like and how to carry out their roles and legal responsibilities. This text addresses the how of working with students and their parents within the school community, ensuring that the framework of transition planning, team collaboration, and student participation advances students' smooth transitions to adulthood. A system of communication is provided in this text to promote movement through the curriculum, and the activities of transition aid in understanding the process of transition planning. Whether or not you ultimately work in the area of transition, this text will also help you in the areas of collaboration and student engagement, which are applicable to any teaching and administrative role. You will also learn about school- and community-based transition services and in-school activities that widen the range of inclusion in the life of the school community.

To broaden your understanding of how transition planning is implemented, the 13 categories of disability under the Individuals with Disabilities Education Act (IDEA) are addressed. Each category of disability affects the individual student in unique ways. Therefore, student needs are addressed using a transition framework to advance each student through the transition to adulthood with a focus on the impact of the specific disability. It also guides you to work with students who are diagnosed with two or more learning or medical disabilities.

This text also provides an overall perspective about programs that may inform the work with school administrators and other stakeholders on the special education team. Another area addressed is the role of the secondary school teachers in general education and special education in the Child Find process, which continues through secondary school. These often-missed disabilities, including emergent mental health disorders and recent cognitive changes from accidents or another source, become apparent during middle and high school and may only be evidenced by academic failure and truancy. This is addressed in the chapters on specific learning disabilities and mental health disorders.

You will also learn about children and youth who have more than one disability and how they can substantially improve a student's overall functioning from the services of well-trained professionals, such as related service staff, community counselors, vision therapists, sign language interpreters, occupational therapists, assistive technology specialists, and nurses. The resolution of challenges is a primary role when working with students with disabilities in order to guide them from high school to living more independently during the transitional years and beyond.

Culture and bias are also discussed. This text presents in a general way how various cultures define independence. The text guides teachers to look at personal bias and how individual and the dominant culture's beliefs are applied to students with disabilities. Discussion about bias and culture assists teachers of students in special education to seek information from students and their families about culture and family living situations, rather than assuming that all students have the same living goals as the dominant culture. Families are key stakeholders during the transition planning process. Therefore, the text provides educators with a means to collaborate with students and their families to develop a pathway to post-school life, which includes what parents and students desire based on cultural aspects of their daily lives.

Transition planning specialists require interviewing skills. This text teaches special educators the initial steps to creating the first transition plan by practicing interview skills that enable them to learn about the students from their points of view. Collecting information on students' current preferences, abilities, and self-knowledge, as well as providing students with ongoing opportunities to learn about career and community choices, is challenging, and case studies are presented to demonstrate the challenges of transition planning.

This text provides examples of educational, social, independent, and career-planning activities within the specialized curriculum that are meant to be results oriented, in keeping with the direction of the legislation that underpins transition planning. An emphasis on a transition curriculum incorporates practices that guide students to develop self-determination, self-knowledge, independence skills, social skills, and advocacy skills, which are foundational skills that advance post-school success.

Assistive technology, which is often required for communication, is discussed, as well as the latest court cases that support the use of an assistive program or any program that can increase student learning and participation in educational tasks, such as the use of assistive technology, including for students with the most severe disabilities.

Transition also involves a change in the roles of the special educator. A new role means a change of perspective. The IEP contains goals and areas of improvement directed by school-based IEP teams. During transition planning, special educators take on a new role where they support students in planning their future directions and continue to facilitate ongoing learning.

To the greatest extent possible, regardless of the disability, all students with disabilities are encouraged to self-determine their outcomes while addressing their disabilities. This text shows the team how students can participate partially, with support, or fully on the IEP team. The skill development instruction provided in this text guides educators to facilitate and instruct students to take a primary role in their outcomes as they transition to post-school life.

ORGANIZATION OF THIS TEXT

This book begins with an overview of transition planning and current special education law, providing practical guidance on how to develop transition plans. It explains the special education teacher's role in the transition process and how it blends with that of parents, the school, and community agencies. Included is a detailed discussion of the myriad considerations that special education teachers may encounter in the normal scope of their responsibilities, including transition planning for students with severe mental health disorders, specific learning disabilities, autism spectrum disorder (ASD), neurological conditions, and the eligibility categories covered in Part 6. It also covers specific age-level considerations that facilitate transition practices to help families and students successfully through the various educational levels, from early intervention and preschool, to school-age programs, middle school, high school, and beyond.

Part 1: Introduction to Transition Planning

Chapter 1: Transition Planning and Special Education Law

This chapter discusses the legislative support and direction of transition planning in special education and civil rights law. The content includes how the Americans with Disabilities Act, the IDEA, and the Rehabilitation Act support the educational and community inclusion of children and youth with disabilities.

Part 2: Transition Planning Practices

Part 2 is about evidence-based strategies and the involvement of families. It further outlines the engagement of parents and the use of research-based practices for the development of transition goals and needed supports and services for the IEP.

Chapter 2: An Interactive Framework of Activities Focusing on Community Access, Student Engagement, and Post-School Goals Selection

This chapter focuses on the components of the transition planning framework. The framework components are organized as a series of "gates" that include specific activities and skill sets to facilitate the transition planning process. Each gate is designed for the transition planning specialist or special education teacher to guide students and their parents through the transition planning process. The transition framework has 10 gates. Eight of the gates include instructional, career-based, and developmental activities, and two others are about evaluating student outcomes and the transition planning team's self-assessment, respectively.

The gates include activities that are meant to engage the students in developing early skills and knowledge in self-advocacy, the transition planning process, and how to collaborate within the family. The gates also address the use of assessments to evaluate future medical and educational needs and how to help students create their own goals for employment, family and social activities, and independent living.

The chapter closes with research-based practices such as helping students to develop self-determination, autonomy, and self-advocacy constructs that are needed to support them as they move from full dependence to partial or complete independence.

Chapter 3: Collaborating With Families During the Transition Planning Process

This chapter discusses the use of the collaborative model for developing transition plans. It includes a process of teaching the family and the student about transition planning. Parents often face barriers to participation in the transition planning collaboration. The chapter discusses how to overcome those barriers, such as physical or intellectual disabilities (intellectual disabilities) or terminal illness, and seek parent participation whenever possible. When those barriers cannot be overcome, guidance is provided on how to work with students when parents are unable to provide the support students need to transition successfully.

Student participation in goal development, IEP attendance, and leading their IEP meeting requires that the student receive instruction and regular communication. Communication is the foundation of effective transition planning, and this chapter outlines a process to engage students and parents in learning about the roles and responsibilities for the collaborative team. Communication letters and brochures are discussed as materials that require ongoing dissemination and updates to reflect current events and opportunities to learn about transition.

Special educator interactions and communications are also of the utmost importance and are discussed in the context of conflict resolution when conflicts adversely affect student progress during transition planning. This chapter contains case studies to aid in the understanding of the concepts.

Part 3: Assessments

Part 3 provides information on medical, academic, behavioral, social, independence, and post-outcome assessments as each is used to support positive outcomes for students with disabilities.

Chapter 4: Medical Conditions, Assessment, and Transition: Implications of Disability and Medical Conditions on Work-Seeking Activities and Educational Progress

Medical conditions and their assessment are an ongoing challenge, and implications for students with disabilities and multiple medical conditions are often seen among children with more severe disabilities. With advancement in health care management, more students are able to come to school. However, to ensure the students' safety and ability to participate, special educators require knowledge about Individual Health Care Plans, which are used to support student attendance. The development of Individual Health Care Plans requires parents and school nurses to collaborate with medical professionals who manage the treatment needs, such as medication management. Ensuring student safety requires use of collaboration and coordination skills.

Medical conditions can complicate the days of students with disabilities. Throughout an adolescent's high school years, he or she may need to leave the classroom to receive medications, such as daily nebulizer treatments for asthma or medications for seizures or mental health disabilities. Special education teachers and transition planning specialists require skills and knowledge about the students' medical needs. Related student needs emerge from medical conditions, such as medication management, self advocacy for treatment, self care goals development, and ongoing communication with school nurses and families to maintain students' health and safety at school. All of these needs complicate work-seeking, as well as the types of employment options.

Chapter 5: Assessment Tools

This chapter describes a range of assessments that serve students by providing them with systematic feedback about their preferences, career and independence readiness, communication skills, and academic readiness for post-school educational programs. The chapter includes information on formal and informal assessments. Multiple tables are available in the chapter and the Student Supplemental Materials with informal and formal assessments, inventories, surveys, questionnaires, and observational assessments.

Part 4: Transition Plan Development

Chapter 6: Transition Plan Frameworks: Creating the Transition Plan

This chapter describes how to use assessments and the transition planning framework to create transition plan goals within the IEP. The chapter demonstrates how to teach students to create measurable goals and meet the requirements of IDEA.

Chapter 7: Career and Employment-Based Learning: Supporting Entry Into the Workforce and Postsecondary Education

This chapter discusses the use of preference surveys and assessments and the conferencing process to plan entry into the workforce. Whether the entry is directly into employment or via vocational training or postsecondary education, the goal is obtaining and maintaining employment. The pathways to entry are described.

Part 5: Special Education Programs: Responsibilities and Resources of Transition Team Members and Community and Governmental Agencies

Part 5 describes the roles of the school administrators, special educators, transition planning specialists, and governmental agencies. The professionals who implement transition requirements work in various capacities and have multiple responsibilities for transition planning. This includes discussion about how they work together in collaboration to facilitate effective transition planning programs and individual transition plans.

Chapter 8: School Leadership and Transition Planning

This chapter addresses the responsibilities of school boards, school superintendents, special education administrators, and supervisors, who are the primary leaders who ensure the requirements of IDEA are met. This chapter includes information about the relationships among school leaders, the transition planning specialist, and the secondary special education team related to maintaining and creating transition planning activities.

Chapter 9: Roles of the Secondary Special Education Team and Community Agencies

This chapter discusses the roles and responsibilities of the transition planning specialist, the special education team, and the special education administration as the roles pertain to the development of competencies to work with students during transition planning. Guidance about how to interact with students to establish meaningful plans is provided.

This chapter also provides a list of agencies that offer in-school and post-school connections to services and employment. Descriptions of each are provided. Also, information on Medicare and Medicaid and the Social Security Administration's role with the most severely disabled youth is included.

Part 6: Special Considerations: Working With Diverse Groups of Students

The chapters in Part 6 describe the disability characteristics of students participating in transition planning. The unique challenges of transitioning youth and their parents depend upon the severity and type of disabilities present. Learning, emotional, behavioral, sensory, and intellectual disabilities; ASD; and medical, neurological, and orthopedic conditions impact choices and training and the ability to complete the activities of transition planning.

Part 6 is divided into two sections. The first part applies to students who have average to above average cognitive functioning. The second part applies to students with autism and intellectual disabilities, when speech is present; it discusses the additional safety and post-school needs that require further consideration when planning for post-school life.

The first half of Part 6 applies to students who can, for the most part, participate fully in their transition plan development. They have an average to above average intelligence quotient but have disabilities that deny full access to academics and the workplace. Students addressed in Chapters 10 through 13 and most of Chapter 14 can complete the framework of activities and self-determine the course of their lives with specially designed instruction and post-school supports.

The second half of Part 6 describes approaches to transition planning for students who will need support to participate or who may only be able to participate partially in the transition planning frameworks. In some cases, youth in these IDEA categories will need their parents or guardians to participate on their behalf and be instrumental in helping to ascertain their preferences. As defined, the IDEA eligibility categories represented in these chapters are adolescents with borderline to substantially below-average intellect and who have been diagnosed as having intellectual disabilities. The activities of transition for these youth are meant to maximize their ability to be independent, to work whenever possible, to self-determine the course of their lives to the maximum extent possible, and to support and include them in the community throughout post-school life.

Chapter 10: Students With Specific Learning Disabilities and Speech and Language Impairments

This chapter gives an overview of the characteristics of specific learning disabilities and speech and language impairments in relation to postsecondary needs. The unique characteristics of students with one or more specific learning disabilities are aligned to supports that will be needed in post-school life.

Chapter 11: Students With Emotional, Behavioral, and Severe Mental Health Disorders

This chapter tackles the complex world of mental health disorders within the context of the characteristics of mental health disorders and post-school outcomes when a lifetime of medical care and mental health monitoring are on the horizons of young people whose mental illnesses emerge during the transition to adulthood. Also included is transition planning for students with low behavioral and impulse control. These students are often served in emotional and behavioral disorders programs as well. This chapter discusses how specialized and early transition planning can guide these students to work instead of to juvenile detention centers.

Chapter 12: Students Who Are Blind, Visually Impaired, Deaf, Hard of Hearing, or Deaf-Blind

This chapter is about the supports needed and the agencies that provide a transition to adulthood services for students who are legally blind, deaf, hard of hearing, or deaf-blind. Also, other communication disorders are described when they require special education or 504 plans to support communication.

Chapter 13: Students With Autism Without Accompanying Language or Intellectual Impairment

This chapter addresses students diagnosed with autism who do not have intellectual disabilities nor lack speech. These significant differences in diagnosis indicate that these students with autism can fully participate in the framework of transition planning with attention to their significant behaviors and are eligible for services under the IDEA category of the autism spectrum. The needs of this group are individualized based on their sensory and communication challenges.

Chapter 14: Students With Other Health Impairments, Chronic Medical and Orthopedic Impairments, and Traumatic Brain Injury

This chapter applies to students who have chronic medical conditions, orthopedic disabilities, traumatic brain injury, and neurological conditions. These students, who need specialized support to access school and work, are discussed individually to give an overview of their needs.

Chapter 15: Students With Mild, Moderate, Severe, Multiple, and Profound Intellectual Disabilities

This chapter is about the wide range of characteristics within the category of intellectual disabilities. Given this range of intellectual, adaptive, and physical abilities, the variability of the transition planning process is addressed. Information about accessing services for students with the most profound degree of disability is included.

Chapter 16: Students With Autism and Accompanying Language and Intellectual Impairment

This chapter addresses the characteristics of students with autism and accompanying intellectual and language disabilities. Youth with ASD and intellectual disabilities typically neither understand or use spoken language or understand or use gestural communication. Due to these significant communication disabilities, transition plans and communication systems that allow increased supported or partial participation in transition planning are discussed. Access to adult services is also included.

Part 7: Special Education Transitions

Chapter 17: The Effectiveness of Transition Planning: Monitoring the Practices of the Special Education Team

Improving practice is the primary goal addressed in this chapter. The text discusses how the special education team and transition planning specialist work directly with students and their parents to carry out a data-based self-assessment. Further, data collection is discussed based on implementation of each component of the transition planning framework.

A self-assessment describes whether and how the transition planning process produced a tangible results-oriented plan for the student's post-school life. The self-assessment and program assessments use the results of three student interviews and address the student's report on their satisfaction with his or her prospects and plans.

The chapter includes a matrix from a transition planning specialist's self-assessment study to show transition activities that were reported as successful for a group of students. Case reports about these students briefly describe how the students perceived transition planning met their needs.

Chapter 18: Special Education Transitions From Birth to Age 21

Although the transition to adulthood is the focus of this text, the use of the word *transition* occurs multiple times as students progress through special education programs and services. Therefore, it is essential that all special educators be aware of and understand the supports that should be in place to smooth the transition process for each student. Also, although it is not often mentioned, each transition brings with it additional challenges for the family. Parents too need support as they negotiate this journey with their children. Teachers' roles as advocates and guides are discussed.

ADDITIONAL FEATURES OF THIS TEXT

Case Reports

This text has a wide range of case reports related to the main topic of each chapter. Each case report is based on actual events, with particulars changed to maintain anonymity. These instructive case studies shed light on the challenges of transition planning and provide both practical guidance and areas for reflection. The author provides professional experiences to discuss the case reports and exercises to reflect on each case. These exercises enable the student to learn about real situations and how they were handled. The cases also give students insight into actual experiences of students in special education.

Digital Resources

The Student Supplemental Materials provides additional forms, guides, discussion prompts, and current events exercises to support learning.

Exercises

The exercises in each chapter are not only to help integrate learning but to stimulate further thought and discussion. Some of the exercises give the reader the opportunity to go out into a real-world situation and learn about the students and the team members who are part of the transition team.

Group Assignments

Special education teams work in a collaborative process. To address the collaborative process and the transition planning specialist's key roles, multiple exercises are provided, as well as field experience assignments that require teamwork. These assignments are crucial to developing collaborative skills.

PowerPoint Presentations

The PowerPoint presentations play a role in further explaining concepts within each chapter. They are not typically an overview of the chapter but rather reinforce some of the most salient topics to provide an additional learning experience. Also, one of the PowerPoint presentations is a sample of a parent training that can serve as a template for the future transition planning specialist.

Research

This text endeavors to meet the spirit and the letter of the law regarding the development of transition plans. Transition planning has been studied extensively, and the evidence-based practices that support better post-school outcomes have gained support from some prominent researchers in the field of transition. Research and evidence-based practices are emphasized in this text, and these works are cited throughout. The results of ongoing research played a significant role in the author's work as a transition planning specialist and the development of the author's dissertation on the topic.

Part 1

Introduction to Transition Planning

Transition Planning and Special Education Law

CHAPTER OBJECTIVES

→ Explain the legislation underpinning transition planning.
→ Describe the two ways a student can participate in transition planning.
→ Identify the requirements of Child Find.
→ Describe eligibility for transition planning under Section 504 of the Rehabilitation Act.
→ Explain why many states legislated starting transition planning at age 14.
→ Outline how to ensure that transition planning is in place by age 14.
→ Describe the differences between research-based, promising, and unsubstantiated practices.

TRANSITION LEGISLATION AND TRANSITION SERVICES

Foundations of Transition Planning

This section contains a brief overview of the federal government's current regulations regarding transition planning and transition planning services required as part of the Individualized Education Plan (IEP) development. A more comprehensive overview is presented in the Student Supplemental Materials.

Rae, J. M. *A Collaborative Approach to Transition Planning for Students With Disabilities* (pp. 3-24).

In 1975, the Education of All Handicapped Children Act (EAHCA) did not include transition planning because the law aimed to bring about educational equity and access to education. The legislation did not address the lives of young adults with disabilities after they left school, even though schooling for typically developing peers is focused on the transition to adult life, adult responsibilities, and postsecondary education.

Two factors instigated the inclusion of transition planning and later the addition of transition services. In the 10 years after the EAHCA of 1975, children with disabilities were leaving the public school system with no mandates to guide them into post-school life. Applying the approaches used with typically developing students are ineffective in the same way that general education instructional practices are ineffectual for students with disabilities. Secondly, students with disabilities were not achieving positive post-school outcomes as expected after they exited from special education programs. Therefore, transition services were added to the law solely to promote positive results for students as they moved through secondary school to post-school activities and into adult life. The following box describes the legislation for transition services that form the foundation for transition planning.

For reference, each law has a number associated with it from the Code of Federal Regulations, which catalogs the laws via codes. Recent updates are published in the Federal Register. The legislative directions for transition services as listed in the Code of Federal Regulations are shown in the following box.

§300.43 Transition services.

(a) Transition services mean a coordinated set of activities for a child with a disability that—

(1) Is designed to be within a results-oriented process, that is focused on improving the academic and functional achievement of the child with a disability to facilitate the child's movement from school to post-school activities, including postsecondary education, vocational education, integrated employment (including supported employment), continuing and adult education, adult services, independent living, or community participation;

(2) Is based on the individual child's needs, taking into account the child's strengths, preferences, and interests; and includes—

(i) Instruction;

(ii) Related services;

(iii) Community experiences;

(iv) The development of employment and other post-school adult living objectives; and

(v) If appropriate, acquisition of daily living skills and provision of functional vocational evaluation.

(b) Transition services for children with disabilities may be special education if provided as specially designed instruction, or a related service if required to assist a child with a disability to benefit from special education.

(Transition services, 34 C.F.R. § 300.43 [2012])

Eligibility for Transition Planning Under the Individuals With Disabilities Education Act

Eligible Children Through Young Adults

Students with disabilities who are eligible under the Individuals with Disabilities Education Act (IDEA, 2004) receive transition services. A comprehensive evaluation is completed to determine eligibility for special education and related services, including transition planning. The comprehensive assessment is conducted by a team of individuals qualified to assess whether a student has a disability. Even if a child has a diagnosis from a medical facility, he or she must be evaluated by the local education agency (LEA; i.e., the school district where he or she resides) and qualify for special education and specially designed instruction to meet his or her needs. A multidisciplinary team (MDT) conducts assessments, makes observations, and interviews parents and others who know the student best. The MDT creates an initial evaluation report based on the multiple evaluations, including parent and teacher reports about the student using evaluative criteria. The MDT reviews all of the information and determines the presence of a disability. An IEP is then developed with goals to help the student with disabilities meet his or her unique needs. The student is reevaluated every 2 to 3 years, depending on the disability type, and, if still eligible, the student will continue to receive special education services.

Eligible Disability Categories

The IDEA disability identification categories were updated in 2017. The following box on page 6 shows the current list, including descriptions of the disability categories. To reduce stigma and better reflect the disabilities, the names of disabilities are changed periodically. This occurred recently when the diagnosis of mental retardation was replaced with the term *intellectual disability*. The next section describes the IDEA definitions of each disability group. The category *development disability* is also used to define eligibility for children with disabilities from birth to age 3 years (under IDEA Part C). It also includes children ages 3 through 9 years (under IDEA Part B). The term *developmental delay* means a delay in one or more of the following areas: physical development, cognitive development, communication, social or emotional development, or adaptive (behavioral) development.

When designing transition plans for each population of eligible students, evidence- and research-based strategies and practices must pertain to the type of disability. Strategies that work with students with autism spectrum disorder (ASD) can be applied to students with Down syndrome only if there is supporting evidence that the practice is effective for both groups of students.

COMPONENTS OF TRANSITION PLANNING

Currently, federal and state laws define what transition planning is and provides some principles and evidence-based practices and predictors that guide implementation. Transition planning activities need to be delivered as a continuum of activities and services, such as receiving instruction on transition skills for adulthood and being given a planned course to participate in learning activities that increase the likelihood of improving post-school life opportunities.

The activities must be results oriented, rather than mere discussions about the future. Activities must be designed to develop skills, such as teaching students how to create their own meaningful goals. The transition planning process is meant to be implemented over several years so that skills can be firmly established as adolescents move through school, beginning in middle school and ending at graduation. Transition planning should focus on developing social, academic, and functional skills to not only support students but also to result in tangible outcomes like employment, postsecondary education, and social and leisure activities that can enrich their lives.

The pathways to improving post-school options and opportunities for inclusion can be participation in a school-to-work plan, which includes, for example, instruction on work, social interaction, academic, organizational, and attendance skills, all of which increase the likelihood of employment. Paths to post-school life can also be supported employment, such as transitioning to work with a job shadow and mentoring. Integrated employment, such as entry-level positions with opportunities for advancement, postsecondary education, vocational education, and continuing adult education, are additional options. Selection of these options is based on each student's needs, strengths, preferences, and interests. Assessments are used to guide the selection of goals, including those goals that the student feels are needed.

§300.8 Child with a disability.

(a) General. (1) Child with a disability means a child evaluated in accordance with §§300.304 through 300.311 as having an intellectual disability, a hearing impairment (including deafness), a speech or language impairment, a visual impairment (including blindness), a serious emotional disturbance (referred to in this part as "emotional disturbance"), an orthopedic impairment, autism, traumatic brain injury, and other health impairment, a specific learning disability, deaf-blindness, or multiple disabilities, and who, by reason thereof, needs special education and related services.

(2)(i) Subject to paragraph (a)(2)(ii) of this section, if it is determined, through an appropriate evaluation under §§300.304 through 300.311, that a child has one of the disabilities identified in paragraph (a)(1) of this section, but only needs a related service and not special education, the child is not a child with a disability under this part.

(ii) If consistent with §300.39(a)(2), the related service required by the child is considered special education rather than a related service under State standards, the child would be determined to be a child with a disability under paragraph (a)(1) of this section.

(c) Definitions of disability terms. The terms used in this definition of a child with a disability are defined as follows:

(1)(i) Autism means a developmental disability is significantly affecting verbal and nonverbal communication and social interaction, generally evident before age three, that adversely affects a child's educational performance. Other characteristics often associated with autism are engagement in repetitive activities and stereotyped movements, resistance to environmental change or change in daily routines, and unusual responses to sensory experiences.

(ii) Autism does not apply if a child's educational performance is adversely affected primarily because the child has an emotional disturbance, as defined in paragraph (c)(4) of this section.

(iii) A child who manifests the characteristics of autism after age three could be identified as having autism if the criteria in paragraph (c)(1)(i) of this section are satisfied.

(2) Deaf-blindness means concomitant hearing and visual impairments, the combination of which causes such severe communication and other developmental and educational needs that they cannot be accommodated in special education programs solely for children with deafness or children with blindness.

(3) Deafness means a hearing impairment that is so severe that the child is impaired in processing linguistic information through hearing, with or without amplification, that adversely affects a child's educational performance.

(4)(i) Emotional disturbance means a condition exhibiting one or more of the following characteristics over a long period of time and to a marked degree that adversely affects a child's educational performance:

(A) An inability to learn that cannot be explained by intellectual, sensory, or health factors.

(B) An inability to build or maintain satisfactory interpersonal relationships with peers and teachers.

(C) Inappropriate types of behavior or feelings under normal circumstances.

(continued)

(D) A general pervasive mood of unhappiness or depression.

(E) A tendency to develop physical symptoms or fears associated with personal or school problems.

(ii) Emotional disturbance includes schizophrenia. The term does not apply to children who are socially maladjusted unless it is determined that they have an emotional disturbance under paragraph (c)(4)(i) of this section.

(5) Hearing impairment means an impairment in hearing, whether permanent or fluctuating, that adversely affects a child's educational performance, but that is not included under the definition of deafness in this section.

(6) Intellectual disability means significantly subaverage general intellectual functioning, existing concurrently with deficits in adaptive behavior and manifested during the developmental period, that adversely affects a child's educational performance. The term "intellectual disability" was formerly termed "mental retardation."

(7) Multiple disabilities mean concomitant impairments (such as intellectual disability-blindness or intellectual disability-orthopedic impairment), the combination of which causes such severe educational needs that they cannot be accommodated in special education programs solely for one of the impairments. Multiple disabilities do not include deaf-blindness.

(8) Orthopedic impairment means a severe orthopedic impairment that adversely affects a child's educational performance. The term includes impairments caused by a congenital anomaly, impairments caused by disease (e.g., poliomyelitis, bone tuberculosis), and impairments from other causes (e.g., cerebral palsy, amputations, and fractures or burns that cause contractures).

(9) Other health impairment means having limited strength, vitality, or alertness including heightened alertness to environmental stimuli, that results in limited alertness with respect to the educational environment, that—

(i) Is due to chronic or acute health problems such as asthma, attention deficit disorder or attention deficit hyperactivity disorder, diabetes, epilepsy, a heart condition, hemophilia, lead poisoning, leukemia, nephritis, rheumatic fever, sickle cell anemia, and Tourette syndrome; and

(ii) Adversely affects a child's educational performance.

(10) Specific learning disability—(i) General. Specific learning disability means a disorder in one or more of the basic psychological processes involved in understanding or in using language, spoken or written, that may manifest itself in the imperfect ability to listen, think, speak, read, write, spell, or to do mathematical calculations, including conditions such as perceptual disabilities, brain injury, minimal brain dysfunction, dyslexia, and developmental aphasia.

(ii) Disorders not included. A specific learning disability does not include learning problems that are primarily the result of visual, hearing, or motor disabilities, of intellectual disability, of emotional disturbance, or of environmental, cultural, or economic disadvantage.

(11) Speech or language impairment means a communication disorder, such as stuttering, impaired articulation, a language impairment, or a voice impairment, that adversely affects a child's educational performance.

(continued)

(12) Traumatic brain injury means an acquired injury to the brain caused by an external physical force, resulting in total or partial functional disability or psychosocial impairment, or both, that adversely affects a child's educational performance. Traumatic brain injury applies to open or closed head injuries resulting in impairments in one or more areas, such as cognition; language; memory; attention; reasoning; abstract thinking; judgment; problem-solving; sensory, perceptual, and motor abilities; psychosocial behavior; physical functions; information processing; and speech. Traumatic brain injury does not apply to brain injuries that are congenital or degenerative, or to brain injuries induced by birth trauma.

(13) Visual impairment including blindness means an impairment in vision that, even with correction, adversely affects a child's educational performance. The term includes both partial sight and blindness.

(§ 300.8 Child with a disability [71 FR 46753, Aug. 14, 2006, as amended at 72 FR 61306, Oct. 30, 2007; 82 FR 31912, July 11, 2017])

Instructional activities are also critical features of transition planning. Curriculum-based activities include career exploration, social development, team-building exercises, interview skills development, and employment skills development. Instruction should also include a focus on personal characteristics such as confidence, task completion, timeliness, and self-advocacy via leadership of the IEP meeting. Other related services can support students in working toward their plans, including job coaching, assistive technology consultation, assistive technology devices, and paratransit services. Finally, community experiences, including in-school opportunities to interact with typical peers and peers with disabilities in after-school programs, job shadowing within the school, and community-based instructional activities, should also be included.

As students go through the process of transition planning, ongoing age-appropriate assessments provide students and transition planning specialists with current information on the students' strengths and needs, such as acquisition of daily living skills and provision of functional vocational evaluation. Academic assessments in reading and math inform students of their progress and where they need to improve, particularly in relation to adult and employment vocabulary. Assessments may also show students what characteristics they may need to feel comfortable and confident in a field of work.

Overall, the primary aims of transition planning are community inclusion, employment in the community, participation in family and community activities, and the ability for each student to be as independent as possible and a contributor within his or her own family.

Statements of Transition Needs and Services

IDEA guides schools to include transition planning as early as possible, when the team decides it is appropriate or, for most states, by age 14. The planning starts at the first IEP meeting when transition is discussed, then after team discussion, which includes students' preferences, wants, and needs, a statement of needed services is written into the IEP using the additional components of transition framework, described in Chapter 2. By age 14, according to many state laws, students will also be guided to create goals. The goals of the transition plan must include appropriate *measurable* postsecondary goals. These goals must be based upon age-appropriate transition assessments and activities related to training, education, employment, social development and social skills, and independent living skills. Transition plans and services include courses of study, such as vocational school, courses, and seminars, to address needed transition skills and other experiences to assist students in their transition into secondary and postsecondary job training, entry-level employment, educational programs and, finally, increased independence.

A course of study will include graduation requirements such as courses and credits needed to earn a diploma or a certificate of completion. The academic coursework in transition courses helps students develop skills and related subskills that are purported to improve post-school outcomes. Instructional modules address goals and include group and direct instruction in independent living skills; self-determination and self-advocacy training; and management of the home, personal finances, and health care needs, to name a few.

Transition Law and Severe Disabilities

Some eligible students may be unable to fully participate in many of the aforementioned activities of transition due to the severity of their intellectual and, in some cases, physical disabilities. The severity of physical and cognitive impairments indicates whether life-long supervised support and financial assistance are warranted. However, to increase the self-determination of the young people in the activities of importance to them, all efforts should be directed to practices that will include the students' preferences and ensure the highest level of participation across environments.

To encourage input from students who have limited communication and severe disabilities, assistive technology and a plan of communication will be a necessary component for students who cannot communicate through the sensory systems because of deafness and hearing impairment, blindness and vision impairment, and the inability to respond to evaluation questions that require physical movement. According to IDEA, all children and young persons who have been evaluated, have been determined to have disabilities, and are in need of special education and related services are eligible for transition services under IDEA. Therefore, even students with the most severe disabilities participate in transition planning. If students are not in need of special education services but have disabilities, such as mental health disorders, they too are eligible for transition services through Section 504 plans, which do not require special education eligibility.

Section 504 of the Rehabilitation Act

Transition services and special education are available to identified students under Section 504. A multidisciplinary evaluation is not required to make this determination. The Rehabilitation Act of 1973 primarily addressed discrimination in and access to the workplace. In 1995, Section 504 was added to include schools. This civil rights law gives educational and school program access to students with disabilities who do not require specially designed instruction or special education. This can occur when students with disabilities can learn within the general education setting with methods afforded typical peers but are unable to access their education due to conditions or disabilities that may or may not be hidden. Table 1-1 contains examples of circumstances when a student may warrant a 504 transition plan. These conditions often require transition activities to support the transition to post-school life because, without accommodations, the student's ability to access post-school options are diminished. The table lists just some of those conditions.

The service needs of students with hidden disabilities, such as social anxiety, are often misunderstood and falsely attributed to negative personal character traits. Bateman, Bright, O'Shea, O'Shea, and Algozzine (2007) posit that students with these disabilities may be considered problem students who are regarded as lazy. School districts identify students who require transition services even when they may not be eligible under IDEA. The following section discusses the LEA's requirements and the underlying legislation for both IDEA and Section 504 of the Rehabilitation Act. Students with *parents* with disabilities or other severe impairments can be eligible for support to decrease their likelihood of dropping out. In the next section, the IDEA eligibility category other health impairments is discussed.

Transition Planning Eligibility and Other Health Impairments

If a student with a disability has, for example, a mental health disorder under the diagnosis of anxiety, he or she would have a disability under the IDEA eligibility category of other health impairment. If that same child excelled at academics and was not in need of specially designed instruction

TABLE 1-1. MEDICAL CONDITIONS AND TRANSITION PLANS

1. Medical conditions such as seizure disorders and diabetes are often unnoticed and most often cause loss of in-class time.

2. Mental health disorders such as selective mutism and social anxiety disorder diminish or prevent participation in typical oral presentations and normal everyday interactions.

3. Severe depression impairs planning ability and motivation and impairs the interaction skills needed to advocate and plan new life directions.

4. Orthopedic disabilities require pre-planning to ensure attendance and access to events.

5. Attention deficit disorder impairs the ability of the brain to ignore extraneous noise and concentrate on the task at hand.

6. Autism spectrum disorder level 1 or level 2 support (formally known as *Asperger's disorder*) impairs social reciprocity and understanding of gestural cues used in everyday communicative exchanges.

throughout his or her career, he or she could become eligible for transition services and planning under special education, if the parents or the student alerted the school because the child was not able to make the necessary steps toward independence due to severe social anxiety. An evaluation would be done, and the student could receive services via special education.

Alternatively, the same student could opt for a 504 transition plan. This type of plan is relatively flexible, and because it does not require a multidisciplinary evaluation, services can be implemented quickly. In both situations, the local Office of Vocational Rehabilitation becomes involved, and, in this manner, both agencies work together to develop a transition plan. As stated previously, academic success does not unilaterally mean the student is not eligible for special education or transition planning. The transition planning specialist is typically responsible for the transition planning of students who have 504 transition plans.

Child Find and Section 504

Acquired and Emergent Disabilities

School districts' attempts to find children with disabilities continue through secondary school, and schools must make ongoing efforts to find students who may have disabilities. School systems must advertise and seek to determine whether students may be eligible under 504 or IDEA. By creating public awareness and in-school awareness, schools must also attempt to find children and youth who may have become disabled well after childhood. Examples of students with acquired disabilities are those who have had head injuries, emerging mental health disorders, or emerging inherited or congenital medical conditions.

Secondary-age students with late-onset disabilities or acquired disabilities will most likely need and be eligible for transition services. In the case of mental health disorders, these typically emerge between the ages of 14 and 24 years, with symptoms that are manifested in an episodic pattern. These can be difficult to see because symptoms may change in intensity during different periods of time. Other serious conditions, such as severe social anxiety, become more prominent in middle and high school and often result in school elopement or absences when school activities and tasks, such as eating in front of peers or participating in group presentations or interactions, are required. Social judgement spurs excess anxiety and school refusals. Another example is if a head injury resulted in a memory impairment. Some teachers see this only in classes that require a high level of recall. Therefore, these acquired disabilities are often missed or are viewed as behavior problems, and the lack of recognition can have deleterious outcomes in a students' academic and social lives.

The federal government's Child Find requirements address these late-emergent disabilities. This law (described in the following box) is crucial to support this group of students. The transition planning specialist and the special education team need to know the requirements outlined in this statue. Under this statute, the school district develops procedures for finding students suspected of having a disability, and school personnel who suspect a student of having a disability must make a referral to the special education program. (Note: IDEA uses the words, *child* and *children* to describe all school-age students from preschool through high school graduation or when the student ages out of special education programs and services.)

§ 300.111 Child find.

(a) General

(1) The State must have in effect policies and procedures to ensure that—

(i) All children with disabilities residing in the State, including children with disabilities who are homeless children or are wards of the State, and children with disabilities attending private schools, regardless of the severity of their disability, and who are in need of special education and related services, are identified, located, and evaluated; and

(ii) A practical method is developed and implemented to determine which children are currently receiving needed special education and related services.

(c) Other children in child find. Child find also must include—

(1) Children who are suspected of being a child with a disability under § 300.8 and in need of special education, even though they are advancing from grade to grade; and

(2) Highly mobile children, including migrant children.

(d) Construction. Nothing in the Act requires that children be classified by their disability so long as each child who has a disability that is listed in § 300.8 and who, by reason of that disability, needs special education and related services are regarded as a child with a disability under Part B of the Act.

(Child find, 34 C.F.R. § 300.111 [2012])

Exercises

1. Find your state's Department of Special Education website, usually listed under the Department of Education. Review the website and describe the information provided about transition planning. If it is not present, determine, by contacting the school, where they provide the information.

2. Describe how your local district implements Child Find procedures.

TRANSITION EDUCATION

To help students with disabilities, their parents, and the special and general education teams understand the goals and processes of transition planning, transition education is needed; each group of stakeholders should be trained and knowledgeable about curriculum-based transition activities and vocational, post-school educational opportunities and independence goals. Stakeholders should understand that each of these activities and their related strategies must be tangible and clearly defined rather than merely a series of discussions between the transition planning specialist and the student. In previous IDEA authorizations, special education teams and school administration could cover the letter of the law through discussing the transition to adulthood in the way that it is done with typically developing students. However, using the approach used with students without disabilities resulted in few positive outcomes for students with disabilities.

Students with disabilities need well-developed instructional support and career guidance to find work and educational experiences where they can succeed. School-wide understanding and knowledge about comprehensive transition planning supports students with complex learning and disability-related needs. Students also need to understand the focus and need for transition planning at a time in their lives when they are trying to be independent. To develop the overarching skills and related subskills needed for post-school success, adolescents with disabilities will need direct instruction to enable them to transition between school and work and acquire adult living skills. The school's professional and support staff, community, and the student will need to learn that the complex learning, medical, and physical supports needed by these students will preclude learning these skills easily or incidentally. Therefore, to attain improved post-school outcomes, it is first of utmost importance to improve transition education and services (Test et al., 2009).

Special education teachers and supervisors select and implement the curriculum, and for students with disabilities, the required skills are initially embedded in a curriculum that addresses adult life skills and should guide students as they move through their secondary educational program. Furthermore, the school community should focus on transition planning as transition-focused education rather than one that occurs outside of class (Kohler, Gothberg, Fowler, & Coyle, 2016). Structured teaching modules delivered via curriculum-based instructional programs in a long-term framework can form the basis of career education and adult life skills development with implementation beginning in middle school. This foundational approach to transition planning is realistic given the expectations of transition services legislation and the needs of students with disabilities.

Transition Planning Timelines

There has been some debate over when to begin transition activities. In fact, the federal government changed the age for services in two reauthorizations. In 1990, the federal government required that an Individual Transition Plan must be part of a student's IEP no later than age 16. In the original legislation, the transition plan was to direct a coordinated set of activities and interagency linkages designed to promote the student's movement to post-school activities such as independent living, vocational training, and additional educational experiences (IDEA, 1990). IDEA clearly laid out the direction of transition planning but only required that the goals be promoted. No results were needed in the letter of the law, but were rather hoped for in the spirit of the law. In the IDEA amendments of 1997, the age of transition planning was lowered to 14 years old. In IDEA (2004), the timeline to begin transition services was again changed to age 16. Many states are still using age 14 despite the change.

Currently, federal law mandates that transition planning services must begin during the year before the student turns 16 years old. The federal law requires that the student attend the IEP meeting if transition is going to be discussed. The federal guideline states that the LEA (i.e., the school district):

> [M]ust invite a child with a disability to attend the child's IEP Team meeting if a purpose of the meeting will be the consideration of the postsecondary goals for the child and the transition services needed to assist the child in reaching those goals under §300.320(b). (IEP team, 2006)

The Transition Timeline Controversy

As stated previously, federal legislation requires that IEP teams consider the transitional needs of students with disabilities at the age of 16 (Transition services, 2012). Many educators believe that age 16 is too late to begin a successful transition for students with disabilities (Philbin, 2009), and research suggests that the earlier provision of transition services significantly increases employment rates for people with disabilities, such as those with ASD (Cimera, Burgess, & Wiley, 2013). In a study by Cimera, Burgess, and Bedesem (2014) about the potential impact of early transition services for students with intellectual disabilities, two groups were compared. Both groups had 7520 individuals. One group included only individuals from states requiring services be addressed by age 14, and the other group comprised individuals from states that required services by age 16. Students from states that implemented transition planning by age 14 were more likely to be employed than their peers from states with implementation at age 16. Over a 4-year period, 58.8% of participants from the early transition states became employed, compared with 45.6% for individuals from later transition states. Given the complexity and the many goals to be accomplished, the age 16 timeline is not as conducive to post-school success.

For some students, typically young persons with moderate, severe, and profound intellectual disabilities, special educators may be content with beginning at age 16 because young people with intellectual disabilities may stay in school until age 21 and therefore have many years to go through the transition planning process. However, these students are transitioning to adult services and supported employment, rather than unsupported employment and post-school vocational and educational programs. For this reason, more research about available programs and services and advance planning are needed in preparation for accessing adult services. There are waiting lists for adult services, financial planning, and medical plan changes at age 18 that must be addressed. Therefore, for those students, beginning planning by 16 years old, and preferably before, is warranted so that the team is fully aware and can plan appropriate supports for their unique transition needs.

Although students may not be aging out of school-age services, they are in fact aging out of children's services. Interagency attendance at IEP meetings is needed to plan supports to manage the coming changes. Given the complexity of services needed for the most intellectually disabled students and the often-concomitant medical needs and physical disabilities, transition planning discussion should begin by age 14 to prepare for the age-of-majority changes that will impact them and to ensure that they are on waiting lists for housing and medical care if need be. Parents and other IEP team members should be knowledgeable of coming changes and be prepared to include these changes on the IEP discussion agenda. Documentation of the discussions should be kept in the student's confidential file and noted in the parent information section of the IEP.

Inviting Students to Their Individualized Education Plan Meetings

Transition planning legislation initiated the practice of inviting young people to their IEP meetings for a few reasons. For students with disabilities, it is a mark of passage signaling to them that things are changing: they are becoming young adults. Now students can communicate directly to the team about their preferences, hopes, dreams, and needs for the future. From the first IEP meeting they attend, they will learn to share their perspectives with the team members. They will also learn to lead their IEP meetings. The theoretical underpinning for this practice is that students who participate in the IEP process and who select their own goals are more likely to reach those goals.

Voicing preferences, setting goals, making choices, exploring options, and actively participating in developing plans are steps that increase student self-determination. Research supports the development of self-determination as a predictor of post-school success for persons with disabilities, and it also underpins legislation requiring that students be invited to their IEP meetings when transition is being discussed. Research suggests that there are increased positive outcomes for students who take an active role to set goals and self-determine the course of their lives. A self-determined person is better able to control his or her own destiny (Wehmeyer & Webb, 2012).

This concept will be discussed in more detail in Chapter 2 and throughout this text. It is the intent of the legislation that young persons with disabilities become more self-determined as they go through the process of transition planning, become better able to act independently, and become causal agents in their own lives. During IEP meetings, students will also be given the opportunity to advocate for themselves when, at times, a team may not be supportive of students' chosen goals. This level of involvement in the IEP is encouraged because it is a predictor of post-school success.

Exercises

1. Define self-determination according to current research. Research should be within the last 4 years. Use only peer-reviewed articles.
2. Describe why a student benefits from inclusion in the IEP meeting.

INDEPENDENCE AND AGE OF MAJORITY

Control of School Records

The transition planning specialist must be aware of students' age-of-majority rights. As students go through the process of transition, it will be possible that some students who plan to graduate on time may be a year behind their same-age peers or may need to earn some credits to graduate. If this is the case, it is possible that these students will turn 18 years old, and full control of the IEP team decisions will be turned over to the students. However, in some states, such as Pennsylvania and Mississippi, this would not occur because parents maintain control of the IEP until students are 21 years old, the age when services are no longer provided under IDEA. However, students, despite special education law, are in control of Section 504 plans, and schools can develop transition plans under this plan.

The age of majority for special education varies by state, even though nationally the age of majority is 18 years old. This is more relevant when students are significantly disabled. If not significantly disabled, delaying the age of majority decreases students' abilities to be independent and more self-determined while they are still in school. IDEA gives states the authority to elect transfer of educational decision-making rights to students. The following two boxes describe the age of majority law and provide the legal definition of a parent.

§ 300.520 Transfer of parental rights at the age of majority.

General. A State may provide that, when a child with a disability reaches the age of majority under State law that applies to all children (except for a child with a disability who has been determined to be incompetent under State law)—

(1)(i) The public agency must provide any notice required by this part to both the child and the parents; and

(ii) All rights accorded to parents under Part B of the Act transfer to the child;

(2) All rights accorded to parents under Part B of the Act transfer to children who are incarcerated in an adult or juvenile, State or local correctional institution; and

(3) Whenever a State provides for the transfer of rights under this part pursuant to paragraph (a)(1) or (a)(2) of this section, the agency must notify the child and the parents of the transfer of rights.

(b) Special rule. A State must establish procedures for appointing the parent of a child with a disability, or, if the parent is not available, another appropriate individual, to represent the educational interests of the child throughout the period of the child's eligibility under Part B of the Act if, under State law, a child who has reached the age of majority, but has not been determined to be incompetent, can be determined not to have the ability to provide informed consent with respect to the child's educational program.

(Transfer of parental rights at the age of majority, 34 C.F.R. § 300.520 [2011])

§300.30 Parent.

(a) Parent means—

(1) A biological or adoptive parent of a child;

(2) A foster parent, unless State law, regulations, or contractual obligations with a State or local entity prohibit a foster parent from acting as a parent;

(3) A guardian generally authorized to act as the child's parent, or authorized to make educational decisions for the child (but not the State if the child is a ward of the State);

(4) An individual acting in the place of a biological or adoptive parent (including a grandparent, stepparent, or other relative) with whom the child lives, or an individual who is legally responsible for the child's welfare; or

(5) A surrogate parent who has been appointed in accordance with § 300.519 or section 639(a)(5) of the Act.

(Parent, 34 C.F.R. § 300.30 [2012])

Table 1-2 shows the state-by-state breakdown for the age of majority. In special education, the age of majority is the age when a student can take full legal rights for his or her IEP. For example, if a student believes that he or she is not getting the special education services that he or she is eligible for, the student can ask for mediation and the continuum of due process rights provided by federal and state law. The student can also agree or disagree with the IEP's contents and ask for additional services for the transition to adulthood.

A student must be informed that he or she is going to reach the age of majority as follows:

§300.320 Definition of individualized education program.

Beginning not later than one year before the child reaches the age of majority under State law, the IEP must include a statement that the child has been informed of the child's rights under Part B of the IDEA, if any, that will, consistent with 34 C.F.R. §300.520, transfer to the child on reaching the age of majority.

(Definition of individualized education program, 2006)

Medical and Mental Health

The age-of-majority control of mental health treatment varies by state but is never older than age 18. The age of majority for mental health treatment may be also be significantly younger depending on the state law. In addition, some states, such as Pennsylvania, permit adolescents by age 14 to seek and consent to mental health treatment, including in-patient treatment. Parents of children through age 18 can also consent for their child to receive treatment. Neither parent nor child can revoke the consent of the other. This allows the parent/child to secure treatment for their child/themselves. Each state has different ways of designating responsibilities.

Mental health disorders have a significant stigma attached to them, and stigma can reduce or block parents' support when their children need treatment. Because of the impact of stigma on treatment seeking, some states do not require parental permission, and children can seek mental health treatment without notifying their parents who may be ashamed that their children are facing mental health difficulties. Alternatively, parents can seek treatment for their adolescent who may refuse treatment as a result of a suicide attempt or a psychotic episode.

In states where parents must grant permission for treatment, the content of the therapeutic sessions is confidential unless the child becomes a threat to him- or herself or others.

TABLE 1-2. AGE OF MAJORITY BY STATE

STATE	AGE (IN YEARS)	STATE	AGE (IN YEARS)
Alabama	19	Montana	18
Alaska	18	Nebraska	19
Arizona	18	New Hampshire	18
Arkansas	18	New Jersey	18
California	18	New Mexico	18
Colorado	18	New York	18
Connecticut	18	Nevada	19 or graduation
Delaware	19	North Carolina	18
Florida	18	North Dakota	18
Georgia	18	Ohio	18 or graduation
Hawaii	18	Oklahoma	18
Idaho	18	Oregon	18
Illinois	18	Pennsylvania	21
Indiana	18	Rhode Island	18
Iowa	18	South Carolina	18
Kentucky	18	South Dakota	18
Louisiana	18	Tennessee	The later of 18 or graduation from high school
Kansas	18	Texas	18
Maine	18	Utah	The earlier of 18 or graduation from high school
Maryland	18	Vermont	18
Massachusetts	18	Washington	18
Michigan	18	West Virginia	18
Minnesota	18	Wyoming	18
Mississippi	21	Wisconsin	18, or, if still in high school, the later of 19 or graduation
Missouri	18	Virginia	18 or end of high school

Transition planning specialists, though they may be privy to mental health information shared by students or their families, are bound by confidentiality and the student's right to access mental health services. The special education team must know about their state laws regarding mental health confidentiality. It is crucial to have a clear understanding of the transition planning specialist's role in relation to the student and parents with regard to mental health laws.

USING EFFECTIVE PRACTICES IN TRANSITION PLANNING

Federal legislation requires that schools be charged with implementing programs, practices, methods of instruction, and well-designed transition plans that have scientific evidence of effectiveness. The use of evidence- and research-based practices underpins the framework of the transition planning process. Multiple concepts and practices have empirical evidence supporting their use. Test et al. (2009) assert the following:

> [G]iven the current emphasis on evidence-based practices in education, the field of secondary transition can now say that we have a set of evidence-based predictors of post-school success based on criteria for quality correlational research suggested by Thompson et al. (2005).

Key examples of evidence- or research-based practices and predictors of success include self-determination, self-advocacy, goal setting, inclusion with typical peers, community access, career exploration, direct participation in IEP development and IEP meetings, and, most importantly, embedding transition planning skills development within the curriculum. Effective practices are the foundation of student involvement in transition planning.

Evidence- and Research-Based Practices and Predictors

In the No Child Left Behind Act (NCLB, 2001), federal law requires that teachers use practices and programs that predict success based on scientifically based research. Scientifically based research is a systematic effort to discover or confirm facts or to investigate a problem or topic, most often by scientific methods of observation or experiment. A study is designed using a research design and uses high-quality data analyses. Studies are rigorously reviewed by a group of people with expertise in the field of inquiry under investigation. If the study meets the standards of the peer review, the study is conducted. Data analysis of the study results determines whether the practice does what it says it is supposed to do. For example, does a student's self-determination predict better employment? For transition planning, several practices and predictors have been studied to determine the correlation between practice and positive post-school outcomes. To be considered evidence based, the practice must do the following:

- Demonstrate a positive effect on post-school outcomes
- Allow one to infer that the practice led to improvement
- Be replicated and supported by multiple high-quality studies
- Have been peer-reviewed and published in an academic journal in the field
- Have been reviewed by a reputable organization (e.g., What Works Clearinghouse, National Technical Assistance Center on Transition; IRIS Center, n.d.)

Defining evidence-based practice can be difficult because the standards for what qualifies as evidence based can vary across different fields. According to Cook and Odom (2013), research for evidence-based practices must meet certain standards in terms of research design, quality, and quantity. Usually, it is expected that, for a practice to be evidence based, it should be supported by more than one high-quality experimental study showing that practice has a significant effect on outcomes. An evidence-based practice in the context of transition planning should be supported by both evidence in practice and peer-reviewed research by specialists in the field of special education and transition planning.

When discussing research, the terminology is important. Evidence-based practices and evidence-based programs are not the same. Evidence-based programs are a collection of practices when used together are defined as skills, techniques, and strategies that have been proven to work through experimental research studies and large-scale research field studies.

Applicability of a given study is an important consideration as well. A practice is only evidence-based for the category of students being examined by the study in question. For example, a study on practices for students with ASD would not apply to a student with emotional and behavioral disorders unless students with emotional and behavioral disorders were one of the research groups. It is crucial that transition planning specialists not assume that all students with disabilities benefit from the same programs and practices (Mazzotti, Rowe, Cameto, Test, & Morningstar, 2013).

Research-Based Practices

Research-based practices use less rigorous standards, and a moderate number of studies show that the strategies are effective for the population studied. Research-based studies must use research designs and be reviewed for quality by persons with the qualifications to review and judge research. They do not require as many participants as in studies that resulted in evidence-based practices.

Promising Practices

Promising practices are practices still going through the research process that may become research-based practices. Some studies may already demonstrate some success for improving outcomes. They may use rigorous research designs and adhere to indicators of quality research (Bremer, Kachgal, & Schoeller, 2003). However, more studies replicated with fidelity need to be conducted to ensure efficacy. Promising practices include those practices that predict improved outcomes through correlational studies.

Unsubstantiated Practices

Special education law requires the use of evidence-based practice (Every Student Succeeds Act, 2015; NCLB, 2001). This was not always the case. Practices that demonstrated limited success for improving outcomes were often implemented without any systematic review to see whether the practices helped students make progress. Unsubstantiated practices are based on no qualifying studies, unpublished research, anecdotal evidence, or professional judgment. Also, some programs endorse their own products by publishing studies that support efficacy without following scientific research design (Test et al., 2009).

Advocacy and Teacher Bias:
Impact on Transition Planning

Prior to working with students on their transition plans, special education teams should educate themselves on advocacy and its relationship to program development for students. The following section is a brief overview of attitudes toward children and youth with disabilities and the long history of discrimination that both they and their families have had to contend with.

To effectively develop transition plans for students, educators must overcome negative perspectives of children with disabilities and the related stigma of disability. Teachers, who play the role of advocate, must confront with rigorous honesty personal views about disability. Determining how effective a transition planning specialist can be in advocating for educational opportunities, materials, services, and employment opportunities includes some reflection and self-assessment. Therefore, a review of personal bias is prudent. Before reviewing bias, educators should consider the perspectives of their cultures of origin, as well as their commitment to supporting educational rights for students with disabilities and their ability to advocate for educational and community equity.

The denial of an education based on disability, gender, race, or any other immutable characteristic exposes explicitly stated or implicitly applied societal beliefs. These beliefs can underlie our actions about who should be educated, how this should happen, who receives the financial support using pooled community resources, and who does not. Therefore, educators must consider questions such as, what beliefs underlie the denial of education to children and youth with disabilities while giving opportunities and education to typical peers? Why is there ever a need for high-level due process hearings and court interventions to attain educational rights that are granted to typically developing children? The President's Committee on Excellence in Education (2002) brought this problem to light. This commission report points out that children with disabilities now have access to education, but they do not always have access to the quality of education they deserve to succeed in school and later life. It is significant to note that this report comes 27 years after the doors of schools were first opened to children with disabilities and reflects the slow progress of educational development.

The courts further institutionalized a low standard for special education in the *Hendrick Hudson District Board of Education v. Rowley* (1982). When it stated "Thus, the intent of the Education of All Handicapped Children's Act (1975) was more to open the door of public education to handicapped children on appropriate terms than to guarantee any particular level of education once inside" (*Hendrick Hudson District Board of Education v. Rowley,* 1982). Low-quality educational programs for children with disabilities expose societal attitudes toward children and youth with disabilities. Such educational discrepancies became evident in 1996, when a court ruling about special education stated that a school district should know that a child has an inappropriate IEP or is not receiving more than a de minimis educational benefit (*M. C. and G. C., on Behalf of Their Son, J. C. v. Central Regional School District,* 1996). In 2008, rather than overturn this low bar for the education of a special education student, the judge in *Thompson R2-J School District v. Luke P., et al.* supported the previous ruling and called this low standard a precedent. The ruling in the Luke P. case reinforced but added that a "merely de minimis" education is adequate for students with disabilities and that IDEA only opened the door to education. This ruling was overturned 9 years later in the spring of 2017 (*Endrew F. v. Douglas County School District*). The dates on these rulings indicate that 21 years had passed before this low standard for the education for children and youth with disabilities was finally overturned by the U.S. Supreme Court in March 2017.

The continued social and cultural acceptance of educational discrepancies that exist for children with disabilities, and the relevant judicial decisions, have reinforced low expectations for children with disabilities that can cow teachers into being unable to advocate for better options and services for their students. This societal bias and a transition planning specialist's own biases may thwart a teacher's work with youth with disabilities. A critical examination of personal biases, as well as the laws and ideologies that underlie ever-evolving beliefs about what students with disabilities can achieve or should be entitled to, is prerequisite to beginning work in transition planning. As a result of the Endrew ruling, time will reveal whether this ruling will make a difference in the opportunities and educational programs and materials provided for students with disabilities. Additional discussion on the history of cultural and historical views that underpin bias and discrimination appears in the section on worldviews and discrimination.

Transition specialists and special education team members: The following assignment is meant to open an intimate and reflective journey for the work with students with disabilities. Reflect on these questions and analyze personal viewpoints that might be sources of bias.

Self-Reflection Exercise

1. Please complete the following personal reflections before reading the next section.
   a. Have you ever judged a person's intelligence based upon his or her physical appearance?
   b. Have you ever discussed the limits of education of a group of individuals with disabilities?
   c. Have you ever, based on vague or overly general information about a child with a disability, made a decision regarding whether assistive technology would be beneficial to that child (without sufficient data to support you)?
   d. Have you ever been uneasy in a social situation where a person with a disability was present?
   e. Have you ever asked a child with a disability what he or she may need to be able to learn?
   f. Have you ever wondered what a parent did that may have "caused" a disability?

g. What do you know about work options for persons with disabilities?

h. Do you have any friends who have disabilities?

i. What shared beliefs or experiences among your family and friends might affect how you think about disabilities?

j. Have you ever said or thought, "The apple doesn't fall far from the tree" about a student with a behavioral disability?

k. How might reflecting on personal biases regarding disabilities impact your work with students?

Teacher Bias and Identity Discrimination

The preceding self-reflection exercise should begin an ongoing process of review and analysis about personal biases that may impact a transition planning specialist's or special education team member's commitment to and understanding of a student's capabilities, strengths, and needs. Personal biases have their roots in many years of shared familial, societal, and personal views, beliefs, and judgments about groups or individuals.

It is important that educators be aware of how they might inadvertently convey their own biases during their conversations with others and to think about how these social interactions impact their work with students. This is especially important if those interactions could potentially lead to life-changing consequences for students, such as the reduction or denial of technology, services, supports, curriculum development, and educational equity. Educators must also ask themselves how personal and shared thoughts, feelings, and prejudices reduce their commitment to any student through negative judgments of inability, character, race, sex, gender orientation, religion, privilege, or poverty. Educators' personal biases and rigid perspectives can distort students' abilities to share who they are and what they think and to have their messages accurately perceived. Rigid and biased perspectives impair an educator's ability to adequately understand the content of a child's or youth's conversation (Rubin & Rubin, 2005) or behaviors during the student-teacher/transition planning specialist conferencing process discussed in this text.

Teachers and transition planning specialists, as part of IEP teams, must strive to note and ameliorate biases so that biases do not affect their ability to work effectively with students. The effect of these biases can be especially limiting for students during transition planning, when cultural stereotypes and personal prejudices may project onto the students based on what the transition planning specialists think people with those characteristics might want to do, should do, or could do.

In short, students must be met with an open, unbiased mind and solutions-oriented approach about their capabilities, strengths, and needs so that useful, student-centered plans can be developed. Reflecting on biased perceptions is the first step in successful and fair transition planning. To further shed light on societal views, the next section addresses the background of societal beliefs.

Self-Reflection Exercise

1. Using the personal information from the previous reflection questions, analyze and discuss what impact your beliefs or the beliefs of others may have had on your work with a student. Also, write about other thoughts you become aware of during this reflection.

WORLDVIEWS, DISABILITY, AND DISCRIMINATION

Each special education professional holds a personal worldview, a professional viewpoint, and a general mind-set about how well any child with a disability or other characteristic will perform academically, adaptively, and socially. Two prominent sociologists, Peter L. Berger and Thomas

Luckmann (1991), first identified the presence of fixed professional views when they discussed self-identity, asserting that the self-identity of any group evolves from a combination of formal and informal beliefs. These beliefs, together with the daily work routine, formulate a worldview for workers in each profession (McCord, 1983). Berger and Luckmann's work further postulates that people and groups interacting within a social system will create concepts and cognitive representations of the actions of others—in this case, of those with disabilities. These ideas become habituated, replayed, and made available to other members of society.

Leaders in the field of disability consistently view disabilities as disorders and conditions in need of a medically oriented approach (Braginski & Braginski, 1971). This viewpoint has continued, and teachers' beliefs continue to be generally consistent with medical model perspectives on disability as biologically defined (Lalvani, 2015). Although progress has been made through litigation, civil rights law, special education, health care provision, and advocacy, the stigma associated with disability has continued to lead to the marginalization of persons with disabilities, as well as their families. Persons with mental health disabilities continue to be the subjects of significant discrimination because society still holds the worldview that they are dangerous despite research to the contrary (Yeh, Jewell, & Thomas, 2017).

Teachers in special education, as representatives of the field of special education, must examine their professional biases as they relate directly to the students they teach. In the role of special education expert, a teacher's negative professional attributions about a disability impart a negative perspective on the child as an individual. Lalvani (2015) asserts that to combat this negative viewpoint, teachers must challenge dominant discourses about families of children with disabilities and problematize the medical–model-based assumptions of negative outcomes and pathological functioning among this group (p. 391). "The medical model of disability, which has historically predominated in the public imagination, depicts disability as a deficit from the norm, a malady to be fixed through physical therapy, technological devices, and personal willpower" (Oliver & Barnes, 2012, p. 170). In contrast, parents of children with disabilities resist the medicalized tragedy perspective and focus on social barriers such as access to strong educational programs and services, social acceptance, and inclusion. Therefore, parents who have moved past the personal tragedy to acceptance feel the impact when teachers view them as needing sympathy (Oliver & Barnes, 2012).

Wolfensberger, Nirje, Olshansky, Perske, and Roos (1972); Wolfensberger (1980); and Mutua (2001) discussed social perceptions of persons with disabilities and found that persons with disabilities have historically been viewed as deviant in that they do not reflect the social view of normal. Before civil rights legislation, the social norm in the United States had been to reject persons and children with intellectual, behavioral, mental health, or other disabilities from our schools, communities, workplaces, and even homes. Wolfensberger et al. (1972); Wolfensberger (1980); and Mutua (2001) further discussed how deviant status activates societal devaluation and rejection and has led to the physical separation of disabled persons from their families and communities. Social devaluation compounds the mark of disability, and a secondary stigma is projected onto the mother of the child. This devaluation, directed toward the mother of a child with a disability, is well-documented and is a long-standing interpersonal dynamic in the United States (Colker, 2015). Prejudicial ideas about the mother can reduce teacher perceptions of the mother's contributions to her children. During transition planning, parents are included in decisions, and minimizing parental suggestions and parental contributions reduces options for post-school employment. For example, at one school, a mother was not included in decision making because the transition planning team felt the mother was "too disorganized to get it together." When notified of the meeting, the mother reported that she had found a job for the student in a family business.

It is important to be critical and aware of one's own personal biases and ensure that parents are included in the transition planning process. Even if a family member seems overwhelmed or otherwise not engaged, the transition planning specialist must overcome "mother bias" and prejudices about a parent's suitability to give input for planning. Family members do think about their children's future and, in most cases, can contribute valuable information. In a study on mothers of children with disabilities, mothers, as compared with fathers, bear the brunt of blame and shame due to deeply held traditional beliefs that assign mothers to childhood social development. These beliefs, coupled with scientific discourses that connect children's well-being to mothers' bodies and gestational practices, devalue and blame the mother of the child with a disability (Blum, 2007). Devaluation of the mother can play out in habituated discriminatory sayings such as "the apple doesn't fall far from the tree," a pat phrase that devalues the parents as well as the child with a disability. Therefore, bias can impact the educator's work not only with the student but also with the parent and can impair the ability of the transition planning specialist to develop effective plans as part of the IEP team. This will be examined further in the section on families.

Summary

Transition planning specialists need to have a thorough understanding of the legislative goals of transition planning, federal mandates, and state laws that support implementation. The transition planning specialist, along with special education team members, ensures that the legal mandates are met. The team must stay current in the field so that they know about changes being discussed and those being finalized for later implementation.

Special education is based on eligibility as the result of a multidisciplinary evaluation. Under special education law, students and their families are ensured that a transition plan including the student will be developed. Students with acquired or emergent disabilities may be determined eligible for special education, or they can secure transition plans via 504 plans. The 504 plans can be implemented without parental oversight, and this process is more expedient when seeking immediately needed services. Emergent and acquired disabilities often become evident during secondary school. Up until graduation, Child Find legislative requirements are still in place. If functional, behavioral, or academic performance declines, referrals are required to determine whether the behavioral changes are the result of emergent or acquired conditions.

Carrying out the requirements of transition planning takes time, and the timeline for implementing transition plans has been a source of controversy. However, waiting until a student in a special education program is 16 years old to implement a transition plan is well past the ideal time to begin attending vocational training or preparing for college. Therefore, many states begin transition planning at age 14 or sooner to carry out transition in a way that research suggests is best practice.

Another legislative mandate is inviting students to their IEP meetings. This practice is the result of research that indicates that student involvement by age 14 and participation as an IEP team member is best practice for developing essential skills such as self-advocacy and self-determination.

Legislation such as the IDEA (2004) and Every Student Succeeds Act (2015) requires the use of evidence-based practices. Technical support is provided to the schools via state and national agencies to assist in disseminating and reviewing the latest research. Looking for best practices and predictors of post-school success is paramount to the establishment of strong transition activities. This also includes knowing what the unsubstantiated practices are and ensuring that those practices are not used in educational practice. Finally, in order to work with students, an in-depth examination of personal bias is necessary so that societal and personal bias does not result in limited services to students as they transition to post-school life.

References

Bateman, D. F., Bright, K. L., O'Shea, D. J., O'Shea, L. J., & Algozzine, B. (2007). *The special education program administrator's handbook*. Boston, MA: Pearson Education, Inc.

Berger, P. L., & Luckmann, T. (1991). *The social construction of reality: A treatise in the sociology of knowledge*. London, United Kingdom: Penguin Books.

Blum, L. (2007) Mother-blame in the prozac nation: Raising kids with invisible disabilities. *Gender & Society,* 21(2), 202-226.

Braginski, D., & Braginski, B. (1971). *Hansels and Gretels.* New York, NY: Holt, Reinhart & Winston.

Bremer, C. D., Kachgal, M., & Schoeller, K. (April 2003). Self-determination: Supporting successful transition (Research to Practice Brief, Vol. 2, Issue 1). Minneapolis, MN: National Center on Secondary Education and Transition.

Child find, 34 C.F.R. § 300.111 (2012).

Child with a disability, 34 C.F.R. § 300.8 (2017).

Cimera, R. E., Burgess, S., & Bedesem, P. L. (2014). Does providing transition services by age 14 produce better vocational outcomes for students with intellectual disability? *Research and Practice for Persons with Severe Disabilities,* 39(1), 47-54.

Cimera, R. E., Burgess, S., & Wiley, A. (2013). Does providing transition services early enable students with ASD to achieve better vocational outcomes as adults? *Research and Practice for Persons with Severe Disabilities,* 38, 88-93.

Colker, R. (2015). Blaming mothers: A disability perspective. *Boston University Law Review,* 95(3), 1205-1224.

Cook, B. G., & Odom, S. L. (2013). Evidence-based practices and implementation science in special education. *Exceptional Children,* 79(2), 135-144.

Definition of individualized education program, 34 C.F.R. § 300.320 (2006).

Education of all Handicapped Children Act of 1975, Pub. L. No. 94-142, 20 U.S.C. § 1401 (1975).

Endrew F. v. Douglas County School District, 137 S.Ct. 988 (2017).

Every Student Succeeds Act of 2015, Pub. L. No. 114-95, 20 U.S.C. § 1601 *et seq.* (2015).

Hendrick Hudson District Board of Education v. Rowley, 458 U.S. 176, 102 S. Ct. 3034, 73 L. Ed. 2d 690 (1982).

IEP team, 34 C.F.R. § 300.321 (2006).

Individuals with Disabilities Education Act Amendments of 1997, Pub. L. No. 105-17, 20 U.S.C. § 1400 *et seq.* (1997).

Individuals with Disabilities Education Act of 1990, Pub. L. No. 101-476, 20 U.S.C. § 1400 *et seq.* (1990).

Individuals with Disabilities Education Act of 2004, Pub. L. No. 108-446, 20 U.S.C. § 1400 *et seq.* (2004).

IRIS Center. (n.d.). Evidence-Based Practices (Part 1): Identifying and Selecting a Practice or Program. Retrieved from https://iris.peabody.vanderbilt.edu/module/ebp_01/

Kohler, P. D., Gothberg, J. E., Fowler, C., & Coyle, J. (2016). Taxonomy for transition programming 2.0: A model for planning, organizing and evaluating transition education, services, and programs. Western Michigan University. Retrieved from http://www.transitionta.org/

Lalvani, P. (2015). Disability, stigma and otherness: Perspectives of parents and teachers. *International Journal of Disability, Development and Education,* 62(4), 379-393.

Mazzotti, V. L., Rowe, D. A., Cameto, R., Test, D. W., & Morningstar, M. E. (2013). Identifying and promoting transition evidence-based practices and predictors of success: A position paper of the division on career development and transition. Career Development and Transition for Exceptional Individuals, 36(3), 140-151. https://doi.org/10.1177/2165143413503365s

M. C. and G. C., on Behalf of Their Son, J. C. v. Central Regional School District, 108 Ed. Law Rep. 522 (3rd Cir. 1996).

McCord, W. T. (1983). The outcome of normalization: Strengthened bonds between handicapped persons and their communities. *Education and Training of the Mentally Retarded,* 18(3), 153-157.

Mutua, N. K. (2001). Policied identities: Children with disabilities. *Educational Studies,* 32(3), 289-300.

No Child Left Behind Act of 2001, Pub. L. No. 107–110, 20 U.S.C. § 6319 (2001).

Oliver, M., & Barnes, C. (2012). *The new politics of disablement.* New York, NY: Palgrave Macmillan.

Parent, 34 C.F.R. § 300.30 (2012).

Philbin, K. M. (2009). Do students with disabilities successfully transition into the work force or postsecondary education? *Education Masters.* Paper 288. Retrieved from https://core.ac.uk/download/pdf/48616879.pdf

The President's Commission on Excellence in Special Education: Hearing before the Committee on Health, Education, Labor, and Pensions, United States Senate, One Hundred Seventh Congress, second session on examining recommendations of the President's Commission on Excellence in Special Education regarding the Individuals with Disabilities Act of 1997 (IDEA), July 9, 2002. (2003). Washington: U.S. G.P.O.: For sale by the Supt. of Docs., U.S. G.P.O., [Congressional Sales Office], 2003. Retrieved from http://search.ebscohost.com.ezproxy.sju.edu/login.aspx?direct=true&db=edsgpr&AN=edsgpr.000549299&site=eds-live

Rubin, H. J., & Rubin, I. S. (2005). *Qualitative Interviewing: The Art of Hearing Data* (2nd ed.). Thousand Oaks, CA: Sage Publications.

Test, D. W., Mazzotti, V. L., Mustian, A. L., Fowler, C. H., Kortering, L., & Kohler, P. (2009). Evidence-based secondary transition predictors for improving postschool outcomes for students with disabilities. *Career Development for Exceptional Individuals,* 32(3), 160-181.

Thompson, B., Diamond, K. E., McWilliam, R., Snyder, P., & Snyder, S. W. (2005). Evaluating the quality of evidence from correlational research for evidence-based practice. *Exceptional Children,* 71(2), 181-194.

Thompson R2-J School District v. Luke P., et al., 540 F.3d 1143 (10th Cir. 2008).

Transfer of parental rights at the age of majority, 34 C.F.R. § 300.520 (2011).

Transition services, 34 C.F.R. § 300.43 (2012).

Wehmeyer, M., & Webb, K. W. (Eds.). (2012). *Handbook of adolescent transition education for youth with disabilities.* New York, NY: Routledge.

Wolfensberger, W. (1980) The definition of normalization: Update, problems, disagreements and misunderstandings. In R. J. Flynn & K. E. Nitsch (Eds.), *Normalization, social integration and community services.* Baltimore, MD: University Park Press.

Wolfensberger, W. P., Nirje, B., Olshansky, S., Perske, R., & Roos, P. (1972). *Normalization: The principle of normalization in human services.* Toronto, Canada: National Institue on Mental Retardation.

Yeh, M. A., Jewell, R. D., & Thomas, V. L. (2017). The stigma of mental illness: Using segmentation for social change. *Journal of Public Policy & Marketing, 36*(1), 97-116.

Part 2

Transition Planning Practices

An Interactive Framework of Activities Focusing on Community Access, Student Engagement, and Post-School Goals Selection

OVERVIEW OF THE TRANSITION PLANNING FRAMEWORK

Transition planning requires a global viewpoint about how to proceed. The transition planning specialist must be able to communicate transition planning goals when working with individual students, groups of students, and their parents. In collaboration with families, community members, organizations, and students, the transition planning process provides resources that help students develop needed skills over time (Kohler, Gothberg, Fowler, & Coyle, 2016). The components of the

Rae, J. M. *A Collaborative Approach to Transition Planning for Students With Disabilities* (pp. 27-46).
© 2020 SLACK Incorporated.

transition planning framework, when implemented during late middle school and secondary school, guide and educate students to choose goals and complete the multiple steps to prepare them for post-school life.

Curriculum-based instructional activities are the first student transition activities that lay the groundwork for students to play an integral part in developing their post-school plans. Therefore, the transition planning specialist and the special education team choose an up-to-date transition-based curriculum, instructional activities, and foundational lessons that focus on career exploration, as well as related courses of study, in-school assignments, and activities to build interaction skills. In concert with parents, they plan activities that increase self-responsibility and future autonomy in adult relationships.

As part of the framework goals and to the greatest extent possible, students of transition age are expected to participate in their IEP meetings whenever transition is discussed. Students need instruction and practice to participate, and the transition planning specialist works with IEP team members to educate students about their new role as an IEP team member in transition plan development. The transition planning specialist, as part of the special education team, plans instruction to guide each student to understand the role he or she will play as the primary person who will determine what his or her needs and preferences may be for adult life.

As part of a transition framework, the transition planning specialist meets with the parents and the student through a series of trainings and scheduled conferences to ascertain the student's preferences, family constraints, strengths, and needs.

To prepare for face-to-face trainings and conferences, communication tools, age-appropriate assessments, parent and student introductory letters, and questionnaires are the initial steps in creating a transition plan. From these tools, an outline of needs helps the student design goals for initial and subsequent transition plans, which include activities and instruction.

Teaching students about the process of transition planning "is the fundamental basis of education that guides development of students' educational programs—including strategies that keep them in school—rather than an 'add-on' activity for students with disabilities when they turn age 14 or 16" (Kohler et al., 2016, p. 1).

Students benefit from the transition framework and the continuum of planned instructional activities, which, when individualized per the student's preferences, underlie the creation of measurable goals in four primary skill development areas: (1) in-school and post-school education, (2) entry-level employment, (3) independent living, and (4) interaction skills.

The following framework guides how the transition planning process progresses and divides the framework components into a system of "gates." It is a process that extends over 5 years, so although the process may appear daunting, in practice it can be accomplished.

A FRAMEWORK OF TRANSITION ACTIVITIES

Gate 1, Part 1: An Introduction to the Student

The following is a list of communication tools and introductory lessons that should be part of the introduction process.

1. Letter of introduction
2. Invitation to transition planning training
3. Group orientation for transition planning overview: Its basis in special education and civil rights law
4. PowerPoint presentation about the goals of transition planning in the IEP

5. PowerPoint presentation about the student and the transition planning team
6. Group instruction on self-determination: What is it?
7. Group instruction on person-centered planning (PCP): What is it and how is it done?
8. Group instruction on advocacy training: Special education and civil rights law
9. Group instruction on self-monitoring
10. Group instruction on choice making and goal writing for the future
11. Group instruction on talking about goals: Student-teacher role-playing activities
12. Group instruction on the importance of IEP meeting attendance
13. Group social skills development: Guidelines for group activities
    a. Curriculum-based skills for conflict resolution and social interactions
    b. Career curriculum: Ongoing presentations on jobs
    c. Independence skills
    d. Health, mental health, and safety skills
14. Writing the disability narrative: Students learn about their own and others' disabilities and finally write their own narrative for the IEP on how their disability affects them academically, socially, physically, or in any other ways.

Gate 1, Part 2: Learning About Transition Planning and the Individualized Education Plan

In the second phase of Gate 1, group activities are meant to teach students the entire process of writing an IEP by using a hypothetical student or themselves. In this group of activities, teachers/transition planning specialists work with the students in small groups to create an IEP for their hypothetical classmate with a disability. These activities are also meant to instruct students in goal selection and construction.

1. Group instruction: Introducing the IEP meeting
2. The transition planning IEP: Why is the student involved?
3. Group instruction on the IEP documents
4. Group instruction and discussion: Parent-teacher-student collaboration: How can parents help?
5. Working with your parents to reach your goals or working independently with the transition planning specialist
6. Writing a practice IEP with transition goals
7. Developing goals for a hypothetical student
8. Drafting a mock IEP
9. Drafting a meeting agenda checklist
10. Meeting format
11. Mock IEP practice session with peers

Gate 2: Introducing Parents to Transition Planning

In Gate 2, the steps to introducing parents to transition planning are shown. (Chapter 4 addresses working with parents during transition planning.)

1. Parent invitation to transition introduction training (based on level of support student needs to participate in the IEP meeting [see Chapter 4])
2. Introductory meeting and PowerPoint presentation on the transition process

3. Introduction to assessments and post-school goals
4. Guidance and support to the parent
5. Explanation of the types of student participation
   a. Input only
   b. Partial participation: They are at the meeting but only observe, and teachers, family, and friends provide observed preferences
   c. Supported participation: They attend part of the meeting and need support to share preferences
   d. Full participation: They share about their disability and their goals and interests, and they lead the meeting
      i. Transition planning meeting and student leadership: A culminating goal for self-determination
6. Parent training in the preceding four types, including ways to encourage students to attend and voice their preferences, hopes, and dreams
7. Parental instruction: Self-determination and PCP
8. Sample letter to prepare parents for the legally required invitation
9. Introducing parents to post-school support agencies

Gate 3: Action Planning and the Individual Health Care Plan

Gate 3 is the development of an Individual Health Care Plan (IHP). Whether a student has an active medical condition or not, attention to medical care is essential for success in post-school life. In Chapter 4, the management of common types of medical conditions and the development of an IHP are discussed.

Gate 4: Transition Planning Assessments

In Gate 4, students learn about the assessments that will help them set goals for transition. The transition planning specialist or school psychologist can interpret relevant assessment scores, and students can collaborate with the transition planning specialist and self-select initial academic, independence, career, social, and behavioral goals.

Later, using follow-up assessments and checklists, students can see if their IEP translated into increased reading and math levels; increased self-determination, self-advocacy, and autonomy; more access to social and community experiences both in school and out; and more independence in the activities of daily living.

The assessments are also the basis for eligibility to adult services that students may need in adulthood. If students are not progressing but are maintaining skills, this will need to be addressed in teacher-student conferences, and action will be initiated to change this course. The types of assessments are discussed in Chapter 6.

Student Assessment Battery

- Formal assessments
  - Receptive language assessment
  - Expressive language assessment
  - Behavioral assessment
  - Reading grade-level attainment
  - Math grade-level attainment

- Informal assessments
  - Self-determination assessment
  - Self-advocacy assessment
  - Career interests assessment: Accessible to all students with disabilities
  - Behavioral needs interview: Student self-assessment of needs
  - Temperament inventories and instruments
  - Social assessment: Student self-assessment
  - Student preference assessment
  - Environmental inventory: Student self-assessment
  - Observational assessment
  - Adaptive behavior/daily living skills
  - Related services assessment
  - Additional remediation student preferred

Gate 5: Creating Measurable Goals: The Individualized Education Plan and Transition

Using Gate 1 (instructional tasks), Gate 2 (parent involvement tasks), Gate 3 (personal health care tasks), Gate 4 (assessment information), and Gate 6 (conferencing), the student will create goals with the transition planning specialist and keep a record of completion of those goals using a checklist format. In Chapter 7, concrete examples demonstrate how to create measurable goals from each gate using the student's preferences, strengths, and needs. Also, in Gate 6, goals will be more schedule based and revolve around actions rather than the skill development tasks used in Gates 1 through 5.

Gate 6: Conferencing in Transition Planning Is a Longitudinal and Action-Based Planning Process

Throughout the transition planning process, the transition planning specialist regularly schedules individual transition planning conferences. It is during these conferences that assessments, preferences, and more personal needs are discussed, IEP content is reviewed, current goal progress is reviewed, and future efforts are provided with supports as needed. Students should know who their transition planning specialist is and have a schedule of meetings planned. Conferences with the transition planning specialist are described in detail in Chapter 10. The following is a general overview of the topics discussed during the student and transition planning specialist conferences.

Planning for Post-School Life: Discussing Independent Living and Post-School Goals

CONFERENCE 1 EXAMPLE

- Student reflections: Preparing for the future. Surveys, questionnaires, and a personal disability narrative explaining the student's experiences as follows:
  - School experiences
    - Academic: Course of study
    - Student preferences: Use questionnaire (See Chapter 10 on how to interview in the conference setting.)
    - Social skills
    - Disability experiences
    - Medical care awareness and planning

- Cultural and family of origin considerations addressed
- Current and possible post-school directions

CONFERENCE 2 EXAMPLE

- Supports needed: Community-based experiences
- Community living choices and goals
  - Developing leisure activities
  - Developing independence skills
  - School-based activities
  - Navigating financial considerations: Social Security Administration and waivers
  - Financial instruction and goals
  - Using community-based instruction (CBI)
  - Community access: Paratransit and using public transportation
  - Training in the community
  - Making connections: Office of Vocational Rehabilitation
  - Company training programs
  - Disability specific support agencies

CONFERENCE 3 EXAMPLE

- Upcoming goals, activities, and directions: Longitudinal data collection
  - Academic assessment: Yearly
  - Behavioral assessments (student self-assessment): Yearly
  - Social assessments (student self-assessment): Yearly
  - Student preference assessment: Yearly
  - Environmental inventory (student self-assessment): Yearly
  - Physical environment needs, school, and community: Yearly

Gate 7: Communication: Maintaining Student Conference Records

The transition planning specialist alerts the student, team, and parents to the schedule of conferences, trainings, and assessments. The transition planning specialist reviews the activities of transition and how they will be carried out over the school year. Transition events should be posted and shared on a school-based transition website and in hard copy form, should be posted on a school bulletin board, and should be made available to the student.

Respecting the student's need for notice is addressed by scheduling dates in advance and informing the student of changes to the meetings in a timely fashion. If rescheduling is needed, it should be done at the time of cancellation. At each conference, records are reviewed and updated, and the transition planning specialist and student can make comments. Records are for determining the completeness of planning for each student.

Gate 8: Implementation of Career Action Plans

How a student will be prepared for a career is the focus of Gate 8 (also see Chapter 7). There are multiple pathways that address training, internships, job trials, intensive training, and integrated and entry-level employment.

Gate 9: Action Plan: Teacher Self-Assessment and Student Perspectives About Transition Planning

Gate 9 addresses whether the activities of transition were completed. In this gate, the transition planning specialist and the secondary special education team review the data from pending graduates to determine whether the students are meeting their transition plan goals and whether all gates were completed. A series of questions, discussed in Chapter 18, asks students to evaluate whether they reached their goals, what else they may need, and what recommendations they would suggest that may help future students with disabilities.

Gate 10: Permission for and Follow-Up on Post-School Outcomes: Indicators 13 and 14

Gate 10 addresses federal evaluation Indicators 13 and 14, which include a series of questions that the federal government asks to determine the effectiveness of transition planning.

Each school district, typically via the special education transition team, follows up with students 1 year post-graduation to see if the transition plan resulted in employment, greater independence, post-school education, and greater community involvement and whether the IEP helped students meet their postsecondary goals.

Upon reviewing Gates 1 through 8, it is evident that the preferences and perspectives of the student must be included. Attention to the student as a unique individual is a deliberate plan to guide transition planning specialists and secondary special education teams to be instrumental in not just teaching what self-determination, self-advocacy, and independence are, but also giving the student the playing field to develop these skills in real-life scenarios. Developing these characteristics and adult skills through practice places students in a better position to find post-school satisfaction and opportunities for inclusion.

Participation in the activities of transition will vary based on the unique disability, needs, and preferences of an individual student. Throughout this text, the degree of participation and how to make the transition planning process available to all students is described. Even for the most significantly disabled, giving opportunities to increase self-determination and participate in transition planning is of primary importance.

Summary of the Gates

The preceding sections gave an overview of the 10 gates. Each gate includes activities that combine to create a framework for the transition plan. Gates 1 through 4 include instruction about transition planning, developing personal characteristics and skills that are predictors of success, including and involving parents, developing knowledge of and managing health care needs, and using assessments to guide students about their strengths and needs. In Gates 4 and 5, students learn to create measurable goals and participate in a system of self-monitoring. In Gates 7 and 8, students meet with the transition planning specialist and discuss progress, changes, and additions to the plan; plan to practice and self-assess skills; and explore interests, careers, and entry-level and long-term employment options, community agency supports, and the related educational pathways to each. An action plan is developed for entry-level employment, long-range educational plans, and community inclusion. Finally, in Gates 9 and 10, students and the transition planning specialist review the effectiveness of the transition planning activities and the process. In the following section, the component parts of Gates 1 through 10 are described.

COMPONENTS OF TRANSITION PLANNING AND PREDICTORS OF POST-SCHOOL SUCCESS

Self-Determination and Self-Advocacy

Thinking about and acting on one's plans by creating and accomplishing goals is crucial to post-school success. One of the most proposed personal characteristics students will need for post-school success is the development of self-determination. The theoretical assumption behind student participation in transition planning and the IEP meeting is that being part of the process enhances the student's ability to assume some responsibility for his or her future, thereby facilitating the transition from the school community to inclusion into the community at large (Wehmeyer & Schwartz, 1998).

Self-determination theory is a theory involving the development of intrinsic motivation and the problem of amotivation. In self-determination theory it is posited that if the activity is not integrated into the person's sense of self, motivation does not occur. The theory also focuses on types, rather than just amounts of motivation, paying particular attention to autonomous motivation and controlled motivation as predictors of motivated action, performance, relational and well-being outcomes (Deci & Ryan, 1985).

According to Deci and Ryan (2008), self-determination also addresses the social conditions that enhance vs. diminish motivation, and they propose a finding that the degrees to which basic psychological needs for autonomy, competence, and relatedness are supported vs. thwarted needs affect both the type and strength of motivation. Self-determination theory also examines people's life goals or aspirations, showing differential relations of intrinsic vs. extrinsic life goals to performance and psychological health, with intrinsic motivation being related to psychological health (Deci & Ryan, 2008, p. 183).

In the social context of transition planning, the activities of transition integrate the student into a process where they are guided to be autonomous and accomplish their goals. When goal accomplishment is supported the individual develops an increase in self-determined action. "In other words, when the social context," such as the transition planning process, "supports autonomy, the level of people's identified and integrated motivation for the target activity or domain will increase" (Gagné & Deci, 2005). Transition planning success depends upon the ability of the team to facilitate the student's success, by providing experiences that foster self-determination.

Developing Self-Determination

Self-determination is gained via the development of a set of component elements of self-determined behavior, including simple choice making; more complex decision making; problem solving, goal setting, and task performance; self-observation, evaluation, and self-reward; developing an internal locus of control; positive attributions of efficacy and outcome expectancy; and self-awareness and self-knowledge. Being able to develop and use these skills can be learned during the transition planning years.

Additional skills and personal characteristics support improved post-school outcomes, and other researchers have seen other success-related skills manifested by acquiring self-determined behavior. Ryan and Deci (2013) assert that self-determination theory proposes three basic psychological needs—autonomy, competence, and relatedness—that are being fulfilled via the social context, and they are essential for optimal growth and functioning for all humans throughout their lifespan. The primary psychological need, autonomy, is defined as freedom from external control or influence (i.e., independence). Self-determination theory researchers differentiate autonomous behaviors, which are internally motivated by a sense of volition, from controlled behaviors, which are externally motivated often through a sense of obligation, pressure, or anticipated rewards (Vansteenkiste, Zhou, Lens, & Soenens, 2005). It is worthy of note, however, that persons can be self-determined even when acting in accord with an external demand, provided "the person fully concurs with or endorses doing so" (Ryan & Deci, 2006, p. 1560).

Rowe et al. (2014) add an additional construct for self-determination that is important to address during the adolescent years: awareness of and acceptance of the consequences of one's choices.

Adolescents who are beginning to make decisions can benefit from ongoing guidance about the possible unintended consequences of decisions when they make decisions without carefully examining possible outcomes. Poor decisions can derail all positive outcomes and must be an essential part of transition planning within the context of the decision-making activities.

Self-Determination, Culture, and Family

Family support and the need for autonomy and self-determination are not exclusive to one culture, regardless of whether a person lives in an individualistic vs. collectivistic or vertical vs. horizontal society; if that person acts autonomously, in accordance with his or her values, he or she is likely to experience a greater sense of well-being (Wichmann, 2011). Typically, cultural differences reflect a difference in perspectives and needs, but the quest for autonomy is shared.

Parents play a primary role in either supporting autonomy or not. Their attention to their child's need for autonomy will support the child's feelings of competence and relatedness (Ryan & Deci, 2013). Some parents do not support the autonomy of their adolescent, and self-determination theory asserts that unless the parenting approach provides empathy, a rationale, and choice and minimizes the use of controlling parenting techniques, the adolescent has difficulty dysregulating emotions (Ryan & Deci, 2006). Chapter 3 of this text discusses how to be part of a collaborative team with parents when facilitating their child's independence.

Self-Determination, Autonomy, and Self-Advocacy: Dependence to Independence

During the elementary and middle school years, IEP goals are selected by a team of professionals who scrutinize all areas of a child's weaknesses and strengths and then develop goals based on the weaknesses. Information is collected from all the team members about the child. The child has no control over any of the contents of an IEP, nor does the child have a say in what he or she is expected to do. During transition planning, this approach is expected to change, and, for the first time, young persons with disabilities are asked what they want to do. When the student is included in IEP decisions, there is now an opportunity for the child to develop a sense of volition by internal values (i.e., what the child thinks) instead of through coercion or pressure (i.e., what the adults think; Grolnick & Raftery-Helmer, 2013).

In addition, the natural life course for any adolescent is that parents begin to shift more responsibility onto the child. Within the context of IEP development and with adult guidance, the IEP meeting is a structured place for young people with disabilities to begin to assert goals of their own. Commencement of transition planning at the age of 14 helps the development of self-determination because there are a few years ahead to learn to make choices, share perspectives and preferences, and develop needed young adult skills.

Through the process of transition planning, making these steps with a supportive group of adults can inspire a student's confidence as he or she takes those first unsteady steps toward independence. For students with disabilities to grow into adults who can successfully function in society, secondary school educators, such as the transition planning specialist, are needed to guide and encourage students along the continuum of instructional activities and provide in-school services that prepare them to meet the challenges of adult living. Without the support of the transition planning specialist, adolescents with disabilities and additional family constraints will have few supports to help them move toward self-determination, competence, independence, and satisfactory life outcomes.

Self-Determination Through Person-Centered Planning

Some students with disabilities will not be called upon to make multiple autonomous decisions. They will, however, be able to participate in selecting their preferences and activities to give them more say in their own lives. PCP was designed for students with moderate to profound intellectual disabilities and with autism, intellectual disabilities, and communication disabilities. Students with moderate intellectual disabilities can participate in more advanced transition planning activities, and this can be determined individually. The assessment gives the transition planning specialist a better idea of hidden safety and disability severity needs that would place the student within the PCP structure.

Students with severe, multiple, or profound intellectual disabilities also have a framework for transition, and the process has the same legal requirements. However, differentiated modes of participation are used based on the needs of students with severe disabilities (Browder, 2011).

Students with the most severe intellectual and communication disabilities can participate in the transition planning process, even if they only contribute their preferences. This type of participation is known as *partial participation,* and students are involved in some or many but not all parts of IEP development and transition planning activities. For instance, there are several ways to increase self-determination and involve a student with severe to profound intellectual disabilities and autism, who are typically also nonverbal. Test et al. (2004) conducted a review of the literature to investigate interventions designed to increase students' involvement in their IEP planning processes. Findings showed that students with widely varying disabilities have been able to demonstrate active involvement in their IEP planning. Rowe et al. (2014) includes ensuring all students, including those with significant disabilities, have a functional communication system to engage in decision making, problem solving, goal setting, taking the initiative to reach goals, and accepting the consequences for one's actions.

According to Arndt, Konrad, and Test (2006), participation in the planning process of an IEP meeting can be to suggest making a list of the student's preferences. There several ways to determine student preferences. The teacher can compile a list based on previous experiences with the student, interview past teachers, or use a systematic preference assessment. Creating a visual representation of student preferences using a picture-based system can help the student communicate. In this way, the transition planning specialist can determine the student's wants and needs and include them in the transition IEP.

In a review of the literature on IEP participation, Kelley, Bartholomew, and Test (2013) indicated that both published curricula and PCP strategies are effective ways to increase students' involvement in their IEP meetings.

The practice of fostering the development of student leadership skills by including students as active participants in developing the IEP plans and teaching them how to be engaged in IEP development during transition planning underpins the development of self-determination (Rowe et al., 2014).

STUDENT ENGAGEMENT IN TRANSITION PLANNING

Individualized Education Plans Versus Individualized Education Plans With Transition Plans

The approach to IEP development, as discussed in Chapter 1, is based on a medical model with medical model perspectives on disability as biologically defined (Lalvani, 2015). This approach is diagnostic and then prescriptive. IEPs are developed based on the following conditions: after the initial evaluation, after required periodic reevaluations, and annually.

The student does not attend or participate in IEP development, and the leader of the IEP team is a special education teacher, or, during secondary school, the transition planning specialist can lead as well. Other related services staff are team members, and based on the student's eligibility for services, these may include a speech therapist, an occupational therapist, and/or a physical therapist.

Each professional working with the student reviews current and previous assessments, which reveal the student's strengths, needs, and growth areas. Then, the IEP team members decide the goals that will go into each IEP. The parents can also add goals for the student to meet.

This approach does not involve the student, either in the meeting or in the decision making. Children under age 13 generally would not understand the IEP process unless someone explained it. However, there is no obligation for anyone to do so prior to the decision to discuss transition planning. By age 13, preparation for inclusion in transition planning should begin by including the student. This requires interactions between the transition planning specialist, the student, and the student's family to participate in the process together. An example of an interactive transition planning approach is discussed in the following case report about Sam, provided to demonstrate how giving leadership to the student can be difficult even when all the components of a quality transition plan have been implemented. The following section begins with a novice transition planning specialist's story about a transition plan that did not work out as envisioned, even though the plan was developed with fidelity using all evidence-based practices of a transition framework.

The student in this story was the center of the transition process. The transition plan facilitated the student along a path to reach his post-school goals. The transition plan framework followed legislative guidelines and included the required components of the transition plan, including a course of study, career exploration, social skills development, ongoing assessment for progress monitoring for a language-based learning disability, employment skills development, and instruction on how to participate in an interview. However, the initial employment plan failed, and the student advocated for himself, self-determining his outcome despite the model plan his transition planning specialist had envisioned.

Case Report: Sam

Sam was in a class for students with mental health disorders. The program fell under the Individuals with Disabilities Education Act (IDEA, 2004) and was for students determined to have an emotional disturbance. Sam was shy and withdrawn and had depression, a learning disability, a reading level of sixth grade by the time of graduation, and an average intelligent quotient score. He did not have an intellectual disability, and his disturbance was that he was depressed and had a school elopement history. He rarely spoke after his placement in a program, and when he did, he was so soft-spoken it was difficult to hear him, and he had difficulty expressing his thoughts. Even with these disabilities, he was calm and caring with his peers. He never acted out in any way in this setting but was known to walk out of his general education classes when he was unable to do the work. The school staff viewed him as hostile and possibly a threat to school safety.

Sam's classroom location was at a behavioral health facility; he spent 2 years there. His transition planning specialist there was also his teacher. Sam had a longitudinal plan for transition. This plan included a series of teacher-student and teacher-parent conferences to develop a framework for his transition to adulthood. Sam had an academic course of study (although modified so he could also address his significant emotional needs), participated in a career exploration curriculum, learned social and behavioral strategies, and participated in ongoing language-based assessments. He explored careers and employment settings, visited vocational technical schools and colleges, worked on interpersonal interaction goals, worked on passing his driver's permit test, and had learned to dress for an interview, as well as how to interact during an interview. By 12th grade, he was feeling better about himself. He was feeling the confidence he needed to work; he wanted to work. He had decided against additional training.

One of Sam's abilities was strong organizational skills. He often volunteered to organize the various staff areas around the building, most noticeably the storage areas of his teacher. His teacher allowed him to do this during his lunch breaks. He had a remarkable skill and a mind for organization. Everything he did had a logic to it that added to classroom management. Based on the IEP team's observations of his skills, there were many workplace niches that Sam fit. He was given vocational assessments that also supported the view the teachers held that he had the skills to work in an office. The team found Sam several office and office supply store positions. He selected a position in a local office supply company. However, he quit within 2 weeks, apologizing and saying that it was not for him.

His transition planning specialist, who was also his special education teacher for part of the day, was very disappointed and began suggesting other options, thought to be perfect. Then, given the earlier failure of the work placement, the transition planning specialist reconsidered making any more suggestions and decided to conference with Sam again, deciding to ask more in-depth questions about why he left the position rather than what he should try next. Upon reflection, the transition planning conferences had fallen short of bringing Sam in as a full participant who could self-determine his life course. The transition planning specialist realized that it was the team's ideas that were the basis of the plan, not Sam's ideas. The transition planning specialist was still caught in the medical model, observing, assessing, and telling Sam what he could and should do.

By playing the role of teacher and IEP team member who assessed and prescribed, the transition planning specialist and the IEP team continued to act toward Sam in the way a teacher acts toward a younger student. Instead of listening to what he truly wanted, the transition planning specialist looked at his abilities and assessments and guided his goals and his employment. Sam did not share what he felt he would or could do for his workforce entry employment.

Sam's transition planning specialist invited him to a follow-up conference. During the conference, Sam reported that he did not want to work with people. He said he did not understand people, and the negative infighting he saw in his first 2 weeks on the job reinforced this perspective.

This, of course, led to some concern. What kind of job does not involve people? Sam also shared his desire to travel, and he could not see how that would be possible with the job he had due to the wages and scheduling. He wanted to travel now. His teacher could not envision what type of employment would have no people and enable travel. Then she asked if he had any idea of such a job. He said yes, but he did not think his teacher/transition planning specialist would like the job he thought would give him what he wanted. His transition planning specialist was able to encourage him to share his thoughts, willing herself to listen without judgment of any kind. Sam explained that there was a bus company near him. He said that he had heard that at night they have workers who clean the buses. He said that being a cleaning person was the part he thought the team would not like. So, instead of saying anything about this, the transition planning specialist asked what else he liked about the job. He reported that he would be in the buses alone at night, even though a few other workers would also be there. It would be quiet, and that quiet was essential to him. He also said the employees received substantial discounts on bus tickets because it was a travel bus company.

His vital work finding something he wanted and determining his own future had developed his ability to determine what was right for him and to advocate for it. The transition planning specialist's vision for Sam was based on a personal perspective about what he could do, without understanding how his mental health, learning disability, and personal dreams would ultimately determine his actions. The transition planning specialist's push for an outcome she determined could have derailed his self-determination. Even though the transition planning specialist had taught the class how to self-advocate, she had made it difficult for Sam to do so. She had somehow communicated, without explicitly stating it, a personal preference for Sam's employment. Sam perceived that the job he preferred was not one that would ever have been offered as an option by his transition planning specialist, perhaps because of a general bias against maintenance professions.

Because of this transition planning relationship, the transition planning specialist saw the essence of self-determination. The student's preferences, skills, wants, needs, and emotional, social, and communication skills are the drivers for developing a successful transition plan.

Sam asked the team for references and set up an interview. He was offered the position. He accepted it immediately because he wanted to conference with his transition planning specialist to find out if the salary and benefits would be enough to support himself. He described the position offered as he had reported earlier: the night shift cleaning the busses. The salary offered was $35,000 a year with health and education benefits and trip discounts. The insurance benefits would pay for his ongoing mental health care, and the education benefits would help him to take classes should he so desire, and of course he would be able to travel.

Exercise

1. Explore your thoughts about Sam's chosen path. Do you have value judgements about his path? Given the importance of employment and its relation to post-school success, does your personal experience provide students with enough knowledge about job options? What would you need to do to improve your knowledge of the current work marketplace for entry-level employment and post-school options?

Discussion

The transition planning specialist needed to redirect the focus from her ideas for Sam's success and refocus on Sam's perspective. Once she did this, he spoke more from his heart. He admitted that he became very nervous around people to the point of wanting to escape, just as he had in high school, and, after long periods of anxiety, his depression deepened. He felt battling the urge to escape would continually keep him in an upsetting psychological state while trying to work. He had been through many medication trials, and none had helped. So he knew himself and his disability, and he knew what he could and could not do. The quiet and calm shell that he kept about him in his current placement was how he needed to manage his life to decrease the negative impact of his mental health disorder. He also spoke more about the infighting at work. He reported that he was unable to interpret rapid conversational speech. Although his slow auditory language processing speed was noted in his multidisciplinary evaluation, the information was not analyzed by the team. Sam was able to apply it to a work situation where he would be unable to communicate using the normal pace of verbal directions and social interaction information. He felt his inability to process could be confusing and would limit his social acceptance, an experience from high school he did not want to repeat.

The transition planning specialist realized that language-based disabilities are a crucial factor in workplace success. His neurological development, anxiety about his verbal abilities, and depression required a job to match Sam's skills and needs. Also, only Sam could explain how his disabilities impacted him in the workplace. At age 19, armed with self-knowledge, self-advocacy, and self-determination, he became part of the adult world.

A significant underpinning of transition planning is that the student trust the transition planning specialist to listen and encourage the student to examine his or her wants and needs for transition. The student must also be able to report his or her own needs and feel safe doing so. It is hard to admit disabilities, such as mental health disabilities, which carry a significant public stigma and self-stigma (Corrigan, Larson, & Ruesch, 2009). If the transition planning specialist had continued to match Sam with job prospects based on what were positive perceptions of him, his career assessments, and his classroom performance, the team most likely would have seen him continually leave jobs, not because he could not work but because the team's evaluation of him did not adequately reflect his innermost hopes, dreams, strengths, and needs.

An IEP meeting followed Sam's job offer. The transition planning specialist needed to be present and supportive as he presented his plan to the team and the special education supervisor from his school district. He wrote a personal narrative about himself and how his disabilities affected him in school and at work, and this was put into his IEP to document his participation and encourage the team's acceptance of his goals. Sam wanted to work part-time until he graduated and then transition directly into full-time employment. The team and the school district supervisor of special education developed the last semester course of study and an attendance plan that supported Sam's choices. However, the work hours and sleep schedule change caused him to fall asleep in school. He asked to be able to move into full-time work and attend school 2 hours a day, earning the rest of his credits as work study. A revision to the IEP was developed, and he transitioned to full-time employment.

This enabled him to come to school in the afternoon. Sam graduated while employed full-time. He returned to his high school to walk at graduation. Sam had grown from a failing sophomore who repeatedly ran from the school building to a young man with a diploma and a job he enjoyed.

The following year, Sam returned to visit, and he wanted to show the team his new car. It was the same model and color as the transition planning specialist's car. He also shared his travels and his ability to help his family at home.

Sam's employment outcome gave him access to health care, post-school education, robust leisure activities, and the finances to be an adult member of the family. He was able to find pride in the activities of adult life and enjoy outings while having the money to do so.

Engaging the Parents

In Sam's planning, his father was unavailable, and his mother felt that at age 19 he was able to make his own decisions. She did attend the meetings, and after many years of contention over her son's marginalization at his school as a behavior problem, she was very grateful for the help provided by the transition team.

In Chapter 3, the development of a collaborative team, including the student, is discussed. Parents can be instrumental in facilitating the tasks needed for entry-level employment. In addition, many parents are resources for job experiences. When parents cannot be supports to their children, other options are planned.

Facilitating Community Access

Using a Transition Curriculum for Skill Development

To develop the overarching skills and related subskills needed for post-school success in the community at large, adolescents with disabilities will need direct instruction. The complex learning needs of students with disabilities preclude learning these skills easily or incidentally, as students without disabilities might.

Therefore, structured teaching modules, delivered via curriculum-based instructional programs and in a long-term framework, can form the basis of career education and adult life skills development, with implementation beginning during middle school. This curriculum-based foundational approach to transition planning is realistic given the expectations of transition services legislation and the needs of students with disabilities (Kohler et al., 2016).

Community-Based Instruction: Creating Community Connections

CBI is typically in the community. In this text, it can refer to both in-school and out-of-school activities, social interactions, educational and leisure activities, and cultural events that increase students' understanding of different environments and the diverse people they will meet. Community experiences are planned to increase the ability to work, learn, live, and play in multiple settings like peers and adults without disabilities.

Part of transition planning includes the use of CBI, which gives students with disabilities the chance to habituate to multiple out-of-school environments and to function within those environments for multiple purposes, such as work; maintaining survival skills, such as food shopping; and social and leisure activities. CBI is operationally defined as "activities occurring outside of the school setting, supported with in-class instruction, where students apply academic, social, and/or general work behaviors and skills" (Rowe et al., 2014, p. 120).

For example, the use of CBI is supported by classroom instruction to prepare for activities in the community. Please refer to Case Report: Donny and Dean in Chapter 15.

School-Based Transition Activities: Developing In-School Connections

Transition activities provide opportunities for students with disabilities to work in groups as they learn about their roles and responsibilities in the transition planning process. In this section, some subgoals are addressed, which can lead to more advanced functioning in the school and later in the workplace.

Some examples of preliminary skills are as follows:

- Participating in assignments of transition
- Interacting with a small group to complete transition group assignments
- Developing a planning process for the small group projects
- Developing pro-work habits such as strong school attendance records and average to above-average grades

These subgoals are foundational goals that will be needed in any workplace condition. When students are given a goal-setting task and successfully complete that task, they become more self-directed in their approach to work and may even become more interested in less desirable tasks. The effects of the development of competence, self-efficacy, and intrinsic interest are well-grounded in the research. As early as 1981, Bandura and Schunk replicated earlier studies and asserted that proximal subgoals are more motivating and sustain more interest than distal (faraway) goals. Therefore, taking students through a series of subgoals increases competence, and self-motivation will continue over time.

During middle and secondary school, peer relationships become more important and can have both positive and negative effects, especially when academic confidence is low (Ryan, 2001). Creating a cohesive student transition planning group, where members are connected to one another through the common theme of transition planning, can support the acquisition of skills and the completion of transition activities in a positive, socially constructed, interactive milieu.

Working on subgoals in social groups can support students in gaining competence within their peer groups when activities are planned and students are instructed on how to manage their group process. Careful attention is given to avoiding hierarchical group structures, which is negatively related to individual achievement (Wilson, Karimpour, & Rodkin, 2011).

The goal of all transition planning is not only that each student has knowledge, work, and social skills for employment but also that they have developed a number of prerequisite competencies that give them the competence they need to grow and learn new skills when needed in the world of work and within their social experiences.

CAREER EXPLORATIONS

As discussed in the previous section, an essential feature of employment is the ability to work with individuals or groups of people. The school setting is an excellent place to develop interaction skills. Therefore, when assigning career explorations, students work in groups. The group work develops social skills and knowledge of career options. Socialization activities, not social skills lessons, are a better fit for middle and high school students, who are drawn to their peers during this developmental period. Researching and familiarizing themselves with careers and entry-level jobs is a subgoal that undergirds later searches for an entry-level job. Developing social interaction skills is also crucial to finding an entry-level position. Establishing subgoals, such as expanding on career knowledge and career skill development, widens students' worldviews and their spheres of conversation.

In Sam's story, even though he ultimately chose a setting with few people, he had completed crucial subgoals and understood positive social interactions, such as how to job search, ask for job leads, and interview, as well as knowing to ask for the team's commentary when he wanted feedback about accepting the position.

There are many career curriculums for career awareness and career-based skill development. These programs must be reviewed often and updated. Use digital media and curricular materials that are less than 3 years old.

The Student Supplemental Materials has a list of current curricular materials.

Identifying and Exploring Careers

Career Curriculums

Career curriculums are used to introduce students to a wide variety of jobs. Career curriculums are available through publishers and special education organizations. The transition planning specialist should provide introductory sources that are both visual and auditory programs about employment. A continuum of internet links from the transition planning specialist should be designed to reveal a wide range of employment situations, not for selection but to widen employment vocabulary and educate students about what other people do for a living. By seeing what other people do, students can develop schemas of their interests.

Most students with disabilities need curricular programs that introduce them to careers. The transition plan requires a statement about curriculum and career explorations, as well as goals on social, academic, and job-seeking skills. The curriculum also includes life skills instruction, career and vocational skills, a career-based curriculum, ideas about structured work experiences, various assessments, and support services and plans for more intensive supports and placements.

Community Career Connections

Family members are also good sources of knowledge about various job experiences. Parents, for the most part, are in the world of work. Students can open a dialogue with their parents about work and workplace challenges. Early career explorations in their environment is a way for students to talk to their parents about jobs in the family.

Interviewing family members about their jobs is an interactive way for students to explore ideas and share what they learned with their peers. Students can be assigned people to interview within the school and out. In a small seminar group, presentations about the results of their interviews further extend social experiences with their peers. This type of shared experience is a subskill that develops social connections and gives students a framework with which to interact with adults and peers. The students can demonstrate their knowledge of careers and social interactions as well as organize their thoughts through the development of a PowerPoint presentation. Sharing their knowledge increases feelings of self-competency. The transition planning specialist and IEP team can develop a group of volunteer interviewees in the community. The transition planning specialist's tasks include gathering the appropriate people and resources to create a set of experiences and assignments.

Every community has a local tax collection structure. Those agencies have lists of businesses in the community. Students can actively research local businesses to find out what types of work environments are available in their local communities. Depending upon the degree of a student's disability and the family of origin structure, some students may want to stay in the local area.

Larger local companies may have multiple locations that could be of interest. Exploration assignments about company websites can provide multiple opportunities to expand the students' and the secondary transition team's connections. Knowledge of opportunities developed via planned activities develops multiple skills in research, organization, and oral presentations about those local companies.

Programs for Post-School Support

There are supported care programs for young adults with disabilities, such as Social Security and waivers. Supported employment will be detailed in the chapters which define the students who are eligible for these programs. Typically, the students most affected by severe disabilities are the young adults who are eligible. Navigating financial considerations for secondary transition will also be discussed in the sections on specific disabilities.

Community Living and Independent Adult Living Skills

Both students with disabilities and without disabilities need support to develop adult living skills and to practice and plan for adulthood. However, the impact of disability limits options for students with disadvantages, and multiple supports must be given to including students with disabilities. The school programs that are accessible to children and youth with disabilities are limited in comparison to the experiences afforded peers without disabilities. To develop social skills in school-age programs, participation is necessary, just as it is for other children and youth. After-school and community activities help students with disabilities be with friends and have the same social, community, and leisure activities that other students may take for granted. Choosing what they would like to do should begin during middle school.

By high school, some patterns of behavior and social groups have been established. Lack of social skills development decreases their comfort level in joining activities.

Adult living skills are necessary for full or partial independence, participation, and contribution to the family. It is crucial for the transition planning specialist to communicate with the parents about developing adult living skills both at home and at school.

The following is a detailed checklist of needed skills. Chapter 7 provides guidance on creating transition goals using these categories:

- Self-determination
- Self-care
- Organization
- Clothing care
- Medical care
- Financial management
- Cooking
- Maintaining the home's cleanliness
- Outside home maintenance
- Using multiple forms of transportation
- Accessing community services

Decision Making

Practicing decision making begins in school with curricular activities and participation in school activities that promote self-determination and social interactions. Out of these experiences, making choices begins the process of self-determination. Students with high-incidence disabilities often have difficulty organizing materials, reviewing options, and making selections. These challenges, as well as having other sensory and intellectual disabilities, require that planning for post-school life be within an organized framework of instructional activities for the teacher, students, parents, and faculty. Also, school and community activities and instruction are included in the framework and are specific to each student and his or her ability to participate. Therefore, decision making and goal selection require direct instruction for all students with disabilities.

Engaging Students in Making Choices and Selecting Goals: Writing Measurable Transition Goals

Students participate in the development of post-school goals, and transition planning specialists mentor students in the process of determining their goals for the future.

In the past, educators and families talked about the student rather than to the student, thus controlling all supports to address his or her disability. With the legislative direction in IDEA (2004), the student with a disability is now involved rather than a sidelined player. During adolescence, the previous strategy for adult–team member decision making becomes inappropriate for many adolescents with disabilities. Goal generation without the agreement of the student can fail to facilitate independence. The student, over the course of his or her school life, has relied on adults to help him or her succeed in school, and adults make most of the choices about his or her future.

If an adult-controlled approach to transition planning and IEP development continued, it could remove the student's ability to make the choices that will shape his or her future. In short, he or she has had no prior experience choosing goals and now must be given a chance to do so. He or she also must be taught how to participate and develop goals. The insistence of adults to maintain control of their child's choices can infantilize the child and make him or her overly dependent and ineffective in planning his or her life. Students with disabilities, like their peers, want autonomy. They see other students becoming independent, and they want to do that as well but lack the skills to make a self-determined action.

However, inviting students to plan and attend their IEP meetings without prerequisite skills will stymie participation. Attending the IEP meeting and having adults ask them about their wishes is a significant change in self-perception. Students know little about the IEP process or goal selection and construction. The lack of involvement and choice encourages passiveness about making choices for themselves. For example, when invited to the IEP meeting, one student said, "I don't go to that meeting; my mother does all that." This perspective can be overcome for students to reap the benefits from their involvement. Therefore, students should be included as early as possible so that they have time to develop the skills they will need to learn to set goals that are necessary to have satisfactory adult experiences.

Preparing for Entry-Level Employment

Entry-Level Jobs, Early Job Experiences, and Later Advances

Early job experiences provide social and work skills that students with disabilities need. The attitude of the transition planning specialist should be that of an explorer who, with the students, looks for a range of current options. As noted earlier in the chapter, the early part of the voyage starts with career exploration. The transition planning specialist works in multiple roles as a teacher, mentor, and guide who will explore options with the students. It is critical for the transition planning specialist to develop accurate listening and interview skills and a framework for decision making to help the student organize their thoughts while learning about various careers. They also must help students with disabilities to explore interests and glean a broader perspective. Additional knowledge of students' options and needs forms the basis of early employment experiences. By working to gain an in-depth understanding of the students, a transition planning specialist can mitigate unfounded perspectives on individual students and focus on the students' needs for postsecondary life.

Post-School Success

If all the components in each gate are completed, then the plan is constructed and carried out with fidelity, and it can be reasonably hoped that a post-school plan is in place. A follow-up review would determine whether the completion of the activities of transition led to employment, further education, and greater independence. The federal government uses two measures—Indicators 13 and 14—and the special education drop-out rate to determine the success of the transition planning process.

Throughout the rest of this text, details are provided on developing the transition planning specialist's skills and knowledge so that transition planning can be implemented effectively.

EXERCISES

1. Create a PowerPoint presentation on the concept of self-determination and its place in the research.

2. Interview a student with a disability. Have the student write or dictate a narrative for you to explain how the student thinks he or she learns best.

3. Do exercise 3 about yourself. Identify your and your student's strengths and needs. Use the information you find to write about yourself as if you have the disability you researched. Use your real family and home and place yourself in that setting as you write about your hypothetical disability, how it affects you, and what you will need to be independent in your activities, not necessarily your living situation. Suggestions: Tell your audience about how you see yourself in comparison to others. Tell how your hypothetical disability affects your schoolwork. Tell about the difficulties brought on by your temporary or permanent disability. Share your struggles with a classmate.

4. Describe the following: Agency invitation/participation, student invitation to IEP, age-appropriate assessment, post-secondary goals for education/training, employment, and independent living.

5. Explain why post-secondary goals are updated annually or sooner.

6. Describe a course of study.

7. Describe transition activities.

8. Write five measurable goals.

SUMMARY

The evidence-based activities described in this chapter can expand students' vision and determine what their lives could look like based on their knowledge of themselves; their skills; their preferences; and additional training, education, and community options for employment and leisure activities.

Under the guidance of the transition planning specialist and their parents (as able), students can learn to recognize the need for additional skills and training as they explore a career or post-school educational options. Research has supported that for post-school outcomes to be successful, students must not just have an active role but must be fully involved in determining a life plan. A self-determined life course is related directly to the sustained motivation to follow through on completing the activities needed to reach planned goals. This framework addresses comprehensive activities of transition planning and will help the transition planning specialist to form a conceptual structure for practice as well as a guide for implementation.

The transition planning specialist also needs a structure to document the provision of services and the adherence to special education transition law.

REFERENCES

Arndt, S. A., Konrad, M., & Test, D. W. (2006). Effects of the self-directed IEP on student participation in planning meetings. *Remedial and Special Education, 27*(4), 194-207.

Bandura, A., & Schunk, D. H. (1981). Cultivating competence, self-efficacy, and intrinsic interest through proximal self-motivation. *Journal of Personality and Social Psychology, 41*(3), 586.

Browder, D. M. (2011). *Teaching students with moderate and severe disabilities.* New York, NY: Guilford Press.

Corrigan, P. W., Larson, J. E., & Ruesch, N. (2009). Self-stigma and the "why try" effect: Impact on life goals and evidence-based practices. *World Psychiatry, 8*(2), 75-81.

Deci, E. L., & Ryan, R. M. (1985). Intrinsic motivation and self-determination in human behavior. New York, NY: Plenum.

Deci, E. L., & Ryan, R. M. (2008). Self-determination theory: A macrotheory of human motivation, development, and health. *Canadian Psychology/Psychologie Canadienne, 49*(3), 182-185.

Gagné, M., & Deci, E. L. (2005). Self-determination theory and work motivation. *Journal of Organizational behavior, 26*(4), 331-362.

Grolnick, W. S., & Raftery-Helmer, J. N. (2013). Facilitating autonomy in the family: Supporting intrinsic motivation and self-regulation. In B. W. Sokol, F. M. E. Grouzet, & U. Müller (Eds.), *Self-regulation and autonomy: Social and developmental dimensions of human conduct* (pp. 141-164). Cambridge, United Kingdom: Cambridge University Press.

Individuals with Disabilities Education Act of 2004, Pub. L. No. 108-446, 20 USC § 1400 *et seq.* (2004).

Kelley, K. R., Bartholomew, A., & Test, D. W. (2013). Effects of the self-directed IEP delivered using computer-assisted instruction on student participation in educational planning meetings. *Remedial and Special Education, 34*(2), 67-77.

Kohler, P. D., Gothberg, J. E., Fowler, C., & Coyle, J. (2016). Taxonomy for transition programming 2.0: A model for planning, organizing and evaluating transition education, services, and programs. Western Michigan University. Retrieved from http://www.transitionta.org/

Lalvani, P. (2015). Disability, stigma and otherness: Perspectives of parents and teachers. *International Journal of Disability, Development and Education, 62*(4), 379-393.

Rowe, D. A., Alverson, C. Y., Unruh, D. K., Fowler, C. H., Kellems, R., & Test, D. W. (2014). A Delphi study to operationalize evidence-based predictors in secondary transition. *Career Development and Transition for Exceptional Individuals, 38*(2), 113-126.

Ryan, A. M. (2001). The peer group as a context for the development of young adolescents' motivation and achievement. *Child Development, 72*, 1135-1150.

Ryan, R. M., & Deci, E. L. (2006). Self-regulation and the problem of human autonomy: Does psychology need choice, self-determination, and will? *Journal of Personality, 74*, 1557-1585. doi:10.1111/j.l467-6494.2006.00420.x

Ryan, R. M., & Deci, E. L. (2013). The importance of autonomy for development and well-being. In B. W. Sokol, F. M. E. Grouzet, & U. Müller (Eds.), *Self-regulation and autonomy: Social and developmental dimensions of human conduct* (pp. 19-46). Cambridge, United Kingdom: Cambridge University Press.

Test, D. W., Mason, C., Hughes, C., Konrad, M., Neale, M., & Wood, W. M. (2004). Student involvement in individualized education program meetings. *Exceptional Children, 70*, 391-412.

Vansteenkiste, M., Zhou, M., Lens, W., & Soenens, B. (2005). Experiences of autonomy and control among Chinese learners: Vitalizing or immobilizing? *Journal of Educational Psychology, 97*, 468-483.

Wehmeyer, M., & Schwartz, M. (1998). The relationship between self-determination and quality of life for adults with mental retardation. *Education and Training in Mental Retardation and Developmental Disabilities, 33*(1), 3-12.

Wichmann, S. S. (2011). Self-determination theory: The importance of autonomy to well-being across cultures. *Journal of Humanistic Counseling, 50*(1), 16-26.

Wilson, T., Karimpour, R., & Rodkin, P. C. (2011). African American and European American students' peer groups during early adolescence: Structure, status, and academic achievement. *Journal of Early Adolescence, 31*(1), 74-98.

Collaborating With Families During the Transition Planning Process

CHAPTER OBJECTIVES

- → Describe the term collaboration.
- → Create parent training modules on adolescent development and transition planning.
- → Create letters of communication about transition planning for parents.
- → Describe the roles of the transition planning specialist, parents, and student in the development of independence.
- → Describe the challenges that parents face during the transition planning period and its effect on their child's progress during transition planning.
- → Explain the ways to enable parents to participate in transition planning by overcoming barriers to Individualized Education Plan (IEP) meeting attendance.

PARENTAL INVOLVEMENT IN TRANSITION PLANNING

Teachers engage parents when they contact them for events and encourage their attendance at meetings. To ensure parental involvement, "educators must make a conscious effort to ensure that parents have the opportunity to meaningfully participate in the IEP process" (Bartlett, Etscheidt, & Weisenstein, 2007, p. 67). These proactive teacher behaviors influence the parents' decision to become involved (Browder & Spooner, 2011). Parental involvement in transition planning is also a predictor of improved post-school outcomes for students with disabilities (Hirano & Rowe, 2016).

Rae, J. M. *A Collaborative Approach to Transition Planning for Students With Disabilities* (pp. 47-81).
© 2020 SLACK Incorporated.

However, existing research contends that parents of transition-age children often report limited knowledge about the process of transition, indicating a need for additional training (Young, Morgan, Callow-Heusser, & Lindstrom, 2016).

Developing a collaborative relationship ensures the parents a role as they share their knowledge about themselves, the student, family barriers, and family resources. Understanding the family's needs and constraints, cultural background, economic situations, and even the health status of family members is crucial when working collaboratively on transition plans for the student. The transition planning specialist's commitment to communicating with the parents encourages ongoing collaboration.

To improve collaboration, the transition planning specialist should be aware that previous experiences, such as being an IEP team member, their child's progress, or the special education program may not have always been positive, and parents may have lost motivation to come to IEP meetings. As one parent said, "I just got tired of hearing what is wrong with my child." Parental concerns about bringing their child into a meeting where the child's shortcomings have been openly discussed in the past can serve as an objection to including their child in an IEP meeting.

The reasons for limited or no participation with their child's IEP and other school meetings are variable, and the transition planning specialist or special education teacher must respectfully probe to find what barriers may need to be overcome due to a history of limited communication.

To facilitate collaboration, Hall (2013) asserts that there are seven principles guiding family partnerships that can create positive outcomes for families from all backgrounds. Those principals are communication, professional competence, respect, trust, commitment, equality, and advocacy.

When all members of the IEP team have these objectives, parents and the student will be better able to express their views and trust that their views are heard. Commitment to demonstrating the principles of partnership honors cultural diversity and treats students with families and dignity (Hall, 2013, p. 57). Weaknesses in any of the seven principles are likely to result in conflict or disinterest. If trust is lost, which often occurs when a student is not making progress, district-parent contention can result. Parents may disengage, and conflicts can arise when they feel their views are not heard or when they feel they are not part of the team (Browder & Spooner, 2011).

Transition Education: Building Relationships Through Communication

Introductory Materials

For parents, transition planning is a new way of interacting with their child and the program staff. For the transition planning process to be effective, parents need to understand the rationale and the process. The formal process begins when an informational packet is sent to the home with an introductory letter, parent questionnaire, and brochure containing the rationale for transition planning, the goals of transition legislation, and information about parent and student training and the transition planning process.

A parent questionnaire is a communication tool that includes questions, such as how the student functions at home and the student's preferences, independence level, and at-home responsibilities. It is not meant to be a private communication between the parent and the teacher. In keeping with the inclusion of the student in selecting preferences, this document should be completed by the parent with the student to start a conversation about the student's preferences, visions, and plans. Family contention can arise when parents present a competing view of their child to school staff, especially during the adolescent years.

The informational packet includes questions about the parents' need for special accommodations to access the training materials, such as a technology to convert text to speech, a sign language interpreter, a translator, or paperwork written in Braille. Schools may send commercial surveys home as well. These can provide a list of skills their child already has, and those commercial products are often tied to a curriculum with lessons to teach the skills they need.

The student should also receive an informational packet with an introductory letter and questionnaire. The questionnaire asks about the student's thoughts about career interests, preferences, and needs. A sample student questionnaire appears in the Student Supplemental Materials.

A written brochure should provide necessary information on transition planning and the goals of transition planning. It should give information about the transition planning specialist and the school district's transition website if they have one about transition. The following information is helpful to communicate:

- Transition planning specialist contact numbers
- Transition website address
- Accommodations provided for parents with disabilities or medical barriers
- Second language translation services
- A glossary of transition terms
- A transition planning overview

Parent Training

Parent training can be provided via face-to-face training or informational materials about the rationale for student attendance at the IEP meeting. Introductory activities provide access to the parents' training materials:

- Face-to-face training
  - Presentation on transition planning
  - Breakout groups to discuss the presentation
  - Explanation of transition vocabulary that may not be familiar
  - Provide parent contacts: Community groups based on disability
  - Provide linkages and descriptions of post-school services
  - Provide agency contacts such as the Office of Vocational Rehabilitation (see Chapter 9)
- Informational materials about the rationale for student attendance at the IEP meeting
  - A list of skills and activities for the student
  - A sample of career curriculum activities
  - A PowerPoint or podcast format with long-term information on the transition

Getting Started: Informative Introductory Letters

To formally introduce the process of transition planning, sample introductory letters are provided in this chapter and the Student Supplemental Materials. One is for parents of students with typical communicative functioning and disabilities, and the other is for parents of students with more severe intellectual and communication disabilities. The rationale behind the differences is that parents with students with more severe medical and intellectual disabilities have additional needs that require multiple trainings about agency support and life-long dependence on families.

SHIFTING PERSPECTIVES ABOUT THE STUDENT

Engaging the Student in Transition Planning and the Individualized Education Plan Meeting

Legislation spearheaded the practice of inviting the young person to his or her IEP meeting for several reasons. For a student with disabilities, attendance at the meeting is a mark of passage that things are changing; he or she is becoming a young adult. Now the student can communicate directly to the team about his or her preferences, hopes, dreams, and needs for the future. For the first IEP meeting the student attends, he or she will have been prepared to share his or her perspectives with the team members. Before this, the student's parents should have participated in a parent information night and received information that will help them encourage their child's attendance at the IEP meeting.

If the parents agree to their child's participation, the transition planning specialist and special education faculty will work with the student and the parents to prepare them to participate in developing the transition plan. This process begins with goal setting.

Student Participation in Goal Setting for the Individualized Education Plan Meeting

The theoretical underpinning for this practice is that the student who participates in the IEP process, as well as in the process of selecting goals, is more likely to reach those goals. Creating goals he or she wants to reach, exploring job preferences, voicing personal preferences, making choices, and actively participating in developing a plan are complex skills; when developed over a long-range period, it significantly increases these skills and the student's self-determination. Research predicts that post-school success is grounded, in part, on these goal-setting skills. Research also supports increased positive outcomes for students who take an active role to set goals and self-determine the course of their lives (Williams-Diehm, Wehmeyer, Palmer, Soukup, & Garner, 2008). A self-determined person is better able to control his or her destiny (Wehmeyer & Webb, 2012). The legislation intends that young persons with disabilities develop increased self-determination, independence, and prosocial behavior. This begins by teaching them together, both the parents and the student, and including them as a team members with the student being the central player in the collaborative process.

COLLABORATION MODEL AND SCHOOL-BASED PROFESSIONALS

In order for the transition process to be successful, the special education team will need additional training on collaborative skills and IEP meeting management.

Collaboration Skills

There are four models that teams may have used while planning IEPs:
1. Multidisciplinary model
2. Interdisciplinary model
3. Transdisciplinary model
4. Collaborative model

The collaborative model is the best practice for transition planning. In the collaborative model, the student becomes a team member who chooses goals based on a self-evaluation of his or her needs.

To be effective when working with the student and the parents, the most effective teams must be able to resolve conflicts, communicate clearly, remain stable and open to parent and student information, take risks by listening to other viewpoints, establish roles and responsibilities, keep meetings minutes to update progress, and establish adequate meeting times and places (Westling & Fox, 2009). Collaboration is the most effective practice when long-term goals are being pursued, such as with transition planning. Collaboration plans can be adjusted throughout the year if need be to reflect the mastery of a student's short-term goals.

Conflict Resolution

Prior to meetings, a team must be able to resolve internal conflicts. Internal conflicts do little to guide students and their parents through transition and must be resolved. The same process can be used if a conflict arises between the student and their parents as well. The following steps can be taken to resolve conflicts at the team level:

1. Develop a statement of the problem.
2. Identify the issues that are barriers to solving the problem.
3. Discuss the points for and against the competing positions and solutions.
4. Agree while trying to get consensus.
5. Keep a log of the issue and resolutions
6. Create a system of addressing conflicts as they arise.

All team-based conflicts must be resolved well before the transition IEP meetings so that the goals of transition planning can be the focus. When school-based team members are unable to resolve a conflict, the team may need the special education supervisor's assistance to avoid any errors in the implementation of the IEP. An administrator can set up training on team self-awareness about group processes and how individual behaviors can prevent their team from collaborating and solving problems.

EFFECTIVE PRINCIPLES FOR COLLABORATION

Collaboration is defined as a process of participation through which people, groups, and organizations form relationships and work together to achieve a set of agreed-upon results (Kochhar-Bryant, 2008). The following sections demonstrate the collaboration needed during transition planning.

Collaborating for Career Exploration and Work Connections

Systems Collaboration

Most students, unless they can drive, cannot arrange to do community-based activities on their own. Trips can be planned in collaboration with their parents, other families, or the school, which can set up on community-based instruction (CBI) trips. CBI is especially helpful when students are taken to, for instance, a local community college when they want to attend information nights when disability services are the topic. Learning about how colleges support students through their Office of Disability requires that schools share the opportunities and parents and families work together to ensure their children's interests, access to the school's campuses, and post-school options are explored. The following are examples of activities that will require adult involvement and collaboration. The transition planning specialist provides the structure for the overall plan:

- Transition planning specialist
  - Organizes college or vocational school visits
  - Requests transportation and secures funding through the school district for trips

- ◦ Shares college visit guidelines, tour times, and dates
  - ◦ Shares continuing education information with all students with disabilities and their parents
- Transition planning specialist or parents
  - ◦ Guide student to get working papers
  - ◦ Introduce student to college's Office of Disability
- Parents
  - ◦ Discuss possibilities they have found with their child
  - ◦ Search Medicaid and Social Security support
  - ◦ Join a parent transition planning committee
  - ◦ Visit and evaluate the appropriateness of post-school day placements
  - ◦ If relevant, look at a supported apartment living
  - ◦ Be put on waiting lists, even if graduation is a number of years away
- Student
  - ◦ Determines preferences for job exploration
  - ◦ Explores Careerlink to look at employment opportunities
  - ◦ Makes choices for job shadowing
- Office of Vocational Rehabilitation
  - ◦ Meets with eligible students
  - ◦ Invites spokesperson to speak to the students they serve

Visiting a community college or vocational education site is an example of system coordination initiatives that are used to achieve change in a student's self-perception of possibilities, develop a student's knowledge of the processes of accessing post-school education, and increase the student's and parents' knowledge of institutions and systems of support within institutions.

Challenges to Collaboration

Although IEP team members may demonstrate a desire to collaborate, the fact remains that "team members typically lack the skills, tools, and support structures that would allow them to orchestrate significant pedagogical and curriculum changes through the collaborative work of the team" (Troen & Boles, 2011, p. 1). Setting team guidelines, keeping records of meetings and responsibilities, and creating agendas, as well as having access to conflict resolution, are helpful in building collaborative team skills. Conflict resolution is also a learned skill and can be acquired through ongoing professional development and school-based practices.

Team training can help extinguish negative team behaviors, such as going off task or blocking discussion by interrupting. These, as well as other behaviors, often lead to prolonged meetings and delays in completing the meeting goals. It is crucial that the collaborative process with the student and the parent not be derailed by limited collaboration skills on the parts of individual professionals involved in the planning process.

Community Collaboration

The transition planning specialist and the school's parent transition committee may work with a community organization that focuses on post-school life. Parents and school-based leaders can establish relationships with large and small companies that employ individuals with disabilities.

The transition planning specialist and parents can also provide support and suggestions to other parents for options for post-school life. Young adults with disabilities can also participate in organizations and committees that advocate for access to employment and community opportunities.

Parental awareness and involvement are vital to the strength of these efforts, especially when parents are knowledgeable about local community job and service learning opportunities. Their presence in the community makes them best able to see what is accessible to the student. Parents can be a crucial part of communication and collaboration efforts. For instance, having students create a school newsletter to which parents and students can contribute to can provide awareness of what is happening in the school around issues of disability and post-school outcomes.

THE STUDENT EXPERIENCE: INCREASING THE STUDENT'S ROLE

The transition planning specialist is instrumental in guiding the student to participate in the IEP meeting. Research supports that students who participate in IEP development are more likely to have positive outcomes (Mason, McGahee-Kovac, & Johnson, 2004). In the past, educators and families talked about the student rather than to the student, thus controlling all aspects of the IEP. With the legislative direction in the Individuals with Disabilities Education Act (IDEA, 2004), the student with a disability is now expected to be a leader on the team. At this stage of adolescent development, if parents and teachers create the goals that the student pursues, those goals have meaning only to the professionals, and the aspirations behind those goals may better match those of the adults. If this approach to the transition planning continues, it will remove the student's ability to determine his or her life choices. The insistence of adults to maintain control of their child's choices can result in learned helplessness, rendering them ineffective in planning his or her own life.

Students with disabilities, like their peers, want autonomy. They see other students becoming independent, and they want to attain that goal as well. Inviting students to plan for and attend their IEP meetings without prerequisite skills will limit their responsiveness to participation.

Transition planning specialists support students to participate through direct instruction, with opportunities to practice advocating for themselves, voicing their questions, asking for support, and describing their preferences, needs, and future aspirations.

For students with disabilities, having adults ask them about their preferences and needs leads to a significant change in self-perception. Historically, IEPs stem from a professional (medical) model of disability, where professional viewpoints and recommendations are derived from assessments of strengths and needs. The needs are then remediated or not. The students know little about this process or how the goals are chosen. Lack of understanding or inclusion in the goal creation process can produce a passive attitude about making choices for themselves. Undoing this passivity is difficult. For example, when invited to the IEP meeting, one student said, "I do not go to that meeting. My mother does all that." This perspective must be overcome for students to reap the benefits of their involvement.

Barnard-Brak and Lechtenberger (2010) studied the association of student IEP participation with academic achievement across time. The study included 3912 students across all IDEA disability categories and suggests that involving students with disabilities in the IEP process should begin during elementary school. In their national longitudinal study, participants were between 7 and 12 years old. For this group of students, there was "a significant correlational path between initial statuses and demonstrated growth between initial achievement and later achievement" (Barnard-Brak & Lechtenberger, 2010, p. 349). Further, "the results of the study indicate a significant, positive association between student IEP participation and academic achievement across time" (Barnard-Brak & Lechtenberger, 2010, p. 346). Their study suggests that achievement is enhanced when students with disabilities begin to shape their futures during elementary school.

To increase a student's engagement in transition planning, the transition planning specialist, student, parents, community members, and organizations can come together to listen to the student's needs and accomplishments. They help the student with the logistics, so activities are developed that will help the student reach his or her goals throughout the longitudinal transition planning process (Kohler, Gothberg, Fowler, & Coyle, 2016). IEP team membership requires that the transition planning specialist teach the student to work with the parents and teach the parents to shift their focus to the child as the child learns how to be the pivotal person to determine the path he or she wants to take. The team focus will shift from talking about fixing the child's deficits to learning about what the student may want to learn and do. This shift also entails that the student take on responsibilities and plan for him- or herself how he or she will accomplish the goals the student set for him- or herself. Although this text begins with the inclusion of students in earnest by middle school, research supports an earlier focus, starting in elementary school, on goal setting participation for students with disabilities.

Parents also benefit from their child's participation. Studies show that parents contributed more, perhaps because of the less intimidating climate, or perhaps because their child's speaking encouraged it. IEP meetings where parents and children participated were more of a team effort rather than a teacher-directed meeting with the IEP shared as if no further discussion was necessary (Hawbaker, 2007).

Communication Challenges: The Nonverbal Student

Communication is important when including or determining the preferences of nonverbal students. Parents of students with severe disabilities must provide crucial information for transition plans because their children cannot do it on their own. Of significance is the fact that many students with severe to profound intellectual disabilities and autism spectrum disorder cannot speak. Parents experience different settings and activities with their children and often recognize nonverbal communication that is essential for their children's well-being. They can provide information that would otherwise be difficult for other team members to gather. These students should have plans that improve their inclusion in the activities of daily living and access to communication devices at an early age.

In the past, students with severe disabilities were still excluded until the late 1980s, unlike their less disabled peers (see the Student Supplemental Materials). As institutions began closing, they went to settings such as group homes away from their local communities. Many school buildings could not accommodate wheelchairs, and little was known about how to teach the most severely impaired, so exclusionary practices continued. Once school buildings were made accessible, these students began to come to school. However, there was no obligation on the part of schools to provide any communication devices due to the de minimis standard. Using assessments standardized for students without disabilities made assessment inadequate. The most severely impaired could not access the assessments due to lack of speech or physical movement, both of which are required in standardized assessments. This locked children into a life in which they were unable to communicate. Due to little attention to this group of adolescents, their cognitive functioning cannot be fully known. Some researchers assert that the gap between aspirations and outcomes is especially apparent among students with intellectual disabilities, autism spectrum disorder, and multiple disabilities in the early years after high school (Carter, Austin, & Trainor, 2012) and throughout adulthood (Siperstein,

Parker, & Drascher, 2013). This gap is not surprising given the profound effect of their disabilities on speech and movement. However, this history should not prevent transition teams and parents from finding assistive technology that allows them to communicate their preferences.

Matching a child to a transition plan for successful outcomes has been challenging when there were few options or limited provisions for children and adolescents who cannot communicate verbally. Therefore, every effort must be made to assist the student to communicate. For example, in the following case report, collaboration did not occur for many years until technology was used to include this student.

Case Report: Jason

A new transition plan was written for Jason, a 14-year-old boy. A new teacher came to his class, a program for nonverbal students with severe intellectual and physical disabilities. The new teacher observed her class to familiarize herself with her new students. Once she began to work, she talked to her new supervisor about a child in the class who seemed to be following the conversation and laughing at appropriate times. During an introductory phone call with the parent, the parent said that the child seemed to understand what was talked about, even though the child's evaluation described him as being at the intellectual level of a toddler.

In the parent information section of the IEP, the parents said that they wanted their son to have a high quality of life, and they were happy to be able to provide him that. No other goals were requested. The new teacher asked for an assistive technology assessment for a head control or eye tracking device because the child could move his head to indicate yes and no answers and he could laugh. An eye tracking device was trialed and later approved. The child was evaluated using the eye tracking device that was fitted for him. He received instruction on how to use it. It allowed him to answer questions by looking at pictures of objects on a computer screen. Then he was evaluated again using testing designed for users of eye tracking devices. He would use his eye gaze to select answers to a school psychologist's questions from an array of four choices. The results of his receptive language test were that he was functioning receptively at the fourth-grade level, considerably higher than the previous diagnosis. This moved him from the intellectual ability of a 2-year-old to a fourth grader, or, for IDEA eligibility, from profound intellectual disability to moderate intellectual disability. If he had been included and had received assistive technology sooner, a higher vocabulary could have been reached, and he would have received greater opportunities for interaction and at least partial placement in a general education class.

Later, the child was given an electronic wheelchair to enable him to be more independent. He learned how to use a head control device to move the wheelchair. By pressing back on the head control for left and right, the wheelchair moved forward. He no longer needed staff to push his wheelchair, a step in developing independence skills. The therapist who taught him to use the head control device complained that he thought it was funny to hit the wall from time to time or to speed up away from her. This, however, was to be expected as the student had gained some independence for the first time at age 14. As part of the transition plan, more appropriate educational activities included instruction in reading and the provision of assistive technology such as text-to-speech literature.

Access to literature or picture-based receptive language activities is included in transition plans. The literature falls under academic skills in the IEP and addresses leisure activities for post-school life in the transition section. For parents, projecting too far forward and imagining that their child is too disabled to be employed or interact with others can sometimes result in their child having no chance to become more involved and self-determined in their own lives. This child was able to participate in his IEP meeting with the use of technology. Although he could not understand adult vocabulary, his teacher was able to prepare him to use his technology to show his preferences, experiences, and new skills.

EXERCISES

1. Research two forms of assistive technology that can increase a student's comprehension and communication.
2. Describe how to monitor progress on receptive vocabulary.

DISCUSSION

Although the teacher advocated for this child and encouraged the parents to ask for this change, parents do not always want to get into a situation where there may be contention between them and the school district, as is often the outcome when the parent requests additional services. A fear of contention for this family caused a missed opportunity for their child with the most severe disabilities. Parents at times need to be guided to get the correct services for their child. In this case, a new teacher advocated for the child but had to get the parents' agreement to pursue this.

Parents and school staff can underestimate the students with the most severe to profound disabilities. This leads to limited provision of services. Previously, there were no requirements to provide for the child with a disability beyond the de minimis standard until *Endrew F. v. Douglas County School District* (2017). This case provides direction for parents who are now legally able to find appropriate supports for their children.

GUIDING PARENTS

Parental Background on Disability

A student without disabilities typically plans for postsecondary life with the help of parents, family, and school counselors. Schools provide significant guidance counseling, but they do not provide or use a directive approach to their role. Most parents are involved and support and encourage their children's future directions. Parents of students with disabilities have various challenges that make this style of planning for the transition to adulthood less likely to translate into positive post-school opportunities. There are no existing norms or models for parents to follow. Many parents do not feel prepared to find options for the future when they cannot draw from their own experience because they did not, most likely, have a disability. There are resources to support parents in helping their children with disabilities; knowledge about where to find these resources can be provided by those experienced in working with students with disabilities. Depending on the severity of the disability, many parents have concerns, and rightly so, about whether and how much independence is safe for their children. Therefore, the period of transition is fraught with parental challenges around what is possible and available to their children. Transition planning activities help parents negotiate the passage to adulthood by answering specific questions about their child and their child's specific needs.

Language and Culture

The family's individual situation may play a part in how involved parents become. Including parents as much as possible and giving them opportunities to share their expertise as caregivers may make them feel more comfortable in the group (Westling & Fox, 2009). Contact with parents may require communication via their first language.

For very brief communications, there are free translating programs online. These programs allow users to type a message in one language and produce the translation in the language of choice. However, always use a translator for complex messages.

All parent contact using a translator should be followed by a survey to determine whether the communications met the family's needs. Asking the parents if the translation was understood is important when services are needed again. Establishing multiple means to interact with parents provides the teacher with a consistent way to communicate with them. Teacher behavior, such as using transition programs and arranging for translators for parent training and IEP meetings, should remove some cultural and personal barriers originating in a lack of communication.

When working with families during the transition planning process, be aware of the importance of respecting another's origins and language in the formation of a child's cultural identity and well-being (De Houwer, 2015; Puig, 2010). Helping culturally diverse parents feel welcomed requires sensitivity and awareness of their cultural values (Browder & Spooner, 2011, p. 60). Cultural background might influence how open parents are to propositions or professional assessments given during IEP meetings (Browder & Spooner, 2011). This may be evident during discussions about independence. In many families, there is no pressure to move away. Many family members stay at home unless they marry and start a family, and sometimes not even then. When getting information from the parents, it is important to understand how culture impacts their vision of schooling. By finding out about how a family views family life, educators are in a better position to help the student plan. Educators should aim to level power relations by understanding every family's individual strengths (Beneke & Cheatham, 2016).

Schools and teachers should not be making efforts to change a students' or parents' values or ignore their cultural backgrounds. Respecting families facilitates cooperative relationships and can lead to higher expectations for success. The school-based members of the IEP team should discuss the expectations and determine what cultural differences might exist (West, Leon-Geurero, & Stevens, 2007).

Benefits of Student Autonomy and Parental Guidance

As their children participate in the IEP process, parents will express legitimate concerns and at times considerations around circumstances such as the family money constraints and safety concerns. Young persons are not free to act unilaterally but are directed by their parents' concern for their welfare during this developmental period.

The developmental period of adolescence is a time when young people require adult guidance to avoid pitfalls that may cause them to be a person other than the one they had hoped to be. Impulsivity is a well-known characteristic of adolescence. Taylor, Barker, Heavey, and McHale (2013) reported that even among typically developing youth, 18-year-olds performed more poorly on strategy generation and concept formation during adolescence than their younger counterparts. The ramifications of the inability to plan might not occur because of injury or disability alone but rather as a natural consequence of neuronal reorganization. It is plausible that specific functions might be temporarily diminished or abolished, "going offline" during periods of steep maturational change. This cognitive stage can partially explain increased risk-taking, poorer behavioral inhibition, and reduced impulse control in adolescents when compared with later adulthood. The possible unintended consequences of adolescent behavior should be part of the transition planning curriculum.

In fact, although adolescents may assert otherwise, they still need their parents for the provision of food, clothing, shelter, medical care, and other survival needs. Early independence skills develop, for the most part, in supervised settings. Despite this level of dependence, young persons take on increasing levels of participation in their survival within their family group. As noted in Chapter 2, young persons can be self-determined even when acting in accord with an external demand, provided "the person fully concurs with or endorses doing so" (Ryan & Deci, 2006, p. 1560).

Many adolescents recognize their parents' good intentions and hopes for them and take their guidance seriously while naturally asserting their own beliefs and wants, which are often at odds with

those of their parents. During this formative period of adolescence, the drive to be more independent becomes a powerful motivator, and with guidance, parents can help their children to navigate
this period more effectively and help them produce better adult outcomes. Parental support for their
child's participation in the IEP meeting is a safe and effective way to:

- Open the lines of communication with their child
- Support of their child's need to be more self-determined
- Guide their child to finish his or her education
- Increase their child's participation in adult skills and employment development
- Support their child's search for entry-level employment
- Support their child's participation in further educational programs or courses
- Utilize the transition planning specialist's support to continue to build literacy prior to and after
  graduation
- Develop family goals that increase independence
- Help their child's transition into an adult role in the family
- Help their child develop knowledge of the potential destructive outcomes related to premature
  involvement in sexual activities
- Help their child develop knowledge about how decisions to drink and take drugs can produce
  poor outcomes in becoming a mature adult

Parents play a primary role in supporting the development of responsibility, self-determination,
and independence by creating a continuum of increasing responsibilities and behavioral imperatives.
Parents can help their children gain independence while still maintaining age-appropriate boundaries. Therefore, self-determination can be supported both at home and at school.

Helping parents and students understand the process delineated throughout the transition framework in Chapter 2 along with the supports discussed in this chapter is an IEP team collaborative
process that guides students toward increased understanding of self-determination, advocacy, and
the outcomes they want for themselves. Being included in the IEP process, selecting their own goals,
and completing goals create motivation and movement toward greater responsibility. However, transition planning outcomes cannot be accomplished without parents' help, such as when they provide
students with transportation to jobs or contribute details about their children's disabilities.

Parent Information About the Student

When developing an IEP, information from parents is crucial. Parents have significant information about their child and may have taught them many responsibilities. Services of transition,
such as instruction in self-care, should not be continued in school if already mastered at home.
Independence skills should be documented in an assessment and added to the transition planning
information. Instruction in goal setting, as explained in Chapter 2, gives students the opportunity to
self-assess to determine what they think they would like to learn or do. Making students with disabilities redo goals already mastered can be demoralizing. Parents are excellent resources for ruling
out goals that have already been accomplished.

Parents and their adolescent child can also give two very important pieces of information—what
the child can do and what the child wants to learn—by completing a questionnaire (Westling &
Fox, 2009). These answers will give the planning team insight as to what the parents and their child
envision in terms of community living, housing, employment, and leisure activities. The parents
can provide current information about the student's activities, such as community groups, physical
activities, social activities, friends, and church.

A parent interview following the questionnaire is an excellent way to determine the availability
of outside resources, such as jobs and job shadowing experiences, that may be available through

the family. Parents can provide information on family members or other community members with whom they have a relationship and with whom they may have first discussed job opportunities. Westling and Fox (2009) report that follow-up studies indicate that family members can play an important role in helping to find employment for students.

The transition planning specialist should always be cognizant of the demands on parents' time and plan to interview by teleconference. The interview needs to be done with as little intrusion into the family's privacy as possible. Westling and Fox (2009) suggest the interview should be done at a convenient time for the parents and the interviewer, and it should not use professional jargon.

Parents who are English language learners will need the services of a translator who can join a teleconference remotely or in person. Those parents who cannot come to school, due to the remoteness of school, can be provided with transportation, at the expense of the school district, or meet at an alternate location close to the students home. IDEA (2004) gives additional directives:

- Assessment and other evaluation materials should not be racially or culturally discriminatory.
- Assessment and other evaluation materials are to be provided in the child's native language or another mode of communication unless it is clearly not feasible to do so.
- A child must not be determined to be a child with a disability if the determinant factor is lack of appropriate instruction in reading or math or limited English proficiency.
- Parents are entitled to an interpreter at the IEP meeting, if needed, to ensure that the parents understand the proceedings.
- When developing an IEP, in the case of a child with limited English proficiency, the language needs of the child as they relate to their IEP must be considered.

Parent Information and Students With Emergent and Severe Disabilities

Due to the generality of what is considered a successful outcome, little attention is given to some of the challenges of adolescents with severe mental illness or intellectual and multiple disabilities. A student with a mild reading-based specific learning disability, with the use of assistive technology and other accommodations, can attend college. A student with emotional disabilities can advocate for a Section 504 plan to help recover credit or submit an assignment late due to absences when he or she has an episode of bipolar depression. These students can succeed in these situations and many others with appropriate supports in place. Parents can assist their children in learning to advocate for themselves and becoming employed or going to post-school training and/or college.

However, for many parents, the disabilities of their children may be acquired and not come until later in life, or they are not clearly understood. For example, a student who was without an academic disability but had some distractibility under IDEA eligibility and other health impairment begins to lose his ability to express his thoughts. He is in ninth grade and will continue to lose the ability to communicate. This difficulty with speech may be a symptom of schizophrenia or another degenerative brain disease. For this discussion, we will assume his behavior is the result of schizophrenia. Schizophrenia is a degenerative process that will impact the type of environment a person can live in and be educated in and the type of job the person can perform. Sometimes paranoia can occur, where the student may become pervasively fearful and avoid other people and all fearful situations that may be real or unreal. This form of the illness disables the student and develops over a period of a few years. For these students, a more supportive and safe post-school supportive living situation may be needed. School attendance and task completion may or may not be possible or may be sporadic depending on the mental health disorder episode frequency or type or the effectiveness of medication. For students with emergent and acquired severe disabilities, transition will take a different path and parents will need to be guided through the changes, even after the initial parent trainings, with additional information on local mental health services and ongoing contact with the school psychologist. Students can participate if the transition planning specialist and parents provide students with additional support to complete a preference assessment and facilitate planning involvement. The student's attention and organizational difficulties will require more frequent parent meetings and student conferences, attention to the plan goals, and access to local mental health service organizations.

Therefore, it is important to consider how to plan with students who have severe intellectual disabilities, mental health disorders, or traumatic brain injury whose post-school outcomes will have a different trajectory that, although an excellent outcome for them, may not fit the success paradigm suggested by the culture at large. Despite differences in post-school trajectories, teams should avoid the following pitfalls. Lack of action due to the degree of a student's disability is not permitted under IDEA. Here are some problem responses that should be avoided:

- Not always advocating for a change of course when a disability such as a mental health disorder, psychological trauma, acquired physical disability, traumatic brain injury, severe intellectual disability, or neurologically based progressive illness causes further decline in functioning
- Not looking for supplementary aids and services that support higher functioning
- Deciding a student will not benefit from a communication system
- Not contacting the Office of Rehabilitation in a timely fashion
- Not maintaining current contact with parents
- Not updating current functioning levels

Failing to consider other options for outcomes, that may be less culturally successful may result in a poor quality of life as a disability becomes more disabling or when the parents can no longer care for their significantly disabled child.

Regardless of the severity of the student's disability or late onset of disability, team members and parents who work directly with the student must have recent assessments and information about the child. The methods of data collection require adaptation to the student's communication, physical, and intellectual needs.

As part of the assessment process parent information is important. Parents' concerns about changes in their child should never be ignored, nor should the transition planning specialist or special education team assume a student's abilities prior to the completion of all assessments. During assessment and the assessment review, before the IEP meeting, parents should be called to talk about the information section in the IEP. In this section of the IEP, the parents provide information about what is happening at home and the preferences, activities, and skills to give a more comprehensive understanding of the student.

The team should also avoid assumptions about how parents may feel about their child, their child's disabilities, and the future. Even with progressive conditions like muscular dystrophy, parents need to talk to the transition planning specialist about the changes that are to come in a plan. Even in the face of severe disabilities and progressive illness, do not assume a static perception about the student's future. In addition, according to Blustein, Carter, and McMillan (2016):

> No two parents are likely to hold the same expectations, priorities, or concerns for their children with intellectual disabilities. Transition teams should consider how best to solicit

from individual families' information about the expectations they hold, the outcomes they prioritize, and the concerns they have, especially for the most severely impaired. Transition services and supports can then be strategically aligned to address these individualized perspectives. (p. 175)

Therefore, each year and biweekly for students with progressive loss of functioning, the parent information section of the IEP must be updated. "Parents know their children best. They can provide information that no other person can about the student's background, positive and negative experiences, major moves, critical events, current situation and the family's issues" (Westling & Fox, 2009, p. 122). The following case report is an example of when the parent information was not provided.

Case Report: Gracie

Gracie, 15 years old, came to school in a wheelchair; she was diagnosed with autism and a physical disability. One of her IEP goals was to increase her independence skills. She was nonverbal and had an intellectual disability. For students like Gracie, developing independence skills can help her get into adult services. The more assistance she needed, the more restrictive a setting she would be placed in.

A new supervisor attended an IEP meeting for Gracie. The special education teacher, physical therapist, and occupational therapist had been working with this student for 3 years. As the meeting began and the IEP was reviewed, the supervisor noticed the parent information section was not filled out. The supervisor asked the team why it was blank, and the special education teacher said the parent did not have anything to add to it. The supervisor responded that IDEA requires that this section cannot be blank, and the parent must have something to let the team know regarding how Gracie functions at home. The parent was asked to tell the team about Gracie's day-to-day life at home. The parent went through her child's day. Then the teacher asked about her child's independence skills. The parent stated, "Gracie is independent in the bathroom."

She continued, "I just need to be there in case she falls." The supervisor was puzzled, and even though she was new to the supervisory position, she did not want to admit not knowing that Gracie could walk. The IEP had no information that Gracie was ambulatory. Gracie was at the meeting, so the supervisor asked the parent if she could ask Gracie to use the bathroom. Gracie stood up, and the parent helped her from the wheelchair. Gracie stood on unsteady feet and held onto the table, walked a few feet independently, and leaned against the blackboard. She then made her way to the bathroom in the corner of the room. As she reached the bathroom door, she reached for the sink for support. She closed the door partially, and she could be heard using the toilet, flushing the toilet, and then turning on the water in the sink. At this point, the parent said, "She will just run the water to trick you, so you have to tell her to use the soap and water (prompts required) and then dry with the paper towels." The supervisor asked the parent why Gracie was in a wheelchair. She said, "Gracie takes so long to walk places, and she would need someone with her because she will fall due to the balance problems. I did not want to inconvenience the staff, so I got her the wheelchair." Gracie came back to the wheelchair, albeit slowly, and sat down.

The teacher, physical therapist, and occupational therapist were all speechless and professionally embarrassed.

EXERCISE

1. When a student is not given the services he or she needs, the student can be given a compensatory education agreement. Research compensatory agreements and describe two situations where they were used.

DISCUSSION

The team completed the new IEP without interviewing the parent, leaving the parent information section blank. This situation was the direct result of the team's failure to interview the parent. Also, the physical therapist assumed the child could not walk since she came to school in a wheelchair. However, a weightbearing assessment was not done. In addition, the team did not maintain the entry of data previously gathered from the parent. This information should also have been in the present levels of independence skills. There is an important reason that IDEA mandates a section with parent information. It is to include the parent, who knows the child best, in providing information. The parent in this case could have provided essential information, but she was excluded. Digressions in this area, which directly resulted in the provision of inadequate services, are the basis of due process cases, as well as deprivation of services. Gracie was entitled to and given compensatory physical therapy to make up for her loss of services.

Parents have intimate knowledge of their child, and the team needs information about the child's current functioning to plan effectively and develop appropriate goals.

Exercises

1. Develop a brochure using the information from this text to teach parents about transition planning.
2. Create a PowerPoint presentation on transition education activities with your class and the parents.
3. Some schools give students with disabilities an assigned school counselor, as is done with students without disabilities. If this is the case, how might the transition planning specialist coordinate transition planning with the assigned counselor?
4. What differences and commonalities do you see between counseling available for students and transition planning programs available for special education students? You will need to interview a school counselor for this information.
5. Most parents of students with disabilities worry about social experiences. How can you work with a parent to increase options for after-school activities? Develop an after-school activity designed for students with moderate intellectual disabilities.
6. A parent of the only deaf student in the high school would like her child to be included in after-school activities. How might you find an after-school activity that would provide the most inclusive setting?

STARTING THE TRANSITION PLANNING PROCESS: INDIVIDUALIZED EDUCATION PLAN TIMELINES

Helping the Parent Stay Organized

By age 13, at the annual IEP, transition should be discussed. A productive IEP meeting for the student and the family should include several steps. The transition planning specialist sends a letter to introduce transition planning. The transition planning specialist or a designated special education teacher who teaches the student may take the lead in organizing the meeting and preparing the IEP paperwork.

Students must be invited to the IEP at age 14. Parent and student preparation for attendance at the IEP meeting and student participation in a transition course of study must be included in the IEP before the child reaches age 14. As mentioned previously, the number of activities of transition, starting during the year the child turns 16 years old is ill-advised. Most students with disabilities who have been struggling through school and have multiple academic failures have typically decided to drop out by then. The purpose of transition planning is to prevent this, and parents must be informed about transition planning at an early age so they can advocate for earlier services, particularly if their child is failing academically. Not informing parents about services and supports would be akin to not informing the parents of college-bound students about the necessity for after-school activities to college acceptance. Transition planning is the guidance plan for students with disabilities.

The timeline of the annual IEP depends on when transition planning is included in the IEP. By not carefully considering when to discuss transition, there is a high likelihood that it will be difficult to ensure that the plan is implemented with fidelity. IEPs are developed annually. To stay in compliance with special education law, the annual IEP meeting must occur 1 day before the date of the last annual IEP meeting. The only time this can be delayed is with parental written consent. Annual IEPs with initial transition statements or plans are tied to the child's year of transition eligibility. Each student in special education will have a different timeline for commencing transition planning. For example, there are four conditions that trigger the commencement of transition planning in the annual IEP:

1. The special education school-based team wants to discuss transition.
2. The parent or the student wants to discuss transition.
3. The state of residence mandates a transition plan be present in the IEP by age 14.
4. The state of residence mandates a transition plan be present in the IEP by age 16.

Annual IEPs rarely fall on or near the child's birthday, and transition plans must be implemented by his or her birthday. In the third condition mentioned earlier, the transition plan must be implemented during the year the child will turn 14 years old. If the IEP was developed in the spring and the student turns 14 years old in September, transition should have been planned in the spring and the child should have attended that IEP meeting. Then the IEP would comply with transition planning law because it was implemented during the school year when the child will turn 14 or 16 years old, respectively, depending on the state. This timeline requires that transition planning be addressed during the annual IEP before the child turns 14 or 16 years old. This guarantees that a plan is in place when the child reaches transition age. Therefore, the transition plan may begin with a statement of transition, and the contents of the framework will begin well before the child's 14th birthday. Table 3-1 is a hypothetical example of how an IEP can become out of compliance with special education law.

A plan of transition, using an evidence-based curriculum and a confirmed course of action and study for high school, can help the parents feel confident that the local education agency, also known as the *school district*, is attentive to the needs of their child. Having the plan in place before 14 years old is a demonstration of transition planning specialist and special education team competence. Delays and out-of-compliance IEPs encourage the parents to lose trust and feel they need to advocate for their child, a very laborious process. This can bring ill will that is hard to overcome and perpetrates tension in future IEP meetings.

Table 3-1 illustrates how waiting until the 14th birthday to write the transition plan makes a simple process more difficult to carry out. In the less desirable timeline, Timeline #1, transition activities will not be implemented until after the hypothetical student, Peter, turns 14 years old. In the second, desirable timeline, the meeting to discuss transition takes place while Peter is 13 years old.

The process in Timeline #2 supports a smooth transition and provides more clarity to the transition planning process. Curricular activities can be part of a transition course that begins at the start of the school year with other peers who have transition plans. This plan structure gives a consistency that aids in communication between all stakeholders.

Table 3-1. Planning for Transition

STUDENT NAME: PETER JONES
AGE: 13
IEP ANNUAL MEETING DATE: 5/1

Timeline #1

1. Peter's annual IEP is on May 1, 2018. A transition plan was not discussed.

2. On October 15, 2018, Peter turns 14 years old. Transition services are now required.

3. Prior to his 14th birthday, parental permission was needed for transition activities.

4. IEP must be revised either in person or via a phone conference to add the transition statement or services.

Timeline #2

1. Peter's annual IEP is on May 1, 2018. A transition plan is discussed.

2. The IEP is developed with a transition plan.

3. School year begins September 2018.

4. Peter is 13 years old. Peter begins transition curriculum with his peers.

5. Beginning plans are in place by age 14. An additional revision is not needed.

6. Parents begin the school year being able to access the full year of transition activities.

Pitfalls of Timeline #1

- Timeline #1 requires that the parents participate in a revision IEP when the IEP is in effect for only 2.5 months.

- Parents miss work time twice.

- Timeline #1 causes piecemeal delivery of transition services instead of providing them an organized pathway to participating and understanding how transition is carried out.

- This timeline risks noncompliance because implementation may not be in place by age 14.

Timeline #2 Example of Best Practices

Timeline #2 is a more systematic way to begin writing a transition plan, and it includes the parents in the activities of transition planning. The next part of the chart includes examples of what the first transition year can include.

(continued)

TABLE 3-1. PLANNING FOR TRANSITION (CONTINUED)
TRANSITION PLANNING FRAMEWORK: PARENT AND STUDENT TRAINING
Transition Plan Services Year 1

- September: Parent and student introduction: Parent engagement in parent training
- September: Framework of transition activities introduced
- Fall through spring
  - Module 1: Career explorations
  - Module 2: Social engagement: Transition activities and assignments
  - Module 3: Self-determination, self-advocacy, goal construction, and goal action plans
  - Module 4: Introduction to the IEP and goal selection
  - Module 5: Reading and writing transition goals: Writing the personal narrative
  - Module 6: Individual conference with transition planning specialist: Schedule review
  - Module 7: Assessments review: Course of study determined
  - Module 8: Mock IEP meeting
    - Peter participates in his IEP by providing goals and sharing his narrative about his disability.

Student Introductory Letter About Transition Planning

After the introductory letter is sent to the parent and the child, the parent gives permission for the child to:

1. Attend the entire IEP meeting
2. Attend the part of the IEP meeting where transition is discussed
3. Exclude the child and follow federal regulations to ensure preferences and interests are provided

Written Introduction to Transition

The following is an introductory letter to the student and a list of the types of activities that can go into the IEP with an implementation date for the fall. This should be sent prior to the first IEP meeting where transition is discussed. This letter captures the spirit of collaboration and inclusion that can be communicated to the student. (See the Student Supplemental Materials for other examples.)

Derry School District
1015 Washington Lane
Derry, New Hampshire 03038

Dear Student,

You may already be thinking about what you would like to do during high school, and perhaps you think about your life after high school. At this time, it is important that you begin to think about what you would like to do to plan for post–high school life. There are activities and studies you can be involved in to help you prepare.

Transition planning is a process to help you prepare for your post–high school life. It is a set of activities for any student who is eligible because he or she has a disability. Your current educational program and IEP are designed to meet your academic and other needs related to your disability. During your next IEP meeting, we will discuss transition planning and how it can help you plan for life after high school. Transition planning serves to give additional help with employment skills, education, community involvement, and self-advocacy skills that can benefit you as a young adult.

To help you learn more about transition planning, you will be asked to participate by answering questionnaires and participating in training, school courses, and activities that will make you knowledgeable about yourself and possible choices you would like to pursue. As part of the program, you will gain the skills to participate in and even lead your IEP meetings. Your participation is a step toward taking on young adult responsibilities. There will be introductory training for you in school as well. Your parent will be sent an invitation to the training.

Your parent will be formally introduced to transition planning and your inclusion in the IEP meeting, which is a significant change for both of you, but one that can help you reach your goals for graduation and beyond.

At your upcoming IEP meeting, you will talk about a career exploration course with classmates in your grade. You will also participate with peers in small group classes to develop skills and goals you want to reach now. Along with career explorations and other activities of transition, you will be assigned a transition planning specialist who will meet with you regularly to help you with your plans.

So, welcome to transition planning! We look forward to teaching you how to participate in your IEP meeting, as well as how to gain skills and knowledge that will help you in adult life.

Information about the parent-student transition planning introduction is attached. Please respond by sending back the attached form. There is also a questionnaire that you can fill out in school and go over with your primary special education teacher.

Thank you.
Best regards,
Ms. Barnes
Transition Planning Specialist
jbarnes@schooldistrict.com
Phone: 215-555-5555

Transition Activities: Developing a Parent Action Plan

Many students turn 14 years old during middle school. Transition curricular goals and supports to the student are best accomplished if begun during the beginning of eighth grade and continued during ninth and tenth grade. The following is an example of the activities.

Inviting and Informing the Parents About the Student's Activities of Transition

The following information and training topics should be provided to the parents:
- A calendar of planned transition activities
- A calendar of their child's transition conferences
- A calendar of parent trainings
- Information on career-research activities
- Information about vocational-technical programs
- An overview of the career curriculum
- An overview of a possible transition planning continuum

Parental Consent for Attendance at the Individualized Education Plan Meeting

Inviting the Student to Plan for Transition

The parent assists in the student's participation in the IEP meeting. One barrier is that some parents do not want their child to attend the IEP meetings. This objection about their child's inclusion in the IEP meeting can be mediated through parent training about the evidence-based practices and why including the child in planning his or her future is important. Parent training that includes real stories about students attending their IEP meetings can help parents shift their perspectives to include their children. Not knowing enough about why transition planning can help students is a barrier that creates an exclusionary practice.

Federal Law and Student Attendance at Individualized Education Plan Meetings

Although transition planning is grounded in the notion that student attendance and active participation in the IEP meeting is a significant driver of student success, there is a caveat. According to federal law, if the child is under 18 years of age, the parents may decide whether the child will attend the meeting. Therefore, it is essential to the success of the planning process and the child that the transition planning specialist help the parents and their child be active participants. To encourage attendance, the special education teams typically inform the parents about the benefits of their child's inclusion via transition planning information and training. Inclusion is important even if the student can only participate to a partial degree. If parents are informed about what is available to their child and how it is going to be implemented, they may be more likely to include the child in the IEP meeting.

The Invitation

As stated previously, the school district:

> [M]ust invite a child with a disability to attend the child's IEP Team meeting if a purpose of the meeting will be the consideration of the postsecondary goals for the child and the transition services needed to assist the child in reaching those goals under §300.320(b). (IEP team, 2006)

However, the parents make the final decision regarding attendance. Section 614(d)(1)(B)(vii) of the act clearly states that the IEP team includes the child with a disability whenever appropriate. Generally, a child with a disability should attend the IEP meeting if the parent decides that it is appropriate for the child to do so. If possible, the agency and parent should discuss the appropriateness of the child's participation before a decision is made in order to help the parent determine whether the child's attendance would be helpful in developing the IEP, would be directly beneficial to the child, or both. Until the child reaches the age of majority under state law, unless the rights of the parent to act for the child are extinguished or otherwise limited, only the parent has the authority to make educational decisions for the child under Part B of the act, including whether the child should attend an IEP meeting.

This regulation regarding the implementation of IDEA establishes that the parent must be fully informed about the practices related to transition planning, how the process proceeds, and whether they want to include their child. Therefore, gaining parental support is necessary to create a successful plan, and it rests upon the special education team to set up a system to instruct the parent on the school and legislative requirements, as well as the basis for the practices in the research.

If the parent decides not to allow the child to attend the IEP meeting, the IEP team "must take other steps to ensure that the child's preferences and interests are considered" (IEP team, 2006). However, as mentioned earlier, excluding the student, who can fully or partially participate, defeats the underlying purpose of transition planning and the principle of inclusion.

STEPS TO EFFECTIVE TRANSITION PLANNING MEETINGS

When preparing for the IEP meeting where transition is discussed, following consistent procedures enhances the ability for team members to be prepared, organized, professional, and on time.

Individualized Education Plan Team Organization

1. The team facilitator must be a transition planning specialist, transition coordinator, special education teacher, or special education administrator, all of whom can work with the student who can be part of the facilitation activities. A certified administrator is also present to ensure that the law is followed and approve the plan. They also confirm appropriate funding.

2. The team members, including related service staff, input current levels of student academic and functional achievement IEP and recommended next step goals into the web-based IEP system.

3. The facilitator/transition planning specialist develops the meeting agenda.

4. The facilitator designates someone to keep meeting records, also known as minutes.

5. The facilitator resolves group conflicts, such as goal recommendations, ahead of the IEP meeting.

6. The team reviews previous goals both mastered and revised.

7. The team members interview the student and parent to plan the mastered, revised, and new goals for the IEP.

8. The facilitator sends the agenda to team members, the parent, and the student to add additional thoughts and questions. (Even if the student does not attend, his or her preferences are added here.)

9. The facilitator includes additional parent questions and concerns and family transition goals that they may want to discuss.

10. The facilitator assigns a speaking order to each team member and the plan for the parent and student to ask questions and present ideas.

11. The team reviews parent and student questionnaires.

12. The transition planning specialist meets with the student to review the pre-transition planning questionnaire.

13. The transition planning specialist reviews current assessment data with the student.

14. The transition planning specialist and special education teacher, along with any general education teachers who are on the team, meet to discuss the student's involvement in transition planning as well as his or her progress in their classrooms.

15. The facilitator reviews the IEP draft for the meeting.

16. The facilitator sends a draft of IEP goals and recommended and potential services to the team for further collaboration. The team asks the questions: Will the student be able to logistically accomplish these goals? If not, what are the student's priorities?

17. The facilitator determines with the student, who is part of the team, what their priorities are; how they want to accomplish them; and what goals are not longer significant to them, including team member goals.

Parent-Student Communications

1. The transition planning specialist will send out a transition introductory letter. This includes parent information and questionnaire, meeting agenda, and student questionnaire.

2. The facilitator sends an IEP meeting invitation to the parent and the student.

3. The transition planning specialist contacts the parent upon receipt of the letter and gains permission to invite the student. Whether the parent permits attendance or not, an invitation must be sent to the student.

4. The transition planning specialist and the parent confirm attendance and the level of student participation: partial, supported, or full participation.

5. Via teleconference or phone call, the transition planning specialist contacts the parent, updates the parent information section, and goes over any questions about the questionnaire.

6. The transition planning specialist prepares the student transition activity list for the first year.

This level of preorganization ensures that everyone knows the format of the meeting and that the family understands the process.

Preparing the Parent for the Child to Lead or Participate in the Meeting

As noted previously, all special education students are to be formally invited to attend their IEP meetings at age 14. The invitation requires documentation. In some cases, such as those children and adolescents with severe intellectual and behavior disorders, full, supported, or even partial participation in the IEP meeting may not be possible. However, there are other ways of participating. Some examples regarding the process are provided in the following list:

- Parent invitation to transition planning introduction
- Introductory meeting and PowerPoint presentation on the transition process
- Introduction to assessments and post-school goals
- Guidance and support to the parent
- Explanation of the types of student participation:
  - ◦ Input only: Preferences are gathered through observation and from those who know the student.
  - ◦ Partial participation: The student attends the meeting but only observes and gives preferences using a communication device.
  - ◦ Supported participation: The student attends part of the meeting and needs support to share preferences.
  - ◦ Full participation: The student shares goals and interests and information about his or her disability and learns to lead the meeting. He or she also learns to lead the meeting and to do so by graduation.
- Parent receives information on the four types of participation, including ways to encourage the child to attend and voice his or her preferences, hopes, and dreams.
- Parent receives instruction about the importance of self-determination and person-centered planning as it relates to the ways to participate.

Transition Planning Introduction Letter to the Parent

This letter is for the parent of a student who plans to follow the full participation framework for transition. Other examples more relevant to other students with disabilities are located in the Student Supplemental Materials.

Derry School District
1015 Washington Lane
Derry, New Hampshire 03038

Dear Parent,

Federal special education law requires that your child be invited to his or her IEP meeting. In the state of _____, a process called transition planning begins during the school year when your child is going to turn _____, or before if the IEP team recommends it. Here at school, we have a program to help your child learn skills and to provide guidance on reaching employment or educational goals.

To help you learn more about transition planning, you will be asked to participate in initial training that will increase your knowledge about your child's transition to post–high school life. You will also be prepared to work with your child and the special education team during IEP development and during the IEP meeting.

Your participation and your child's participation is a step toward helping your child take on young adult responsibilities as his or her ability and maturity allow.

As noted in your child's most recent IEP meeting, your child will begin participating in multiple activities to help him or her take on more adult responsibilities, explore courses of study, create goals for the future, and participate in a transition curriculum and in career exploration courses with classmates. Your child will also be assigned a transition planning specialist to meet with throughout the year.

We look forward to working with you and your child.

Information about the parent-student transition planning is attached. Please respond by sending back the attached form.

Thank you.

Best regards,

Ms. Barnes
Transition Planning Specialist
mbarnes@schooldistrict.com
Phone: 215-555-5555

The Student Who Declines to Attend

In some cases, the child will resist attending. The process of motivating the student to participate in his or her IEP meeting and begin transition planning will benefit from parental support, and the parental role in encouraging attendance is integral to the child's success.

When the student declines to attend, the team meets with the student and about his or her selected goals, preferences, and career training or interests. After the information is put into a transition plan format (see Chapter 6), the transition planning specialist and the student can meet with the parent in a conference call. The student's ideas for the transition plan are reviewed with the parent, who can collaborate with additional ideas. This meeting can review upcoming events and instruction, such as information on curriculum-based activities, CBI activities, and the dates for parent training (see Chapters 2 and 3).

Teacher Bias and Student Attendance

The transition planning specialist and the special education teacher can best help the student and the family by careful planning, education about transition planning, and ongoing communication with the family and the student. Students often decline the meeting because they are inadequately trained or do not want to participate due to various concerns. The reasons for avoidance may be discovered during the individual conferences. By building rapport with the student and providing the student with opportunities to practice participation, the transition planning specialist can guide the student to participate.

At times, the transition planning specialist may have a personal bias about the student's ability to be the key player in the meeting, and the transition planning specialist's reasoning must be examined. Bias can limit children and youth because of teachers' perspectives on what they can do or not do. The attention given to recognizing the student as a team member requires that the transition planning specialist should fully understand how to implement the types of student participation that are possible. Most likely it will be very different based on the student. However, the student should be guided to attend as much as possible. In the next section is a sample for the student and the parent about how a meeting can proceed.

Student Attends and Leads the Individualized Education Plan Meeting

When the collaborative team prepares a meeting plan, has an agenda, and uses inclusive behaviors, trust can be established with both the parent and the student. The parents and the child feel more confident when they have a clear plan and when they fully understand what they will be doing in the meeting. An easy place to begin including the student is by giving the student time on the agenda to share his or her preferences with the team. The student will be prepared to tell about him- or herself and be better able to share preferences and goals. Sharing some self-selected goals and supports the student may feel he or she needs can be a stepping stone to increasing confidence in eventually leading the IEP meeting.

The student and the parent can be prepared first by understanding the format of the transition planning meeting. A student who is trained can lead his or her IEP meeting. The following is an example of a meeting format to teach the student how to be a leader in the meeting.

Preparation for the Meeting

- Arrival time: Informal greetings
  - Participants sit at assigned seats.
  - Anyone attending via conference call or virtual attendance is brought in.
  - Student reads participants from a list.
  - Student introduces the IEP attendance signature sheet.
  - Informs group the signature is for attendance only.
  - Order of discussion is announced, and an updated agenda is given out.
  - IEP contact information is reviewed and confirmed.
- Meeting content
  - Student hands out current IEP.
  - Review of eligibility needs page.
- IEP discussion
  - Student reviews strengths and needs.
  - Student shares current transition goals.
  - Parent shares the current supports to the student.
  - Transition planning specialist describes current supports he or she is providing.
  - Team members review current academic progress.
- IEP goals
  - Student presents a narrative about his or her disability and how it affects him or her in the following experiences:
    - Academic
    - Social
    - Disability experiences
    - Current and possible post-school concerns about the disability
  - Student can ask for help accessing his or her choice of the following:
    - Community-based experiences
      - Community living choices and goals
      - Developing independence skills
      - Developing leisure activities

- School-based activities
  - After-school clubs
  - Sports/intramural sports
  - Access to after-school noncompetitive sports
- Student can advocate for and receive instruction with his or her parent about access to public and private services:
  - Navigating financial considerations: Social Security and waivers
  - Using CBI
  - Community access/paratransit
  - Using public transportation
  - Training in the community
  - Making connections: Office of Vocational Rehabilitation
- Student can read his or her list of prepared goals from the IEP draft.
- Team members and student discuss or agree on goals. In follow-up transition planning conferences between the student and the transition planning specialist, a plan for accomplishing goals can be carried out.
- Post-IEP meeting goals
  - Transition planning specialist and student review results of transition activities.
  - Transition planning specialist and student create additional personal goals or review student-created new goals.
  - Transition planning specialist and student review the following:
    - Calendar of immediate activities
    - Calendar of planning conferences
    - Career-research schedules/assignment template
    - Visiting vocational-technical schools
    - Reviewing training programs to support student goals
    - Post-school living, community living, and leisure opportunities
    - Evaluating workplace settings and personal needs
    - Developing the self, such as developing living and work skills
    - Using assessments for self-knowledge
    - Planning visits to career centers
    - Reviewing schedule for next transition planning specialist–student conference

FAMILIES THAT DO NOT OR CANNOT PARTICIPATE: SCHOOL AND TEACHER RESPONSIBILITIES

Although family engagement is related to positive student outcomes in special education (Wilder, 2014) and the inclusion of parents at IEP meetings is explicitly stated as promoting success, it must be noted here that at times, due to mental illness, physical illness, incarceration of the parent, lack of financial resources, addiction, terminal illness, or other events, some parents must or do relinquish their role in planning. This is often done without the parent explicitly stating so. However, some parents will welcome a more intensive role lead by the transition planning specialist. It can be expected that in some situations, parents may not respond to meeting requests or do so sporadically.

Family beliefs and cultural constraints may also determine parental involvement. Teachers may define these problems and the situation as untenable due to family problems. Moreover, the transition team may be tempted to relinquish responsibility. This stance defeats the spirit and the requirements of the law. These circumstances mean that the educator in the role of transition planning specialist must be especially diligent in making sure the students trust his or her interest in their success and see him or her as someone who believes that the students can make progress and will provide them needed supports. In these situations, the transition planning specialist may feel more like a mentor than a special educator.

The inability to take on transition planning does not mean the parent should be excluded. A parent who cannot participate wants to hear about the progress the child is making, and updates to the parent can be surprisingly helpful to a student who may feel the absence of the parent. Regular communication with the parent via phone will keep him or her abreast of plans, as well as provide the parent opportunities to give useful information. At times, however, a minor level of participation may not result in a positive outcome. The following section provides an example of this.

Family Belief Systems

At times, families develop a specific worldview and their place in it. For example, some families believe their children should only be doctors or teachers. There are also families who have had little academic success or have had multiple family members who have not graduated from high school. The following case report addresses the latter example.

Case Report: Billy

A student in a program for emotional and behavioral disorders (EBD) came from a family in which no one had graduated from high school. He had received encouragement to graduate from his special education teacher and transition planning specialist, who were unaware of the family's beliefs about education. He decided to share his background with a trusted teacher. He believed his situation was hopeless because his family was actively deterring him. They made it difficult if not impossible to do homework and teased him about doing anything that resembled academics. Bringing books home had become impossible because they were often grabbed from him and tossed back and forth between family members.

The special education team met, and a plan was developed to encourage him. Billy's homework requirements were changed to inspire him to work hard in school to meet his new graduation requirements. The plan was as follows:

- Work diligently and participate throughout each class period.
- Comply with all classroom rules.
- Use study hall to read an economics text (course needed for graduation) and answer all chapter questions.
- Finish all other texts by reading them in school in place of homework.
- Stay after school to keep up.
- Begin looking for work.

The team consulted with the principal about this, and the team agreed that because he had both specific learning disabilities and EBDs and was at high risk for dropping out, this was a way to help him graduate without him bringing it to the attention of his father, who reminded him often that he had not graduated either.

Billy felt he could keep up with the high demands, which was difficult because of his own social projection as a student who bragged to friends about dropping out at 17 years old, the legal age to drop out in his state.

Billy was graded each day based on both productivity and compliance. If all the criteria were achieved, he would receive a grade of A. He found striving for the A each day to be motivating, and it enabled him to focus on an immediate goal rather than a long-term goal. Compliance was also rewarded as it was for his entire EBD class, with preferred food items once a month. The transition planning specialist helped him find a job; like Sam's job in an earlier case report, it lacked prestige but gave him benefits and tuition reimbursement.

Soon he was saying, "If I graduate, I will be the first one." He did graduate. His transition plan included an intensive school-based plan for graduation.

EXERCISES

1. Research family barriers to graduation. Use only peer-reviewed studies.
2. Research the current dropout rate in the United States among students with disabilities and their general education peers.

DISCUSSION

In this case report, Billy met with familial, cultural, and psychological beliefs about education. The family put several barriers in place to support their child not to graduate. These included deterring him from studying and failing to provide a home life conducive to learning. His parents were also alcoholics, and Billy had a mild intellectual disability due to fetal alcohol syndrome.

Although the staff wanted to encourage the parents to support their son, the daily use of alcohol, the negativity, and the threat to the family story would have put the student in a stressful situation rather than help him make progress toward his goal to graduate.

MENTAL HEALTH DISORDERS IN THE FAMILY: EFFECTS ON LEARNING AND EMPLOYMENT

The Parent With Mental Illness and Addiction

Mental health disorders have a significant impact on learning and attendance, but when the parent has the same disorder, family routines are difficult to establish. The following types of mental illnesses are most frequently seen. A parent with a mental health disorder may be unable to manage the complexity of the IEP and transition planning process. The illnesses listed here often require medications that are very sedating, and if the parent also works, the medication significantly cuts into his or her waking hours. Many persons with these illnesses withdraw from life periodically and are unable to provide the parenting their children need.

- Bipolar I
- Bipolar depression/bipolar II
- Cyclothymic disorder
- Schizophrenia spectrum/paranoid schizophrenia
- Psychotic disorders
- Anxiety disorders
- Major depressive disorder
- Agoraphobia conduct disorders
- Drug-induced mental health disorders
- Posttraumatic stress disorder

Each illness has a tremendous effect on emotionally stable and consistent family functioning. Students with parents with mental illness rarely share this information because stigma often reduces the student's willingness to seek help. The children of parents on the schizophrenia spectrum, or those whose parents have periodic psychotic breaks, can often be removed from their homes to emergency foster care overnight. Schools only see this as an absence because there is no clear path to share these overnight or few-day events. Repeated absences require the intervention of the home-school visitor, school social worker, or person designated to that role. In these situations, when parent involvement will be sporadic, it is important to include the parent wherever possible.

Many students who live in these conditions need strong independence skills, and many often have these skills due to years of being on their own during their parents' mental health disorder episodes.

Parents who have degenerative brain diseases like severe schizophrenia often cannot plan or organize their thoughts or speech, and they often have an overwhelming fear of being harmed, to the point of feeling they need to defend themselves. These parents rarely if ever attend IEP meetings, and these students will need counseling and academic support to avoid becoming at risk for dropping out. Repeated absences of a special education student or any student should be examined.

In some families, both parents may have a mental health disorder. When students do not share that their parents are mentally ill, other signs can indicate high stress at home. In the following case report, the mental illness of the mother adversely affected her daughter socially and emotionally. She was placed in an EBD class due to withdrawn behavior. However, the students in the class had many behavioral issues, and the team did not think the placement appropriate, but the student did not seem to be disturbed by all the behaviors.

Case Report: Aileen

Aileen's transition planning focused on academics and pre-employment skills. With the focus on academics, she was able to move from being in an EBD class with academic support to general education. During the period of transition, the transition planning specialist would call to set up conferences or IEP meetings. Each time, there was music playing so loudly that the transition planning specialist could not hear the parent. There were loud verbal interactions going on in the background as well. On one occasion, being unsure that this was the correct number, the transition planning specialist asked if Aileen lived there, and the woman hung up on her. At the time, the transition planning specialist was concerned that the student might be in an abusive situation and met with Aileen about it. Aileen reported that no one ever hurt her there.

The transition planning specialist and the team decided that they would support her but continue to invite her mother. However, her mother never came to school. Eventually, Aileen graduated, had a job in place, and married. Later, she told the transition planning specialist that her mother was mentally ill and would become very boisterous and would "blast her music and sing really loudly." Her mother had many friends in and out of the house. It was not a home Aileen could bring friends to. Eventually, the mother went into mental health treatment, and Aileen and she became very close.

Additional information on mental health disorders will be provided in Chapters 4 and 11.

Early Release of Parental Responsibility

Each school can promote:

> [T]he ways in which each parent will be responsible for supporting their children's learning, such as monitoring attendance, homework completion, and television watching; and participating, as appropriate, in decisions relating to the education of their children and positive use of extracurricular time. (No Child Left Behind Act, 2001)

Although the above quote seems like a positive guide, involvement does not happen in some families, and, in fact, the opposite may be seen. For example, involvement can reflect the family history with education or the health of the parent, as seen in Billy's and Aileen's case reports. Also, when the child starts to rebel during the middle school years, he or she may be given a high level of independence and freedom. This level of freedom, where the child can come and go as he or she pleases before the development of his or her ability to make good choices, can result in deleterious outcomes. A child who can come and go from home with complete freedom may have difficulty planning. Some of these students do not want adult direction, and they become so autonomous that they have not set boundaries for themselves. Students like this usually need to develop a strong rapport with the transition planning specialist. Goal setting and school attendance is the priority. Many of these students only come to school after a court order. This is typically the first boundary that is set. The transition planning specialist can break this cycle by working with the student to develop a transition plan and motivate the student to graduate. Part of the plan can include extended family members the student is close to. These relationships can set up supports for post-school life. Most students have someone who cares for them and provides them with supportive direction. So, even when the parent has relinquished responsibility, other in-school adults and extended family members can step in to help.

Supportive Relationships With Parents

Parental Grief

Parental grief is an ever-present reality for parents of students with severe disorders and disabilities. Mental illness often emerges during the adolescent's transition to adulthood. As mentioned previously, it is marked by an inability to think or speak coherently, and, upon onset, the student will only appear withdrawn and unmotivated. Parents recognize signs of lower functioning behavior and deterioration of speech before the professionals do. They may suspect they are somehow losing the child they know. Parents need multiple levels of support in negotiating the loss of the child they know and in creating a new transition plan to help their child. Circumstances like emergent mental illness, when parents slowly realize that their child will not be doing what he or she was able to do before, are traumatic, and they will begin going through a grief process. The transition planning specialist can collaborate with the school psychologist and attend a grief support training if he or she has not done so already. Those working in special education need to be prepared for the loss of a child or the child the parents knew due to severe mental illness, degenerative diseases, severe and multiple disabilities, and traumatic accidents. To meet this need, there is a parent support section in the IEP, and consultation to the parent can be added to promote communication during crisis periods. Referrals to community agencies can be provided within the IEP as well.

Some parents can be visibly depressed, and the intervention of the school psychologist to provide direction toward support groups may help these parents considerably. Transition planning specialists and special education teachers are not counselors or doctors, and their role is to make a referral to the school psychologist, who is trained to help the parents and classroom teachers in these situations. Parents differ widely on how they express grief, and the primary role of the transition planning specialist is to seek support from the school psychologist and ensure that the connections are made to enable the child to get the needed care through the appropriate governmental agencies. However, a special education team, whose members are sensitive and well-trained in the challenges parents and families face, can provide emotional support, and in-school counselors can be included in a support team to ensure the student remains engaged in their education and understood during challenging times.

The Terminally Ill Parent

You may have a student whose parent is terminally ill, and the student may not talk about it in school. It is helpful to provide in-school counseling to support the student. In addition, the surviving parent will need to meet with the transition team so the student can move forward during this difficult time. Some illnesses, such as cancer, can have prolonged survival with considerable disability. The transition planning specialist will need to take on a more significant role during this time. The student may not be able to see past the time beyond the parent's death, so keeping the focus on the activities of the day is probably helpful. A schedule of phone conferences with the parents, including the ill parent, if able, can be continued so that the parents can be included in their child's life and encourage the child. When a parent dies, children often come back to school very quickly. A 504 plan can be developed to give the student accommodations that allow the child to talk to a counselor as needed. In one case, when a student's mother had died, the teacher told her she could draw or write or read until she was ready to do her work. She wrote a little book about her mother. After 3 days, she quietly said, "I am ready now," and returned to her work.

The Terminally Ill Student

Students can also have terminal illnesses or conditions resulting in shortened lifespans. These students and their parents need special consideration, especially when an illness is degenerative, such as muscular dystrophy. Changes in the transition plan will address how to help these students stay engaged in school, often with the use of assistive technology. Toward the end phases of muscular dystrophy, a student may appear at school less, and the transition planning specialist will need more contact with the family and the general education teachers to make changes to how grades are handled. Students with illnesses like muscular dystrophy often want to continue to come to school and attend their general education classes and physical support classrooms; parents and students will need the academic class program to eventually give grades based on attendance. Children with muscular dystrophy are living longer in some cases, but many pass on by their late teens and early twenties. Parents know that the death of their child is coming, but when it does, the tragedy of it is felt the same, especially since they are gone at the prime of their lives. Attending a funeral is an important way to support the family, who often wants to be with others who knew their child well. Providing solace after the death of a child by sending flowers and making personal visits provides support to the parents and is a help to the entire family.

Parental Physical or Cognitive Disability

Additional considerations and planning are required when the parent also has a disability. Arrangements can be made for transportation to the school and classroom visits, and IEP meetings can be held on the same day to help the parent have more access to the school. Also, the room where the IEP meeting is held must be accessible to the parent. The school can designate an accessible room, and the transition planning specialist must let the parent know that arrangements have been made for him or her.

Another concern is parents who are unable to read or have limited reading ability. By being sensitive to the stigma around lack of reading ability, the transition planning specialist can address this by asking if text-to-speech access to the IEP is needed.

Some parents have a cognitive word blindness or visual problems, such as strabismus, that impair the ability to read. Word blindness, or the inability to convert letter symbols to sounds, is significantly disabling. Therefore, it is important to establish whether any barriers to participation exist and include supports to enable the parents to access the school, the IEP, and other required communications.

Incarcerated Parents

Incarceration of a parent can be particularly challenging, especially if it is the mother who had custody. However, it is important to know when the parent will be returning home because he or she will be getting the child back in most situations. The person who is responsible for the child during the incarceration, as well as the child's social worker, can let you know if the parent will be home and whether he or she wants a copy of the IEP sent via the person acting on his or her behalf. In some cases, the parent may be able to attend the meeting via conference call when his or her release is imminent. Alternatively, the parent may want an update on the child, and prison staff may allow him or her to speak to the special education program supervisor. Confidentiality is imperative, and no reference to any illness, incarceration, or other personal matter should be discussed outside a confidential setting, nor should it be added to an evaluation report or IEP because legal consequences can result. In most cases, the courts have designated a family member as the foster care parent to act in the parent's stead. As defined by special education law, they can act as the parent and be the only contact person for school personnel. Members of the IEP team do not contact incarcerated parents independently. This is the role of the special education supervisor and chief school administrator, who will better know the situation and be able to guide the team on what is appropriate. Once the parent is home, they become the contact for all school communications unless a court order indicates otherwise.

Youth.gov has a number of resources for children and youth who have incarcerated parents. Providing resources and working with other teachers to support the student is a significant protective factor.

Overinvolved and Negatively Involved Parents

Parents may negatively affect their child's path to post-school success, through no fault of their own, due to illness, lack of understanding of their family dynamics, or the disability itself. The following case reports are examples of two such situations.

Case Report: Eve

Eve was a high school student with selective mutism: she could speak but would do so only in the presence of people she knew well. However, it was always difficult to hear her. This is typically a severe anxiety disorder. Eve also had a specific learning disability and had difficulty remembering information presented orally. In Eve's case, the parent had many demands of the IEP team. She believed her daughter had some disabilities. She did have difficulty with word closure, which meant that although she could hear the beginnings of words, the endings were often missed, such as hearing close instead of closed, two words with significantly different meanings. In conversation, processing meaning is delayed, and comprehension of real-time social conversations was difficult, a problem similar to Sam's language processing difficulty. Although she had an excellent vocabulary and read well, she just could not process spoken language for social interaction.

In Eve's relationship with her parent, whom she trusted implicitly, it was never clear whether Eve stopped speaking because the mother was controlling or whether the mother became controlling because Eve was not speaking. Maybe Eve did not fully comprehend what her mother or others were saying, and she allowed her mother to speak for her. This remains unknown.

The transition planning specialist built a rapport with Eve through the conference and interview process. By having a speech processing assessment and writing her narrative about her hopes and dreams, Eve was able to share a side of herself never seen. She wanted to drive and get a job. This was a surprise to the team; because the selective mutism related to anxiety, she had been unable to say this before. Eve did learn to drive, got a car with the help of her parents, got a job, and went on to fulfill other dreams, which she is currently living.

DISCUSSION

Eve's situation was not intentional, and she was able to effectively plan to be independent. She wrote and used her disability narrative to "speak for her" and to get her needs met. She took her academic disabilities into consideration, and she now works in a profession that does not require intensive reading or a lot of complicated discussion. She was able to pursue her preferences with success.

Case Report: Karolyn

Karolyn's mother had moved in with an unsavory person. When Karolyn was home in the evenings, he spent a great deal of time criticizing her. He told Karolyn she was a loser, she was ugly, and she would never amount to anything, as well as other things that cannot be expressed here. Although Karolyn had an intelligent quotient of 130, she became convinced she was unworthy to live. Although her grades were outstanding before this man's arrival in her life, she began to fail and planned to drop out of high school. She also had made a suicide attempt that would have been successful had her mother not gotten a call from school about her daughter's absence and went home to find Karolyn near death. She was placed in a hospital and then a school to help students who are actively suicidal. Although it was a rough start and she was still expressing the intent to die, the counseling program worked on helping her talk about her sadness and make some goals. She did nothing in class, only coming to school to stay out of her home. She repeatedly told her teacher to "just flunk me." She was frozen in the words of the man in her house and the lack of anyone to protect her from him.

Meanwhile, the transition planning specialist for this program, with the support of the school counselor, thought of a plan for her school failure. When the school sent for her grades, the transition planning specialist wrote all As. Karolyn stood by the teacher's desk as she showed Karolyn that she was putting in all As. Karolyn insisted that this not be allowed. She was stunned for a few days and decided to earn those grades she was given freely, telling the teacher, "I am going to make that up to you." Although she never really moved past the negative words of her mother's boyfriend, she did begin to do well, and she worked hard enough to earn the credits to graduate and begin working.

DISCUSSION

Although this is not a typical intervention, the depth of Karolyn's despair required a break into her negative reality. She needed some intervention to override the verbal abuse of this fellow and the lack of protection she received from her mother.

Transition planning for this student moved forward and revolved around her planning a new life elsewhere, graduating, and getting a job. Unfortunately, at times the students with negatively involved parents seek to create real families by having children, and Karolyn did just that.

EXERCISES

1. Describe the possible derailment to self-determination and self-esteem in Eve's and Karolyn's case reports.

2. Go to the Student Supplemental Materials and locate Chapter 3. Read each form and describe 10 things you have learned about transition planning from the forms.

3. Field experience project: Using the interview form from the Student Supplemental Materials, interview a high school student from general education and a student from special education. Describe your results and what you learned about the interview. Prior to the interview, read Chapter 9, which discusses how to establish meaning when interviewing a student.

4. After reading each parent letter, work with at least three other teachers to design an introductory letter that describes your district's parent introduction to transition planning, or work with your classmates and research a district where you reside.

SUMMARY

This chapter addressed collaboration with parents and their children. With training, parents can help their children move toward self-determination by encouraging their children's attendance at IEP meetings and supporting the development of their independence and employment and training skills.

This chapter demonstrates strategies to help parents understand transition, such as sending informative introduction letters to parents and students, collecting information from parents and students via questionnaires, explaining the rationale for planning at age 13, providing a sample outline of activities, and introducing parents and students to participation in IEP meetings. Parent and student training on what transition is and how they can work together on establishing goals is the foundation for developing a plan.

At times, parents may not want to or be able to participate for any number of reasons that they may never share. For example, some parents may not want to participate because they feel they lack the knowledge or experience of teachers and other professionals. There are situations when parents cannot participate. Transition planning specialists and special education teachers must address these situations and find alternative means of inclusion. Inviting parents to regular teleconferences or phone conferences is a proactive strategy to collect important information and to encourage parental participation to the greatest extent possible.

Collaborating with parents and students entails educating them together and individually about the goals and process of transition, developing meeting procedures for them that are communicated and easily understood, providing them with information on transition activities, and seeking to include them both in the decision-making process whenever possible. The transition planning specialist and the secondary special education team are the communicators of the information, processes, and procedures that enhance the parents' ability to be team members who can support their child's journey to adulthood.

References

Barnard-Brak, L., & Lechtenberger, D. (2010). Student IEP participation and academic achievement across time. *Remedial and Special Education, 31*(5), 343-349.

Bartlett, L. D., Etscheidt, S. L., & Weisenstein, G. R. (2007). *Special education law and practice in public schools.* Upper Saddle River, NJ: Pearson/Merrill Prentice Hall.

Beneke, M. R., & Cheatham, G. A. (2016). Inclusive, democratic family-professional partnerships: (Re)conceptualizing culture and language in teacher preparation. *Topics in Early Childhood Special Education, 35*(4), 234-244.

Blustein, C. L., Carter, E. W., & McMillan, E. D. (2016). The voices of parents: Post-high school expectations, priorities, and concerns for children with intellectual and developmental disabilities. *Journal of Special Education, 50*(3), 164-177.

Browder, D. M., & Spooner, F. (2011). *Teaching students with moderate and severe disabilities.* New York, NY: Guilford Press.

Carter, E. W., Austin, D., & Trainor, A. A. (2012). Predictors of postschool employment outcomes for young adults with severe disabilities. *Journal of Disability Policy Studies, 23*, 50-63.

De Houwer, A. (2015). Harmonious bilingual development: Young families' well-being in language contact situations. *International Journal of Bilingualism, 19*(2), 169-184.

Endrew F. v. Douglas County School District, 137 S.Ct. 988 (2017).

Hall, L. J. (2013). *Autism spectrum disorders: From theory to practice.* Boston, MA: Pearson Education.

Hawbaker, B. W. (2007). Student-led IEP meetings: Planning and implementation strategies. *TEACHING Exceptional Children Plus, 3*(5), Article 4.

Hirano, K. A., & Rowe, D. A. (2016). A conceptual model for parent involvement in secondary special education. *Journal of Disability Policy Studies, 27*(1), 43-53. https://doi-org.ezproxy.sju.edu/10.1177/1044207315583901

IEP team, 34 C.F.R. § 300.321 (2006).

Individuals with Disabilities Education Act of 2004, Pub. L. No. 108-446, 20 U.S.C. § 1400 *et seq.* (2004).

Kochhar-Bryant, C. (2008). *Collaboration and system coordination for students with special needs: From early childhood to the postsecondary years.* Columbus, OH: Prentice Hall.

Kohler, P. D., Gothberg, J. E., Fowler, C., & Coyle, J. (2016). Taxonomy for transition programming 2.0: A model for planning, organizing and evaluating transition education, services, and programs. Western Michigan University. Retrieved from http://www.transitionta.org/

Mason, C. Y., McGahee-Kovac, M., & Johnson, L. (2004). How to help students lead their IEP meetings. *TEACHING Exceptional Children, 36*(3), 18-24.

No Child Left Behind Act of 2001, Pub. L. No. 107–110, 20 U.S.C. § 6319 (2001).

Puig, V. I. (2010). Are early intervention services placing home languages and cultures "at risk"? *Early Childhood Research and Practice, 12*, 1-19.

Ryan, R. M., & Deci, E. L. (2006). Self-regulation and the problem of human autonomy: Does psychology need choice, self-determination, and will? *Journal of Personality, 74*, 1557-1585. doi:10.1111/j.l467-6494.2006.00420.x

Siperstein, G. N., Parker, R. C., & Drascher, M. (2013). National snapshot of adults with intellectual disabilities in the labor force. *Journal of Vocational Rehabilitation, 39*, 157-165.

Taylor, S. J., Barker, L. A., Heavey, L., & McHale, S. (2013). The typical developmental trajectory of social and executive functions in late adolescence and early adulthood. *Developmental Psychology, 49*(7), 1253-1265.

Troen, V., & Boles, K. C. (2011). *Rating your teacher team: Five conditions for effective teams.* Thousand Oaks, CA: Corwin Press.

West, E., Leon-Geurero, R., & Stevens, D. (2007). Establishing codes of acceptable schoolwide behavior in a multicultural society. *Beyond Behavior, 16*(2), 32-38.

Westling, D. L., & Fox, L. (2009). *Teaching students with severe disabilities* (4th ed.). Upper Saddle River, NJ: Pearson Education.

Wehmeyer, M., & Webb, K. W. (Eds.). (2012). *Handbook of adolescent transition education for youth with disabilities.* New York, NY: Routledge.

Wilder, S. (2014). Effects of parental involvement on academic achievement: A meta-synthesis. *Educational Review, 66,* 377-397.

Williams-Diehm, K., Wehmeyer, M. L., Palmer, S. B., Soukup, J. H., & Garner, N. (2008). Self-determination and student involvement in transition planning: A multivariate analysis. *Journal on Developmental Disabilities, 14*(1), 25-36.

Young, J., Morgan, R. L., Callow-Heusser, C. A., & Lindstrom, L. (2016). The effects of parent training on knowledge of transition services for students with disabilities. *Career Development and Transition for Exceptional Individuals, 39*(2), 79-87.

Part 3

Assessments

Medical Conditions, Assessment, and Transition

Implications of Disability and Medical Conditions on Work-Seeking Activities and Educational Progress

CHAPTER OBJECTIVES

- → List the primary medical conditions seen in students with disabilities.
- → Describe the contents of an Individual Health Care Plan (IHP).
- → Explain how the school nurse leads in the development of an IHP.
- → Explain why regular comprehensive medical examinations are crucial to the health of nonverbal students.
- → Describe how side effects of medication affect learning.
- → Describe how educational time is lost due to medical conditions.
- → Describe how an undiagnosed seizure disorder may change a student's educational trajectory.

MEDICAL CARE AND DISABILITY

Medical conditions can be a cause of disability because of heredity conditions; the age of the parents; external environmental conditions; and in utero environmental conditions, such as viruses, the use of antibiotics, or the maternal ingestion of toxins (e.g., in the form of certain medications or alcohol).

A medical condition may also be a second disability unrelated or related to the primary disability, such as heart defects that are often present as part of Down syndrome. The combination of both intellectual disabilities and a medical condition further challenges the student. To address the multiple medical diagnoses and their influence on intellectual, physical, and emotional characteristics of disability requires ongoing medical management and medical analysis. Over the course of a student's

Rae, J. M. *A Collaborative Approach to Transition Planning for Students With Disabilities* (pp. 85-103).

life, medical needs will change. Both physical growth and puberty instigate changes in medication effectiveness. Physical growth might require new wheelchairs and standers to accommodate the growing student. Therefore, health care professionals (e.g., physicians, nurse practitioners, school nurses) and parents continually analyze changing health disorders. Teachers and health care professionals monitor the student's daily health condition and alert the nurse to perceived changes in the student's behavior. For life-threatening conditions, such as anaphylactic reactions and unremitting seizures, Medical Crisis Plans (MCPs) are developed with the help of the parents and shared with the school staff and the special education team.

MANAGING STUDENT HEALTH CARE NEEDS

Individual Health Care Plans

Although not required by law, IHPs are highly recommended to avoid errors in the care of students with disabilities who also have medical conditions. The IHP is updated yearly by the parents with their physician, and medical information is then communicated to the school nurse, who with parental permission, can contact the physician. Once an IHP is written, the school nurse reviews it with the special education team and it becomes part of the school and IEP records. Information such as seizure disorders are also noted in the IEP.

Each year, before school starts, the special education administrator or the principal send out medical forms to parents. The updated medical information is compiled, new prescriptions are prepared, and the student's current medical status is reported to the parents by the family physician. Medical forms are returned, and prescriptions are brought in by the parents or sent or faxed directly to the nurse from the physician's office. The school nurse can only administer medication if she has permission forms and prescriptions. Upon receipt of prescriptions and an updated medical history form, the student's current medical status (if there have been changes), an updated IHP, and a new MCP are added to the student's Individualized Education Plan (IEP), nursing records, and permanent special education file. Through these ongoing health records reviews, a longitudinal plan allows monitoring over the student's school years. Longitudinal information is crucial for students with medical conditions and medical complications and disabilities. School nurses are the professionals who organize student health care information. One concern is that at times, medical conditions can be confused with behavioral problems. When a student with cognitive ability ranging from mild intellectual disability to gifted intellectual functioning is in secondary school and begins transition planning, the family and their physician should review medical information directly with the student. This helps the student take on more responsibility for his or her care, which can increase self-determination. When the school nurse develops the in-school IHP, the student should meet with the transition planning specialist and the nurse to review the documents.

The MCP is an emergency plan to communicate procedures when a student has a life-threatening condition, such as intractable seizures or anaphylaxis due to food allergies such as peanuts or fish. The transition planning specialist, along with the school nurse, manages and shares the information so effective transition and Section 504 plans can be developed to support the student's safety. The transition planning specialist has a responsibility to maintain confidentiality. In protecting confidentiality, the school nurse and the transition planning specialist keep student medical records and IHPs secured in a password-protected file and a hard copy in a secured area. Although this level of confidentiality is required, the faculty are expected to provide emergency care and are therefore not bound by the Health Insurance Portability and Accountability Act (HIPAA) because they need to be informed of important medical information and must be trained to know when students may need their help. They must also be trained to carry out life-saving measures in case of emergencies.

Medical Needs and 504 Plans

A 504 plan is both a general education intervention and a special education plan for a student with medical needs. Any student who needs support to access his or her education due to a temporary medical illness is eligible for a 504 plan designed to make changes to his or her program. An IHP can also be developed.

Medical Care and Transition Planning

Due to the impact of medical conditions on job acquisition, employment, and independence, the transition planning specialist must include medical conditions as part of the assessments and job experience placement process. Any medical needs will need to be addressed for all activities of transition.

As the transition planning specialist and student review assessment information, they also discuss medical information. During a conference, it may become evident that a student may not be able to carry out the essential duties of a preferred job. For example, sedating medication, often used for mental health disorders, can challenge some career and employment options.

Alternatively, students may be able to do the job with appropriate accommodations, such as a work schedule adjustment. As mentioned previously, student medical information is protected via HIPAA. The transition planning specialist's responsibility for the privacy of health records requires procedures to maintain confidentiality and prevent other students and other unauthorized persons from gaining access to private information. The student should be informed of his or her rights regarding privacy. However, students should understand that if they have a medical crisis plan, school staff members must know what to do to help them. Otherwise, their privacy is ensured because information protected by HIPAA must be securely handled to prevent access by those without clearance, and all staff members must ensure that the students' information is not shared beyond those who need to know.

To assist students in understanding their medical status and disabilities, special educators refer students to the school nurse, parents, and physicians who guide students to understanding and managing their medical needs.

Parental and Student Consent

Parents, except in families with multiple constraints (discussed in Chapter 3), are responsible for the care of their children, which typically involves taking them to appointments and ensuring they have medical insurance, among other responsibilities. To put together an IHP, parents must supply essential information, medical prescriptions, and medical follow-up with their family physician or clinic-based services. Parents must provide a list of inoculations and important medical information for their child to enter the school program. For students who receive medication in school, a doctor must have signed a release of information so that the school can keep medication and manage its administration at the school. The school nurse shares information regarding how the student is doing on the current prescription.

In some states, prior to the age of majority, a student can give permission for the sharing of relevant psychiatric information. Parents no longer have complete control over their child's access to psychiatric medication or therapy, which may be the case when a child returns to school after a mental health short-term placement. Schools are often informed regarding therapy and medication when a child returns to school. However, depending on the return-to-school plan, some certified staff will be informed, but the student is included in those meetings. Including the student in discussion about their medical care is in keeping with their independence goals. Although parents and students can ask for care, students, without their parents consent, can share their information either verbally or in writing by giving permission to share their records.

The school nurse collects information about what medication is administered at school or home. Behavior monitoring, if the student and parent agree to it, provides information to the doctor about a medication's effectiveness. Charts are used to monitor the times and dates of medication administration, daily alertness, energy levels, agitation, and mood changes. The student, the teacher, and the parents can track the effectiveness of the medicine across settings, or the student may opt only to self-monitor. Daily monitoring provides data to the physician, who determines whether changes need to be made.

The school nurse establishes a preferred mode of scheduled communication with parents to facilitate coordination of medical treatment and to alert parents when medical issues arise. A questionnaire and sample medical form in the Student Supplemental Materials represent examples of medical information documents for the student and parents to complete together. During secondary school, as part of independence goals, the student should be starting the process of learning his or her medical history whenever possible.

Depending on the degree of a student's intellectual disability, independence in filling in these forms will vary. Students with the most severe intellectual disabilities and students with autism who require substantial support, who are typically nonverbal, will need parents, as defined by the Individuals with Disabilities Education Act, to handle all medical information. Students with moderate intellectual disabilities can be part of this process with the full support of parents and staff.

Students with vision disabilities may need to have medical documents in preferred modalities, such as a text-to-speech/speech-to-text program or Braille. However, these students must be asked their preferred reading or communication tools.

Students of transition age who are deaf or hard of hearing need a way to communicate to the school nurse and other professionals. Therefore, communication occurs with the support of an interpreter or the use a text-based communication program. Telecommunications systems for the deaf such as teletypewriters and video relay services (e.g., Sorenson VRS) allow them to interact with medical professionals via phone.

As mentioned throughout this text, one of the components of transition planning includes discussion of the student's disability and how it affects overall functioning in school and out. Arranging conferences to discuss the impact of a disability should also include private discussion with the student about medical care. During these discussions, a school nurse can be very helpful to the student for guidance. Medical goals can be established, such as instruction about health and safety issues, that can help students learn to avoid people who may encourage the use of drugs and alcohol or initiate behaviors that may result in pregnancy, as well as other harmful behaviors that could derail their futures. Parents are partners in health management and are crucially important in providing opportunities to engage their adolescents in positive activities with their families and in the community.

As discussed in Chapter 2, the curricular components of transition planning include medical care education. Students should know how to do things such as set an appointment, manage their medications, and understand their medical needs. They also need to make connections between medical needs, such as medication, and how these needs affect their learning.

In Chapter 3, there was also discussion about parents who were unable or unwilling to be involved in their children's lives. In these situations, the special education team, the transition planning specialist, and the administration should develop programs to ensure these students receive ongoing medical assistance to ensure they know how to access health care. Contact with community agencies through a home school visitor can direct students about securing services.

Exercises

1. What is the parent's role in medical management when a student has an intellectual disability and a medical condition?
2. Explain the consultation and collaboration roles between the parent, school nurse, and special education team.

HEALTH CARE MANAGEMENT

Students who are beginning to manage their medical and health care and treatment may find it useful to identify health care goals. However, without guidance, they may not know where to start. The following choices may help these students understand and take over some aspects of self-management of health, medical care, and mental health care. Students can create and select goals to initiate the process of learning about medical management. The following are potential transition goals.

Self-Care Goals

The student can begin to select goals. A few goals at a time would be most appropriate:
- Go to the nurse's office daily to take prescribed medications.
- Report side effects of medication.
- Self-monitor behavior related to medication.
- Set cellphone or watch alarm to take medicine.
- Attend his or her IHP meetings.
- Participate in lessons on frustration management.
- Set physical activity goals.
- Identify, use, or create school and community activities to participate in.
- Develop a weekly behavior goal.
- Demonstrate a reduction in self-critical comments.
- Obtain counseling as needed.
- With adult assistance, identify early signs and symptoms of depression. Set up a response plan.
- Use community resources to assist with reintegration into school after hospitalization.
- Decrease anxiety by learning and implementing strategies.
- Report thoughts of suicide and homicide.
- Report unusual sensory experiences, such as voices.
- Report problems that are difficult to solve alone.

Self-Advocacy Goals

Learning to manage medical needs is vital to the student's future. Understanding his or her medical conditions helps the student to set goals around health care needs and to prepare to manage medical care postsecondary school:
- Review the IHP and bring the report to review with the current family doctor.
- Find physicians who work with people with disabilities.
- Be able to explain the disability to the doctor and bring a list of needs and concerns.
- Discuss auditory comprehension problems.
- Determine how the doctor will communicate reliably so the information is understood.
- Have written or typed questions prepared for appointments. (For example, a student with disabilities can ask: "I cannot write easily or remember. I need our discussions written down or recorded or I do not recall what we talked about.")
- Get a prescription filled.
- Learn about medical insurance and Medicaid. Apply for Medicaid when needed.
- Keep medical care up to date.

Student and School Nurse Collaboration

The student should be aware of the nurse's role when helping to manage health care during secondary school. The following is a list of services the nurse provides that are helpful to the student. Each of these are reviewed with the student:

- Provides information for student's medical needs
- Facilitates inclusion in general education for students with significant medical needs
- Responds to seizures, and debriefs and provides documentation to the student regarding the time of, type of, and length of the seizure
- Provides emergency care, including determining the need for emergency medical assistance
- Collects doctors' orders
- Monitors and secures medications
- Collects student feedback about affects of medication
- Provides catheterization and tube feeding
- Provides routine diagnoses
- Makes referrals for medical evaluations
- Takes reports about mental health
- Confers with parents to guide student concerns

By being aware of the services nurses provide, students with disabilities can learn to seek the nurse's assistance and see the nurse, the transition planning specialist, and the special education team as resources.

Students With Severe Intellectual and Medical Needs

The roles of the nurse and transition planning team have a significantly different focus for the most impaired and medically fragile adolescents. The following are examples of nurses' responsibilities:

- Teaches and monitors suctioning
- Treats asthma
- Provides emergency life-saving care
- Reviews medical information of students with severe disabilities
- Confers with other medical professionals and teachers to maintain student's daily health
- Confers with private nurses
- Attends IEP meetings for students with severe medical needs
- Contacts parents about medical concerns and updates prescriptions
- Consults with teachers and physical therapist regarding health needs of students with severe physical disabilities who typically have no verbal language
- Follows the state's nurse practice act as well as guidelines established by state departments of education
- Consults with the parents, transition planning specialist, and special education team about medication monitoring
- Performs supervision of medical care to enhance the student's ability to attend school

SCHOOL NURSE AND TRANSITION PLANNING SPECIALIST CONSULTATION AND COLLABORATION

There are areas of medical intervention where the special education team and school counselors consult with the school nurse to best help the transitioning student. Consider the following examples that can be part of an IHP and a 504 plan:

- Physical conditions and classroom access
  - Recovery after physical injuries, such as concussions
  - Impaired mobility
  - Depression, medication management, and side effects
  - Lack of physical stamina due to depression, medication, and muscular dystrophies (MDs) and other health disorders
- Neurological conditions and missed classroom time
  - Uncontrolled movements of seizures
  - Visual perceptual changes post-seizure
  - Impaired problem-solving abilities
- Impact of medical status
  - Time involved with therapy for mental health
  - Access to therapy
  - Monitoring of medication and medical condition
- Inability to cope
  - Inadequate social support
  - Lack of family cohesion in a crisis
  - Ineffective parental coping
  - Anxiety disorders
  - Emergent mental illness
- Inability to complete the role of student
  - Absences from school due to therapy and rehabilitation
  - Impaired coping
  - Cognitive deficits (e.g., memory loss, poor organizational skills)
  - Mood disturbance
  - Impaired self-esteem
  - Transition into a new school environment

The nurse, school counselors, and special educators can include the student in a pre-IEP meeting to consider options and problem-solving approaches that can help with the issues listed previously. For instance, medication may be an issue if a student feels his or her privacy is compromised by multiple students arriving for medication at the same time. When this is a student concern, arrangements are made to manage this more confidentially. If nursing facilities need to be reorganized to accommodate this, then that should be done. Fearing disclosure of mental illness can impair medication compliance. Respecting the student's needs includes having the transition planning specialist and school administration give an expedient response to these needs and protect the privacy needs and rights of students with disabilities and medical needs.

ACCURATE AND COMPREHENSIVE
MEDICAL DIAGNOSIS AND ANALYSIS

Student involvement is crucial when reviewing medical status and resolving concerns such as privacy and confidentiality and overall medical- and disability-based needs. As mentioned in the previous section, for students with multiple physical, sensory, and intellectual disabilities, discerning medical conditions, and even pain, is a significant challenge.

Medical Care and the Nonverbal Student With Severe Intellectual Disabilities

For students with the most severe intellectual and physical disabilities, medical conditions can account for changes in behavior. For this reason, medical considerations, especially for students who are nonverbal or lack self-advocacy skills, must be the first consideration. Ignoring medical history or the possibility of a new condition can result in a failure to impart best practices in medical care. Observations often focus on behavior, and this can delay medical review, such as in the following case report.

Case Report: Parson

Parson is nonverbal, uses a picture-based communication system, and has an intellectual disability. Due to a drug raid at his home when he was 8 years old, he became excessively anxious as well. The anxiety resulted in a refusal to transition or difficulty with transitions between teachers and classrooms. After the drug raid, the Department of Human Services placed him in a residential community and made him a ward of the state. In residential facilities, high staff turnover is often the norm. Few residential staff knew Parson well enough to notice his behavioral changes. In school, the changes were apparent because there were long-term staff members who knew him for 8 years.

At age 16, Parson began falling asleep in school after lunch. Upon awakening, he would wet himself. He became distraught, having long been toilet trained, and he wanted to go home even though there were extra clothes and facilities to wash the soiled items.

Using a picture communication board, he asked to go home. Asking to go home was a change in his behavior. His teacher wanted to do a functional behavior assessment (FBA), which may indicate what is happening to cause the behavior. However, staff were unable to determine an antecedent to the wetting other than sleeping, which was also a new behavior.

Another observation was planned. The team members, the nurse, the teacher/transition planning specialist, and the supervisor observed him when he fell asleep. Upon awakening him, there were some mild, full-body tremors. The nurse and supervisor had seen many types of seizures and believed the brief period of shaking to be a seizure. However, the student's medical records at school did not indicate a seizure disorder history. The school nurse made a request of the residential program doctor for an electroencephalogram (EEG) to detect seizure activity.

However, that did not explain the wetting. Parson's teacher had also been collecting data on his toileting habits. He noticed an increase in urination, and he provided previous urination records to compare with current records. The data demonstrated doubling of his urination. The teacher, who had adult-onset diabetes, related this to his experience and expressed further concern. The nurse was unconvinced of the need for another referral, but a full special education team review indicated that his recent behavior changes, the wetting, and the sleeping were all uncharacteristic.

After discussion and team advocacy, the residential home medical director ordered another medical assessment and a records review. A review of his 8-year-old records at the group home revealed that the student did, at one time, have a diagnosis of epilepsy, and because at age 8 he had been seizure free, medication was discontinued. Now, at age 16, due to puberty, he could again experience seizures. The EEG revealed that this was indeed the situation. The medical assessment also revealed diabetes. Seizures made him fall asleep and he had a seizure upon awakening, while diabetes caused the urinary incontinence. Although his early school records noted the seizure disorder, the information was not noted in subsequent IEPs and IHPs.

EXERCISE

1. How would the use of an IHP and improved record keeping have helped the diagnosis of Parson's medical conditions?

DISCUSSION

It is imperative to include a comprehensive list of previous medical information in each IHP and IEP. When a medical disability has gone into remission, there is always a possibility for a reoccurrence. Nonverbal students cannot tell adults how they feel, and at times, even those who can speak have difficulty seeking help.

Although a communication board would not have helped in this situation, for students who are nonverbal, it is crucial to develop a picture communication board that includes illness so that the nonverbal student can advocate in this way. When there are physical, ritualistic activity changes or behavioral changes, these can be signs of illness or pain. When a child is a ward of the state, schools and the residential facility or foster family must be vigilant in ensuring medical information is handled correctly.

However, even with a communication board, a student with an intellectual disability will have impaired communication. The transition planning specialist and school nurse can ensure optimum care by following up on these issues, providing communication tools, and involving the student's caretakers. The transition planning specialist ensures all information is included in the IEP and IHP so that future placements can ensure his health and safety.

MEDICAL CONDITIONS AND DISABILITY

According to the Centers for Disease Control and Prevention (2018), medical status is a known cause of disability. The following medical conditions and diseases cause functional and cognitive disabilities. They also compound the effects of the primary disability. The student with medical conditions and disabilities, the transition planning specialist, and the special education team should know each student's medical condition so that employment and educational plans can be developed with any adaptations needed to address constraints on the student. The following section contains the more typical, prevalent medical conditions that compound or cause disability.

Neurological Conditions

Epilepsy and Seizures

Epilepsy is a neurological condition, and it is the most chronic condition encountered by school personnel (Barnett & Gay, 2015). Epilepsy is characterized by recurrent seizures. Seizures are caused by temporary unregulated electrical charges in the brain (Shorvon, Guerrini, Cook, & Lhatoo, 2012). A seizure is epilepsy when the generation of seizures is long-term or involves recurring, unprovoked seizures (Camfield & Camfield, 2003). There are two key times during the lifespan when epilepsy can develop: early childhood and during puberty, with 75% occurring by age 20 (Barrett & Sachs, 2006).

Seizures are not synonymous with epilepsy. In the school setting, this may be confusing. Often the phrase *having seizures* is the description used to report epilepsy. Seizures can cause changes in a student's behavior, movements, feelings, and level of consciousness. If a student has two or more seizures or a tendency to have recurrent seizures, a physician typically does an EEG to confirm the diagnosis of epilepsy. Video EEG is one of the most effective ways to determine the presence of ongoing seizure activity. In the following case report, a video EEG monitor was used for diagnosis.

Case Report: Henry

Henry was placed in a special education class for emotional and behavioral disorders (EBDs) during kindergarten. By the time he was 15, he had spent his entire school life in a class for students with emotional disturbance. Finally, he was placed in an EBD class in a partial hospital program. He was placed for depression and periodic and disruptive behavioral outbursts. On a number of occasions, Henry would suddenly jump up and have an angry outburst. An FBA was completed, but no antecedent for each behavior was seen. In other words, nothing at all precipitated the events. A staff member with some experiences with seizures suggested maybe he was having an absence seizure of some type that caused the outbursts.

After this, Henry had one last outburst in which he started confronting a peer, saying he was going to kill him. The targeted student was a student who had been reported to frequently provoke other students. A crisis procedure was initiated, and Henry left the building to a calm-down area. Staff implemented a de-escalation protocol and asked him to place the scissors he used for the threat on the steps. He began talking as if nothing had happened, and the teacher believed he really did not know what had just transpired.

It was then suggested that testing be done to determine if he was having seizures. His placement was in jeopardy because the setting could not handle that level of violent behavior. Henry was put on a monitor for 24 hours. The result was that he had 32 seizures of the absent type over a 24-hour period. He was put on seizure medicine and was able to return to general education.

EXERCISE

1. How did carrying out the FBA change the course of assessment from a behavioral explanation to seeking an alternative medical explanation?

DISCUSSION

Henry's case report is an example of the need for full medical assessments for all students with learning and emotional disorders. Clearing medical problems is the first step to providing appropriate services for students to benefit from their education and to successfully make the transition to adulthood.

Muscular Dystrophies

MDs cause a variety of disabilities depending on the type of MD. The disabilities are physical, but in some types an intellectual disability is present as well. MD causes progressive muscle weakness and muscle wasting (atrophy). Decreases in mobility make the tasks of daily living difficult. MDs are a group of conditions in which voluntary movement weakens over time. They can develop at any time from infancy to adulthood.

There are a number of MDs, and studies are being done about the effects on children from birth to late adolescence (Centers for Disease Control and Prevention, 2018). In the school setting students with any of the MDs require an IHP and related services such as consultation between the school nurse and the student's medical team, in school medical supervision, and an IEP that makes ongoing modifications to the student's program as the MD progresses.

The significant needs of adolescents with MDs require ongoing parent–special education team and school nurse contact. Eventually, respiratory problems and changing orthopedic problems occur. In the end stages, the special education team will increase the supports to the student to help him or her transition to end-stage care. The lifespan of a student with MD depends on the type of MD and can range from the teens to age 30. Research has made some progress in improving longevity. Special education teams and the transition planning specialist should develop knowledge of the type of MD and the emergence of increasing physical disability and be prepared to make appropriate accommodations and modifications as needed.

Problems related to congenital brain malformation, which occurs in some forms of congenital MD, include intellectual disabilities, vision problems, behavioral and learning problems, and seizures.

Spina Bifida

Spina bifida is a neural tube defect of the spine. Typically, it is diagnosed at birth. The spinal cord is open or split meaning the closure of the neural tube was not completed. In more severe cases the spinal cord protrudes through the back and can be damaged in utero or via trauma to the spine during delivery (Burns et al., 2017). Spina bifida can include physical and intellectual disabilities from mild to severe, an inability to feel legs and feet, and an inability to move the legs. Also, difficulty releasing urine can result in toxicity and organ failure. Two types of spina bifida cause disabilities: myelomeningocele and meningocele.

Cerebral Palsy

Cerebral palsy (CP) can be congenital, when brain damage occurs before birth, or acquired, when brain damage occurs after birth. Brain damage affects the ability to control muscle movement. There are four types of CP: spastic, dyskinetic, ataxic, and mixed. Some children have more than one type. CP is caused by infection; injury; or decreased blood flow to the brain from trauma, such as a car accident, stroke, heart problems, or sickle cell disease (Smithers-Sheedy et al., 2013). CP can result from multiple births or premature births, and mothers who have epilepsy have a slightly higher risk. Children and adolescents with CP require ongoing medical monitoring related to the effects of CP. Children with CP are represented significantly in special education programs, and they may have accompanying intellectual disabilities or learning disabilities.

Scoliosis

Scoliosis is a curve in the spine and includes a permanent rotation of the spine that can advance and become disabling and painful (Rousseau & Bessette, 2012). Those with CP or MD can also have scoliosis. In severe cases, the rib cage will press on the lungs and heart, making it difficult to breathe and for the heart to pump. In severe cases, a titanium rod is used to straighten the spinal column to correct the curve and improve the functioning of the heart and lungs.

Respiratory Conditions

Asthma

Asthma is the periodic restriction of the bronchi and bronchioles that makes it difficult to breathe. It ranges in severity. Childhood asthma is a common chronic condition. Often asthma is triggered during exertion. Asthma can adversely affect school performance because of absences due to asthma attacks. School support for the treatment of asthma requires consultation among the school nurse, the family, and the physician to coordinate the treatment protocol across settings. The IHP for a student with asthma contains an asthma emergency treatment plan for emergency management of asthma symptoms and an individualized asthma action plan (American Academy of Asthma Allergy & Immunology, 2016).

Anaphylactic Shock

Anaphylactic shock or anaphylaxis, as noted previously, is life threatening because it causes internal swelling, which closes the breathing passages.

Anaphylactic shock results from consumption of, for example, peanuts, fish, and aspirin (Eigenmann et al., 2018). Most students who are anaphylactic have epinephrine on their person. If the affected student recognizes the reaction soon enough, he or she can self-administer the shot. If not, school personnel should be trained during their biyearly Red Cross life-saving trainings. Under either condition, the student will need immediate hospitalization. It takes several days after a severe reaction to return to typical functioning. Many of these students will experience ongoing lesser symptoms that require monitoring. Although there are no known cognitive effects of this type of allergy, severe allergies can result in skin and breathing problems that impact educational access. Students with this condition will need an IHP and a 504 plan for the required emergency care after hospitalization. School-wide training is paramount to avoid panicked or negligent responses, which may result in the loss of life-saving care.

Cystic Fibrosis

Cystic fibrosis (CF) is an inherited and fatal genetic disease that requires ongoing medical treatment. There are no intellectual disabilities caused by CF; however, complex medical treatments are warranted, and quality of life and school attendance are adversely affected due to the health impact of CF. CF most often affects the lungs, but it can also affect the sinuses, digestive system, liver, pancreas, and reproductive organs (Thomson & Harris, 2008). CF leads to progressive loss of lung function. The IHP of a student with CF will include inhaled medicines, daily airway clearance techniques, and pancreatic enzyme supplements. Exposure to colds and other respiratory infections require long recovery periods and extensive absences, putting the student significantly behind his or her peers.

Pneumonia

Pneumonia and other illness may also affect students. Students with the most severe disabilities usually have a greater propensity toward contracting infectious diseases such as pneumonia and influenza. Additionally, many also have difficulty clearing their lungs and require suctioning throughout the school day. The inability to clear the lungs leads to pneumonia and lung infections. Pneumonia leads to acute respiratory distress, and if not treated, death (Ventura, Bonsignore, Gentile, & De Stefano, 2010). Therefore, ongoing monitoring and interventions such as suctioning and airway clearance techniques are used to keep the lungs and throat clear of mucus.

Congenital Complications

Anencephaly, Microcephaly, and Hydrocephaly

Anencephaly is a type of neural tube birth defect that prevents formation of the brain and skull. The baby is born without the front of the brain and the cerebrum, causing profound disabilities. Microcephaly is when the brain does not grow. It results in multiple and severe disabilities, including intellectual disability, feeding and swallowing issues, balance issues, hearing loss, and vision problems. Seizures are often present as well. Hydrocephaly occurs when there is a buildup of cerebrospinal fluid in the brain. Depending on the amount of fluid, brain damage or other symptoms such as difficulty walking can occur. This condition may or may not cause intellectual disability, as long as the fluid does not create too much pressure on the brain. However, it often causes severe pressure on the brain. It is treated with a shunt, a tube that drains the fluid from the brain. If not treated, severe to profound intellectual disability can occur, as well as an enlarged and disfiguring head size. Hematomas can also cause hydrocephaly. When this occurs, a head injury or child abuse must be considered.

Congenital Heart Defects

Congenital heart defects (CHDs) can be present in children with disabilities. CHDs are typically present in children with Down syndrome. Some children with Down syndrome do not have these defects repaired, and these children receive medical monitoring over their lifespan. CHDs do not cause disability, but along with a disability, they impact future care.

Jaundice and Kernicterus

Jaundice is a condition that results when a chemical called bilirubin builds up in the blood (Gazzin, Masutti, Vitek, & Tiribelli, 2017). This happens when, after birth, a baby's liver cannot remove the bilirubin and causes a yellow color in the skin. Kernicterus is a type of brain damage that occurs if jaundice is not treated. It also causes CP, hearing loss, vision loss, teeth problems, and sometimes intellectual disabilities.

Anoxia and Hypoxia

Anoxia is a complete lack of oxygen to the brain, and hypoxia is a reduced supply of oxygen. During birth, compression, twisting, or knotting of the cord cuts off an infant's oxygen supply. A doctor may also cause this by mistakenly cutting the umbilical cord too soon before the baby is breathing on its own. A baby that moves around actively in the womb can get tangled in the cord. The cord can wrap around the neck, leg, or ankle. As the baby tries to move, it compresses and constricts the cord, depriving the baby of oxygen. Heart rate monitoring can detect this, but without prenatal care, this is missed and results in anoxia or hypoxia and brain damage.

Drowning, near drowning, and asthma strangulation also cause anoxia and hypoxia. Recovery from near drowning without brain damage is rare. The brain damage from each situation can range from mild to profound (Hypoxia, n.d.).

Environmental Toxins

Fetal Alcohol Syndrome

Fetal alcohol syndrome causes a wide range in the degree of impairment. This syndrome occurs when the mother drinks during pregnancy. Alcohol causes multiple developmental problems such as small head size, abnormal facial features, shorter than average height, low body weight, and poor coordination. Other behaviors that affect school success are hyperactive behavior, attention difficulties, poor memory, learning disabilities, speech and language delays, and intellectual disabilities. Adolescents with fetal alcohol syndrome can demonstrate poor judgment. Other disabilities and medical issues are vision and hearing problems and heart, kidney, and bone problems. These limitations and the concomitant medical issues require ongoing monitoring when the medical conditions are present or when the student complains about physical pain (Fetal alcohol syndrome, n.d.).

Gastrointestinal Conditions

Gastroesophageal reflux is chronic and life-threatening for many children with severe disabilities. Contents from the stomach regurgitate into the esophagus, which leads to direct aspiration of food. This causes infections and pneumonia. Oral-motor and pharyngeal motor problems reduce the child's ability to swallow and masticate food. Many times, this is the instigation for inserting a feeding tube. This avoids damage to the throat due to stomach acids and reduces food aspiration and choking. Students who are not tube fed must not be prone post-meals for therapies. One full hour for digestion is required to prevent aspiration (Gastroesophageal reflux, n.d.).

Psychological Illnesses

Mental illnesses and mental health conditions, also known as *mental health disorders*, can be present in any person with a disability. They cause psychological symptoms and atypical behaviors that vary in intensity. There are multiple mental health disorders, such as anxiety disorders, depression, bipolar disorder, schizophrenia spectrum disorder, obsessive-compulsive disorder, trauma and stress-related disorders, and dissociative disorders (American Psychiatric Association, 2013). These disorders often

TABLE 4-1. GRADE 9 REPORT CARD			
MAJORS	**GRADES**	**ELECTIVES**	**GRADES**
English	B+	Health	A-
American History	B	Child Health	B-
Physical Science	B	Marching Band	A
Algebra	B	Band	A+
French 2	B+	Orchestra	A
Intro to Business	B+	Phys Ed	A-

emerge between age 14 and 24, during the transition to adulthood. Each of these disorders typically results in the need for mental health care and complicates the transition to adulthood. The effects of mental illness interfere with the ability to cope with social and academic pressures. The medication for decreasing mental health disorder symptoms can be very sedating.

Students with any disability are not immune from having a mental health disorder as well. Having a learning disability and a mental health disorder requires special education, an IHP, and a 504 plan. A 504 plan expedites changes in schedules and academic requirements when the symptoms of the mental health disorder impair academic and physical ability. A shortened school day or a chance to rest may lessen the impact of the sedation. If a hospitalization occurs, a part-time transition back to school can be helpful.

The following case from Rae (2011) reflects the needs of a young girl who, due to the emergence of bipolar disorder, began to fail in school.

Case Report: Ms. Smith

Ms. Smith received the diagnosis of bipolar disorder during the ninth grade through private treatment with a psychiatrist. She reports having no memory of this year, and she is unclear about the cause of this memory loss. However, she does know that her grades were good up until 10th grade, but that knowledge could have come from her transcript review with the researcher during transition planning. Her school records during ninth grade indicate a high level of performance. Her high school transcripts reflected a challenging schedule and included the courses and grades shown in Table 4-1.

On the 10th-grade transcript, a marked decline was evident in the first semester. She earned only two grades in general education: a B+ in geometry and a D in biology. During the summer after her ninth-grade year, she was hospitalized for the first time. She reported that she was then put on "a lot" of medication and that the disorder and the medication side effects affected both her academic and social-emotional performance. She reported the following:

> At that point, I was unable to stay awake in class because of the side effects. I was falling asleep, and the teachers were calling my parents saying, "What is the matter with your kid? She is unable to stay awake during the day." [The teachers] made me stand in the back of the room so I would stay awake. I did really badly in tenth grade. [The diagnosis] makes it difficult for me to concentrate. I get frustrated easily. I get overwhelmed when under stress, and I have difficulty completing tasks, which is why it is so important for me to be in a small school with therapists where they let me take a little break when I start to get really upset. If I cannot escape my stress, I begin to cut myself.

She also described her moods as unstable and emotionally intense: "The instability of my mood was difficult for students in general education to understand, causing social problems that are confusing and distracting to me."

EXERCISE

1. How did teacher bias or assumption interfere with the education and medical care of this student?

DISCUSSION

In this story, it is easy to see and extrapolate to other students how hard it is to meet the expectations of the academic program with a mental health disorder. With detailed transition planning, this student went to college, graduated with honors, and is now working at a job that suits her intellect while providing medical insurance to meet her ongoing mental health needs.

MEDICATION SIDE EFFECTS

Medications have side effects that can cause significant discomfort to the student. Often, as in the case of seizure medications, the cognitive effects are detrimental to alertness and, in many cases, memory. Medication to treat mental health disorders can also impair functioning. The following are only a few possible side effects of mental health disorder medication, such as antianxiety medications, benzodiazepines, antipsychotics, and mood stabilizers. Medication can cause the following side effects:

- Sleep problems
- Decreased appetite
- Delayed growth
- Headaches and stomachaches
- Rebound irritability when the medication wears off
- Mood and behavior changes
- Constipation
- Stomach pain
- Nausea
- Breast swelling
- Severe drowsiness
- Missed periods
- Excessive weight gain

The symptoms listed previously lead to difficulties across settings. In addition, they often lead to noncompliance to medication protocols set by the student's psychiatrist or physician.

Medication Management and Documentation

To help with establishing the correct dose, medication monitoring is crucial. This is especially important for the medications used for mental health stabilization. As in Ms. Smith's case report, the medication that controlled the symptoms made it impossible to her to function in school. Medication charting and the student's self-monitoring could have helped Ms. Smith function in school. A personalized charting system that applies to the individual student should be designed. Table 4-2 shows an example, and see the Student Supplemental Materials for another example. A transition planning specialist can work with the student and the school nurse to add to an existing format to better reflect the needs of the individual student. Understanding how medication affects school, employment, and social interactions is essential during the transition to adulthood. The transition planning specialist and school nurse are crucial to the development of self-care skills for students with medical illnesses.

TABLE 4-2. MEDICATION CHARTING

MEDICATION CHARTING WEEK OF _____	MONDAY	TUESDAY	WEDNESDAY	THURSDAY	FRIDAY
Time					
Medication					
Dosage					
Teacher observation					
Side effects Yes/No Describe:	YES				
Drowsy					
Inattentive					
Irritable					
Disorganized					
Speech disorganized					
Other					

Life-Sustaining Interventions

The following medical supports are commonly used with students who have the most severe disabilities. These medical interventions increase life expectancy by sustaining life through alternate feeding, breathing, and the maintenance of bodily functions:

- Feeding tubes, which provide a form of liquid sustenance
- Breathing tubes, which are placed in the nose or throat
- Nebulizers, which are used to treat severe asthma
- Tracheostomy (trach), which is a curved tube that is inserted into a tracheostomy hole made in the neck and windpipe (trachea). There are different types of tracheostomy tubes that vary in certain features for different purposes (Browder & Spooner, 2011).
- Oxygen, which is used to keep the blood oxygenated when the body can no longer do it on its own
- Braces or other physical supports, which are placed on the legs and hands to prevent muscle atrophy, improve circulation, and prevent sores developing from immobility

EFFECTS OF MEDICAL CONDITIONS AND WORK SEEKING

As mentioned earlier in the chapter, medical conditions have a significant effect on the type of employment students will seek. Some conditions prohibit driving, heavy labor, or supervision of children due to physical conditions or sedation. Therefore, meeting with students and developing trust is crucial to developing plans when medical illness and disability prevent full employment. Other options are available such as part-time work, working from home, or positions that can be handled with or without accommodations. There are employment risk assessments that can help the student and the transition planning specialist develop transition plans that are most likely to result in an outcome that will create inclusion and satisfaction in adult life.

Risk Assessment and the Americans With Disabilities Act

According to the Equal Employment Opportunity Commission, an individual with a disability must also be qualified to perform the essential functions of the job with or without reasonable accommodation in order to be protected by the Americans with Disabilities Act (ADA). This means that the applicant or employee must:

- Satisfy the job requirements for educational background, employment experience, skills, licenses, and any other qualification standards that are job related
- Be able to perform those tasks that are essential to the job, with or without reasonable accommodation

The ADA does not interfere with an employer's right to hire the most qualified applicant, nor does the ADA impose any Affirmative Action obligations. The ADA simply prohibits employers from discriminating against a qualified applicant or employee because of his or her disability.

Essential Functions for Employment

The student and the transition planning specialist should carefully examine each job to determine which functions or tasks are essential to performance and which can be managed with accommodations. Employers have lists of essential functions for each job position. For instance, if a student wants to drive a delivery truck, he or she may have to carry up to 60 pounds from the truck to the front door. The essential functions are typically listed on the company's website. At times they are part of the job description.

Factors to consider when selecting work include the following:

- Does the student feel he or she can perform the job that is being advertised and described?
- What is the degree of expertise or skill required to perform the function of the job?
- Is it an entry-level position?
- What kind of time commitment does the job require?
- Can the student be transported there, and how will this be achieved?

The student must have an understanding of what employment would provide satisfactory life experiences and how the disability may require attention to how they can participate in employment. There are agencies that help with employment. Organizations such as the MDA work with people with MD to find employment. The transition planning specialist can guide the student to research organizations that can support his or her employment efforts. In addition, there are options for employment listed in the Student Supplemental Materials for the chapters on individual disabilities. Students can also use the essential functions as a guideline to learn what skills they will need to perform jobs of interest and use the transition planning process to develop those skills.

EXERCISES

1. Interview a student with a medical disability about how having a medical condition affects his or her education.
2. Interview a student with a physical disability about supports in place for moving around the building.
3. Describe the purpose of an IHP.
4. What is medication monitoring, and what is its purpose?
5. What are self-care goals?
6. What is self-advocacy in the context of medical care?
7. What are essential job skills, and how do they affect students with medical disabilities?

SUMMARY

This chapter discusses the effects of medical conditions and the needs of students with these conditions. Consideration is given to how these conditions influence transition programs and employment. Some of these are profound and life-long conditions that require the transition planning specialist and family to plan for employment in relation to the student's life course while creating as many opportunities as possible. Schools, colleges, and employers can support inclusion of youth with disabilities and health care needs. However, even with the severity of a given medical condition, employment, post-school education, and lifestyle satisfaction can be expected with proper supports in place. In cases when students cannot speak for themselves, substantial effort on the part of the school-based team can result in far better outcomes for students with disabilities and medical conditions.

The transition planning specialist, the school nurse, and the parents are pivotal in guiding the student to understand and participate in his or her health management or to coordinate post-school care. Medical professionals are also key contacts for parents whose children require ongoing life-sustaining support.

The special education team and medical support professionals are also involved in the day-to-day concerns regarding the impact of the medical condition(s) on academic, social, and independence needs. Health management is crucial to the student's school performance and workplace inclusion.

In two of the case reports in this chapter, the disintegration and disruption of academic progress and normal inclusion in the community derailed the students' success and made it unlikely for them to find in-school or post-school success. Henry's medical condition resulted in a life in the most restrictive school environment, and Ms. Smith's mental illness resulted in school failure and a loss of her academic status and her school activities. Without medical intervention and the support of the transition planning specialist, both would have been in and out of school and work, and in Henry's case, his outcome could have been incarceration. The medical conditions of students with disabilities should always be the first line of support.

REFERENCES

American Academy of Allergy Asthma & Immunology. (2016). School-Based Asthma Management Program. University of Wisconsin – Madison Department of Medicine. Retrieved from http://hipxchange.org/SAMPRO

American Psychiatric Association. (2013). *Diagnostic and statistical manual of mental disorders* (5th ed.). Washington, DC: American Psychiatric Association Publishing.

Barnett, J. E. H., & Gay, C. (2015). Accommodating students with epilepsy or seizure disorders: Effective strategies for teachers. *Physical Disabilities: Education and Related Services, 34*(1), 1-13.

Barrett, R. P., & Sachs, H. T. (2006). Epilepsy and seizures. In L. Phelps (Ed.), *Chronic health-related disorders in children: Collaborative medical and psychoeducational interventions* (pp. 91-110). Washington, DC: American Psychological Association.

Burns, C. E., Dunn, A. M., Brady, M. A., Starr, N. B., Blosser, C. G., & Garzon, D. L. (2017). *Pediatric primary care* (6th ed.). St. Louis, MO: Elsevier.

Browder, D. M., & Spooner, F. (2011). Teaching students with moderate and severe disabilities. New York, NY: Guilford Press.

Camfield, P., & Camfield, C. (2003). Childhood epilepsy: What is the evidence for what we think and what we do? *Journal of Child Neurology, 18*(4), 272-287. https://doi.org/10.1177/08830738030180041401

Centers for Disease Control and Prevention. (2018). CDC Organization and Roles. Centers for Disease Control and Prevention. Retrieved from: https://www.cdc.gov/about/organization/mission.htm

Eigenmann, P. A., Akdis, C., Bousquet, J., Grattan, C. E., Hoffmann-Sommergruber, K., Hellings, P. W., & Agache, I. (2018). Highlights and recent developments in food and drug allergy, and anaphylaxis in EAACI Journals (2017). *Pediatric Allergy and Immunology, 29*(8), 801-807.

Fetal alcohol syndrome. (n.d.) *Gale Encyclopedia of Medicine.* Retrieved from https://medical-dictionary.thefreedictionary.com/fetal+alcohol+syndrome

Gastroesophageal reflux. (n.d.) *Miller-Keane Encyclopedia and Dictionary of Medicine, Nursing, and Allied Health* (7th Ed.). Retrieved from https://medical-dictionary.thefreedictionary.com/gastroesophageal+reflux

Gazzin, S., Masutti, F., Vitek, L., & Tiribelli, C. (2017). The molecular basis of jaundice: An old symptom revisited. *Liver International: Official Journal Of The International Association For The Study Of The Liver, 37*(8), 1094-1102. https://doi-org.ezproxy.sju.edu/10.1111/liv.13351

Hypoxia. (n.d.) *McGraw-Hill Concise Dictionary of Modern Medicine.* Retrieved from https://medical-dictionary.thefreedictionary.com/hypoxia

Rae, J. M. (2011). Post Transition Planning–Young Adult Stories—Perspectives on School and Life: A Case Study of Employment, Social, Family and Mental Health Management Outcomes of Three Young Adults Who Completed Two or More Years of High School in an Emotional and Behavioral Special Education Program in Partial Hospitalization 1 Setting (Doctoral dissertation). Retrieved from Proquest. (3448164).

Rousseau, C. M., & Bessette, A. (2012). *Scoliosis: Causes, symptoms & treatment.* Hauppauge, NY: Nova Biomedical.

Shorvon, S., Guerrini, R., Cook, M., & Lhatoo, S. (Eds.). (2012). *Oxford textbook of epilepsy and epileptic seizures.* Oxford, United Kingdom: Oxford University Press.

Smithers-Sheedy, H., Badawi, N., Blair, E., Cans, C., Himmelmann, K., Krägeloh-Mann, I., … Wilson, M. (2013). What constitutes cerebral palsy in the twenty-first century? *Developmental Medicine And Child Neurology, 56*(4), 323-328. https://doi-org.ezproxy.sju.edu/10.1111/dmcn.12262

Thomson, A. H., & Harris, A. (2008). *Cystic fibrosis* (Vol. Updated and rev. 4th ed). Oxford, United Kingdom: OUP Oxford.

Ventura, F., Bonsignore, A., Gentile, R., & De Stefano, F. (2010). Two fatal cases of hidden pneumonia in young people. *Journal of Forensic Sciences, 55*(5), 1380-1383.

Assessment Tools

CHAPTER OBJECTIVES

→ Describe the difference between the use of eligibility assessments and transition assessments.

→ Identify a variety of formal and informal transition assessments and procedures.

→ Identify student strengths, preferences, and interests as they relate to post-school settings.

→ Distinguish between age-appropriate transition assessments and those assessments that are not age-appropriate.

→ Describe a framework of assessments for a student who is nonverbal.

→ Describe a framework of transition for a student with learning disabilities who is college bound.

→ Describe how language impacts interaction in the workplace and how assessments are used to identify expressive and receptive language development.

→ Use the results of living skills analysis to develop goals in natural environments.

→ Use valid and reliable assessment practices to minimize bias based on disability.

TRANSITION ASSESSMENT

Assessment is an ongoing and coordinated process of collecting information about a student's strengths, needs, preferences, and interests as they relate to the demands of current and future living, learning, and working environments (Sitlington, Neubert, Begun, Lombard, & Leconte, 2007;

Rae, J. M. *A Collaborative Approach to Transition Planning for Students With Disabilities* (pp. 105-122).
© 2020 SLACK Incorporated.

Tidwell, Fleming, Kraska, & Alderman, 2016). Transition assessment serves students by providing them with a systematic process to define their preferences, career and independence readiness, communication skills, and academic readiness for post-school life and educational programs and employment. Initial self-assessments and self-disclosure of their thoughts about their future underpin assessments. In conferences with the transition planning specialist, the student uses existing assessment information about current achievements as the foundation to learn about where he or she functions currently and to make choices on the goals the student wants to pursue as he or she begins to take on more adult responsibilities.

Transition assessments also inform students, the transition planning specialist, and special and general education teachers about the transition services the students will need. During their conferences, students can advocate for the services they will need to achieve their selected goals. To make informed choices about their goals, students will need to be knowledgeable about their progress on the goals they have set and how each goal applies to other nonacademic environments, such as managing personal health and being independent (or as independent as possible) in independent living either at home or in the community.

To do this, an adolescent needs adult guidance. During adolescence, most students do not know what they will need to live as young adults. The process of self-assessment of their current independence skills underpins what the needed transition services will be. Academic assessment guides their needs in reading, math, and face-to-face communication when using spoken language, sign language, or assistive devices.

Transition assessment should result in a baseline of acquired skills and provide a picture of skills they will need for increased or full independence. As mentioned in Chapters 3 and 4, the process of goal setting requires knowledge of current performance as well as a vision for the future.

Parental involvement is part of the assessment process, and its importance should not be underestimated. Parental knowledge about the student's skills is crucial to prevent duplication of efforts, particularly in independence skills.

INITIAL EVALUATIONS, REEVALUATIONS, AND TRANSITION ASSESSMENTS

Assessment Purposes

Distinguishing the purposes of transition assessment from eligibility assessment is crucial to selecting assessment tools for transition planning. In Chapter 2, eligibility for special education and related special education services was introduced. When a school-age child is brought to the attention of the school via Child Find or teacher or parental referral, a diagnostic screening starts the process. Instructional strategies are reviewed, interventions are put in place, and ongoing assessment monitors progress in the general education setting. If after intensive instruction progress is not made in the area of concern, a referral is made, and the parent, if in agreement, initiates the completion of initial evaluation assessments. These assessments are completed by a multidisciplinary team, including a school psychologist and special education team members who are qualified to administer diagnostic assessments. Examples of diagnostic assessments include intelligence quotient (IQ) tests, current independence skills, expressive and receptive language assessments, mathematics assessments, and other cognitive and physical tests to determine whether the child has one or more disabilities. The results, if indicative of a disability, result in the student being classified as eligible for special education services.

The school psychologist is the person who analyzes the assessments, determines if there is a disability, and makes recommendations for programs or services that will meet the child's needs. As part of the diagnosis, the student may be determined eligible to receive special education and related services, such as speech therapy, physical therapy, occupational therapy, and special transportation. If the student is diagnosed with autism spectrum disorder, for example, a program using research-based practices for students with autism spectrum disorder will be recommended. When the details of the recommended initial program and services are completed, the multidisciplinary team reviews the final evaluation report to ensure the information reflects the team's professional assessments. The multidisciplinary team evaluation is sent to the parent, and an Individualized Education Plan (IEP) meeting is scheduled, again with the parent's permission, based on the individual needs of the child. Based on the assessments and the resulting profile of strengths and needs, the IEP is developed and updated annually. This is the basis of special education eligibility. Evaluations to determine continued eligibility as a child with a disability are called *reevaluations*.

Reevaluations

Initial diagnosis is not the end of the evaluation process. The eligible student will be reevaluated at regular intervals, but not less than 1 year and not longer than 3 years, depending on their disability category. The reevaluation is to determine whether the student is still eligible for special education and related services and in need of specially designed instruction in a special education program. The reevaluations confirm or disconfirm that the child continues to be eligible for special education. The reevaluation reports often rely on the student's academic, social, and behavioral history and longitudinal information, including how long the child has had a disability and the severity of the disability. Information from the reevaluation reports may contain older and sometimes out-of-date academic achievement data or IEP goals for progress monitoring and may not be relevant as a baseline upon which to develop an IEP because the baselines are dated. If old data is used, the student will not be given activities and educational experiences at his or her current stage of development.

Conducting Useful Assessments

To be useful, assessments must result in activities that increase educational options, develop independent living skills, increase self-advocacy and self-determination, expand employment opportunities, and open the door to increased social inclusion. In short, assessments should lead to growth and improve options for adult life.

To be useful to the student, the assessment scoring must be in a simple format that has meaning to them. The student requires information such as his or her actual reading and math levels in order to get the assistance he or she needs. Also, if the student wants to go to college, assessments that give useful information to support his or her success are needed. For example, if the student wants to attend trainings or college, his or her reading speed is crucial to understanding whether he or she will be able to complete reading assignments in a timely fashion. The transition planning specialist and the student need to know how the student compares to the average student to inform future accommodations for college and to find, for example, alternative ways for the student to learn information more rapidly.

Transition planning requires multiple assessments. Transition assessments are particularly helpful when a baseline for academic, social, emotional, independence, and behavioral skills is established at age 13, but only when it is done in a way that enables the student to create goals. Providing education in needed skills and helping the student set goals to develop these skills is useful. During middle school, students see the future as far off and can begin planning without being overwhelmed by the things they need to learn.

OVERVIEW OF TRANSITION SKILLS AND RELATED ASSESSMENTS

Areas of Assessment

It is important that the transition planning specialist know the types of tests available and the areas that need to be assessed. Table 5-1 is an overview of the assessment areas that the transition planning specialist will need to keep up to date for each student. A schedule of assessment is set up for each of the five major areas included for transition planning. One assessment should be completed for each area:

1. Cognitive development
2. Knowledge and skills for employment
3. Knowledge of careers and vocations (and, when appropriate, college or vocational readiness)
4. Social and emotional skills
5. Activities of daily living

These five areas will be the focus areas when the transition planning specialist meets with the student during the transition planning conferences.

For example, if the student is below grade level and needs to attain a seventh-grade reading and comprehension level, then the team needs to focus on employing the best methods to increase vocabulary and reading comprehension. To see if the student is acquiring new vocabulary, a standardized measure can be done yearly. For instance, the Kaufmann Test of Educational Achievement (KTEA) has a long form. Initially, the long form is used because it reports more detail about the student's reading and math needs. After the implementation of an intensive vocabulary development program, the short form can be used to see if progress has been made each year. If progress is not made, the team must find a research-based program and deliver a more effective reading intervention.

The transition planning specialist's and special education team's role is to facilitate lifelong learning, continue to encourage students, and provide students who are not reading yet with audio and digital texts.

Arguably, reading, language usage, and social behavior are critical to any employment situation and therefore must be a primary focus in the education and transition planning of students with disabilities.

Additional assessments in these areas are also paramount in helping the student define what he or she will need because adolescents often do not know what they need to know for adulthood.

Students should be informed about the multiple assessments they will use and how to self-assess. Self-assessment, in keeping with the spirit of self-determination development, is better accomplished when the student uses a checklist to select needs and goals and tracks assessment results. Assessment checklists help guide the student's plan plus help students reflect upon upcoming needs, such as getting working papers or applying for an identity card. Table 5-1 lists assessment areas.

Social and emotional assessments are also used by students to self-monitor. These can be done more frequently and can help students to seek assistance when they consistently have difficulty overcoming personal challenges such as argumentative behavior or depressive symptoms that can hurt them socially or on the job.

The following case report is provided to share the assessment used in the case of Sam, who was discussed in Chapter 2.

Case Report: Sam

Sam first entered the emotional support program as an 11th grader, a very late start for transition planning. He was evaluated using the KTEA, and the results gave his reading, reading comprehension, spelling, and math levels. His reading comprehension was at the fourth-grade level. His math was at the 10th-grade level. He was then put on an intensive receptive oral language program and

TABLE 5-1. OVERVIEW OF ASSESSMENTS: INITIAL ASSESSMENTS FOR TRANSITION PLANNING

COGNITIVE DEVELOPMENT

- Language Development Domain
  - Overall and occupational language development assessment
  - Reading comprehension and math application assessment
  - Receptive language development assessment
  - Picture-based receptive language assessment
  - Assistive devices and communication development

Repeated measures to provide ongoing data collection from 7th to 12th grade. During 12th grade, a final report called the Summary of Performance will have the final assessment results. It can be used to acquire adult services.

KNOWLEDGE AND SKILLS FOR EMPLOYMENT

- Career Readiness Domain
  - Money management
  - Work-seeking skills
  - Self-advocacy
  - Self-determination
  - Employment goal setting
  - Stamina for part- or full-time employment
  - Medical barrier assessments

KNOWLEDGE OF EDUCATIONAL AND VOCATIONAL OPTIONS

- Post-School Academic Domain
  - Certification programs, such as in the medical fields
  - Part-time community college
  - Employment and evening school
  - Employment and evening leisure programs
- College Readiness Domain
  - College preparation skills assessments
  - Accommodations and modifications needed for college success

SOCIAL AND EMOTIONAL KNOWLEDGE AND SKILLS

- Psychological Needs Domain
  - Temperament
  - Interaction skills
  - Social comfort level

(continued)

TABLE 5-1. OVERVIEW OF ASSESSMENTS: INITIAL ASSESSMENTS FOR TRANSITION PLANNING (CONTINUED)

- Psychological Needs Domain (continued)
  - Anxiety
  - Depression
  - Serious mental illness
  - Understanding of environmental needs
  - Argumentative or provocative behavioral assessments and interventions

ACTIVITIES OF DAILY LIVING

- Self-Help Domain
  - Self-care domain
  - Level of independence
  - Interpersonal skills
  - Safety training
  - Social interaction skills
  - Medical care

given time to read each day. He read age-appropriate, grade-level classics written at the fourth- to fifth-grade level, aligning his work with his peers. Aligning his reading program with his peers improved his ability to have a common background of educational experiences. At the end of 11th grade, he was given the KTEA using the short form, and he had made progress. When assessed again at the end of 12th grade using the KTEA short form, he was on a 6th-grade reading level. Sam also used self-assessments provided to him and worked on his independence, social, behavioral, and mental health needs. He completed a class where he learned about careers and met with the transition planning specialist in ongoing conferences to make plans and set goals. For Sam's plan, multiple assessments over time were used to help him self-monitor his progress.

EXERCISES

1. Select a student and choose assessments that assess cognitive, academic, social, emotional, and career preferences. Research the assessment choices and determine if they are appropriate for the student.

2. Describe two reading assessments. Compare whether both assessments provide a comprehensive picture of the students reading abilities and areas of need. Describe what you think would enhance the value of your selected assessments.

Informing the Student About Progress

Assessments for transition planning include both quantitative data, such as achievement tests like the KTEA, and qualitative data, such as checklists, transition planning specialist–student conference information, and direct observation. Throughout each assessment process, the transition planning specialist is the person who explains the assessment data to the student. Although there is a team, the student can be overwhelmed if assessment data are reported to him or her by multiple people. Students with disabilities often have problems with both material and mental organization, and many students with disabilities do not process language in the same way as their peers without disabilities. Therefore, the student should be given the respect of receiving assessment information in a private forum in writing, not at an IEP meeting. Privacy avoids a situation where, because of multiple voices, distractions, and social anxiety in the group setting, the student is unable to comprehend the assessment information. Social behaviors also sidetrack the student's focus and can prevent understanding of the information, such as being concerned that the team may be inconvenienced because student wants to ask many questions.

Emotional Considerations for Late Readers

Many students become emotionally fragile about academic assessments, often refusing to take them by high school. As one student reported, "Why should I find out one more time that I am dumber than everyone else?" Being told year after year how far behind they are can only be demoralizing.

Reporting to a middle or high school student that his or her reading score is at the fourth-grade level can be very upsetting. Far more disturbing is telling them that 90% of their class is doing better at reading than they are, an assessment that is not useful. Therefore, the transition planning specialist must use a communication style that encourages growth and finds a method of instruction that changes this trajectory. Some students, such as Sam, do not feel distressed but are relieved to know their reading level. Sam was buoyed by the fact that our newspapers are written at the sixth-grade level. However, his response may not be a typical response. Discussing low-level reading scores and implementing an intensive reading program while continuing to plan to increase receptive vocabulary and language comprehension is a responsible approach. Helping the student to understand how to use his or her assessments to guide his or her progress and to advocate for better instruction can redirect the emotional trauma of the slow development or nondevelopment of reading. Students need encouragement and the understanding that being literate is not accomplished by reading alone but by accessing information in multiple ways.

A Word About Career Interest Assessments

Career interest assessments and inventories often have a list of questions about a student's preferences, interests, and skills. These questions are meant to create a list of career options that the student may not have thought of or knew were options. They often suggest career clusters that have a wider variety of options for further research. An excellent career assessment should provide more options for exploration. However, some generate a small list that can be so limiting that the career interest assessments may be discouraging. For example, one student said he was interested in law. His only suggestion related to the law was a career as a security guard. Another student answered questions about being interested in working with animals, and one of her four recommendations was to be a fish farmer. Another student said he wanted a job that was active, and his assessment suggested working on a sanitation truck. If any of these suggestions were one of 20 possible explorations, then it may not have been so discouraging to these students. However, in each case, it was one of four suggestions. Also, other than the fish farmer suggestion, most students searching for jobs know what those jobs are and would be able to seek information about those positions without a career assessment. Such a limited number of results may lead some students to decide that an unknown authority in the field has determined they have few options for their jobs of interest. Limitations imposed in career assessments may narrow down a student's interests for entry-level, volunteer, or internship positions. When looking at assessments, the goal of career interest inventories should be to actively encourage students to consider careers outside of their social learning experiences and that of their school-based teams in order to avoid limiting explorations. Interest inventories should not tie students to specific areas when they have not developed career skills. The purpose of career assessments is to assess what careers students know about and plan early exposure to work and additional careers. Early and often exposure is the standard for better outcomes (Luecking, 2009).

Academic Assessment Specificity

Assessments should demonstrate reliability in what they assess. It is important that the student understand why he or she struggled and in which academic and social areas. Also, through interviewing the student, he or she can report on the subjects he or she dislikes. Subject preference is an immediate assessment of where the student is struggling, as well as the reasons the student is struggling. For instance, if a student struggled with completing homework and is college bound, then reading speed may need to be assessed. A student with a reading speed in the 14th percentile will not be able to keep up with the required reading because it will take him or her many more hours to read than a student in the 90th percentile. Therefore, a student with slow reading speed in high school may need modified assignments to make the due dates, or, if enrolling in college, may need to take fewer college courses per semester than students with higher reading speeds.

Introducing the student to disability resources, such as college or vocational school Office of Disability, is a way to develop the student's autonomy and increase the student's ability to both understand his or her disability and seek solutions to aid in his or her success. For instance, most colleges require a full-time class schedule to live in the dormitories. In the case of a student with slow reading speed, if the student wants to go to college and live in the dorms, the student will need to ask for a change in this rule. The student can also ask for extended time in testing. Students who are college bound and have learning disabilities can use assessment results to research and find colleges that encourage students with disabilities by providing additional services to support their success.

The transition planning specialist can use the assessment process to guide the student to search and advocate for accommodations and modifications to ensure success in postsecondary school and life. The student needs to have specific information about, as mentioned in the example, reading speed to address what to do and how to do it. Without detailed knowledge like this, the student will never really know that he or she could do the work but must take another pathway to succeed.

Conferences and Progress Toward Goals

Ongoing conferences are an assessment for both the student and the transition planning specialist. During transition planning specialist–student conferences, the transition planning specialist keeps the timeline data on the completed activities of transition, both what the transitions planning specialist has carried out and what the student has completed. This information includes updated questionnaires to document any new options the student wants to discuss, the results of new transition assessments, and the often-changing personal preferences. Ongoing conferences can also help students verbalize their thoughts about how they think they are doing in the quest for preferred employment, post-school continuing education goals, social and independence skills.

The conference assessment process can inform the transition planning specialist about other skills and whether the activities of transition have:

- Increased the student's ability to share events where he or she has used self-determination, self-advocacy, and autonomy
- Increased receptive and expressive language as evidenced in yearly reading assessments and conversation skills
- Increased employment-based vocabulary and skills
- Developed knowledge of interaction skills for the workplace
- Helped the student delineate future areas of study
- Helped the student delineate areas or leisure activities within the school and community at large
- Increased independence skills such as personal healthy living activities, food preparation, home and money management, understanding of personal safety, and other self-care activities
- Encouraged goals for lifelong learning

When addressing these criteria, assessments can give the student a more comprehensive view of foundations for positive lifelong experiences. During the conference, the student can assess him- or herself and how his or her current goal planning can move forward. The following section includes multiple formal and informal assessment measures, such as standardized and unstandardized assessments, curriculum-based assessments (CBAs), checklists, teacher observations, and situational assessments.

TYPES OF ASSESSMENTS

Formal and Informal Assessments

Assessments can be either formal or informal. Formal assessments involve establishment of grade-level performance and a comparison with other students in the general population. Formal assessment for grade-level performance in reading, math, and receptive and expressive language is helpful to set a starting point for additional study and activities in these areas, as well as to determine whether additional accommodations and modifications are needed. They assess both verbal and performance levels and are administered once per year. Formal assessments are standardized instruments that include descriptions of their norming process, reliability, validity, and recommended uses (Walker, Kortering, Fowler, & Rowe, 2010).

Federal law requires the use of "appropriate measurable postsecondary goals based upon age-appropriate transition assessments related to training, education, employment, and, where appropriate, independent living skills" (Definition of individualized education program, 2006). In contrast, informal assessments provide descriptive information and are not normed to the general population of same-age students. Formal assessments such as IQ tests are typically administered early in a child's school career. For example, they are informative for the transition planning specialist when a student, due to mental illness or the family's sudden instability, has earned poor grades. A student who has an aptitude for college may appear otherwise, and the IQ is an indicator that the academic grades may not reflect the student's potential. Formal assessments are a significant component of transition planning in the areas of written, oral, spoken, receptive performance; math; and progress monitoring. All assessments must be accessible to the students who are being tested, such as delivering the test in sign language or providing ways for students who are blind to be tested. If an IQ test or any formal or informal instrument is not accessible and is not adapted for physical and sensory disabilities, then the measure can not assess intellect accurately and should not be part of the data. The following sections contain examples of formal assessments.

Formal Assessments of Intelligence and Aptitude

Intelligence Tests

Intelligence tests assess a person's cognitive ability to think and reason rather than assessing knowledge achieved through learning. IQs are used as a data point to determine the level of intellectual disabilities, normal intellectual functioning, and superior to gifted abilities.

General and Specific Aptitude Tests

Aptitude tests measure specific skills or ability. They can measure a variety of skills specific to academic performance and the ability to do well in specific employment situations. They can measure skills and behaviors that are necessary for specific jobs.

Behavior Assessments and Observations

These are a wide variety of techniques for studying and evaluating behavior, including data collection tools, direct observation, interviews, psychological tests, and a sampling of attitudes and beliefs that lead to specific behavioral interventions (VandenBos, 2007). These assessments can be used to assess a student's self-control and behavioral responses in social and work situations and plan instruction in prosocial skill development. The BASC-3 (Behavior Assessment System for Children, Third Edition) is an example of a standardized measure that contains a student self-assessment.

Achievement Tests

These tests measure learning of general or specific academic skills, such as receptive language, expressive language, math, spelling, and phonemic awareness. Schools use achievement tests as guides for determining the occupational skills needed for secondary school vocational programs. Achievement tests can show where the student is and what adult life communication skills and mathematical skills are needed and when to use assistive technology. They are norm-referenced and standardized.

Aptitude Tests

Aptitude tests are norm-referenced and standardized. They measure innate potential, and they are used in a variety of professional, vocational, and diagnostic purposes.

Informal Transition Assessments

Informal assessments also show evidence of a student's improvement over time. They are student centered and are part of the instruction and learning process. They have real-world applications and are useful for assessing completion of goals. Informal assessment includes multiple people and the student. They also measure the effectiveness of the transition curriculum, community-based instruction, and the other activities of transition planning (Spinelli, 2002). The following are examples of informal assessments.

Adaptive Behavior/Daily Living Skills Assessments

Also known as *adaptive daily living skills*, these assessments indicate the type and amount of assistance that a student will need. For students with disabilities, the assistance may be in school or in a simulated community setting, such as an apartment. Curriculum-based special education activities, vocational training, and supported work experiences in and out of school can teach skills such as using public transportation or paratransit systems. Progress on these activities is documented using observational data and task analysis data. Each assessment can also indicate the need for a personal care assistant. A review of the level of functioning a student demonstrates also tells the team what type of living skills will be needed for post-school life.

Behavior Checklists

Behavior checklists guide the development and delineate behavioral needs that may impair the student's ability to function in a job, home, or community setting. Multiple areas can be assessed, such as acceptable community behavior, social interaction skills, mental health, and the ability to complete responsibilities. Deficits in these areas are often addressed through cognitive therapy and goal setting. Resources to guide access to behavior health supports, such as cognitive therapy, can be added to the area in the IEP that indicates these resources and where they are available. Social interaction goals, such as greeting others, decreasing smoking, and planning social or leisure activities, can be the focus of self-monitored behavioral interventions.

Communication Assessments

Communication assessments, both formal and informal, can help students understand why they may not understand social interactions. The use of communication assessments establishes a baseline of performance and guides future training and skill development for interactions. The level of language development is crucial here as well because the student must be able to comprehend spoken language in many different scenarios, conversations, and instructions. Although not often mentioned, receptive vocabulary development is often truncated when reading is delayed. In other words, the focus on reading the words becomes paramount for both reading and vocabulary development, often neglecting comprehension and use in the social language. Receptive language vocabulary development enhances cognitive processes and interaction skills and requires continued development.

For students with low reading grade levels, attention should be paid to developing a more advanced receptive vocabulary. Opportunities to use vocabulary in spoken language can help social and task interactions needed within social and work contexts. Attempts to develop vocabulary must be more than memorizing a list of words, which are typically soon forgotten. Receptive language acquisition must be addressed, and a group discussion about word meaning can further enhance a student's interaction capabilities. Yearly assessments in language usage are imperative for students with language and reading delays.

Curriculum-Based Assessments

CBAs may be designed by educators or be part of a commercial transition curriculum. For instance, a student may have completed a unit on goal setting and developed a goal. Once completed, the student provides evidence via teacher assessment or CBA that he or she has mastered a more complicated goal, such as learning to use online banking. Curriculums such as the Brigance Life Skills Inventory, Comprehensive Inventory of Basic Skills (reading and math), and Transition Skills Inventory are comprehensive curriculum and assessment measures. The Transition Skills Inventory contains checklists that provide a comprehensive list of skills and instructional materials for all the areas listed in Table 5-1.

Direct Observations

Direct observations can be very helpful to the student. For example, a student who is having social difficulty can ask for an observation about what behaviors may be alienating other students. These kinds of observations are more clandestine, meaning that the purpose of the observation should not be evident. If done in multiple observations, they are a significant aid to students with interaction problems. Also, observations done in other natural environments can help students. For instance, what students sit alone in the lunch room or face bullies while waiting to leave for home?

Direct observations by job coaches inform work supervisors and the transition planning specialist about how a job placement is going. Direct observation at times may indicate a need for additional training or instruction. Direct observation can also help determine supports the student may need when executive functioning is impaired and the student appears to have difficulty with creating plans and goals. The transition planning specialist can offer this to assist the student with strategies to address the areas of concern for the student. In order to be effective and increase self-determination, the student should not be observed without his or her permission.

Environmental Analysis

This analysis is also referred to as an *ecological assessment*. It is an examination of the places where the student is educated, lives, and hopes to work. If a student expresses an interest in a job, then learning about the work environment provides data that can match the student's comfort level. For instance, a student with mild hearing loss may find the background noise of the environment prohibits him or her from hearing the spoken language of coworkers. If the student demonstrates the ability to do the job, a solution such as a desk placement, if possible, can accommodate his or her need. Using websites such as Job Accommodation Network (askjan.org) can assist in finding information about accommodations.

Self-Determination Assessments

These assessments can be given in a pre- and post-instruction format, because unlike preferences, which are inherent in characteristics in the student, self-determination activities assist in making those preferences come to fruition. These assessments help the student set goals he or she wants to accomplish rather than goals set by the IEP team.

Transition Planning Inventories

Transition planning inventories assist in identifying multiple transition strengths and needs in various aspects of adult living, including employment, postsecondary schooling and training, independent living, interpersonal relationships, and community living. Rather than using multiple tests, these assessments cover multiple areas. A student's goals, self-advocacy, and self-determination are often assessed as well. A student's performance on self-awareness of his or her preferences and an ability to select goals can also be determined. Ultimately, this type of assessment belongs to the student. From the results, the student can plan what to work on. This is an area where self-determination can be developed.

Parents or guardians and educators can provide additional information about current activities and help the student avoid redundant activities in order to choose activities that will increase his or her ability to create satisfying life experiences.

Interviews and Questionnaires

Interviews and questionnaires are informal assessments that can be face-to-face or via a data collection instrument. These tools gather information to determine the student's vision of his or her life after secondary school. Information from questionnaires helps the transition planning specialist take steps to help the student participate in the course of study to reach his or her goals. Collecting information about the student's vision can begin with a preference assessment and future vision questionnaires located in the Student Supplemental Materials.

Student Conferences

Student conferences are ongoing meetings with the student's transition planning specialist regarding movement through the framework of transition activities. During conferences, continual reassessment occurs as the student evolves in age and maturity. Student conferences can inform the transition planning specialist when a student requires needed services and supports to transition to his or her selected post-school outcomes. Student conferences also provide data regarding the need for parental and community agency involvement.

Activities of Daily Living

Adaptive behavior assessments and independent living tests help the student and IEP team discuss whether the student will be able to live independently as a young adult. These tests also help the transition planning specialist and the student determine the type and amount of needed instruction for independence. For example, safety skills checklists, behavioral checklists, and independent living skills checklists are informal measures that can be used to develop goals. They include dressing, feeding, grooming, hygiene, toileting, home skills, school skills, and work skills.

Assessment Tools

In the Student Supplemental Materials are specific assessment tools. Educational publishing companies or testing services are the sources for these, and links to the company websites are provided.

The transition planning specialist and special educators should be knowledgeable about these assessments. A schedule of assessment is part of transition planning. Refer to the Student Supplemental Materials for a table with a list of assessments. Table 5-2 has a proposed long-range schedule of assessment.

Age-Appropriate Assessment

The focus on age-appropriate assessments also includes age-appropriate activities. Attention to this comes from categorizing students by a measure called developmental age. For instance, a child may have slowly developed to function as a 2-year-old but failed to make progress past that level. Programming for these students often included toddler books and toys. Even if a student could progress, the education level often did not move past the use of toddler toys and activities. It was believed that the student's level of performance was fixed. As the child aged, he or she continued to be attached to children's toys and activities. Upon entering a high school special education classroom, multiple preschool activities were evident. Although some students have such severe cognitive damage that they will not pass a preschool level, academic and functional progress is now the focus and age-appropriate activities are required. Age-appropriate testing includes using assessments that do not have a ceiling, such as using the Brigance Preschool Inventory. An inventory that has a ceiling of 5 years old may not be able to assess children appropriately, especially when they may need modifications to access the testing instrument. In Jason's case, he was diagnosed to be at a preschool level, but with assistive technology, it was determined he was at the fourth-grade level for receptive language. If the school psychologist had used the Brigance Preschool Assessment and had assumed a preschool level of functioning, then Jason's full potential would not have been found. Age-appropriate means a student's chronological, rather than developmental, age (Wehmeyer, 2002).

Using Assessments

A strategy that can help a student use self-assessments is reading the descriptions to the student. The assessment descriptions are worded in a way that can pique a student's interest. Assessments can be fun, especially if a group of students take them together. The social aspect makes it a positive experience.

Most assessments can be accessed via the computer which enables accommodations for nonreaders. The information in an assessment sheds light on whether a student is prepared to meet an advanced transition goal, such as entry-level employment. The student and the transition planning specialist can collaborate about securing employment training as well as a narrowing down of employment options. However, assessments alone cannot replace ongoing student–transition planning specialist communication and conferencing. Assessments can be used to form a template of strengths and needs that the student uses to guide his or her choices (see Table 5-2).

The student can use these topics and related assessments to determine their needs and select goals in any area. For instance, a student may want to go to the doctor on their own. The student would

TABLE 5-2. A PLAN OF ASSESSMENTS BY GRADE: ASSESSMENT SCHEDULE EXAMPLE

ACADEMIC/EDUCATION	7TH GRADE	8TH GRADE	9TH GRADE	10TH GRADE	11TH GRADE	EXIT ASSESSMENT
Reading and Math Assessments						
Alternate assessments for student with severe intellectual disabilities	X	X	X	X	X	
Receptive vocabulary using standardized testing—individual	X	X	X	X	X	X
Expressive vocabulary standardized testing—individual	X	X	X	X	X	X
Reading speed—individual	X		X		X	
Reading comprehension—individual	X	X	X	X	X	X
Standardized tests (e.g., KTEA)	Long form	Short form	Short form	Short form	Short form	X
Environmental inventories/assessments/checklists	X	X	X	X	X	X
Picture communication assessments for receptive and expressive language	X	X	X	X	X	
Person-centered planning for IEP—severe disabilities (data collection from people with knowledge of the student)	X	X	X	X	X	X
Career Assessments						
Career interests preferences assessments/questionnaires—groups		X	X	X	X	X
Career skills CBA—groups	X		X	X	X	
Career development preferences assessments—individual	X	X	X	X	X	
Vocational school preferences assessments—groups	X	X	X	X	X	
Work preferences—individual/parent involvement				X	X	X

(continued)

TABLE 5-2. A PLAN OF ASSESSMENTS BY GRADE: ASSESSMENT SCHEDULE EXAMPLE (CONTINUED)

ACADEMIC/EDUCATION	7TH GRADE	8TH GRADE	9TH GRADE	10TH GRADE	11TH GRADE	EXIT ASSESSMENT
Social Skills Assessments						
Social skills assessments—group practice and observation			X	X	X	X
Situational assessment in general education—individual	X	X	X	X	X	
Behavioral assessments (CBA)—individual			X	X	X	
Tests of executive functioning—individual	X				X	
Interview preparation (CBA)—small groups			X	X	X	
Work skills CBA	X	X	X	X	X	X
Living Skills Assessments						
Independence skills CBA and checklists						
Self-determination CBA	Sets goals	Sets goals	Sets goals	Sets goals	Sets goals	Sets goals
Self-advocacy CBA		Reports	Reports	Reports	Reports	Reports
IEP leadership—group and individual instruction	Student attends IEP meeting	Student attends IEP meeting	Student attends IEP meeting	Student leads IEP meeting	Student leads IEP meeting	Student leads IEP meeting
College readiness assessment			X	X	X	X
Conferences—transition planning specialist/student portfolio preference assessments repeated	2	3	3	4	5	Exit summary

develop a skills list to initiate managing his or her own health care. Or a student may want to be more social and have a get together. In this case, they may choose a cooking goal. Multiple areas can be selected and are based on the student's perception of goals they want to reach. In transition planning all assessments are used so the student can select the goals for transition.

- Student preferences
- Medical status
- Physical stamina
- Fine motor development
- Gross motor development
- Independence
- Emotional status
- Behavioral compliance
- Attention span
- Academic grade-level achievement in math and reading
- Academic subject interests
- Academic successes (or not)
- Activity preferences
- After-school activities
- Amount of inclusion in general education
- Specially designed instruction and IEP goals

Each of these areas can be used by the student to develop long-term plans. Assessments for transition enable the student to determine what he or she may want to develop or learn.

Effective Student Assessment

There are factors that may impact the successful completion and management of student assessments and the timely completion of a planned course of assessment. The transition planning specialist's failure to stay on task, maintain accurate records, and update the framework regularly interferes with giving the student the information he or she needs. These delays and lack of commitment to completing this will slow the trajectory of goal completion.

Illness and medication changes are other roadblocks that, if not included in the planning, can adversely affect the movement toward goals. Therefore, this should be addressed proactively.

Testing environments can adversely affect the results of the assessments. Poor lighting, lack of ventilation, background distractions, and poor implementation of the assessment protocols can reduce scores. As mentioned earlier, some students refuse to take the assessments. However, if the transition planning specialist is effective at communicating the student planning focus of assessments, there should be less resistance. Determining the reason for refusal is the first step in overcoming assessment objections. If the student never agrees to assessment, transition planning can continue without assessments.

Transition Action Plan Assessments Checklist

Maintaining a transition planning framework checklist of assessments documents the collaborative work and keeps the transition planning team organized. Figure 5-1 contains the list of assessments that should be included over the 5-year transition planning period. A measure of each is chosen and a long-term plan of assessment is developed, just as is done with any school testing.

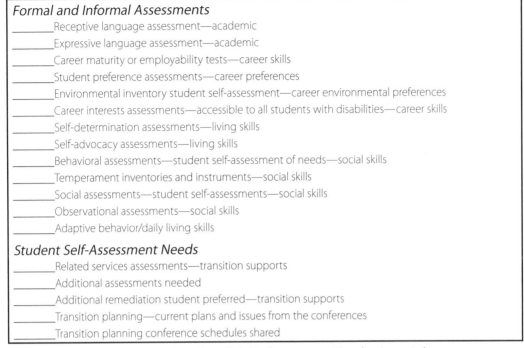

Formal and Informal Assessments

_____Receptive language assessment—academic

_____Expressive language assessment—academic

_____Career maturity or employability tests—career skills

_____Student preference assessments—career preferences

_____Environmental inventory student self-assessment—career environmental preferences

_____Career interests assessments—accessible to all students with disabilities—career skills

_____Self-determination assessments—living skills

_____Self-advocacy assessments—living skills

_____Behavioral assessments—student self-assessment of needs—social skills

_____Temperament inventories and instruments—social skills

_____Social assessments—student self-assessments—social skills

_____Observational assessments—social skills

_____Adaptive behavior/daily living skills

Student Self-Assessment Needs

_____Related services assessments—transition supports

_____Additional assessments needed

_____Additional remediation student preferred—transition supports

_____Transition planning—current plans and issues from the conferences

_____Transition planning conference schedules shared

Figure 5-1. A list of assessments that should be included in the 5-year transition planning period.

Assessment Results and Assessment Framework

Table 5-2 is an example of a group of assessments and a sample timeline for administration. A schedule of testing should be given to the parents in the introductory training or via the mail system. Assessments are student driven and the student determines what assessments they want.

Putting It All Together

Refer to the Student Supplemental Materials for a chart that can be used to organize which assessments the team and student decide to use. The special education team, including the student, can choose a group of assessments and ensure they meet the needs of the student. The transition planning specialist documents the dates of each assessment used. Although a student may also use many of the personality, skills, and career searches on the internet, these should not replace those in the table. However, if the student wants to use them and discuss them, it is recommended to do so.

This framework is designed from the table in the Student Supplemental Materials that contains a list of assessments. The master list is not a comprehensive list, but it has age-appropriate measures and recent revisions.

Students with severe intellectual disabilities will need other types of assessment, and these are discussed in the chapters on autism and intellectual disabilities. Appropriate assessments take the severity of the disability into account, and adaptations and modifications are used to make these assessments accessible to the students with severe and multiple disabilities. There are assessments for students with severe intellectual disabilities in the Student Supplemental Materials.

EXERCISES

1. Describe three behavior assessments.
2. Describe the readiness skills needed for college.
3. Describe how self-determination is assessed using the American Institutes for Research Self-Determination Assessment.
4. Explain the use of Choice Maker Life-Centered Career Education. How can educators access it, and what is its purpose?
5. Work in a group and divide assessments from the charts provided in the Student Supplemental Materials. Research one assessment from each of the following areas: interests, goal setting, reading, mathematics, behavior, environmental, preferences, self-determination and self-advocacy, careers, vocational, cognitive, college readiness, and social skills. Discuss each in your group and write a brief report on each.

SUMMARY

This chapter provides information about the types of assessment used for transition planning. A plan of assessment is used to provide baselines for academic achievement, social, behavioral, independence, and career readiness. Transition assessment is primarily to inform the student of where he or she stands currently and to guide him or her to select goals to prepare for the future. The transition planning specialist and special education team members must be well-trained in the administration of both formal and informal measures of assessment and know how to help students with unique developmental characteristics use the results of assessments to help them meet their goals and follow their aspirations.

REFERENCES

Definition of individualized education program, 34 C.F.R. § 300.320 (2006).

Luecking, R. G. (2009). *The way to work: How to facilitate work experiences for youth in transition.* Baltimore, MD: Brookes Publishing Company.

Sitlington, P. L., Neubert, D. A., Begun, W. H., Lombard, R. C., & Leconte, P. J. (2007). *Assess for success: A practitioner's handbook on transition assessment* (2nd ed.). Thousand Oaks, CA: Corwin Press.

Spinelli, C. G. (2002). *Classroom assessment for students with special needs.* Upper Saddle River, NJ: Pearson Education.

Tidwell, P., Fleming, C., Kraska, M., & Alderman, L. (2016). Identifying the referral process, practices, knowledge, training and technical assistance needed for quality transition assessments. *Journal of Rehabilitation, 82*(1), 3-11.

VandenBos, G. R. (Ed.). (2007). *APA dictionary of psychology.* Washington, DC: American Psychological Association.

Walker, A. R., Kortering, L. J., Fowler, C. H., & Rowe, D. (2010). *Age appropriate transition assessment guide* (2nd ed.). Charlotte, NC: National Secondary Transition Technical Assistance Center, University of North Carolina Charlotte. Retrieved from https://www.wcu.edu/WebFiles/PDFs/Tag.pdf

Wehmeyer, M. (2002). Self-determination and the education of students with disabilities. ERIC Digest E632. The Educational Resources Information Center. Retrieved from https://files.eric.ed.gov/fulltext/ED470036.pdf

Part 4

Transition Plan Development

Transition Plan Frameworks
Creating the Transition Plan

CHAPTER OBJECTIVES

- → Describe the contents of the Individualized Education Plan (IEP).
- → Describe the content of the transition form.
- → Identify the contributions the student can make to the transition portion and the IEP goals.
- → Describe the difference between transition planning and transition services.
- → Explain why IEP goals are aligned to grade-level standards.

INDIVIDUALIZED EDUCATION PLAN CONTENTS

The IEP has content that is required by law and mandated by the Individuals with Disabilities Education Act (IDEA, 2004) legislation, so it is a legal document containing an agreement between the school district and parents about their child's educational plan. The transition plan within the IEP includes documentation that ensures the transition activities and services are present and are being completed as determined during the annual review and via progress reporting. The required contents are listed in the IEP. Along with the content are suggestions for how the student can participate in the development of the IEP. The following pages are the content sections of the IEP.

Rae, J. M. *A Collaborative Approach to Transition Planning for Students With Disabilities* (pp. 125-150).
© 2020 SLACK Incorporated.

Contact Information, Student Disabilities, and Signature Page Section

Each state has some flexibility regarding how the IEP and the transition plan form are visually designed. However, the contents of the IEP and its transition section have multiple legal requirements outlined in the next section. The IEP opens with contact information, the student's current areas of need, and a place to document any revisions. It also includes documentation for transition-age students stating that an invitation to the IEP meeting was sent to the student and that the parents agreed or disagreed to the student's attendance. In addition, a signature page records attendance at an IEP meeting.

Revision Section

There are activities and services to support the student's transition into adulthood. The course of study, completion of a transition curriculum, and the accomplishment of all goals cannot be documented in the annual IEP. Therefore, between annual IEP meetings, IDEA allows revisions to goals to be made with the student and confirmed with the parent via conference calls. The practice of revising the IEP encourages attention to goal completion and offers a solution to tracking the completion of goals over the course of the year. These are usually done 6 months after the annual IEP.

Information From the Parent Section

This section is where parents provide information that may help the student. Completion requires a formal interview with the parent or questionnaire. In this section, any changes in the student's or family's status can be noted. During this parent interview is an opportunity to add new topics, needed permissions, and concerns before the annual IEP meeting.

Present Levels of Academic and Functional Performance

This section includes information about the student's disability, all assessment updates, in-school and community inclusion status, and strengths and needs that must be addressed. The student's participation in transition planning should also be noted here.

Student Contribution to Present Levels of Academic and Functional Performance

A statement of the child's present levels of academic and functional performance includes how the child with a disability's current performance affects participation in general education. Although the evaluation report establishes eligibility for special education, this section of the IEP explains the impact of the disability on learning.

This section includes current curriculum-based and standardized grade-level assessments and teacher observation data from current assessments and those assessments that are located in the most recent evaluation report. Evaluation report assessments that are not up to date should not be used when they are over 1 year old. Important information is to include academic grade-level performance in reading and math, behavioral performance, task completion, timeliness, social ability, and the impact of the disability on performance. It is used to demonstrate progress from the previous year.

As of transition age, a student narrative expands this section to give the secondary transition team information about supports the student may want. Before this age, most children rely on adults to tell them what the problem is and how to fix it. By age 13, many students have enough introspection and self-observation skills and vocabulary to express their perspectives about what they need or want to learn. With this added maturity, the student can contribute to this section according to his or her own perspective.

Annual Goals

Annual goals are written each year. The transition goals used in this section measure progress and are written so that they can be accomplished during the current IEP. Goals can be short term or long term, with short-term goals being required for students with intellectual disabilities who take alternate assessments.

Legal Description: A statement of measurable annual goals, including academic and functional goals designed to:

- Meet the child's needs that result from the child's disability to enable the child to be involved in and make progress in the general education curriculum [34 C.F.R. § 300.320(a)(2)(i)(A)]
- Meet each of the child's other educational needs that result from the child's disability [34 C.F.R. § 300.320(a)(2)(i)(B)]
- A description of:
- Benchmarks or short-term objectives for children with disabilities who take alternate assessments aligned to alternate achievement standards (in addition to the annual goals) [34 C.F.R. § 300.320(a)(2)(ii)]
- How the child's progress toward meeting the annual goals will be measured. [34 C.F.R. § 300.320(a)(3)(i)]
- When periodic reports on the progress the child is making toward meeting the annual goals will be provided such as through the use of quarterly or other periodic reports, concurrent with the issuance of report cards [34 C.F.R. § 300.320(a)(3)(ii)]

(Definition of individualized education program, 2006)

Student Contribution to Annual Goals

For this section, the student can self-select goals under the areas of focus for transition planning, and when the goals are academic they are aligned to state standards for the student's age and grade level. Using age-appropriate standards is required practice when setting goals. Nonacademic goals are also included in the IEP.

In the past, the practice was to select goals using the student's developmental age, which ensured limited improvement in intellectual or general functioning. This is the underpinning of the current requirement that goals are aligned to grade level. This requirement ends the practice of limiting a student's instruction based on intelligence quotient (IQ) or standardized tests, which are normed to students without disabilities but were routinely administered to students with disabilities. Each state provides the grade-level standards for each academic content area, such as social studies and math. Each standard is given an identification code. Goals in the IEP are related to general content standards and are identified by the standard number. In the examples provided here, career awareness has numbered standards. So if the student wants to research entry-level jobs or jobs that match personal preferences, then when a goal is created, its related standard must be included.

In the following list are five state goals and the standards aligned to state career standards for an eighth-grade student.

1. Career awareness and preparation: Students build awareness of the variety of careers available and begin identifying areas of interest.

   1.1 Relate interests and abilities to careers

   1.2 Relate interests and preferences for leisure or work

   1.3 Determine local entry-level jobs that may prepare for later more advanced employment

Measurable goal: Aligned to career state standard 1.1

The student will self-select three areas of interest and research two jobs that may relate to that interest. Questions to be answered are: Describe the three areas of interest and explain what is attractive about each, then answer if this is this something to pursue as a job or a personal interest. The student will submit completed task by a date he or she selects.

2. Career exploration: Students explore one personal career interests by seeking adults and community resources to expand options and inform their decision making.

    2.1 Use and identify effective speaking and listening skills

    2.2 Identify and use multiple sources in the community and online for researching job opportunities

    2.3 Prepare a resume and letter of introduction

Measurable goal: Aligned to career state standard 2.1

While observing a classmate during a mock interview, the student will use a checklist assessment provided by the teacher to determine whether the classmate used effective communication skills.

3. Career placement retention and advancement

    3.1 Identify attitudes and work habits that support continued employment and advancement

    3.2 Complete application and interview process for entry-level positions

    3.3 Define constructive criticism, group dynamics, management and leadership, negotiation and problem solving

Measurable goal: Aligned to career state standard 3.2

Students will apply to the school-based job-shadowing program and complete the application and interview process within 1 week of their decision to apply.

4. Independent living skills and increasing autonomy

    4.1 Participate in skills self-assessments

    4.2 Make choices for prioritizing goals

    4.3 Meet with transition planning specialists according to personal schedule and update progress

Measurable goal: Aligned to career state standard 4.2

Students will take a self-assessment about independent living skills and select three goals for completion within 1 week of transition planning specialist–student conferences. As each goal is completed, students will self-select two more and create a timeline for completion.

5. Social and community activities

    5.1 Research after-school activities and clubs

    5.2 Advocate for transition planning clubs that visit additional worksites for community-based instruction (CBI)

    5.3 Observe a student advocacy group for students with disabilities

Measurable goal: Aligned to career state standard 5.3

Students will attend a self-selected number of advocacy training or advocacy group meetings by the end of the first semester. Students will use speech-to-text technology or write a written report aligned with the meeting agenda and submit it within 1 week after attendance.

Legal Description: A statement of the special education and related services and supplementary aids and services, based on peer-reviewed research to the extent practicable, to be provided to the child, or on behalf of the child, and a statement of the program modifications or supports for school personnel that will be provided to enable the child to:

- Advance appropriately toward attaining the annual goals [34 C.F.R. § 300.320(a)(4)(i)]
- Be involved in and make progress in the general education curriculum and to participate in extracurricular and other nonacademic activities [34 C.F.R. § 300.320(a)(4)(ii)]
- Be educated and participate with other children with disabilities and nondisabled children in extracurricular and other nonacademic activities [34 C.F.R. § 300.320(a)(4)(iii)]

(Definition of individualized education program, 2006)

Special Education–Related Services and Specially Designed Instruction

To help a student make academic and functional progress and progress to post-school life, this section includes information about how the student's program is modified and supported to enable the student to meet annual IEP and transition goals and, when included, objectives. As noted earlier, objectives are required for students who take alternate assessments (typically students with the most severe disabilities).

Student Contribution to Specially Designed Instruction and Related Services

Students and their parents should be apprised of the types of related transition services available to them. If they have concerns about an undiagnosed disability, students can request an updated evaluation. Services they can ask for include audiology services, counseling services, identification and assessment of disabilities, medical services, occupational therapy, orientation and mobility services, parent counseling training, physical therapy, psychological services, recreation therapy, rehabilitation counseling services, school health services, social work services in schools, speech-language pathology services, and transportation training. Services can be ongoing, temporarily intensified, or time limited to enable students to overcome a temporary roadblock to employment.

Participation With Nondisabled Students

In order to ensure that each student is receiving his or her education in the least restrictive educational environment, the federal government requires that a calculation is completed describing the amount of time the student is educated or included in academic and nonacademic activities with same-age peers in the general education environment.

Legal Description: An explanation of the extent, if any, to which the child will not participate with nondisabled children in the regular classroom and in extracurricular and other nonacademic activities [34 C.F.R. §300.320(a)(5)]

(Definition of individualized education program, 2006)

Student Contribution to Participation in the General Education Setting

The student can discuss the number of inclusion opportunities and work with the secondary transition planning team to increase the amount or add supports for success in the general education classroom. If necessary, the student can advocate for after-school programs to meet the needs of students with disabilities in clubs with barriers to participation.

Participation in State and Districtwide Assessments

Participation in assessments is a way to indicate whether the programs are meeting the learning needs of students. There are alternative assessments for students with the most severe disabilities. For students without severe intellectual disabilities, they take the same assessments as their nondisabled peers. Typically, they are given some accommodations to complete them. If a student is eligible for the alternative assessment, it is stated in the IEP.

Legal Description: A statement of any individual appropriate accommodations that are necessary to measure the academic achievement and functional performance of the child on state and districtwide assessments [34 C.F.R. §300.320(a)(6)(i)]

If the IEP team determines that the child must take an alternate assessment instead of a particular regular state or districtwide assessment of student achievement, a statement of why:

- The child cannot participate in the regular assessment [34 C.F.R. § 300.320(a)(6)(ii)(A)]
- The particular alternate assessment selected is appropriate for the child [34 C.F.R. § 300.320(a)(6)(ii)(B)]

(Definition of individualized education program, 2006)

Student Contribution to Participation in Assessments

By high school, many students may have opted out or had their parents opt them out due to the ongoing embarrassment of being a low performer. Opting out of standardized testing is an area of controversy.

However, in the spirit of improving outcomes for students with disabilities, the use of individual achievement tests in math, reading, and social and behavioral skills provides the most useful information for this age group given their disabilities and post-school needs. Students with disabilities know that standardized assessments do not take them where they need to go for post-school life. In keeping with the students self-advocacy, self-determination, and self-esteem, students at transition age may not benefit and, indeed, may even be hurt by the ever present reminders about what they cannot do.

Location and Timelines for Services

The transition services provided can be dated with an annual date or time-limited date. These dates are noted with each specially designed instruction, related service, and transition service.

Legal Description: The projected date for the beginning of the services and modifications and the anticipated frequency, location, and duration of special education and related services and supplementary aids and services and modifications and supports [34 C.F.R. §300.320(a)(7)]

(Definition of individualized education program, 2006)

Student Contribution to Location and Timelines for Services

The student can be part of the discussion about how long some services may be needed. For instance, if travel instruction is provided to ride a bus to work, once the student feels confident to travel on his or her own, he or she can end the service. The student also may add some ideas on where he or she may need support in the community, suggest a CBI plan, and report when the need for the services ends.

Needed Transition Services

Transition services are part of providing students with a free, appropriate public education under IDEA. In addition, transition services are provided to transition-age youth through the Rehabilitation Act of 1973, which authorizes services such as preemployment transition services, job placement, placement assessments, supported employment, and other Office of Vocational Rehabilitation (OVR) services. These supports connect students with employment and careers. Earlier in the history of transition planning, students had to graduate from high school or end their right to education prior to age 21 to start the eligibility application to the OVR. This has changed and this agency is now involved earlier, before graduation, so that the process is completed and the student knows whether they are eligible for OVR services well before graduation. In keeping with the goals of transition planning, attention to post-school outcomes before graduation is essential for a successful transition to post-school settings. Service coordinators from OVR and other workplace settings are more easily accessible when students are in school and their schedules can be adjusted. Students without parental support benefit as well when the school can arrange transportation options when families are unable to drive, read, or otherwise participate. In addition, OVR representatives and local agencies funded by the Department of Health and Human Services supports coordinators typically come to schools and help transition students to group home settings and day programs for adults with disabilities.

> Legal Description: Beginning not later than the first IEP to be in effect when the child turns 16 years old, or younger if determined appropriate by the IEP team, and updated annually thereafter, the IEP must include:
> - Appropriate measurable postsecondary goals based upon age-appropriate transition assessments related to training, education, employment, and where appropriate, independent living skills [34 C.F.R. §300.320(b)(1)]
> - The transition services (including courses of study) needed to assist the child in reaching those goals [34 C.F.R. §300.320(b)(2)]
>
> (Definition of individualized education program, 2006)

Student Contribution to Transition Services

Transition services are funded under IDEA and the Rehabilitation Act, and together, the school district and the OVR provide services such as preemployment services (e.g., job placement, supportive employment), job counseling, and workplace readiness skills. The student can receive these services, which are the responsibility of the schools and the state vocational rehabilitation services.

An interagency agreement governs these services by state. Referrals to other services can also be provided. Services selected must be in the IEP by age 16 but can also go in prior to age 16 when the team agrees it is expedient for the child. Additional services are supports to the student to help them complete the needed credits to graduate: creating of alternate pathways to graduation, such as work programs where credits are received based on successful inclusion in a work setting; enrollment and support in technical school; or classes with accessible testing for students with disabilities; support to find colleges that provide services to students with learning disabilities; and finally, providing options for continued opportunities to learn after graduation.

INTRODUCTION TO THE TRANSITION PLANNING FORM

Student Preferences

A formal transition plan is designed by each state to document the transition planning process. The school district must keep documentation that a transition plan is written and implemented according to federal guidelines. The transition plan documents the student's needs, vision, and preferences not only at the beginning of transition planning but throughout the period when transition planning is in effect, beginning when transition is first discussed until graduation. The transition planning specialist must discuss transition and document the discussion annually in the IEP and via a record of meetings and transition services for the student. A transition form is part of the IEP, and it is revisited throughout or revised each year to ensure that current needs are met, changes in plans are noted, and services are provided. All documentation regarding the student's participation must be kept as part of the main file for the student, to verify the student's participation and the special education team's facilitation and attention to promoting the student's involvement in planning their post-school life.

Writing the Postsecondary Vision

A case report about a student named Carrie follows and then a transition plan outline based on her needs. This is an example of a potential plan for Carrie. It includes her preferences and interests and the desired outcomes for postsecondary education/training, employment, and adult living. The information about her perspectives and experiences is based on the student questionnaire provided in the Student Supplemental Materials and additional information from a student–transition planning specialist conference.

Case Report: Carrie

Carrie is a ninth grader and in special education for a learning disability. Her assessments indicate she has an average IQ, reads at the sixth-grade level, and has a reading speed in the fifth percentile. She had many absences during seventh and eighth grade, bordering on truancy, for which her parent wrote absence notes. This practice is reaching its permitted limit, and the parent will soon be called into court for Carrie's absences.

The IEP team and the transition planning specialist have decided to discuss her vision for the future in order to begin transition services. Her absences are a predictor of early school leaving (i.e., dropping out), and the special education team plan to use the services of transition planning to reset her trajectory.

Carrie tells the team she always wanted to work in a pet store. She describes her social anxiety disorder, a diagnosis that the parent had not shared, and her delays in learning to read. She believes that working in a pet store is something she can do but thinks her anxiety may prevent her from taking the steps to apply for a job. She also does not think that working in a pet store will provide her enough money later in life. Carrie says she often "freezes" and cannot speak in front of individuals and small or large groups.

Carrie has been participating in a transition curriculum. For a recent assignment she looked at careers in small animal care. This exploration revealed options she did not know existed.

The transition planning specialist begins intensive conferencing with Carrie. This includes the student questionnaire and a request that she write about her disabilities for the IEP transition plan narrative. This belongs in the disability-related needs section of the IEP to further delineate needed supports.

DISABILITY-RELATED NEEDS

This section contains the student's perspectives about his or her disability-related needs that require IEP goals and/or related services. This section is where the student can include his or her narrative about how his or her disability affects education, social, and employment needs. The narrative can also go in the present levels section.

Other disability-related needs include any technology, transportation, academic, counseling, or other need that can help the student gain employment and post-school education under the Americans with Disabilities Act. The student may also need an Individual Plan of Employment through the OVR, whose services include assessment, guidance, job search support, and family services in addition to other individually determined needs.

PERSONAL DISABILITY NARRATIVE (CARRIE'S NARRATIVE)

I will leave places without getting what I need rather than ask for help. If I go to a restaurant, I do not go alone. If I do go with someone, I will not mention it if I did not get a condiment, my drink, or something I ordered. If I am with a friend, I hope they notice and speak for me. If not, I will just eat, unhappy about paying for something I did not get or want.

I am always afraid I will make a mistake, so I know working is going to be hard for me. I feel comfortable being with animals, not people, but people will always be around.

My reading has gotten better, but I am still so slow at it. I can barely keep up in my regular education classes. I have to do hours of homework at night and on the weekends. Really, my life is not that much fun. I like learning, but the way I have to do it, like they do in my regular classes, feels impossible; I just want to give up, just stop everything, if that makes sense. Frankly, school has been so hard, trying to keep up and never being really good at it, well, I just want to graduate and never look back.

My transition planner says it does not have to be this way in adult life, but I have been getting help since second grade and I am afraid I have too many problems to ever be able to do the things I want, like working with animals and learning about them.

EXERCISES

1. Reflect on Carrie's situation. Do you think a ninth-grade student can advocate for needs without intervention? What curriculum materials and instruction would you provide?
2. Research adolescent development and determine if there is research to describe advocacy abilities for that age student. Use peer-reviewed articles or texts for your sources.
3. How did you feel when you read Carrie's narrative?

DISCUSSION

Carrie expressed several difficulties in academics and social interactions that qualify her for services from the OVR and counseling via the local mental health program. Carrie, with the help of the transition planning specialist, decided that further exploration would be worthwhile. She saw that the vocational technical school has a small animal care program. She also found that there is an agricultural college nearby with a program on small animal care. Table 6-1 shows the transition plan designed by Carrie and her transition planning specialist with her mother's permission. Table 6-2 provides a list of services and supports. This information underpins the supports and services that will go into the transition section of the IEP. This chart represents the first conference outcome and will be updated as new services are needed.

Carrie's absences during ninth grade were the impetus for an intensive level of intervention via transition planning services. Although the needed transition services must be in place by age 16, that would have been too late for Carrie, who was losing faith in her motivation to continue. By meeting with Carrie, interviewing her, and finding out about her challenges, the team was able to redirect her trajectory and plan new ways for Carrie to learn and pursue her goals.

Student Contribution and Age of Majority

Although students are at the age of majority at age 18, as noted in Chapter 1, the age of majority can be older for special education than for state law. Therefore, students will need to know about these differences and be given a chance to express their thoughts about control of the IEP content (see Chapter 1).

TABLE 6-1. CARRIE'S TRANSITION PLAN

TRANSITION PLAN NEEDS

Instruction

Courses of study: Carrie is in a general studies program and will graduate by earning credits in required courses. She will also be in a transition education program. In 10th grade she will decide if she will attend vocational school.

- Formal transition program
  - Transition curriculum
- Possible vocational training
- Continued career exploration
- Supports to overcome learning delays due to slow processing of reading materials
- Exploring other certificate programs and vocational school
- An intensive reading program

Related Services

- Assistive technology: Explore alternate ways to learn course content to speed up learning and increase cognitive and intellectual development
- Environmental assessments: Self-assess comfort level in various situations and environments
- Work with transition planning specialist to set up goals to address social fears; consider a work-based learning experience

Community Experiences

- Public transit training
- Access to community leisure activities

Employment

- Employment: Entry-level employment
- Job shadowing: In pet store, veterinary clinic
- Internship: Veterinary clinic

DAILY LIVING SKILLS

- Daily living skills assessments
- Stress-reduction strategies for environmental and social anxiety
- Self-selected independence goal plan
- Self-advocacy and self-determination skills related to independence and job seeking
- Exploring postsecondary education supports for persons with disabilities.

Post-School Objective Plan

- Work and take one class a semester
- Two-year program for animal sciences
- Employment: Interests
- Animal sciences
- Veterinary assistant/technician

Post-School Education

- Part-time community college
- Agricultural college
- Vocational technical program
- Ongoing self-development through adult education programs

Additional: Carrie wants to drive but has been too anxious to begin the steps to take the tests.

Additional assessment: Not needed at this time.

- Functional vocational evaluation if anxiety is too pervasive for meaningful progress
- Eligibility for Medicaid to seek mental health services

Needed Services: Based on the student's plan, a list of transition services was compiled (see Table 6-2).

TABLE 6-2. INSTRUCTION, SERVICES, AND SUPPORTS FOR CARRIE'S TRANSITION PLAN

INSTRUCTION: EXPLORE AND LEARN

- Transition planning curriculum with direct instruction on employment preparation
- Work-based learning application
- Career exploration
- Exploration of local animal science programs and certificate programs
- Community options seminar about local businesses to explore other options
- Instruction about community experiences/post-school adult living
- Are there certain types of community and/or adult living experiences that will help the student reach his/her postsecondary vision?

SERVICES

- Vocational education program tour for students with disabilities
- Job coach via OVR to access part-time employment, supported job placement, service learning projects, participation in work experience program, job shadowing, and internships
- Transition planning after-school club support for practice in resume writing/ interviewing skills, the use of a one-stop resource center, and job-specific skills in areas such as customer service, technology, etc.
- Coach for mental health strategy for self-advocacy
- Parent meeting and encouragement to attend mental health counseling because of pervasive social anxiety and low self-esteem

INDEPENDENT LIVING: COMMUNITY-BASED ACTIVITIES

- Visits to community resources
- Participation in community-based experiences to learn how to independently access community resources, visit restaurants, build social relationships, manage money, understand health care needs, use transportation options, and practice organizational skills
- Learn about mental health counseling agency and how to apply for Medicaid to cover treatment costs
- Learn about recreational therapy providers
- Explore community clubs such as athletics, horticultural, animal interests

Student Contribution to Transition Services

A student, such as Carrie, can request any of the services listed in Table 6-2 through the OVR or through the school district under IDEA. The student may also ask for help with other services, such as getting working papers and a Social Security card. In addition, the transition conferences become part of the specially designed instruction because the student will need this type of intensive intervention to access instruction and other services for post-school life.

Goals

After the plan is designed, goals are developed and placed in the IEP. The transition planning specialist works with the student to develop the goals so the legal requirements are met, but the student must be able to carry out the goals. Examples of how to goal set are addressed in the section called Student Goal Setting. Table 6-1 shows a plan for Carrie.

Measuring Progress and How Parents Will Be Informed

School districts must report on both academic progress in general education, if the student is included, and IEP goal progress. Therefore, students in academic programs and who have an IEP receive reports for both. Report card distribution and IEP progress monitoring are determined by district, but it is typically done quarterly. Progress on IEP goals is typically reported on the same dates as the report cards, or a school district may select an alternate date.

Student Contribution to Monitoring Progress Toward Goals

The student will know about his or her progress on the IEP goals via ongoing conferencing with the transition planning specialist, secondary special education teachers, and general teachers, as well as in reports issued on the same schedule as general education peers.

Transition Planning Specialist Reflection Exercise

1. Carrie's plan and the information that would become her disability narrative revealed key information about her preferences and needs requires some post-plan reflection. Complete the following exercise and determine whether this plan reflected Carrie's needs. With Carrie in mind, the transition planning specialist must know whether the plan captured the key questions in the exercises. By reviewing the following questions, the team can quality check their performance and determine whether they need more information:
   a. Who is the student currently, and what is his or her vision for the future?
   b. Where does the student want to be in the future?
   c. What will the student need to do and want to do to get there?
   d. What are the student's current demands, and what will the student need to do to overcome them? If the student cannot do this alone, what supports does he or she need?
   e. What does the student view as options under his or her current conditions?
   f. What attitudes and beliefs can impair the student's ability to avoid behaviors that can derail his or her future?
   g. What academic subjects does the student struggle with, and why?
   h. What social situations does the student struggle with, and why?
   i. Does the student have difficulty declining to participate in activities that he or she does not want to do?
   j. What knowledge can the transition planning specialist provide to facilitate more options for the student?

ESTABLISHING STUDENT PREFERENCES

The Foundation of Transition Plans

The student's vision, dreams, preferences, and skills needed to help him or her reach his or her goals are the building blocks of the transition plan. Like Carrie, students with disabilities think about what they want to do but do not have enough knowledge and often lack the communication skills to explain their thoughts. Also, like Carrie, students may have a clear picture of what they see as their barriers. Once students reach adolescence, if their receptive vocabulary has been developed, the more advanced vocabulary can be used to explain their learning, psychological, and performance fears that will affect their ability to pursue goals. From the interactive interview conferences, Carrie developed a narrative about her barriers, and from that, a plan to address her employment, wishes, and concerns developed.

To effectively assemble the building blocks for a plan, preliminary information gathering requires that the transition planning specialist develop specialized interview skills and, when needed, communication tools to guide the student to express him- or herself. In Chapter 9, the process of conferencing with the student using effective interviewing to establish his or her meaning is explained. It is essential to establish the student's meaning, which is in the context of his or her abilities and disability. This type of information cannot be gathered from a preference assessment. The essential information that the student provides about him- or herself is the foundation of the plan.

Changing Choices, Preferences, and Needs

Changing choices and preferences is a natural part of transition planning, and decision making and preferences are viewed as both changeable and static. The transition planning specialist, when conferencing with the student, keeps up-to-date on the results of choices and encourages the student to research a range of options, such as those noted in Carrie's initial plan while continuing to develop her employment skills and give her tools to increase learning speed. As the student explores and learns, choices are culled or tried and discarded, as in Sam's case (see Chapter 2).

Although preferences for a preferred job are motivating, job choices, especially entry-level positions, can be motivated by other preferred rewards. Students with disabilities do pick and remain in jobs they do not prefer. They see a job as a means to other outcomes, such as getting a car or making other purchases. Earning money gives the student buying power and independence. Job preference may not matter once the student begins to see the new freedom and power in earning, as well as the pride of contributing to the family by carrying his or her own expenses and becoming less dependent on parents.

Therefore, students who are going to work can be guided to look at their entry-level job choices and preferences as not only about what they want to do but also as a path to both short-term goals, such as meeting friends for dinner, and long-term goals, such as going on vacation or accessing further education. These social, learning, and leisure motivators are mediators that ground students in the realities of everyday life and enable them to make compromises to get their needs met. In this way, entry-level employment during high school is a playing field for the decision-making process, helping students learn workplace skills and develop independence while learning skills for future full-time employment.

Many negative comments are made about the types of jobs a student may take. Often those most available are the ones that receive the most derision. These comments should be avoided because deciding a student's outcome by his or her entry-level job is rather short-sighted and can deter a student from getting important workplace skills.

As stated throughout this text, a student who chooses the goal is more likely to be engaged, self-determined, and motivated to complete the task. Although preferences increase motivation, choosing a preferred goal or situation is not necessarily going to maintain continued interest. As with any untried choice, a preference may be discarded once the experience becomes a reality. So, choosing something does not mean the student will maintain the motivation to continue choosing it. Preferences can also be discarded when they are viewed as too difficult to accomplish. The concept of persistence is difficult for many students, and the transition team can encourage a student to continue through those more challenging goals, but the student should also feel free to stop. However, a student may also return to a previously discarded goal with new energy. This process is to be expected and does not reflect on the transition planning specialist's effectiveness.

Student Goal Setting

Developing and Setting Goals

This is where the responsibilities of the transition planning specialist and the special education team mesh with the student's goals. The transition planning specialist ensures that there is a process in place to teach the student how to develop and reach goals. Parents are also involved in providing planned activities outside of the school schedule.

Defining Measurable Goals

The student needs to be informed that goals have both an educational and legal purpose. To meet the goals of the special education law, a goal must meet five criteria. The goal must be specific, measurable, attainable, results-oriented and time-bound. To be specific, it must name the skill or subject area and the expected result. To be measurable, it has to be written in such a way that the progress on the goal can be measured for documentation. The goal must also be attainable by the student based on the student's ability. The goal must clearly state what the student will do to accomplish the goal and include the time frame in which it is to be accomplished. Each goal should lead to an outcome that advances progress toward employment, post-school education, and increased independence.

Developing Career, Post-School Education, and Employment Goals

Once a target activity is chosen, the objectives are developed to break the task down into measurable, attainable steps. For example, if a student tells the transition planning specialist that he or she wants to attain a driver's license, the student will need to find out information about getting the license.

As an example, let us look at Phil's vision. Phil wants to learn to drive. Phil wants to take classes at community college. Phil wants a part-time job. The three goals for this illustration are community access, education, and employment. Each of these can be accomplished while Phil is still in high school. Phil can get his license, get into a job-shadow position, and take summer classes at the local community college before high school graduation (Table 6-3).

Completion of these goals is reported in the quarterly reports on progress, and new goals are added on the revision page of the IEP. Developing independence goals can be more complex due to the number of tasks to be completed.

Constructing Independence Goals

Palmer and Wehmeyer (2003) suggest the following steps to structure the teaching of goal setting:
1. Identify the goal: What do you want to learn or do?
2. What do you already know?
3. What do you need to learn?
4. Write the goal: Is the goal clear, concise, measurable, short term/long term?
5. Create an action plan: How will you begin to work on this goal, and when?
6. What problems or barriers may be encountered?
7. Evaluate progress and adjust the plan or goal. How are you doing? What have you done?

This process can be used to create individual goals or multiple goals for more comprehensive transition activities. A comprehensive transition activity is one where the activity draws on the student to make more than one choice, organize the task, create a checklist of needs and an overall plan, include adults and peers, lead the group involved, and result in a product. The student should write the goals. In this way, they increase their self-determination and ability to plan and use executive functioning using a motivating activity.

TABLE 6-3. CREATING ATTAINABLE, MEASURABLE GOALS: PHIL'S COMMUNITY ACCESS TRANSITION GOALS

CAREER: COMMUNITY ACCESS GOALS

Specify Goal	Make It Measurable	Make It Attainable	Name the Result	Define the Period
Phil will learn the information he needs to pass the learner's permit test.	Phil will go online and print out the steps to getting a license and download or order the driver's manual.	Phil will use the classroom computer and printer to go to the Department of Motor Vehicles website.	Phil will choose how he wants to access the driver's manual.	Phil will have the manual and begin to study by Monday, September 7. Progress will be measured on September 7.
Phil will learn the content of the manual to pass the permit test.	Each day Phil will study one section topic.	Phil will set aside 1 hour to read and answer section questions. He will register with the in-school afternoon resource room and use the computer there.	Phil will complete the manual practice tests by September 30.	By September 30 Phil will schedule his test and complete the test by October 15.

POST-SCHOOL EDUCATION

Specify Goal	Make It Measurable	Make It Attainable	Name the Result	Define the Period
Phil has anxiety about going to college and negotiating a campus due to issues with executive functioning. He wants to try one course in a subject that is not high demand such as physical education. He wants to take it in the summer and use the credit to make up a gym credit he needs	Phil will explore the college website for information on summer classes for high school students. Phil will visit the community college with his parents.	Phil will print out a list of summer classes and their descriptions. Phil will decide which one he would like to take. Phil will find out the costs and get parental support for attendance.	Phil will take one community college course in a preferred subject.	Phil will register by March of the same year.
Phil wants to get a job in a retail business but feels he will need some support to learn the job.	Phil will participate in on-the-job training at Party Supplies to learn how to properly take orders for balloons, organize products on the shelves, and work at a cash register.	Phil will follow the job coach's lead and learn each task.	Phil will apply for a position at Party Supplies or participate in another training opportunity.	Phil will complete 3 hours of training, 2 days a week for 4 weeks.

Analyzing Tasks and Setting Subgoals

Complex plans and their subgoals should be broken down into their component parts. This is a process called *task analysis*. Breaking a plan into a checklist is particularly useful for students with autism or memory and organizational problems.

The process of task analysis is important for students with disabilities and is effective for any student with a disability. Although it is often identified as part of systematic instruction for students with intellectual disabilities, it is also quite applicable to developing goal-setting and goal-completion behaviors. A task analysis is more specifically defined as "breaking up the complex task into smaller tasks" (Cooper, Heron, & Heward, 2007). The task analysis process involves generating relevant tasks that should be considered for instruction (Johnassen, 2009) and, in this text, constructing transition goals.

The ability to carry out the complex processes involved in planning requires opportunities to practice making plans for transition activities, plans that are to be carried through to completion. The process of developing an activity of transition includes "the ability to make choices, solve problems, set goals, evaluate options, take initiative to reach one's goals, and accept consequences of one's actions" (Morningstar & Mazzotti, 2014, p. 9). Taking responsibility by reviewing one's plans and making adjustments prior to plan initiation can lead the student to greater self-efficacy in his or her ability to act independently or in collaboration with others. According to Bandura (1994), "the most effective way of creating a strong sense of efficacy is through mastery experiences. Successes build a robust belief in one's personal efficacy. Failures undermine it, especially if failures occur before a sense of efficacy is firmly established" (p. 71).

The goal of the activities of transition are to develop not only skills but also feelings of competence and self-efficacy by going through the process independently and successfully. Creating his or her own task analysis gives the student new skills to plan and complete tasks using a task analysis approach.

Table 6-4 illustrates the development of multiple skills such as leadership, social interaction, and post-activity self-evaluation for a student, Jack, who wants to be able to cook for himself. Table 6-4 is a breakdown of how this activity supports independence and autonomy. The table is broken into how the student is engaged in leading the plan and setting the goals and how the transition planning specialist and the student delineate the types of skills that will be developed and the supports needed to plan and carry out the process of cooking three breakfasts for friends over a designated time period. The plan includes a tangible product to self-assess and to share with peers. In column 3 there is a task analysis about what steps need to be done. This section is developed by Jack and followed by discussion with the transition planning specialist for any questions or suggestions he may ask, such as engaging his parents in the plan. This comprehensive approach and the evaluation of each part is a foundation for future novel activity plans.

Finally, plans are a task analysis, and therefore this type of goal setting can engage students on multiple levels and create skills that will help students plan during adulthood.

Another use of this type of task analysis for goal setting is to create group plans for CBI. Students can become efficacious in created and preferred social activities and learning to gain consensus around where to go and what to do. Self-determination is furthered by selecting educational, social, and self-CBI experiences. These group activities can create group cohesion, organizational skills, and the ability to plan a social course of action.

See Figure 6-1 for an example of how to track completion of the plan.

TABLE 6-4. JACK'S PLAN FOR INDEPENDENCE: A TASK ANALYSIS TO DEVELOP MULTIPLE SKILLS

INDEPENDENCE AND AUTONOMY GOALS

Student Leads Plan	Student Sets Goals	Student Develops Skills	Possible Supports Needed
Self-assesses wants and needs	• Increase independence • Self-care • Food • Meal planning • Money management • Task planning • Social experiences • Clothing • Transportation	Independence skills and personal development • Choice selections • Decision making • Self-awareness • Goal development • Communicating needs: Self-advocacy • Goal completion • Increased independent living skills • Self-determination • Social skills • Leadership skills	• Transportation • Money • Food • Select time • Select date • Directions • School personnel • Family • Peers
Identifies needs Sets goals	Explores desires	Decision making • Goal: I want to learn to make three breakfasts. • Self-awareness and advocacy	• Transportation • Money • Food • Select time • Select date • Directions • School personnel • Family • Peers
Makes choices	Identifies goals	Decision making • Cooking • Fried eggs and bacon • Pancakes • Hot cereal	• Asks family for support to buy the products • Invites family or friends to come eat

(continued)

TABLE 6-4. JACK'S PLAN FOR INDEPENDENCE: A TASK ANALYSIS TO DEVELOP MULTIPLE SKILLS (CONTINUED)

INDEPENDENCE AND AUTONOMY GOALS

Student Leads Plan	Student Sets Goals	Skill Development	Possible Supports Needed
Considers action plans using task analysis Enlists a peer to video the cooking task	Creates an action plan	Decision making • Watch cooking videos with peer participants for homework Self-advocacy • Enlist peers to record cooking activity in a step-by-step process. • Tell parents about the plan. Self-efficacy • Enter project with knowledge of cooking process Independent performance • Set up shopping list • Secure transportation • Pick up supplies • Cook as per directions created from recipe or videos • Set table • Serve family	• Asks family for support to buy the products • Invites extended family or friends to come eat
Student evaluation	Evaluates progress Reviews the video of cooking breakfast	Self-evaluation • Creates evaluation. Checklist evaluates: 　◦ Utensils cleaned 　◦ Food cooked 　◦ Food proper temperature 　◦ Table set	Reviews progress using the checklist with supervising teacher Shows video to class and teacher. Reports on the experience. Was the experience successful? Did Jack learn to cook one breakfast? Did he coordinate the video project with his peers? Was the experience social?
Student adjustments	Adjusts plan and considers next goals	Reviews plan with guests for suggestions	Edits and shares project with tech team and supervising transition planning specialist for review.

EXAMPLE MEASURABLE GOAL FOR SELF-MONITORING

Goal: Jack will complete a series of activities to learn to cook three breakfasts by _____.

Evaluation: Jack will record himself cooking and share it as a media model for sharing the new skill with peers within 2 weeks after the breakfast.

Task Analysis Checklist

- I will view videos that teach how to cook the three breakfasts for homework.
- I will choose assistants to create a video/digital record of the project.
- I will choose the food, plan, and cook three breakfasts by _____.
- I will plan a shopping list, secure transportation and money, purchase what I need, and invite people to eat the breakfast.
- I will create and use a checklist to track my progress.
- I will develop and use the checklist to evaluate the meal.
- I will report my progress to my peers via my recording.

Date for goal completion _____

Figure 6-1. Preliminary activity plan.

THE STUDENT NARRATIVE AND GOAL SETTING

Professionals who work with students with disabilities may not be aware of a student's thoughts about his or her experiences in the classroom or how the student may have felt about the impact of his or her disability on his or her academic, functional, and social performance.

As discussed earlier, for the first time, the student can make these experiences known to the IEP team. Creating a narrative in writing, using text-to-speech, or an interpreter is the starting point for the student to self-determine the best fit for future work environments. This process is the foundation for the future, and educator input should not stymie the information provided by the student in this first self-reflective activity.

Team members should look at the narrative not as a source for developing goals for the student but rather as the student's example of what he or she may need for the transition services, education, training, and the beginning of employment. In the narrative, the student can include how he or she wants his or her needs addressed, and the examples of student contributions for the IEP in this chapter can guide him or her.

Giving the student the IEP process as a forum to describe his or her school experience can help the student end what has not worked for him or her. Through this process, the student can begin to know themselves, their disability-related needs, and their hopes and dreams.

The Transition Planning Specialist's Role

In the following review of a written narrative, the transition planning specialist begins the balancing act of guiding, encouraging, and structuring the process so this student can design her goals. Once this narrative is completed, the transition planning specialist should go over it and use the interviewing techniques described in Chapter 10, not to change the story, but rather to probe for further self-perceptions that will help guide the first IEP and the transition section. This narrative was written by a student with bipolar disorder who was in an emotional and behavioral disorder program. The diagnosis and history makes this a narrative with significant complexity. This report was partially included in Chapter 5 about medical assessments.

Case Report: Ms. Smith

My diagnosis makes it difficult for me to concentrate. I get frustrated more easily than the other kids at school. I can do well for a while and then I start to feel agitated and anxious. I feel like I cannot do the work, and I think I am stupid; my mind feels disorganized. When I get like this, I cannot concentrate on all the social interactions of my friends. I often misunderstand things and think they want to hurt my feelings or something, which is completely untrue. I get overwhelmed when under stress, and I have difficulty completing tasks. Even the noise of the large school distracts me. I really need a small setting for school or to be in a situation where there is not much social involvement to do my work like I used to be able to do. Before this illness started, I was a good student; now I am not. I lose things when I am like this and feel like a scatterbrain who never gets anything in order. This is what bipolar disorder did to me. I am not the person I was before.

I have found that when I get overwhelmed from this, if I can walk away from the schoolwork for a bit, take a little break when I start to get really upset, then I can start back again feeling more organized inside. If I cannot escape my stress, I want to hurt myself to distract from my emotional anguish—anguish is the only word I can think of to describe the feeling. I can go from feeling happy to anguished and suicidal on the same day. This instability of my mood was difficult for students in regular education to understand, causing social problems that are confusing and distracting to me. After I moved to this smaller school where they gave me therapy, I have not been in the hospital once, and I am not suicidal anymore, nor have I hurt myself in a long time.

EXERCISES

1. How would you define the terms *distracting, emotional anguish,* and *scatterbrain* to effectively understand the problems this student is trying to communicate?
2. How would you establish the meaning of this communication? (Establishing meaning is further discussed in Chapter 9.)

DISCUSSION

This is a transcript written to be put into Ms. Smith's IEP. In this case, the student was advocating for a small school setting or to graduate from there and go right into a small community college part-time in nonpressured classes. This was one of a few plans floated within transition idea sessions. The final plan was to go to a small community college to get her back into a more normal setting and to help her gain more insight into what level of work and school she could handle.

This is an example of developing self-determination, and the student was able to steer her IEP team to understand her needs and to equip them better to help her meet her goals. She was taught how to participate in her IEP and to write her perspective; she felt she was able to tell the team about her illness challenges as a permanent disability in a before-and-after way. She could express and talk to the IEP team about her disability in a way that helped the IEP team members develop an understanding that did not include returning to her school district. Instead, she later left the small school in a partial hospital setting, considered the most restrictive setting under IDEA, and she did go to a local community college. Then she graduated from a university with honors. However, she did have to leave for 1 year; when feeling better, she went off her medication, had an episode, dropped out, went for treatment, and returned to college.

The transition planning specialist was able to look at her strengths (academics) and her needs (mental health medical care) and discuss them with her so she could guide the team about her limitations regarding retuning to high school. Although some viewed this as the end of her school career, the transition planning specialist saw it as the beginning. Being a transition planning specialist often requires the creativity to find a path not thought of before. This student had no belief in her intelligence and even though she had a high aptitude and a 130 IQ, she had lost hope. In situations like this one, a transition planning specialist may be the first person to believe in the student as the student takes the logical, though not conventional, steps forward.

In the following case report, a student came up against two situations when the team did not have a process of gathering relevant student information about academics or preferences.

Case Report: Peter

Peter was a seventh-grade student with a disability under the category of other health impairment. His IQ was in the high 80 range. He received speech and occupational therapy and special education in a program for students with learning disabilities.

Peter's parents were attending their son's IEP meeting. During the meeting, the teacher reported that Peter was still on a second-grade reading level. Peter's parents became concerned when the teacher said that Peter had plateaued and would no longer benefit from reading instruction and that the IEP should now focus on functional goals. Despite his parents' concerns, a transition plan was developed with other more functional rather than academic goals.

Peter's parents believed that not enough intensive reading instruction was provided, and they felt Peter could improve his reading. The family asked for a due process hearing to ask for a more appropriate program with intensive reading instruction, something he was never provided with before.

The parents won the hearing, and Peter was placed in a school that provided intensive reading instruction. By the end of 10th grade, Peter was able to read at the 7th-grade level. His family returned Peter to his home school district so he could receive transition planning services to prepare him for employment. He is currently employed in a job of his choice. Leading the IEP helped Peter be more of a leader and helped him figure out what he wanted to do after high school. The transition planning process helped him look for jobs and participate in mock interviews with classmates.

EXERCISES

1. Based on this case report, what information was used to determine the shift from academic to functional goals?

2. Using only peer-reviewed studies, research delayed reading acquisition and reading plateaus. What is known about breaking through plateaus and is there more research that needs to be done?

3. Using peer-reviewed research, identify five intensive reading programs and their effectiveness for students with reading disabilities.

4. How could a student narrative have helped Peter? Write a disability narrative from Peter's perspective.

DISCUSSION

Peter reported that his teachers did not understand his disability. He reported that he was not given other ways to overcome the disability and that teachers kept repeating the same interventions over and over. In addition to the reading delay, his handwriting did not develop into legibility. Due to his physical disability in the area of fine motor skills, he was unable to finish written assignments. Although he had occupational therapy, it did not correct the physical disability. Peter reported that he had to advocate for technology that would help him complete his assignments. He stated that the following issues presented difficulties.

1. Teachers did not understand what his disabilities were.

2. He could not find any other alternatives to reading and writing

3. Teachers kept repeating the same interventions

4. What did not work? Handwriting and learning cursive.

Peter stated that things that helped him were public speaking, switching to typing (although he wished they had switched sooner), assistive technology, the computer, and an IPAD, which were provided at his private placement. Once he returned to his local school district, he advocated for himself. His advocacy enabled him to get a book share program with books in a auditory format, and he was able to use a computer to write.

ORGANIZATION AND PLAN DEVELOPMENT

Previous conferences must be reviewed by the transition planning specialist before meeting a student because each meeting should build upon the previous one. Knowledge of the details of former and current aspirations demonstrates the transition planning specialist's willingness to work with the student. The student will appreciate that the transition planning specialist detailed those earlier conversations. Remembering the details of every conversation is difficult given that the transition planning specialist will be working with multiple students. Therefore, the transition planning specialist should regularly reread notes and the narrative. Demonstrating a lack of knowledge about the student is evident when a student arrives to the conference and the transition planning specialist is seen fumbling through papers trying to remember the plan. Students who are neglected or have low-self-esteem are particularly vulnerable when treated with this type of disregard. Respecting the student means demonstrating that respect. The transition planning specialist should have contacted the student, read previous discussions ahead of the meeting, and had him- or herself and the student prepared with the conference talking points. It is essential to impress on students that their transition planning specialist cared enough to be ready for the meeting. The transition planning specialist should have a hard copy and a digital record of the student's plans available at every meeting to further reassure the student that the transition plan is an organized process meant for his or her success.

EXERCISE

1. Pick two disability categories under mental health and specific learning disabilities. Research each one. Use the information you find to write about yourself as if you have the disability you researched. Use your real family and home and place yourself in that setting as you write about your hypothetical disability and how it affects home, school, friends, and the ability to live on your own. Suggestions:
   a. Tell your audience about how you see yourself in comparison to others.
   b. Tell your audience how it affects your schoolwork, your family, and your friends.
   c. Tell about the difficulties brought on by your disability.
   d. Talk about an injury, vision problem, or other issue that further affected your movement or sensory system. Share your struggles with a classmate.

SUMMARY

Through the creative, interactive, and collaborative transition planning process, the student becomes part of the adult community for the first time. To effectively participate in adult life, the student learns that he or she is also part of multiple communities. The student will be an adult member of a family community, a workplace community, a further education community, and a neighborhood community. In each community where the student will be a member, he or she will have responsibilities where he or she can play a vital role. To play these vital roles, the goals in the transition plan are crucial steps to the student's autonomy and inclusion in multiple settings. Through instructing the student, giving the student autonomy, respecting the student, and including the student in the process of IEP development, the transition planning specialist and secondary special education team give the student the skills to direct his or her own life. Building a transition plan with an adolescent who is becoming a young adult appears to be a complex process. It entails many updates and revisions as the student learns new skills and advances in maturity. The transition plan documents a continuum of efforts to facilitate special education and encourage the student's journey to adulthood. When the last transition plan is completed and the team attends graduation, the result of the work becomes visible. Seeing the students graduate is the culmination of the transition process; it is life-changing for the student who, like Carrie and Ms. Smith, may have given up without the transition planning process and the work of the special education team.

REFERENCES

Bandura, A. (1994). Self-efficacy. In V. S. Ramachaudran (Ed.), *Encyclopedia of human behavior* (Vol. 4, pp. 71-81). New York, NY: Academic Press.

Cooper, J. O., Heron, T. E., & Heward, W. L. (2007). *Applied behavior analysis* (2nd ed.). Upper Saddle River, NJ: Pearson Merrill Prentice Hall.

Definition of individualized education program, 34 C.F.R. § 300.320 (2006).

Individuals with Disabilities Education Act of 2004, Pub. L. No. 108-446, 20 U.S.C. § 1400 *et seq.* (2004).

Johnassen, D. (2009). *Task analysis methods for instructional design.* New York, NY: Routledge Press.

Morningstar, M., & Mazzotti, V. (2014). *Teacher Preparation to Deliver Evidence-Based Transition Planning and Services to Youth with Disabilities.* (Document No. IC-1). University of Florida and Collaboration for Effective Educator, Development, Accountability, and Reform Center. Retrieved from ceedar.education.ufl.edu/wp-content/up-loads/2014/08/transition-planning.pdf

Palmer, S. B., & Wehmeyer, M. L. (2003). Promoting self-determination in early elementary school: Teaching self-regulated problem-solving and goal-setting skills. *Remedial and Special Education, 24*(2), 115-126.

Rehabilitation Act of 1973, Pub. L. No. 93-112, 29 U.S.C. § 701 *et seq.* (1973).

APPENDIX: STUDENT QUESTIONNAIRE FOR TRANSITION PLANNING

Transition Conference 1

Student: _____ Date: _____

School: _____ Grade: _____

Age: _____ Annual IEP Due Date: _____ Phone Number: _____

Transition Planning Specialist Contact Extension: _____

This form has 25 questions. If you cannot answer any of these, please come see me before the conference date.

Transition Planning Specialist's Name: _____

1. Now is the time to think about what you like to do. What interests and preferences do you have?

    Current interests: _____

    _____

    _____

    Preferences: _____

    _____

    _____

    What do you do or are you learning to do well? _____

    _____

    Anything else you would like to mention? _____

    _____

    _____

2. When you graduate from high school, what do you think about doing?

    _____ Begin competitive employment, working full-time or part-time

    _____ Work in a job with a job coach available to assist when needed

    _____ Attend a local community college or trade school

    _____Attend a local community college taking subjects I want to learn about

    _____Work part-time and go to community college or vocational school

    _____ Enlist in the military

    _____Work full-time and attend community or 4-year college in the evening

    _____ Attend a 4-year college

3. What other ideas have you thought about that are not listed? _____

    _____

    _____

4. Do you think you will need help getting and keeping a job? _____ YES _____ NO

    Do you know how to interview? _____ YES _____ NO

    Do you know how to dress for an interview? _____ YES _____ NO

    Do you know how to look for your first job? _____ YES _____ NO

    Have you ever been paid for work before? _____ YES _____ NO

    Have you learned about a first job you would like to do? _____ YES _____ NO

    What would you like to learn about getting a first job? _____

    _____

    _____

5. Following graduation, do you plan to live at home or one of the following?

   _____ Live with my parents and help support myself

   _____ Live in our home or the home of a relative

   _____ Live in an apartment with a friend(s) and need no extra help

   _____ I am in foster care

   _____ I am not sure

   _____ Other (please specify) _____

6. In the future, do you anticipate you will need to live on your own? _____ YES _____ NO

7. What coursework and activities would you like to take in high school?_____

   _____

   _____

   _____

8. What kind of work experience (paid or unpaid) do you have? _____

   _____

   _____

9. Do your parents have preferences regarding the type of work they would like you to do now and in the future? If so, what do you think about those ideas? _____

   _____

   _____

10. What leisure/recreational activities do you enjoy? _____

    _____

    _____

11. Are there other leisure/recreational activities in which you would like to participate? If so, please name them. _____

    _____

    _____

12. Do you want to obtain a driver's license? _____ YES _____ NO

    Do you think you will need transportation to work? _____ YES _____ NO

    How will you get there? _____

    Do you know how to take a train or a bus? _____ YES _____ NO

    Do you want to learn? _____ YES _____ NO

13. In which of the following areas, if any, do you feel you need to improve?

_____ Clothing care	_____ Meal preparation and nutrition
_____ Hygiene/grooming	_____ Home care (cleaning/maintenance)
_____ Health/first aid	_____ Shopping and making purchases
_____ Crossing streets	_____ Time management
_____ Sex education	_____ Measurement
_____ Money management	_____ Safety in the home
_____ Driver's education	_____ Parenting/child development
_____ General safety	
_____ Other (please specify)	

    _____

    _____

14. Do you receive assistance from any public or private agency? If so, what service or assistance is provided, and which agency provides the service? _____

    _____

    _____

15. Do you have a legal guardian? _____ YES _____ NO

16. If not, do you know when you might need a guardian before you turn 18? _____ YES _____ NO

17. Would you like information on guardianship? _____ YES _____ NO

18. Do you have a medical concern? _____ YES _____ NO

19. Do you have an Individual Health Plan? _____ YES _____ NO

20. Do you have any other personal concerns that you need help with or that may make it difficult for you to graduate on time? _____ YES _____ NO

21. Is any family member ill and you will need extra help for meeting your goals? _____ YES _____ NO

22. Do you feel safe in school and in the community? _____ YES _____ NO

23. What subject do you dislike? _____

24. What subject do you want help with? _____

25. Do you think we can do more to help you learn? If so, describe: _____
_____
_____

Please bring this form with you to the first transition planning meeting.

Career and Employment-Based Learning
Supporting Entry Into the Workforce and Postsecondary Education

PREPARING THE STUDENT FOR EMPLOYMENT

School-Based Preparatory Experiences

Career explorations were previously discussed as instructional activities for individuals or small groups of students. Between 8th and 10th grade (or ages 13 to the later of 15), students are participating in a transition career curriculum, most likely aligned to state standards. They have researched many careers as a part of an Individualized Education Plan (IEP) goal for transition planning.

Rae, J. M. *A Collaborative Approach to Transition Planning for Students With Disabilities* (pp. 151-168).
© 2020 SLACK Incorporated.

By 10th grade, setting up additional in-depth experiences can begin. Students with disabilities should have begun participation in school-based clubs and planned career explorations to define their current choices. The goal now is for students to be more detailed as they learn about the marketplace and local community and school opportunities. They will need to see the most current options in employment and decide if there are experiences that may be available in their area of interests.

Many students with disabilities have difficulty with executive functioning. In a conference with the transition planning specialist, the planning process is structured, and students learn how to define a small group of choices. Students begin to look at specific companies of interest, the goals of the companies, and how the students can be an asset to the workplace. The students will define what skills they have and what skills are needed. Students may also decide that they want to participate in a vocational program, and as they progress through the program, they will work with the transition planning specialist and a vocational school placement counselor who will provide guidance on the application process. Students will decide on part-time work and what other skills or schooling they want or need.

As students progress through Gate 8 of the plan (conferencing with the student; defining career selections, training, post-school education, and transition services), the goal is they will have a plan of activities to apply to other job search efforts that arise later in life.

Workplace Environments

Career explorations should include a review of the company environment and environmental conditions. Personal preferences, such as tolerance of settings without windows or settings where the employee will experience extremes of weather, should be examined. A well-developed environmental inventory is used by students to analyze environmental issues they will need to consider. Although there is no perfect environment, teaching students to evaluate potential working conditions can help them define their preferences and rule out or narrow down employment settings.

If they discover there is no exact fit for what they had hoped to find, students can develop skills and participate in preferred employment that does not match every preference. Discussions about preferences for the employment environment, if addressed early, can lead to a more realistic career plan.

As students explore employment and career interests, they may or may not become consciously aware that places of employment have missions and goals. Each employer wants the employee to complete tasks that carry out its company's mission for the delivery of its products and services, be it food, clothing, or other services. Students must understand that the employer expects its vision to be carried out and that the company has a role it expects the employee to play. An employer's vision and goals include an expectation that the employee carries its message of quality services and a quality product to the customer.

In the process of company exploration, students should be getting to know themselves as people with preferences, tolerances, and reasons behind their quest for employment. They need to know if their strengths and needs align with those of their chosen companies.

Preparing for Social Interactions at Work

Students need to prepare for social interactions at work. These include social greetings, work-related communication, work task roles, and even social exchanges in the lunch room. Students with disabilities need a more extensive range of social experiences in preparation for the workplace. After-school clubs, either those already in existence or those proposed by the students, are a place to develop strong interpersonal skills, and they help students decide what after-school activities may align with a career or are areas better chosen as social activities.

Interest Clubs

Interest clubs are a way to explore interests or find leisure and social activities with same-age peers. Table 7-1 contains examples of clubs that students with disabilities may benefit from. Naturally, participation for students with disabilities can bring about inclusion with their peers and provide them a practice ground for the development of social skills and skills related to their interests. One benefit for students with disabilities who have been in special education for over 60% of the school day is to be able to see how students interact. For students with low coping skills, such as students with emotional and behavioral disorders, these can be valuable preliminary employment learning experiences (Schunk, 2003). By seeing multiple types of interactions, students with disabilities can be prepared for the various social interactions that occur in the workplace. Being members in a learning environment and developing a sense of belonging with peers and adults through engagement in extracurricular activities engages and motivates struggling students to believe they can succeed (Margolis & McCabe, 2006). Engaging students in successful social experiences that are moderately challenging facilitates student engagement and improved self-efficacy. The ongoing struggle in academics can result in a decreased belief in their ability to achieve in any environment. Teachers and the transition planning specialist need to encourage students to try the learning experiences provided in school activities (Margolis & McCabe, 2006).

Exercises

1. Pick five of the clubs listed in Table 7-1 and contact your local school district advisors. Ask for information about how students with disabilities participate.
2. Research whether a local school district has clubs that include students with disabilities.
3. Research whether the school district has clubs that are specifically for students with disabilities.

WORK-BASED LEARNING

School-Based Job Observations, Internships, Work Sampling, and Service Learning

The most important factors associated with successful post-school employment are paid and unpaid work experiences during the last years of high school, along with a high school diploma (Benz, Lindstrom, & Yovanoff, 2000; Luecking, 2009). High schools provide preliminary career preparation experiences in the form of work-based learning experiences. Work-based learning refers to a program of work experiences that occur in a bona fide workplace (Hamilton & Hamilton, 1997), including interviews, tours, job shadowing, internships, apprenticeships, and service learning. They can be on site or through a contracted experience in the community. For example, job shadowing can include career planning events when students can interview or shadow a school employee. School-based career experiences may also be a positive first foray into learning about careers. In addition, many teachers have other forms of employment during the summer months and can provide students with ideas about other areas of employment.

Other unpaid experiences could include working in the school library or following the technology staff as they fix school computers and provide technical support. (Chapter 8 discusses how to work with the administration to set up this type of program.)

Job shadowing should also include an evaluation for students to analyze what they may like or dislike about a particular position. Discussion with peers should follow the visits to create interest and opportunities for social experiences and career interest sharing.

TABLE 7-1. HIGH SCHOOL AFTER-SCHOOL CLUBS

CAREER EXPLORATIONS

Transition-planning club	Career exploration club
Community marketplace club	School store
Career preparation club	Career projects and clubs
Career search club	Self-exploration
Business skills development club	

PLANNING AND LEADERSHIP COMMITTEES

Senior prom	Student council for students with disabilities
Junior prom	
School activities	Yearbook

MUSIC

Orchestra	A cappella club
Jazz band	Choral ensembles and musical
Marching band	Music club
Spring musical	Dance club
Stage crew	

LEARNING

Art club	Special education school honor society
Photography club	TV media club
Acting club	Homework club
One-act plays club	Library

CULTURAL

No Place for Hate	Cooking club
Sign language learning	Gay-straight alliance
Fellowship club	

SCIENCE

Experiential science club	Science newspaper club
Robotics	Assistive technology research club
Science writing club	Robotics club
Computer club	

ACTIVITY CLUBS

Friday sports club	Environmental club
Yoga club	Law and advocacy for students with disabilities
Fitness club	
Ultimate frisbee	

Internships

Internships are another way for students to earn practical experience. These positions may be paid or unpaid, but they do not typically result in employment but can lead to employment. Internships are rotating, meaning they are temporary opportunities for young persons to earn experience. Setting up an internship can be done in the local community by using local resources on a contract basis. However, any outside organization would need to go through background clearances because most students are under 18 years old.

Work Sampling Experiences

Work sampling experiences involve spending time in multiple work environments, such as working in the school store or participating in school fundraising events. Volunteer work can also be a work experience, and it also builds upon a young person's resume and experiences. Examples of in-school volunteer opportunities may be giving directions for programs or events, managing technology for the classroom, or doing volunteer work for a teacher.

Service learning is another experience done for a longer term that provides students with hands-on volunteer service opportunities in their community, such as planning food drives for the local community cupboard or collecting and donating books to a low-income school. Yearly service learning opportunities can help students see themselves in different roles and help them learn leadership and management skills.

Work-based learning provides students multiple avenues to learn about various career areas and different work styles, as well as helping them discover the work they enjoy (Cease-Cook, Fowler, & Test, 2015).

Entry-Level Job Explorations

When a student begins planning to work part-time during high school or full-time after high school, discussion will center around jobs. There are two types of entry-level employment. The first type is full- or part-time workforce entry-level employment. Entry-level employment encompasses jobs that need work skills but without significant training. These positions are sought out by students in school or right out of high school. During the transition planning period, young persons interested in these positions are those who want to work part-time while in high school, students who want only part-time employment, and students who, due to disability, do not have the stamina for full-time employment and advancement. During high school, these jobs help students gain experience in business or service industries where they can develop employment skills.

The second type of entry-level employment is employment for persons with training and skills related to the job. These employees are looking to learn about their chosen field, and they may want to advance in knowledge and skills. For instance, a job as a bank teller can be an entry-level position for someone seeking to advance in banking, or the person may decide to remain in that role as a career.

MARKETPLACE EMPLOYMENT OPPORTUNITIES AND EDUCATION

Some schools have career centers that are specialized areas equipped with resources and materials used to research occupational opportunities. These areas provide a place to do career research via computers. Job search websites are designed to provide information about a much wider variety of fields. For instance, by putting in a search for human resource jobs, a list of companies and various jobs under that title appear. Each job description will tell the responsibilities and the training needed. Larger companies can have 10 or more entry-level positions with detailed information on the specifics of each job. A search for the word *animal technician* will bring multiple options in the field.

Banking is another area where an employee search will generate a number of positions where a college degree is unnecessary for entry-level positions. Providing students with the time to explore careers is essential. Most students with disabilities, and even some adults, have little knowledge of the marketplace outside their field. Widening students' understanding of the marketplace creates choices and allows them to assess needed skills.

Many students want both jobs and school, and therefore seek employment with a consistent work schedule. A consistent schedule is crucial for continuing education if students want to seek additional training or personal enrichment.

Company websites provide excellent information about employment and job descriptions, and other websites post reviews by employees about the pros and cons of working for the company and at specific locations. General employment sites such as CareerOneStop.org, Indeed.com, and USAJobs. gov have job links to explore specific careers and requirements. Also, some sites such as Indeed.com include employment guides about how to succeed in the workplace.

The transition planning specialist should guide students in the current marketplace, and students should not be limited to the discrete contents of commercial programs about employment. They should have experiences, see current employment training films, and have access to resources that increase their understanding of what is available in today's marketplace.

Career Preference Assessments Versus Career Explorations

Students and their teachers are often encouraged to use preference assessments. Preference assessments may be based on a minimal time period when employment data are collected. The data may be aligned only to profiles of persons in those jobs. Students answer assessment questions, and if their answers match others in a job, they receive career suggestions. They then receive job matches. Some students are unhappy with the results of their preference assessments. One student reported on her disappointing feedback from her assessment:

> I think the bleak outcomes of a particular assessment could be especially detrimental to a group of teens who have issues with low self-esteem or be vulnerable to it. I think most teens suffer from esteem fragility, but using preference assessments when the group has known esteem issues ... it's very damaging.

As mentioned in the previous chapter, using questions about student preferences to show students limited options is not useful. It is essential to reflect on whether preference assessments are helpful to the student. The transition planning specialist must consider the individual student to understand potential unintended consequences of an assessment, such as whether it lowers an already-struggling student's self-esteem. Using the logic of self-determination, using an assessment to indicate what one is good at, and then providing options that the student does not prefer may not reflect the spirit of self-determination.

Additional questions about how well preference assessments match the current marketplace are of considerable importance. If the assessment was last updated in 2009, then new technology positions are not represented. Moreover, questions such as how students perceive their sex roles and cultural roles may not be reflected in the assessment design. There are many sex-type self-beliefs that may also render preference assessments as a reflection of culture and bias rather than a useful tool to match a student to a career that represents his or her best option (Correll, 2001).

Creating Career Portfolios

Students can create career portfolios to structure their process. Career portfolios keep information that students have already reviewed so that they can revisit their research later. Otherwise, valuable time will be wasted looking for the information again. They can cut and paste information about their interests into a document (including the website address), label them, and provide some brief information in a graphic organizer designed by the transition planning specialist. Table 7-2 is an example of a graphic organizer used to set up a career portfolio quick list. Card 1 is an example of

TABLE 7-2. GRAPHIC ORGANIZERS: CAREER EXPLORATIONS AND CAREER KNOWLEDGE

EXPLORATION AND CAREER KNOWLEDGE PORTFOLIO FILE CARD 1

Job 1 Ultrasound Technician

Type of work	Ultrasound technicians use specialized equipment to create images of muscles, organs, and tissues that provide physicians information for identifying disease and injuries.
Location for work	Hospital or clinic
Preparation and training needed	Associates (2-year) degree in medical sonography
Specific job exploration opportunities (job shadowing, internships, job coaching)	Attend allied health at vocational technical school Attend an exploration day at vocational technical school
Positive aspects	Working independently Flexible hours
Negative aspects	Weekend work
Does this job match my need for a job now? If not, what do I need to do?	No. Volunteer in a hospital to see other hospital-based employment.

↓↑

SELF-KNOWLEDGE: WHAT THEY NEED TO KNOW CARD 2

Who am I?	Profile: Age, interests, timeline to reach my goals
What type of environment is best for me at this time in my life?	Indoors, outdoors, clean, organized, etc.
What type of environmental access and supports may I need to work now?	Accessible building, enlarged print, and enlarged keyboard
What kind of stamina do I have?	I need to go to bed early. Otherwise, during the day, I do not have energy.
What is my medication schedule, and how does it affect my day?	After I take my medicine at 8:00 p.m., I go to sleep. It is sedating.
What do I want to learn and do after high school to continue to grow as a person?	I want to work and take classes at the high school night school.

↓

MY SHORT- AND LONG-TERM CAREER PREFERENCES CARD 3

Narrow down options	Hospital-based employment Additional training
First job experience	Volunteer in a hospital
Later entry-level	Register for vocational technical school and search certification programs
Short-term job plans	Apply to work in a nursing home
Long-term employment plan	A career working in a hospital

how to organize the results of one exploration, and card 2 is a comparison of the job information to the self-knowledge chart. It is better to keep it short like this, so students can quickly collect some career cards and their priorities. In card 3, they choose results from their card 1 and card 2 files and write their options.

A student's career portfolio is a tool to increase options that may be beyond the experiences of teaching staff or student. Searching for careers can produce new ideas and future considerations and lead students to consider training and employment that may not have been readily apparent.

Using the Conference System to Seek Employment and Training

As the student creates a career portfolio, the transition planning specialist can meet with the student and go over what he or she has been discovering. The transition planning specialist can add to the conversation by asking additional questions such as why a job appeals to the student. The transition planning specialist will also begin structuring what services the student may need to seek and secure employment or training.

Chapter 9 outlines the process of effectively interviewing a student to establish meaning from the discussion. As the transition planning specialist asks the questions listed here, the interview process is implemented. Once the student makes his or her choices, the transition planning specialist creates the service plan and asks the following questions:

- Where does the student want to work in the future?
- What will the student need to do and want to do to secure these careers?
- What are the student's current demands, and what will the student need to do to overcome them? If the student cannot do this alone, what supports does he or she need?
- What does the student view as options under his or her current conditions?
- What social situations does the student struggle with, and why?
- Does the student have difficulty declining to participate in activities that might compromise his or her integrity?
- What knowledge can the transition planning specialist provide to facilitate more options for the student?
- What training does the student need?
- What attitudes and beliefs or behaviors can impair the student's ability to avoid behaviors that can derail his or her future?

As the student discusses his or her career portfolio employment interests, the student's needs, such as social skills training, driver's training, the use of paratransit, college or community college admittance, and vocational school admittance, will become apparent. Throughout the conference process, the transition planning specialist will need to guide the student toward planning such things as how to get a college or certification program loan, how to find the requirements for their choices, and how to research what kind of experience and references they will need.

HOUSING NEEDS

Before graduation, the transition planning specialist should be sure the student has housing. Many students are in foster care or have families who are unwilling to care for them after graduation. In these cases, plans need to be in place for them. Here are some questions to ask by age 16:

- After graduation, what are the student's plans for housing?
  - The student will reside in the family home or the home of a relative.
  - The student will reside in an apartment with a friend(s) and needs no extra help.
  - The student is in foster care and needs new plans.

- ○ The student is not sure.
- ○ Other (please specify).
- In the future, does the student anticipate the need for assistance in managing any adult living needs? (e.g., medical insurance, attaining Medicaid, or how to continue to receive mental health counseling)
- Do the student's parents have preferences regarding the type of work the student does? Does the student agree with this preference?
- Are there other leisure/recreational activities in which the student would like to participate?
- Does the student want to obtain a driver's license?
- Does the student have or need working papers and an identification card?
- Does the student need transportation to work?
- Does the student know how to take a train or bus?

CAREER TRAINING AND EDUCATION

Students should have developed the following competencies via the transition planning process demonstrating career-decision readiness:

- The student knows a wide array of employment situations.
- The student has developed options for independence or partial independence.
- The student has begun to apply for jobs, vocational programs, or colleges that have supports for students with disabilities.
- The student has chosen the type of employment supports he or she needs, such as employment or supported employment.
- The student has opportunities for part-time post-school education and college placements and work.
- The student participates or leads the IEP meeting, demonstrating leadership skills.
- The student participates in after-school and leisure activities and has developed social skills and connections.
- The student and the parents are actively involved in the transition planning process.

By 11th grade, the student is actively leading or is present at his or her IEP meeting. The student knows about the age of majority and self-advocacy is understood. Male students register for selective service. Many teachers note a change in activity levels, particularly by the midpoint of 11th grade. At that time, students begin to see that graduation is on the horizon and are looking forward to it.

ACQUISITION AND RETENTION OF EMPLOYMENT

Job Search Safety

Although students look and act more mature, they still need guidance. Students should be taught to do job searches safely so they know they are on a legitimate website. Larger, established companies have domain names, and students should be taught to recognize them when they search and distinguish them from ads and unsecured sites. Currently, official sites have a green check indicating they are secure, use "https" to indicate encryption, have a privacy policy and contact information, and have a verified or trust seal. Most school settings have security features that limit the problem.

All contacts should come from the company's human resources department, not a personal email. Many large companies have supports for persons with disabilities to add to the legitimacy of the site.

Students should be taught about scams and that they should never pay to apply for a job. For example, many pyramid schemes ask people to buy and stockpile products to sell. The idea is that people will recruit others to sell under them. These jobs mean an immediate and ongoing outlay of the recruit's money before making any sales or money. There are no benefits, days off, or any other employee perks. The people who recruit for these positions can be skilled at convincing their recruits that much money can be made selling their products. Students who want to go into sales should consider starting in retail sales as part of a company where they can advance.

Also, students should avoid applying for any job that requires reshipping, meaning that products are first shipped to their homes and they are asked to forward them to another location. Most often these shipping jobs are sending illegal items. Also, jobs that ask students to transfer money are most likely illegal enterprises. Most questionable jobs make offers of pay and flexibility that are too good to be true, and students need to know that these pitfalls exist before going through the embarrassment of being scammed or losing money rather than making it. Most employment websites have a system to report bogus or questionable advertisements for jobs. However, once a student has been misled by one, it may be hard to feel confident again.

By being aware of the possible negative consequences of the employment search, the transition planning specialist and the parents can protect the student from poor search experiences that may negatively affect his or her motivation. Job searching is not an area where a student should learn from mistakes. Parents must be intimately involved with the job searches of their minor children. Safety must be addressed in the parent training. Parents can help their children when they search by reviewing the employers and going with them to interviews. All companies must have a building location with prominent signage. Until the student has some on-site work experiences, larger companies or well-known local job opportunities are a good starting place.

Workplace Dress and Company Identity

Students need to distinguish between their identity and the company identity. Students are at an age when they are learning about themselves. They often choose clothing that reflects their preferences about who they are and how they want others to perceive them. If how they dress aligns with the job they want, they may not be fully cognizant that most companies have an identity, and the identity is not the employee's identity.

Many schools tend to be very informal in dress code, so there are few opportunities to learn workplace clothing needs. Therefore, a seminar on appropriate clothes for various company settings can focus on function and company identity. Students can also learn how clothing can relate to career advancement.

If comfortable dress or a certain style of dress is essential to students, working for a company like United Parcel Service (UPS), with its very strict uniform, may unfortunately stymie their perceived unique individuality. Students who do not understand work dress codes or are unduly embarrassed by them can benefit from learning about how a company develops its image.

If they do not understand that the uniform is not their property and that it represents the company, they might alter the uniforms and jeopardize their employment.

Attendance, Timeliness, and Work Completion

Dress, attendance, timeliness, and task completion are all aspects of a student's reputation as an employee. Valuing these personal characteristics begins in school, and the student should understand the importance of school attendance. The special education team can be instrumental in making the student feel wanted and welcomed to increase his or her attendance and to feel part of the classroom community. If school attendance is not stellar, the student may have misconceptions about the importance of attendance.

The high school report card is a significant and underused tool for employment preparation and acquisition. Information such as attendance, grades, completed coursework, and activity participation creates a strong first impression for an employer. It is crucial that students view their high school transcripts as a tool, and schools should do more to promote the use of high school records in the job search.

If a student's course load is too heavy to succeed, careful consideration should be given to this so the student can build a school record that will help and not hurt him or her. A student who has been guided appropriately in credit acquisition and the importance of creating a good school record is in a better position to not give up on his or her education or on him- or herself.

Students must develop three habits in particular: attendance, handing in completed work, and doing so on time. Establishing patterns of schoolwork behavior using these three constructs is crucial, not just for immediate employment success but for later in life when marketplace conditions change and the student needs these patterns of behavior to succeed in new situations.

A student can be taught to understand that he or she is selling not just his or her skills and the work itself, but his or her work habits too. A student who can submit a resume and a copy of a report card, dresses well, interviews well, and understands the company is in an excellent position to become employed.

Some students may feel their grades earned in a special education program are not as valuable as grades earned by their peers, and they may feel compelled to share that they are in a special education program. For example, students with learning disabilities have reported lower academic self-efficacy, as well as decreased academic competence (Lackaye & Margalit, 2008). Good grades in any program indicate a strong work ethic in an individual who may need some accommodations (Luecking, 2009). However, attendance, timeliness, work completion, and work ethic are significant concerns for employers, and they can be very accommodating to students who demonstrate these valued work characteristics.

Criminal Records and Collateral Consequences

It is essential that students with disabilities have direct instruction on activities that may impact their work reputation, such as stealing, drinking alcohol, or being involved in petty crime. The financial devastation for students with disabilities who participate in activities that are dangerous, costly, and redirect the life path cannot be understated. Sadly, there are many students with disabilities who are taken advantage of and misled when they do not understand the cost of their participation in certain behaviors. Adolescents with disabilities can also be misguided when they discuss the consequences of various choices with their peers or when they gather information from the media. Students with intellectual and social disabilities are vulnerable to being misguided by peers (see Chapter 17 for more discussion on this).

Unfortunately, the media and adolescent misperceptions may promote negative outcomes, such as the cavalier use of some drugs or alcohol, a juvenile record, a destroyed workplace reputation, and the solicitation of new users under the guise of it is going to be legal. One misguided belief is that arrest will be erased when the student turns 18 years old. This depends; in some states, it is not expunged until age 19, 3 years after when an adolescent will want to be employed. Also, some records are never removed depending on the crime. The transition planning specialist and high school administration should spend orientation time updating students, especially those with disabilities who benefit from explicit instruction, on the criminal prosecution of juveniles and those students who are over 18 years old.

Depending on the state, the consequences for alcohol and drug violations can widely vary. The most significant and immediate impact is incarceration in a juvenile facility, and students need to understand how hard it is to plan for post-school life from there. In many states, there are set sentences for possession of marijuana and driving under the influence (DUI) or driving while intoxicated (DWI). DUI and DWI cases are considered serious offenses and include alcohol, illegal drugs, and prescription drugs. The student and the family bear the burden and associated costs of a loss of the driver's license, substantial fines, counseling, and community service. In one state, carrying a small amount of marijuana is up to 30 days in jail, or a year on probation and a $500 fine. A DUI charge and a second offense can be loss of a license for up to 10 years. For second offenses, a house arrest with an ankle bracelet is typically part of life postsentencing.

A state may be more forgiving by placing the accused in a first offender program, but that still carries a juvenile criminal record. However, some states may have no tolerance policies. The transition planning specialist must be aware of the laws of the state and be able to guide students away from this financial disaster, including the requirement of an SR-22 insurance form, tripled auto insurance rates, and registration as a high-risk driver.

In 2015, 2333 teens were killed and 235,845 were treated for injuries sustained in motor vehicle accidents (Cooper, 2018). The rate of teen death in this country remains substantially high based on higher rates for the three most prevalent causes of death among adolescents and young adults: motor vehicle accidents, homicide, and suicide (Lawrence, Gootman, & Sim, 2009). Adults continue to have a wide reality gap with their adolescent children, grossly underestimating their children's risk-taking behavior (Shore & Shore, 2009).

Parents and students should be knowledgeable about the effect of a criminal record of any kind on their career-seeking efforts. Most employers do not want to risk injury to their employees when a young person has already begun using drugs and alcohol and has demonstrated disrespect for the safety of others by driving while intoxicated. They do not want theft or vandalism either. Employees who come in with these problems are risks. Therefore, attention to direct instruction about juvenile behavior records is of primary importance. What students do and say is important in a way that they may not be cognizant of at this age.

TEACHING WORKPLACE SKILLS

Formal and Informal Communications

Formal communication styles, including the use of respectful interactions, are required in most companies where there is direct work with the public. The employee represents the goals of the company, and interactions with customers or clients are expected to be done in a way to carry out the company's customer service ideals. Instruction with video demonstrations can be used to illustrate the differences between conversational speech with a friend, a coworker, a boss, and a customer. Many companies will teach their employee customer scripts, but students should have a clear understanding of the company's identity and the reason for the scripts. Community trips can be used to evaluate companies and their advertised and operational identities.

Informal interactions can also be problematic due to the varied work styles of potential coworkers. Even in the lunchroom, where informal conversation may occur, some employees keep their formal style of interaction with coworkers. Students with autism without intellectual disability or speech and language-based or emotional behavior disabilities in particular will need direct instruction about the types of interactions appropriate in the workplace.

Communication Skills

Practice is a meaningful exercise to equip students with communication skills for the workplace. Students should develop a formal greeting style for workplace situations. They should be able to communicate that they have received a direction and be at ease providing compliant responses. Communicating information either verbally or via email or notes should follow the formal interaction style. Students should understand that they should interact, write, and email in a way that most people perceive as respectful. Appropriate speaking volume, giving the other person the appropriate space, and using attentive posture to imply interest in the other person's workplace requests are essential. Other practice areas are eye contact and facial expressions that demonstrate that the student is listening.

Cooperation is a communication skill. Knowing how to promote the completion of tasks as a team requires working and planning together. Most tasks in the workplace have procedures in place, and teams often share the completion of tasks using those procedures.

Working closely with others requires good hygiene. Hygiene communicates respect for the team. Signs and signals of respect for others is a valuable lesson that students need to learn. Sometimes students develop fears of deodorants. When this happens, there is little the transition planning specialist or the family can do to change this behavior, and lack of self-care will end chances for most jobs during the interview. A resourceful transition planning specialist can work with parents and switch out bathroom soap for deodorant soap. This is one of the critical issues that arise more than one would hope or expect.

Areas that indicate respect and that also require communication are arriving to work on time, calling in sick to work rather than just not showing up, and requesting vacation time. Each of these areas, if taught explicitly, can help students focus on work and not be distracted trying to learn and recall this type of information.

Participating in clubs and leisure activities provides a firm foundation for work-based social skills. Coworkers rarely talk about what they learned in class during high school. Having topics to discuss during breaks requires appropriate topics for discussion in the workplace. Knowing what to talk about and when not to socialize on the job are important social skills. Having well-developed interests encourages appropriate conversations during break periods.

Students can be protected from victimization at work by avoiding specific off-task conversations. Some conversations are testing situations to bring a student into reputation-damaging situations, such as stealing, taking drugs after work, or participating in other illicit activities. Sexual harassment can also arise, and students need some background discussion and instruction on how to deal with the problem.

Most places of employment provide training on all workplace policies, including harassment, but some smaller companies may not. Employers with more than 50 employees most likely have training that gives the employees clear directives regarding problematic workplace conversations. However, the transition planning process should prepare students for proper interactions in the workplace and use a coaching model to help students learn the structure of the job when information is presented verbally. Role-playing challenging situations can address these uncomfortable workplace situations before they arise.

Accommodations

Students who cannot read or who have slow processing speed will need to inform their employers, and a job coach can help students use their self-advocacy skills to get any adjustments they may need, such as the following:

- Students can ask coworkers to speak slowly when there is difficulty in understanding or processing information.
- Students can create a plan for requesting assistance.
- Students can ask for task lists to clarify what they are to do.
- Students can ask a resource person to handle conflicts or requests.

Universal Design

Some large employers are committed to universal design. Universal design is founded on the principle of universal access. Universal design is a focus on creating environments that are accessible to people with a wide range of abilities, disabilities, and needs. Application of universal design principles reduces the need for assistive technology because products developed using universal design theory account for all possible communication needs. The products are more usable by everyone, not just people with disabilities (Button, 2007). Students can benefit from researching larger companies that are committed to universal design.

The Office of Disability Employment Policy assists both employers and employees through nonregulatory agencies to help in the provision of workplace accommodations and to help retain workers with disabilities. These agencies include the following:

- Job Accommodation Network
- National Collaborative on Workforce and Disability for Youth
- Partnership on Employment and Accessible Technology

Exercises

1. Research the environmental modifications of three employment situations that may be available to a student using a wheelchair.
2. Research companies that design their workspaces according to universal design. Describe two space designs that reflect the principle.
3. Research federal and state work initiatives for transitioning students and adults.

ADDITIONAL TRAINING AND EMPLOYMENT OPTIONS

Students can search for temporary and per diem employment when medical conditions or disability result in episodic medical events. Staffing agencies have websites that list and describe available employment. These agencies can be good sources of exploration. Registering with these companies enables employees to create their availability schedules. These agencies can also be instrumental if there is a lapse in employment, such as when a company relocates, and the young person does not want to be unemployed. Students need to know that employment status may change and they can have a recourse to address those changes through temporary or per diem employment.

Career Changes and Learning New Skills

At times there will be less opportunity to work in a preferred area of employment, and students should be prepared to develop new skills by participating in additional training. Researchers project that 63% of jobs in the United States will require additional education or training (Carnevale, Smith, & Strohl, 2010). To address this, students should be knowledgeable about community-based certification programs and online educational programs that can help them move forward to a new career or employment.

The most important thing about education is students learn to learn. They should leave school learning to study and acquire new skills. If they have a reliable strategy for learning, they will be able to learn a new career or job at any point in their lives and avoid long-term unemployment. Certification programs on the job trainings are available and lead to new experiences and future income, and even new places to live.

Given that students with disabilities have difficulty learning new material, educators and researchers can open the discussion about technology and learning strategies that enable students to learn information using technology and other strategies that expedite learning.

Post-School Diploma Options

Unfortunately, the last 2 years of high school is also a time when students may feel they will not be able to complete their requirements and graduate, and they may plan to drop out. If they have a job and can minimally care for themselves, this can also pull them in this direction. If the transition planning specialist has been working with students and engaging them in the transition planning process, this trajectory can be redirected. If a student has a job and is not going to graduate with peers because they do not have enough credits, an intervention strategy to recoup credit or develop a work-based learning program is needed to help the student earn credits. For instance, writing about their work day, social experiences at work, or their training can be the basis of earning English writing credits. Although these changes may not align directly with requirements, alternate assignments can keep the students engaged to earn credits and help them graduate. There are also other options for earning a diploma at local community college as well as participating in online learning through the high school or community college. There is really no reason that a student should not be able to recoup credits with the myriad of technological supports and online learning opportunities.

Community Colleges and State Diplomas

One intervention strategy is that some states allow students to take an entrance test to attend community college. If they do not pass the reading and math sections, they can take two remedial classes. The school district can give credit for those classes. Once the remedial classes are completed, the community college can allow students to attend a prescribed number of classes and receive a state diploma. The credits they earn can go toward a 4-year college degree program.

There are programs and organizations to help students who have left high school. Organizations such as the Boys and Girls Clubs of America, Gateway to College, Job Corps, the National Dropout Prevention Center, and the National Guard are some resources that help students earn their diplomas. The transition planning specialist and secondary education team work with the most at-risk students with disabilities to encourage the completion of their programs and their successful transition to post-school life. A high school diploma is required for most jobs, so the transition to post-school life must have a clear path to graduation. Supports can be written into the transition plan to support attention to graduation. Most students will work to graduate with the proper supports. Many who drop out have to work to provide some support to their families and themselves when there is little money or a sick parent. Therefore, schools can be instrumental by not putting the student or their family at further risk by sending the student into post-school life without a diploma.

College Attendance Versus Employment

There are many paths to postsecondary education. Strict adherence to the promotion of full-time college without a clear career path can bring about financial challenges that may be detrimental.

The special education team and the transition planning specialist should be able to hear the student's preferences and concerns and show the student how to reach his or her goals with realistic plans that address finances. If the student comes from a family with few resources, helping him or her apply for grants and financial aid may be a pathway. In some families with no history of attending college, this process is unknown. When families have few financial resources but their income is not low enough for grants, students can apply for school loans. The transition planning specialist must have plans in place to guide the student through the process by collaborating with the guidance counselor (guidance counselors can be trained to learn about college supports for students with disabilities). However, taking a college loan is a long-term commitment. Families and the students with disabilities should not feel obligated to attend 4-year colleges right out of high school if it is a significant family burden. There are multiple ways to earn college degrees. The student needs to understand the finances required to pay back large sums of money, the life of the loan, and its effect on independence. When parents are signers on educational loans, they are important stakeholders about where a student attends college. Therefore, their voices on college are required.

If the student has the resources in place, securing college supports for his or her disability should be done before enrollment. Each term, college professors are sent lists of students who need extended time on tests or homework submission when, for example, a medical condition flares or a mental health disorder results in hospitalization. Students with disabilities must set up a meeting or communication with the Disability Office at their preferred colleges to see what supports are in place and to find out the accessibility of the college campus. Colleges do not have the same legal obligations, such as extending a free appropriate public education. They need to ensure appropriate academic adjustments to prevent discrimination based on a disability. The Office of Civil Rights provides information for students with disabilities entering postsecondary institutions, which provides information for post-school life. Employment and education is also an option. For some students, participating in both part-time college and a job gives them valuable job skills so that when they do enter the world of full-time work, they have additional preparation. Ultimately, college or employment does not need to be an either or situation, but a careful blending of the two options.

Other Considerations and Laws

Child Labor Laws

Before embarking on a career search, the transition planning specialist must know the laws regarding employment, particularly for students under 18 years old. Students and their parents need to know what they may need to be employed, such as identity cards and working papers for minors. There are many laws via the Department of Labor and Industry that regulate the employment of minors. The U.S. Department of Labor has a website that describes what can be done at what age. The following section contains the age-related employment rules.

The Youth Worker and Employment

At ages 14 and 15, students can work in homes and family businesses with little restriction. All work must be outside of the school day. These students may not work more than 3 hours a day or over 18 hours a week during the school year. During holidays, 8 hours a day is permitted, but not later than 7:00 p.m. during the school year and 9:00 p.m. during the summer.

Before age 16, some employment is permitted. Students can work in retail, creative jobs like singing or playing instruments, computer programming, yardwork without the use of machinery, delivery work, food service with limited cooking, working on cars, and some work at amusement parks.

At ages 16 and 17, students may work unlimited hours. However, there are certain workplace hazard restrictions, such as they may not use meat slicers or drive machinery.

There are some exemptions to these restrictions. Apprentice or student learner programs are permitted if specific guidelines are followed. The transition planning specialist must be aware of employment policies and be able to provide information on attaining working papers for workers under age 18. Most school districts have this process established in their secondary school programs.

Exemptions to Work Laws

Exemptions to the hours and time limits for employment are available, such as when a family owns a business. In those cases, there are no limitations on the number of hours worked.

Other exceptions to this are special programs, such as the Work and Career Exploration Program designed for 14- and 15-year-olds who are at risk for leaving school. The Work and Career Exploration Program is a planned work experience and career exploration program that allows students to work up to 23 hours a week. Programs like this can help students from families in poverty who often leave school to be able to feed themselves or who need more support to remain engaged in their education.

EXERCISES

1. Research the graduation requirements of three local school districts. Compare and contrast them.
2. Research local secondary and postsecondary school vocational training programs. List the options for training.
3. Reflect on your knowledge about these careers.
4. Research the number of Americans in four states who go to college, vocational training, or unskilled work.
5. Research alternatives to earning a diploma in your state.

SUMMARY

Students with disabilities need explicit instruction about workplace conditions, including preparing them to explore environments and to evaluate workplaces of interest. However, students need to be prepared to enter workplaces and training programs. Students can underestimate the importance of their schoolwork, work completion, study habits, and attendance. The transition planning specialist and secondary special education team are key team players as they guide students to develop study and schoolwork habits as foundations for employment.

As students mature through the process of transition planning, they are learning about many types of jobs and careers and the training they will need. From those explorations, a group of interests is selected. Students take their selections and begin planning for their next steps. They make decisions about what type of work-based learning experiences, after-school activities, work environments, and skills they want to pursue.

As students go through a process of career discernment during career conferences, they need to develop awareness of their work reputation and every aspect of becoming an asset to the workplace or their chosen career.

The transition planning specialist will help students as they select many types of employment, training, and postsecondary education. Multiple paths lead to successful lives that do not include going directly into full-time college after high school. The individual preferences, culture, resources, and disability can come together in an intricate pattern that can produce fulfilling results as students pursue their hopes and dreams.

REFERENCES

Benz, M. R., Lindstrom, L., & Yovanoff, P. (2000). Improving graduation and employment outcomes of students with disabilities: Predictive factors and student perspectives. *Exceptional Children, 66*(4), 509.

Button, C. (2007). Universal Design. U.S. Department of Labor: Office of Disability Employment Policy. Retrieved from https://www.dol.gov/odep/media/newsroom/universal.htm

Carnevale, A. P., Smith, N., & Strohl, J. (2010). *Help wanted: Projections of jobs and education requirements through 2018.* Washington, DC: Center on Education and the Workforce.

Cease-Cook, J., Fowler, C., & Test, D. W. (2015). Strategies for creating work-based learning experiences in schools for secondary students with disabilities. *TEACHING Exceptional Children, 47*(6), 352-358.

Cooper, T. (2018). Risky motor vehicle behaviors among Rhode Island high school students. *Rhode Island Medical Journal, 101*(7), 47-50.

Correll, S. J. (2001). Gender and the career choice process: The role of biased self-assessments. *American Journal of Sociology, 106*(6), 1691-1730.

Hamilton, M., & Hamilton, S. (1997). *Learning well at work: Choices for quality.* New York, NY: Cornell University Press.

Lackaye, T., & Margalit, M. (2008). Self-efficacy, loneliness, effort, and hope: Developmental differences in the experiences of students with learning disabilities and their non-learning disabled peers at two age groups. *Learning Disabilities: A Contemporary Journal, 6*(2), 1-20.

Lawrence, R. S., Gootman, J. A., & Sim, L. J. (Eds.). (2009). *Adolescent health services: Missing opportunities.* Washington, DC: National Academies Press.

Luecking, R. G. (2009). *The way to work: How to facilitate work experiences for youth in transition.* Baltimore, MD: Brookes Publishing.

Margolis, H., & McCabe, P. P. (2006). Improving self-efficacy and motivation: What to do, what to say. *Intervention in School and Clinic, 41*, 218-227.

Schunk, D. H. (2003). Self-efficacy for reading and writing: Influence of modeling, goal setting, and self-evaluation. *Reading and Writing Quarterly, 19*, 159-172.

Shore, R., & Shore, B. (2009). Reducing the teen death rate. KIDS COUNT Indicator Brief. The Annie E. Casey Foundation. Retrieved from https://files.eric.ed.gov/fulltext/ED507782.pdf

Part 5

Special Education Programs

Responsibilities and Resources
of Transition Team Members and
Community and Governmental
Agencies

School Leadership and Transition Planning

CHAPTER OBJECTIVES

→ Describe the roles of the school board and superintendent in transition planning.

→ Identify key responsibilities of the administrative team when developing in-school activities for students with disabilities.

→ Define the roles of special education administrators for implementing a transition curriculum.

→ Describe how to develop an after-school program for students with disabilities that encompasses the social needs for students during transition.

→ Explain the steps used to monitor the effectiveness of transition planning.

→ Explain the components of a legally defensible transition Individualized Education Plan (IEP).

EFFECTIVE COMMUNICATION WITH CENTRAL ADMINISTRATION

The Role of the Superintendent

Each school has a system of governance that supports all aspects of day-to-day school operations. The superintendent is the school board's appointed leader of the school district. Superintendents, who also may have other titles, are licensed under the State Department of Education regulations and hold certifications and letters of eligibility that enable them to lead public schools. Superintendents may hold a doctoral degree or a master's degree that qualifies them for the role, and an administrative certification permits them to direct the school district and its programs, as well as interpret the

Rae, J. M. *A Collaborative Approach to Transition Planning for Students With Disabilities* (pp. 171-185).
© 2020 SLACK Incorporated.

research and identify evidence-based practices used to determine the suitability for curriculum and instructional practices.

The primary responsibility of the superintendent includes leading all administrative and school-based administrative teams. The superintendent meets regularly with school board members and communicates policy to the board, the schools, and the public. In this role, the superintendent meets with directors who oversee the day-to-day affairs of running a school district. The superintendent also works together with the administrative team to advance the school's mission within the context of federal and state education law. The superintendent's ability to set the tone of the school suggests that his or her support for special education is crucial for the success of the special education program.

The governance hierarchy within a district may vary from one local education agency (LEA), also known as a *school district*, to another, with rural districts being less staffed and having less of a hierarchy. The following is an example of a school governance structure. Beneath roles 2 and 3 are the employees that they supervise who have a direct connection to supporting the policies, procedures, and school and community activities for special education.

(1) Superintendent—school board

(2) Director of Pupil Personnel Services

    (A) Nurses (B) Speech therapists (C) Physical therapists (D) School psychologists

(3) Director of Special Education   Director of Curriculum and Instruction

    (A) Supervisor of Special Education   (B) Building Principal

       (i) Transition planning specialist   (i) Vice Principal, Assistant Principal

       (ii) Special education teachers   (ii) Teachers and staff

          (a) Paraprofessionals

(4) Director of Technology

(5) Director of Food Services

(6) Director of Athletics

(7) Director of Facilities

Special Education In-School Collaboration

Having knowledge of special education law is part of a superintendent's duties. In addition, the superintendent should have background on the characteristics of students with disabilities. The superintendent's knowledge of the characteristics and needs of students with disabilities depends on previous work with students with disabilities or college- and master's-level courses in special education. However, some superintendents do not have any background in special education. Superintendents, knowledgeable about general education, may be less familiar with special education and, for example, may not know the benefits and uses of assistive technology; the transition planning specialist may be required to work with the special education supervisor to develop information sessions that inform superintendents about current special education innovations and research-based practices. Providing information and informing superintendents about disabilities, transition planning, and improved curricular and transition activities can lead to the provision of additional funding for technology in the classroom. The transition planning specialist and supervisor of special education must be well-grounded in current research that supports effective programs and services. The superintendent oversees special education programs and must rely heavily upon the special education administrative team, special educators, and transition planning specialists to inform him or her, for example, about the needs and requirements of the Individuals with Disabilities Education Act (IDEA, 2004) as it relates to assistive technology. The oversight and collaboration among multiple stakeholders ensures that students with disabilities are protected through the implementation of legally defensible IEPs, evidence-based practices, and quality transition plans.

The School Board

Superintendents and school board directors meet regularly. Local school boards are also known as *boards of education*, *school committees*, *school directors*, or *trustees*; they undertake certain key responsibilities such as, but not limited to, the following:

- Searching for and hiring the superintendent
- Reviewing and adopting policies, curriculum, and the budget
- Overseeing facilities issues
- Adopting collective bargaining agreements
- Working with the superintendent to stay in compliance with state, federal, and IDEA law

Typically, school board members are citizens who volunteer and who have been voted in or appointed to the school board. The board members provide citizen governance to the school. Their role is to represent the voices of the community who want to express their concerns about school district matters. In their role, they are accessible to the community. If schools do not perform well or if they proceed in a direction unfavorable to the community, board members can be removed or voted out (Bateman, Bright, O'Shea, O'Shea, & Algozzine, 2007).

School board members, unless they are special educators or have a child or family member with a disability, may find special education practices and regulations a challenge to comprehend. The special education department may benefit from meeting with board members to present information about the secondary special education programs and transition planning. This type of communication can help the department of special education to develop a positive reputation community-wide. It can also help board members develop a knowledge base, equipping them to respond when funding proposals for transition activities are submitted for consideration and approval. If board members know about everyday activities and they trust the team's expertise, then proposals and additional funding requests can be more easily understood.

At times, school board members may resign or be voted out of office. When turnovers occur, the superintendent may enlist the special education director or supervisor to reintroduce the transition planning and special education program. When a board member orientation is planned, being a program ambassador will be important for continuing the support of existing transition activities and the development of new activities.

Central Office Administrators

Special education administrators for larger districts (i.e., LEAs) typically include the director of pupil personnel services, director of special education, and the supervisors of special education. For transition planning, the director of special education is the person to whom the special education supervisor reports. The directors and supervisors of special education are required by federal law to be certified to perform their duties. Their certification qualifies them to employ, supervise, and evaluate special education teachers and transition planning specialists, and they direct special education programs.

Each program for children with disabilities should be under the general supervision of people responsible for educational programs for children with disabilities in the state education agency (SEA) and meet the educational standards of the SEA (State eligibility, 2017; SEA responsibility for general and special education programs supervision, 2018).

The central office administrators report to the superintendent. The director of special education oversees the work of the special education supervisor and program staff to ensure the implementation of the legal requirements of special education. Knowing the school governance hierarchy can help the transition planning specialist support the goals of the administrators and vice versa. Understanding the administrator's decision-making process in a school district is essential to success when working to provide in-school and community activities of transition. Various directors in the administrative hierarchy have a role when the special education team needs updated transition assessments, curricular materials, assistive technology devices, school-based training activities, community-based activities, or other prized additions to the transition planning activity program.

Directors of Curriculum, Instruction, and Special Education

When proposing educational products and services, all requests must have research to support their efficacy or the proposal will not be in keeping with the intent of the No Child Left Behind Act (2001), IDEA (2004), or the Every Student Succeeds Act (2015). Therefore, under the oversight of the SEA, the LEA is responsible for ensuring that those under its direction also strive to meet the standards of practice as they are aligned to these education acts, such as the use of practices and curricular and instructional materials that are grounded in the current research.

Using research- and evidence-based practices requires a commitment by all staff to use the curriculum, practices, and procedures that can best accomplish the education of students with disabilities. It is an ethical and legal imperative that the special education department comprehensively examines the efficacy and has information about the curriculum and strategies they use for instruction. By supporting and advocating for best practices, educators protect the educational equity rights of children with disabilities. The special education administrators review all proposed curricular and program requests. It has taken some years and a few legislative acts to establish that whatever schools use to promote learning must have solid research behind it before it can be implemented in schools. Therefore, the framework, curriculum, instructional practices, and activities of transition planning must also be evidence based and approved by the director of special education and sometimes by the director of curriculum and instruction.

Another duty of the special education administrators is to remain informed about the legal changes at both the state and federal levels regarding special education. They keep the superintendent, school board, faculty, and staff informed about all changes and pending changes. The state Office of Special Education updates them about all changes in state and federal law. The special education administrators, in turn, update the special educators. However, the transition planning specialist is expected to stay current with changes that may be pending by reading state and federal communications about special education, which are available on their websites.

Although special education directors or special education supervisors provide oversight to the work of the transition planning specialist, it is secondary and middle school transition planning specialists, in concert with secondary special educators, who are primarily responsible for carrying out the day-to-day instruction, transition planning activities, data collection, IEP development, and IEP implementation. Together they are charged with ongoing data collection to comply with federal and state laws meant to ensure students with disabilities are making progress and are participating in the activities of transition. The director submits data to the respective SEA to indicate that the school district (LEA) is meeting its obligations under special education law and that the special education programs, transition plans, and IEPs are doing what they are designed to do.

School Service Directors

The special education director is the primary contact for the special education department at the school administration central office. Typically, the special education director's office is there, along with the following school directors:

- Superintendent—school board
- Director of pupil personnel services

- Supervisor of special education
- Director of technology
- Director of food services
- Director of buildings, grounds, and maintenance
- Chief Financial Officer and school accounting department
- Director of transportation
- School attorney

Each of these leaders are involved in implementing services for students in special education. In smaller school districts, some of these roles are combined.

Ongoing meetings about the special education department may involve the leaders of school services departments, depending on the transition activities or an activity proposal. As the list indicates, the team would have to work with the special education supervisor and a director to develop, for instance, on-campus job services. Also, other directors, such as the director of technology, would be involved if the job site was in the media department and entailed the use of technology equipment.

The director of building and grounds plans for school events by assigning staff to provide supervision during transition events for the family introduction to transition planning, doing the setup, and keeping a schedule of classroom and large meeting space use. The director of transportation is also involved in supporting inclusion of special education students by, for example, ensuring access to wheelchair-accessible buses for community-based instruction and after-school events, such as attendance at away games. An attorney provides legal advice so that all events and activities are covered under school district policies and insurances. This collaboration between departments is less daunting than it may seem because after an activity has received approval and any additional guidelines, the activity tends to be institutionalized and repeated yearly as part of the school program.

The special education supervisor and special education director will need reports from the transition planning specialist at regular intervals about the success of or needed improvements to any new or preexisting activity of transition. Regular written communication reporting on the success of transition planning activities and supporting activities can smooth the way for future changes and additional needed supports or funding voted on by school directors. For instance, if an after-school activity is highly attended, this would be evidence of the future need and use of the program. Ongoing collaboration about school-based and community-based transition activities establishes and validates attention to the needs of students with disabilities, thereby helping them to become an integral part of the school's culture.

EFFECTIVE COMMUNICATION WITH MIDDLE AND HIGH SCHOOL LEADERS

Principals

High school and middle school principals are the leaders of their respective buildings. Regarding transition, they perform primary roles in facilitating collaboration, mediating conversations, and developing school community. They set the tone of the school building by encouraging school-based teams to work together effectively as they pursue team goals. They can also provide training on how to run productive meetings to promote positive interactions between building personnel as they resolve differences. The principal meets and has an ongoing dialog with the secondary special education supervisor, assistant principal in larger schools, and transition planning specialist when student concerns arise. Like the superintendent and special education supervisors, the principal must know all the activities and issues that occur in the building and must be informed about transition planning programs, meetings, and ongoing activities both on and off campus. The principal is provided with all the information that belongs in the school calendar, such as parent introductory meetings for transition planning. The principal is provided with ongoing reports about students, both with and without disabilities, who are at risk for dropping out.

Students in both regular education and special education who are at risk of dropping out are often in the principal's sight early on because of course failure and because attendance data reports show high absenteeism. Because principals play a pivotal role in encouraging academic attainment, there is more involvement with special education teachers regarding attendance and course failure. Principals aim to improve graduation rates. The principal and transition planning specialist work together to handle special education student issues that foreshadow dropping out. Together the school-based special education team and the principal address student issues and resolve roadblocks that may cause the student to exit school without a diploma.

The principal's primary contact is the superintendent who, along with the special education director and supervisor, also wants to improve graduation rates. These administrators work together to review special education student issues that rise above typical school-based problems and to address issues that may spur a student with a disability to exit school without a diploma.

If there are assistant principals, the transition planning specialist will primarily communicate day-to-day concerns to the assistant principals, one of which will most likely be the contact person for transition planning and the special education department in the building. It is important to remember that although a principal may have limited direct interactions with the transition planning specialist, the principal's favorable view of the special education department is important to ensure his or her support of school-based activities.

Principals play an important role with the faculty, and professional development is a core responsibility for principals (Billingsley, McLeskey, & Crockett, 2014). Professional interaction and development are meant to deepen teacher knowledge and improve practice and academic achievement (Benedict, Brownell, Griffin, Wang, & Myers, 2016). Providing professional development and the opportunity to collaborate on academic improvement requires facilitation by the principal. Formerly, and sometimes still, special education has functioned like a school within a school. Opportunities for combined special education and general education departmental meetings can help move away from a parallel play approach, meaning they are in the building but rarely move through the building; instead, they may be in self-contained classes (placed in special education classes more than 60% of the school day) for educating only students with disabilities. However, special education teachers must now hold content area certifications, which means students in special education are or may be in the same hallways, moving from class to class, like students in general education, but their teachers hold special education and regular education certifications.

Learning about general education requirements and lesson design and sharing concepts of partial participation can improve understanding between departments and improve general education inclusion. To build school-based support and positive alliances, the special education supervisor and the principal can support communication. This can be facilitated by the creation of learning communities where faculty get together to discuss topics about special education and regular education practice. By getting to know other teachers, the transition planning specialist can better determine where additional supporters for transition planning activities may be. The transition planning specialist who seeks out productive school-based relationships is in a better position to shed light on the challenges of disability. The principal is the key leader to support those faculty connections through the facilitation of learning communities, grade-level and departmental faculty meetings, and faculty training.

Assistant Principals

As mentioned previously, in the day-to-day operations within the school, the transition planning specialist most likely reports to an on-site assistant principal, with larger schools having more than one assistant principal. The assistant principal is in the position of coordinating sports, after-school activities, in-school work programs, and parent meetings. In smaller LEAs, there may be one principal who carries out these duties.

The transition planning specialist must have a positive professional relationship with the assistant principal, who supervises programs related to the program the transition planning specialist may want to develop. For instance, if the transition planning specialist wants to set up an after-school noncompetitive sports club, get student volunteers, and secure funding, he or she will need to collaborate with the special education administrators and the assistant principal to introduce a proposal. An outline of the proposal will include information about the activity and a plan for implementation, including a list of school partners who may need to be involved. A list of challenges will also be built into it. The proposal is completed with the assistant principal in charge of after school programs. An example of the process is as follows:

1. The first contact is the special education supervisor, who would contact both the building principal and the special education director about the proposed after-school activity.
2. The special education director and school principal would see what funds were available.
3. The special education supervisor would facilitate the plan by securing the principal's approval for the transition planning specialist to explore what possibilities may exist.
4. The principal would alert the assistant principals about the pending transition planning specialist contact.
5. The transition planning specialist will have already discussed this with the special education faculty.
6. A confirmation email from the special education supervisor to the stakeholders would need to be sent to indicate the commencement of the first stage, the gathering of information.
7. Once the activity plan is completed, it is shared in an email so that the special education supervisor can reply affirmatively or suggest changes if necessary and include the principal for other suggestions and ideas.
8. If suggested, the transition planning specialist will conduct further fact-finding or rewrite parts of the plan that are unclear to the administrative team.
9. After the principal's approval, the most likely contact will be the assistant principal in charge of after-school programs.
10. The assistant principal in charge of after-school programs and the transition planning specialist will set up a meeting; determine logistics; discuss how to organize; and prepare a proposed plan of action, including possible costs.
11. All parties will approve the proposal.
12. A finalized plan with the benefits of the program will then go through the administrative hierarchy and finally the superintendent. Prior to this stage, it is expected that the superintendent is being informed by the special education administrator.
13. The chief financial officer will determine the funding stream for the proposal.
14. The superintendent and special education administrators, who are highly qualified to evaluate the proposal and the research to support its use and consult with the director of special education, determine whether the proposal meets submission criteria and is ready to go before the school board for final approval.

School governance requires this level of clarity and detail to comply with all board policies, and most districts will have a template to submit the final proposal to the board. The plan will include funding, staffing, after-school transportation, and other supporting needs.

Although there may be a significant need for after-school programs that can uniquely meet the needs of students with disabilities, the school governance process can seem cumbersome to the neophyte transition planning specialist. Given the complexity of the approval processes and the intricacies of professional relationships, it is fundamental that the transition planning specialist develop relationships within his or her sphere and expect that once the proposal is handed off to the director of special education, the transition planning specialist will need to wait as the central office administrators complete their procedures. The transition planning specialist should stay in touch with the special education supervisor and follow up on whether the proposals have received preliminary approval and subsequently have made it into the board agenda for final approval.

The transition planning specialist is prepared and knowledgeable to develop such a proposal and be aware that the special education administrators must follow a board policy to develop new programs or activities. If approved at the central administration stage, it is put on the board agenda and approved, denied, or returned for more information. Once approved by the board, the program's name will go on the board minutes, which are shared with the public. Therefore, proposals must be in excellent form. As mentioned previously, programs and services are reviewed every year. Data must be collected on the number of students who participated and the attendance at each week's after-school sports event, including spectators and volunteers. If there are not sufficient data to demonstrate benefit, then a review of continued funding will be undertaken. Therefore, it is important to remember that activities such as after-school sports programs use qualitative (e.g., How did the students benefit?) and quantitative (e.g., How many students participated?) data to justify continuing the activity.

The role of the special education supervisor in the secondary setting is outlined in detail in Chapter 10.

General Education Teachers

General education teachers are key players in the success of students with disabilities who are in their general education classrooms. Therefore, the transition planning specialist and the special education team must increase faculty understanding of special education eligibility, programs, and services. Of high concern to the faculty will be teaching students with language delays and specific learning disabilities. Going to each teacher who has a student with a disability is a cumbersome way to communicate about transition planning and its goals. Therefore, inviting teachers to be in learning communities and including training about disability is a positive step toward expanding faculty competence for working with students who have disabilities. Setting up faculty observations of new students may also be a welcome way for the general education teacher to get to know a new or existing student who will be entering the class. Teacher learning communities can be used to discuss evidence-based practice on transition planning, inclusion, and the general education teacher's importance in working with students who are at risk for dropping out.

Participating in learning communities and special education trainings can positively affect special and general educational practice.

School District Compliance Monitoring and Transition Planning

As discussed throughout this text, the unfortunate outcomes of students with disabilities have increased attention to transition planning results. Students with specific learning disabilities, emotional and behavioral disabilities, and mild intellectual disabilities are at significant risk for dropping out of secondary school.

Students with more severe intellectual disabilities and autism, who are often entirely dependent on family for their care, stay enrolled and complete their programs. Most have a lack of mobility and planning ability to carry out their wishes. In short, they need a high level of protection, care, and attention to where they will receive programming after programs through IDEA end at age 21.

Therefore, students with specific learning disabilities, mild intellectual disabilities, and emotional disabilities are of primary concern. It is hoped that by intervening with these students by middle school using transition planning, the percentage of those students dropping out will be decreased, and timely graduation, increased post-school training, and employment will be the ultimate result. The federal government monitors the outcomes of students with disabilities with the intent of improving their post-school outcomes and reducing dropout rates.

FEDERAL AND STATE IDEA DATA
COLLECTION AND MONITORING STRUCTURE

Our federal and state governments are involved in helping to reduce the dropout rate across the United States and to address this for students with disabilities; it is believed that transition planning, done with fidelity, will help improve both graduation rates and post-school outcomes. Our federal and state governments want to collect quantitative and qualitative data about the efficacy of transition plans, including whether IEPs are implemented with fidelity, and whether they did, in fact, improve post-school outcomes. Data collection and analysis help legislators use this information to make informed decisions to determine what changes or additions to legislation may be warranted. SEAs collect the transition information from LEAs/school districts, which are responsible for collecting data. That data is submitted by filing monitoring reports, which include indicators about the implementation of transition plans, student graduation, and post-school outcomes and other indicator data. The state's Office of Special Education Programs reports the data to the U.S. Department of Education, which is within the U.S. Department of Education. That information is included in a later report to Congress.

State Performance Plans

The submission of transition planning data is part of the IDEA (2004) requirement that every state develop a State Performance Plan (SPP). The SPP provides targets to focus schools on areas of need and assists states in compliance with IDEA. Previously, states submitted special education data, such as the number of students served and the disability categories represented in the population of special education students. As of 2015, both an SPP and an Annual Performance Report (APR) describe the state's current success in meeting SPP targets. These targets are known as *indicators*. Each state must report annually to the Secretary of the U.S. Department of Education on its performance under its SPP. Specifically, the state must report in its APR the progress it has made in meeting the measurable and rigorous targets established in its SPP (U.S. Department of Education, 2017). Performance of each LEA in the state on several indicators is reported through special education data reports are analyzed via a management information system. Each state has a system for how it inputs the data using the federal guidelines. The Secretary of the U.S. Department of Education reviews and reports on the indicators and issues an annual determination to each state on its progress in meeting the requirements of the statute. The determinations are part of the ongoing efforts to improve education for America's 7 million children with disabilities (Office of Special Education and Rehabilitative Services, 2017; U.S. Department of Education, 2017).

State Performance Indicators

Transition planning and later improvement efforts are requirements of IDEA (2004). As mentioned in the previous paragraph, indicators determine compliance to federal directives and the success of transition plans. Twenty performance indicators determine compliance with IDEA, but in this chapter, only the transition planning indicators are discussed. Other indicators are discussed in the Student Supplemental Materials.

Transition Indicators 1, 2, 13, and 14 are monitored to provide data about the success of special education students as a result of their involvement in a transition planning program. These indicators are used during student file reviews to ensure the student's transition plan has everything required as a result of transition legislation (discussed in Chapters 2 and 3 of this text). The federal and state governments want to know whether the inclusion of all the transition requirements within the IEP resulted in better outcomes for students. The following indicators are monitored to answer those questions:

- Indicator 1: Graduation rates
  - Percent of youth with IEPs graduating from high school with a regular diploma.
- Indicator 2: Dropout rates
  - Percent of youth with IEPs dropping out of high school.
- Indicator 13: IEP postsecondary transition goals and services
  - Percent of youth with IEPs aged 16 and above with an IEP that includes the following components of transition:
    - Appropriate, measurable postsecondary goals
    - Annually updated
    - Based upon an age-appropriate transition assessment
    - Includes transition services
    - Includes courses of study
    - Will reasonably enable the student to meet those postsecondary goals
    - Has annual IEP goals related to the student's transition services needs
    - Has evidence that the student was invited to the IEP meeting
    - Has evidence that a representative of a community agency that provides transition support invited with parental consent? (Monitoring, technical assistance, and enforcement, 2017)
  - The transition planning specialist and the special education team keep student records documenting that the IEP contains the required provisions. Each data set is analyzed by each state by comparing them with special education students' post-school outcomes and whether those activities led to positive post-school outcomes. This analysis of the data sets is used to determine whether positive post-school outcomes are related to the process of transition planning. The data are collected and compiled by the special education team and submitted by the special education administrator. Each state is required to collect and report indicator data along with their performance in the other SPP indicators. The data in the state APR is due in February each year.
  - Indicator 14 follows up on the student and requires that the student's address, phone number, and email address be up to date so a designated special education teacher can collect follow-up data about what they are doing post-school. In the next section is the information collected for Indicator 14.
- Indicator 14: Postsecondary outcomes
  - Percent of youth who are no longer in secondary school, had IEPs in effect at the time they left school, and were:
    - Enrolled in higher education within 1 year of leaving high school
    - Enrolled in higher education or competitively employed within 1 year of leaving high school
    - Enrolled in higher education or some other postsecondary education or training program; or competitively employed or in some other employment within 1 year of leaving high school

Beginning in 2015, the IDEA Part B SPP/APR and IDEA Part C SPP/APR include a State Systemic Improvement Plan through which each state focuses its efforts on improving a state-selected child or family outcome. When new indicators are added, the special education administrator meets with the special education team to update the requirements, such as a recent indicator including information on the families of children and youth receiving transition services and participating in transition planning (U.S. Department of Education, 2017).

State Performance Plan Ratings on IDEA and Transition

States are rated on their reports and given one of the four following ratings. Each special education department will want the transition plans to meet the aims of IDEA:

1. Meets the requirements and purposes of IDEA
2. Needs assistance in implementing the requirements of IDEA
3. Needs intervention in implementing the requirements of IDEA
4. Needs substantial intervention in implementing the requirements of IDEA

States that do not meet the requirements will need to take corrective actions.

Reports to Congress

After states submit their data about their post-school outcomes to the U.S. Department of Education, each state's plan is reviewed, and receives one of the ratings noted in the previous section. Then a letter is sent to each state to confirm whether the state met the requirements of IDEA (2004). States post this information on their Department of Education websites. The state's SPP/APR are usually posted on these websites in July.

The federal government reports to Congress about the results of the data analysis for the nation. The federal government wants to know whether the state does the following:

- Provides a free appropriate public education for children with disabilities under IDEA Part B (school-age programs) and early intervention services to infants and toddlers with disabilities and their families under IDEA Part C
- Ensures that the rights of these children with disabilities and their parents are protected
- Assists states and localities in providing for the education of all children with disabilities, and
- Assesses the effectiveness of efforts to educate children with disabilities (U.S. Department of Education, 2013)

Section 616(a)(1)(A) of IDEA requires the secretary of the U.S. Department of Education (Department) to monitor the implementation of IDEA through oversight of general supervision by the states and through the State Performance Plans (SPP) described in section 616(b). To fulfill these requirements, the Office of Special Education Programs (OSEP), on behalf of the secretary, has implemented the Continuous Improvement and Focused Monitoring System (CIFMS), which focuses resources on critical compliance and performance areas in IDEA. Under IDEA sections 616(d) and 642, the Department performs an annual review of each state's SPP and the associated Annual Performance Report (APR) (collectively, the SPP/APR) under Parts B and C of IDEA and other publicly available information to make an annual determination of the extent to which the state is meeting the requirements and purposes of Parts B and C of IDEA. The SPPs/APRs and the Department's annual determinations are components of CIFMS.
(IDEA, 2004)

Transition planning is examined to assess the effectiveness of an LEA's efforts to educate children with disabilities as well as whether those efforts reasonably ensured community participation, further education, training, and/or employment. At the LEA level, the special education department is a vital player in ensuring that free appropriate public education leads to better post-school outcomes for students with disabilities.

Exercises

1. Choose an area of disability. Interview a secondary special education teacher or the designated transition specialist about two students who have dropped out. Define the reasons for leaving school. Interview the teacher about strategies that can aid similar students to stay in school.
2. Interview two special education students in the 10th grade. Determine what they are thinking or planning for post–high school life. Then determine what supports they have in place to work toward those goals.
3. Go to the U.S. Department of Education website. Search the Part B SPP letters and APR letters and find two states. Compare the results of those two states.

WRITING LEGALLY DEFENSIBLE TRANSITION PLANS

Every IEP must be legally defensible. This means that the IEP must be filled out, with all questions answered and evidence that the parent provided information, was sent an invitation, and attended the meeting either in person or via conference call. The goals within the IEP must be measurable and advance the student toward post-school outcomes that are tangible, and there must be evidence that the student has an established place in employment or post-school education (Yell, Katsiyannis, Ennis, Losinski, & Christle, 2016). There should also be evidence in the student's file that the targeted outcomes from his or her preferences and the transition skills have been developed so that independence is facilitated. If a post-school placement is not settled upon graduation, a parent can ask for mediation to ensure that the goals of transition planning have been met. Mediation does not include the responsibilities that fall to outside agencies and their transition services to students over 18 years old. Although schools invite the agencies, the school district cannot compel them to act, nor are their services under IDEA. When mediation does not result in a plan outlining a post-school placement, parents can request a due process hearing. Due process requests are less likely if the transition planning specialist, special education team, family, and student work through the transition planning process as a collaborative team. When the team works with the student and the family, and they are timely and focused on the outcomes, the plan will most likely meet the criteria and thereby avoid a due process hearing.

To maintain fidelity to the transition planning process, the special education team and the transition planning specialist must review each student's file and check that every requirement for the IEP and the transition plan are present throughout the transition planning process. As stated in the previous section, there are a number of indicators that the state uses to assess school districts for compliance and performance for special education programs. Altogether there are 20 performance indicators for which data are collected, and although all 20 indicators are monitored, the transition planning specialist is most intensively involved in Indicators 1, 2, 8, 13, and 14.

Two indicators are used to address that all requirements for the IEP are met. Indicators 1 and 2 concern data on the number of students with IEPs who graduated with a diploma and who dropped out. This information is kept by the special education team and the high school administration. Indicator 8 is also used to determine whether schools facilitated parent involvement for transition planning.

Indicator 13 is the most comprehensive transition data set collected. It is the checklist to ensure that the IEP meets the requirements of a legally defensible transition plan. As mentioned, it measures that the plan's activities, which this text defined in the recommended framework, meet the requirements of the law as well as providing direction and goals based on evidenced- or research-based practices that will result in positive post-school outcomes. To determine whether the transition plan in the IEP is legally defensible, eight factors must be present. The following eight questions guide the file review process:

1. Are there appropriate, measurable postsecondary goals in the areas of training, education, employment, and independent living skills?
2. Are postsecondary goals updated annually or more when each goal is accomplished?
3. Are measurable postsecondary goals based on age-appropriate transition assessment(s)?
4. Will transition services reasonably enable the student to meet his or her postsecondary goals?
5. Do transition services include courses of study that will reasonably enable the student to meet his or her postsecondary goals?
6. Do annual goal(s) relate to the student's transition services needs?
7. Was the student and the parent invited to the IEP team meeting where transition services were discussed?
8. With the prior consent of the parent (or student who has reached the age of majority), was a representative of any participating agency invited to the IEP team meeting?

Indicator 14 is the follow-up information that will be used to determine whether the design and implementation of the transition plan resulted in a positive outcome for each student (see the Appendix at the end of Chapter 6).

- Indicator 14. Percent of youth who are no longer in secondary school, had IEPs in effect at the time they left school, and are:
  - Higher education
    - Enrolled in higher education within 1 year of leaving high school
      - Enrolled full- or part-time
      - Community college (2-year program)
      - College/university (4-year or more program)
      - Completed at least one term
  - Competitive employment
    - Enrolled in higher education or competitively employed within 1 year of leaving high school
      - Worked for pay at or above the minimum wage
      - Worked in a setting with others who are nondisabled
      - Average of 20 hours a week
      - 90 days at any time in the year since leaving high school
      - Includes military employment
  - Other postsecondary education or training
    - Enrolled full- or part-time in higher education or training program (e.g., adult education or vocational technical school that is less than a 2-year program)
    - Completed at least one term other employment
      - Worked for compensation below minimum wage other employment
      - 90 days at any time since leaving high school

States that do not meet the goals set for special education programs in the indicators are expected to take corrective action. To avoid due process or a corrective action from the state, all the contents listed previously, including the post-graduation assessment, must be accounted for. Though this list may seem short compared to the transition framework, the path to the goals is carrying out longitudinal transition framework activities and trainings.

THE TRANSITION PLANNING SPECIALIST, STATE MONITORING, AND SYSTEMATIC IMPROVEMENT

For the follow-up post-school outcome data, the school district will have a procedure will in place to survey students who have graduated. Please see Table 17-1 for an example of this.

Both special educators and transition planning specialists must be aware of and work to address the legal requirements of data collection regarding the quality of transition planning. Transition IEPs are monitored to support efforts to ameliorate the problems that are the causes of unsuccessful post-school outcomes. According to the National Technical Assistance Center on Transition (2012), the indicators help LEAs by informing program improvement. The indicators look at whether former students are doing well under a number of different criteria, including the drop out rate and post-school outcomes, and where improvement could be made based on the post-school outcomes of the students. Data may be disaggregated by gender, race/ethnicity, disability category, or exit status. LEAs can see how effective the transition planning is for various groups of students. This can shed light on adaptations that may be needed when the needs of those students are not met. In this way, both SEAs and LEAs can explore what in-school experiences influenced their students' post-school outcomes.

MONITORING OUTCOMES VIA THE EXIT SURVEY

Legislation requires data collection and analysis to determine whether the strategies of transition resulted in positive post-school outcomes for students with disabilities. The student, unless he or she cannot participate due to the severity of his or her disability, is the participant, and the transition planning specialist or designee will need to acquire the student's signed permission to be contacted and interviewed upon graduation and 1 year after graduation. Parent participation is needed when the child's disability is too severe to provide information. Districts typically have their own permission form that has been reviewed to ensure it aligns with the requirements of legislation. If any other surveys are required by the school district or the team, and as noted in the previous section, the post-school survey must be a single survey, not combined with any other, and additional information is noted in another survey, as demonstrated in Chapter 17.

EXERCISES

1. Interview an administrator regarding practices for carrying out Indicator 13.
2. Interview a high school–level educator responsible for transition. Ask how he or she supports the administrative requirements of Indicator 13 data collection for post-school outcomes.
3. Interview a transition planning specialist about how he or she lays the groundwork for data collection for Indicator 13.
4. Research Indicators 1 through 20 via the Office of Special Education and Rehabilitation Services.
5. Use three LEA Department of Special Education websites. Read about how they monitor Indicators 13 and 14. Pick from various geographical locations. Report findings to the class.

SUMMARY

This chapter discussed the complex interworkings of law, policy, and procedure. It discussed the roles of the administrative team, transition planning specialist, and special education team as they participate in and complete the goals of the local community, state, and federal governments. Monitoring the results of special education legislation is an ongoing process, with new criteria for evaluation being added periodically. The transition planning specialist and special education team are in a unique position to ensure that the monitoring data are collected each year while also putting forward transition activities that can result in positive post-school outcomes and decrease the drop-out rate for special education students. The process of monitoring and improving transition services is complicated because of the multiple people in multiple roles who must be involved in the process. It is through the work of the transition planning specialist and special education team that transition services and plans are implemented using a framework for transition that is organized and organized in a way that can provide data and bring about improved post-school outcomes in all areas addressed in the transition plans.

REFERENCES

Bateman, D. F., Bright, K. L., O'Shea, D. J., O'Shea, L. J., & Algozzine, B. F. (2007). *The special education program administrator's handbook*. Boston, MA: Pearson Education.

Benedict, A. E., Brownell, M. T., Griffin, C. C., Wang, J., & Myers, J. A. (2016). Leveraging professional development to prepare general and special education teachers to teach within response to intervention frameworks. In T. Petty, A. Good, & S. M. Putman (Eds.), *Handbook of research on professional development for quality teaching and learning* (pp. 42-61). Hershey, PA: IGI Global.

Billingsley, B. S., McLeskey, J., & Crockett, J. B. (2014). Principal leadership: Moving toward inclusive and high-achieving schools for students with disabilities (CEEDAR Document No. IC-8). University of Florida, Collaboration for Effective Educator, Development, Accountability, and Reform Center. Retrieved from http://www.smcoe.org/assets/files/about-smcoe/superintendents-office/statewide-special-education-task-force/Principal-Leadership-Moving-Toward-Inclusive-and-High-Achieving-Schools-for-Students-With-Disabilities%20copy.pdf

Every Student Succeeds Act of 2015, Pub. L. No. 114-95, 20 U.S.C. § 1601 *et seq.* (2015).

Individuals with Disabilities Education Act of 2004, Pub. L. No. 108-446, 20 U.S.C. § 1400 *et seq.* (2004).

Monitoring, technical assistance, and enforcement, 20 U.S.C. § 1416 (2017).

National Technical Assistance Center on Transition. (2012). Transition indicators. Retrieved from https://transitionta.org/indicatorb

No Child Left Behind Act of 2001, Pub. L. No. 107-110, 20 U.S.C. § 6319 (2001).

Office of Special Education and Rehabilitative Services. (2017). Department releases 2017 Determination Letters on state implementation of IDEA. Retrieved from https://sites.ed.gov/idea/department-releases-2017-determination-letters-on-state-implementation-of-idea/

State eligibility, 20 U.S.C. § 1412 (2017).

SEA responsibility for general supervision, 34 C.F.R. § 300.149 (2018).

U.S. Department of Education. Office of Special Education Programs. (2013). Part B State Performance Plan (SPP) and Annual Performance Report (APR): Part B Indicator Measurement Table, 2013-14. Retrieved from http://www2.ed.gov/policy/speced/guid/idea/bapr/2015/partbmeasurementtable5-14-14.pdf.

U.S. Department of Education. (2017). 2017 Determination letters on state implementation of IDEA. Retrieved from https://www2.ed.gov/fund/data/report/idea/ideafactsheet-determinations-2017.pdf

Yell, M. L., Katsiyannis, A., Ennis, R. P., Losinski, M., & Christle, C. A. (2016). Avoiding substantive errors in individualized education program development. *TEACHING Exceptional Children, 49*(1), 31-40.

9

Roles of the Secondary Special Education Team and Community Agencies

CHAPTER OBJECTIVES

- → Describe the role of the special education supervisor in transition planning.
- → Describe the roles of the transition planning specialist and special education teachers in transition planning.
- → Describe the role of the school psychologist working with students with disabilities.
- → Identify what expertise is needed to interact with the students effectively.
- → Identify the beginning steps in developing optimal teacher attitudes to be efficient transition planning specialists.
- → Describe effective student–transition planning specialist interactions using a conference approach to transition planning.
- → Describe how the transition planning specialist establishes meaning during student conferences.
- → Demonstrate how to interview students to elicit rich information to help them design their immediate goals for transition.
- → Articulate why a continuous review of teacher bias is necessary.
- → Describe how the transition planning specialist and team can ensure cohesion through the use of a team checklist.
- → Describe the intersection of the U.S. Office of Special Education and the Rehabilitative Services Administration and how it affects transition services.

Rae, J. M. *A Collaborative Approach to Transition Planning for Students With Disabilities* (pp. 187-206).
© 2020 SLACK Incorporated.

ROLE OF THE SECONDARY SPECIAL EDUCATION SUPERVISOR

The special education supervisor works with the special education team and transition planning specialist to support the implementation of transition supports and services. Ideally, they are instrumental in facilitating the program's successful implementation and improved outcomes for students. The team members who direct and implement programs and related services for transition—the special education administrator, the transition planning specialist, and those who teach secondary students in special education and general education classes—work together in a collaborative process to advance the student's goals. As the last school district personnel who will see special education students off into adulthood, they guide transition through a dynamic and organized interactive process. The special education supervisor plays a crucial role in the overall design of the transition procedures and processes. They work with the transition planning specialist and secondary special education teachers, as the administrative leader. Overseeing transition, providing guidance, and supporting student independence is as important as the work of medical professionals who support a patient's health by providing health care. With the same seriousness of purpose, the secondary special education supervisor and special and general educators, in collaboration with the transition planning specialist, provide support to the student. The special education supervisor guides the program by completing activities throughout the course of the school year as follows:

- Work with central office administrators, communicating activities of the special education transition team.
- Attend Individualized Education Plan (IEP) meetings.
- Maintain oversight of the transition planning school-based team.
- Review faculty email communications daily.
- Review faculty, parent, and introductory student information.
- Review existing invitations to faculty, parents, and students.
- Meet with high school administrator(s) and special education director to address the development of new and existing programs.
- Meet with special education director to stay current about what funding is included in the budget.
- Provide continuing education and learning community forums to review case studies at in-services and special education faculty meetings during the school year.
- Review and approve faculty professional development about, for example, the impact of disability on learning and the effect on post-school life.
- Be present as a leader and participate in general education faculty in-services during the first faculty in-service on the district's opening day.
- Plan with the transition planning specialist to extend professional development to middle school faculty.
- Plan with the transition planning specialist and review presentations for parents about transition planning.
- Review calendar of community-based instruction activities and current transition curriculum for transition-age students.
- Review all frameworks and forms used to collect data, and create plans for transition.
- Work with the transition planning specialist and the secondary special education team to talk about additions and deletions to the current forms.
- Approve and implement new forms.
- Evaluate teacher IEP performance using periodic checks and file reviews.
- Organize due process materials.
- Review the effectiveness of transition planning by establishing data collection on graduates and school leavers (i.e., dropouts) with disabilities.

- Ensure that the secondary special education team has a system of documentation for transition activities.
- Provide reviews of the submitted data.
- Observe special education teachers regularly and discuss observations.
- Evaluate all special education staff yearly and provide feedback on the transition planning process.
- Create agenda templates with the help of the special education team about informational meetings for faculty, parents, and students.
- Maintain records of activities, and meet with central office administrators to keep them included in progress and needs throughout the school year.
- Update the special education and transition planning manuals.

Special education supervisors are the key persons who provide leadership and ensure all the requirements of transition planning are completed. They are instrumental in ensuring that community connections are developed and parents are informed of post-school programs. They must have knowledge of changes in adult services programs under the auspices of the Department of Health and Human Services.

The special education supervisor liaisons with the district and community agencies, such as the local mental health counseling center. They are involved in developing interagency agreements for purposes such as having a mental health therapist come to the school to run groups for students to address coping with the death of a family member, overcoming self-stigma about their disability, developing strategies for graduating when there is a family history of dropping out, and developing strategies for living in families where drug and alcohol abuse and mental health disorders are present. The special education supervisor will work with the director of special services, sometimes called the director of pupil and personnel services, playing an instrumental role in collecting information on whether special education students accessed this assistance and found it helpful.

The special education supervisor and the transition planning specialist review current transition curriculum, transition activities, school-to-work programs and transition procedures and practices. As students access multiple options during transition, the special education supervisor meets with teachers and the transition planning specialist to ensure the plans are following the law.

Special education supervisors have many responsibilities that support improved post-school outcomes. The special education supervisor is a key player, interacting and collaborating with the secondary special education team and all school and community stakeholders.

ROLE OF THE TRANSITION PLANNING SPECIALIST

The transition planning specialist must have skills to support direct interactions with the students, the special education team, families, and the staff. The following are major requirements for transition planning specialists:

- Implement an interactive and collaborative approach to transition planning.
- Strive to understand the student's perspectives.
- Know how to validate the student.
- Effectively interview the student.
- Know where the student is developmentally and how it affects the ability to plan post-school life.
- Know how to conference with students given a wide range of ability and disability.
- Know when to increase the conference meetings when a student is struggling.
- Work with the special education supervisor, team members, and the student's general education teachers to address challenges that might sideline a student's success, and include community-based or in-school counselors when necessary.

- Plan meetings and follow through on the plans generated at the student's transition planning conferences.

- Generate solutions so the goals of transition are being expedited.

- Ensure legal mandates are followed and IEPs are in compliance.

For instance, an IEP meeting for initial transition planning is coming up, and one special education teacher has not tested the student or asks for an extension for the IEP meeting because his or her part is incomplete. At times, a teacher may miss deadlines, creating significant stress to all team members, most significantly the transition planning specialist, who is responsible for leading the transition planning process with the student. To facilitate the completion of transition tasks, a process must be in place to monitor the submission of needed information. Ultimately, the transition planning specialist will be called into any due process meeting if an IEP falls out of compliance in violation of special education law. Compliance with the special education legal requirements and, of particular concern, meeting timelines might be ignored, but if the parents address this via a due process case, these cases can last a long time at considerable expense to the school district. For example, one case lasted 10 years. Therefore, continuous monitoring is needed to ensure compliance with special education time lines and transition plan development and implementation. The transition planning specialist, the special education supervisor, and secondary special educators should regularly attend training to institutionalize procedures to avoid noncompliance with special education law.

Transition Planning Student Study Team Meetings

Transition planning student study team meetings are a positive strategy for having regular communication between the IEP team members about the student's pending services needs and the team's role in securing transition services. Information discussed includes supports needed to advance the student, the student's class performance, emotional and social issues, credit acquisition and the student's course of study, and other transition planning needs as they arise through the transition planning specialist–student conference process.

With knowledge of the student's current status, the team will be aware of ways they can further encourage and implement the use of effective instructional strategies that will help the student acquire new skills. The following meetings are part of this structure.

Creating a schedule and abiding by it is important to the success of the student's plans. Forgotten staff meetings result in forgotten and significantly delayed plans. Three meetings capture different aspects of transition planning. Study team meeting 1 keeps the special education director up to date with the secondary special education and transition planning as well as future proposed plans or existing transition plan reviews. Study team meeting 2 is to maintain compliance by reviewing each student's transition plan and files. Study team meeting 3 is the weekly or biweekly update for each student receiving transition services and the roles being completed by individual team members. The following is an example of how collaborative meetings can be organized.

1. Monthly communication meeting: Special education supervisor, transition planning specialist, and secondary special education team
   a. Team leader: Transition planning specialist reports on transition planning program needs.
   b. Keep meeting records
   c. Discuss student's progress and needs
2. Monthly compliance team meeting: Review of upcoming IEP, transition plans, Individual Career Plans, leisure plan/school activities, and academic documents
   a. Team leader: Special education supervisor or transition planning specialist
   b. Keep meeting records
   c. Discuss student's progress and needs

3. Weekly transition student study team meetings
   a. Team leader: Special educator
   b. Keep meeting records
   c. Discuss student's updates, successes, and needs

General Meeting Practices

Meetings must have accurate records, called *minutes*, and team members who are not the leader are assigned to keep minutes. Keeping minutes is required for a few reasons. They provide a structure to completing activities, and they facilitate the scheduling and timely completion of team responsibilities and team improvement goals.

Prior to each transition planning meeting, agendas are emailed by the team leader to the team members for additions, the agenda is updated with the additions, and finalized versions are sent. Meetings 1 and 3 are the transition planning specialist's responsibility. After the meetings, the transition planning specialist adds changes, and a PDF version is emailed to staff.

At each meeting, previous topics and assignments are reviewed and next actions are planned; using a new business and old business pattern to end and begin new actions is an organized way to run the meeting. Trainings on how to run an organized meeting will help the team stay on task.

The transition planning specialist keeps a hard copy and a digital copy of the meeting minutes. The meeting minutes may be needed to document team activities and are used for compliance monitoring.

TRANSITION PLANNING SPECIALIST INTERACTIONS WITH THE STUDENT

Student Conferencing as an Interactive Approach to Transition Planning

This text supports the use of a student and transition planning specialist interactive and collaborative approach to helping students reach their goals. An interactive approach entails the use of transition planning conferences. Using a system of ongoing conferences increases student and transition planning specialist knowledge about the strengths and needs of the student. It enables the student and transition planning specialist to work out the unique problems that arise that may stymie an individual's success. It is a form of ongoing individual attention that increases chances for the student to engage in and complete the activities of transition successfully. Students with disabilities need support to manage transitions as do students without disabilities. However, they need professionals and parents who can provide additional help to address their needs because of their disabilities. Students with high incidence disabilities and students who are served in classes for students with emotional and behavioral disorders are at high risk for leaving school early without graduating, have difficulty attending post-school educational programs, and have difficulty securing employment without direct support.

Students with learning disabilities, speech delays, other health impairments, emotional conditions, and mild intellectual disabilities make up approximately 90% of special education students (McFarland et al., 2017). These same students can, within the structure of transition planning, develop the skills to secure employment and participate in the community at large.

As part of the conferencing process, students will be able to benefit from the implementation of the three-pronged approach to transition planning discussed in Chapter 7:

1. Individual Career Development Planning
2. Transition Plan in the IEP additionally focuses on academic and cognitive development, a course of student credit attainment and literacy.
3. Independence and Leisure Plan

Structuring the interactive approach organizes the student who has difficulty planning or executing plans and encourages the student to view the transition planning specialist as the primary resource person on the path to taking on his or her own responsibilities.

Meeting With the Student

Through conferences with the student, which occur as planned sessions over the school year, the student adjusts his or her plan by striking off goals as they are completed and constructing new ones. Meeting with the student helps the student to stay focused on each goal and continue to plan the next goals. In order to be effective, the transition planning specialist will need to interact effectively with the student using a listening strategy when interviewing the student. This strategy will be addressed in the section on the conference. By talking about their thoughts on their futures, students learn about themselves, their needs, and their goals. The transition planning specialist can strive to understand their goals and challenges as well. Because the student does not typically have a clear picture of his or her future or may not even think of the future as they struggle with existing challenges of learning, the transition planning specialist is the pivot point where interactions with the student become the change agent for the student's life. The following is an example of a student who was guided via conferencing.

Case Report: Ms. Smith

In a qualitative study by Rae (2011), Ms. Smith recalled transition planning meetings and working with her teacher to figure out what credits she needed and how she could complete her senior year at the community college. She did not know why her teacher encouraged that direction other than that her teacher felt she would be "ready to go." She also recalled figuring out the social situation and how to "handle people" (Rae, 2011, p. 43). She talked about learning that a community college could lead to a 4-year college, which was an option she was unaware of. She believed that this option would be "a good transition to figure out what you wanted to do" (Rae, 2011, p. 44).

DISCUSSION

The field notes from the study indicated that whenever Ms. Smith was having a difficult time working with peers in the academic setting, the researcher would wait "no less than 4 days" to discuss the academic issues that may affect her job or school life in the social area. The researcher also noted that "ongoing, caring conferencing is a productive way to encourage intrinsic change" (Rae, 2011). In this case, the transition planning specialist reviewed student records, provided meaningful information to the student, and provided a nonthreatening environment to discuss her social challenges. In a review of earlier school records, an aptitude test revealed a college-level aptitude and an intelligence quotient score of 128, more than adequate to comprehend college material. However, the student's status at that time included a full year of school failure and multiple inpatient hospitalizations for a mental health disorder. After setting up a credit recoupment strategy, both in the emotional support program and at the community college, this student graduated from high school by finishing her high school credits at a community college as part of her transition plan. Later she matriculated at a 4-year college, graduated, and won a history award. She is currently employed and maintains her mental health treatment.

This is an example of how a conferencing approach was used to review records and provide information about unknown options and social supports that led to a student's university success.

TRANSITION PLANNING SPECIALIST AS LEARNER

Collaborating With the Student: Challenges

Identity is formed during adolescence, and during this period, every effort must be made not only to validate the student's planning process but also to avoid invalidating his or her hopes and dreams. Transition planning specialists must view this as a developmental process that requires an understanding of how current hopes, dreams, and self-perceived needs and skills will develop and change. Previous studies have found that communicating acceptance and understanding (i.e., validation) enhances the recipient's psychological and physiological well-being when compared with receiving nonunderstanding feedback (i.e., invalidation; Greville-Harris, Hempel, Karl, Dieppe, & Lynch, 2016). Therefore, the student's goals and aspirations should be explored, and teachers should not be dismissive of a student's perspectives or emotions.

Recognition of student perceived needs and teacher understanding of those needs establishes the foundation of an interactive and collaborative approach to transition planning, which serves to validate the student as an individual. Positive interactions establish trust for future transition planning conferences. If the transition planning specialist is critical or otherwise fails to accept the student's current self-knowledge, wishes, and dreams, then invalidation is the outcome. Invalidation affects student confidence and detracts from feelings of competence. Invalidating the student occurs when the teacher devalues the student's thoughts, positive or negative. Another way to devalue a student is to fail to train the student to participate in the IEP goal selection and time lines, a decision that undermines the student's self-determination. Also, not accounting for the student's normal fear of speaking in front of the team and putting in place strategies to help with nervousness, invalidates the student's emotions and can lead to inhibition of the ability to assert their goals in an IEP meeting. Another example of devaluation is pointing out that the student's aspiration to be a teacher may not be the best option when the student does not like large groups of people. Most students, via the conferencing process and using environmental inventories for preferred settings, determine this for themselves. So, rather than focusing on telling the student what he or she cannot do, the transition planning specialist should provide opportunities to show the student what jobs entail without implying that he or she cannot or should not do it.

According to a study by Greville-Harris et al. (2016), the effects of invalidating feedback have adverse social outcomes, including a significant reduction in social engagement behaviors. Interestingly, it was found that invalidation is more detrimental to social behavior than validating feedback is. This surprising discrepancy was also found in earlier work in Porges' theory (1995, 2007), which suggests that under conditions of perceived threat, our ability to engage socially is reduced, decreasing the ability to display behaviors such as reciprocal eye gaze and positive affect displays. These prosocial skills are necessary to succeed in social situations such as school and work. Therefore, transition planning specialists must demonstrate support for and delve into the expressed wants and needs of the student and create a forum for the student to discern and plan best choices for him- or herself. In short, the transition planning specialist should not diminish a student's feelings of competence but rather enhance them.

The Conference

Ongoing discussions about personal and career explorations are a critical part of conferencing with the student. It is through longitudinal conferencing that an essential understanding of the student begins to emerge. The initial meeting includes a get-to-know-the-student questionnaire, which requires interview skills. Effective interviewing is a process of eliciting in-depth information by using a questioning technique. This technique provides rich data to inform the student's direction for the future.

With this strategy, the transition planning specialist asks a question, the student responds, the transition planning specialist clarifies the student's answers, and the student confirms that the transition planning specialist understood. The transition planning specialist is not advising. The transition

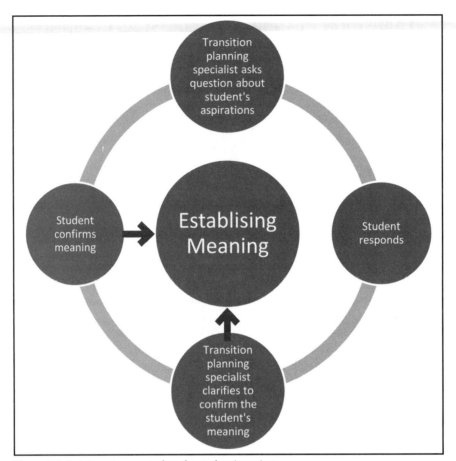

Figure 9-1. An interactive approach to the student interview.

planning specialist is the learner, learning about the student in an interactive way that leads to a deeper understanding. The transition planning specialist does so without adding personal or professional thoughts. Figure 9-1 is a schematic about how meaning is established in an interactive process.

The process of establishing meaning, learning about the student, and becoming a skilled listener and learner is essential to the interactive approach. Establishing meaning in the first conference is essential to being someone the student believes will strive to understand who he or she is as a person. The process of continual discussion, clarifying the student's communicative intent, and expressing that the transition planning specialist (i.e., the listener) understands the message is crucial to transition planning success.

The Interview Strategy

Teacher Interview Skill Development

When interviewing a student in the conference setting, it is essential to follow a planned course of action to establish meaning. Through the interactive process of the conference, the transition planning specialist makes sense of the interview responses using the cycle described in Figure 9-1.

During the interview, clarification is needed. The student is only beginning to talk about goals, often leaving out the things that are important to him or her or the things that are constraining his or her progress. For instance, although the transition planning specialist may be aware of a lack of family cohesion, most likely they do not know any of the underlying factors that are derailing the student's goals. For example, the student discussed earlier reported that if he graduated, which was not likely due to lack of credit attainment, he would be the first in his family to graduate. Based on his history and his report, the transition planning specialist could have viewed the parent history of school leaving prior to graduation as inherent in the family system, and thus an insurmountable problem in credit acquisition. By sharing the family history, the student provided evidence that at age 16, although he was behind, he did want to graduate but could not see how he would make it.

To find the more nuanced meaning, the transition planning specialist can use a technique called *data source triangulation* to ensure the information provides an accurate understanding of the student's goals. Information is said to be more reliable when three pieces of information are typically used to see how a student may function in a given environment. Triangulating, or providing three sources, helps the educator develop a more complete picture about what a student will need. In short, it helps the educator in the transition planning specialist role develop a more global view of options for each student.

The transition planning specialist uses the student's self-reports, aspirations, interviews, observations, and school records to communicate with the student to clarify and review themes and concepts about the student's goals. For example, the same student tells the transition planning specialist that he has difficulty sitting for long periods of time. The transition planning specialist thinks about this and gives a probe such as, "Tell me more about that," a request for information that will further establish meaning. Probing further will elicit more information, such as asking if there are any times of the day when this is not a problem. The transition planning specialist can also ask the student's permission to gather more information about his classroom difficulty from his other teachers. From this data, information may emerge to specify when this problem is evident. Through the reports of at least three other teachers, the student gains additional perspectives and matches the classroom teacher's observations to his or her own. For example, although a given teacher might not see the student as overly active, it may be that the student may be struggling to hide it. Having this nuanced understanding can help the student generate ideas about how he wants to handle the problem. A student who has severe difficulty sitting for long periods of time is facing a tremendous roadblock because more sitting is required in high school due to lengthy assignments. When another observer does not share the student's self-perception, this does not change the student's subjective experience but rather supports that the student is currently fighting to prevent movement and is successful but at a cost of losing focus on the task because all his or her energy is going to sitting still.

A student's daily experiences are guides to what he or she will need to do to reach his or her goals. Finding and expressing deep-seated concerns pulls those concerns into consciousness. Once brought into consciousness, they can be part of a plan for graduation. As the student and the transition planning specialist continue to conference, career exploration should include positions where the student with a high activity level could use his or her considerable energy.

Other information is often revealed as the transition planning specialist and the student meet in the conference setting. The transition planning specialist uses interviews, observations, and school records to communicate with the student to clarify and review previous thoughts and dreams and emergent themes and concepts about the student's life situation and goals.

After the initial conference, the following questions help the transition planning specialist analyze what the student has shared. Table 9-1 illustrates the use of the sources linked to transition planning questions. The use of the interactive approach to conferencing provides information supporting the transition interview process with efforts to "minimize misperception" (Stake, 1995, p. 134). The goal in transition planning is to establish meaning and to provide and exchange information with the student and the team, creating opportunities to revise transition plans when exploration creates new options. The information that the student shares requires that the transition planning specialist ask questions as he or she interacts with the student in an open and ongoing process to establish meaning about both the student's new and preexisting daily practices, family constraints, goals, and aspirations. Each of these student revelations provides the foundation for discovering what the transition planning specialist believes may be viable supports under the student's circumstances. In short, the information provided is the impetus for the plan. When working with students, it is important to

TABLE 9-1. TEAM COLLABORATION TO SUPPORT STUDENT GOALS

SAMPLE QUESTIONS	DATA SOURCE #1	DATA SOURCE #2	DATA SOURCE #3
	Student–Transition Planning Specialist Conferences	*Transition Planning Specialist and Classroom Teachers*	*File Reviews, Course of Study Documents, and Report Cards*
What is the nature of this student's current life? What roadblocks are there to graduation?	Parental serious mental health disorder Student's long working hours Behind in credit acquisition Low-income family No possibility of tutoring	Classroom observation as part of the interview process Interviews of teachers Collaboration with administrators to support credit recoupment	Assessments Credit acquisition review Current status Past academic success and decline Increase in absenteeism
What is the student's recollection of both general education and the special experience? What does the student need to complete or recoup credits? What is the student willing to do?	Interview Under what circumstances did the student learn best? What changes need to be made to adjust to current circumstances?	Semester and grading period records Other ways to earn credit	Interview teachers about student's learning strengths

(continued)

TABLE 9-1. TEAM COLLABORATION TO SUPPORT STUDENT GOALS (CONTINUED)

SAMPLE QUESTIONS	DATA SOURCE #1	DATA SOURCE #2	DATA SOURCE #3
	Student–Transition Planning Specialist Conferences	*Transition Planning Specialist and Classroom Teachers*	*File Reviews, Course of Study Documents, and Report Cards*
What supports will he or she need to graduate? What skills can this student learn and take with him or her?	Review history with the student Review strengths (in this case, previous attendance data) Discuss whether the parent will support graduation What does the student consider the greatest roadblock to graduation?	Conference call to the parent with the student Ascertain current support for graduation (never assume the parent cannot become supportive despite history) Determine the level of support available Prepare to initiate intensive conferencing as a protective factor when it is clear the parent can give no support	Conference with the student Develop a plan for credit recoupment Make recoupment plan have active components, such as a community services elective Part-time workforce entry job with job coaching at the restaurant to earn credit Begin career explorations, scholarships, and cooking classes according to student's vision

WORK WITH THE STUDENT TO DOCUMENT THE NEED FOR TRANSITION ACTIVITIES

Design an Outline of Wants and Needs for the Transition Plan

Student-generated graduation goals	Additional transition activities	Projected outcomes
• Handling money effectively • Budgeting and reserving money for future independence • Securing a job coach • Setting up the credit recoupment strategy by using current employment and a job coach to earn work study credits	• What would he or she like to do or try? • Participation in a school-to-work program • Explore post-school options • Prepare a plan to review options as part of the credit recoupment strategy	• Earn enough credits to graduate • Full-time employment • Leisure outcome • Additional education, such as one class at community college in an area of interest • Cooking classes • Health preservation activities due to overwork conditions

realize that each student is unique, and each student will bring unique experiences and special stories to tell. The purpose of the interview is not to get simple yes or no answers but a description of an episode, a linkage, and an explanation (Stake, 1995, p. 65). By taking the student's goals and constraints into consideration, the transition planning specialist can collaborate with the transition team to find options that support the student.

Responsive Interviewing

The interactive approach in the conference setting is guided by responsive interview techniques (Rubin & Rubin, 2005). Rubin and Rubin assert that, in the responsive interview model, the transition planning specialist is looking for "depth and detail, and vivid and nuanced answers, rich with thematic material" (2005, p. 129). During the interviews, the educator employs probes to "manage the conversation by keeping it on topic, signaling the desired level of depth and asking for examples or clarification" (Rubin & Rubin, 2005, p. 129). Probes are used to ask for examples or further clarification of points and to elicit more detail without changing the focus of the questions. The transition planning specialist should expect that inconsistencies will arise during an interview, especially over the longitudinal process of transition planning. The student's inconsistencies can revolve around instances of the student holding two opposing viewpoints about the same aspirations during the conferences. The educator should be aware that most students will have those competing perspectives within themselves. Follow-up questions and probes help clarify the basis for inconsistent responses and allow more "nuanced answers" (Rubin & Rubin, 2005, p. 136). Effective interviewing supports the ongoing attention needed to guide the student to positive post-school outcomes.

Over time, the transition planning specialist will carry out multiple conferences with the student. The transition planning specialist and special education teachers should keep not just the current perspectives of the student but also the past perspectives. These documents provide educators with guidance to understand that transition planning is a fluid process. Figure 9-2 demonstrates how the conference process can progress.

THE CONFERENCE ENVIRONMENT

The interview and conferences tend to be more like casual conversations about the student's life. Making the student comfortable, the transition planning specialist approaches the conferences sincerely and with an attitude of concern. An upbeat yet serious approach to the student as an independent person develops trust further. The transition planning specialist makes the entire interview and conferencing process a positive event for the student and listens as the student shares thoughts and opinions about the circumstances of his or her past or present. The transition planning specialist must see the student as competent to select needed goals they would like to pursue for independence, training, and options for post-school education.

After an initial conference, it is expected that there may be a need to clarify points made by the student. The transition planning specialist must be aware too that although initial questions have been answered, the student may think of other information in response to earlier questions. This backtracking is to be expected. It is always possible that even in the same interview, a meaning or communication the transition planning specialist believed was understood changes when the student remembers new information that alters the original information or context.

Upon closing the conference, there may be questions in the transition planning specialist's mind. These questions can be brought to the next conference after a careful review of the original questions is complete. More complex questions are covered during the second interview.

Maintaining written information and remembering the student's concerns fosters trust and future conversations that will provide a deeper level of communication. Follow-up questions remain specific to the comments made by the student during the interview process. The transition planning specialist

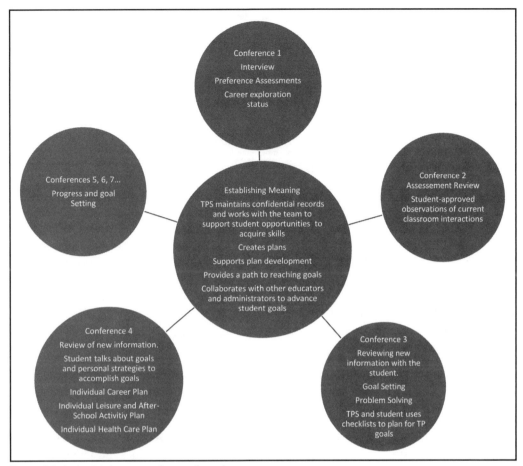

Figure 9-2. An interactive approach to conferencing.

documents the information provided by the student, picking up nuance, particular themes and concepts, and a more vicarious experience of the student's life (Rubin & Rubin, 2005; Stake, 1995).

Eligibility Labels and Student Identity

Students with disabilities have eligibility labels that give a narrow view of who the students are and how they will function in a given situation. The label detracts from transition planning and often results in a general list of accommodations and career suggestions. The transition planning process requires more. Transition conferencing strives to circumvent self-stigma and public stigma that can emerge when the discussion turns to the nebulous profile of a student with learning disabilities or a student from a "dysfunctional family." Focusing on these labels will not support positive outcomes.

The valuable information is how a student learns and how his or her learning patterns affect him or her in classes. Regarding the dysfunctional family stigma, the transition planning specialist and special education team need to know what constraints are present and work to address options for student achievement. Most adults have enough self-knowledge to know that there are careers and activities that they will not be able to do. Everyone faces this eventually, but students with disabilities may believe early in life that there have been many things they cannot do that they saw their peers do easily, and there have been few opportunities to see themselves as competent. Transition planning is the time to show them otherwise by guiding them to find their first job, providing them rewarding educational experiences, and providing them social and leisure activities that will lead them to a full independent life. By getting to know a student's deeper concerns and anxieties about living and learning, the secondary special education team can help the student to be a self-determined person who, with the support and backing of adults in their school and life, can find the path to a satisfying post–high school life.

Conferences as Protective Factors

Many articles have been written about protective factors that increase the likelihood of post-school success. By being an involved and supportive adult, the transition planning team can be a protective factor for students with family and their own constraints. To further the transition planning specialist's competence, see the following suggestions:

- Be a fact finder for the student when he or she needs resources.
- Realize that you do not need to respond immediately to every question, but follow-up is essential.
- Thoughtfully consider each concern. Helping the student consider alternatives can model problem-solving behaviors and avoid the pitfall of impulsively responding with poorly constructed responses.
- Tell the student when more information is needed.
- Demonstrate an attitude of caring and respect.
- Communicate commitment that the transition planning specialist–student team works together to move the student to the next steps in life.
- Value the student and demonstrate respect by being early for scheduled transition planning conferences.
- Demonstrate a caring attitude by being prepared for all student conferences and IEP meetings.
- Do not cancel your appointments with the student. If you are sick, call the school and communicate your absence directly to a team member who should inform the student upon arrival.
- Understand that students will change over time through the interactions and activities and because developmentally their identity is forming. Avoid demonstrating frustration; frustration is to be expected.

The relationship between the transition planning specialist, the special education teacher, and the student requires confidentiality, patience, and instruction so that the student, over the course of the process, develops a sense of self-identity relative to his or her age, characteristics, and maturity. Remember that students are not adults; they are in a developmental stage that is fraught with impulsivity and developmental problems with planning, and they still benefit from adult support during transition.

The role of the team is critical, and striving to guide students through the process to self-determination and positive post-school outcome is a trust given to you, the transition planning specialist and team. A line from by J. McGovern (personal communication, 2019) expressed this well, "And I know for sure that teachers make a difference, they always have and they always will and we should never be afraid of doing good."

ROLES OF THE SECONDARY SPECIAL EDUCATION TEAM

Role of the Special Education Secondary School Teacher

The special education teachers and transition planning specialist must know the range of functional and academic skills of each student. Each special education classroom teacher is tasked with knowing the student's academic and social and emotional behavior in the classroom.

The student comes to the transition planning process with a limited amount of self-knowledge about how he or she may behave under multiple conditions in and out of the school setting.

The student comes with diverse strengths, needs, and skills. He or she exhibits various levels of maturity, adolescent development, physical disabilities, intellectual disabilities, and psychological and psychosocial skills. By knowing the student in a classroom-based relationship, the special education teacher plays a primary role in making the process student centered. The special educator is with the student every day and is integral in constructing the student's current status, especially when social and classroom behavioral challenges may become roadblocks to post-school success.

The transition planning specialist and special educators, within the context of the student study team, review the current information and together construct a document of current strengths and needs for transition. They organize assessments and ensure that the transition planning specialist has a full picture of the student's current level of functioning. Prior to IEP meetings, they test all reading and math levels to ensure that the student is making progress on language usage and mathematics so crucial to communication and independence. The special educators are also the teachers of the transition curriculum, and they should have a checklist of information about what the student has completed and needs to complete.

Special education teachers must collect data on the student's progress in addition to data on IEP goal progress, just as general education teachers do. Data the special educators provide include:

- Academic achievement in the classroom
- Academic achievement via curriculum-based assessment
- IEP goal achievement
- Yearly reading assessments
- Yearly math assessments
- Social and emotional performance assessment

All data collected are reviewed with the student to guide future goals. The special education teachers are also the general education liaisons. They communicate the information they gather from other educators. Assessment forms can be used the compile the information for the team and the student. The role of special education teachers, as opposed to that of transition planning specialists, is to focus on students in their classrooms, and they are the academic specialists for the students they teach.

During transition, the transition planning specialist along with the special educator may meet together with the student to review credit acquisition and the course of study. If the student is in general education classes, then the special educator works with the student and the general education teacher to advance the student's success in the classroom; this information is shared with the transition planning specialist. Oftentimes, the special educator is instrumental in making adaptations and improvising in collaboration with the general education teacher and transition planning specialist to find alternate pathways to completing class requirements.

Role of the School Psychologist

School psychologists function in multiple roles. They meet with parents when more complex issues arise, such as when a student is suicidal or exhibits early signs of a serious mental health disorder. They also perform the district's evaluations to determine eligibility for special education. As part of the evaluation, they triangulate data sources to derive a diagnosis using multiple psychometric and academic assessment tools; standardized tests; student observation; and parent, student, and teacher questionnaires and interviews. They are trained in applied behavior analysis, can conduct functional behavioral assessments, and develop positive behavior plans to decrease problem behaviors and increase adaptive behaviors.

Their role in transition planning can be to attend parent meetings to discuss issues related to self-esteem and mental health. They also meet with families in need of clarity about supports for their child or their child's mental health status in the classroom. In addition, they play a crucial role by consulting with the transition team. In particular, this support is given and noted in the IEP to support special education teachers who work directly with the students.

MISSION STATEMENTS AND LEARNING COMMUNITIES

One way to advance the goals of the transition planning team is to create a transition mission statement. When secondary teams work together to create a mission statement, group compliance with that mission statement is more likely. As the team develops a transition mission statement, they work out viewpoint conflicts and develop a common approach to transition planning.

The Council for Exceptional Children has examples of mission statements that can guide the process specifically for transition planning. The Council for Exceptional Children also has transition standards to guide practice.

Creating a Learning Community

The special education supervisor, transition planning specialist, and general and special education teachers have a professional and legal responsibility to follow current research. Because research can be challenging to read and can be misconstrued, learning communities are forums where current research can be reviewed, discussed, and placed in the continuum of research in the field. Through meeting in learning communities, knowledge about current evidence-based practices relevant to students in the special education program can increase professional skills and eliminate professional stagnation. To address the search for and use of evidence-based practices, some administrators provide support for these forums and may participate in them as well. Learning forums are places where teachers get together to review research articles and professional publications about current trends in both special and general education. Because not everyone can interpret statistics, it can be helpful to have someone in the school assigned to answer questions about the data analysis. However, it is not always necessary to do that because reputable journals have already reviewed the article. Teachers can read the narrative sections, which can be easily understood.

Confidentiality

The transition team is responsible for confidentiality. The confidentiality of all students is to be protected. Students have the right to expect that when they give permission to be observed and interviewed, the special education team will preserve their anonymity (Glesne, 1999). Therefore, conferencing information must be kept in a confidential file. Personal family information is not written down.

A system of handling and storing the information from the conferences must be done procedurally, and storage in locking files is required. Storing private information on computer desktops and personal computer files is not conducive to protecting confidentiality.

Although most IEPs are written on the computer, they are typically done in platform-based IEP writer systems, which have security features. Therefore, the team must ensure that their practices do not unwittingly expose their student's personal communications to public scrutiny. Emailing any personal information or messages should also be avoided so as not to expose staff's or student's personal communications.

The Most Severely Impaired

For students whose disabilities prevent this level of interaction, the transition planning specialist will be involved with the family in helping develop a plan that will develop increased independence and communication of the student's needs and wants. The differences in cognitive and behavioral styles is discussed in the chapters on disabilities.

Whatever the impact of the disability, the transition team must facilitate the highest level of engagement and avoid entirely controlling the student's program; instead, they should develop the student's ability to be as self-determined as possible. Transition planning for the most severe intellectual disabilities is discussed in Chapter 15.

Transition Programs and Services: Major Challenges

Secondary school special education teachers are often diverted from the goals of transition planning by the demands of helping students with disabilities succeed in general education classes. For students with high-incidence disabilities, a number of hours each week are spent in resource rooms to help them keep up with their general education studies. When most of the special education teachers' time is spent in resource room activities, completing transition activities is difficult. However, school districts have some leeway with students who have IEPs, and they can design alternative programs that meet students' transition needs. The transition team will be called upon to develop programs that support inclusion in general education but also to create other avenues that support transition goals, such as after-school programs (e.g., career exploration) where students can earn credits toward graduation. Some students will have multiple issues to address.

Working in collaboration, the secondary special education team, special education supervisor, and central school administrators, including the superintendent, can develop transition planning and educational strategies that assist students to earn credits to graduate, learn social and work skills, and transition to work successfully. The special education team must address issues that prevent graduation for students with disabilities.

As mentioned, schools have a significant degree of latitude in programmatic decisions. Therefore, program development in special education can be a significant boost to graduation rates, a problem that has plagued special education since its inception.

Agency Involvement: Making Connections

The following case report is an example of how the Office of Vocational Rehabilitation (OVR) provided a post-school service that was essential to Declan's independence. In the following case report, the driving lessons began after graduation. The school district contacted to the OVR before graduation with the plan of implementing supports to Declan when he transitioned to adult services. Declan was also transitioned to adult services at a local agency funded under the Department of Health and Human Services, which also assisted him in accessing other mental health services since he had reached the age of majority.

Case Report: Declan

Declan has a mental health disorder. Upon placement in an emotional and behavioral disorder class in an alternative setting, he no longer spoke in the classroom and refused to attend school in the general education setting. His diagnoses were selective mutism and agoraphobia, and he heard voices of the nondirective type. His transition plan included learning to ask for assistance, going out in public, eating in public, talking to peers, and gaining independence skills. After a year in his emotional and behavioral disorder placement for non–acting-out students, he began to speak and was able to go out and do most typical activities. However, Declan was not making progress on getting his driver's license or taking driving lessons. Declan lived in a rural area, far from centers of employment. He needed support to transition to the workplace, and at the age of 18, the year of his graduation, he and his family had not been able to initiate private or family instruction for driving; however, they had secured a car. A number of months went by and there was no progress. Even with his family's urging, Declan was unable to take the driver's test, allow his parents to teach him, or in turn make attempts to complete these independence tasks, so the transition planning specialist notified the home school district that had responsibility for contacting the OVR, and a request for services was initiated. Declan's alternative school set up his registration for the driver's test, and studying for it became part of his school program.

Students in the program earned elective credits through transition seminars for independence skills, such as taking the driver's license test. Declan's included obtaining a license as part of his independence goals. Through the OVR, Declan received driving lessons and went on to interview successfully at a small rural restaurant, which he later went on to manage.

This is an example of how the transition planning specialist from his alternative school setting, the school district, and the OVR, collaborated to make Declan's transition to adulthood a success.

To be effective, a transition planning specialist understands the background and perspectives of the student. In Declan's situation, he, through meeting his needs, was able to go out into the world. Just prior to graduation the school district did push him to go to community college, but he did not finish. He later told his transition planning specialist he felt like a failure because he could not do it. So, although he felt good about what he was doing, going to college before he was ready was not advantageous to him. Sometimes we push values onto students when their own circumstances require a different approach.

OVERVIEW OF FEDERAL RESOURCES AND STRUCTURE

In the Student Supplemental Materials, there is a list of agencies and the supports they provide for transition planning. To effectively plan for the last 2 years of transition, contacts are set up during the 10th-grade year for students who plan to graduate in 12th grade. Agencies also provide case managers, called *supports coordinators*, for youth who are severely impaired, have moderate to profound intellectual disabilities, or have nonverbal autism and provide a plan to finalize transition by age 21. Secondary special education teams and the transition planning specialist need to have a working knowledge of the adult services organizations in the areas where their students reside. In the Student Supplemental Materials are some of the major government funded agencies and supports the team and administrators should be more than familiar with.

Self-Reflection Exercise

The following questionnaire is a reflective exercise to help special educators self-assess their current level of expertise.

Knowledge Self-Assessment

1. What is your overall understanding of adolescent development?
2. When did you last read a peer-reviewed article about adolescent development?
3. What steps will you take to update your knowledge about adolescent development?

Adolescent Identity Formation

1. What do you know about the development of adolescent identity?
2. What is the effect of self-determination on adolescent identity?

School Social Experiences for Adolescents With Disabilities

1. Do you believe students with disabilities should be provided after-school programs that provide supports for inclusion?
2. Do you know how many students with disabilities participate in after-school activities in your school?
3. Do you know if a wheelchair-accessible bus is provided for students with disabilities who would like to participate in after-school activities?
4. Do any students who are deaf attend your school?
5. What social experiences are available for them?

Previous Experiences

1. Have you ever given a student the opportunity to create an IEP goal?
2. Do you feel willing to let a student develop at least two goals?
3. Are you prepared to teach a student to be a member of the IEP team?

Perspectives on Employment

1. Do you believe college is the best career path?
2. Have you had any family members who have not attended college?
3. What do you think when a student says he or she does not want to go to college?
4. What do you know about opportunities in vocational and technical fields?
5. What do you know about lifelong learning?
6. Would you guide a student to post-school learning opportunities?
7. What do you know about post-school learning opportunities?

EXERCISES

Use the Student Supplemental Materials to answer these questions:

1. Describe the functions of the Office of Special Education.
2. Describe the functions of the Rehabilitative Services Administration.
3. Identify the acts that a student with a disability will need to know about to advocate for access.
4. What do you know about the Department of Health and Human Services?
5. How does this agency lead post-school services for students with disabilities?
6. What is the OVR? What type of student do they work with? Are there students who they do not serve? If not, explain.
7. Do you know where students with moderate to profound disabilities go after they age out of school programs?
8. What do you think about the provision of post-school services for persons with disabilities?

SUMMARY

This chapter discussed the roles and responsibilities of the special education supervisor, the transition planning specialist, the special education teachers, and community agencies. Together, they work to ensure the student receives care and attention to create a plan of transition. Each professional needs the others to provide resources, gather data, and develop student strengths through a carefully designed, supportive, and collaborative approach to one another and to the student. Everything a teacher says to a student resonates. Therefore, the secondary transition team crafts interactions so that the student becomes confident that the team can be trusted to help him or her with his or her plans. The development of successful plans includes attention to the attitudes of the school-based teams. The team's outcome-focused attitude, preparation, and follow-up are crucial for the student.

Many significant family problems are masked until the conferencing process begins. The act of ongoing conferencing helps students reveal and work through or around their roadblocks to graduation, employment, and post-school education and independence. The team's responsiveness to each student's challenges can help students create solutions to personal situations that may inhibit their success.

The secondary special education transition team process is a face-to-face cycle of interactions that underpin the construction of fruitful plans. Professional submission to the greater good of the student commits each team member to pull together to support the student to the next stage of life. As teams and community agencies work together, guiding students to plan or participate in the construction of their future, their dynamic interactions form the foundations of student success.

REFERENCES

Glesne, C. (1999). *Becoming qualitative researchers.* New York, NY: Longman.

Greville-Harris, M., Hempel, R., Karl, A., Dieppe, P., & Lynch, T. R. (2016). The power of invalidating communication: Receiving invalidating feedback predicts threat-related emotional, physiological, and social responses. *Journal of Social and Clinical Psychology, 35*(6), 471-493.

McFarland, J., Hussar, B., de Brey, C., Snyder, T., Wang, X., Wilkinson-Flicker, S., ... Hinz, S. (2017). Children and youth with disabilities. In *The condition of education 2017.* Washington, DC: National Center for Education Statistics, U.S. Department of Education. Retrieved from https://nces.ed.gov/programs/coe/pdf/Indicator_CGG/coe_cgg_2017_05.pdf

Porges, S. W. (1995). Orienting in a defensive world: Mammalian modifications of our evolutionary heritage. A Polyvagal Theory. *Psychophysiology, 32,* 301-318.

Porges, S. W. (2007). The Polyvagal Perspective. *Biological Psychology, 74,* 116-143.

Rae, J. M. (2011). Post Transition Planning–Young Adult Stories—Perspectives on School and Life: A Case Study of Employment, Social, Family and Mental Health Management Outcomes of Three Young Adults Who Completed Two or More Years of High School in an Emotional and Behavioral Special Education Program in Partial Hospitalization 1 Setting (Doctoral dissertation). Retrieved from Proquest. (3448164).

Rubin, H. J., & Rubin, I. S. (2005). *Qualitative interviewing: The art of hearing data* (2nd ed.). Thousand Oaks, CA: Sage Publications.

Stake, R. E. (1995). *The art of case study research.* Thousand Oaks, CA: Sage Publications.

Part 6

Special Considerations
Working With Diverse Groups of Students

Full, Supported, and Partial Participation in Transition Planning

The chapters in Part 6 discuss how eligible students can participate in transition planning. Each young person's disability and abilities have bearing upon what supports he or she will need in order to participate in the transition plan development. Instruction on how to participate, how to develop goals, and how to complete transition instructional activities. Each the student's level of participation, will vary depending on a number of variables. Despite students individual constraints and challenges, the transition planning specialist and special education team are charged with ensuring student participation in transition planning to the greatest extent.

Students will generally fall into three levels of transition planning participation: full participation, supported participation, and partial participation. These levels of participation are not predetermined levels where students are designated to each. The framework structure and the gates of transition provide a path for the transition planning specialist, the special education team, the student, and the parents to understand and engage in the process. Each disability is defined in its respective chapter, including the characteristics of disability that affect a student's ability to fully participate in each area of the framework of transition. Examples of the original and differentiated frameworks are provided as guidelines.

The levels of participation are meant as a guide to transition planning specialists and special education teachers working on transition planning teams to implement a wide range of supports so students can participate. The type of participation is not a fixed set of requirements based on disability.

High- and Low-Incidence Disabilities

This section has been added to clarify the use of the terms *high-incidence* and *low-incidence* disabilities, which often appear in discussions about students with disabilities. Disabilities are often described as low or high incidence. Deaf-blindness, visual impairments, orthopedic impairments, and hearing impairments have a very low incidence within the population of school-age students with disabilities, hence the name *low incidence*.

The others listed make up a much higher proportion of the total number of students with disabilities and include specific learning disabilities, speech and language impairments, emotional disturbance, and other health impairments. For instance, students with multiple disabilities have a significant number of disabilities. They are low incidence within the population of students with disabilities. They also are of low incidence within the group of students with intellectual disabilities who represent 6.1% of students in special education, whereas students with multiple disabilities represent 1.9% of students with intellectual disabilities.

Transition Planning Participation and the Dropout Rate

One of the purposes of transition planning is to redirect students with disabilities who may eventually drop out to positive post-school outcomes. The dropout rate among students with disabilities remains high. Two groups, students with emotional and behavioral disorders and those with specific learning disabilities, leave school at a much higher rate than their same-age peers. In 2012, the dropout rate for adolescents and youth with specific learning disabilities between 16 and 24 years old was roughly twice that of their peers without disabilities (14.4% vs. 6.3%, respectively; Cortiella & Horowitz, 2014).

The graduation rate for students with specific learning disabilities has been gradually rising for a decade, with 68% receiving a general high school diploma in 2011 vs. 57% a decade ago (Cortiella & Horowitz, 2014). However, it is well below the graduation rate of their nondisabled peers, indicating that more work needs to be done.

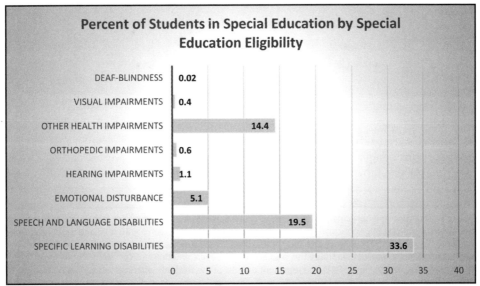

Figure P6-1. Percent of students in special education by special education eligibility. These students, when they do not have intellectual disabilities, will be full participants while receiving ongoing guidance and can complete all of the gates of the transition planning framework. (Source: Snyder, T. D., de Brey, C., & Dillow, S. A. [2019]. *Digest of Education Statistics 2017* [53rd ed.]. Washington, D.C.: National Center for Education Statistics.)

Further "statistics reveal that dropping out of high school is related to negative outcomes. For example, the median income of persons aged 18 through 67 who had not completed high school was roughly $25,000 in 2012. By comparison, the median income of persons aged 18 through 67 who had completed their education with at least a high school credential, including a General Educational Development certificate, was approximately $46,000" (Stark & Noel, 2015, p. 1). Among adults in the labor force, a higher percentage of dropouts are unemployed than are adults who earned a high school credential (McFarland, Cui, & Stark, 2018).

Students with specific learning disabilities are also disproportionately represented in the juvenile justice system, indicating additional needs for explicit instruction to establish positive social outcomes behaviors as part of transition planning. The graduation and employment of students with disabilities requires a commitment to transition planning to circumvent undesirable outcomes and to create better quality outcomes for these students. Engagement of students in transition planning leads to engagement in life.

PARTICIPATION IN TRANSITION PLANNING

In Figures P6-1 through P6-3 are the Individuals with Disabilities Education Act (2004) categories of disability. The three figures are provided to show how students can benefit from three ways to participate in transition planning: full participation, supported participation and partial participation. The students represented in Figure P6-1 will be able to fully participate in the continuum of activities for transition. They will be able to develop career vocabulary, learn to self-advocate, and become more self-determined; they will be able to increase social, academic, vocational, and independence skills. These eligible students will have average to gifted intellectual abilities, but many, because of the severity of their disabilities, have significant difficulty negotiating the steps to adulthood (see Figure P6-1). The following students can be taught to recognize danger and learn how to stay safe, with some individual exceptions that will be discussed in their respective chapters later in

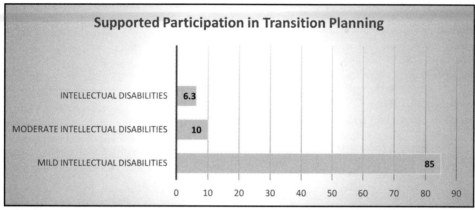

Figure P6-2. Supported participation. Students who can participate in the complete framework of transition but require significant supervision and assistance. This chart is about students with mild and moderate intellectual disabilities. Of students with intellectual disability, 85% have mild intellectual disabilities and 10% have moderate intellectual disabilities, and those with severe, multiple, and profound intellectual disabilities are shown in Figure P6-3 and represent the rest of the students with intellectual disability. (Source: Snyder, T. D., de Brey, C., & Dillow, S. A. [2019]. *Digest of Education Statistics 2017* [53rd ed.]. Washington, D.C.: National Center for Education Statistics.)

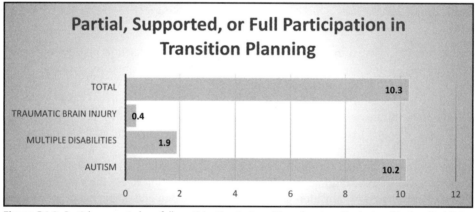

Figure P6-3. Partial, supported, or full participation in transition planning. Students with the disabilities represented here will need special assistance to be engaged in transition planning. Special education teams will use a supported or partial participation approach (see Chapter 15). Students with a traumatic brain injury may be able to fully understand the concepts. Students with autism without intellectual or language disabilities will be able to understand the concepts but will need significant support to successfully transition to post-school life. (Source: Snyder, T. D., de Brey, C., & Dillow, S. A. [2019]. *Digest of Education Statistics 2017* [53rd ed.]. Washington, D.C.: National Center for Education Statistics.)

the text. Some of these students may have other mild disabilities. They may or may not have various degrees of the following disabilities:

- Blindness or visual impairment
- Hearing impairments
- Hard of hearing, deaf, or hearing impaired
- Autism without intellectual or speech and language disabilities
- Attention-deficit disorder
- Inability to read or speak fluently
- Mild to severe mental health disorder
- Multiple mild disabilities

Although these disabilities range from mild to severe, these students can fully participate in the activities of transition.

Students with disabilities who are the most highly represented (i.e., high incidence) in special education have speech and language impairments and specific learning disabilities. Typically, unless they are deaf or cannot speak, they communicate verbally, and they are taught to go through the full continuum of transition activities with support for their learning, communication, or emotional needs. However, each student is unique in how they are affected by their disability, and no assumptions should be made by their disability category.

As the most highly represented students in special education, the size and general characteristics of the group lends itself to using a small-group transition curriculum and activities that are recommended in this text. Full participation in transition planning, including leading their Individualized Education Plan (IEP) meetings, is a goal that the students in this group complete using a series of conferences where the students interact with the transition planning specialist and often other members of the special education team and general education teachers who provide supports to assist them in reaching their goals.

Students who can participate with support in each gate or who may not be able to actively participate are listed by disability in Figure P6-2. This is not meant to confine any group to a list and be a way to carry out transition planning but rather to provide guidance to the transition planning specialist and special education team to avoid an all or none approach to transition planning.

Figure P6-2 includes students who have mild to moderate intellectual disabilities. Students with mild intellectual disabilities may appear to be like peers, whereas those with moderate intellectual disabilities often have characteristics indicative of a syndrome, but both have characteristics that make them vulnerable in the community (American Psychiatric Association, 2013). Socially, both groups have difficulties that are addressed during transition planning, especially for employment placement and community activities. These students can benefit from supported participation because they either need complete supervision to engage, as may be evident for students with moderate intellectual disabilities who have significant intellectual and adaptive skill needs.

Students with the most severe intellectual disabilities are represented in Figure P6-3. These students can be guided through transition planning using the partial participation model. The autism spectrum is indicated on two lists, and within the autism spectrum, the levels of participation can vary considerably. Therefore, students with autism without intellectual or speech and language disabilities, formerly called *Asperger's disorder*, may or may not be able to participate fully. The characteristics of autism and the variability within the spectrum are discussed in Chapters 13 and 16 to further address transition needs of these students.

Students with traumatic brain injury also have a wide range in the ability to participate fully, depending on the area of brain insult. Working with the student as an individual and consulting with knowledgeable professionals, the parents, and the student can best determine how the student wants to or can participate.

REFERENCES

American Psychiatric Association. (2013). *Diagnostic and statistical manual of mental disorders* (5th ed.). Washington, DC: American Psychiatric Association Publishing.

Cortiella, C., & Horowitz, S. H. (2014). *The state of learning disabilities: Facts, trends and emerging issues* (3rd ed.). New York, NY: National Center for Learning Disabilities.

Individuals with Disabilities Education Act of 2004, Pub. L. No. 108-446, 20 U.S.C. § 1400 *et seq.* (2004).

McFarland, J., Cui, J., & Stark, P. (2018). *Trends in High School Dropout and Completion Rates in the United States: 2014 (NCES 2018-117). U.S. Department of Education.* Washington, DC: National Center for Education Statistics.

Snyder, T. D., de Brey, C., & Dillow, S. A. (2019). *Digest of Education Statistics 2017* (53rd ed.). Washington, D.C.: National Center for Education Statistics.

Stark, P., & Noel, A. M. (2015). *Trends in high school dropout and completion rates in the United States: 1972–2012 (NCES 2015-015). U.S. Department of Education.* Washington, DC: National Center for Education Statistics. Retrieved from http://nces.ed.gov/pubsearch

Students With Specific Learning Disabilities and Speech and Language Impairments

CHAPTER OBJECTIVES

→ Identify the characteristics of specific learning disabilities.

→ Identify the characteristics of speech and language impairments.

→ Identify the impact of a disability on the learning process and post-school employment.

→ Identify and describe the possible forms of assistive technology that may be appropriate for post-school education.

→ Describe the dropout rate and post-school outcomes of students with specific learning disabilities.

SPECIFIC LEARNING DISABILITIES

Students who have specific learning disabilities or speech and language impairments are in the largest category of students receiving special education services. According to the National Center for Educational Statistics, approximately 2.3 million students have specific learning disabilities, and 1.3 million have speech impairments (Stark & Noel, 2015). Specific learning disabilities and speech and language impairments can vary from mild to severe and can originate from genetic and environmental causes. The following box describes the characteristics that define specific learning disabilities and speech and language impairments.

Rae, J. M. *A Collaborative Approach to Transition Planning for Students With Disabilities* (pp. 213-227).
© 2020 SLACK Incorporated.

§300.8 Child with a disability.

(10) Specific learning disability—(i) General. Specific learning disability means a disorder in one or more of the basic psychological processes involved in understanding or in using language, spoken or written, that may manifest itself in the imperfect ability to listen, think, speak, read, write, spell, or to do mathematical calculations, including conditions such as perceptual disabilities, brain injury, minimal brain dysfunction, dyslexia, and developmental aphasia.

(ii) Disorders not included. A specific learning disability does not include learning problems that are primarily the result of visual, hearing, or motor disabilities, of intellectual disability, of emotional disturbance, or of environmental, cultural, or economic disadvantage.

(11) Speech or language impairment means a communication disorder, such as stuttering, impaired articulation, a language impairment, or a voice impairment, that adversely affects a child's educational performance.

(§300.8 Child with a disability [71 FR 46753, Aug. 14, 2006, as amended at 72 FR 61306, Oct. 30, 2007; 82 FR 31912, July 11, 2017])

Specific learning disabilities and speech and language impairments become evident when a student does not achieve along the same developmental continuum as his or her same-age peers, even when the student has commensurate intellectual abilities. Despite the student's age, ability levels, and age-appropriate instruction, he or she demonstrates delays in one or more of the following areas, ranging from mild to severe:

- Expressive language
- Receptive language
- Auditory processing
- Written expression
- Age-appropriate reading
- Reading fluency
- Reading comprehension
- Spelling accuracy
- Mathematics calculations
- Arithmetic facts
- Mathematical reasoning (American Psychiatric Association, 2013)

When students demonstrate delays in reading acquisition and communication development, school professionals and certified assessment professionals use empirically based and age-appropriate formal and informal assessments to identify patterns of weakness in the areas listed previously. Further assessment is completed with a battery of psychometric tests, including an intelligence quotient test to rule out an intellectual disability. Sensory testing is scheduled by the parents, including advanced vision testing to rule out convergence disorders and hearing and auditory processing assessment via the school (administered by a qualified audiologist) to determine whether the student is processing entire words or parts of words. Upon completion of assessments, a complete battery of reading tests is used to delineate where the reading deficits lie to create specific areas to address in order to provide appropriate instruction. Assessment is only useful when it helps the student to understand his or her strengths and needs.

TYPES OF SPECIFIC LEARNING DISABILITIES

Dyslexia

Adolescents with dyslexia have a history of difficulty with accurate decoding, word recognition, and spelling despite adequate instruction and normal vision and hearing (Lyon, Shaywitz, & Shaywitz, 2003). Dyslexia describes a neurologically based dysfunction in the phoneme-sound connection, sound binding, word recognition, and reading comprehension. Reading is difficult to acquire and delayed beyond the expectations of age and intelligence.

Dyslexia is caused by multiple genetic and environmental risk factors, and several genes have been linked to dyslexia (Kaminen et al., 2003). The brain involvement in dyslexia is related to the left hemisphere, where reading and language are processed. Neuroimaging of the brains of people with specific learning disabilities indicate structural differences when compared with the brains of people without specific learning disabilities. For persons with dyslexia, underactivations are reported in two posterior left hemisphere regions: the temporoparietal region, an area that is crucial in language processing, and the occipitotemporal region, an area thought responsible for the whole word recognition (Raschle, Chang, & Gaab, 2011).

Specific environmental and heredity factors may increase children's risk for dyslexia or specific learning disabilities generally, and although there are some differences across languages and orthographies, there is also evidence for common underlying brain basis (Peterson & Pennington, 2015). Less is known about how the manifestation of dyslexia may vary across levels of socioeconomic status and ethnic/racial groups (Peterson & Pennington, 2015).

The neurocognitive causes of dyslexia are also multifactorial, and dyslexia is commonly comorbid with attention-deficit hyperactivity disorder (ADHD) and speech and language impairments. Evidence-based treatments for dyslexia emphasize intensive, explicit instruction in phoneme awareness, phonics, word analysis, reading fluency, and reading comprehension, and a growing number of intervention-imaging studies are investigating how remediation of dyslexia alters brain activity (Gabrieli, 2009). Effective remediation of reading problems in younger children is better established than in older children, and less is known overall about the successful treatment for reading fluency in older children. However, research on the development of receptive and expressive vocabulary in older students has had some promising results (Ebbers & Denton, 2008).

It is important to know that there is also a subset of children who do not respond well to existing interventions (Peterson & Pennington, 2015). These children need to have alternate means to learn subject matter, such as access to Bookshare, which provides books in electronic format to those who are dyslexic, blind, or visually impaired.

Dyscalculia

Dyscalculia is defined as persistent difficulty acquiring arithmetic facts and processing numerical information, and the deficits are not explained by low intelligence (American Psychiatric Association, 2013). Dyscalculia includes deficits in multiple mathematical abilities, reflecting a delay based on the student's age and education level.

Difficulties include counting mentally; seeing number patterns; performing mathematical operations; adding; subtracting; dividing; multiplying; and measuring area, shape, and size. Students with pure dyscalculia without dyslexia have problems within the right hemisphere. Children with dyscalculia lag behind their peers in mathematics performance, but otherwise, their general cognitive ability, reading, and writing skills are average or above average (Butterworth, 2005). In a study on families and students, Shalev and Gross-Tsur (2001) found a familial connection, with a significant number of siblings also having dyscalculia.

Many adolescents with dyscalculia have other cognitive dysfunctions, such as impaired working memory and visuospatial skills. Dyscalculia can be comorbid with dyslexia and ADHD (Kaufmann & von Aster, 2012).

Dysgraphia

Dysgraphia is a specific learning disability where students continue to have illegible handwriting, inconsistent spacing and spelling, missing and unfinished words, and difficulty copying or planning on paper despite instruction. Dysgraphia is also the inability to write coherently as a symptom of brain disease or damage. It causes significant emotional frustration for students, is negatively associated with academic functioning, and interferes with the ability to learn. Intervention studies attempting to remediate dysgraphia are few and report only small gains in letter shape but not speed or number legibility (Case-Smith, 2002).

Dysgraphia often persists despite proper instruction and practice (Smits-Engelsman & Van Galen, 1997). Although efforts to improve handwriting continue in school, dysgraphia is a neurologically based weakness that is resistant to remediation and is present at all ages (Mayes, Breaux, Calhoun, & Frye, 2019). Neuroimaging supports this view, and studies show dysgraphia is associated with acquired neurological damage and brain abnormalities (Berninger & Richards, 2010; Rapcsak et al., 2009).

To reduce frustration, schools should provide accommodations to circumvent and compensate for dysgraphia in order to improve academic success. Educational time and therapy should be in different time periods. When the goal in school is learning, producing text, and measuring knowledge (vs. writing per se), educators should teach to the student's strengths and not rely on the student's weak graphomotor skills to provide a learning activity.

Visual Perceptual/Visual Motor Deficit

Visual perceptual/visual motor deficits affect the understanding of information that a person sees or the ability to draw or copy. *The Diagnostic and Statistical Manual of Mental Disorders, Fifth Edition* (American Psychiatric Association, 2013) describes this as a developmental coordination disorder. In this disorder, multiple tasks requiring eye-hand coordination are difficult for the student, and these difficulties persist well after the developmental period. A characteristic seen in students with specific learning disabilities is subtle differences when the student draws shapes or prints letters. During reading, they will lose their place frequently; they struggle with cutting; they hold their pencil too tightly or have poor eye-hand coordination. They may also have problems with maintaining their position in space and appear clumsy and bang into things at times.

TYPES OF SPEECH AND LANGUAGE IMPAIRMENTS

Speech and language impairments are both classified as communication disorders. Speech impairments deal with the production of sound, and they cause difficulty pronouncing words fluently or intelligibly. They can be due to neurological or oral motor problems. Children and youth with language impairments have trouble understanding what people say or have difficulty expressing themselves. Causes of speech and language impairments vary from diagnosed medical problems to the unknown. It is possible for a person, adult or child, to have both conditions; the disorders range from mild to severe.

Speech Impairments

Speech impairments include articulation, voice, fluency, and motor-speech impairments (Hallahan & Kauffman, 1991). Articulation disorders occur at the phonemic level and are structural or motor based. One cause of articulation disorders is a cleft palate, which leads to incorrect tongue placement and apraxia of speech (a weakness or paralysis of the speech muscles). Other causes are biological and nerve factors (Hallahan & Kauffman, 1991; Rosenberg, Westling, & McLeskey, 2011).

Fluency disorders, also known as *stuttering*, are evident when there are a high number of repeating sounds or syllable repetitions and prolongations (Rosenberg et al., 2011). The flow of normal speech has some interruptions such as repetitions, speaking too quickly to be understood, reversing word order, pausing at wrong places, stumbling, or using inappropriate patterns of stress, but these examples do not point to a fluency disorder. However, when a speaker's persistent efforts cannot change the pattern of the interruptions or the flow of speech prevents the listener from understanding, then a disorder must be considered (Hallahan & Kauffman, 1991). A child who appears to have a stuttering problem should be evaluated by a speech-language pathologist. The student is less likely to experience problems with an early diagnosis. Persistent stuttering that goes untreated can result in a lifelong disorder, and unfortunately, many educators and physicians do not refer potential stutterers because they assume that stuttering is a normal part of speech and language development (Hallahan & Kauffman, 1991).

Voice disorders refer to how a voice sounds and focuses on the pitch, intensity (loudness or softness), and phonatory quality. A disorder can be determined if it differs significantly from the range of voices within the student' family or community.

Phonological errors, also known as *developmental speech sound disorder,* are a persistent difficulty with speech sound production. The errors interfere with speech intelligibility or prevent verbal communication that cannot be explained in terms of sensory problems, motoric difficulties, or other physical conditions. Phonological errors include systematic omissions, substitutions, or distortions of phonemes within words, despite being able to repeat these phonemes in isolation (Hayiou-Thomas, Carroll, Leavett, Hulme, & Snowling, 2017). It appears in early childhood in 3% to 6% of the population (Eadie et al., 2015).

The three types of phonological disorders are substitution, omission, and addition. In a substitution error, the speaker replaces one phoneme with another (e.g., the word *bear* becomes *tear*). With an omission error, the speaker deletes a phoneme (e.g., the speaker says *stai* instead of *stair*). In an addition error, the speaker adds an extra phoneme (e.g., instead of *stair,* the speaker may say *sta air*) (Rosenberg et al., 2011).

Children who have this disorder have trouble differentiating phonemes or sounds of language to construct words, causing a problem with emergent literacy, but if no other language problems are present, literacy will proceed (Hayiou-Thomas et al., 2017).

Oral-Motor Problems

Oral-motor problems include dysarthria, developmental apraxia, and acquired apraxia. Dysarthria is characterized by slow, labored, slurred, and imprecise speech (Hallahan & Kauffman, 1991). Sounds may not be able to be produced due to muscle weakness (Solomon, Makashay, Helou, & Clark, 2017). Developmental apraxia is a disorder of motor planning sequencing rather than weakness of the muscles (Botha et al., 2014). The use of the word developmental is a misnomer because it is not something that changes with development. The problem is not in receiving information, as the child can hear and understand the message. The problem originates in the brain. The brain does not adequately enable the child to respond to the message even though they know what to say. Acquired apraxia is similar but occurs because of brain damage or stroke. In apraxia, the speaker knows a mistake has been made, but he or she cannot correct it (Hallahan & Kauffman, 1991).

Voice Disorders

Voice disorders can be organic disorders caused by physical conditions that have affected the structure or function of the larynx. The growth of nodules, polyps, or cancerous tissues are examples. Neurological disorders can cause voice disorders as a result of nervous system dysfunction. Problems with the nervous system can include paralysis or weakness of the vocal cords or tremors. This disorder may also cause difficulty swallowing.

There are many causes of voice disorders: physical abnormalities, infections, or a failure to learn to speak appropriately.

Language Impairments

According to the *Diagnostic and Statistical Manual of Mental Disorders, Fifth Edition*, the core difficulties in language impairments are deficits in the comprehension of spoken language or the production of spoken language, conversational speech, or discourse (American Psychiatric Association, 2013). Deficits are also evident in written communication. The quantity and quality of spoken and written language are not age-equivalent and interfere with academic success.

Language impairments are disorders of knowledge and cognitive understanding of sounds that make up a word, change the meaning of a word, and determine how the word is used both in a sentence and in communication. Language impairments are also separated into primary language impairment, meaning no known cause, and secondary language impairment, caused by another condition. Speech impairments are heterogeneous. There are different types, degrees, and combinations (Hallahan & Kauffman, 1991). There are three types of language impairments, some of which can co-occur: form, content (semantics), and use (pragmatics).

A form disorder refers to phonology, morphology, and syntax. *Phonology* is the sounds of the language used to make the words. Phonemes are the smallest unit of sound that can affect word meaning. For example, the word mat is made up of three phonemes: m, a, t (Rosenberg et al., 2011). Morphology is the rules for constructing words and parts. For example, morphemes are the rules for constructing words and parts and their ascribed meanings. The meaning of the word *walk* changes when the ending changes: walk, walked, walking, walker. Syntax is the rules for connecting words together. He was *walking* with a *walker*.

A content disorder is a disorder of vocabulary and occurs when the speaker uses words that are not meaningful or are invalid. Use disorders relate to the social aspects of language and include conversational language. The speaker must understand how to engage with greetings, requests, commenting, taking turns, initiating conversations, and engaging in a wide range of other language uses in specific situations (Rosenberg et al., 2011). Language impairments can improve over time as a result of maturity, educational experiences, and speech-language intervention (Rosenberg et al., 2011).

READING, MATHEMATICS, AND LEARNING

As can be seen by the number and scope of learning, language, and speech disabilities, the way professionals think and communicate about these disabilities in their respective fields can lead to confusion for the families and students who receive therapy or instruction. The processes of learning to read, perform mathematical computations and problem solving, and learn subject matter are complex and difficult to describe. Adding to the confusion for parents and professionals is the lack of common terminology to discuss specific learning disabilities.

Currently, investigations into the identification and causes of disabilities and their remediation cross multiple fields of inquiry. For instance, although the U.S. National Library of Medicine, under the auspices of the National Institutes of Health, has current studies on specific learning disabilities, those studies use the terms *dyslexia, dyscalculia, dysgraphia,* and *dysarthria,* whereas states may have been reluctant to use those terms in evaluations and instead used terms like, a specific learning disability in math as indicated by a discrepancy between intellectual disability and expected grade-level performance. The American Psychiatric Association uses the word *disorder* rather than *disability.*

As discussed in Chapter 2, eligibility category definitions do not define the instructional needs of the student. When eligibility criteria are being used in the IEP to define present levels, it is more difficult for team members, including parents and general education teachers, to identify the deficit specifically. There is a lack of a common language to describe the details of the deficit, such as "Jon does not voice the sound of the *t* in the words like *mat, hat, bat.*" This type of specificity guides instruction for late readers. Also, addressing how they will learn when reading is not functional enough to learn subject matter is part of the remedial strategy.

The avoidance of specific terms and descriptions of deficits is not in conflict with the Individuals with Disabilities Education Act (2004). When it became a concern for parents, advocacy and disability groups from the U.S. Department of Special Education and Rehabilitative Services (Yudin, 2015) responded with a letter that clarified that the use of descriptive terms is permitted but, according to federal law, the decisions on what programs are used stays with the local education agency, which is the school district. Whatever terms used to describe the disability, the student and the parents should find them informative and a guide to helping the student to learn. When thinking about what parents want to know about their children's disabilities and the professional focus on the deficits that are deterring learning, example questions are provided below. Each of the students in the following prompts has been diagnosed with a specific learning disability in reading or math.

By secondary school, if reading is not productive for learning, reading for literacy and enjoyment is encouraged. Other means of learning content should be implemented. Parents should know what their child needs as should the transition planning specialist so that the student can receive the correct supports such as online learning, text to speech and speech to text technology.

By secondary school, if reading is not productive for learning, reading for literacy and enjoyment is encouraged. Other means of learning content should be implemented. Parents should know what their child needs as should the transition planning specialist so that the student can receive the correct supports, such as online learning, text to speech, and speech-to-text technology.

Prompt 1

- Special education teacher question: What are the possible connections between the speech delay and my student's literacy acquisition?
- Parent question: I was told that speech therapy would correct my child's speech problem, and it has, but now my child is reading at the second-grade level but is in sixth grade. Was there something else I could have done to help prepare my child to read? When will my child read?

Prompt 1 Exercises

1. Define the underlying concerns of the team members.
2. What immediate transition strategy will you begin?

Prompt 2

- Special education teacher and speech therapist question: My student is 12 years old now and getting ready for transition planning. Is this a hereditary condition, and how does that affect the student's prognosis?
- Parent question: My father never learned to read. Is this going to happen to my child? When will we know if my child will learn to read?

Prompt 2 Exercises

1. Given what you have learned, how will you describe this student's need and develop a transition plan for the student, who is 12 years old and cannot read?
2. How will you discuss this with the parents? What professionals will be involved?

Prompt 3

- Special education teacher question: One of my students, age 12, is not learning to read. What intensive programs are available, and how long should I continue to use the current program that my student has not benefitted from in 8 months?

- Parent question: My child has not learned in a new reading program for the past 8 months. What do I have to do to get a better program that will help her?

Prompt 3 Exercise

1. Given what you have learned about special education programs and services, how will you address the student's lack of progress with the special education team and the parents?

Prompt 4

- General education teacher question: My student is 13 years old. It is the end of sixth grade, and he is unable to multiply. He will not use the calculator and has stopped functioning in the group. The special education teacher has recommended we set up a positive behavior support plan, but I think it is not about rewards.
- Parent question: My son cannot multiply. Now he takes two math classes in the resource room working at his own level, but he still cannot remember a number of multiplication facts. In general education, the rest of the class is moving on to more difficult math. He says he cannot learn and is refusing to go to school. What do we do? We have begun bribing him to go, but he seems depressed.

Prompt 4 Exercises

1. Given the psychological overtones in this prompt and the math needs, how would you go about helping this student?
2. In each of these prompts, the student, who has a specific learning disability, is unable to participate or learn due to the effects of his or her specific learning disability. How will a student or educator describe the disability?

The purpose of this terminology discussion is threefold:

1. It promotes the use of a common language so that educators can communicate with their students.
2. Parents and the student need knowledge about themselves to advocate for services.
3. When educational practices do not result in learning, the language of the disability is used to defend the student against the continued use of ineffective practices and to ensure the student has tools to learn in another modality.

In order to decrease early school leaving, students and their parents must have access to and teachers must be knowledgeable about the most current and effective tools for reading acquisition. In American culture, when a child does not learn to read, he or she is going to have great difficulty during transition. The teachers, parents, and student need to know the root cause of the disability and how to meet learning, social, and employment needs that they will need throughout adulthood.

TRANSITION PLANNING

The Disability Narrative

As discussed in previous chapters, the disability narrative is the student's first foray into planning for inclusion in the IEP meeting. It is most likely the first time the student will describe what it is like for him or her to be a person with a disability.

The disability narrative gives the student a chance to share his or her preferences and needs and to be a collaborative member of the IEP team. It can be empowering for the student with specific learning disabilities to spend time in self-reflection about his or her learning experiences and how he or she learns currently.

Given the wide range of disabilities represented under the title *specific learning disabilities* and the difficulty in describing them specifically, it is vital for the student to begin to focus on the situations that are conducive to learning and those that are not. Understanding of the disability underpins goal development and self-determination. If the student knows his or her strengths and limitations in clearly defined terms, the student has a starting point to create future plans to use strengths and address his or her needs.

The disability narrative is a tool for change where the student with a specific learning disability can self-initiate the team's support in helping the student to reach his or her goals. The student needs to know if he or she has dyslexia and how the dyslexia is preventing learning. The student needs to understand disability to effectively advocate for learning tools.

Motivation and Engagement to Stay in School

As the transition planning specialist works with a student with specific learning disabilities, a question that is raised is: How has the disability and the student's perspective about the disability affected motivation to stay in school? For example, does the student want to continue learning, or is he or she thinking about dropping out? Students with specific learning disabilities have a concerning dropout rate, and a significant number of students with specific learning disabilities are in juvenile detention centers (Stark & Noel, 2015). Transition planning seeks to change these trajectories, so the transition planning specialist and secondary educators should be aware of the student's perspectives. Transition planning is meant to motivate students to develop visions and dreams for the future and provides funding and in- and out-of-school supports to enable students to access education, independence skills, and employment. Research shows that the transition team can help by giving feedback that can increase students' expectancy of success and task value (Brophy, 2010). Teachers initiate multiple interactions per day. However, this process is complicated for students with specific learning disabilities, who are far behind peers in performance. They benefit from a different approach for praise. Deci, Koestner, and Ryan (1999), in a meta-analysis of 128 studies using extrinsic rewards, found that a teacher's use of praise and extrinsic reward often led to increases in students' intrinsic motivation. Hattie and Timperley (2007) suggest that there are four types of feedback:

1. Feedback about the task
2. Feedback about the processing of the task
3. Feedback about self-regulation
4. Feedback about the self as a person

Use of feedback about the person is often used in general education classrooms, where the stellar work of one student is lauded. A student who has difficulty with sentence structure or even an average student will not benefit from comparative praise because he or she knows how the other student is performing in comparison to his or her own performance. Students with specific learning disabilities can distinguish how they perform in relation to peers. Using feedback about the task, the processing of the task, and the student's self-regulation provides a better platform for motivation. Motivating older students to stay in school and to strive toward their best performance requires direct feedback about the task, the process of the task, and self-regulation.

This type of feedback uses comments about the student's school and work habits to tell the student that he or she is making progress and making an effort. For instance, the following are utterances about the work. As simple as they are, they identify three things:

1. "I see you working." (Feedback about effort)
2. "I see you have 10 items correct." (Feedback about the process)
3. "I see you are finished." (Feedback to guide self-reward)

Using phrases like "great work" or other effusive pronouncements is subjective and does not necessarily inform the student with a specific learning disability that he or she is making progress. Statements about steps toward completion of tasks and comments on work completed are effort motivators.

The goal is for the student to become intrinsically motivated to make concerted efforts to complete assigned tasks. When the teacher is unavailable, the student needs to have a self-regulating motivational system in place to maintain motivation and effort. This process is essential for students with specific learning disabilities to develop productive work and school behaviors. As mentioned previously (Chapter 7), attendance, completion of tasks, and report cards that indicate educational participation and engagement are tools for the future. Often special education teachers help students develop these skills using direct instruction or comments on the task, rather than general comments that do not define the successful action.

Exercise

1. Use the following types of feedback to reward a student or a family member. Do not use any qualifiers such as "great job." When a job is done, simply say, "I see you are done" and refer to how the person feels about being done, not how you, the teacher, feel or think.

   a. Week 1: Track how often you must ask the student to stay on task and how many total students completed the task.

   b. Week 2: Implement the following and count how many times you redirected the student to tasks.

      i. Feedback about the task: "I see you started."

      ii. Feedback about the processing of the task: "I see you have gotten three done."

      iii. Feedback about self-regulation: "I see you are persisting to complete that assignment."

   c. Describe your observations about student productivity.

The transition planning specialist would use this same type of feedback system on the activities of transition. It is the process that is the important work. As the students go through the transition activities, they should become more self-regulating, and the team should use strategies for all students that assist them to develop characteristics that improve their overall functioning and abilities.

Learning, Self-Regulation, and Motivation

Self-regulation is the process students must use to monitor or keep track of their own learning and completion of tasks. Most often, self-regulation strategies will emerge from transition goal setting and completion. Self-regulation occurs as students do the following activities (Reid, Lienemann, & Hagaman, 2013):

1. Set their own learning and performance goals.

2. Track the completion of their behavior and/or performance on goals.

3. Monitor their success through self-evaluation.

4. Develop a system of self-talk to help them self-regulate and direct learning, such as by asking themselves what they need to do next, when to check their calendars, and how to use technology to meet their goals.

5. Set up a system to reward themselves for completing tasks or steps in a group of tasks.

Parental Involvement and Motivation

When a student with a specific learning disability enters the 10th grade, parents and the transition planning specialist become actively involved in working with the student, who is narrowing down options for career training, entry-level employment, and college. Between 10th and 11th grade, the student will go through multiple changes and may become more settled in his or her approach to planning for post-school life. If the student has gone through the activities outlined in the framework and met with the transition planning specialist in his or her conferences, the collaborative relationship should be well established.

Parents, if there are no barriers, will begin to spend some time talking with the transition plan-ning specialist and their child about the logistics of looking at options. If the student plans to attend a training program post-high school, the parents should be involved and visit community colleges or training programs that may be farther away.

There are multiple colleges that have extensive supports for students with specific learning dis-abilities. They are places that have tutoring, student groups, and specialists. These are different from colleges that only have an Office of Disability. Many of these colleges are reasonably priced and have financial aid. Costs of these programs should be reviewed, and a preliminary discussion about how costs can be covered is a positive step in adult responsibility.

Although their child may be trying to assert their independence, the parents' attention to their child's studies, attendance, and future goals is necessary for graduation. Students with disabilities tend to have twice the absences as their typical peer (Wagner, Newman, Cameto, & Levine, 2005). This practice needs correction, and the reason for avoidance needs to be addressed so avoidance does not become a coping skill. Parents and the school can work together with the student to promote pro-work skills such as attendance. Research supports that increased parent involvement translates to higher attendance and graduation rates for students (Landmark, Zhang, & Montoya, 2007).

By 10th grade, the parents and the student should be attending the IEP meeting, and there is no bona fide reason why this research-based practice should not be well established. Barriers to imple-menting this practice need to be addressed. Despite legislation and policies that encourage collabora-tion with the parent and student, parent and youth attendance in IEP meetings may not occur when school personnel do not view parents as equals (Park, 2008). This may indicate that school teams may not take the step of establishing a collaborative team for transition planning.

Students with specific learning disabilities benefit significantly from involvement and under-standing of how to participate and even lead the IEP meeting. Making the student a leader in the IEP meeting also has some history of being ignored (Martin, Marshall, & Sale, 2004). However, it is the transition planning specialist's responsibility to avoid this pitfall, especially with students in this high-risk group. Further, the barriers to school support for student involvement include lack of training or preparation for students to practice self-advocacy prior to the IEP or transition meet-ing (Wehmeyer et al., 2011). Therefore, adequate time must be given prior to the meeting. As stated previously, because students with specific learning disabilities are the largest population of students in special education and the group with the highest dropout and unemployment rates, they are also the students who can fully participate in all the activities of transition planning and are ideally suited to reap the benefits of full access to a life where they can find a satisfactory and rewarding lifestyle.

Parents' participation in a training with their child prior to the IEP meeting via a web-based conferencing system can help remove pre-meeting nervousness. Use of technology such as Skype (Microsoft), FaceTime (Apple Inc.), and similar programs can prove useful in synchronizing practice meetings when parents cannot attend meetings in person (Cavendish & Connor, 2018). With the support of parents, the transition planning specialist, and the secondary special education team, this time of life can be a positive time for the student.

Students with specific learning disabilities are able individuals with learning difficulties. However, they need guidance and patience; explicit instruction on the pitfalls of poor choices; the tools to help them learn; and support to guide them into positive social, vocational, career, and educational experiences.

Disability Documentation

Documentation of a disability is needed in a number of circumstances. The following name a few. Students who are going to need the support of the Office of Vocational Rehabilitation (OVR) will require documentation of their disability. If the family is seeking support, such as Medicaid, Social

Security or placement in a supported apartment setting, they also need documentation. When a student is going to college, they are required to provide documentation to access assistance from the Office of Disability and any scholarships based on a disability. Documentation of household income includes the following information:

- Tax return
- W2
- Pay stubs
- If the student receives Social Security Income or Social Security Disability Income, a copy of the award letter or monthly benefit statement is required.

OVR (see Student Supplemental Materials for the agencies title by state) provides diagnostic and evaluation services, vocational counseling and guidance, rehabilitation teaching, orientation and mobility training, and job placement assistance are always provided regardless of the student's and/ or family's income.

If a student received a monetary settlement because the disability is the result of negligence, the settlement may be charged based on a financial needs test to determine the extent the student's funds contribute toward the cost of certain OVR services and college. These services will be outlined in the Individual Employment Plan and are provided to the college.

If the student is asking for testing accommodations for college entrance exams, the following information needs to be submitted:

- Existence of an impairment
- Diagnosis of the disability and its impact on functioning
- Rationale or why the accommodations are being requested
- Documentation of accommodations granted in the past

To receive services, the student should keep his or her diagnosis up to date on a yearly basis, including having a secure place to keep disability documentation. After the student submits the documentation, he or she will be approved or denied, or there will be a request for more information. Denial is typically based on incomplete information.

Education

Students with specific learning disabilities can be lifelong learners. Through the use of assistive technology and social strategies, language and learning can be continued, and other means of acquiring knowledge can be a regular part of high school and post-school life. High-interest, age-appropriate books and magazines with instructional vocabulary are available. Some educational magazine companies sell monthly and bimonthly magazines on a wide range of topics. The magazines are professionally produced, include current events, and provide content at the young adult level. An ongoing effort to expand vocabulary and increase literacy includes small-group discussion, which has been shown to increase expressive and receptive vocabulary. When attending post-school education, the student should know how to buy online texts and be able to download them onto a device that provides text-to-speech technology. Text-to-speech programs have a pause feature that allows the student to review what they missed. Most programs have a feature that will slow the speed of the speech to suit the needs of the student who may benefit from increased or decreased speed in order to comprehend the spoken word. Multiple tools for educating oneself support the student during transition and beyond.

Expressive and Receptive Vocabulary

Students with specific learning disabilities have a unique capacity to participate in programs that develop receptive and expressive vocabulary to an advanced degree. Attention to interactive discussions about word meaning in small groups and ongoing assessment can demonstrate growth in these areas.

Developing receptive vocabulary is also crucial to inferring meaning from texts. Continuing to work on receptive vocabulary primes the student for better word identification and comprehension when more advanced vocabulary has already been developed. Activities where students can discuss topics using teacher-selected prompts can perform the same function as the use of pre-teaching (Coulter & Lambert, 2015).

Learning Tools and Technology

Learning tools are essential to giving delayed or nonreaders access to reading. Therefore, ongoing attention to the provision of tools that help students learn is essential to best practice. The following are used to help students with disabilities speed up their learning. Because the reading process is often slow and labored, other means of access are necessary to keep these young persons at an age-appropriate level conversationally:

- Reading: Assistive technology enlarged print
- Bookshare: Translates textbooks to speech
- Project Gutenberg: Classic books in digital format can be read with text-to-speech apps. These are especially important when general education students are reading the classics. Students with specific learning disabilities miss valuable social and classroom opportunities when their reading speed and fluency disables them from moving through the readings along with their peers.
- Text-to-speech software
- Speech-to-text software
- Screen-reading software
- Audiobooks
- Portable word processors
- Auditory word processing software
- Word prediction programs
- Graphical word processors
- Onscreen keyboards
- Voice recognition software
- Organizational/outlining programs
- Online writing support

Establishing a consistent plan of technology use should be part of the transition plan for students with specific learning disabilities. A list of colleges that provide special programs for students with specific learning disabilities is available in the Student Supplemental Materials. The transition planning specialist and special education team should be knowledgeable about colleges that provide support to these students.

EXERCISES

1. Research five agencies that support students with learning disabilities. Identify the services they provide, how they provide them, and how they help the students to succeed.
2. Explain why is it essential that students with a specific learning disability have alternative ways to learn.
3. Give examples of how disabilities may effect job performance.
4. Work with a group and create a PowerPoint presentation about all of the learning and technology tools listed in the previous section.

SUMMARY

This chapter discusses students with specific learning disabilities, speech and language impairments, and the impact of disability on learning and communication. Students with specific learning disabilities have multiple challenges as they reach transition age. They must continue to struggle to improve their reading and/or math level while simultaneously trying to complete subject matter easily accessible to same-age peers.

Students with specific learning disabilities benefit from understanding the basis of their disabilities. In order to participate in their IEP meetings and advocate for themselves, they need to use the recognized names of their disabilities. They will need to keep documentation to access services and receive accommodations in the workplace and in college. Therefore, clearly identifying the nature of their disability and its impact on their independence and learning is important to their self-advocacy efforts.

Students with specific learning disabilities can participate fully in all of the activities of transition described in this text. Given the high dropout rate, low wages associated with dropping out, high rate of placement in juvenile detention centers, and high unemployment levels, students with specific learning disabilities need a well-planned intensive process of transition planning.

There are many college programs that assist students with disabilities. Careful review of these programs during middle school can facilitate dreams of success for a young person with specific learning disabilities. Early attention to career, vocational, and post-school education can lead to employment and advancement.

REFERENCES

American Psychiatric Association. (2013). *Diagnostic and statistical manual of mental disorders* (5th ed.). Washington, DC: American Psychiatric Association Publishing.

Berninger, V., & Richards, T. (2010). Inter-relationships among behavioral markers, genes, brain and treatment in dyslexia and dysgraphia. *Future Neurology, 5,* 597-617.

Botha, H., Duffy, J. R., Strand, E. A., Machulda, M. M., Whitwell, J. L., & Josephs, K. A. (2014). Nonverbal oral apraxia in primary progressive aphasia and apraxia of speech. *Neurology, 82*(19), 1729-1735.

Brophy, J. (2010). *Motivating students to learn.* New York, NY: Routledge.

Butterworth, B. (2005). The development of arithmetical abilities. *Journal of Child Psychology and Psychiatry, and Allied Disciplines, 46*(1), 3-18.

Case-Smith, J. (2002). Effectiveness of school-based occupational therapy intervention on handwriting. *American Journal of Occupational Therapy, 56,* 17-25.

Cavendish, W., & Connor, D. (2018). Toward authentic IEPs and transition plans: Student, parent, and teacher perspectives. *Learning Disability Quarterly, 41*(1), 32-43.

Child with a disability, 34 C.F.R. § 300.8 (2017).

Coulter, G. A., & Lambert, M. C. (2015). Access to general education curriculum: The effect of preteaching key words upon fluency and accuracy in expository text. *Learning Disability Quarterly, 38*(4), 248-256.

Deci, E. L., Koestner, R., & Ryan, R. M. (1999). A meta-analytic review of experiments examining the effects of extrinsic rewards on intrinsic motivation. *Psychological Bulletin, 125*(6), 627-668.

Eadie, P., Morgan, A., Ukoumunne, O. C., Ttofari Eecen, K., Wake, M., & Reilly, S. (2015). Speech sound disorder at 4 years: Prevalence, comorbidities, and predictors in a community cohort of children. *Developmental Medicine and Child Neurology, 57,* 578-584.

Ebbers, S. M., & Denton, C. A. (2008). A root awakening: Vocabulary instruction for older students with reading difficulties. *Learning Disabilities Research & Practice, 23*(2), 90-102.

Gabrieli, J. D. (2009). Dyslexia: A new synergy between education and cognitive neuroscience. *Science, 325*(5938), 280-283.

Hallahan, D. P., & Kauffman, J. M. (1991). *Exceptional children: Introduction to special education.* Boston, MA: Allyn & Bacon.

Hattie, J., & Timperley, H. (2007). The power of feedback. *Review of Educational Research, 77*(1), 81-112.

Hayiou-Thomas, M. E., Carroll, J. M., Leavett, R., Hulme, C., & Snowling, M. J. (2017). When does speech sound disorder matter for literacy? The role of disordered speech errors, co-occurring language impairment and family risk of dyslexia. *Journal of Child Psychology and Psychiatry, and Allied Disciplines, 58*(2), 197-205.

Individuals with Disabilities Education Act of 2004, Pub. L. No. 108-446, 20 U.S.C. § 1400 *et seq.* (2004).

Kaminen, N., Hannula-Jouppi, K., Kestilä, M., Lahermo, P., Muller, K., Kaaranen, M., ... Kere, J. (2003). A genome scan for developmental dyslexia confirms linkage to chromosome 2p11 and suggests a new locus on 7q32. *Journal of Medical Genetics, 40*(5), 340-345.

Kaufmann, L., & von Aster, M. (2012). The diagnosis and management of dyscalculia. *Deutsches Ärzteblatt International, 109*(45), 767-778.

Landmark, L. J., Zhang, D. D., & Montoya, L. (2007). Culturally diverse parents' experiences in their children's transition: Knowledge and involvement. *Career Development and Transition for Exceptional Individuals, 30*(2), 68-79.

Lyon, G. R., Shaywitz, S. E., & Shaywitz, B. A. (2003). A definition of dyslexia. *Annals of Dyslexia, 53*(1), 1-14.

Martin, J. E., Marshall, L. H., & Sale, P. (2004). A 3-year study of middle, junior high, and high school IEP meetings. *Exceptional Children, 70,* 285-297.

Mayes, S. D., Breaux, R. P., Calhoun, S. L., & Frye, S. S. (2019). High prevalence of dysgraphia in elementary through high school students with ADHD and autism. *Journal of Attention Disorders, 23*(8), 787-796. doi:10.1177/1087054717720721

Park, Y. (2008). Transition services for high school students with disabilities: Perspectives of special education teachers. *Exceptionality Education International, 18*(3), 95-111.

Peterson, R. L., & Pennington, B. F. (2015). Developmental dyslexia. *Annual Review of Clinical Psychology, 11,* 283-307.

Rapcsak, S. Z., Beeson, P. M., Henry, M. L., Leyden, A., Kim, E., Rising, K., ... Cho, H. (2009). Phonological dyslexia and dysgraphia: Cognitive mechanisms and neural substrates. *Cortex, 45*(5), 575-591.

Raschle, N. M., Chang, M., & Gaab, N. (2011). Structural brain alterations associated with dyslexia predate reading onset. *NeuroImage, 57*(3), 742-749.

Reid, R., Lienemann, T. O., & Hagaman, J. L. (2013). *Strategy instruction for students with learning disabilities.* New York, NY: Guilford Press.

Rosenberg, M. S., Westling, D. L., & McLeskey, J. (2011). *Special education for today's teachers: An introduction* (2nd ed.). New York, NY: Pearson.

Shalev, R. S., & Gross-Tsur, V. (2001). Developmental dyscalculia. *Pediatric Neurology, 24*(5), 337-342.

Smits-Engelsman, B. C. M., & Van Galen, G. P. (1997). Dysgraphia in children: Lasting psychomotor deficiency or transient developmental delay? *Journal of Experimental Child Psychology, 67*(2), 164-184.

Solomon, N. P., Makashay, M. J., Helou, L. B., & Clark, H. M. (2017). Neurogenic orofacial weakness and speech in adults with dysarthria. *American Journal of Speech-Language Pathology, 26*(3), 951-960.

Stark, P., & Noel, A. M. (2015). Trends in high school dropout and completion rates in the United States: 1972-2012. NCES Compendium Report 2015-015. Washington, DC: U.S. Department of Education, National Center for Education Statistics. Retrieved from https://nces.ed.gov/pubs2015/2015015.pdf

Wagner, M., Newman, L., Cameto, R., & Levine, P. (2005). Changes over Time in the Early Postschool Outcomes of Youth with Disabilities. A Report of Findings from the National Longitudinal Transition Study (NLTS) and the National Longitudinal Transition Study-2 (NLTS2). Retrieved from https://nlts2.sri.com/reports/2005_06/nlts2_report_2005_06_execsum.pdf

Wehmeyer, M. L., Palmer, S. B., Williams-Diehm, K., Shogren, K. A., Davies, D. K., & Stock, S. (2011). Technology and self-determination in transition planning: The impact of technology use in transition planning on student self-determination. *Journal of Special Education Technology, 26*(1), 13-24.

Yudin, M. K. (2015). Guidance on dyslexia. United States Department of Education. Retrieved from https://www2.ed.gov/policy/speced/guid/idea/memosdcltrs/guidance-on-dyslexia-10-2015.pdf

Students With Emotional, Behavioral, and Severe Mental Health Disorders

STUDENTS WITH MENTAL HEALTH DISORDERS AND BEHAVIORAL CHALLENGES

Adolescents, who under the Individuals with Disabilities Education Act (IDEA), are eligible for special education under a category called *emotional disturbance* and are typically in the normal to gifted range of intelligence. However, students with mild intellectual disabilities and conduct

Rae, J. M. *A Collaborative Approach to Transition Planning for Students With Disabilities* (pp. 229-254).
© 2020 SLACK Incorporated.

problems are often placed in these programs as well. In addition, mental health disorders can be present with any disability. For the purpose of this chapter, the discussion is centered around students with mental health disorders.

The label of emotional disturbance, used by IDEA, is problematic for students with these disabilities. These students, like the community at large, view emotional disturbance in a variety of negative ways. Students categorized with this label are aware of their diagnostic label, as are adults. Stigma from the community arises from this label and shame and self-stigma become part of the students everyday perspective of themselves (Walker, Geddes, Lever, Andrews, & Weist, 2010).

Although the term *mental retardation* was changed to *intellectual disability* because of its derogatory connotations, as of this book's writing, the label emotional disturbance has not been changed to a less stigmatizing term. Nor has it been further refined to reflect students with mental health disorders that do not stem from an emotional trauma, nor those students with volatile behaviors.

Although the special education program label and the student diagnostic label are not publicly shared in the school buildings, the faculty and the administration know the designation. Therefore, these students come to school with a psychological burden and must wrestle with perceptions of themselves, the teachers, and, if the secret is revealed, their peers. In addition, as they become older concerns about the perspectives of their peers become more prominent and their placement, if in a single classroom all day, marks them as different. Fortunately the practice of secluding students with this label in self-contained classes in remote areas of the school is changing.

The following box includes the description of the IDEA eligibility criteria under the label of emotional disturbance.

§300.8 Child with a disability.

(4)(i) Emotional disturbance means a condition exhibiting one or more of the following characteristics over a long period of time and to a marked degree that adversely affects a child's educational performance:

(4a) An inability to learn that cannot be explained by intellectual, sensory, or health factors.

(4b) An inability to build or maintain satisfactory interpersonal relationships with peers and teachers.

(4c) Inappropriate types of behavior or feelings under normal circumstances.

(4d) A general pervasive mood of unhappiness or depression.

(4e) A tendency to develop physical symptoms or fears associated with personal or school problems.

(4f) Emotional disturbance includes schizophrenia. The term does not apply to children who are socially maladjusted unless it is determined that they have an emotional disturbance under paragraph (c)(4)(i) of this section.

(§300.8 Child with a disability [71 FR 46753, Aug. 14, 2006, as amended at 72 FR 61306, Oct. 30, 2007; 82 FR 31912, July 11, 2017])

Characteristics and Criteria of Students With Emotional Disturbances and Behavioral Disorders

Special education eligibility under emotional disturbance means a condition exhibiting one or more of the following characteristics "over a long period" and to a marked degree that adversely affects a child's educational performance.

These criteria for special education eligibility primarily focus on behaviors and feelings that are part of the diagnostic profile for a youth with a mental health disorder. In two sections, depression and schizophrenia are noted explicitly. There is no indication in this description of any aggressive behaviors. All of the behaviors noted adversely affect the child's educational performance to such an extent that they are eligible for special education, related services, and at times 504 plans.

Despite IDEA's clearly referenced criteria, many classes for students classified under emotional disturbance have been used to place students with conduct disorders, which include aggressive and disruptive behaviors that do not stem from a mental illness. For the most aggressive students who participate in ongoing stealing, lying, bullying, and other socially unacceptable behaviors, help is indeed warranted, but not necessarily in an emotional disturbance program.

Aggressive behaviors can arise from schizophrenia and paranoid schizophrenia. Bipolar disorder combined with alcohol and drug abuse is of concern when they instigate aggression. However, the aggression arises from symptoms of the illness or duress as opposed to personality disorders or conduct disorders, such as oppositional behavior unrelated to another diagnostic category.

The diagnostic criteria for mental health disorders require observations and data collection over time. Students with these disorders are under considerable duress as they try to manage their difficult-to-understand symptoms alone. Typically, schoolwork suffers and failure begins well before a diagnosis is made. These signs are visible to their teachers, who can look at these behaviors as indicators to a much deeper problem. Although teachers are the primary persons to refer students, referral is not the end of the teacher's role. Engaging with students in a positive manner and meeting with the school psychologist underpins better outcomes.

In the next sections mental health disorders are described. Each section is by no means meant to encourage general education teachers, special education teachers, or transition planning specialists to give or suppose a diagnosis. A licensed psychologist or psychiatrist is a person who is highly qualified to diagnose; psychologists and psychiatrists work within the confines of their profession as do teachers. It is, however, important for teachers to know that some behaviors should be referred to the school psychologist and student assistance teams because behavioral changes possibly related to mental health, left unaddressed, can be detrimental or even devastating for the student.

Through observations and interactions, teachers play an ongoing role in collecting observational information, student self-reports (e.g., suicidal thoughts), and when appropriate, student writing assignments to provide immediate notice and information for referrals to school-based student assistance teams. Once parents are alerted, the student will be involved in meetings to address his or her needs, including having an on site counselor and a 504 plan to help the student. Moreover, after a student is diagnosed, the special education team better serves in the collaborative team format in consult with the student, counselors, and school psychologists via daily contact during class and during transition planning conferences, whether through an IEP or a 504 plan.

To facilitate self-determination, the special education team must include the student in meetings in which he or she is the subject of discussion, particularly when it is about the student's mental health disorders. Self-determination is not just about the student's Individualized Education Plan (IEP) and transition plan. Allowing the student to be self-determined also includes the student's perspectives and skills in managing his or her mental health care and taking responsibility for him- or herself and any behavior related to a mental health disorder to the greatest degree possible. Every state has rules about the student's control of mental health information and treatment; some of which was addressed in Chapter 1. Teams involved should personally read that information and avoid relying on second-hand information. School districts can train staff regarding the state guidelines.

Emergence of Mental Health Disorders

Teachers and parents are typically the first to see changes in the child, whether in middle or high school or in general or special education classes. Some changes develop gradually, and some develop dramatically. The emergence of mental health disorders occurs very early in life. Half of all lifetime cases begin by age 14, and three-quarters of cases have begun by age 24 (Kessler, Berglund, Demler, Jin, & Walters, 2005), a period corresponding to the transition to adulthood. Early emergence is particularly significant given the inability of a young adolescent to recognize and seek treatment for a mental health disorder (Kazdin, 1997).

Studies reveal that anxiety disorders often begin in late childhood, mood disorders in late adolescence, and substance abuse in the early 20s. However, anxiety disorders, such as selective mutism, are seen by kindergarten. Young people with mental health disorders experience this disability when they are in the prime of life, a time when they would normally be the most productive (Kessler et al., 2005; Kessler & Wang, 2008; Paus, Keshavan, & Giedd, 2008). Thus, mental health disorders are a chronic disease of the young (New Freedom Commission on Mental Health, 2005).

Symptoms and Educational Attainment

Multiple symptoms of mental health disorders can interfere with educational attainment. The symptoms include problems with nighttime sleep; evening and nighttime psychomotor agitation; lack of sustained attention, hyperactivity, and active alerting mechanism; impulsiveness, poor social interactions, and emotionally labile responses; pervasive feelings of hopelessness; and negative feelings about their ability to participate (Beck, Wenzel, Riskind, Brown, & Steer, 2006; Brozina & Abela, 2006). Affective disorders, such as bipolar disorders, anxiety disorders, and/or depressive disorders, may impair an adolescent's ability to sustain such productive activities as school-related tasks. Those with anxiety disorders often struggle with the diversion of their attention from how to best proceed to overwhelming concerns of failure and mishap (Bandura, 1982). Anxiety related to social phobia affects the social interactions necessary to perform academic tasks in groups and to form and sustain friendships (American Psychiatric Association, 2013). Bipolar I and II disorders and related depression interfere with an adolescent's ability to sleep as do periods of high (manic) or hypomanic activity and agitation (American Psychiatric Association, 2013). Poor sleep interferes with the alertness required for academic success. Further confounding referral, normal mood and behavior can appear between depressive and manic episodes. Also, negative predictions about their ability to manage social and educational tasks, related to low mood, depression, and major depression, affect a student's school performance (Beck et al., 2006). Symptoms of mental health disorders cause an unstable pattern of school performance as the bipolar symptoms start, escalate, decline, and stabilize. In bipolar II, the upward positive behavior happens more frequently, followed by longer periods of depression and accompanying suicidal thoughts. An adolescent's capacity to function academically is diminished, including the inability to complete school requirements on a consistent basis or on time.

Many students whose illnesses emerge in high school are hospitalized on a short-term basis to implement a plan for medication and to stabilize the young person after a suicide attempt or psychotic or bipolar I manic episode. Students who need hospitalizations or partial hospital programs often miss a significant amount of class and can fall far behind in school. Many do not want to reveal their illness due to stigma because they do not want to have this disability, and in the early phases, they may see it as a temporary aberration. When facing these emergent disorders, the need for ongoing treatment, such as medication and counseling, to adjust to the change in life course and medication monitoring and the associated stigma of mental illness are barriers to treatment and pose treatment challenges.

Treatment Stigma

The inability of significant others to recognize behavior changes as mental illness signs, as well as family and adolescent feelings about stigma, can have serious consequences for educational, social, and employment outcomes for the adolescent. The seriousness of the personal and social effects of mental health disorders has been established. In 1999, a study by Link, Phelan, Bresnahan, Stueve, and Pescosolido suggested that there has been some improvement in the way the public perceives mental health disorders. However, the stigma still surrounds these disorders, and more work needs to be done to alleviate this perspective (Corrigan, Larson, & Rüsch, 2009; Corrigan, Druss, & Perlick, 2014). Self-stigma, or negative beliefs about oneself because of mental illness, causes several problems such as harm to a person's sense of self-esteem and efficacy (Livingston & Boyd, 2010). Mental health disorder categories carry stigma, and research indicates that persons with mental health disabilities do not seek out mental health services so as to avoid stigmatizing labels (Corrigan et al., 2014). Clement et al. (2015) also assert that label avoidance, the phenomenon that people opt not to engage in treatment to escape the stigma commensurate with diagnosis and labels, leads to lack of treatment. In a 2015 study of college-aged students, Jennings et al. concluded that when there are negative perceptions toward seeking help by an individual's significant other, the individual with a mental health disorder may "endorse similar stigmatizing beliefs toward themselves, and subsequently prefer handling problems on their own rather than seek treatment" (p. 113). Mental illness in contemporary society continues to be plagued by social stigma (Corrigan et al., 2014), even though most people will, at some point in their developmental trajectory, experience mental distress severe enough to qualify as a diagnosable mental illness. Another challenge to treatment is the shortage of psychiatrists to treat children and youth who require medication (Gabel & Sarvet, 2011).

To help students recognize and seek treatment, the age of majority for mental health treatment was changed to prior to age 18, with one state going as low as age 12. This change was meant to improve help seeking and treatment. Parental fear of stigma was a roadblock to treatment. To resolve this and remove the variable of parental stigma interfering with treatment, mental health counseling intervention can be accessed by the student without permission. The following section describes mental health disorders to inform school personnel who may work with students diagnosed with these disorders.

MENTAL HEALTH DISORDERS

Anxiety

Anxiety is a future-oriented state in which an individual experiences the possibility of a threat occurring that invariably will result in a negative outcome (American Psychiatric Association, 2013). Approximately 40 million Americans suffer from some form of anxiety disorder that significantly interferes with their ability to participate in school, work, and social activities (Kessler et al., 2005). A specific form of anxiety known as *social anxiety disorder* (SAD) especially challenges a young person's ability to perform academically. Those affected by this disorder may avoid important activities, such as attending classes or extracurricular activities. Others with SAD may attend activities but avoid active participation, thereby achieving less in school and work. According to Burnham, Schaefer, and Giesen (2006), SAD contributes to poor functioning. Nonetheless, most cases go untreated.

Social Phobia

Another anxiety disorder, social phobia, usually begins in early childhood or adolescence, after a childhood marked by shyness and social inhibition (American Psychiatric Association, 2000). Shyness and inhibition affect social functioning during a time when the formation of relationships is necessary for both school success and personal satisfaction. If a social phobia is comorbid, the other disorders are usually secondary to the social phobia; this combination of disorders significantly increases the disabling effects of the condition (Brunello et al., 2000).

Comorbid Anxiety Disorders

Anxiety disorders, when occurring in isolation, are the most prevalent and treatable form of mental health disorders. However, anxiety disorders frequently co-occur with other anxiety disorders, such as panic disorder with and without agoraphobia, specific phobia posttraumatic stress disorder, and generalized anxiety disorder. Anxiety disorders can also be comorbid with depressive disorders and substance abuse as well, thus confounding the treatment for the disorder (Kessler et al., 2005).

Emergence of Anxiety Disorders

According to the International Consortium in Psychiatric Epidemiology, anxiety disorders in the United States first appear before age 5, with 50% occurring by age 14 and 75% occurring by age 25

(First, France, & Pincus, 2004). Also, the United States ranks first for recent and lifetime prevalence for this disorder. Anxiety disorders have consistently been shown to be highly persistent. Sixty percent to 70% of adult survey respondents who have a lifetime anxiety disorder reported that the disorder was active in the prior 6 to 12 months (Kessler, 2007). Anxiety disorders are often comorbid, and more than half of those with anxiety have been found to have a mood disorder as well. Also, anxiety has been found to be the primary disorder in people with anxious depression. American adults aged 18 and older, or about 18.1% of Americans 18 to 24 years old, are diagnosed with an anxiety disorder, compared with 11.0% for the 25 and older age group (Kessler et al., 2005).

Cognitive Theory of Social Anxiety

The *Diagnostic and Statistical Manual of Mental Disorders, 4th Edition, Text Revision* (DSM-IV-TR; First et al., 2004) describes SAD as a marked and persistent fear of situations in which the person is exposed to unfamiliar people or possible scrutiny by others. The individual fears that he or she will act in a way that will be embarrassing or humiliating (American Psychiatric Association, 2013). The disorder may result in avoidance of the feared situation (or other social or performance situations) or the person will endure the situation with intense anxiety or distress. Examples of feared situations include public speaking, informal conversations in small or large groups, eating in public, writing, public performances, dating, and interactions with authority figures (American Psychiatric Association, 2000, 2013).

Studies support significant cognitive and physical differences in children with anxiety disorders from those without anxiety disorders. In a study of high school students with stable low, stable high, and escalating anxiety, those with the latter two, respectively, predicted another anxiety disorder, panic disorder (Weems, Hayward, Killen, & Taylor, 2002). According to Field (2006), "Cognitive explanations of anxiety suppose that high-level cognitive processes cause and maintain anxiety" (p. 431). Cognitive models of anxiety also suggest that negative thoughts affect the anxious individual's ability to cope with fear in two ways: They overestimate the danger or threat and they underestimate their ability to cope with the threats (Beck, Emery, & Greenberg, 1985).

Physiological and Behavioral Manifestations

A 1985 comparison study by Beck et al. found that anxious and nonanxious people responded differently to repeated exposure to one or more moderately frightening stimuli. Nonanxious people became habituated to the threatening situation, but anxious people became more anxious. According to Beck et al. (1985), the nonanxious person can determine what a threat is; the anxious person is not able to make that distinction. Although the specific physical manifestations of anxiety vary for individuals, general signs are motor tension, autonomic hyperactivity, expectation, vigilance, and scanning while often mild depressive symptoms are usually present. The actual symptoms are not different from the symptoms of persons with typical development as they undertake performance tasks. However, the individual with an anxiety disorder does not habituate (i.e., get used to); instead, he or she begins cognitive distortions about catastrophic outcomes of the situation (Weems et al., 2002).

The cognitive distortions in anxiety create strong physiological responses. In a study on autonomic recovery and habituation in SAD, the reported responses from anxiety-inducing situations differed little between high-trait anxious and low-trait anxious individuals (Mauss, Wilhelm, & Gross, 2003). However, during repeated exposure to impromptu speech activity, low-trait anxious reported reduced anxiety, in contrast to those with high-trait social anxiety, who did not habituate but did report ongoing anxiety. The actual autonomic response between the groups showed no significant difference; the difference was in habituation (Mauss et al., 2003). The authors of the study reported that this outcome supported the theories of social anxiety that indicate cognitive factors as a root cause.

In an earlier comparison study of autonomic response during test taking, Beidel, Turner, and Dancu (1985) found that pulse rates of anxious children were moderately stable and twice as high as nonanxious children with test anxiety and four times as high as the nonanxious test group. Similarly, the correlation for the "socially anxious" children during the read-aloud task was twice as high as for the entire group. In a later study, Beidel, Turner, and Morris (1999) suggested that future investigations should determine if the 6-month retest period represents a sufficiently lengthy period to discriminate "disorders" from "reactions" and determine the characteristics of those children for whom the disorder does not "go away." Unfortunately, treatment for this is exposure to the feared situation (Benito & Walther, 2015) and to reduce the behaviors that are used to calm the reaction to the feared stimuli. Since it is unknown what the depth of the fear is, it would be hard to determine the level of fear one caused to the child. In some textbooks, teachers have been given in-school strategies to "help" the student, all with good intention; however, the student must agree to all suggestions for public performance, or the teacher can risk more severe responses. If an in-school strategy is going to be used, the school psychologist and treating psychologist, if there is one, the parent, and the child are to be the people who recommend or agree to the strategy.

Somatic Symptoms in Anxiety

Somatic symptoms that may also interfere with daily functioning, such as muscle tension and stomachaches, are hallmarks of the clinical features of anxiety disorders. Somatic symptoms are often the reason for absences from school, calls to the pediatrician, and, in extreme cases, visits to hospital emergency departments (Ginsburg, Riddle, & Davies, 2006). Ginsburg et al. (2006) also reported that children with an anxiety disorder report at least one somatic symptom and the majority reported more than one somatic symptom. In a study by Beidel et al. (1999), children with anxiety disorders reported they were in substantial distress across many social situations. The situations reported could significantly affect a young student's performance in school. Such situations as reciting in front of others, experiencing ordinary social interactions, and performing in athletics are examples of skills essential for school success but not within the cognitive abilities of children with SAD.

Obsessive-Compulsive Disorder

Obsessive-compulsive disorder (OCD) is described on the American Psychiatric Association (2019) website as an anxiety disorder. However, it is listed as its own disorder in the *Diagnostic and Statistical Manual of Mental Disorders, Fifth Edition* (DSM-5; American Psychiatric Association, 2013). OCD is a syndrome in which patients report intrusive, recurrent, and unwanted ideas and thoughts that are difficult to dismiss and disturbing in nature and degree. Compulsions are repetitive behaviors meant to reduce the anxiety created by the obsessive thoughts. Repetitive behaviors such as hand washing, counting, and repeating words are actions originally taken to reassure and reduce the distress, but often begin to cause distress. The behaviors often take a significant amount of time to perform and significantly interfere with a person's routine (American Psychiatric Association, 2000). The first symptoms of OCD appear during childhood or adolescence, with a median age of onset of 19 years. It affects about 1% of the adult population older than 18 years old.

Behavioral therapy is an effective treatment for OCD. Patients are asked to "gradually endure the anxiety that the obsessional fear provokes while refraining from compulsions that allay that anxiety" (American Psychiatric Association, 2013).

Treatment and Course of Anxiety Disorders

The main goals of treatment for social phobia are to reduce phobic avoidance of social situations, reduce distress, and improve role functioning. Treatment may include social skills training (American Psychiatric Association, 2013). Ollendick and King (2004) assert that there are only two well-established psychosocial treatments for children with specific phobias: participant modeling and reinforced practice. The strategies designed by clinicians may include exposure techniques, where the client is gradually exposed to or is required to complete tasks requiring assertiveness in social situations. The client may practice these situations before actual immersion in the experience. Pre-immersion strategies include modeling, reinforced practice, and rehearsal (American Psychiatric Association, 2013). Cognitive-behavioral therapy is also used for these disorders, and clients may be encouraged to explore their thoughts behind their behavior. Pharmacological treatment is also considered efficacious for *adults* along with cognitive therapy for the remission of symptoms for social phobias, but not for specific phobias. Although many phobias begin after a traumatic event (American Psychiatric Association, 2013), many individuals do not recall the onset of the fears and reports of fears are individually based. Phobias begin at an average of 9 years of age and increase in intensity over time regarding additional stress and traumatic events. There are trained therapists who work with children, youth, and adults to handle feared situations using reacher-based methodology.

Normal Fears

Many studies have shown that fears normally decrease from childhood to adolescence, and more than 100 studies have been completed to delineate normal fears from fears that interfere with functioning (Gullone, as cited in Burnham et al., 2006). A study about normal and clinical fear (Burnham et al., 2006) found that 1 in 10 school-age students had significant school-related fears. Fears associated with school-related stimuli can precipitate and maintain school refusal. In a major investigation of anxiety-based school refusal, Last and Strauss (1990) identified that the average age of onset for social phobia was 12.4 years. This is the age when most students make the transition to middle school and may be in classes with new classmates and teachers. In a study by Weems et al. (2002), children were assessed for their level of worry. They found that, on average, children reported 5.74 worries, with the most being in the areas of health, school, disasters, personal harm, and future events. When compared with the clinic children (those with anxiety disorders), the intensity of the clinic children's worries was significantly higher.

Self-Efficacy and Anxiety

A major function of thought is to enable people to predict events and to develop ways to control those events that affect their lives. Predicting events requires effective cognitive processing of information including information that contains many ambiguities and uncertainties about the outcomes of activities. It involves skill in managing aversive emotional reactions, which can impair the quality of thinking and action. There is a marked difference between possessing knowledge and skills and being able to use them well under pressing situational demands (Bandura, 1994, p. 73).

In his 1982 study of people with social phobia, Bandura measured coping behavior. His study demonstrated that performances varied as a function of perceived efficacy. Increased levels of perceived self-efficacy both across and within the same subjects gave rise to progressively higher performance accomplishment. Those who judge themselves inefficacious in coping with environmental demands imagine potential difficulties as more formidable than they are (Beck, 1967). This self-referent negativity creates stress, which impairs performance by diverting attention from how best to proceed with the undertaking to concerns over failings and mishaps (Bandura, 1982). In preliminary explorations of cognitive processing of enactive experiences, people register notable increases in self-efficacy when their experiences disconfirm misbeliefs about what they fear and when they gain new skills to manage threatening activities. Using competent models teaches effective strategies for dealing with challenging situations; the self-efficacy of a person with a phobia could be influenced by that person observing the experiences of others performing the task he or she would soon perform. Persuasiveness also boosted the self-efficacy of people with phobias, but only when it was within realistic bounds. Bandura (1982) also noted that cognitive appraisal and an aversive arousal state also mediate self-efficacy, because high arousal, present in anxiety disorders, usually debilitates performance; people are more inclined to expect success when not beset by aversive arousal. People avoid activities and situations they believe exceed their coping capabilities. When people try to cope with threats for which they distrust their personal efficacy, their stress mounts: their heart rate accelerates, their blood pressure rises, and they activate stress-related hormones (Bandura, 1982). Bandura's 1982 study confirmed that different modes of influence strengthen self-precepts of efficacy: the higher the level of self-efficacy, the greater the performance accomplishments in academic and social behavior. An efficacious outlook produces personal accomplishments, reduces stress, and lowers vulnerability to depression. "Self-efficacy beliefs are the product of a complex process of self-persuasion that relies on cognitive processing of diverse sources of efficacy information conveyed enactively, vicariously, socially, and physiologically" (Bandura, 1986, p. 1390). Once formed, efficacy beliefs contribute significantly to the level and quality of human functioning. When applying this to transition planning, small student-created goals facilitate success. The transition planning conferences underpin setting up goals that are doable and result in successful outcomes.

Selective Mutism

In most cases, selective mutism is a form of social anxiety. Selective mutism often persists into high school, significantly impairing academic and social progress. Many students with selective mutism will refuse to go to school. Kotrba (2014) described children who have SM as exhibiting the following traits:

- Show difficulty responding and initiating verbally, if they respond at all
- Have difficulty communicating nonverbally
- Typically have average to above-average intelligence
- Are perceptive and sensitive
- May freeze and/or have awkward movements when anxious
- Demonstrate poor eye contact

A student has selective mutism when there is an absence of speech in settings where they are expected to speak. It manifests in two ways: either they do not speak of their own volition or they have a physical response that prevents them from speaking (American Psychiatric Association, 2013).

Students with selective mutism can speak and will do so in at least one place. Also, they may be quite different at home if they feel safe and secure there (American Psychiatric Association, 2013). Traumatic mutism can occur too, typically when a child has witnessed a traumatic event, such as the death of an important person in his or her life. This type of mutism comes on suddenly. In relation to shy or timid children, they are at the furthest end of the spectrum.

There are many times that teachers can contribute negatively and increase the anxiety level in children with selective mutism. As a result, these children feel trapped or forced to retreat even deeper. Examples include teachers trying to force a child to talk, giving up on a child if he or she does not talk, trying to entice a child to talk with rewards, punishing a child for not talking, and not keeping other kids from bothering the child.

A progressive reward system can help a child by starting with private opportunities to show his or her work to the teacher, nodding his or her head for yes and no answers, and having his or her parents tape an oral report at home. Teachers and the family must not give negative feedback about speaking because doing that is what the student fears. Teachers can accept any kind of nonverbal communication and should continue to talk to the child but with topics that do not expect an answer.

The right circumstances will help prevent worsening of the condition. The most ideal conditions will help increase confidence and reduce anxiety. "If intervention is initiated, then it's important for the teacher to work with other professionals, and those involved with the student's family" (Kauffman & Landrum, 2013, p. 281).

Employment and Anxiety

The transition planning process can be helpful to a student with selective mutism. Typically, he or she wants to be finished school and have more control over his or her life. If a student is not speaking in high school and has frequent absenteeism, a setting with intensive therapy, such as a partial behavioral support program or a therapist that can work with students without behavioral problems and who want to intensively address anxiety and absence of speech, may be needed. Construction of the transition plan gives the student direct control over his or her life and can help the student gain self-efficacy as he or she addresses his or her therapeutic needs. The following case report demonstrates how transition planning helped a student make progress.

Case Report: June

June had selective mutism for her entire school career. She did spend her final years in a small group setting for students with internalizing mental health disorders. When transition planning began, she created her narrative about the effects of her disability, and an IEP transition meeting was planned. The idea of graduating and leaving school motivated her to participate. Prior to the meeting, she began to speak, and one of the first things she said was that she wanted to learn to drive. Given her fear of speaking and her request to learn to drive, the transition planning specialist encouraged her to talk about it in the IEP. The transition planning specialist also said she would support her in this goal. June wrote her disability narrative, which outlined her goals for a job working with horses and the need to learn to drive so she could work.

She participated in her IEP transition meeting and was able to tell the team what she wanted. Her parents were surprised and supportive. June found her niche in life working on a horse farm, a retreat center for adults.

DISCUSSION

It is important that students with anxiety examine their needs for employment settings. The transition planning for students served in emotional support classrooms (IDEA category) can be more intensive. With anxiety, the correct setting is important. June had no learning disabilities or other health impairment, but she, like Sam, knew herself well enough to pick the correct employment situation. Intensive planning with a transition planning specialist, behavioral specialist, and her parents, who had faith in her abilities underpinned, her courage to plan her future.

Mood Disorders

Major Depression

Depressive disorders are episodic and chronic; children, adolescents, and adults who develop these disorders have a lifelong vulnerability. Additional symptoms include weight loss or gain, feelings of worthlessness, inappropriate guilt, inability to concentrate, indecisiveness, and recurrent thoughts of dying or suicide; in children and adolescents, the persistent mood may be irritable (American Psychiatric Association, 2013).

EMERGENCE OF DEPRESSION

In childhood, boys and girls experience depression equally; however, after puberty, females have a higher rate of depression than males (American Psychiatric Association, 2013). In 2007, 8% of the population aged 12 to 17 had a major depressive episode (MDE) during the past year (Substance Abuse and Mental Health Services Administration [SAMHSA], 2008). If onset occurs during adolescence, both a vulnerability to major depression and risk for continued impairment and future disorder exist. If a reoccurrence or relapse occurs during the transition to adulthood, continued risk of persistence into adulthood exists. When an episode occurs during adolescence, with no relapse or recurrence during the transition to adulthood, the expectation of normal function during adulthood results (Reinherz, Giaconia, Hauf, Wasserman, & Silverman, 1999).

Depressive illnesses often interfere with normal functioning and can negatively impact productivity and performance in the workplace (Kessler et al., 2003). According to the Kessler study, role impairment is substantial: 59.6% of the participants with major depression experienced severe or very severe role impairment (2003). A study about the recurrence of depression reassessed 274 young adults for depression after their 24th birthday. Lewinsohn, Rohde, Seeley, Klein, and Gotlib (2000) found that only one-quarter of the participants remained depression free. A second quarter experienced a subsequent MDE, and a third quarter experienced a comorbid disorder and depression (Lewinsohn et al., 2000). In a study by Reinherz et al. (1999), depressed participants demonstrated poorer psychosocial functioning evidenced by self-reports of poor self-esteem and self-mastery, more interpersonal problems, higher need for social support, and dissatisfaction with career progress, as well as heightened risk for suicidal behavior.

PHYSIOLOGICAL AND BEHAVIORAL MANIFESTATIONS

Major depression is part of a group of depressive disorders marked by diminished interest or pleasure in all or almost all activities for all day or most of the day, every day (American Psychiatric Association, 2013). Periods of depression, recovery (also called *remission*), and relapse (also called *reoccurrence*) mark the course of major depression (Abramson, Alloy, & Metalsky, 1989). Multiple factors influence the onset of depression; genetic factors may be evident when onset occurs in early childhood and when depression is evident in other family members. Major depression is also influenced by environmental and physiological risks (American Psychiatric Association, 2013). Abnormalities in sleep electroencephalograms are evident in 90% of inpatients with an MDE and 40% to 60% of outpatients. Sleep continuity disturbances, intermittent wakefulness, and early-morning wakefulness all affect the quality of sleep. These sleep patterns may persist between episodes of major depressive disorder (American Psychiatric Association, 2000).

COGNITIVE THEORY OF DEPRESSION

The cognitive perspective originally developed by Beck (1967) emphasizes a primary triad in depression. Beck posited that an individual with depression has a "negative view of the world, a negative view of self, and a negative view of the future" (1967, p. 256). Based on Beck's study of depression in clinical patients, he discovered that, because of the negative views and the thoughts arising from those viewpoints, an affective state arose because of the way the individual viewed him- or herself or the environment. Because of depression, study participants demonstrated changes in motivation under five groupings: loss of motivation, escapism, avoidance, suicidal wishes, and intensified dependency wishes. Physical symptoms such as mental slowness, fatigue, and agitation were evident.

The cognitive theory asserts that the distortions regarding themselves and the world make individuals vulnerable to depression. Furthermore, a specific set of conditions may activate depressive symptomatology (Beck, 1967). In childhood and adolescence, the depression-vulnerable individual becomes sensitized to specific situations; prototypes of these situations may surface later in life, triggering depression (Beck, 1967, p. 278). This cognitive perspective of depression was further developed through learned helplessness models and hopelessness theory (Abramson et al., 1989; Seligman, 1975). The hopelessness theory specifies a chain of contributory causes hypothesized to cause the symptoms of depression. In hopelessness theory, adverse events are the occasion setters for people to become hopeless, the precursor to depression. Negative thoughts about potential outcomes lead to inaction and hopelessness. "This specific vulnerability hypothesis requires that there be a match between the content areas of an individual's depressive attribution style and the negative life events encountered for the attribution 'diathesis-stress' interaction to predict future symptoms of 'hopeless depression'" (Abramson et al., 1989, p. 361). "Beck's cognitive perspective, as well as the contributions from the helplessness-hopelessness models, formed an empirical basis for cognitive-behavioral therapy initially developed by Beck (1979) and colleagues" (American Psychiatric Association, 2013, p. 762; Beck, Rush, Shaw, & Emery, 1979). These studies give the special education team insight into the hopeless thinking of students with depression. Many students with and without disabilities are in situations that are significantly stressful beyond what most people experience. When in these inescapable situations, hopelessness would be a natural outcome. Through transition planning, the special education team can provide hope by guiding the student to independence to facilitate movement into a satisfactory and positive post-school situation, and as the student plans and completes plans to move on from hostile settings, things appear less hopeless.

TREATMENT OF DEPRESSION

Both pharmacologic and cognitive-behavioral therapies have been proven to be efficacious treatment. The goal of treatment is full remission of symptoms and return to social and workplace functioning. A patient's knowledge and awareness of the early signs of relapse can help him or her maintain control over the symptoms of this disorder throughout the lifespan (American Psychiatric Association, 2013). Some students are on medication for depression. Students may or may not share that they are on medication. Medication self-monitoring, which students report to their doctor, is part of the student's medical treatment. If there is a sharing of mental health treatment, an Individual Health Care Plan can be designed to help the student determine whether the medication is helping. Although teachers do not have the medical degree to diagnose or recommend medication, they are essential for reporting changes in behavior that may indicate a life threatening condition like depression. In addition, they are instrumental in supporting students with depression to reach their goals.

Bipolar Disorder

During diagnosis and treatment, it is significant to note that if there is an episode of major depressive disorder during adolescence, this also predicts an increased risk for onset of bipolar disorder (Rao, Ryan, Birmaher, & Dahl, 1995). "Bipolar disorder, marked by severe and cyclical mood, cognition, and activity changes, is usually discussed as an adult condition and it is indeed rare in childhood" (Weisz & Hawley, 2002). However, rates increase during adolescence, and bipolar disorder generally has its onset between the ages of 15 and 30 years old (American Psychiatric Association, 2013, p. 811). Cyclical activation periods are known as the *manic phase* in bipolar I and the *hypomanic phase* in bipolar II. Depressive episodes alternate with the activation periods (American Psychiatric Association, 2013). The manic phase can lead to individuals believing they are above the law as well as fueling participation in life-threatening behaviors (Weisz & Hawley, 2002). In juveniles, irritability, explosiveness, and mixed manic-depressive features are observed more so than periods of euphoria, which is often part of bipolar 1 symptomatology.

Diagnoses of bipolar I and II require both cross-sectional and longitudinal data. This form of diagnosis prevents the misdiagnosis of major depression when individuals with bipolar disorder only present for treatment of depression.

Persons who experience a manic, hypomanic, or mixed episode, virtually all whom have a history of one or more depressive episodes, are diagnosed with bipolar disorder. Those who experience major depressive and manic episodes are diagnosed with bipolar I disorder, and those with major depressive and hypomanic episodes are diagnosed with bipolar II disorder (American Psychiatric Association, 2000, p. 797).

Lifetime prevalence estimates are at 1.0% for bipolar I, 1.1% for bipolar II, 2.4% for subthreshold bipolar disorder, and 4.45% for overall prevalence. Sex-specific rates for males and females, respectively, occur at 0.8% and 1.1% for bipolar I, 0.9% and 1.3% for bipolar II, and 2.6% and 2.1% for a subthreshold bipolar disorder such as cyclothymia (Merikangas et al., 2007). These statistics indicate there is not a significant gender difference in rates of bipolar disorder.

In a study by Kim, Miklowitz, Biuckians, and Mullen (2006), stressors from various areas correlated with the severity of bipolar mood symptoms over time, even for adolescents receiving pharmacologic and psychosocial interventions. However, the DSM-IV-TR refutes this argument, noting that there is no single paradigm that explains the occurrence and variability of bipolar disorder, and successful treatment of bipolar disorder with medications has made the biological basis of this disorder incontrovertible (First et al., 2004, p. 824). Family genetics may better explain the biological basis for this disorder. "Available evidence indicates familial factors are important determinants of who develops bipolar disorder" (American Psychiatric Association, 2013, p. 816). Studies using relatives of identified cases have higher rates of bipolar disorder than control groups or subjects with unipolar depression (American Psychiatric Association, 2013). Although there are studies that point to stressful life events as a precipitator of an episode in established bipolar diagnosis, there are also studies that have failed to find significant associations (American Psychiatric Association, 2013). It is also significant to note that "completed suicide occurs in 10-15% of individuals with bipolar disorder," making this a life-threatening disorder (American Psychiatric Association, 2000, p. 384).

TREATMENT AND COURSE OF BIPOLAR DISORDER

Pediatric bipolar disorder appears to affect children and adolescents more severely than adults. Regardless of the differences between research groups regarding how bipolar disorder in children is defined, it is agreed that pediatric bipolarity is a serious and pernicious illness (Demeter, Townsend, Wilson, & Findling, 2008). "The refractory nature of pediatric-onset bipolar (PBD) warrants a comprehensive and immediate approach to treatment" (Pavuluri et al., 2004).

The first report to describe the psychopathological course of bipolar disorder in children and adolescents studied 263 children and adolescents between the ages of 7 and 17 years old. This study indicated that 70% of the participants recovered from an index episode and 50% had at least one recurrence, particularly of depressive episodes. During a weekly analysis of mood symptoms, 60% of the time participants had numerous changes in symptoms and shifts of polarity, subsyndromal symptoms, and 3% of the time psychosis (Birmaher, Axelson, Strober, & Gill, 2006, p. 180). Due to the rapidly changing mood states, some research suggests that children and adults with bipolar disorder are not ready for psychosocial treatments until their medication has stabilized the symptoms (Kowatch et al., 2005).

"Limited research has been devoted to developing and testing psychosocial treatments for bipolar disorder" (Young & Fristad, 2007). Treatment for bipolar disorder includes a specific episode's resolution or the maintenance of a stable mood. Professionals in the field recommend partial hospital treatment programs for individuals who are a danger to themselves or others, and these programs provide support during intensive episodes. Pharmacologic medications may be used to stabilize the individual, and there may be a need to monitor related blood tests during the implementation of the treatment. Medications and psychotherapeutic treatment goals include improvement of symptoms and functioning (American Psychiatric Association, 2013). Choices of medication need to reflect the individual's ability to manage compliance in a potentially chaotic environment. Also, because of the cycling and potential for sudden onset of suicidality, medications should be administered that would not be as lethal in the event of an overdose (Geller & Luby, 1997).

The course of this disorder is lifelong, and bipolar disorder requires ongoing education of both the individual and his or her family so they can recognize early warning signs and identify triggers of episodes, as well as develop action plans to address those developments (American Psychiatric Association, 2013). Recently, treatments have been developed or adapted for use in the pediatric bipolar population. Young and Fristad (2007) studied the components of four treatments: family-focused treatment (FFT), the RAINBOW program, multifamily psychoeducation groups (MFGs), and individual family psychoeducation. These evidence-based treatments include psychoeducation; skill building; communication; and problem solving regarding symptom management, emotional regulation, and impulse control. Randomized, controlled trials have demonstrated the effectiveness of psychoeducation and FFT. Studies of 101 recently hospitalized adult patients with bipolar disorder indicated an association with lower relapse rates, lower rehospitalization rates, better medication adherence, and reductions in mood symptoms up to 15 months after treatment (Miklowitz, George, Richards, Simoneau, & Suddath, 2003). A smaller study of adolescents yielded similar results. A sample of 20 adolescents who participated in FFT with their parents demonstrates that the participants experienced a 38% average reduction in manic symptoms and a 46% improvement at their 12-month follow-up (Pavuluri et al., 2004).

Another psychosocial intervention, the RAINBOW program, has been adapted from FFT for use with children aged 8 to 12. In an open trial of the program with 34 children and adolescents, significant improvement was observed in not only bipolar symptoms, but also aggression, attention-deficit hyperactivity disorder (ADHD) symptoms, and global functioning (Pavuluri et al., 2004).

MFPGs constitute a technique like FFT and RAINBOW. These psychoeducational groups focus on educating families about their children's illness and its treatment. This treatment includes both the reduction of expressed emotion (e.g., anger and criticism) and the improvement of problem solving and communication. In contrast to these treatments, MFPG is designed for children with pediatric bipolar disorder or depressive disorder. Parents meet other parents of children with mood disorders, and children meet other children with a "similar illness" (Young & Fristad, 2007, p. 159). The program teaches children how to identify their mood symptoms, and they develop a toolkit for managing the symptoms. In a pilot study conducted with 35 families with children aged 8 to 11, families were assigned randomly to a group or were wait-listed. Parents and children assigned to an intervention group reported improved social support from parents and peers (Fristad, Goldberg-Arnold, & Gavazzi, 2002). In a meta-analysis of the effectiveness of psycho-education Miziou et al. (2015) reported on the effectiveness of psychosocial treatment for bipolar disorder for specific interventions in selected groups who benefited when applied as early as possible. The authors also asserted that more research needs to be done on effective treatments.

Bipolar disorder can derail students from their successful path to adulthood, therefore treatment is essential and the special education team is alert to behaviors that become disruptive or will contribute to negative outcomes and refer students for an intervention.

Suicide Risk for Depressive Disorders and Bipolar Disorders

Suicide is the second leading cause of death among persons aged 10 to 14 and the second among persons aged 15 to 24 years (Sullivan, Annest, Simon, Luo, & Dahlberg, 2015). Suicide risk related to the symptoms of mental health disorders remains a management challenge. Although suicide is uncommon in childhood, its occurrence increases markedly in the late teens and continues to rise in the early twenties, peaking in adulthood. Suicide was the second leading cause of death for age group 10 to 24 years old (17.3% of deaths) and the third leading cause of death for age group 25 to 44 years old (Heron, 2018, p. 34). Suicide has been linked to mental health disorders. However, not all suicides can be directly linked to a mental health disorder. In a study of victims of completed suicide, it was reported that more than 90% had a significant psychiatric illness at the time of their death (Shaffer et al., 1996). Although there has been a decrease in the overall suicide rate in the United States since 2000, the overall suicide decrease does not reflect the suicide rates for youth and adolescents. Suicide for youth and adolescents between the ages of 10 and 14 years old increased 51% between 1981 and 2004 (Centers for Disease Control and Prevention, 2004).

During 2004, 283 children between the ages of 10 and 14 years old completed suicides in the United States (Centers for Disease Control and Prevention, 2004). In the African American population, the growth in suicide is most significant, and, although the rates are lower than for white children, African American children (aged 10 to 14 years old) showed the most significant increase in suicide rates between 1980 and 1995 of all ethnic groups (233%). White children were far more likely to complete suicide than African American children. Before puberty, attempted suicides and suicide completion associated with depression are quite rare. Rates typically increase with puberty, peaking among 15- to 19-year-olds (Brown, Cohen, Johnson, & Smailes, 1999). These statistics indicate a long-term significant problem with suicide in American youth. Currently, females are more likely than males to attempt suicide (Ivey-Stephenson, Crosby, Jack, Haileyesus, & Kresnow-Sedacca, 2017), but males are five times more likely to complete their attempts. Suicide rates increased in 44 states between 1999 and 2016, and 25 states had a 30% increase. Approximately half had known mental health disorders (Stone et al., 2018). However, without a review of medical files, there is no method to see if undiagnosed medical conditions were present. Fortunately, for people with these disorders, treatment can reduce this risk.

Schizophrenia and Psychotic Disorders

Schizophrenia, as with most disabilities, has a spectrum of symptoms from mild to severe. The most severe form becomes noticeable when there is an inability to focus on and comprehend the realities of everyday life. In daily life, the ability to organize the thoughts, set a course of action, and act on plans is diminished or not present. Because there are hallucinations present, individuals with schizophrenia cannot organize themselves enough to seek treatment. Often they are viewed as lazy, but in fact, they cannot carry out the advocacy needed to seek help. Due to its symptoms of psychosis, schizophrenia prevents the organized thought that underpins planning. When young persons demonstrate pervasive and resistant psychotic symptoms, the disability and side effects of the medication will have a significant impact on employment and learning.

Psychosis is usually described as a split from reality. There are two major types of psychosis in schizophrenia: hallucinations and delusions. Both are signs that the condition is escalating. The person with schizophrenia can be taught to recognize early signs and be taught to seek help. The following are early signs of psychosis:

- Trouble concentrating
- Hearing, seeing, tasting, or believing things that others do not
- Unusual thoughts or beliefs that are fixed regardless of what others believe
- Strong emotions, often inappropriate
- Withdrawing from family and friends
- Decline in self-care

Psychosis involves hallucinations and delusions that include more pervasive symptoms that infer or prevent normal interactions. They can be drug induced or a part of a mental health disorder. The following case report is an example. Haley refused to go to high school. She spoke little unless spoken to and often had a fearful look on her face. Finally, she was placed in a partial hospital program.

Case Report: Haley

Haley was sitting with her peers and her teacher. A student revealed that he had smoked some sort of marijuana and became convinced his friend's dog was speaking to him and was going to tell his parents that they had been smoking pot. He then said he began thinking of ways to get rid of the dog or keep him from talking. Luckily, he asked his peers if the dog was talking and they decided he should go home, assuring him that the dog could not talk. He then said he decided not to take drugs anymore. The young man asked the group if that had ever happened to them. All except Haley said no. Haley said, "I hear voices but not from dogs and not from drugs. Mine speak to me all the time, or they sing. I can see them in my head, they look like a Greek choir in Greek togas."

The teacher asked Haley what they sang or said. She said they told her the kids in the high school were talking about her or they told her she was ugly and stupid. One of the students asked if the voices ever told her anything good about herself. Haley said, "No, only upsetting things." After that, she began to talk more openly and said she felt she could talk about it now. She shared that when she first heard the voices, she became terrified that she was crazy and that if her classmates found out they would not like her. She was in the fourth grade. So, she withdrew rather than risk discovery.

In this case report, the boy's psychosis was drug induced, and Haley was later diagnosed with schizophrenia. She never sought medication for it because she said she had become used to it.

DISCUSSION

Haley was very frightened of her own sensory experiences and was able to identify them as something that was not normal. What she described were auditory hallucinations that distracted her throughout her school years. She appeared as a student who was very slow at completing her work, although she was compliant and did so. Another symptom of schizophrenia is delusions, when the person imagines him- or herself to be something or someone he or she is not.

Hallucinations comprise the following:

- Hearing voices (auditory)
  - Voices are of known or unknown people
  - Voices are not the person's thoughts
- Inexplicable feelings (sensory)
- Seeing glimpses of objects or people that are not present (visual)
- Catatonic symptoms
- Disorganized speech
- Switches from one topic to another

Freedom to get treatment is also necessary when voices or delusions start.

Schizophrenia and Employment Planning

Schizophrenia is a spectrum mental health disorder with a wide range of functioning. At the highest functioning level, employment will most likely be where the student may assert he or she can best function. Persons with schizophrenia can hold jobs such as the following:

- June became a manager at a fast food restaurant.
- Kyle, a young man with paranoid schizophrenia, worked monitoring cable salespersons doing telephone sales. When he had a more intrusive episode, his employer allowed him to take time off until his medication was adapted and he improved enough to return.
- Mary liked to clean houses. She had delusions that someone from the government was following her but was able to work if she could control her hours and days. She knew when she could work and when she could not and would adjust her schedule accordingly.

People with schizophrenia can learn and perform in many areas of life. John F. Nash was a brilliant mathematician who was hospitalized over a long period of time, but when his condition slowly improved, he returned to work at Princeton (Nasar, 1994). These are examples of people who sought treatment.

Others have not been as successful. In these cases, some people with untreated schizophrenia will begin to wander. This can be because the brain cannot organize thought. In addition, some forms of schizophrenia are far more severe and become lower on the spectrum due to a lack of treatment. Adolescents with schizophrenia need intensive therapy and treatment to monitor the effectiveness of their medication and to help them deal intellectually and emotionally with the life change caused by this significant disability.

When staff are degreed professionals, partial hospital programs are positive options for those with schizophrenia who are supervised by both a psychologist and a psychiatrist. The best programs for people with schizophrenia have hotlines to provide support to the student and the family if issues arise at home. Also, these programs have mandatory counseling for the parents without the student. A student with this condition should have Medicaid to cover health care so he or she can access counseling and psychiatric care prior to an acute episode. He or she may also require a supports coordinator to check on and assist the student with home care services. Transition planning can revolve around the same areas of those for other students except more intensive supports for post-school life will need to be coordinated with local agencies that provide care and support.

Treatment Considerations

Schizophrenia is usually progressive. Antipsychotic medications are taken in a few forms but can also be given in injections once or twice a month. Psychoeducation, such as learning about the condition, is not usually possible before finding a medication that will decrease the symptoms to a level where the person can function in reality.

Families are involved in the student's care because severe schizophrenia makes independent living difficult if not impossible. Support to access education and employment services are needed. When medication becomes ineffective, the student may have a psychotic episode, which requires immediate hospitalization until medication can be adjusted. People with schizophrenia can monitor their own symptoms and request to go to their psychiatrist or the hospital to get stabilized. Transition planning will be quite different in that more supports will be needed and more outside agencies will be involved in the student's care. Person-centered planning underpins the transition plan and includes input from the treatment team and student. Even though schizophrenia is a severe disorder, the student's preferences, strengths, needs, and involvement are important for his or her transition to adulthood.

Governmental Agencies

Governmental services through the Department of Health and Human Services are typically needed by persons with schizophrenia. As they get older, the ability to care for themselves diminishes.

However, there is also a range of impairment in schizophrenia. With this understanding, they can participate in work and school. Employment may vary from part-time to full-time, and short-term hospitalizations may be needed at times to adjust medication, which can affect liver function. With supports in place to plan for episodes, people with less severe forms of schizophrenia can work. They can participate fully in transition planning unless in advanced stages of the condition. Over time, this condition can improve significantly if it is treated early and consistently. Maintaining a consistent schedule and creating a school plan that limits stress and academic pressure supports inclusion and a smooth transition planning experience.

FRAMEWORK FOR TRANSITION PLANNING

Students with mental health disorders need additional supports for their emotional and behavioral needs. Although they can very successfully participate in the full participation transition framework, special considerations around their interaction challenges and the episodic nature of the condition are warranted. The transition planning specialist must also ensure their needs are met and to what degree they may need to add additional supports. The transition planning specialist needs to ask the following questions when planning with students with mental health disorders and behavioral disorders. To begin they should examine the following topics and answer the questions related to each topic:

- Protective factors
    - What family, social, and financial supports are available to the student?
- Resilience factors
    - Does the student show persistence when facing difficult situations?
    - Does the student share concerns?
    - Does the student know when a problem needs to be discussed with an adult or friend?
    - Does the student know his or her own weaknesses and strengths?
- Goal-setting skills
    - Does the student set goals and complete them?
    - If not, what prevents the student from doing so?
- Intensive conferencing
    - Identify why this student requires intensive conferencing (e.g., executive functioning or depression impairs planning).
    - Do the parents have mental health, addiction, financial, or extended family constraints? Most likely you will only know this second-hand from the student if they share. Does the student need psychoeducation to learn about the condition?
    - Does the student need preparation for the meeting leadership training to address anxiety and social withdraw behaviors?
    - How are anxiety, depression, and bipolar disorders affecting employment possibilities?
- Preferences for employment
    - Did the student learn how to do an environmental assessment?
    - Did the transition planning specialist remember not to use preferences assessments? Preferences assessments cannot capture the emotional-social aspects of mental health disorders or any disability.
    - Did the student interview include the interview process to establish meaning and understanding about the student's strengths and needs in the current environments?
    - Is the conference setting a place where the student is comfortable writing or talking about the effects of the mental health disorder or behavior issues on the goals?

- ○ Did the student share mental health treatment and current stamina related to work and school tasks?
- ○ Is there a review of Individual Health Plans, academic courses, independence, and future medical access?
- Follow-up services
  - ○ Does the student need community mental health supports?
- Parent transition education and support counseling
  - ○ Does the student's parent need help to access the transition trainings?
  - ○ Is the parent aware of community-based supports?
  - ○ Does the parent need school psychologist periodic meetings?
- Transition planning team
  - ○ Has the team developed student-teacher trust?
  - ○ Has the team maintained confidentiality among the student, teacher, transition planning specialist, and school psychologist?
  - ○ Has the transition planning team met the support goals they were to provide to the student?

Transition planning with this population of students entails multiple complex considerations. School-based teams include the student, parent, school psychologist, school counselor, special education and general education teachers, and transition planning specialist. With careful attention to the student's needs, strengths, and preferences, and by giving the student the opportunity to work, continue training, or pursue education, the student, unless a severe and pervasive disability is present, can find satisfactory post-school employment and education. Students with mental health disorders can develop self-determination and autonomy as they grow in self-knowledge about their conditions with the support of the transition team.

Best-Fit Practices

The first consideration for students with mental health disorders is that early referral for students who begin to fail in school is paramount because failure is an indicator of an emergent mental health disorder. Also, high absenteeism can be the result of these problems. Students with mental health disorders must receive quality educational programs with differentiated instruction and adaptations. Adaptations to existing requirements can help them as they go through early treatment, mental health stabilization, and early medication adjustment.

When working with students who have long histories of mental health disorder symptoms, disruptive home lives, and poor treatment fidelity, it may be unrealistic for large-scale public schools to facilitate more positive outcomes. If a school district is unprepared to deal with complex mental health issues, placement in small school settings or very small classes in the public school setting with support may be a better fit. Furthermore, students with severe mental health disorders who are exhibiting suicidal gestures, behavioral acting out, and school failure eventually require hospitalization and a stepdown program in a partial hospital. As mentioned previously, partial hospital programs, following acute hospitalization, are uniquely designed to combine child goal-setting therapy, parent counseling as a requirement of placement, and an educational program. The intensive support provided there includes intensive small-group and confidential programming. This type of intensive programming is optimum and is beyond the training and expertise of general education settings. The goal of these settings is to gradually return the student to the general education setting or to another inclusive placement such as a school-to-work setting.

The second consideration is that there must be both social skills and therapeutic support to students with these disorders once they return to their school district of origin. Schools need to scrutinize their programs and supports to determine if they are research based, implemented with fidelity, and oriented toward improving outcomes for the individuals in that program rather than just housing them in special education emotional support classrooms.

A third consideration is that school districts have little incentive to continue programming for students with mental health disorders during their hospital stays, which can be brief and intermittent and may occur and end before the districts become aware of them. These repeated placements disrupt semester courses, and schools may assign failing grades to students rather than provide intensive educational interventions during those periods. Transition planing with these students indicates the need for extraordinary attention to the student's and parents' needs, as the student will also no longer be the child they have always known.

These conditions, once emerged, are lifelong and require ongoing treatment but can be managed and result in satisfactory life experiences. That these conditions occur during school age indicate that school districts need to plan for an increase in responsibility for students who were previously of no serious concern.

Finally, collaboration and coordination by schools and mental health services can establish improved directions for educational programming and mental health treatment during school age. If students with these disorders are to receive appropriate treatment as well as a free appropriate public education, steps must be taken to provide supports and services during mental health disorder emergence, episodic return during treatment, and treatment monitoring such as medication monitoring in the form of the Individual Health Care Plan. Perhaps addressing the development of differentiated educational programs and computer-based learning programs that allow individual advancement in addition to treatment will result in improved post-school outcomes for young adults with these disorders.

Navigating the Mental Health Behavioral Health System

School districts typically provide contact and services information about their local mental health services. The agencies also advertise their services in newspapers and on the internet. Where students live determines where they receive services. Each area has a system of services provided through contracted agencies. The agencies provide mental health support to the community in the form of counseling, emergency hospitalization, 24-hour suicide prevention hotlines and family crisis hotlines, alcohol and drug addiction counseling, and referrals to more intensive services such as long-term hospitalization for acute manifestations of a mental health disorder episode.

These local agencies, which receive their payments through private insurance and Medicaid, have therapists, psychologists, and psychiatrists on staff whose services for adolescents are covered via Medicare funds or private insurance. The student can access these services on his or her own in some states as early as age 12. The student receives a Medicaid card in his or her own name at the age that services are requested. Intake workers meet with the student alone or with the parents and fill out the paperwork for funding. Currently, if there is no health insurance, mental health services are provided for through Medicaid based on the provisions of each state. The transition planning specialist and the secondary special education team should be knowledgeable about the mental health options available to students in their state and local communities. Although the school psychologist makes these referrals because they are the specialists representing the school districts, the transition planning specialist should be able to work with the school psychologist and know the procedures and timelines for securing mental health services. School districts can develop a memorandum of understanding with an agency to provide in-school counseling or special programs for their students.

SAMHSA, under the direction of the Department of Health and Human Services, is the lead government agency funding comprehensive mental health services for children with emotional disturbances. The Comprehensive Community Mental Health Services for Children with Serious Emotional Disturbances Program (also called the *Children's Mental Health Initiative* [CMHI]) is administered by the Child, Adolescent and Family Branch Center for Mental Health Services. There are currently grants available to develop an evidence-based, family-driven system of care that is grounded in planning that is individualized, youth guided, culturally competent, in the least restrictive environment, community based, accessible, and a collaborative effort across agencies.

A significant problem reported is that 71.9% of children and adolescents receiving care had a parent with depression, 55.3% had a parent with addiction, and 39.6% were exposed to domestic abuse and violence. Research regarding the CMHI services and programs reported fewer behavioral and emotional problems, fewer suicides and suicide attempts, improved school attendance and academic performance, fewer law enforcement contacts, reduced hospitalizations, and reduced caregiver strain (SAMHSA, 2016).

Behavioral Disorders

Conduct Disorders

These disorders, which include violent and aggressive behavior, as mentioned in the Introduction, are not covered under IDEA. However, many students with conduct disorders are placed in programs for students with depression, anxiety, bipolar, and schizophrenia. This is done due to the disruption they cause in general education environments. In classes for students, they often continue the same behavior, along side their peers with mental health disorders. Eventually, if behavior is not changed through the use of strategies for students with these behaviors, these students demonstrate the same disruptive behavior in the community. In the community these behaviors are considered crimes. The result is, depending on the severity and the student's age, incarceration in a juvenile detention center or alternative schools, and if over 18 years old, incarceration.

Oppositional Defiant Disorder

According to the DSM-5 (American Psychiatric Association, 2013), oppositional defiant disorder (ODD) is identified by a group of behaviors. These behaviors are more severe than those one would see with a strong-willed child who battles a parent for preferred items and activities. Correcting the behaviors requires in-home and in-school strategies that rise above what is required for typical parenting. The following behaviors are exhibited:

- Often and easily loses temper
- Is easily annoyed by others
- Is often angry and resentful
- Often argues with adults or people in authority
- Refuses to comply to adult requests or rules
- Deliberately annoys others
- Blames others for own mistakes and misbehavior

ODD emerges in childhood and, if given intensive intervention during preschool, can be remediated. There are three levels of severity: mild, moderate, and severe. Mild indicates it occurs in only one setting, such as home or school. Moderate severity means it occurs in two settings, and severe is when it occurs in all settings. Parents feel duress when the child's ODD falls in any level of severity because this pattern of behavior indicates parental interventions were not sufficient to change the child's behavior.

School Problems

Due to the behaviors described in the moderate to severe range, poor school performance will be evident, including refusals to do schoolwork or speak appropriately to their peers. Children and adolescents with ODD often speak and act on impulse without considering the effects of their behavior or the feelings of others.

Students with ODD have difficulty making friends. Although they may demonstrate typical behaviors when interacting with peers, they are not predictable in their interaction styles. Other students may be unable to determine what may make the student with ODD angry or when they will be the target of the anger. Students with ODD may have other disorders or mental health disorders, such as ADHD, conduct disorders, depression, anxiety, and learning and communication disabilities.

Environmental Causes

Environmental conditions can cause poor behaviors in children and adolescents. The style of family communication and the family's respect for the law and authority guides the child. Therefore, some children are communicating the messages they have received from the parents.

Case Report: Andrew

Andrew lived with his family. The family did not work but would steal and then sell the stolen items. From a young age, Andrew would be put in the back seat of the car each night while the parents drove around to steal things.

Andrew had a mild intellectual disability and a long history of absenteeism, refusing to come to school. He also never did homework. He did not display aggression toward his peers. His oppositional behavior was around attendance and schoolwork. In this case, he was not viewed as oppositional because his oppositional behavior interfered with his own progress and not the progress of others. In 10th grade, Andrew moved in with his uncle and was placed in a program for students with emotional disturbance and learning needs. In his new placement, the special education teacher saw him talking to the students in the life skills class. As a result, he was given an in-school work experience in a special education class for students with moderate to severe intellectual disabilities. He went to the class every day, earning credit for his work there.

EXERCISE

1. Describe a student who has mild oppositional behaviors like Andrew. What could be done to help the student come to school and engage in transition planning?

DISCUSSION

According to his school records, Andrew refused to attend school or do homework and was diagnosed with ODD, a DSM-5 category, not an IDEA eligibility category. However, he was placed in the school district class for students with emotional disturbance. During his placement in this class, he shared his reason for not doing his work and being absent. Because he was in the back of the car all night, he did not get much sleep and was not able to do homework. On the mornings after the parents were stealing, they did not make him go to school.

Andrew did not follow in his parents footsteps and knew that what they were doing was wrong; he was able to leave them with a positive character. This is not always the case, and some students take their lead from the parents and participate in the same behavior, defying the rights of others. In Andrew's situation, he did receive benefit from his placement, even though he really did not have a mental health or behavioral disorder but he needed support and guidance to complete school.

Students with autism without intellectual or speech and language disabilities can look like ODD or like they have a behavioral disorder; however, their defiance and outbursts are based on their rigidity about how things should be or because of sensory issues that they cannot tolerate but also cannot articulate.

Case Report: Faith

Throughout middle school, Faith did not get on the bus in the morning but rather played in the woods. Her absenteeism and her parent's inability to monitor her school attendance resulted in a series of placements in mental health facilities and alternative schools for conduct disordered students. She was ultimately placed in a program for students with mental health disorders even though her behavior was not the result of the depression she reported. There she participated in an intensive transition planning program and counseling, and the team gave her references to work in a local library. Some women mentored her at the library, and she earned credit through the school credit recoupment program. Faith had an intelligence quotient of 117, and at 16 years old to graduate from a general public school would mean attending for 3 more years. Her transition planning specialist contacted the five previous placements and collected her grades from each. By putting together a transition and graduation plan, she made up credits and graduated. In the following excerpt, she talks about the programs she was in and how the academics fell far short of her needs:

> I remember, at my last long-term placement, we didn't start (sic) around with the academics with them pretending like we were dumb or giving us elementary math assignments all day, like nine plus two and things like that. I really appreciated that I did not have to go back to kindergarten like at the other hospitals (sic). We had algebra and things like that. The other places had basic math, science, social studies; I do not even know why they bother calling it academics. It was like kindergarten work without the naps. My brain was not ... my brain is not stupid, I am having emotional problems. I am normal that way, that part of me is a normal person. (Rae, 2011, p. 41)

DISCUSSION

When students have mental health and behavioral conditions, whether due to their environment or mental health disorders, their academics are often an add-on to the behavior intervention and counseling programs.

Faith was in four placements prior to the final one she describes here. Students with emotional and behavioral problems, whether they stem from genetic or environmental conditions, need the academics to continue using methods of credit recoupment and accommodations so they can access treatment. This student missed most of middle school due to absenteeism and lost academic programing in high school because alternative settings did not track and maintain grades. By adjusting her program, contacting all her programs for attendance, piecemealing her transcripts, and transitioning her into work, she was able to graduate. After high school, she married, had children, and is now attending school for accounting.

Brain Injury Causes of Behavior

Case Report: Harold and Rome

Both Harold and Rome had mild intellectual disabilities. They were in car accidents during first grade, and neither boy had a seat belt on. Both of them hit the windshield and sustained frontal lobe injuries. Each was affected by learning and organizational problems. Harry, at 14 years old, had a history of behavioral outbursts, and Rome did not learn to read. Neither had any medical tests or a full battery of assessments to determine which interventions would be effective. After placement, there was no academic progress.

DISCUSSION

Students like Harold and Rome need full assessment to effectively plan for their transition needs. If they have not learned to read, intensive intervention is necessary, and a complete neurological evaluation to determine if a medical need was causing the unprovoked outbursts. As discussed in the chapter on medical assessments, treatment may be warranted, especially in situations when the student's behavior may eventually result in imprisonment. Students with mental health disorders require treatment and specialized academic programs, and students with behavioral needs can benefit from medical assessment, routine monitoring to establish the underlying origin of problems with behavior, and behavior support plans to improve their social interactions.

TRANSITION PLANNING: MENTAL HEALTH DISORDERS AND BEHAVIORAL DISORDERS

Students within this eligibility category for special education can complete all parts of the framework of transition. Involving them and focusing on managing themselves in preparation for adult life is crucial. Students in these programs may come from families where illness, addiction, criminal behavior, or abuse have been part of the family or extended family history. In these situations, family cohesion is diminished, and the transition planning specialist and the team intensify the transition process because often these students attempt to leave and live on their own without being prepared. For some students, the transition planning specialist is helping them plan to leave families when they need to do so to survive. Whether they are in the public school setting or an alternative setting, it is crucial that the service of transition planning is available to help students who have lived or currently live in conditions that increase the impact of disability.

EXERCISE

1. Review the websites of five of the resources for Chapter 11, located in the Student Supplemental Materials.

SUMMARY

This chapter described the specific diagnoses for a group of students whose behaviors can significantly alter the trajectory to graduation, post-school education, and employment. Students with mental health disorders are eligible for special education through the designation of emotional disturbance or other health impairments or 504 plans. Students with mental health disorders often receive delayed treatment because their behaviors, such as school avoidance or incomplete assignments, are not disruptive to the classroom. Students who disrupt the educational environment, such as students with conduct problems, are often the first recipients of special education programming.

Mental health disorders have a deleterious effect on school functioning. Therefore, an immediate treatment plan is warranted. Many of these students have good academic skills. If the emergence of the condition has taken a significant toll on their high school achievement, these students can benefit from participation in summer community college courses to make up for high school credit. Self-esteem gains and the chance to see that they can succeed in post-school education can set them on the path to a positive outcome.

Conduct disorders and oppositional behavior are evident in students who have difficulty managing their conduct to align with social mores or who have undiagnosed autism without intellectual or speech and language disabilities/Asperger's disorder. Also, students who may have an undiagnosed medical problem, such as seizures, may exhibit extreme behavioral outbursts as well. For this group of students, transition planning can be highly effective when complete diagnostics and medical assessments are completed to rule out a medical problem and intensive planning, supports, and counseling are prominent features of the plan. Students with maladjusted behavior are not eligible for special education. However, special consideration should go to programs for these students who are often placed in programs for students with emotional disturbance who come from life situations where they are being sexually, emotionally, and physically abused; have suffered neglect; do not have enough food or any medical care; have parents with alcoholism or drug dependencies; and do not receive the love and support of their parents. They also have nongenetic or genetically based mental conditions (e.g., anxiety, depression). Students who are socially or behaviorally maladjusted are often disruptive to the community, and an educational and treatment program to mediate the environmental or thinking errors that underpin the behavior of these students may be warranted.

REFERENCES

Abramson, L. Y., Alloy, L. B., & Metalsky, G. I. (1989). Hopelessness depression: A theory-based subtype of depression. *Psychological Review, 96*(2), 358-372.

American Psychiatric Association. (2000). *Diagnostic and statistical manual of mental disorders* (4th ed., text revision). Washington, DC: American Psychiatric Association Publishing.

American Psychiatric Association. (2013). *Diagnostic and statistical manual of mental disorders* (5th ed.). Washington, DC: American Psychiatric Association Publishing.

American Psychiatric Association. (2019). What is obsessive-compulsive disorder? Retrieved from https://www.psychiatry.org/patients-families/ocd/what-is-obsessive-compulsive-disorder

Bandura, A. (1982). Self-efficacy mechanism in human agency. *American Psychologist, 37*(2), 122-147.

Bandura, A. (1986). Fearful expectations and avoidant actions as coeffects of perceived self-inefficacy. *American Psychologist, 41*(12), 1389-1391.

Bandura, A. (1994). Self-efficacy. In V. S. Ramachaudran (Ed.), *Encyclopedia of human behavior* (Vol. 4, pp. 71-81). New York, NY: Academic Press.

Beck, A. T. (1967). *Depression: Causes and treatment.* Philadelphia, PA: First University of Pennsylvania Press.

Beck, A. T., Emery, G., & Greenberg, R. L. (1985). *Anxiety disorders and phobias: A cognitive perspective.* New York, NY: HarperCollins Publishers.

Beck, A. T., & Rush, A. J., Shaw, B. F, & Emery, G.(1979). *Cognitive therapy of depression.* New York, NY: Guilford.

Beck, A. T., Wenzel, A., Riskind, J. H., Brown, G., & Steer, R. A. (2006). Specificity of hopelessness about resolving life problems: Another test of the cognitive model of depression. *Cognitive Therapy Research, 30,* 773-781.

Beidel, D. C., Turner, S. M., & Dancu, C. V. (1985). Physiological, cognitive and behavioral aspects of social anxiety. *Behavior Research and Therapy, 23*(2), 109-117.

Beidel, D. C., Turner, S. M., & Morris, T. L. (1999). Psychopathology of childhood social phobia. *Journal of American Academy of Child and Adolescent Psychiatry, 38*(6), 643-650.

Benito, K. G., & Walther, M. (2015). Therapeutic process during exposure: Habituation model. *Journal of Obsessive-Compulsive and Related Disorders, 6,* 147-157.

Birmaher, B., Axelson, D., Strober, M., & Gill, M. (2006). Clinical course of children and adolescents with bipolar spectrum disorders. *Archives of General Psychiatry, 63*(2), 175-183.

Brown, J., Cohen, P., Johnson, J. G., & Smailes, E. M. (1999). Childhood abuse and neglect: Specificity of effects on adolescent and young adult depression and suicidality. *Journal of the American Academy of Child and Adolescent Psychiatry, 38*(12), 1490-1496.

Brozina, K., & Abela, R. Z. (2006). Symptoms of depression and anxiety in children: Specificity of the hopelessness theory. *Journal of Clinical Child and Adolescent Psychology, 35*(4), 515-527.

Brunello, N., den Boer, J. A., Judd, L. L., Kasper, S., Kelsey, J. E., Lader, M., … Wittchen, H. U. (2000). Social phobia: Diagnosis and epidemiology, neurobiology and pharmacology, comorbidity and treatment. *Journal of Affective Disorders, 60*(1), 61-74.

Burnham, J. J., Schaefer, B. A., & Giesen, J. (2006). An empirical taxonomy of youths' fears: Cluster analysis of the American fear survey schedule. *Psychology in Schools, 43*(6), 673-683.

Centers for Disease Control and Prevention. (2004). *Morbidity and mortality weekly report, 53*(22), 471-474.

Child with a disability, 34 C.F.R. § 300.8 (2017).

Clement, S., Schauman, O., Graham, T., Maggioni, F., Evans-Lacko, S., Bezborodovs, N., … Thornicroft, G. (2015). What is the impact of mental health-related stigma on help-seeking? A systematic review of quantitative and qualitative studies. *Psychological Medicine, 45*(1), 11-27.

Corrigan, P. W., Druss, B. G., & Perlick, D. A. (2014). The impact of mental illness stigma on seeking and participating in mental health care. *Psychological Science in the Public Interest, 15,* 37-70.

Corrigan, P. W., Larson, J. E., & Rüsch, N. (2009). Self-stigma and the "why try" effect: Impact on life goals and evidence-based practices. *World Psychiatry, 8*(2), 75-81.

Demeter, C. A., Townsend, L. D., Wilson, M., & Findling, R. L. (2008). Current research in child and adolescent bipolar disorder. *Dialogues in Clinical Neuroscience, 10*(2), 215-228.

Field, A. P. (2006). Watch out for the beast: Fear information and attentional bias in children. *Journal of Clinical Child & Adolescent Psychology, 35*(3), 431-439. Https://doi-org.ezproxy.sju.edu/10.1207/s15374424jccp3503_8

First, M. B., France, A., & Pincus, H. A. (2004). *DSM-IV-TR guidebook*. Arlington, VA: American Psychiatric Publishing.

Fristad, M. A., Goldberg-Arnold, J. S., & Gavazzi, S. M. (2002). Multifamily psychoeducation groups (MFPG) for families of Children with bipolar disorder. *Bipolar Disorders, 4,* 254–262.

Gabel, S., & Sarvet, B. (2011). Public-academic partnerships: Public-academic partnerships to address the need for child and adolescent psychiatric services. *Psychiatric Services, 62*(8), 827-829.

Geller, B., & Luby, J. (1997). Child and adolescent bipolar disorder: A review of the past ten years. *Journal of the American Academy of Child and Adolescent Psychiatry, 36,* 1168-1176.

Ginsburg, G. S., Riddle, M. A., & Davies, M. (2006). Somatic symptoms in children and adolescents with anxiety disorders. *Journal of the American Child and Adolescent Psychiatry, 45*(10), 1179-1187.

Heron M. (2018). Deaths: Leading causes for 2016. *National Vital Statistics Reports*; vol 67 no 6. Hyattsville, MD: National Center for Health Statistics.

Ivey-Stephenson, A. Z., Crosby, A. E., Jack, S. P. D., Haileyesus, T., Kresnow-Sedacca, M. J. (2017). Suicide trends among and within urbanization levels by sex, race/ethnicity, age group, and mechanism of death—United States, 2001–2015. *Morbidity and Mortality Weekly Report. Surveillance Summaries, 66*(18), 1-16. doi:10.15585/mmwr.ss6618a1

Jennings, K. S., Cheung, J. H., Britt, T. W., Goguen, K. N., Jeffirs, S. M., Peasley, A. L., & Lee, A. C. (2015). How are perceived stigma, self-stigma, and self-reliance related to treatment-seeking? A three-path model. *Psychiatric Rehabilitation Journal, 38*(2), 109.

Kauffman, J. M., & Landrum, T. J. (2013). *Characteristics of emotional and behavioral disorders of children and youth* (10th ed.). New York, NY: Pearson.

Kazdin, A. E. (1997). A model for developing effective treatments: Progression and interplay of theory, research and practice. *Journal of Clinical Child Psychology, 26*(2), 114-129.

Kessler, R. C. (2007). The global burden of anxiety and mood disorders: Putting the European Study of the Epidemiology of Mental Disorders (ESEMeD) findings into perspective. *Journal of Clinical Psychiatry, 68,* 10-19.

Kessler, R. C., Berglund, P., Demler, O., Jin, R., Koretz, D., Merikangas, K. R., ... Wang, P. S. (2003). The epidemiology of major depressive disorder. *Journal of the American Medical Association, 289*(23), 3095-3105.

Kessler, R. C., Berglund, P. A., Demler, O., Jin, R., & Walters, E. E. (2005). Lifetime prevalence and age-of-onset distributions of DSM-IV disorders in the National Comorbidity Survey Replication (NCS-R). *Archives of General Psychiatry, 62*(6), 593-602.

Kessler, R. C., & Wang, P. S. (2008). The descriptive epidemiology of commonly occurring mental disorders in the United States. *Annual Review of Public Health, 29,* 115-129.

Kim, E. Y., Miklowitz, D. J., Biuckians, A., & Mullen, K. (2006). Life stress and course of early-onset bipolar disorder. *Journal of Affective Disorders, 99*(1-3), 37-44.

Kotrba, A. (2014). *Selective mutism: An assessment and intervention guide for therapists, educators & parents*. Eau Claire, WI: Pesi Publishing & Media.

Kowatch, R. A., Fristad, M., Birmaher, B., & Wagner, K. D., Findling, R. L., & Hellander, M. (2005). Treatment guidelines for children and adolescents with bipolar disorder. *Journal of the American Academy of Child and Adolescent Psychiatry, 44*(3), 213-235.

Last, C. G., & Strauss, C. C. (1990). School refusal in anxiety-disordered children and adolescents. *Journal of the American Academy of Child and Adolescent Psychiatry, 29*(1), 31-35.

Lewinsohn, P. M., Rohde, P., Seeley, J. R., Klein, D. N., & Gotlib, I. H. (2000). Natural course of adolescent major depressive disorder in a community sample: Predictors of recurrence in young adults. *American Journal of Psychiatry, 157*(10), 1584-1591.

Link, B. G., Phelan, J. C., Bresnahan, M., Stueve, A., & Pescosolido, B. A. (1999). Public conception of mental illness: Labels, causes, dangerousness, and social distance. *American Journal of Public Health, 89*(9), 1328-1333.

Livingston, J. D., & Boyd, J. E. (2010). Correlates and consequences of internalized stigma for people living with mental illness: A systematic review and meta-analysis. *Social Science & Medicine, 71*(12), 2150-2161.

Mauss, I. B., Wilhelm, F. H., & Gross, J. J. (2003). Autonomic recovery and habituation in social anxiety. *Psychophysiology, 40*(4), 648-653.

Merikangas, K. R., Akiskal, H., Angst, J., Greenberg, P. E., Hirschfeld, R. M. A., Petukhova, M., & Kessler, R. C. (2007). Lifetime and 12 month prevalence of bipolar spectrum disorder in the National Comorbidity Survey Replication. *Archives of General Psychology, 64*(5), 543-552.

Miklowitz, D. J., George, E. L., Richards, J. A., Simoneau, T. L., & Suddath, R. L. (2003). A randomized study of family-focused psychoeducation and pharmacotherapy in the outpatient management of bipolar disorder. *Archives of General Psychiatry, 60*(9), 904-912.

Miziou, S., Tsitsipa, E., Moysidou, S., Karavelas, V., Dimelis, D., Polyzoidou, V., & Fountoulakis, K. N. (2015). Psychosocial treatment and interventions for bipolar disorder: A systematic review. *Annals of General Psychiatry, 14*(1), 19.

Nasar, S. (1994, November 13). The Lost Years of a Nobel Laureate. *The New York Times*. Retrieved from https://www. nytimes.com/1994/11/13/business/the-lost-years-of-a-nobel-laureate.html

New Freedom Commission on Mental Health. (2005). Subcommittee on Evidence-Based Practices: Background paper. DHHS Pub. No. SMA 05 4007. Rockville, MD: Department of Health and Human Services.

Ollendick, T. H., & King, N. J. (2004). Empirically supported treatments for children and adolescents: Advances toward evidence-based practice. In P. M. Barrett & T. H. Ollendick (Eds.), *Handbook of interventions that work with children and adolescents: Prevention and treatment*. Chichester, England: John Wiley and Sons, Ltd.

Paus, T., Keshavan, M., & Giedd, J. N. (2008). Why do many psychiatric disorders emerge during adolescence?. Nature reviews. *Neuroscience, 9*(12), 947-957. doi:10.1038/nrn2513

Pavuluri, M. N., Graczyk, P. A., Henry, D. B., Carbray, J. A., Heidenreich, J., & Miklowitz, D. J. (2004). Child- and family-focused cognitive-behavioral therapy for pediatric bipolar disorder: Development and preliminary results. *Journal of the American Academy of Child and Adolescent Psychiatry, 43*(5), 528-537.

Rae, J. M. (2011). Post Transition Planning–Young Adult Stories—Perspectives on School and Life: A Case Study of Employment, Social, Family and Mental Health Management Outcomes of Three Young Adults Who Completed Two or More Years of High School in an Emotional and Behavioral Special Education Program in Partial Hospitalization 1 Setting (Doctoral dissertation). Retrieved from Proquest. (3448164).

Rao, U., Ryan, N. D., Birmaher, B., & Dahl, R. E. (1995). Unipolar depression in adolescents: Clinical outcome in adulthood. *Journal of the American Academy of Child & Adolescent Psychiatry, 34*(5), 566-578.

Reinherz, H. Z., Giaconia, R. M., Hauf, A. M., Wasserman, M. S., & Silverman, A. B. (1999). Major depression in the transition to adulthood: Risks and impairments. *Journal of Abnormal Psychology, 108*(3), 500-510.

Seligman, M. E. (1975). *Helplessness: On depression, development, and death. A series of books in psychology*. New York, NY: WH Freeman/Times Books/Henry Holt & Co.

Shaffer, D., Gould, M. S., Fisher, P., Trautman, P., Moreau, D., Kleinman, M., & Flory, M. (1996). Psychiatric diagnosis in child and adolescent suicide. *Archives of General Psychiatry, 53*(4), 339-348.

Stone, D. M., Simon, T. R., Fowler, K. A., Kegler, S. R., Yuan, K., Holland, K. M., ... & Crosby, A. E. (2018). Vital signs: Trends in state suicide rates—United States, 1999–2016 and circumstances contributing to suicide—27 states, 2015. *Morbidity and Mortality Weekly Report, 67*(22), 617.

Sullivan, E. M., Annest, J. L., Simon, T. R., Luo, F., & Dahlberg, L. L. (2015). Suicide trends among persons aged 10-24 years—United States, 1994–2012. *Morbidity and Mortality Weekly Report, 64*(8), 201.

Substance Abuse and Mental Health Services Administration. (2008). *Results from the 2007 National Survey on Drug Use and Health: national findings*. NSDUH Series H-34, DHHS Publication No. SMA 08-4343. Rockville, MD: Department of Health and Human Services.

Substance Abuse and Mental Health Services Administration. (2016). The Comprehensive Community Mental Health Services for Children with Serious Emotional Disturbances Program, Report to Congress 2016. Rockville, MD: Author. Retrieved from https://store.samhsa.gov/system/files/pep18-cmhi2016.pdf

Walker, J., Geddes, A., Lever, N., Andrews, C., & Weist, M. (2010). Reconsidering the term 'emotional disturbance': A report from Maryland. *Advances in School Mental Health Promotion, 3*(2), 46.

Weems, C. F., Hayward, C., Killen, J., & Taylor, C. B. (2002). A longitudinal study of anxiety sensitivity in adolescence. *Journal of Abnormal Psychology, 111*(3), 471-477.

Weisz, J. R., & Hawley, K. M. (2002) Developmental factors in the treatment of adolescents. *Journal of Consulting and Clinical Psychology, 70*(1), 21-43.

Young, M. E., & Fristad, M. A. (2007). Evidence-based treatments for bipolar disorder in children and adolescents. *Journal of Contemporary Psychotherapy, 37*(3), 157-164.

Students Who Are Blind, Visually Impaired, Deaf, Hard of Hearing, or Deaf-Blind

SECTION 1: STUDENTS WHO ARE BLIND OR VISUALLY IMPAIRED

OBJECTIVES

- → Describe the difference between legal blindness and visual impairment used in the Individuals with Disabilities Education Act (IDEA) definition.
- → Describe three vision impairments.
- → Describe how Braille expedites learning and use current research to support contentions.
- → Describe how visual field affects learning.
- → Research three current technological advancements to support persons who are blind in college and at work.

BLINDNESS AND VISUAL IMPAIRMENTS

§ 300.8 Child with a disability.

(13) Visual impairment including blindness means an impairment in vision that, even with correction, adversely affects a child's educational performance. The term includes both partial sight and blindness.

(§ 300.8 Child with a disability [71 FR 46753, Aug. 14, 2006, as amended at 72 FR 61306, Oct. 30, 2007; 82 FR 31912, July 11, 2017])

Rae, J. M. *A Collaborative Approach to Transition Planning for Students With Disabilities* (pp. 255-283).

Students with a visual impairment can have various degrees of vision loss that significantly affect learning. A medical assessment is used to diagnose a student with legal blindness or low vision. *Legal blindness* is a term many are familiar with. Legal blindness is used to label the degree of visual acuity or visual field in order to determine qualifications for government benefits. Low vision is another descriptor to describe a significant reduction of visual acuity that ordinary eyeglasses, contact lenses, and medical treatment cannot entirely correct.

Vision impairment rather than legal blindness is the IDEA (2004) category for special education eligibility, and a student does not need to be legally blind or have low vision to receive services under IDEA. A visual impairment that affects the ability to learn is the qualifying criteria. In the next section, some visual impairments that affect learning are described.

TYPES OF VISION IMPAIRMENT

Congenital Cataracts

Congenital cataracts are present at birth or acquired (also known as *pediatric cataracts)*. A cataract is cloudiness or opacity apparent in the usually transparent crystalline lens of the eye. It causes blurry vision. If undiscovered, it can lead to abnormal connections between the brain and eye. Cloudiness can also cause a decrease in vision that may lead to eventual blindness. If a cataract is large enough, it blocks the light from reaching the retina, and the retina cannot send the signal to the brain. Congenital cataracts are the "most treatable cause of blindness and cause half of vision impairments" (Messina-Baas & Cuevas-Covarrubias, 2017).

Cortical Vision and Cerebral Vision Impairment

Visual impairment for these types of impairments can range from mild to blindness (Roman-Lantzy, 2007).

Cortical vision impairment is historically associated with brain injury, neurological vision loss, and loss due to traumatic brain injury. The injury occurs in the visual cortex and the occipital lobe, so the brain cannot interpret the visual input, even though both eyes are intact. The loss is bilateral with normal pupil responses. Eye examination shows no abnormalities. Although the term *cortical vision impairment* is not precise, it is widely used (Hoyt, 2003).

Philip and Dutton (2014) describe *cerebral vision impairment* (CVI) as another term used to define brain injury to the more complex processing sites in the brain. There are multiple causes, and it is common in children with cerebral palsy (p. 196). No damage to eye structures is seen in CVI. Individuals with CVI may have a variety of visual impairments, including decreased visual acuity and visual field deficits.

Visual processing impairments can interfere with the individual's ability to, for example, identify faces or find objects in a cluttered environment and lead to functional limitations that affect an individual's learning, mobility, development, independence, and quality of life. There are a number of causes of CVI, including infection, but the most common cause of CVI-related brain damage is hypoxia (when the brain does not get enough oxygen), such as in near-drowning or choking. The condition is also caused by head injury, abnormalities in brain formation, hydrocephalus (increased fluid and pressure in the brain), seizures, metabolic diseases, infection, or neurologic disorders (Philip & Dutton, 2014).

Glaucoma

Glaucoma is any of a group of eye diseases characterized by abnormally high intraocular fluid pressure, damaged optic disc, hardening of the eyeball, and partial to complete loss of vision (National Eye Institute [NEI], 2015).

Figure 12-1. Peripheral vision loss image.

Nystagmus

The term *nystagmus* describes fast, involuntary movements of the eyes that may be side to side, up and down, or in a rotation. It can occur in one or both eyes and be present at birth or as a result of an injury. The back-and-forth movement may be minuscule or more pronounced (NEI, 2018).

Optic Nerve Atrophy

Optic nerve atrophy is degeneration of the optic nerve. It can be mild to severe, and it adversely affects central, peripheral, and color vision. Nystagmus can cause this type of degeneration, as can trauma, tumor, decreased blood flow or oxygen, toxins, infections, and hydrocephalus. Vision loss can be mild or severe (NEI, 2018).

Retinopathy of Prematurity

Retinopathy of prematurity is damage to the retina due to the high oxygen levels given after a premature delivery. The use of oxygen to treat premature infants for respiratory distress is associated with damage to the retina (Hartnett & Lane, 2013).

FIELD OF VISION

Field Loss

Glaucoma originates in unrelieved pressure inside the eye as a result of fluid buildup. Permanent impairment can range from loss of peripheral vision to severe vision loss (Figure 12-1). Individuals with glaucoma may experience increased frequency of headaches, blurred vision, halos around lights, difficulty seeing in the dark, and sometimes a nonreactive pupil, pain, or even a swollen eye.

Retinitis pigmentosa is a progressive visual impairment with various end results, ranging from significant vision loss to total blindness. It also causes loss of peripheral vision. One common symptom is night blindness. Retinitis pigmentosa is one of the most common forms of inherited retinal degeneration (Retinitis pigmentosa, 2010).

Figure 12-2. Central vision loss image of retinal detachment.

Figure 12-3. Hemianopsia (also called *hemianopia*). Image of left and right field vision loss.

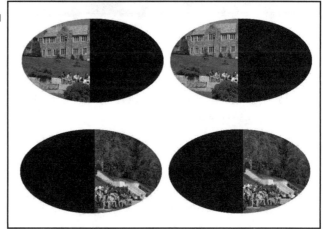

Retinal Detachment

The most common type of retinal detachment is a tear or hole in the retina. Eye fluids may leak through this opening. The fluid leakage causes the retina to separate from the underlying tissues. Causes of retinal detachment can be diabetes, trauma, and severe nearsightedness. Another type of retinal detachment is called *tractional detachment*. Retinal detachment is seen in people who have uncontrolled diabetes, previous retinal surgery, or chronic inflammation (NEI, 2015). When the retina becomes detached, bleeding from area blood vessels may cloud the inside of the eye, an area normally filled with vitreous fluid. Central vision becomes severely affected if the macula, the part of the retina responsible for fine vision, becomes detached. Figure 12-2 represents field loss and blindness.

Hemianopsia

A right or left side homonymous hemianopsia (also called *hemianopia)* is the loss of half of the field of view on the same side in both eyes (Figure 12-3). It frequently occurs in stroke and traumatic brain injuries due to the connections and wiring of the visual system with the brain. About 55% of the cases resulting from traumatic brain injury improve (Zhang, Kedar, Lynn, Newman, & Biousse, 2006). Therefore, vision services may be temporary.

In hemianopsia, damage to one side of the brain affects vision. The visual images that one sees on the right side travel from both eyes to the left side of the brain, while the visual images one sees on the left side in each eye travels to the right side of the brain. Therefore, damage to the right side of the posterior portion of the brain can cause a loss of the left field of view in both eyes.

Figure 12-4. Upper homonymous hemianopsia. An upper field vision loss.

Figure 12-5. Lower homonymous hemianopsia. A lower field vision loss.

It is difficult to illustrate how the person sees with this impairment. The North American Neuro-Ophthalmology Society suggests turning the head and eyes all the way to the left and then walking backward (2016). If the right arm is extended at shoulder height and brought around, pointing straight ahead until it enters the left side field of vision, this demonstrates the degree of field loss. The person does not see a black field but rather no image is entering the brain.

For students with this visual impairment, reading is a significant challenge. When vision is missing in the right field, tracking is impaired. Tracking from the end of the line to the beginning of the next is inaccurate, and the reader often misses the next line. Using a ruler so that the eye can track the printed word can be useful. Boundary-marking devices can aid in reading for both left and right hemianopsia. They can be electronic, or a hemi reading card is helpful and adaptable for both right and left homonymous hemianopsia.

Visual hallucinations or perceptions of additional objects not actually present in the environment are common with hemianopsia.

Upper Homonymous Hemianopsia

In homonymous hemianopsia, the missing visual input can be in the upper or lower field of vision (Figures 12-4 and 12-5). This type of field loss is infrequent. It does not affect reading, but the placement of texts must be adjusted. However, students with severe physical disabilities may not be able to adjust the texts to the correct position.

Strabismus

Strabismus is a misalignment of the eye. It is often present in children with severe disabilities, but it can be present in children without other disabilities as well. Three cranial nerves responsible for eye movement can cause strabismus. When these nerves are weak or otherwise not aligning the eyes, it creates different types of strabismus. In strabismus, the brain sees two different images. The brain may be able to ignore the second image to avoid seeing two images, but it results in reduced vision in the less dominant eye. Strabismus can prevent normal eye tracking during reading and cause the eyes to see two parts of the sentence simultaneously, or the text may appear to slide to the right or left over the next group of words as the eye tracks the printed words during reading. Strabismus can occur in late childhood or even later, and in that case, the dominant eye does not remove the second image. In strabismus, the eyes may look toward the nose, in the opposite direction from each other, or any other combination in which the eyes do not move in unison (Pineles et al., 2013).

These examples do not represent all vision impairments but are provided to demonstrate the significant impact vision can have on learning and the need for highly trained professionals as transition planning team members.

Students with these impairments need specialized services. Although many students with these impairments can learn to read with technological support, others cannot. Students who are unable to see the printed word with any corrective devices use Braille and other supportive technology, such as text-to-speech applications (Rosenberg, Westling, & McLeskey, 2011).

Case Report: Daniel

Daniel had borderline average intellectual disabilities. At age 13, he was blind in one eye and developed cataracts in his other eye. He had surgery, and sadly, it was unsuccessful, and Daniel was determined legally blind. At age 12 he had a consultation with a teacher of the visually impaired, and his teacher and the consultant worked together to develop a new classroom program in his current placement in a special education program with students with learning disabilities. During an Individualized Education Plan (IEP) team meeting, it was determined that his needs could be met by the classroom teacher. However, when the teacher left on medical leave, the new temporary teacher did not implement the interventions as intended. Daniel became withdrawn and depressed and would not move from one area of the classroom. Daniel was transition age, and it was determined that Daniel should have received mobility training after the loss of his vision. Over the summer he was sent to a nearby school for the blind, where he learned to access the environment. He became active again, and his school district decided that the new environment better suited his needs for transition.

Discussion

Vision therapy, mobility therapy, and improving access to assistive technology to promote independence are lifetime supports for children, adolescents, and adults who are blind. Daniel's loss of vision made him severely depressed, and without the teacher he knew well, he became depressed and afraid. He was dependent upon one individual. Students who are blind or become blind need to develop self-efficacy in their ability to access the environment without dependence on a few individuals. Like adolescents without visual impairment, they want to be as mobile and active as possible. Any student with acquired blindness will also need psychological support in the form of counseling. The parents and the school team need to address the psychological issues and move forward, as in Daniel's case, and teach him to do what he did independently before he lost his vision. Students with visual impairments can develop to be fully self-determined and develop self-efficacy through the transition planning process and the vision and mobility teachers, therapists, and agencies that support students who are blind.

STUDENT GROWTH: LEARNING, LANGUAGE, AND SOCIAL INTERACTIONS

Braille

Braille has been well established as a reading method for the blind. IDEA (1997) ensures that the blind and visually impaired are provided Braille instruction to receive a free appropriate public education. IDEA (2004) reauthorized this requirement. The requirement for Braille also applies when a vision impairment is known as a progressive condition that will result in blindness. There has been some concern that schools are decreasing the use of Braille. In June 2013, a letter from Musgrove and Yudin (2013), Director of the Office of Special Education and Rehabilitative Services was sent to the states to reaffirm the use of Braille instruction as a literacy tool for the blind and visually impaired. "Nearly 90 percent of America's blind children are not learning to read and write because they are not being taught Braille or given access to it. There is a Braille literacy crisis in America" (National Federation of the Blind [NFB], 2009). Research provides evidence that there are many intellectual benefits to using Braille. In a study of blind adults who met multiple criteria for success, the following quotes by two participants in the study describe how Braille was essential to their lives:

> Knowing how to look at your environment with your hands and being encouraged and allowed to do this from a young age is so important. I would make sure that any blind child was encouraged to explore the environment with his hands, and I would put Braille on the refrigerator.
>
> What you really need to do is learn how to read Braille first; you've got to have those basic skills. I couldn't have done the mathematics I've done without Braille, and it helped lead to my advanced degrees. (Goodwyn, Bell, & Singletary, 2009, pp. 10-11)

For the transition planning specialist who will work on transition plans with students who are visually impaired, Braille instruction and access to it are written explicitly in the transition plan and the IEP to ensure students' access to it. Many universities and public libraries provide Braille libraries, and students who are blind or becoming progressively blind benefit from them.

Transition planning specialists can be instrumental in advocating for students by being knowledgeable about technology, including Braille, and working with teachers of the visually impaired to facilitate the development of literacy skills needed for post-school life.

Social Interactions

A student who is blind or has low vision may not be able to see gestures or facial expressions. However, even with the limitations of a vision impairment, a student who is blind or visually impaired has environmental cues that help him or her assess social situations. Voice pitch can provide clues about the conversational message, and persons who are blind can access meaning and judge character using voice tone. There is research to support that assessing others by their vocalizations, specifically by pitch, may require little to no experience, and both sighted and blind people can access reliable information, such as competence and trustworthiness, with this innate skill (Oleszkiewicz, Pisanski, Lachowicz-Tabaczek, & Sorokowska, 2017). The pitch and vocal variations help a student who is blind be aware of environmental activities and enable him or her to judge what is happening contextually. Even with this innate ability, students who are blind miss the incidental learning from social experiences and may respond incorrectly to social situations. Adolescents who are blind benefit from ongoing explicit instruction to understand what they may be missing throughout the transition planning period when conversations become more complex and social interaction contexts change. One way to support secondary students in developing these skills is by providing opportunities to engage with their peers in activities such as school clubs and group projects.

TRANSITION PLANNING: BLIND AND VISUAL IMPAIRMENTS

Depending on the degree of blindness, a student will feel the effect of his or her disability in various ways. The student may not be able to read as quickly or as fluently, or he or she may not be able to read at all. Therefore, the interventions the student receives will be quite diverse and addressed in the transition plan. The plan should include the continued use of Braille or any other support technologies, such as screen enlargement via a portable electronic magnifier, screen lighting, or text-to-speech low vision products. Audio textbooks or programs that convert textbooks to speech and braille help students who are blind progress through school with peers. Ongoing use of technology to support language learning, subject matter, and general education classroom participation is added to the transition plan as better-developed devices come onto the market. Lifelong learning for adolescents with low vision and blindness can significantly improve the quality of life and should be an area of focus of transition planning.

Adolescents who are blind can become leaders in their IEP development, but they will need some supports. The IEP should be in Braille, and they should also have a copy on their computer in the text-to-speech format. Their conferences will need additional participants because they will need guidance to help them access the training and post-school environments that are inaccessible because they are web-based only. School libraries should provide up-to-date Braille sections, and Braille ordering programs can provide students with multiple reading materials about colleges and post-school employment, programs, and services for students who are blind.

Students who are blind should register for vocational rehabilitation services through a local agency designated through the Department of Health and Human Services. These agencies coordinate services for children, adolescents, and young adults who are blind. Every state has an agency designated to assist young persons who are blind or visually impaired who are transitioning from high school. For instance, in Florida, the Florida Division of Blind Services helps the blind and visually impaired reach their transition plan goals through their transition services, independent living, and vocational rehabilitation programs. Florida also provides employer services, a business enterprise program, and a rehabilitation center to provide a temporary residence while young persons learn new skills until they can transition to an independent living situation.

In each state, supports are in place to assist students who are blind with post-school education or employment and with community living, as well as giving them access to leisure activities. Most states provide printed material, Braille, and talking books libraries. Many cities have designed parks to be accessible to the blind to increase inclusion. The transition planning specialist is expected to know the services provided in their state.

Working with the parents to understand and use state services can significantly help advance a student's progress toward post-school goals. The transition planning specialist and the parents must understand the contact and application process for their state for each agency designated to assist students who are visually impaired. The transition planning specialist and the parents should be apprised of what services the Division for the Blind is carrying out, which may include coordinating vocational rehabilitation services and transition services, including assessment for eligibility, referral information, assistive technology, counseling services, and job readiness services, specifically as they relate to students who are blind.

Employment

In most states, the vocational rehabilitation program helps individuals who are blind prepare for or retain employment. Services offered can include, but are not limited to, the following:
- Counseling and guidance
- Vocational evaluation
- Blindness skills training

- Mobility (travel) instruction
- Instruction on performing daily living activities
- Vocational and college training
- Occupational tools and equipment
- Job placement services
- Vocational and situational assessments
- Resume support
- Interviewing skills development
- Job development
- Job placement and retention services
- Job coaching services
- Job accommodation support and employer education
- Travel training to navigate public transportation
- Employer consultation for technology use

Services are based on employment needs and choices, and vocational rehabilitation counselors work directly with the student to determine an employment goal and what services are needed to reach student goals.

The transition planning specialist must be well-versed about in-school and post-school services and options. Typically, a transition planning specialist is not a certified teacher of the visually impaired. Therefore, when a transition planning specialist is involved in transition planning, for a secondary school student with a visual impairment, the transition planning specialist still plays a significant role in ensuring that all the plans are implemented and include post-school agency meetings, the vision therapist, and transition services, such as mobility training on a college campus. The transition planning specialist in collaboration with the vision therapist, teachers of the blind, and the student's family are crucial players who ensure that the student's technology is up to date and that the transition plan and IEP provide the student with the highest level of support.

Community Support

A cohesive group of school personnel, family members, agencies, teachers, support persons, and friends help the student to access resources in the environment. If the student is to access any of the websites for the blind and visually impaired, the first contact will need to be a sighted person, or the student will need to have some supports in place to be able to access a web-based system, such as text-to-speech, to have these programs uploaded to their devices and computers. As mentioned previously, agencies such as the NFB take calls, emails, and chats to assist students, their families, and employers. An individual can contact the agency (in whichever form he or she prefers), explain the purpose of his or her call, and then proceed from there. Agencies such as the Job Accommodation Network (JAN) offer guidance on what the Americans with Disabilities Act requires of employers. This agency also helps employers to make their workplaces more accessible to workers who are blind or visually impaired. Agencies such as JAN are grant funded through the Office of Disability Employment Policy, and JAN is part of the Department of Labor.

Teachers of the Visually Impaired

A teacher of the visually impaired is assigned to a student when a visual impairment is diagnosed and the student is determined eligible for special education and related services. The student must be diagnosed by an ophthalmologist or optometrist to determine the need for vision aids, and the teacher of the visually impaired recommends instructional materials. Teachers of the visually impaired are certified teachers who also have a certification for teaching the visually impaired. Teachers of the visually impaired directly instruct the student and provide additional specially designed instruction. They also support student learning by providing direction to the team about the nature of the visual disability and best practices for the student based on his or her needs and abilities. Teachers of the visually impaired are instrumental in helping the student transition to college or other post-school education. They can help the student develop a list of exploratory options and work with school librarians to ensure reading materials and informational documents are available to the student.

Teachers of the Visually Impaired and Supports for Learning and Communication

Schools are the primary providers of in-school technological supports for students who are blind or visually impaired. The following is a list of supports that the teacher of the visually impaired can ensure are part of the student's learning tools:

- Braille keyboards
- Enlarged computer monitors
- Vision therapist services
- Orientation and mobility (O&M)
- Electronic or optical magnifiers
- Large picture books
- Closed circuit television used to enlarge existing print
- Screen enlargers for computers
- Smartboards
- Talking watch, calculator, or clock
- Raised picture books
- Audiobooks
- Tactile communication boards
- Special illumination
- Placement of pictures and text for visual access
- Contrast and color
- Tactile maps

Other supports are school guides that are placed around the building so the student knows where he or she is in the building. The teacher of the visually impaired and the mobility specialist work together to ensure these needs are met.

All teams must be aware of how the disability affects the student's education, career explorations, and independence and leisure activities. The student should feel free to express his or her needs to the team because he or she knows the effects of their disability the best. The wide variety of visual disabilities requires that students be well aware of their strengths and abilities and how they can use their skills in a work environment. As a student creates his or her disability narrative and goes through the transition planning curriculum and career explorations, the student, his or her transition planning specialist, his or her IEP team, supporting agencies, and his or her family can assist the student to design a program structure and delineate the type of employment he or she would like to pursue based on his or her knowledge of him- or herself. Like their peers, they too can benefit from creating a career portfolio to include the careers they are considering. Additionally, they can create a list of technological and mobility supports they will need to reach their educational and employment goals.

ORIENTATION AND MOBILITY SERVICES

In 1997, IDEA mandated that O&M services be offered to any student who is blind or visually impaired who needs them to access the school environment (Neal, Bigby, & Nicholson, 2004). For example, the O&M specialist teaches students with visual impairments to navigate the school environment. As part of transition planning, orientation to the high school or post-school environments may include O&M instruction to gain the following skills:

- A student may need to adapt to spatial and environmental concepts (e.g., sound, temperature, vibrations, directional indicators) to establish or maintain the student's orientation in multiple school and post-school environments.
- A student may need to develop motor skills and stamina for varied terrains.
- A student may want to learn how to use the human-guide technique training to increase his or her independence.
- A student may desire orientation training to access a future college campus.
- A student may want training to set patterns of travel in his or her town or city.
- A student may want consultation on setting up his or her home or campus environment to increase safety.
- A student may want to use various public transportation systems.
- A student may want instruction in travel training, including how to get to specific places, school, home, a place of employment, or leisure environments.

Orienting to the environment and being mobile in it are independence and employment skills. Instruction in O&M can include how to use a long cane, wheelchairs, and electronic travel devices (Neal et al., 2004). O&M service providers and teachers of the visually impaired attend transition planning meetings, and their services are part of the overall IEP transition services.

Advocacy and Vision-Friendly Environments

The transition planning specialist can encourage students to advocate for themselves and their peers with disabilities by requesting universal design principles for students with vision impairments and other disabilities. Students and the special education team can encourage the elimination of building hazards and ask for the use of nonslip, nonglare products to clean and polish floors. They can encourage the use of color contrast, including door handles that contrast with doors, making them easy to locate.

Marking the edges of all steps and ramps with paint, tape, or a highly contrasting color is supportive of persons with mobility challenges and those who are visually impaired. Stairway railings can contrast with the background and extend beyond the top and bottom steps. Hallways and stairways can have tracking molding along the wall with raised numbers or Braille to identify locations. Braille signs can indicate hallways where there are drinking fountains, fire extinguishers, and emergency exits (NFB, 2009).

Independent Living and Going to College

Adolescents who are blind will want to socialize in their home and college dorm. Many people who are blind do perceive light, and blind persons will have visitors who will need to move easily around the home or dorm room. Therefore, each living location should have an ample number of floor lamps and table lamps in recreation and reading areas. The following suggestions are also beneficial for supporting social experiences and their access to their environment.

Arrange furniture in small groupings so that people can converse easily. Make sure there is adequate lighting near furniture. Select textured upholstery and vary the types of fabric to give the home various textures and, for identical furniture, clues for identification. When purchasing new furniture, use brightly colored accessories, such as vases and lamps, to make furniture easier to locate. Avoid upholstery and floor covering with patterns. Stripes and checks can create confusion for people who are visually impaired. Move large pieces of furniture out of the main traffic areas and create the main traffic flow. Place light objects against a dark background; for example, place a dark table near a white wall or a black switchplate on a white wall. Being part of a social experience will entail the student's awareness of how to create environments that are conducive to his or her social needs.

Transition services from college to employment are available, and parents and the student should maintain contacts with the Office of Vocational Rehabilitation. Also, as they advance through college, ongoing searches for employment opportunities should continue. Many colleges and post-school training schools have placement specialists to help students make the transition into work after they complete their school programs.

EXERCISES

1. Explore two schools for the blind and two general education settings for students who are blind. Interview a transition coordinator or transition planning specialist and compare and contrast the services at each school, specifically their transition services. Try to determine job placement success.
2. Explore services for blind students in a public school, specifically their transition services.
3. Compare and contrast your findings between these two explorations.
4. Research two agencies for the blind (listed in the Student Supplemental Materials). Describe the services they provide.

SUMMARY

Students who are blind or have severe visual impairments require specialized transition planning, which includes the involvement of vision and mobility specialists. However, with the correct technological and instructional programs to develop independence, students can be adept at managing their lives and being as self-sufficient as possible. Students can benefit from career explorations and self-assessment on how they can reach their career goals. They can self-determine their outcomes and develop self-efficacy in environments that are accessible. Students who are blind can register with the Office of Vocational Rehabilitation, where they can also receive employment placement support given by persons who work with persons who are blind. By providing a framework for transition, which includes the supports students will need, ensures students with visual impairments access to multiple opportunities at home, for employment, for leisure, and for independence. The Student Supplemental Materials has information about agencies designated to assist students who are blind or visually impaired.

REFERENCES

Child with a disability, 34 C.F.R. § 300.8 (2017).

Goodwyn, M., Bell, E. C., & Singletary, C. (2009). Factors that contribute to the success of blind adults. Research report of the Professional Development and Research Institute on Blindness. Ruston, LA: Louisiana Tech University.

Hartnett, M. E., & Lane, R. H. (2013). Effects of oxygen on the development and severity of retinopathy of prematurity. *Journal of the American Association for Pediatric Ophthalmology and Strabismus, 17*(3), 229-234.

Hoyt, C. S. (2003). Visual function in the brain-damaged child. *Eye, 17*(3), 369-384.

Individuals with Disabilities Education Act Amendments of 1997, Pub. L. No. 105-17, 20 U.S.C. § 1400 *et seq.* (1997).

Individuals with Disabilities Education Act of 2004, Pub. L. No. 108-446, 20 U.S.C. § 1400 *et seq.* (2004).

Messina-Baas, O., & Cuevas-Covarrubias, S. A. (2017). Inherited congenital cataract: A guide to suspect the genetic etiology in the cataract genesis. *Molecular Syndromology, 8*(2), 58-78. doi:10.1159/000455752

Musgrove, M., & Yudin, M. K. (2013). Dear colleague: Braille instruction. U.S. Department of Education, Office of Special Education and Rehabilitative Services. Retrieved from https://www2.ed.gov/policy/speced/guid/idea/memosdcltrs/brailledcl-6-19-13.pdf

National Eye Institute. (2015). Facts About Glaucoma. National Eye Institute. Retrieved from https://nei.nih.gov/health/glaucoma/glaucoma_facts

National Eye Institute. (2018). Facts about age-related macular degeneration. National Eye Institute. Retrieved from https://nei.nih.gov/health/maculardegen/armd_facts

National Federation of the Blind. (2009). *The Braille literacy crisis in America.* Baltimore, MD: Author. Retrieved from https://nfb.org/images/nfb/documents/pdf/braille_literacy_report_web.pdf

Neal, J., Bigby, L., & Nicholson, R. (2004). Occupational therapy, physical therapy, and orientation and mobility services in public schools. *Intervention in School and Clinic, 39*(4), 218-222.

North American Neuro-Ophthalmology Society. (2016). NANOS Patient brochure: Homonymous and hemianopia [Brochure]. Minneapolis, MN: North American Neuro-Ophthalmology. Retrieved from http://www.nanosweb.org/files/Patient%20Brochures/English/HomonymousHemianopia_English.pdf

Oleszkiewicz, A., Pisanski, K., Lachowicz-Tabaczek, K., & Sorokowska, A. (2017). Voice-based assessments of trustworthiness, competence, and warmth in blind and sighted adults. *Psychonomic Bulletin & Review, 24*(3), 856-862.

Philip, S. S., & Dutton, G. N. (2014). Identifying and characterising cerebral visual impairment in children: A review. *Clinical and Experimental Optometry, 97*(3), 196-208.

Pineles, S. L., Velez, F. G., Isenberg, S. J., Fenoglio, Z., Birch, E., Nusinowitz, S., & Demer, J. L. (2013). Functional burden of strabismus: Decreased binocular summation and binocular inhibition. *JAMA Ophthalmology, 131*(11), 1413-1419.

Retinitis pigmentosa. (2010). *Oxford concise medical dictionary* (8th ed.). Oxford, United Kingdom: Oxford University Press.

Roman-Lantzy, C. A. (2007). *Cortical visual impairment: An approach to assessment and intervention.* New York, NY: AFB Press.

Rosenberg, M. S., Westling, D. L., & McLeskey, J. L. (2011). *Special education for today's teachers: An introduction* (2nd ed.). London, United Kingdom: Pearson.

Zhang, X., Kedar, S., Lynn, M. J., Newman, N. J., & Biousse, V. (2006). Natural history of homonymous hemianopia. *Neurology, 66*(6), 901-905.

SECTION 2: STUDENTS WHO ARE DEAF, HARD OF HEARING, OR DEAF-BLIND

OBJECTIVES

→ Identify the three types of hearing loss.

→ Describe three communication tools for adolescents who are deaf.

→ Identify three organizations and describe how they assist adolescents who are deaf or hard of hearing during the transition to adulthood.

→ Describe three current technological advancements that promote inclusion of persons who are deaf.

→ Explain why people who are deaf prefer to be called *deaf* and *hard of hearing* instead of hearing impaired.

DEAFNESS, HEARING IMPAIRMENTS, HARD OF HEARING, AND DEAF-BLINDNESS

§300.8 Child with a disability.

(2) Deaf-blindness means concomitant hearing and visual impairments, the combination of which causes such severe communication and other developmental and educational needs that they cannot be accommodated in special education programs solely for children with deafness or children with blindness.

(3) Deafness means a hearing impairment that is so severe that the child is impaired in processing linguistic information through hearing, with or without amplification, that adversely affects a child's educational performance.

(5) Hearing impairment means an impairment in hearing, whether permanent or fluctuating, that adversely affects a child's educational performance, but that is not included under the definition of deafness in this section.

(§300.8 Child with a disability [71 FR 46753, Aug. 14, 2006, as amended at 72 FR 61306, Oct. 30, 2007; 82 FR 31912, July 11, 2017])

Types of Hearing Loss

Students who are deaf or hard of hearing have a wide variation in hearing ability, from mild and moderate loss to profound deafness. Hearing loss originates in three locations of the auditory processing center: the outer ear, the middle ear, and the inner ear. There are three types of hearing loss, each based on which part of the auditory mechanism is affected:

1. Conductive
2. Sensorineural
3. Mixed

A conductive hearing loss occurs when air pressure waves from the environment fail to pass through the outer ear into the middle ear and from the middle ear to the cochlea. The outer ear is the ear and the auditory canal, and the middle ear begins at the eardrum (tympanic membrane). Behind the eardrum sit three bones, or ossicles, of the middle ear, which attach to the entry structures of the inner ear and then to the cochlea (Sanders & Gillig, 2010).

If there is impairment in any structures in the outer or middle ear, then sound vibrations cannot reach the inner ear and the snail-shaped cochlea. When the vibrations do not reach through the auditory canal to the brain, the cochlea cannot transform the sound vibrations into nerve impulses and send them to the brain for interpretation. In a conductive loss, the cochlea is functioning but cannot receive the vibrations from the middle ear.

Conductive hearing losses may result from birth or trauma such as eardrum perforation (tympanic membrane), fractured skull, or changes in air pressure (Hallahan & Kauffman, 2018). Other causes of conductive hearing loss may be fluid in the middle ear, wax buildup, problems with the eustachian tube, tumors in the middle ear, ear infections (known as *otis media),* or problems with the three auditory ossicles: the malleus, the incus, and the stapes. For example, malformation or calcification of one of the ossicles will prevent movement of sound vibration. These and other malformations can be complex and diverse (Tang, Zhang, Yang, Han, & Han, 2018). In some cases, the conductive hearing loss can be repaired through surgery or may resolve through medication.

Sensorineural hearing loss occurs in the cochlea, the shell-shaped organ of the inner ear, or the eighth cranial nerve (Sanders & Gillig, 2010). Sensorineural hearing losses cannot be repaired through surgery. Cytomegalovirus infection remains the most common environmental cause of congenital hearing loss (Angeli, Lin, & Liu, 2012). Sensorineural loss can occur from birth due to a mother's exposure to German measles or from illness (e.g., meningitis or very high fever), medications, or exposure to loud noises (Rosenberg, Westling, & McLeskey, 2011). Sensorineural hearing loss can also be inherited (Angeli et al., 2012).

Neurofibromatosis 2 (NF2) also affects hearing. Signs and symptoms of NF2 usually result from the development of benign, slow-growing tumors (acoustic neuromas) in both ears. NF2 symptoms appear during the period of transition to adulthood and result in a gradual hearing loss, ringing in the ears, poor balance, and headaches (Evans, 2009).

Fluctuating and Mixed Hearing Loss

Meniere's disease is considered a triad of three symptoms: vertigo, tinnitus, and fluctuating sensorineural hearing loss. Initial hearing fluctuation is associated with the occurrence of future and more frequent hearing fluctuations (Hoa, Friedman, Fisher, & Derebery, 2015). Meniere's disease includes spells of vertigo lasting minutes to hours, with vestibular nystagmus, tinnitus, and an associated sense of fullness in the ears. There are periods of remission and exacerbation. Its etiology seems to involve edema in the labyrinth of the ear, which is attached to the cochlea (Sanders & Gillig, 2010).

Mixed hearing loss is both conductive and sensorineural (Hallahan & Kauffman, 2018). Hearing loss can also be unilateral (in one ear) and bilateral (in both ears). Hearing loss is not a standard phenomenon. Different people will experience loss at different decibels (i.e., levels of loudness) and different frequencies (i.e., sound vibrations per second; Hallahan & Kauffman, 2018; Rosenberg et al., 2011).

Degrees of Hearing Loss

According to the Gallaudet Research Institute (2011), of the students who identify as having any detectable hearing loss range from mild to profound, 60% have no other conditions. Table 12-1 represents the range of hearing loss in a population of students without other disabilities.

To understand the table, one must understand hearing acuity as charted on an audiogram. Hearing acuity is measured by an audiologist who administers a series of hearing tests in a soundproof testing area. The results of hearing acuity for both ears are displayed on an audiogram. Students who are deaf, hard of hearing, or hearing impaired are tested periodically to check hearing status. The range of hearing on an audiogram defines what sounds a person can hear. The table reflects two measures: loudness and pitch. Loudness is measured in decibels (dB), from 120 dB for the loudest sounds to 10 dB for the softest sounds. Pitch is measured from low-pitched sounds (125 Hz) to high-pitched sounds (8000 Hz).

TABLE 12-1. THE AMERICAN NATIONAL STANDARDS INSTITUTE DEGREES OF HEARING LOSS

TOTAL STUDENTS REPORTED	37,828	100%
INFORMATION NOT REPORTED	6516	17.2%
TOTAL KNOWN INFORMATION	31,312	100%
Normal (< 27 dB, American National Standards Institute [ANSI])	6202	19.8%
Mild (27 to 40 dB, ANSI)	4263	13.6%
Moderate (41 to 55 dB, ANSI)	4526	14.5%
Moderate-severe (56 to 70 dB, ANSI)	3877	12.4%
Severe (71 to 90 dB, ANSI)	4183	13.4%
Profound (91 dB and above, ANSI)	8262	26.4%

Source: Gallaudet Research Institute (2011). *State Summary Report of Data from the 2009-10 Annual Survey of Deaf and Hard of Hearing Children and Youth.* Washington, DC: GRI, Gallaudet University.

People who hear normally can hear from 120 dB to 0 dB of loudness. They can also hear from a low pitch of 125 Hz to a high pitch of 8000 Hz. A person with a profound hearing loss may hear only very loud sounds like a firecracker, a siren, or a jack hammer, and no letter sounds at all.

- Profound hearing loss
  - No letter sounds can be heard. A person with a moderate to severe loss may hear a dog barking, a vacuum running, and a piano playing. Although a person with moderate hearing loss can hear those sounds, he or she cannot hear the sounds of the following listed letters. Students with profound hearing loss most often use sign language to communicate.
- Moderate hearing loss
  - j, m, d, b, n, ng, ee, l, u, sh, ch, z, and v. This is an example only; a person with moderate hearing loss may hear some of these sounds or all of them. An adolescent with a moderate hearing loss could have a mild hearing loss in the opposite ear. Students with mild hearing loss can hear the sounds of the letters listed but cannot hear birds chirping, leaves rustling, water dripping, or whispering. They also cannot hear the following listed letters.
- Mild hearing loss
  - p, h, g, k, f, s, or th. Again, this is an example, because each ear can have a different range of hearing in loudness and pitch. Each range of loss includes the ability to hear only those sounds within that range. Therefore, an adolescent with normal hearing can hear every pitch, from high to low, at a soft level. An adolescent with mild hearing loss can hear most speech sounds from a close distance; a student with normal hearing may be able to do so for sounds farther away from the source.

To illustrate the breakdown of hearing loss from mild to profound, see Table 12-1. The standard types of hearing loss are listed along with the percent of students who have each type. To hear speech sounds, the adolescent must hear all sounds that fall between 10 and 60 decibels and 125 and 8000 Hz.

Other Disabilities and Hearing Loss

A hearing test can find other hearing difficulties in adolescents, such as those who may not hear the endings of words. For instance, an audiologist will go through a list of words with and without background noise and have the student repeat the word. For some children and adolescents, even when they can hear, there is difficulty discriminating the ending, such as *-ed* and *-ing.* Multiple sound discrimination problems can be present even though a student may hear in one ear. These deficits are measured by the following tests:

- Speech-in-Noise Test
- Competing Sentences Test
- Filtered Speech Test
- Binaural Fusion Test
- Alternating Speech Test
- Staggered Spondaic Word Test

See the Glossary for definitions.

Students with other disabilities can have hearing loss as well. Of the population of students with hearing loss, approximately 8.8% have intellectual disabilities, 6% have learning disabilities, 7% have other health impairments, 5% have some vision loss, 2.2% have autism spectrum disorder, and 1% are deaf-blind (Gallaudet Research Institute, 2011). Some of these students, especially those with more severe intellectual disabilities, may have difficulty with the use of technology such as hearing aids or cochlea implants that can help them with learning and communication.

TRANSITION PLANNING: DEAFNESS AND HARD OF HEARING

Teachers of the Deaf

Teachers of the deaf must be certified to do so. They must know how deafness affects the student in multiple setting and teach strategies so students can participate in everyday life. They use instructional strategies relevant to deaf education and seek to advance learning, advanced training, and positive outcomes for adulthood. They are trained to work with families of diverse cultures, and they help families who are not deaf advance students' learning and post-school prospects. Teachers of the deaf work with the transition planning specialist and ensure students have the connections needed for postsecondary success. They advise general education teachers on how to set up a DeafSpace (hbhm architects in conjunction with Gallaudet University) environment for facilitating the learning of students who are participating in general education classes. They are also the language teachers for American Sign Language (ASL).

Cochlear Implant Therapists

Cochlear implants are for the severely and profoundly deaf. They send impulses right into the cochlea to the auditory nerve. In order for cochlear implants to be effective, they need to be functioning, meaning that verbalizations are received and can be mimicked back to the therapist. The child who has not spoken is encouraged to emit sounds, and he or she needs to learn to speak and use the spoken language. Typically a speech therapist provides speech therapy as a related service. Persons with cochlear implants need ongoing implant checks to ensure it is working. Even during transition, the IEP needs to continue to include information on how the implant is performing. A person specially trained in monitoring students with a cochlear implant is typically on the IEP team. Some students with cochlear implants may also learn or use sign language.

Interpreters

An interpreter is usually an independent person rather than the student's teacher of the deaf. They are available to students who are deaf and attending general education classes. They do not sit on the IEP team as a member; however, they do interpret the IEP meeting unless the parents are fluent in sign language and can interpret. The student should be able to give the team feedback on the effectiveness of the interpretation and whether it is meeting his or her needs. It is essential that the interpreter can convey complex meaning to the student so he or she understands and can participate or lead the IEP meeting.

Transition Plan Technological Supports for Learning and Communication

Many deaf and hard of hearing students have some hearing. The remaining hearing is called *residual hearing*. Technology is used to maximize hearing. Technology will not change hearing loss but will help a student to maximize the use of his or her residual hearing. Some aids are hearing aids, cochlear implants, bone-anchored hearing aids, and assistive devices.

One assistive device for the classroom is a frequency modulation system, a device that helps people with hearing loss hear speakers in a larger setting, most notably their teachers. Also, it helps those students with hearing aids to hear when background noise is present or when the speaker moves away from the student. Frequency modulation systems can send sound from a microphone worn by someone speaking to classroom audio systems or directly to a hearing aid. If the student has hearing aids, an extra piece is attached to the hearing aid that works with the frequency modulation system. As the teacher moves around the room, a student with an aid cannot hear the teacher. The frequency modulation system transmits the teacher's words directly to the student, substantially increasing understanding. Bone-anchored hearing aids, on-the-ear hearing aids, and in-the-ear hearing aids can connect to frequency modulation systems.

Captioning is another form of support used for online and classroom meetings and in many television programs, videos, and DVDs.

Another technology in development is avatars. Researchers at the German Center for Artificial Intelligence are working to create avatars to communicate with the deaf online and via other communication platforms (Kipp, Nguyen, Heloir, & Matthes, 2011). Avatars are animated characters that can be used on the internet and in airports and train stations to provide information in sign language.

Employment

The U.S. Equal Opportunity Commission (2002) enforces federal law and makes it illegal to discriminate due to, in this instance, being deaf or hearing impaired. Section 501 of the Rehabilitation Act of 1973 requires federal agencies to provide reasonable accommodation for qualified employees or applicants with disabilities, unless to do so would cause undue hardship.

There are an number of supports and devices available for transitioning youth with hearing loss. Some of these are acceptable part accommodations and can be found on the U.S. Equal Employment Opportunity Commission, see the links in the Student Supplemental Materials. They are used to support the work and safety of deaf employees. The following are some examples.

What accommodations may you ask for?

- A sign language interpreter
- TTY (text telephone or teletypewriter, voice carry-over telephone, or captioned telephone)
- Appropriate emergency notification systems (e.g., strobe lighting on fire alarms or vibrating pagers)
- Written memos and notes (used for brief, simple, or routine communications)
- Work area adjustments (e.g., a desk away from a noisy area or near an emergency alarm with strobe lighting)

- Assistive computer software (e.g., net meetings, voice recognition software)
- Assistive listening devices
- Communication access real-time translation or speech to text, which translates voice into text at real-time speeds
- Text messaging
- Cell phone amplifiers
- Flashing and vibrating alarms
- Infrared listening devices (used in difficult indoor listening situations)
- Portable sound amplifiers
- Augmentative communication devices (e.g., personal captioning in web-based video platforms) that allow users to communicate by typing words to communicate with hearing coworkers
- Altering an employee's marginal (i.e., non-essential) job functions
- Other modifications or adjustments that allow a qualified applicant to work

Students can be assisted and educated about these supports. Representatives from the companies that produce these will provide videos on their use. In addition, as noted throughout the text, the student will need to develop advocacy skills to ensure they can access accommodations by advocating for themselves. Both advocacy skills and accommodations can support their employment and facilitate a smooth transition into the workforce.

U.S. Equal Opportunity Commission. Procedures For Providing Reasonable Accommodation For Individuals With Disabilities: https://www.eeoc.gov/eeoc/internal/reasonable_accommodation.cfm

U.S. Equal Opportunity Commission. Questions and Answers about Deafness and Hearing Impairments in the Workplace and the Americans with Disabilities Act: https://www.eeoc.gov/eeoc/publications/qa_deafness.cfm

Exercise

1. Research the Equal Opportunity Commission website and report on supports provided to deaf and hard of hearing people.

ADVOCACY, DEAFSPACE, AND DEAF-FRIENDLY ENVIRONMENTS

The concept of DeafSpace reflects how deaf persons change their surroundings to fit the use of their language, which includes the need for physical space considerations. In the classroom, DeafSpace entails providing lighting, acoustics, and the ability to see smartboards and other learning materials crucial to the success and inclusion of students who are deaf or hard of hearing.

Lighting is of concern because the student must be able to see the interpreter or other classmates who sign. If the teacher is being captioned, the student must be able to see the captioning. Captioning that is too small to be easily read is another area where the student should not have to struggle. If the teacher or professor is lecturing, glare on the face will obscure facial expressions and nonverbal cues. The deaf student knows his or her needs and can sit near the instructor if he or she is using speech reading to the best advantage.

The physical space should be devoid of equipment that blocks a student's clear line of sight. The safety of the student also needs consideration, and strobe lights that alert the student to fire alarms should be installed in all buildings.

Posting communication rules can help include students who are deaf, such as avoidance of covering the face or mouth when speaking. Many students who are deaf can speak, but it does not mean they can hear, so the teacher should use basic eye contact like they would with any student to check for understanding.

DeafSpace

DeafSpace has five core concepts:

1. Sensory reach includes maintaining awareness of activities in the surroundings that facilitate 360 degrees of awareness. Deaf persons have a sensitivity to tactile and visual cues that are important to their safety and knowledge of the environment and the people around them.

2. Space and proximity are essential to maintain clear visual communication. As a group adds more members, a circle will widen to maintain visual connections.

3. Mobility and proximity are needed. While walking, signers need a wide personal distance for communication, and like everyone, they need to scan for hazards while maintaining communicative contact.

4. Light and color support the visual wayfinding and communication of deaf individuals who continually scan the environment for communication cues and movement cues.

5. Acoustics are important, and the deaf sense sound vibrations. Vibrations often come from electronic devices, such as hearing aids and cochlear implants. The reverberation can be distracting and at times painful. These are some considerations when planning space use that will include persons who are deaf and hard of hearing (Gallaudet University, n.d.).

Exercise

1. Explore a school environment and look for spatial designs that may be barriers to persons who are deaf, blind, or deaf-blind.

Learning Strategies

Students who are deaf or hard of hearing are visual learners out of necessity. As they transition to adulthood, they need to access more complex information as they prepare for careers. A study on adolescents with and without hearing supports showed significantly higher scores when students viewed visuals plus captions vs. seeing either visuals or captions alone (Linebarger, 2001; Nugent, 1983).

In addition to using captions and visuals, there are learning strategies that can help students in the classroom, such as reading the chapters covered in class and creating an outline of information the lecture may address. E-texts have chapter outlines that can be copied and typed onto, making the process easier. Also, if there is captioning of the teacher's lecture or an interpreter video, a copy of each can be made available. Asking the teacher for an overview of topics ahead of time can also help the high school student to compare his or her outline to the classroom teacher's outline to see the key focus of the chapter.

Concept maps are often provided with textbooks, and students can be given copies of concept maps for the course.

COMMUNITY AND INCLUSION

Deaf Culture

Approximately 86% of children born deaf have hearing parents, and a rich deaf culture has arisen among those whose children are deaf and their families and friends who have learned sign language—and more significantly among the deaf themselves (Gallaudet Research Institute, 2011). Deaf culture is a community for persons who are deaf, and its activities arise from the use of their language. Sign language, although it varies by geographic area, is the language of the deaf worldwide.

Deaf culture includes valuing all persons who are deaf as a linguistic and cultural group and supporting them in the use of their language (Baynton, Gannon, & Bergey, 2007). The following case report is about a woman's experiences as a deaf child and her transition into adulthood. Her family of origin was not deaf.

Case Report: Marcie

Though my family and I had several home signs for all the things I needed and wanted, I had no real language to acquire; I did not have an opportunity to learn how to express my feelings or share my thoughts. All I had to do was nod my head and pretend that I understood people when they tried to talk to me. That kind of experience led my personality to being a quiet person. Therefore, I had no rich experience with deaf culture or exposure in my early childhood.

I remember very well how I felt lonely and isolated while I lived with my family the first 9 years of my life. When I saw my family communicating with each other, laughing together … they even sang together. My father and my older sister played the guitar, and every time they played I felt more isolated. The feeling of being left out every day constantly frustrated me. I did not know how to communicate or express my frustrations to my mother. I recall sometimes I got angry and behaved badly when I was frustrated with my family.

I was born deaf because my mother contracted German measles while she was pregnant with me. My parents also had four other hearing girls. My mother had a hard time accepting that I was deaf, and she was urged by the speech therapist to take me to a school for the deaf because I was 9 years old with no formal language. I was severely delayed in language and cognitive development. When I started learning ASL, I felt a burst of excitement inside that I could communicate with all the people that could sign at the school. I had no idea there was a substantial deaf community with rich culture and history until I took a deaf history class in high school. I realized there were many small populations of deaf people existing all over the world, I sometimes I felt like I was not an important person because of my deafness and because I could not communicate with hearing people. My 10 years living at my deaf school dramatically changed my life. I learned who I am, and I also learned to appreciate the many positive experiences I was having with all the aspects of deaf culture, deaf community, deaf sports, deaf events, deaf friends, deaf school community, and deaf Olympics. It still carried through to my college life at Gallaudet University for 5 years then I became an employee at Model Secondary School for the Deaf as a dorm counselor for 2 years. Afterward, I changed my job to admission specialist then registration specialist at Gallaudet for 10 years. It turned out to be the best opportunity for me to grow and become a better-educated person because I can do anything to accomplish in my life, my career, my own family, and my further education.

While I was in school, I only visited my family during the holidays and short summer breaks. I tried to teach my family sign language, but they only used notes to communicate with me. It always frustrated me that I was ignored by them. I decided to move out during my junior year of high school and live with a new family in a different city, where the deaf school was located. The new family was motivated to learn ASL so they could communicate with me.

Exercises

1. Interview a deaf or hard of hearing person about his or her education. Describe his or her model of inclusion and the services provided. Ask the student for his or her opinion on any changes he or she would have liked.

2. Look at video links provided by one of the organizations for the deaf provided in the Student Supplemental Materials. Describe the experiences of deaf people and compare them to a bias you may have held about the deaf.

3. Describe how a disability narrative could help students who are deaf to have improved educational programming.

Discussion

Immersion in a deaf community gave Marcie many opportunities unavailable to her elsewhere, and her narrative reflects a certain joy at finding a place where she was understood. A sense of belonging is a predictor of school success, and the construct of belonging is expressed in Marcie's inclusion in the deaf community. Full inclusion in public schools has led to the dissolution of self-contained deaf education classroom programs in favor of providing sign interpreters in general education settings.

INDEPENDENT LIVING AND GOING TO COLLEGE

Preparation for Employment or College

In most states, the vocational rehabilitation program and school-based transition planning help individuals who are deaf prepare for or retain employment. Services offered can include, but are not limited to, the following:

- High school–based services
  - Counseling and guidance
  - Visit local community colleges and vocational schools
  - Vocational evaluation
  - Deaf safety skills training
  - Mobility (travel) instruction
  - Communicating with hearing persons in school
  - Independence goal setting and self-determination
  - High school, vocational school, and college advocacy training
  - Occupational tools and equipment for accessibility
- Office of Vocational Rehabilitation, agency for the deaf, and special education services
  - Job placement services through college or the Office of Vocational Rehabilitation
  - Vocational and situational assessments
  - Resume support
  - Interviewing skills development
  - Job development
  - Job placement and retention services
  - Job coaching services
  - Job accommodation support and employer education
  - Employer consultation for technology use

Services are based on an individual's employment needs and choices, and vocational rehabilitation counselors work directly with the individual and in collaboration with the transition planning specialist to determine an employment goal and the services needed to reach student goals. The Student Supplemental Materials contains a list of state agencies, and those agencies typically have local area contacts. The transition planning specialist must be well-versed in in-school and post-school services and options, and the local agencies that will work with the student after graduation.

Typically, a transition planning specialist is not certified as a hearing therapist or teacher of the deaf. Therefore, when a transition planning specialist is involved in transition planning for a secondary school student who is deaf, the transition planning specialist still plays a crucial role in ensuring that all the plans are implemented. The transition planning specialist must ensure that a vocational counselor of the local Office of Vocational Rehabilitation is present in person or via video conference system with captioning. The transition planning specialist ensures the teacher of the deaf is present at the meetings to interpret for the Office of Vocational Rehabilitation counselor if necessary.

College Programs for the Deaf

Some colleges provide a first-year transition program to support students. Other universities focus on all aspects of education and post-school supports for employment. Gallaudet University in Washington, DC, provides programs for students who are deaf from all over the United States and internationally. All classes are in ASL, and they have B.A., M.A., and Ph.D. programs. The Laurent Clerc National Deaf Education Center is a division of the university that works together with Gallaudet to promote the advancement of deaf and hard of hearing individuals through ASL, research, and scholarly activities.

Another university, the National Technical Institute for the Deaf (NTID) in Rochester, New York, is one of nine schools in the Rochester Technical Institute. It too is designated to provide college for students who are deaf from all states. NTID has an informational link to each state Office of Vocational Rehabilitation, which includes information on the amount of financial support each state gives to students who are deaf. For instance, Delaware gives funding equivalent to 2 years of community college.

The transition planning specialist and the high school teacher of the deaf ensure these connections are made so that students who are deaf can apply to and secure the financial aid and services they will need for college. NTID support includes instructors who communicate using ASL, spoken language, and finger spelling for the deaf and deaf-blind, as well as printed and visual aids and online resources. Frequency modulation systems are also available, along with tutoring, note taking, real-time captioning services, and interpreting staff. The campus has dozens of smart classrooms with state-of-the-art computers and multimedia-based technologies, as well as engineering labs and digital printing presses.

In 2015, 94% of deaf and hard of hearing NTID graduates found jobs within a year. The more than 8000 alumni are employed with industry leaders such as BNY Mellon, Boeing Aircraft, Inc., Central Intelligence Agency, Google, Microsoft, the U.S. Department of Defense, and Walt Disney Company (NTID, 2018).

Each deaf or hard of hearing student is unique. The type of hearing loss and how it affects his or her everyday life can bring each student challenges that may not be fully understood by anyone but him- or herself. The student will need to be able to understand and communicate those needs with the transition planning specialist and special education team. Through transition planning, the student can develop self-advocacy to promote his or her advancement. Even though the student has the same level of understanding and cognitive ability as individuals who hear, everyday life brings a different set of challenges in multiple settings: in places of education, stores, transportation hubs, and other places that are designed by a hearing world.

Exercises

1. Describe how you would change your current classroom to enable the attendance of a blind or deaf student.
2. Describe the principles of universal design in relation to the plan.

TRANSITION PLANNING: DEAF-BLINDNESS

Deaf-blindness is a combined hearing and vision disorder, which can be caused by trauma, viruses, disease, or inherited syndromes. Children and adults who are deaf-blind experience both hearing and vision loss, although neither may be a complete loss (Zeza & Stavrou, 2015).

IDEA (2004) describes deaf-blindness as a hearing and vision loss "which causes such severe communication and other developmental and educational needs that they cannot be accommodated in special education programs solely for children with deafness or children with blindness" (Child with a disability, 2017; Rosenberg et al., 2011).

Students with deaf-blindness are placed in educational settings across the educational continuum (Grisham-Brown, Değirmenci, Snyder, & Luiselli, 2018). Although the states provide funding for state deaf-blind projects as a result of the rubella epidemic of the 1960s, the population now includes students with deaf-blindness from other causes, and the numbers needing services are higher (Grisham-Brown et al., 2018). Many students with deaf-blindness can be missed during the annual special education child count if they are counted within another category such as multiple disabilities.

Even within special education programs, adolescents with deaf-blindness cannot receive appropriate instruction when teachers typically do not have the credentials they need to provide instruction (Blaha, Cooper, Irby, Montgomery, & Parker, 2009). To overcome this, the educational team and family should be provided accessible, ongoing assistance, support, and training from specialists who have expertise, knowledge, and skills to work with people who are deaf-blind (Snyder, 2016).

Technological advancement and increasing knowledge about teaching students with the most severe disabilities have demonstrated that children and adolescents who are deaf-blind can advance through school. Appropriate assessment is needed, preferences can be determined, and goals can be set for increasing independence. Use of technology such as devices with global positioning apps and computers with Braille keyboards enables the use of email systems. Specialized devices are used to print out emails using Braille printers. As more is known about students with deaf-blindness, more advanced systems can be developed.

DEAF-BLINDNESS DISABILITY SPECTRUM

Within the group of children and youth who are identified as deaf-blind, there is a spectrum of ability and disability. Individuals who work with adolescents who are deaf-blind understand their degree of deafness and blindness and the residual aspects of both losses to ensure they get the service and technology they need. The following statistics give a general overview of the types of losses in the blind-deaf spectrum (Killoran, 2007):

- Vision loss
  - 17% totally blind or light perception only
  - 24% legally blind
  - 21% low vision
  - 17% cortical vision impairment
  - 21% other degrees of vision

- Hearing loss
  - 39% severe to profound hearing loss
  - 13% moderate hearing loss
  - 14% mild hearing loss
  - 6% central auditory processing disorder
  - 28% other

Students with multiple disabilities are also part of the group of youth who are deaf-blind. These adolescents are represented in the chapter on intellectual disabilities. However, the types of vision and hearing support they need can be secured through the agencies discussed in this chapter. The following percentages reflect the percent of each population served under IDEA and who are also on the deaf-blind spectrum:

- Students with deaf-blindness and other disabilities
  - 66% have intellectual disabilities
  - 57% have physical disabilities
  - 38% have complex health care needs
  - 9% have behavior challenges
  - 30% have any combination of these, such as an intellectual disability, physical disability, and deaf-blindness

In 2016, 10,749 children with deaf-blindness were served in special education from age 3 to age 22 programs. Approximately 90% are identified as having one or more additional disabilities. Over 40% have four or more disabilities. There was a steady increase from 2010 to 2015, with a 134% increase in the number of students who are deaf-blind who live at home with their parents and graduated from a high school (Killoran, 2007).

Major Causes of Deaf-Blindness

The degree of loss, like most disabilities, is on a spectrum ranging from moderate to total loss (Zeza & Stavrou, 2015). However, in deaf-blindness, there are acquired and congenital origins, which can vastly change the adolescent's level of independence and learning (Munroe, 2001).

Genetic syndromes such as Down syndrome, Trisomy 13, CHARGE (coloboma [i.e., missing pieces of eye tissue], heart defects, atresia choanae [i.e., the gene that causes CHARGE], growth retardation, genital abnormalities, and ear abnormalities) syndrome, and Usher syndrome cause a pattern of disabilities including intellectual disabilities and deaf-blindness.

Congenital prenatal dysfunction in the maternal environment, including drug and alcohol abuse, a virus, and fetal alcohol syndrome, as well as congenital disabilities such as hydrocephaly and microcephaly can cause deaf-blindness. Illnesses such as herpes, AIDS, and rubella can also cause deaf-blindness. Postnatal causes include events such as asphyxia, encephalitis, head injury/trauma, meningitis, and stroke.

Some conditions, such as Usher's syndrome, begin with hearing loss and often lead to an eye disease called retinitis pigmentosa, which is the gradual loss of peripheral vision loss, in which the person's field of vision (what a person can see in front of him or her without moving the head) narrows. Other adolescents may be adventitiously deaf-blind: born with both sight and hearing but lose some or all of these senses as a result of accident or illness.

PROGRAMS FOR THE DEAF-BLIND
FOR THE TRANSITION TO ADULTHOOD

Students who are deaf-blind will participate in transition planning with communication support. They may use Braille communications via email, fingerspelling, or the use of sign and visual aids. A combination of tools is used to facilitate maximum involvement in transition planning. Communication tools should enable the student to share his or her preferences and set goals. Interviewing the student is an essential process when planning for transition. Students who are deaf-blind, with the help of a communicator using finger spelling, can be present in an IEP meeting to share their thoughts about their future. If students have learned braille or have a scribe, they can share their thoughts in writing.

Students who are deaf-blind are also served via the Office of Vocational Rehabilitation, which refers them to training and residential programs that help each young adult be as independent as possible.

Advocacy and Communication

Many of the agencies that provide support for individuals who are deaf-blind, hard of hearing, or blind support ways to include young persons into mainstream life. They work with local governmental agencies, schools, and communities to support the inclusion of persons with disabilities that affect vision and hearing. Like the efforts that are made to create space where deaf people and blind people can move safely and participate, the needs of the deaf-blind also require awareness of their environmental requirements. Community facilities, parks, schools, and recreation facilities are natural settings to advocate for the inclusion of the deaf-blind.

Specialists for the Deaf-Blind Student

Specialists who are knowledgeable about programs and services for students with deafness and blindness are members of the transition team. Typically, there is a representative teacher from both fields at the IEP meeting. The teacher's assistance and knowledge about post-school programs for the deaf-blind facilitate transition planning activities and services. The teacher is crucial to the student's inclusion in a beneficial plan for post-school life.

The transition planning specialist representing students who are deaf-blind meets with the teachers who provide supports and actively gain the student's preferences, keep student activity records, and meets with the student to address completion and initiation of new goals.

Sometimes the teacher of the deaf or the teacher of the blind may also be the transition planning specialist. He or she would be responsible for the implementation of the IEP and ensuring the goals of transition are met. Many students who are deaf-blind are served in schools designed for students with the same disability.

Transition Planning and Assessment Guides

In 2016, the National Center on Deaf-Blindness Transition Work Group revised the guide on transitioning for students who are deaf-blind. The new guidelines reflect current practices, requirements, and trends in education, transition planning, and vocational rehabilitation. The guide uses Kohler's *Taxonomy for Transition Programming* (Kohler, 1996; Kohler & Coyle, 2009; Kohler, Gothberg, Fowler, & Coyle, 2016) to underpin the practices for students who are deaf-blind. It is called the *READY Tool* (Readiness Evaluation of Transition to Adulthood for Deaf-Blind Youth). The National Center on Deaf-Blindness provides checklists and essential activities tailored to transition-age students who are deaf-blind.

Courses for the Deaf-Blind

Agencies for the blind provide courses to improve understanding of the needs of students and adults who are deaf-blind. Confident living courses, residential learning programs, and courses for vocational rehabilitation counselors, which instruct how to work with individuals who are deaf-blind, are available.

Advocacy for Programs and Services for the Deaf-Blind

An advocacy initiative seeks to address the needs of the deaf-blind. The Alice Cogswell and Anne Sullivan Macy Act has been submitted to the U.S. House of Representatives. The bill was presented to amend IDEA to require each state to identify, evaluate, and provide special education and related services to children who have visual or hearing disabilities (or both).

The rationale is that when students are eligible for special education, for example, students who have multiple disabilities, many of whom have poor vision and may be hard of hearing and deaf as well, must be evaluated for vision and hearing disabilities. When these disabilities are present, each disability must be addressed in the IEP via the related services and specially designed instruction delivered by someone qualified to do so in that field. These professionals are teachers of the visually impaired and blind or teachers of the deaf and hard of hearing.

The bill also requires that states must ensure that there are enough qualified personnel to serve children who are deaf-blind and that a full continuum of alternative placements is available to meet the needs of the deaf-blind (Alice Cogswell and Anne Sullivan Macy Act, 2017).

EXERCISES

1. Explore Gallaudet University, NTID, and another mainstream college and describe the services they provide for students who are deaf.
2. Contact a local high school and interview the transition planning specialist about the range of transition services for students who are deaf, hard of hearing, hearing impaired, or deaf-blind.
3. Explore he Helen Keller National Center for Deaf-Blind Youths & Adults and read two success stories. Describe the current situations of those students.
4. Describe any bias you may have had before reading the stories and after.
5. On the same site, find two technological devices and describe how they are used.
6. Use the resources in the Student Supplemental Materials to contact four agencies that provide services for the deaf, hearing impaired, and hard of hearing. Find out what services they provide.

SUMMARY

This chapter presented three groups of students with sensory disabilities. All three groups can participate fully in the transition planning process. However, unlike students with learning disabilities or emotional or behavioral disabilities, independently seeking employment or post-school education and housing is not an option. Therefore, they will need specialized assistance to enter employment settings and the support of agencies during employment searches and when making independence and community living arrangements. Transition planning and career exploration can support these students as they get ongoing information about employment options.

As technologies have developed, access to education and the workplace has expanded. Also, the premise of self-determination encourages students with sensory disabilities to express their needs and self-advocate to be as independent as possible.

Deaf and blind spaces, universal design, and technologies that promote communication have brought students with sensory disabilities more into mainstream life. With ongoing development of technology such as avatars and signal systems for the blind, independence will become greater.

REFERENCES

Alice Cogswell and Anne Sullivan Macy Act, H.R. 1120, 115th Cong. (2017).

Angeli, S., Lin, X., & Liu, X. Z. (2012). Genetics of hearing and deafness. *Anatomical Record, 295*(11), 1812-1829.

Baynton, D., Gannon, J., & Bergey, J. (2007). *Through deaf eyes.* Washington, DC: Gallaudet University Press.

Blaha, R., Cooper, H., Irby, P., Montgomery, C., & Parker, A. (2009). Teachers of students with deafblindness: professionalizing the field. *Division on Visual Impairments Quarterly, 54,* 49-51.

Child with a disability, 34 C.F.R. § 300.8 (2017).

Evans, D. G. (2009). Neurofibromatosis 2 [bilateral acoustic neurofibromatosis, central neurofibromatosis, NF2, neurofibromatosis type II]. *Genetics in Medicine, 11*(9), 599-610.

Gallaudet University. (n.d.). DeafSpace. Retrieved from https://www.gallaudet.edu/campus-design-and-planning/deafspace

Gallaudet Research Institute. (2011). State Summary Report of Data from the 2009-10 Annual Survey of Deaf and Hard of Hearing Children and Youth. Washington, DC: GRI, Gallaudet University

Grisham-Brown, J., Değirmenci, H. D., Snyder, D., & Luiselli, T. E. (2018). Improving practices for learners with deafblindness: A consultation and coaching model. *TEACHING Exceptional Children, 50*(5), 263-271.

Hallahan, D. P., & Kauffman, J. M. (2018). *Exceptional children: Introduction to special education.* Boston, MA: Allyn & Bacon.

Hoa, M., Friedman, R. A., Fisher, L. M., & Derebery, M. J. (2015). Prognostic implications of and audiometric evidence for hearing fluctuation in Meniere's disease. *The Laryngoscope, 125*(suppl. 12), S1-S12.

Individuals with Disabilities Education Act of 2004, Pub. L. No. 108-446, 20 U.S.C. § 1400 *et seq.* (2004).

Killoran, J. (2007). *The national deaf-blind child count: 1998-2005 in review.* Monmouth, OR: National Technical Assistance Consortium for Children and Young Adults Who are Deaf Blind.

Kipp, M., Nguyen, Q., Heloir, A., & Matthes, S. (2011, October). Assessing the deaf user perspective on sign language avatars. In The proceedings of the 13th international ACM SIGACCESS conference on Computers and accessibility (pp. 107-114). ACM.

Kohler, P. D. (1996). *Taxonomy for transition programming.* Champaign, IL: University of Illinois.

Kohler, P. D., & Coyle, J. L. (2009). Transition Institute toolkit. Kalamazoo, MI: NSTAAC Press. Retrieved from http://www.transitionta.org/sites/default/files/Paper_InstituteTK2nd.pdf.

Kohler, P. D., Gothberg, J. E., Fowler, C., & Coyle, J. (2016). *Taxonomy for transition programming 2.0: A model for planning, organizing, and evaluating transition education, services, and programs.* Kalamazoo, MI: Western Michigan University. Retrieved from https://transitionta.org/sites/default/files/Tax_Trans_Prog_0.pdf

Linebarger, D. (2001). Learning to read from television: The effects of using captions and narration. *Journal of Educational Psychology, 93*(2), 288-298.

Munroe, S. (2001). *Developing a national volunteer registry of persons with deafblindness in Canada: results from the study, 1999-2001.* Port Morien, Nova Scotia: Canadian Deafblind and Rubella Association.

National Center on Deaf-Blindness. (2016). Helen Keller National Center. Retrieved from https://nationaldb.org/

National Technical Institute for the Deaf. (2018). Overview. Retrieved from https://www.rit.edu/ntid/about-ntid

Nugent, G. (1983). Deaf students' learning from captioned instruction: The relationship between the visual and caption display. *Journal of Special Education, 17*(2), 227-34.

Rosenberg, M. S., Westling, D. L., & McLeskey, J. L. (2011). *Special education for today's teachers: An introduction* (2nd ed.). London, United Kingdom: Pearson.

Sanders, R. D., & Gillig, P. M. (2010). Cranial nerve VIII: Hearing and vestibular functions. *Psychiatry (Edgmont), 7*(3), 17-22.

Snyder, D. (2016). *Experiences of families raising a child who is deaf-blind and teacher response to those shared experiences* (Unpublished doctoral dissertation). Northern Kentucky University, Highland Heights, KY.

Tang, C., Zhang, J., Yang, S., Han, D., & Han, W. (2018). Unilateral congenital malformations of middle ear with intact external ear: A review of 64 cases. *European Archives of Oto-Rhino-Laryngology, 275*(10), 2467-2472.

U.S. Equal Employment Opportunity Commission. (2002). Enforcement guidance: reasonable accommodation and undue hardship under the Americans with Disabilities Act. Retrieved from https://www.eeoc.gov/policy/docs/accommodation.html

Zeza, M., & Stavrou, P. D. (2015). Program of educational intervention for deaf-blind students. In Y. Tan, Y. Shi, F. Buarque, A. Gelbukh, S. Das, & A. Engelbrecht (Eds.), *Advances in swarm and computational intelligence* (pp. 472-478). Basingstoke, United Kingdom: Springer.

Students With Autism Without Accompanying Language or Intellectual Impairment

CHAPTER OBJECTIVES

- → Describe the characteristics of students within the autism spectrum disorder level 1 or level 2 (ASDL1-2).
- → Describe the level of supports needed for students within the spectrum of ASDL1-2.
- → Describe parental involvement in transition planning for each spectrum.
- → Describe how students with ASDL1-2 can have improved quality of life through community engagement.
- → Describe the types of goal development for students with ASDL1-2.

Rae, J. M. *A Collaborative Approach to Transition Planning for Students With Disabilities* (pp. 285-296).
© 2020 SLACK Incorporated.

Autism Spectrum Terminology: Autism, Asperger's Disorder, and High-Functioning Autism

§ 300.8 Child with a disability.

(1)(i) Autism means a developmental disability is significantly affecting verbal and nonverbal communication and social interaction, generally evident before age three, that adversely affects a child's educational performance. Other characteristics often associated with autism are engagement in repetitive activities and stereotyped movements, resistance to environmental change or change in daily routines, and unusual responses to sensory experiences.

(ii) Autism does not apply if a child's educational performance is adversely affected primarily because the child has an emotional disturbance, as defined in paragraph (c)(4) of this section.

(iii) A child who manifests the characteristics of autism after age three could be identified as having autism if the criteria in paragraph (c)(1)(i) of this section are satisfied.

(§ 300.8 Child with a disability [71 FR 46753, Aug. 14, 2006, as amended at 72 FR 61306, Oct. 30, 2007; 82 FR 31912, July 11, 2017])

The Individuals with Disabilities Education Act (IDEA) describes autism as a developmental disability and does not delineate levels of functioning. However, within the autism spectrum there are significant differences in intellectual development, language and communication impairment, sensory sensitivities, and adaptive functioning. Discussion and even controversy continue about the use of terminology to describe students on the autism spectrum.

Previously, Asperger's disorder was a clinical diagnosis used to describe children with autism characteristics but without clinically significant delays in language or cognitive development or self-help skills (American Psychiatric Association, 2000). As of the *Diagnostic and Statistical Manual of Mental Disorders, Fifth Edition* (DSM-5; American Psychiatric Association, 2013), Asperger's disorder has been subsumed under autism spectrum disorder (ASD).

The terms *high-functioning autism* (HFA) and *low-functioning autism*, are informally used to delineate some differences in an individual child's strengths and needs. However, neither are medical or diagnostic categories for autism, but they have been used in the research on autism and are part of the body of knowledge on autism.

There is still debate on the placement of Asperger's disorder within the autism spectrum based on the shared characteristics while not addressing their significant differences (de Giambattista et al., 2019).

For the purposes of IDEA, autism is the only diagnostic category, and its definition of autism captures both Asperger's disorder and HFA. For the purposes of this chapter, neither of the terms *HFA* or *Asperger's disorder* will be used, but some research has shown that students categorized as having HFA need the support indicated in level 2 (requiring substantial support) in the DSM-5 and those categorized as Asperger's disorder needed the support level 1 (requiring support); this text will use the term *autism spectrum disorder level 1 or level 2* (ASDL1-2). This is for the sake of communication, but it is not used generally. There is still debate on the placement of Asperger's disorder within the autism spectrum based on the shared characteristics while not addressing their significant differences (de Giambattista et al., 2019).

The removal of Asperger's disorder has caused some researchers to contend that without delineations between autism, HFA, and Asperger's disorder, making progress on research will be difficult. For instance, treatments and strategies cannot be sufficiently studied and applied (de Giambattista et al., 2019)

In this text, there will be some information on a few differences as they apply to transition rather than entirely dismiss heterogeneity between the two disorders (Lai et al., 2013). Another area of concern with the terms *HFA* and *Asperger's disorder* is that they give the idea that individuals with HFA/Asperger's disorder have mild impairment while still being on the autism spectrum. This belief negates the seriousness of the social interaction limitations, sensory sensitivities, need for rituals, and learning implications of HFA and Asperger's disorder, which have been currently investigated as having different levels of impairment. Children and young people with HFA/Asperger's disorder are considered high functioning because they develop language and have average to gifted intelligence quotients (IQs) but at the same rates seen in youth without autism. They are also considered high functioning because they can develop work skills. It is in behavior, where there are commonalities. The behavioral characteristics of HFA and Asperger's disorder, the inability to use skills in social settings because of marked limitations, is the focus of their level of need (American Psychiatric Association, 2013, p. 52).

Communication Challenges and ASDL1-2

In this chapter, HFA will be referred to as ASDL1-2. The acronym ASDL1-2 indicates autism that requires a level of support described in the DSM-5 under Levels of Support. In the following section (American Psychiatric Association, 2013), it is characterized by significant qualitative impairments in social interactions; communication; and repetitive patterns of behavior, interests, and activities (Koyama, Tachimori, Osada, Takeda, & Kurita, 2007). A significant challenge for students with ASDL1-2 is understanding the communicative intent of other children, adolescents, and adults. When peer interaction is typical, one person understands the other's emotions and the intention of the message. To do this, the listener holds a mental picture of the communicative intent in the working memory and responds and adjusts to what is being said or physically communicated. The ability to comprehend the nonverbal and verbal communication of others is called *mentalizing* or *theory of the mind* (Barendse et al., 2018, p. 74). Adolescents with ASDL1-2 are aware that they are seen as different, and they are aware of their inability to understand many aspects of communication. As a result, they are more prone to psychosocial stress than adolescents with ASD and intellectual disabilities because they are more aware of opinions and social judgment of peers (Bauminger, Shulman, & Agam, 2003; Burnett, Bird, Moll, Frith, & Blakemore, 2009).

Adolescents with ASDL1-2 have verbal IQs that can be average, above average, superior, very superior, or gifted. They also earn high scores on information and vocabulary subtests. However, communication scores may be over two standard deviations below their verbal IQ. On the Vineland Socialization assessments, students with ASDL1-2 may be three standard deviations below their full-scale IQ, reflecting the magnitude of adaptive impairments despite cognitive ability (Saulnier & Klin, 2007).

Individuals with ASDL1-2 also have more adaptive skills and language than students with ASD and intellectual disabilities. However, students with ASDL1-2 have communication deficits that require substantial support to help them participate in the school and community.

Level of Support

Students with ASDL1-2 require support to make the transition to post-school employment, education, or vocational training. The DSM-5 (American Psychiatric Association, 2013, p. 52) outlines the following levels of supports that students with autism may require:

Level 1: Requiring support

Without supports in place, deficits in social communication cause noticeable impairments. There are difficulties initiating social interactions and clear examples of atypical or unsuccessful response to the social overtures of others. They may appear to have decreased interest in social interactions. For example, a person who is able to speak in full sentences and engages in communication but whose to-and-fro conversation with others fails, and whose attempts to make friends are odd and typically unsuccessful.

Inflexibility of behavior causes significant interference with functioning in one or more contexts. There is difficulty switching between activities and problems of organization and planning hamper independence.

Level 2: Requiring substantial support

Marked deficits in verbal and nonverbal social communication skills; social impairments apparent even with supports in place; limited initiation of social interactions; and reduced or abnormal responses to social overtures from others. For example, a person who speaks simple sentences, whose interaction is limited to narrow special interests, and who has markedly odd nonverbal communication.

Inflexibility of behavior, difficulty coping with change, or other restricted/repetitive behaviors appear frequently enough to be obvious to the casual observer and interfere with functioning in a variety of contexts. Distress and/or difficulty changing focus or action.

Level 3: Requiring very substantial support

Severe deficits in verbal and nonverbal social communication skills cause severe impairments in functioning, very limited initiation of social interactions, and minimal response to social overtures from others. For example, a person with few words of intelligible speech who rarely initiates interaction and, when he or she does, makes unusual approaches to meet needs only and responds to only very direct social approaches.

Inflexibility of behavior, extreme difficulty coping with change, or other restricted/repetitive behaviors markedly interfere with functioning in all spheres. Great distress/difficulty changing focus or action. These children endure gross deficits in verbal and nonverbal communication skills.

Regarding the differences between people with Asperger's disorder and those with ASD, de Giambattista et al. (2019) contend that people with Asperger's disorder typically function at level 1 support where people with ASDL2 need level 2 support. In Chapter 16, there is some discussion about the group of students with ASD who require this level of support. Researchers, who have been studying the differences in diagnostic criteria along the autism spectrum, have used the terms *Asperger's disorder* and *HFA* to define differences they discovered in the studies. Chapter 16, the chapter on students who require level 3 support, discusses students who require supports between levels 1 through 3. See the DSM-5 for further treatment of the levels of support (American Psychiatric Association, 2013, p. 52)

Neurological Basis of ASDL1-2

ASDL1-2 is considered a neurological condition. Fundamental to neurobiology is that it studies how people sense the world and how they act in the world. Researchers have used neuroimaging techniques to document several affected areas of the brain. The areas of challenge listed reveal many areas of behavior and interaction are affected, and it is posited that it is differences in neural networks with insufficient connectivity, which disrupts cell communications, that create the behaviors seen in ASD (Ellison, 2013). There are several hypotheses being researched that propose alternate causes. However, although there is significant attention to the cause and cure of ASD, this text is focused on the characteristics of ASD and helping those adolescents with ASD to be as independent as possible and included and to create a wider understanding of persons with ASDL1-2. The following sections describe the areas of behavior that will need to be understood to prepare for employment.

BEHAVIORAL CHARACTERISTICS OF ASDL1-2

Physical Behaviors

The physical behaviors that are part of communication are noticeably absent in persons with ASD. Behaviors such as eye-to-eye gaze, changing facial expressions to the message, and the use of body posture and gestures are absent. Other gestural behaviors related to social initiation are also not evident. The absence of these communicative behaviors is first seen during the toddler years, when pointing to initiate a parent's attention to an object in the environment does not emerge. In adolescence and adulthood, this is observed as a lack of spontaneous seeking to share experiences.

Routines and Repetitious Behavior

ASD is marked by the need for routines, and adolescents with ASDL1-2 may appear inflexible and will routinely seek to maintain a schedule of activities. If this cannot be done, it can cause anxiety or severe distress.

The repetitive motor mannerisms seen in students with autism who require very substantial support are also present in ASDL1-2, except that the motor mannerisms may be something more socially accepted, such as pen clicking, finger tapping, or knuckle cracking. Some of these repetitive mannerisms are attributed to anxiety.

Another challenge is that there is some evidence of differences in executive functioning in several cognitive skills, such as attention, working memory, planning, reasoning, sequencing, and flexible thinking. In people with and without ASD, these skills benefit not only social interactions but also academics, learning, self-regulation, and activities of daily living. During adolescence, executive planning difficulties are present in peers without disabilities as well; however, these challenges for students with ASDL1-2 persist throughout their lifetimes.

Social anxiety is a challenge for students with ASDL1-2, and they experience anxiety far more than adolescents without ASDL1-2. When ASD and social anxiety co-occur, it is associated with poorer social skills, competence, and social motivation. Self-rated social anxiety and ASD are positively correlated, and a growing body of research suggests that talk therapies like cognitive-behavioral therapy can reduce anxiety and depression in persons with ASDL1-2 (Spain, Sin, Linder, McMahon, & Happé, 2018).

Many adults without ASD prefer talk therapy over medication due to medication side effects (Deacon & Abramowitz, 2005). However, in a study by Buck et al. (2014), multiple medications used for mental health disorders were commonly prescribed. In another study, the ASD group took almost twice the rate antipsychotic medications, which may reflect a higher rate of agitation, impulsivity, and other challenging behaviors (Tsakanikos, Costello, Holt, Sturmey, & Bouras, 2007).

Therefore, while in secondary school, attention to the medical needs of students with ASDL1-2 indicates a need for an Individual Health Care Plan, which includes medication and self-monitoring to determine its effectiveness, ineffectiveness, and possible negative effects. This is a way to improve self-determination and self-advocacy. Also, consideration for school- or community-based counseling early on may support better employment outcomes.

Quality of Social Language

Personal interests tend to monopolize the conversations of people with ASDL1-2, and although they enjoy the company of others, they do not need to share back-and-forth conversation. For example, they may not report significant information to others. They may also have limited and repetitive behavior, interests, and activities that preoccupy them and on which they demonstrate a more intense focus and persistent perseveration. They are typically unable to respond to emotional communications with empathy, although they do understand the discomfort of others. Typically, severe sensory difficulties result in difficulty with physical displays of caring such as hugging, and physical touch is perceived as uncomfortable.

Using Scripts to Interact

To address a student's delay in social speech, school programs for children and youth with ASDL1-2 teach scripts that give preplanned answers to questions students with ASDL1-2 might encounter in interactions with peers. Those who need scripts can use them in social interactions. However, the scripts do not mask atypical aspects of their speech, such as monotone or hypernasal speech. Students with ASDL1-2 are taught to use scripts to respond to everyday questions. However, when used, the social aspects of speech, such as friendliness or concern, are not communicated. Unemotional conversations do not mean the adolescent is not interested in being with people. Adolescents with ASDL1-2 do want to be with people, and they form attachments, but they are unable to respond to emotional aspects of conversations, and they may not be able to respond to the needs of others adequately. Also, the perspective of the young person with ASDL1-2 is difficult to determine due to the lack of intonation and their limited facial expressions (American Psychiatric Association, 2013). Lack of affect does not appear to reflect lack of caring or poor emotional empathy, but rather differences in understanding others' perspectives (Blair, 2005; Dziobek et al., 2008).

Case Report: Jon

A class was out at a park, and Jon was walking along with his teacher when she tripped in a hole and fell backward onto the grass. Jon did not help her up or ask her if she was hurt but said, "I will get a shovel, Ms. G., so you do not fall again." He showed concern that the teacher had fallen, but he did not know how to react to ask questions about an injury or to help her up. He knew falling was not good, and he wanted to prevent future falls.

Exercises

1. Research the use of visual schedules and visual supports for learning as it pertains to ASD.
2. Read Temple Grandin's book *The Way I See It* to better understand the visual thinking process from the perspective of a person with ASDL1-2.
3. In Jon's story, what is the difference between his assessment of the environmental conditions related to the fall and his assessment of the emotional state of the person who fell?
4. How might visual memory and auditory memory affect Jon's belief about what needed to be done?
5. Read Stephen Shore's *Beyond the Wall: Personal Experiences with Autism and Asperger Syndrome*. Describe five challenges he faced living with ASDL1-2. How do these mirror the information provided?

Discussion

If an analysis was possible, one may conclude that Jon reacted based on what he could see, evaluate, and respond to in the physical world. He used his visual analysis to explain and resolve the problem. He could problem solve the physical situation but not the human situation.

In a workplace setting, the lack of emotional concern may or may not cause a negative response because he showed concern by wanting to fix the problem. In practice, Jon would need explicit instruction using scenarios like this one to add an appropriate response to the person who fell. In this way, scripts and role plays are used to teach socially positive responses.

Recognition and Communication of Supports

Adolescents with ASDL1-2 may have difficulty with working memory, which is involved in the processing of social information, including the recognition of facial expressions of emotion (Phillips, Channon, Tunstall, Hedenstrom, & Lyons, 2008). The lifelong difficulties with new situations and environmental stressors, such as changes in routines and other comorbid neurobiological disorders, can affect adaptive functioning in multiple areas (Llaneza et al., 2010) and raise the level of support needed. The characteristics of ASDL1-2 outlined in the following section may increase the level of support needed.

BEHAVIORAL AND EMOTIONAL
IMPLICATIONS FOR TRANSITION PLANNING

Language and Communication-Based Classroom and Workplace Challenges

This section contains the everyday interaction difficulties that make social acceptance and educational activities a challenge for students with ASDL1-2. It is natural to assume that these interactions would transfer into the workplace setting. Although adolescents with ASDL1-2 may be stereotyped as withdrawn, that may not be the case, and each person with ASDL1-2 is unique. It is often the lack of social acceptance that can result from their attempts at communication and style of speech.

Adolescents with ASDL1-2 may use pedantic speech, meaning they will talk about their favorite topics but become bored with the other person when a nonfavored topic is brought into the conversation. They may also speak like a teacher and instruct others rather than exchanging information. Their vocabulary is usually advanced, and they use it in everyday speech. They may also tend to be primarily reclusive and only seek out others when they are interested in talking about a favored topic. Inability to make friends, communication difficulty, and lack of facial affect give the impression that the student with ASDL1-2 does not need social experiences.

Placement of adolescents with ASDL1-2 in classrooms with their peers can cause significant stress when they lack the commensurate skills to interact with peers. Everyday experiences are difficult to share under these conditions. Bonds with friends are most likely when those peers are involved in shared interests that do not require the give-and-take of conversational speech. Conversations that are successful are typically grounded in the physical world and how things function. A method for dealing with the stress related to ASDL1-2 can be addressed during transition planning conferences to make adjustments to decrease stress while the student attends classes.

Transition Plan Participation

Although multiple differences are present, those differences do not prevent students with ASDL1-2 from having an active role and learning to lead the Individualized Education Plan meeting and the transition planning process. Their understanding of the transition planning process can facilitate the growth of advocacy, self-determination, and self-understanding; in fact, the needs and abilities of students with ASDL1-2 call for full participation in transition planning. Students with ASDL1-2 can learn about their disability and communicate how it affects their school and social performance. They can learn to advocate for themselves and, with instruction, plan for how to handle their social anxiety and sensory over-stimulation needs and participate as an active member of the team. Their average to strong intellectual abilities and challenges of ASDL1-2 indicate that they will benefit from a range of activities to facilitate transition to post-school education and work.

Transition Plan Structure

Handling Environmental Stressors and Post-School Life

A significant difference between students with ASDL1-2 and students with other disabilities is the need to pay careful attention to social and physical environments. Neurologically based overstimulation to certain physical environments is characteristic of ASD. Students with ASDL1-2 need to reflect upon and gain a conscious understanding of the types of environments they find overstimulating as they plan for their post-school life.

For the purpose of this discussion, the use of environmental assessments for students with ASDL1-2 is a necessarily useful tool when seeking places conducive to employment, vocational training, post-school education, and even community and leisure activities. An environmental assessment in this context is a planning and decision-making tool. The purpose of the environmental assessment is to assess an environment for certain conditions that are either aversive or conducive to employment and educational success. Through the use of the assessment, students can analyze those conditions. They can determine if they can work or learn in those environments by developing strategies for themselves or declining to seek employment in environments they find to be aversive. One example is when they are hypersensitive to noise. Although not all adolescents with ASD are hypersensitive to noise, many do have this symptom (Baranek, David, Poe, Stone, & Watson, 2006).

Using an environmental assessment is a structured way to eliminate options and narrow down choices using criteria important to the student with ASDL1-2. The first step is to set up a plan of in-school environmental assessment for the student to practice assessing different places in the school that are environmental comfort zones; each one is coded and analyzed. Other environments can be examined as part of the conferencing goal-setting process. During career exploration, the level of environmental comfort can be analyzed as well. By developing this skill, the student will have a list of places that may suit his or her preferences.

A student may want to participate in an environment that he or she perceives as socially and environmentally stressful and develop strategies to acclimate to those environments or decide that the stress of acclimation may be too great and in some cases may not be possible in the face of the neurological origins of the disability. If the student chooses to try acclimation, it may not result in habituation to an environment. The process of analyzing environments is a discovery process of rejecting settings, acclimating to settings, or finding a less stimulating environment to work or study. As an adolescent with ASDL1-2, the student can make these discernments.

Adolescents without ASD may be able to overcome loud working conditions because another motivation, such as making money, is worth the stress of the work environment. However, for students with ASDL1-2, who may be hypersensitive to sound, the stress of the environment may not be bearable for any reward. For instance, expecting the student to work in a loud environment is akin to expecting someone who is visually impaired to read a 6 point font, believing that with practice he or she will be able to adjust to the small font. In ASDL1-2, aversion to loud sounds and settings is a symptom of the disability, and the disability makes certain environmental conditions untenable. Therefore, selecting the best environmental conditions for the student will be a practice that can encourage the student to succeed in a place in which he or she can feel a sense of control.

Students with ASDL1-2 have the cognitive ability to learn to use environmental inventories to help them with their choices and to analyze novel locations that may be of interest and conducive to their success.

Conferences

Conferences with students with ASDL1-2 should be highly structured and rule based. For instance, person-centered planning is a good tool because it clearly outlines what the guidelines are and how the goals can emerge from the student's preferences. Creating a picture-based plan or graphic organizer is useful because students with ASDL1-2 are often visual learners, and the interactive process of the conferences may be difficult for them when there is an expectation of reciprocal conversation. Having a graphic organizer grounds the process of conferencing and makes it concrete for a student with ASDL1-2.

The conference process should not be a stressful interaction where all the student's resources are going into trying to create a mental picture from the conversation. Therefore, making the conference into an enjoyable and visual process will support the student in creating his or her plan. In the same way that the student will be assessing multiple environments, the conference setting is an environment too. Including the student's preferences in making the conference meeting places and transition process socially and environmentally manageable is a way to help engage him or her in the planning process.

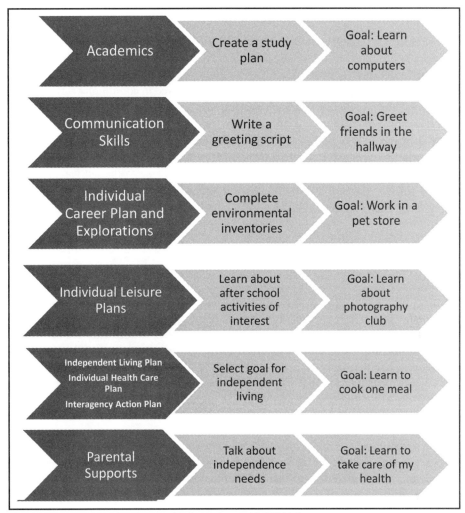

Figure 13-1. Transition planning graphic for students with ASDL1-2.

Setting Goals

Like students with attention-deficit hyperactivity disorder, students with ASDL1-2 have difficulty planning. Students with ASDL1-2 are at some advantage in planning because they like to have patterns in their daily lives. They also like to see linear forms of planning. The transition planning specialist can make the process of transition planning a predictable pattern. An example of how to do this is shown in Figure 13-1. Providing visuals for each goal can give the student a schema or text to process the completion of goals. Once the student suggests his or her goals, putting them in this type of framework helps the student see a pattern toward reaching those goals.

Observations of young children with ASD reveal they enjoy lining objects in a row and they like books with repeating patterns. This is an early learning pattern. Rather than have a student with ASDL1-2 struggle with the process of learning, use the student's pattern of making sense of the world to help him or her make sense of transition planning. Understanding the student's need for patterns and predictability will expedite your understanding of the student and how he or she can thrive in work and school settings.

Transition Planning Challenges

Transition plans for students with ASDL1-2 include high school completion, entry-level employment, participation in postsecondary education, contributing to their households, participating in the community, and experiencing satisfactory personal and social relationships. Youth with ASDL1-2 can transition to college and employment and become involved in community activities. However, staying employed and in college is another challenge due to sensory and social challenges.

During transition, adolescents and young adults with ASDL1-2 require a wide range of services. Throughout their school career, most students with ASDL1-2 benefit from explicit instruction, especially about social conventions. Their adaptive skills are usually strong, and they can learn to manage life in the physical world.

Organizational and social interaction differences and activity-shifting difficulties underpin their need for intensive transition planning. Delineating their needs; motivating goal development; and planning a course of study, services, and supports that match their preferences can be a challenge when change is difficult for them and engenders significant anxiety. Understanding that transition may be met with a rigid response may motivate the transition planning specialist to pay attention to how the plan is communicated and ensure the student the security of a plan he or she can understand and act on with success.

Adolescents with ASDL1-2 look like their peers, and therefore more is expected of them. Social performance, the specter of social anxiety, the effects of sensory overstimulation, and adherence to rigid patterns of behavior are significant challenges for them. In fact, they are self-aware about their difficulties, and the self-scrutiny of adolescence can heighten insecurity of social exchanges and social shortcomings. These same challenges are typically generalized to the workplace and postsecondary settings. It is paramount that the transition planning specialist has a full understanding of the characteristics and needs of students with ASDL1-2, so supports can match their unique needs. Addressing the transition needs of students with ASDL1-2 is a complex and time-intensive effort. Given the limited time during the school day, pursuing academics and significant social needs can result in one supplanting the other. This problem can be addressed by the development of after-school programs, such as clubs for students ASDL1-2, that focus on social development and leisure, artistic, academic, or athletic interests. Planning for college can be facilitated by college visits to see which college has an environment that supports learning and which environments have good supports from the Office of Disability. Calling colleges and talking with the Office of Disability about available supports are self-determination and autonomy activities. Also, getting maps of the campus before the visit and other college information will prepare the student and avoid sensory stress and a disconcerting experience. Because organizing is not a strength, unless it is a specific task, the student will need assistance with filling out applications. In this area, one thinks of a student with ASDL1-2 as one would a student with attention-deficit hyperactivity disorder, and one should provide organizational interventions that can help the student to complete his or her goals.

THE TRANSITION FROM SCHOOL TO EMPLOYMENT

Young people with ASDL1 have skills that are marketable. Companies interested in hiring people with ASD have created programs to bring them into the workforce. Young persons with HFA have a number of positive work behaviors, such as wanting to be on a schedule, appearing for work on time, and being able to focus for an extended period on one task. Also, they often have higher cognitive abilities that support achievement in their field. Studies have shown that adults with ASD are in employed in a range of occupations, including those more counterintuitive to popular conceptions of ASD such as sales, creative arts, and the military (Müller, Schuler, Burton, & Yates, 2003). In addition to their specific job skills, persons with ASDL1 exhibit many characteristics as employees, such as honesty, efficiency, precision, consistency, low absenteeism, and a disinterest in office politics (Müller et al., 2003).

In a study on the occupational activities of 127 adults with HFA, Baldwin, Costley, and Warren (2014) compiled the following list of occupations of the respondents (this is a study that used the terms *HFA* and *Asperger's disorder*):

- Clerical and administrative workers: 22.8%
- Laborers: 22.8%
- Professionals: 22.0%
- Technicians and trade workers: 12.6%
- Community and personal services workers: 9.4%
- Managers: 5.5 %
- Sales workers: 2.4
- Machinery operators and drivers: 2.4%

There is not a rigid type of job preference for persons with ASDL1-2. Therefore, during transition planning, students are given the opportunity to explain their environmental needs and select workplace interests that are most likely not fraught with sensory stimulation. In addition, the needs of students with ASDL2 may require more structure and accommodations to support their higher level of needs.

Although many young people with ASDL1-2 have many positive work characteristics, it is their social characteristics that limit their ability to negotiate social interactions, such as selling themselves on their applications and during interviews.

In preparation for employment, they will need support in negotiating social situations. Some companies have seen the benefits of hiring persons with ASDL1-2. Several companies have programs specifically for them, such as Microsoft, which has a program designed in such a way that individuals with ASD work on various projects on the campus for 2 weeks. During this period, they are observed and participate in informal interviews (Vara, 2016). Opportunities have improved considerably; for example, one company, Specialisterne Foundation reports being the "gold standard" for neurodiversity employment. Other companies, such as Walgreens and Ford Motor Company, have hiring programs as well. See the Student Supplemental Materials for more information on this and other companies, like Spec Al Sterne, that train and support employees with ASD.

EXERCISES

1. Visit each employer website listed in the Student Supplemental Materials. Describe three hiring options and programs for people with ASD.
2. Research two other companies that have programs to employ persons with autism.
3. Interview a student who uses an assistive technology device to help with self-monitoring his or her social communication goals.

SUMMARY

This chapter addressed the characteristics of students with ASDL1-2 and how those characteristics affect their everyday lives. Social and emotional interactions often lack verbal and action-based signs of reciprocity, which makes them appear aloof. Students with ASDL1-2 function well under predictable conditions and need clear visuals to understand the intangible aspects of transition planning. Conversations are often about what can be seen in the physical world, and their memory is largely visual. They have a large fount of knowledge and good recall for what they have learned; however, learning more abstract concepts without supporting visuals is not a strength.

Transitions from middle to high school are significant challenges, and it is to be expected that transitioning to post-school life will need significant support and preliminary visits to adjust to new environments and to structure new patterns for those settings. When planning for the future, helping students with ASDL1-2 visualize and set up new schedules and plans in a tangible manner can facilitate more positive post-school results. Indeed, their reliability and rule-based thinking can be a significant asset in the workplace.

REFERENCES

American Psychiatric Association. (2000). *Diagnostic and statistical manual of mental disorders* (4th ed., text revision). Washington, DC: American Psychiatric Association Publishing.

American Psychiatric Association. (2013). *Diagnostic and statistical manual of mental disorders* (5th ed.). Washington, DC: American Psychiatric Association Publishing.

Baldwin, S., Costley, D., & Warren, A. (2014). Employment activities and experiences of adults with high-functioning autism and Asperger's disorder. *Journal of Autism and Developmental Disorders, 44*(10), 2440-2449.

Baranek, G. T., David, F. J., Poe, M. D., Stone, W. L., & Watson, L. R. (2006). Sensory Experiences Questionnaire: Discriminating sensory features in young children with autism, developmental delays, and typical development. *Journal of Child Psychology and Psychiatry, 47*(6), 591-601.

Barendse, E. M., Schreuder, L. J., Thoonen, G., Hendriks, M. P. H., Kessels, R. P. C., Backes, W. H., … Jansen, J. F. A. (2018). Working memory network alterations in high-functioning adolescents with an autism spectrum disorder. *Psychiatry and Clinical Neurosciences, 72*(2), 73-83.

Bauminger, N., Shulman, C., & Agam, G. (2003). Peer interaction and loneliness in high-functioning children with autism. *Journal of Autism and Developmental Disorders, 33*(5), 489-507.

Blair, R. J. R. (2005). Responding to the emotions of others: Dissociating forms of empathy through the study of typical and psychiatric populations. *Consciousness and Cognition, 14*, 698-718.

Buck, T. R., Viskochil, J., Farley, M., Coon, H., McMahon, W. M., Morgan, J., & Bilder, D. A. (2014). Psychiatric comorbidity and medication use in adults with autism spectrum disorder. *Journal of Autism and Developmental Disorders, 44*(12), 3063-3071.

Burnett, S., Bird, G., Moll, J., Frith, C., & Blakemore, S. J. (2009). Development during adolescence of the neural processing of social emotion. *Journal of Cognitive Neuroscience, 21*(9), 1736-1750.

Child with a disability, 34 C.F.R. § 300.8 (2017).

Deacon, B. J., & Abramowitz, J. S. (2005). Patients' perceptions of pharmacological and cognitive-behavioral treatments for anxiety disorders. *Behavior Therapy, 36*(2), 139-145.

de Giambattista, C., Ventura, P., Trerotoli, P., Margari, M., Palumbi, R., & Margari, L. (2019). Subtyping the autism spectrum disorder: Comparison of children with high functioning autism and Asperger syndrome. *Journal of Autism and Developmental Disorders, 49*(1), 138-150.

Dziobek, I., Rogers, K., Fleck, S., Bahnemann, M., Heekeren, H. R., Wolf, O. T., & Convit, A. (2008). Dissociation of cognitive and emotional empathy in adults with Asperger syndrome using the Multifaceted Empathy Test (MET). *Journal of Autism and Developmental Disorders, 38*(3), 464-473.

Ellison, L. M. (2013). Assessing the readiness of higher education to instruct and support students with Asperger's Disorder (Unpublished doctoral dissertation). Marshall University, Huntington, WV.

Koyama, T., Tachimori, H., Osada, H., Takeda, T., & Kurita, H. (2007). Cognitive and symptom profiles in Asperger's syndrome and high-functioning autism. *Psychiatry and Clinical Neurosciences, 61*(1), 99-104.

Lai, M. C., Lombardo, M. V., Chakrabarti, B., & Baron-Cohen, S. (2013). Subgrouping the autism "Spectrum": Reflection on DSM-5. *PLOS Biology, 11*(4), e1001544. https://doi.org/10.1371/journal.pbio.1001544

Llaneza, D. C., DeLuke, S. V., Batista, M., Crawley, J. N., Christodulue, K. V., & Fry, C. A. (2010). Communication, interventions, and scientific advances in autism: A commentary. *Physiology & Behavior, 100*(3), 268-276.

Müller, E. A., Schuler, A., Burton, B. A., & Yates, G. B. (2003). Meeting the vocational support needs of individuals with Asperger syndrome and other autism spectrum disabilities. *Journal of Vocational Rehabilitation, 18*(3), 163-175.

Phillips, L. H., Channon, S., Tunstall, M., Hedenstrom, A., & Lyons, K. (2008). The role of working memory in decoding emotions. *Emotion, 8*(2), 184-191.

Saulnier, C. A., & Klin, A. (2007). Brief report: Social and communication abilities and disabilities in higher functioning individuals with autism and Asperger syndrome. *Journal of Autism and Developmental Disorders, 37*(4), 788-793.

Spain, D., Sin, J., Linder, K. B., McMahon, J., & Happé, F. (2018). Social anxiety in autism spectrum disorder: A systematic review. *Research in Autism Spectrum Disorders, 52*, 51-68.

Tsakanikos, E., Costello, H., Holt, G., Sturmey, P., & Bouras, N. (2007). Behaviour management problems as predictors of psychotropic medication and use of psychiatric services in adults with autism. *Journal of Autism and Developmental Disorders, 37*, 1080-1085.

Vara, V. (2016). Microsoft wants autistic coders. Can it find them and keep them? *Fast Company.* Retrieved from https://www.fastcompany.com/3062835/microsoft-autism-hiring

Students With Other Health Impairments, Chronic Medical and Orthopedic Impairments, and Traumatic Brain Injury

CHAPTER OBJECTIVES

→ Describe five conditions that are categorized as *other health impairments* (OHIs).
→ Describe the behaviors exhibited for attention-deficit disorder (ADD).
→ Describe the behaviors exhibited for attention-deficit hyperactivity disorder (ADHD).
→ Describe the controversy about medication and ADD/ADHD.
→ Describe accommodations and modifications to assist terminally ill students.
→ Describe the types of traumatic brain injury (TBI).
→ Describe how TBI may affect learning.

CHALLENGES OF OTHER HEALTH IMPAIRMENTS

§ 300.8 Child with a disability.

(9) Other health impairment means having limited strength, vitality, or alertness including heightened alertness to environmental stimuli, that results in limited alertness with respect to the educational environment, that—

(i) Is due to chronic or acute health problems such as asthma, attention deficit disorder or attention deficit hyperactivity disorder, diabetes, epilepsy, a heart condition, hemophilia, lead poisoning, leukemia, nephritis, rheumatic fever, sickle cell anemia, and Tourette syndrome; and

(ii) Adversely affects a child's educational performance.

(§ 300.8 Child with a disability [71 FR 46753, Aug. 14, 2006, as amended at 72 FR 61306, Oct. 30, 2007; 82 FR 31912, July 11, 2017])

Rae, J. M. *A Collaborative Approach to Transition Planning for Students With Disabilities* (pp. 297-311).
© 2020 SLACK Incorporated.

Under the Individuals with Disabilities Education Act (IDEA, 2004), there are multiple conditions that fall under OHI. The following section addresses how the effects of OHIs alter how a student functions in the educational and workplace environment.

Causes of Limited Vitality

Limited vitality due to chronic or acute health conditions can occur with a number of conditions listed under OHI. For example, asthma is a respiratory condition that causes airways to narrow and swell, and the production of extra mucous creates breathing difficulties. ADD or ADHD affect learning because of the extreme difficulty attending to tasks and staying still, as well as having problems with working memory and planning ability. Epilepsy is a medical condition that causes multiple physical and psychological manifestations of atypical brain activity that causes the student to lose awareness (i.e., seizures). The following sections describe how students with OHIs require special education and transition planning. In addition, each section discusses OHI effects on performance and participation in school.

Loss of Instructional Time

Loss of educational time often occurs due to medical treatment or hospitalization, particularly when the condition becomes acute. The student loses instructional time daily when he or she needs treatment during the school day, misses multiple days, or is absent for extended time periods.

Seizures that continue over a period of time are evaluated using electroencephalography, commonly called an *EEG*, to confirm the presence of epilepsy. The effects of seizures, for example, can result in lost educational time. Mild seizures of short duration often result in loss of consciousness, even though the student shows no outward symptoms. Also, there are cognitive effects such as memory impairment that may be present throughout the day. If a seizure is prolonged or is a grand mal seizure, a dose of an emergency medication such as diastat (diazepam) is given. Hospitalization follows to stabilize all vital signs and, in the most extreme events, to prevent death. The seizures that cause the most significant assault on functioning are intractable seizures, also called *refractory* or *uncontrolled seizures*. These seizures are unable to be controlled with any medication, and they are known for causing death or cognitive impairment. At times, students who have intractable seizures may decline in all areas of development. This warrants changes being made to the transition plan so the student can be involved in school to the greatest extent possible. Therefore, those students may need continuous monitoring to keep track of any changes in cognitive status.

Asthma can take from school time as well. More severe cases require treatment with a nebulizer every day. If the treatment cannot control the effects of the current environmental conditions and breathing is impaired, hospitalization and extended absences may occur.

Medications may also result in absences or lack of alertness. The effects of medications and treatments for medical conditions may require special education and related services such as nursing care, Individual Health Care Plans (IHPs), and/or 504 plans.

A student becomes eligible for special education when any condition or its treatment adversely affects his or her educational performance. If educational performance is not affected, then the 504 plan or the IHP informs the faculty involved in teaching the student what will or must be done to meet the student's medical needs and facilitate school attendance.

Need for Homebound Instruction

School districts routinely provide homebound instruction for students with medical illnesses who miss school for extended periods of time. Homebound instruction is a service that has been provided outside of special education services for quite some time. If a student requires special education, a special educator will be assigned. Therefore, there are multiple ways in which children with and without disabilities are provided an educational program when chronic illnesses reduce classroom time. However, the service is limited to a few hours per day and is not meant to replace a full-time educational program.

If a student is in a hospital for an extended period, the hospital may also provide, for example, instruction free of charge. However, unless the school district monitors this closely, students placed in mental health facilities for extended periods of time will have no records of credit acquisition because they typically move from the most restrictive hospital setting to less restrictive mental health settings before they return to school. This makes it difficult to compile course records. Monitoring progress and making modifications will prevent loss of school credit and prevent the frustration of school failure. By assigning a special education teacher to provide homebound instruction, it enables the program to continue transition planning.

Mental Health Disorder Emergence and Episodes

As discussed in Chapter 11, students who have an emerging mental health disorder, a short-term severe episode of their mental health disorder, or mental health disorder medication changes may be eligible for special education under OHI. Depression, bipolar disorder, schizophrenia, and anxiety can affect engagement in academics. Each of these affects attention, motivation, and for some mental health disorders, the understanding of verbal language, and even the will to live. The symptoms of these disorders interfere with learning even when there are no learning or intellectual disabilities present. Students with mental health disorders may require an IHP, Individualized Education Plan (IEP), 504 plan, or all of these to prepare for the diagnostic and treatment phase of their emerging condition.

ATTENTION-DEFICIT DISORDER AND ATTENTION-DEFICIT HYPERACTIVITY DISORDER

ADD and ADHD are neurologically based, and each is identified by a marked pattern of inattention alone (i.e., ADD) or in combination with hyperactivity (i.e., ADHD). Multiple internal symptoms and external behaviors affect learning, and those symptoms and behaviors range from mild to severe. It is the most severe manifestations of ADD and ADHD that will warrant either special education, a 504 plan, or both.

The diagnosis of ADD and ADHD based on data about observed behavior alone limits understanding of these conditions. Other conditions can affect attention, activity, executive functioning, and working memory, such as anxiety, depression, and schizophrenia. In depression and anxiety, feeling restless and the inability to concentrate are present but for different reasons. In anxiety, pervasive worry is an ever-present distraction, and in major depression, agitation is often present, and the ability to think and concentrate is diminished. Therefore, based on behavior alone, these mental health disorders may look like ADD or ADHD to an observer who is unfamiliar with other similarly presenting conditions. Therefore, a comprehensive diagnostic battery of tests given by a trained psychologist or psychiatrist is essential to diagnosis, and the characteristics of ADD and ADHD should be assessed in the psychometric instrument used for testing, which can be used to evaluate each condition.

The behaviors of ADD and ADHD have multiple symptoms and degrees of impairment, as do other disabilities. ADD has a predominantly inattentive presentation but without hyperactivity/impulsivity (American Psychiatric Association, 2013). In ADHD, the student is predominantly hyperactive and impulsive. For diagnosis of either condition, the behavior must be seen over a 6-month period (American Psychiatric Association, 2013), and it is usually seen as early as preschool. Although determining this during preschool is not without controversy.

The diagnostic criteria for ADD and ADHD from the *Diagnostic and Statistical Manual of Mental Disorders, Fifth Edition* (American Psychiatric Association, 2013) follows. Additional descriptions are provided in italics. Symptoms significantly affect the student's educational experiences and learning skills. Categories A and B list symptoms that reflect ADD, and categories A, B, and C represent ADHD:

A. ADD
   a. Often fails to give close attention to details or makes careless mistakes in schoolwork, at work, or with other activities
   b. Often has difficulty sustaining attention in tasks or play *(leisure)* activities
   c. Often does not seem to listen when spoken to directly, even in the absence of any obvious distraction
   d. Often does not follow through on instructions and fails to finish schoolwork, chores, or duties in the workplace and is easily sidetracked and loses focus

B. Attention and Executive Functioning
   a. Often has trouble organizing tasks and activities
   b. Often avoids, dislikes, or is reluctant to do tasks *(that require sustained attention or high working memory load)*
   c. Often loses things necessary for tasks or activities
   d. Is often easily distracted
   e. Is often forgetful in daily activities *(e.g., missed scheduled activities)*
   f. Reading is also affected

C. ADHD
   a. Often fidgets and squirms in seat
   b. Often leaves seat in situations when remaining seated is expected
   c. Often runs and climbs in situations where it is inappropriate (in adolescents or adults, may be limited to feeling restless)
   d. Often unable to play or engage in leisure activities quietly
   e. Is often "on the go," acting as if driven by a motor
   f. Often talks excessively (occurs in bipolar disorder and autism as well)
   g. Often blurts out answers before a question has been completed *(impulsiveness control/lack of planning)*
   h. Often has difficulty waiting his or her turn *(restlessness)*
   i. Often interrupts or intrudes on others *(impulsivity/planning)*
   j. Overlooks or misses details; makes careless mistakes in schoolwork, at work, or during other activities
   k. Displays a persistent pattern of inattention, hyperactivity, and impulsivity that interferes functioning (American Psychiatric Association, 2013)

Problems with working memory are thought to have the most significant effect on post-school success. Kasper, Alderson, and Hudec (2012) found that children with ADHD showed deficits of significant magnitude in working memory in both verbal and visual-spatial working memory compared with peers without disabilities.

Working and Long-Term Memory

A meta-analysis of research on long-term memory performance in adults with ADHD suggests that long-term memory deficits in adult ADHD reflect a learning deficit induced at the stage when the person is encoding information. Long-term memory performance deficits in adults with ADHD are strongly influenced by deficits already present in the stage of memory acquisition (Skodzik, Holling, & Pedersen, 2017). The stage of encoding occurs in the short-term memory, and it is likely that the deficit is not in the long-term memory but rather the short-term memory, also known as *working memory.*

Short-term memory deficits have become the focus of intervention. However, interventions for short-term memory have had very limited success. In a review of 23 studies with 30 group comparisons, a meta-analyses indicated that the programs to improve working memory produced only short-term improvements, and the authors acknowledge that memory training produces the effects that do not generalize (Melby-Lervåg & Hulme, 2013). Therefore, time spent using unreliable methods to increase short-term memory is better designated elsewhere, such as teaching the student evidence-based strategies like using technology with features to enable the student to remember what he or she needs to do. In the same way that glasses are used to replace the function of the eye, technology can be used to replace memory tasks. Accepting that the student's memory will not change, instruction about organizing and inserting daily disability support practices can increase student self-efficacy as the student learns to meet his or her needs that stem from the disability. Creating a system of self-support can increase the student's independence and feelings of autonomy.

Behavior, School, and Employment Success

The significant difficulties discussed here, such as attentional problems, may become more apparent when a student enters the mid-elementary grades. Print size decreases and sentence length increases, requiring that the student be able to hold the sentence in short-term memory long enough for its meaning to be integrated. Difficulty with these tasks may be that the neurobiological differences associated with ADD and ADHD prevent access to working memory. Although the reading skills of these students are usually typical, the increased amount of reading and the more complex concepts taught require an increased load on working memory.

In simple terms, working memory is where information is encoded and then stored in long-term memory for later retrieval. Therefore, the inability to retain information in working memory impedes learning (Mahone, 2011).

Medications are often discussed to increase attention and organization and diminish the student's hyperactive behavior. Medications to treat what appears to be symptoms of ADD and ADHD may be suggested by school personnel as an immediate solution to severe attention, organizational, and hyperactivity problems, with hyperactivity being the most disruptive to learning and classroom management. Schools may have a clear procedure when a child's behavior becomes so provocative that it begins to hurt the educational environment. Most often it becomes a significant problem when it decreases the group's ability to learn even after multiple strategies have been applied; that is when medication enters the discussion.

Prior to addressing stimulants further, it should be noted that medication is approved for the pediatric population. Stimulants used for ADD and ADHD are approved for the following ages: 3 to 16 for amphetamine and dextroamphetamine; ages 6 to 17 for amphetamine salts, atomoxetine, dexmethylphenidate, lisdexamfetamine, and methylphenidate; and ages 12 to 17 for benzenediamine and methamphetamine. Articles about medication will use children or pediatrics to describe the population (Nissen, 2006). Concerns about medication for ADD and ADHD include growth suppression, stimulant abuse, and liver damage. The FDA requires a medication guide for any medication with adverse effects. Therefore, the discussion about stimulants covers children through adolescents.

Transition Planning and Students With Attention-Deficit Disorder and Attention-Deficit Hyperactivity Disorder

The Challenge of Prescription Stimulants

It is important to remember that ADD and ADHD emerge in childhood, although ADD may not be noticed until later because those students are less likely to disrupt the classroom by distracting the teacher and their peers. It is the disruptive classroom behaviors that often lead to formal discussion in the context of a team meeting and informal conversations between teachers, outside of a formal system of child study, about medication. This is a manifestation of frustration and signals that the school psychologist be involved more intensively in the problem solving and begin the process of observation with the parent's permission.

The choice of prescribing stimulant medication is the parent's. In collaboration with the parent, the student can also discuss the benefits and drawbacks of the medication with input from the family physician. The parent may be overwhelmed with the behavior at home as well and be conflicted over what to do.

At times the student and parents, through their family doctor, will agree to trial medication with school and home-based monitoring. This may be done before a hospital- or school-based comprehensive behavioral diagnosis and full medical review is completed. In efforts to solve these neurologically based behavioral problems, medication is often the solution when educational strategies fail to help the child reduce impulsive and inattentive behavior.

The intent of this section is not to discuss the pros and cons of medication but rather to impart the importance of comprehensive medical and psychological testing before medications are prescribed. Side effects from ADD and ADHD medications can be significant, and its use for children and adolescents has not been through a significant number of trials. Clinical trials that are conducted for the approval of many ADHD drugs have not been designed to assess rare adverse events or long-term safety and efficacy. While post-marketing studies on students already taking the medication can fill in some of the gaps, better assurance is needed that the proper trials are conducted, preferably before a new medication is approved (Bourgeois, Kim, & Mandl, 2014).

An issue related to safety is long Q prolongation. Long Q is a change in heartbeat, and it is a life-threatening adverse event from ADD medication and other psychotropic medications. This condition requires an immediate withdrawal from the medication. In addition to long Q prolongation, another reported small but significant rise in blood pressure and heart rate has been seen. Studies completed between 2000 and 2008 on these responses to medication were reviewed by Silva, Skimming, and Muniz (2010). Both placebo-controlled and open-label extension trials have repeatedly shown stimulant-induced increases in mean blood pressure, heart rate, and long QT interval in children, adolescents, and adults. Although these increases seem relatively minor, their existence raises questions regarding whether stimulants could influence the likelihood of sudden death or other serious cardiovascular consequences, especially in patients with underlying undiagnosed heart problems. Questions have been raised regarding making screening patients for unrecognized heart problems a required practice before beginning any stimulant medication. Obtaining a baseline electrocardiogram for any patient starting stimulant treatment is reasonable (Silva et al., 2010). Due to the contraindications for the use of ADD and ADHD medication and the need for intensive medication monitoring, school personnel typically can consider other means of working with each student rather than wait or hope for medication to be prescribed. If the medication has adverse effects, all staff, including coaches, should be provided training and given a crisis plan and an IHP.

Medications may be removed at a moment's notice due to the side effects or danger to a student's life or if they precipitate the emergence of bipolar disorder. Therefore, careful consideration to developing learning strategies, transition plans, and employment training for adolescents with ADD and ADHD is warranted to help them be as independent and self-supporting as possible.

Transition Plan Participation and Supports

Youth with ADD and ADHD can participate fully in transition planning. The focus is on the student giving a full picture of his or her particular struggles with learning, activity levels, impulsiveness, and social interactions. Creating the narrative is essential for the student's self-understanding about how he or she learns and functions and how he or she can best meet the essential functions of a preferred job.

Significant problems with both ADD and ADHD relevant to employment are inattention problems and associated features, as well as delays in executive functioning, memory, and planning ability (American Psychiatric Association, 2013).

For entry-level employment goals, training in the use of assistive technology, and teaching students to create task lists and set alarms as reminders, can make a significant difference in task completion. Job coaching can also be of benefit to assist students when starting a new job. Job coaches can help students set up a system of supports to enable them to do the job as intended. They can also observe students to see how the disability affects all aspects of performance. These supports smooth the transition into the world of work. A job with consistent duties and a consistent work schedule can provide employment that does not tax the student with ADD and ADHD.

For students with more severe impairments, they can learn multiple strategies to manage life and support the completion of workplace tasks. Students with ADD or ADHD have average and above average intelligence. They can read and otherwise participate in the world. They can be taught how to organize and remember what needs to be done. As mentioned previously, students with ADD and ADHD have significant problems with working memory, forgetfulness, and acting impulsively, such as acting before thinking of all the possible negative consequences. Other signs of this can be seen in the chronic loss of school books, pencils, and clothing; forgetting what is said to them in passing; and missing appointments. When you apply the possibility of these problems to the workplace setting, it is clear that multiple supports are needed. Fortunately, for most students with a significant impairment of working memory, establishing routines and methods of planning can work. The important thing is to guide the student not to model his or her peers. The student with ADD or ADHD wants to be like other students, but the disability stops him or her from doing so. The student will not be able to model a peer's organization methods. If the student can understand and accept this, the task will be easier for him or her. The student will need his or her own strategies based on his or her environment and the severity of the memory, organization, and impulsiveness problems. Self-assessment, self-monitoring, and the use behavioral strategies are important, as are identifying thought patterns and finding ways to reduce impulsiveness. Cognitive-behavioral therapy (discussed in Chapter 11) can be an effective way to help with impulsiveness; the student can learn strategies to modify unproductive behaviors and increase productive behaviors.

Assistive Technology

Goals for memory support are essential to organization, independence, and everyday functioning. To address working memory impairment and distractibility, students should have assistive technology and training for its use.

Many smartphones have applications to set up schedules and reminders. However, sometimes students with ADD or ADHD will create a schedule but not remember to look at the calendar. Hourly audio or vibrating reminders can signal the student to look at the calendar. Each of the supports needed for school and work success is put into the IEP under assistive technology needs. As students with ADD and ADHD continue to use these supports, they rely less on teachers to check their plan books or do other teacher-monitoring behaviors that reduce responsibility for the student. Independent and responsible task completion and more responsible social interaction are of primary concern in the transition planning of students with these conditions.

ORTHOPEDIC IMPAIRMENT

§300.8 Child with a disability.

(8) Orthopedic impairment means a severe orthopedic impairment that adversely affects a child's educational performance. The term includes impairments caused by a congenital anomaly, impairments caused by disease (e.g., poliomyelitis, bone tuberculosis), and impairments from other causes (e.g., cerebral palsy, amputations, and fractures or burns that cause contractures).

(§300.8 Child with a disability [71 FR 46753, Aug. 14, 2006, as amended at 72 FR 61306, Oct. 30, 2007; 82 FR 31912, July 11, 2017])

Transition Planning and Accessibility to the Workplace and Postsecondary Education

The Americans with Disabilities Act (ADA, 1990) directs that all students and adults with orthopedic impairments specify physical accommodations necessary to help them navigate school grounds or access classrooms and bathrooms when they use wheelchairs or other technology that helps them with ambulation. Whether the disability is temporary or permanent, any physical disability, such as a broken leg or muscular dystrophy, receives accommodations for access to buildings (see Chapter 4).

The Challenge of Accessibility

Through ADA, many changes have been made to provide accessibility to in-school and post-school environments. Work and post-school educational environments have undergone increasing adaptations that improve educational access for all people with disabilities. For instance, IDEA (2004) requires schools to provide accessible transportation to and from school. Also, ramps and walkways must permit movement inside and outside school buildings. Teachers support students with disabilities when they are knowledgeable about mobility devices (e.g., wheelchairs, walkers, crutches, canes) when arranging classroom furniture and assigning seats. An IEP and/or 504 plan can be developed to document the need more detailed accommodations for ease of mobility. The use of universal design throughout a school building can assist students with orthopedic disabilities in all areas of the school.

College Preparation

For students with orthopedic impairments, credit acquisition can be adjusted during the first term so that adjustment to college life and mobility around an active college campus can be established. This is the student's decision if the student decides to do so. By carefully controlling class scheduling during the first semester, the student can establish movement and study practices to support success at college.

Before selecting a college, it is important to a visit each campus. To prepare, the student can make a virtual visit online. This can add to the student's confidence and ability to move around campus expeditiously. If the campus is far from home, a disability counselor can be of assistance. Connecting with the office of disability at any college being considered is essential to establish a successful plan. Most schools have writing centers and other readily accessible academic supports for all students. Knowledge of those supports and connecting with them is essential to successfully completing an academic program. Determining accessibility and mobility throughout campus can be done in collaboration with the parents and transition planning team by using an environmental inventory.

Assistive Technology

Assistive devices can be instrumental in academic participation for students with orthopedic impairments. Alternative input devices are assistive technology devices, including any piece of equipment, product, or system that has been modified to increase, maintain, or improve the functional capability of a student with disabilities (IDEA, 2004). Some devices include alternative input modifications. Alternative input devices are hardware or software that allow users with mobility impairments or OHIs to interact with a computer without the use of a standard mouse or keyboard. One example is voice-recognition software. Students can bypass the keyboard and speak to the computer. The use of alternative input devices helps students increase, maintain, or improve their functional abilities.

This enables the student who is unable to input information into the device via the common means (e.g., keyboard) has another means to control the device. Students with orthopedic impairments can input information via eye gaze or specialized toggle switches. Another device is an infrared sensor with pneumatic switches that gives access to the computer. The sensor is mounted or worn on the head along with a pneumatic switch. The laser is able to follow and track the student's head movements so that he or she can put the cursor anywhere on the computer screen. To click/use the mouse functions, the student needs to breathe or suck on a plastic tube. The cursor will respond as if being clicked like a mouse (Rosenberg, Westling, & McLeskey, 2011).

Participation in Transition Planning

Types of Individualized Education Plan Participation

Students with orthopedic impairments can take part in the full participation model of transition planning. There is variation in the degree of physical abilities represented in this group of students, but their cognitive abilities enable them to take their place as full collaborators in the planning. Some students with orthopedic impairments will go to college and workplace settings, and others may need a significant level of support, supervision, and possibly 24-hour physical care depending on the severity of the disability. Whatever their plan entails, they can significantly benefit from being full team members.

Students who have a terminal illness can also have an orthopedic impairment, have special considerations, and are given full control of the transition process. Two students, with terminal illnesses who fully participated in transition planning, are described in the following case reports.

Case Report: Miguel

Miguel was diagnosed with muscular dystrophy as a child. Slowly, over a period of 4 years, he became progressively weaker. By the fourth grade he was using a wheelchair, and by the eighth grade he could no longer keep up with the schoolwork and entered a special education program with other students with orthopedic impairments and some mild intellectual disabilities.

Miguel was beloved by his friends and his teachers. During secondary school, he participated in a program called Best Buddies where students with disabilities are paired with high school students who join them in activities in school and the community. Until he was in the 11th grade, Miguel came to school every day. He always had a smile for everyone, even as his health notably declined, making it harder for him to breathe and talk. His friends in the class still wanted to interact with him, but he could only interact via the computer and participate in computer-based activities. The teacher had an assistive technology assessment done of his functioning, and a trackball mouse was recommended because he could only move his index finger. The assistive technology device was approved immediately so he could use it right away. Miguel was able to use it for 6 months, and during that time he was absent more frequently. He wanted to make it through his senior year. However, even with support and a significant amount of sleeping, he eventually could not comfortably ride the bus to school. He did not get to graduate from high school, but the students and staff went to his home to award him his diploma.

Miguel had a transition plan developed that addressed what he would be doing. When the track-ball was purchased, the IEP was rewritten. Multiple other supports for attendance were considered, such as an attendant to support him on the bus and throughout the school day; this was approved. Toward the end, he needed breathing support and the care of a nurse; that too was approved. Although his transition plan goal to walk in graduation was not reached due to his untimely death, he remained happy until he could no longer come to school.

When a student has a terminal illness, transition planning is still about helping him or her reach his or her dreams and the transition planning specialist and team continuing to listen to the student's preferences. Multiple communication and comfort measures are required throughout the process of transition planning for students with declining health and terminal conditions. Until the end, Miguel wanted to be with his peers. He still had social needs; even if he could not interact, it was evident that he just enjoyed being part of his class.

Case Report: Marie

Marie also had muscular dystrophy. However, Marie's condition did not progress as quickly until her 11th-grade year. She was able to participate in general education throughout her school career, and she did well. In her district, there was a support teacher and a classroom for students with orthopedic impairment who were also included in general education classes. Marie attended general education, but during 12th grade, the effects of muscular dystrophy began to affect her breathing. Marie could no longer complete her schoolwork and began to do poorly in her classes. Because of this, she wanted to stop going to school. She did not want to die as a school failure.

The poor grades were brought to the program supervisor's attention. A plan was developed to allow Marie to go to her classes and receive an A for participation on a high school transcript. Although she was skeptical about this, her transition team ensured her it was fair because no other student had the same challenges to learning.

There was concern from a teacher about fairness because a student would get an A on the transcript and not have done the work. This teacher did not understand the situation, and it is essential to fully discuss that when a student has a terminal condition, transcripts are of no consequence.

EXERCISES

1. Research your school's policy on students who are terminally ill. How is it handled with the staff? Are they provided with 504 plans? How is permission granted to talk about a terminal illness? Is the student assigned time with a school psychologist?
2. Work with a group of classmates to write a policy for students with terminal illness, giving students full control over their privacy and a path to continued attendance. Some school districts will give you a copy of their policy, if there is one.

DISCUSSION

During their lifetimes, Marie and Miguel participated fully in the development of their transition plans. The primary goal of the transition plan was that they wanted to participate in school as fully as possible. For students like Miguel and Marie, when coming to school is no longer possible, keeping them connected via a Skype (Microsoft) platform is an inclusive option to meet their needs. Seeing friends and learning was vital to the students' every day quality of life. Attending school in this way is an option for students to decide. When attendance and video conferencing are no longer possible due to deteriorated health, teachers go to the students' homes to visit the student and support the families. A school psychologist can be part of the plan for any family of a terminally ill student under specially designed instruction. This relationship helps the parent by providing emotional support and connections to the school and any agencies that may give the family other supports. Teachers can support the parent just by being there as one of the people who knew their child and cared.

TRAUMATIC BRAIN INJURY

The degree of brain injury may require special education and related services or a 504 plan. However, the degree of impairment may be severe and warrants services such as those given to students with severe and profound intellectual disabilities.

> §300.8 Child with a disability.
>
> (12) Traumatic brain injury means an acquired injury to the brain caused by an external physical force, resulting in total or partial functional disability or psychosocial impairment, or both, that adversely affects a child's educational performance. Traumatic brain injury applies to open or closed head injuries resulting in impairments in one or more areas, such as cognition; language; memory; attention; reasoning; abstract thinking; judgment; problem-solving; sensory, perceptual, and motor abilities; psychosocial behavior; physical functions; information processing; and speech. Traumatic brain injury does not apply to brain injuries that are congenital or degenerative, or to brain injuries induced by birth trauma.
>
> (§300.8 Child with a disability [71 FR 46753, Aug. 14, 2006, as amended at 72 FR 61306, Oct. 30, 2007; 82 FR 31912, July 11, 2017])

Common Types of Traumatic Brain Injuries

Skull Fractures, Contusions, Concussions, and Hematomas

Accidents that affect the skull can cause various injuries that result in TBI. Fractures at the back and base of the skull tear layers of tissue that cover the brain. This heavily protected area can be injured at high impact, and brain damage is more likely. Some fractures break the skin, allowing bacteria to enter the skull through the fracture, causing infection, abscesses, and severe brain damage (Rosenberg et al., 2011).

Another cause of TBI is a contusion, or bruise to the brain. The bruise or bruises are from an impact to the head that causes small blood vessels to leak. The degree of brain damage will depend on how extensive the bruise is. The symptoms of the contusion may worsen for a few days after it occurs (Rosenberg et al., 2011).

Skull fractures can injure blood vessels around the brain and cause blood clots in the brain, known as *hematomas*. There are two types: an epidural hematoma is one that forms between the skull and the outer covering of the brain, and a subdural hematoma forms directly on the brain itself. The subdural hematoma is more severe than an epidural hematoma (Rosenberg et al., 2011).

A concussion is an injury that causes a loss of consciousness or amnesia. It causes damage to nerve fibers in the brain. It is well-known that many athletes in high-contact sports get concussions regularly, but any hit or any fall that causes impact to the brain can result in a concussion. One type of concussion is more severe: a diffuse axonal injury results when nerve fibers throughout the brain are injured through violent motion, such a car accident.

One TBI with long-term consequences is repeated concussions. Microbleeds can occur following a concussion, and these increase the risk for cognitive impairment and dementia (Charidimou & Werring, 2011). Brain injuries cause many problems, dependent on the part of the brain that is injured. Problems include forgetfulness, difficulty learning new information, speech and language problems (e.g., word finding), difficulty sequencing things, unstable moods, and difficulty processing information. These challenges have a direct effect on school and work functioning.

Participation in Transition Planning

A student with an acquired TBI will have a long recovery process, and most likely, over time, he or she will gradually increase the time they spend in school. Students need to recover to the extent that they can return to the school and be psychologically ready to return. Students who have a TBI can be provided with multiple pathways to access the general curriculum and, post-rehabilitation, begin planning for post-school life. The special education team, rehabilitation center, parents, and student will collaborate on two transitions: the transition back to school after rehabilitation and transition to post-school life. Using the student's current level of physical and cognitive needs, and his or her own preferences, the school and rehabilitation agencies will work together with the student and parents to plan the logistics of his or her return to the school post-injury. A pre-return meeting includes meeting with the family, a hospital-based therapist, a special education representative, a special education teacher, and the transition planning specialist. A plan of reentry will include permission to use existing hospital records to develop an IHP and evaluation report to determine what services are needed. Once determined eligible based on TBI, the student's IEP takes the student's current cognitive and learning characteristics into consideration, especially attention, visual and auditory perception, memory, and information-processing abilities (Rosenberg et al., 2011).

As part of transition planning, ongoing updates from outside therapists and the parents provide information about cognitive and physical progress if part-time rehabilitation therapy is ongoing. Both teams will collaborate with the student about the goals that the student may want to set based on learning needs and requested assistive technology supports.

With any acquired TBI, special education and related services and supports will be required to provide the student with an appropriate education. As the student makes progress through therapy, the question of how to best support the student will be expected to change. Transition plans will need to be updated regularly as the staff work to meet the needs of the student and ensure that the IHP is included in the transition IEP and reviewed with the school nurse to plan for daily medical needs. The team will also work to include the student with TBI in completion of a framework of transition.

Independent Living in the Community for Students With Severe Orthopedic Disabilities and Traumatic Brain Injury

Governmental agencies give support to eligible persons with disabilities. Supports are coordinated and plans are developed based on individual needs. An evaluation through Medicaid is required by age 18 for students with TBI, and most families have done so prior to the student's return to school. If the parents have contributed to social security, some funds may be available to the child. Transition to adult services is addressed for students with TBI and orthopedic disabilities. To access their environment, an environmental inventory is completed, a 504 plan for accessing the school building is designed, and time is spent prior to a return to learning to travel around the school building.

Accessibility to the Workplace and School

The ADA and legislation such as the Architectural Barriers Act (1968, as amended 42 U.S.C. §§ 4151 et seq.) increased access to school and employment settings. This has increased work opportunities when the building is supported even partially with federal funds. This is the case for public schools. As a result, educational and work environment redesigns have improved access for all people with disabilities who may have been unable to navigate around the classroom, school hallways, and workplaces.

BEST-FIT PRACTICES FOR STUDENTS WITH OTHER HEALTH IMPAIRMENTS

Career Interests

When developing goals for transition, a number of considerations are present, including academics and social development. Physical stamina and health records need to be reviewed by the student whenever possible and used as a guide to establish what the student may need to advocate for when applied to career interests and opportunities. The student's constraints, preferences, wants, and needs can become part of the narrative where the student discusses the effect of his or her disability on everyday life. It may take some time before the student with an acquired TBI may want to do that. It is plausible he or she may only want to do that with a therapist. Therefore, as the student becomes stronger, career explorations can begin. Understanding the disability constraints and the target employment or school goal will help the student establish goals to pursue.

The School Program

The student and the IEP team must discuss if full participation in general education will help the student with transition goals. For instance, should a course be completed in the summer at a community college so that more time can be spent on activities to prepare the student for college or employment? This is a student-by-student decision. There are few limitations when designing an educational program unless they are artificially applied. The following is a brief list of alternative secondary special education pathways for transition planning:

- A year-round, part-time academic program to give more time to accessing education and transition planning
- Earning community college summer credits to apply toward high school graduation credits
- Accessing general education curriculum with modifications such as the use of assistive technology to facilitate access to learning
- Using online learning
- A general education program that uses text-to-speech and digital resources
- A curriculum designed to fit the learning style the student reports is helpful.
- A life skills curriculum using academic and life skills as required for all students with disabilities. Assumption of inability is no longer included in educational programming.
- Align medical needs with the job. Consider part-time and in-home work such as remote employment with credits earned based on hours of participation.
- Work and school program options for 11th and 12th graders
- Ensure that opportunities to learn in other modalities are provided.
- Provide access to programs, services, technology (e.g., Bookshare, assistive devices), and any other support that increases the options for learning.

Students with ADD, ADHD, orthopedic impairments, medical conditions, and TBI can participate fully in transition planning. They can, after training, take leadership roles in their IEP meetings. With mobility and assistive technology support, they can go on to postsecondary training.

Post-School Options for Students With Other Health Impairments

For students with OHIs, a full range of employment options are available when accommodations and the ability to handle the essential functions of the job are well defined. Seeking employment starts with exploration and opportunities in any given field. Students can work with the transition planning specialist and special education team to learn about supports and accommodations or modifications that may be needed to participate in entry-level employment, training, and further education required for a more preferred job or career. Community-based instruction is important to any student with disabilities who wants to access unfamiliar environments. Access to institutions providing postsecondary education is included in transition plans to give the student practice accessing educational environments.

EXERCISES

1. Use the Student Supplemental Materials to find websites, journals, and organizations/agencies related to OHIs.
2. Design a 20- to 30-minute PowerPoint presentation or online interactive learning module about four OHIs.
3. Include what teachers can do, based on the research, to improve instruction for students with OHIs.
4. Use the university library find three articles on ADD. Describe what the current research says about executive functioning and working memory. Search the university's online library to find articles on how memory affects learning, specifically for students with these conditions. Research must be less than 3 years old.

SUMMARY

Students who are eligible for special education under the designation of OHI receive medical and ongoing educational monitoring, access to instruction and instructional materials, and medication monitoring and medical treatment via an IHP.

Students with ADD or ADHD require strategies and can significantly benefit from assistive technology to facilitate attention to schedules and responsibilities. Independence in meeting self-management responsibilities are essential to future employment. Employment that matches the strengths of students with ADD and ADHD is paramount to removing risks associated with multiple job changes or loss of employment.

Students with medical conditions, TBI, and orthopedic impairment require mobility training and access to all areas of the school that students without disabilities can access. Planning must reflect all of those needs.

Students whose mental health disorders do not warrant placement in an emotional and behavioral support program can also receive 504 plans and in-school emergency and periodic counseling to address the episodic nature of mental health disorders. Even when a student is not in special education, transition planning is available when the mental health disorder is impairing his or her ability to seek employment or participate in everyday activities.

REFERENCES

American Psychiatric Association. (2013). *Diagnostic and statistical manual of mental disorders* (5th ed.). Washington, DC: American Psychiatric Association Publishing.

Americans with Disabilities Act of 1990, Pub. L. No. 101-336, 42 U.S.C. § 12101 *et seq.* (1990).

Architectural Barriers Act of 1968, as amended, 42 U.S.C. §§ 4151 et seq.

Bourgeois, F. T., Kim, J. M., & Mandl, K. D. (2014). Premarket safety and efficacy studies for ADHD medications in children. *PLoS One, 9*(7), e102249.

Charidimou, A., & Werring, D. J. (2011). Cerebral microbleeds: Detection, mechanisms and clinical challenges. *Future Neurology, 6*(5), 587-611.

Child with a disability, 34 C.F.R. § 300.8 (2017).

Individuals with Disabilities Education Act of 2004, Pub. L. No. 108-446, 20 U.S.C. § 1400 *et seq.* (2004).

Kasper, L. J., Alderson, R. M., & Hudec, K. L. (2012). Moderators of working memory deficits in children with attention-deficit/hyperactivity disorder (ADHD): A meta-analytic review. *Clinical Psychology Review, 32*(7), 605-617.

Mahone, E. M. (2011). The effects of ADHD (beyond decoding accuracy) on reading fluency and comprehension. *New Horizons for Learning, IX*(1). Retrieved from http://archive.education.jhu.edu/PD/newhorizons/Journals/Winter2011/Mahone

Melby-Lervåg, M., & Hulme, C. (2013). Is working memory training effective? A meta-analytic review. *Developmental Psychology, 49*(2), 270.

Nissen, S. E. (2006). ADHD drugs and cardiovascular risk. *New England Journal of Medicine, 354*(14), 1445-1448.

Rosenberg, M. S., Westling, D. L., & McLeskey, J. L. (2011). *Special education for today's teachers: An introduction* (2nd ed.). London, United Kingdom: Pearson.

Silva, R. R., Skimming, J. W., & Muniz, R. (2010). Cardiovascular safety of stimulant medications for pediatric attention-deficit hyperactivity disorder. *Clinical Pediatrics, 49*(9), 840-851.

Skodzik, T., Holling, H., & Pedersen, A. (2017). Long-term memory performance in adult ADHD. *Journal of Attention Disorders, 21*(4), 267-283.

15

Students With Mild, Moderate, Severe, Multiple, and Profound Intellectual Disabilities

CHAPTER OBJECTIVES

- → Describe the spectrum of intellectual disability.
- → Describe characteristics of mild, moderate, severe, profound, and multiple intellectual disabilities.
- → Identify the areas of responsibility of a case manager.
- → Describe the key characteristic of a mild intellectual disability that drives the need for case management.
- → Characterize the key issues of communication and intelligence quotient (IQ) testing.
- → Define the need for yearly academic and adaptive assessments.
- → Define the uses of person-centered planning (PCP) and environmental inventories.
- → Define the type of transition planning participation that may be appropriate for each category of disability.

Rae, J. M. *A Collaborative Approach to Transition Planning for Students With Disabilities* (pp. 313-338).
© 2020 SLACK Incorporated.

DEFINING AND DIFFERENTIATING CHARACTERISTICS
FOR YOUTH WITH INTELLECTUAL DISABILITIES

§ 300.8 Child with a disability.

(6) Intellectual disability means significantly subaverage general intellectual functioning, existing concurrently with deficits in adaptive behavior and manifested during the developmental period, that adversely affects a child's educational performance. The term "intellectual disability" was formerly termed "mental retardation."

(7) Multiple disabilities mean concomitant impairments (such as intellectual disability-blindness or intellectual disability-orthopedic impairment), the combination of which causes such severe educational needs that they cannot be accommodated in special education programs solely for one of the impairments. Multiple disabilities do not include deaf-blindness.

(§ 300.8 Child with a disability [71 FR 46753, Aug. 14, 2006, as amended at 72 FR 61306, Oct. 30, 2007; 82 FR 31912, July 11, 2017])

Intellectual disability is a category of developmental disability. Historically, intelligence quotients (IQs) have been used to define the levels of intellectual disability as mild, moderate, severe, multiple, and profound. The most recent update of the *Diagnostic and Statistical Manual of Mental Disorders, Fifth Edition* uses levels of severity to specify need in areas of adaptive functioning. The levels of severity are based on functioning in conceptual, social, and practical domains. In addition to adaptive functioning, multiple assessments and clinical judgment, by persons certified to diagnose, are used to determine the level of intellectual disability (American Psychiatric Association, 2013, p. 35). Adolescents with mild, moderate, severe, and profound intellectual disabilities and multiple disabilities require differentiated transition frameworks. The frameworks, based on the individual student, reflect a spectrum of adaptive functioning in intellectual, cognitive, academic, physical, medical, social, and independent functioning within the overall spectrum of intellectual disabilities, along with each student's personal characteristics and abilities. Like the autistic spectrum, students with intellectual disabilities have a wide range of abilities. This range reflects the abilities of students with the most significant needs in all areas of functioning and those within the spectrum who are able to be more independent, learn skills, and complete academic tasks.

Defining Intellectual Disabilities

Youth with mild intellectual disabilities are the highest functioning group of youth with intellectual disabilities; they are also the most highly represented group among students with intellectual disabilities. Typically, they go unnoticed and appear more like their same-age peers but demonstrate significant learning, cognitive, and social needs, as well as some adaptive needs. They may not have the physical characteristics associated with children and youth with moderate to profound intellectual disabilities, who have chromosomal differences and physical and behavioral characteristics that generally identify or associate them as a person with a disability.

Students with moderate intellectual disabilities function at a higher level than students with severe, multiple, and profound intellectual disabilities but need significant supervision, intensive academic and social instruction, a focus on adaptive behaviors, and some support in all settings. They are served in programs that work primarily on functional skills, which give them increased independence skills. They are also required to have academic instruction. Students within this level of intellectual disability can develop reading skills up to the fifth-grade level, but as reading vocabulary advances for their same-age peers, they cannot keep up and miss the reading that increases more advanced comprehension. With reading programs that focus on literacy and the use of picture supports using age-appropriate readings, higher comprehension levels can be achieved. However, given the expectations of the past, more attention can be given to reading to avoid limiting progress based on assumptions about reading abilities (Shurr & Taber-Doughty, 2012).

The next group within the spectrum of intellectual disability are children and youth who require the most support, have the most severe cognitive disability and physical disabilities, and are defined as having a severe, multiple, or profound intellectual disability. At the level of profound disability there is little use of objects due to severe cognitive and physical disabilities (American Psychiatric Association, 2013, p. 36).

Youth with severe, multiple, and profound intellectual disability most often have limited verbal communication abilities. Their use of expressive language can be unintelligible, minimally intelligible, or echolalic; most are nonverbal. These youth need essential communication tools and assistive technology to take part in transition planning, but their limited cognitive disabilities, physical disabilities, and medical conditions often determine how and whether they can participate directly. For these students, other strategies are used to inform the team about their preferences.

The transition planning specialist and team must have knowledge of transition planning, which includes the ability to meet the needs of students with intellectual disabilities by planning for the agency and family supports they will need in adulthood.

Assessment of Intellectual Disabilities

Multiple factors are used to determine if a student has moderate through profound intellectual disability. Assessment includes measures of adaptive functioning within the context of community environments typical of the individual's age, peers, and culture (Rosenberg, Westling, & McLeskey, 2011, p. 205).

Intellectual ability is delineated into groups via IQs and adaptive assessments. The IQ scores provide a spectrum of intellectual functioning from mild to profound intellectual disabilities.

Concerns prevail about the use of IQ tests as the lone measure to determine ability, with detractors arguing that the exclusion of adaptive functioning creates an inaccurate picture of overall functioning. Another issue with IQ tests is they are normed to children with the ability to see, understand spoken language, move their bodies, solve problems, and complete memory tasks. Because of the severity of orthopedic disabilities and sensory disabilities, such as vision and hearing disabilities, these youth cannot respond to test items. Therefore, specialists contend that the IQ test alone does not indicate actual intellectual functioning for the most severely disabled. New measures, such as the Diagnostic Adaptive Behavior Scale (DABS), which assesses conceptual, social (e.g., the likelihood of being victimized), problem-solving, and practical skills, are used to provide more specific detail about the everyday needs of children and youth with intellectual disabilities. Assessments that measure adaptive skills and basic language comprehension are of primary importance when providing baseline data for instruction. Assessments should guide the addition of evidence-based strategies. From the assessments and the student's preferences, the Individualized Education Plan (IEP) team derives goals, appropriate instructional plans, and related transition services.

Providing appropriate services and improving post-school outcomes includes increasing the level of school and community participation so that needs can best be determined. Overall cognitive functioning and medical and orthopedic challenges must be included so the most effective supports can be implemented.

Despite the level of disability, youth with intellectual disabilities are part of the fabric of life and, as members of humanity, can be educated within their community schools with their same-age peers, enjoying opportunities for inclusion and satisfying life experiences. Transition plans should effectively include students with multiple needs in safe and supportive environments where they are given intensive instruction that can prepare them to the maximum extent possible for post-school life. The following sections generally describe each level of intellectual ability with the understanding that within each designation lies another spectrum of adaptive and intellectual functioning, reflecting the uniqueness of each adolescent with an intellectual disability.

CHARACTERISTICS OF STUDENTS
WITH MILD INTELLECTUAL DISABILITIES

Mild intellectual disabilities can occur at conception, during pregnancy, during birth, or after birth. Those that occur at conception can be the result of hereditary conditions, for example, DNA damage due to advanced paternal age or ingestion of toxins. Those that develop during pregnancy occur due to lack of oxygen from a depressed cord, infections, certain medications, or illnesses such as German measles or meningitis. In the journey down the birth canal, a lack of oxygen can cause intellectual disabilities as well. They can also occur after birth from and environmental toxins, such as when water containing lead is used to cook or make formula.

Other causes of mild intellectual disabilities can be a lack of early exposure to a stimulating environment. Mild intellectual disabilities affect intellectual and adaptive functioning. The following characteristics impair the student's ability to remain safe:

- Gullibility: Easily exploited, trustful, unwary, and little understanding of risk
- Working memory: Difficulty remembering complex strings of information and holding primary information while adding additional information
- Learning: Difficulty learning due to poor short-term memory
- Self-regulation: Difficulty managing emotions and behavior
- Impulsiveness: Impulsive behavior, acting without thinking of future consequences
- Vocabulary development: Low grade-level attainment, and a limited vocabulary impairs communication and comprehension of the social speech of others and social messages (American Psychiatric Association, 2013)

Impact on Learning and Employment

The six aforementioned challenges to learning and satisfactory life experiences are addressed when developing employment plans and IEPs for youth with mild intellectual disability. The six areas of need require a comprehensive plan of instruction and, where applicable, community-based instruction (CBI). Of significant importance is gullibility. Students with mild intellectual disabilities are significantly at risk for social problems due to problems with gullibility. Gullibility is defined as the tendency to believe something highly questionable. The *Diagnostic and Statistical Manual of Mental Disorders, Fifth Edition* (American Psychiatric Association, 2013) elaborates on this by describing students with mild intellectual disability as having a "limited understanding of risk in social situations, social judgement is immature for age, and the person is at risk for being manipulated by others (gullibility)" (American Psychiatric Association, 2013, p. 34).

Being manipulated by others at work or school includes the inability to see consequences. One problem that can have significant ramifications is the case of confessions, youth and young adults can be convinced they did something they did not do. Patton and Keyes (2006) argued that this gullibility makes students with mild intellectual disabilities vulnerable to being tricked into committing crimes because they cannot predict the outcomes.

Other areas of functioning, such as working memory, self-regulation, and vocabulary knowledge also limit the ability to comprehend language and communicate intent in school and in the workplace. These factors make adolescents with mild intellectual disabilities susceptible to putting themselves in dangerous or suspect situations, as well as being unable to negotiate themselves out of these situations.

The issue of gullibility and competence has come to the attention of the courts multiple times. The features of intellectual disability and problems with adaptive functioning, including gullibility, reached the Supreme Court, in 2002, in *Atkins v. Virginia*. The Supreme Court ruled that persons with mild intellectual disabilities cannot be given the death penalty because of their tendency to confess to crimes that they have not committed (Snell et al., 2009). More recently, in 2017, the Supreme Court struck down the method Texas used, relying on IQ alone to judge if an intellectual disability is present (*Moore v. Texas*, 2017). The Court ruled that the method Texas used created an unacceptable risk that persons with intellectual disabilities will be executed (*Moore v. Texas*, 2017).

This social vulnerability puts young people with intellectual disability at risk, and consideration about where they work and how their independence can be supported while maintaining their safety is a primary concern.

Students with mild intellectual disabilities are often placed in classes for students receiving support for specific learning disabilities or in general education classes for inclusion. The students in these classes are average or above-average intellectually. Ongoing immersion in general education or placement in work settings without the establishment of sexual, financial, personal, behavioral, and interpersonal boundaries can result in undesirable and even tragic outcomes. Therefore, developing help-seeking behaviors in confusing social situations at school and in work settings is a necessary part of transition planning.

Using a transition curriculum, the transition planning specialist, the special education team, and the family can address this area by working across environments to provide direct instruction about safety in school with peers, at home, and in the community. Keeping students with mild intellectual disabilities safe should be a significant part of the transition curriculum, as well as a prominent consideration in employment settings.

Youth with mild intellectual disabilities also have strengths and many adaptive skills. Those who can attend to their personal needs and move throughout the school independently, study, manage their materials, and can interact with other students. Mild intellectual disability may not be readily noticed and is only identified upon examining the student's learning and adaptive skills (Rosenberg et al., 2011, p. 204). These students, because they do not stand out significantly, may escape Child Find efforts. This further leaves them in a vulnerable position.

To plan appropriately for adulthood, an evaluation defining them as a person with an intellectual disability should occur as soon as possible so that the student and family can get agency support. Without proper academic, adaptive, cognitive, and vocational assessment the student will be deprived of eligibility for a case manager and vocational rehabilitation services, thereby making supports during childhood and adulthood unavailable. Supports coordinators, at times referred to as *case managers*, engage students and their families to assist students with mild intellectual disabilities as they transition into the workplace. With agency, parental, and in-school supports, these students can participate in the framework of transition as well as a transition plan curriculum that intensively targets their needs both during middle and high school through adulthood. These needs include language development, interpersonal communications, boundaries, safety during recreational activities due to immature judgement, physical safety, home safety, selecting employment in situations where conceptual skills are not needed, support in health care, money management, legal decisions, and finally, help will be needed to raise a family (American Psychiatric Association, 2013).

The following case report is about a student with a mild intellectual disability. Kara was passed through each school grade without being able to read above the second-grade level.

Case Report: Kara

Kara was 18 years old when she was placed in an alternative program for students with emotional disturbance. She had been refusing to do work and was expressing suicidal thoughts. Before placement in this program, Kara had stopped doing any classwork in her general education classroom. She was older than most of her peers, did not have enough credits to graduate, and was being bullied. She began to refuse to attend school but would not drop out.

At home, things were not much better. Kara had been leaving home to meet older boys and "have parties." She was defiant, and her parents could not keep her from staying out late.

In her emotional support classroom, none of the previous defiance was evident. She was very compliant and wanted to please. Teachers and therapy staff quickly ascertained that she had a mild to moderate intellectual disability and she was easily led. When additional records were requested, it was evident that Kara had gone through her entire school program with poor or failing grades. The psychologist from the school district of origin said there were no records to indicate she had an intellectual disability because she was never tested. The district psychologist, who was aware of her problems, believed a general education class was the best placement. Special education placement was not considered for Kara.

Kara was finally tested, at the behest of her school placement, just after her 19th birthday. Because she was not tested for intellectual disability before her 18th birthday, she was not eligible for services provided to children and youth with intellectual disabilities and she missed a childhood of needed services.

During her time at the emotional support placement, Kara shared that during 1 school year she never went out for recess because she had to stay in and do her work. Other years, she said she also spent most recesses inside.

Ultimately, a case manager took Kara's case, and she received services as a person with a mental illness: the depression that brought her to the program. With the depression diagnosis, she did get other support services as a person with a disability. However, she should have been getting those services, including Medicaid and a case manager, well before age 19. Although other supports were being developed, Kara stopped doing schoolwork and remained depressed. Her level of comprehension made it difficult for her to interact with the other peers in the program. She stopped attending school.

Unfortunately, in Kara's case, she became pregnant. Although transition planning was implemented through adult services, Kara's need for a social connection was stronger than her need to continue in a school program, which historically isolated her and hurt her confidence and self-esteem. If Kara had received services as a person with a moderate intellectual disability, Kara's trajectory most likely would have ended with an Office of Vocational Rehabilitation (OVR) placement in a group home or supported living apartment.

EXERCISES

1. How might gullibility affect parenting skills?
2. What statue was ignored that should have initiated testing?
3. In your practice have you ever seen a child like Kara?

DISCUSSION

Students who are failing and consistently being socially secluded from peers to address academic problems need a full evaluation under Child Find legislation. At times, teachers and staff blame personal characteristics, such as laziness or family background, to explain the academic failure, particularly for students who have a typical appearance. The situation is especially dire for students with intellectual disabilities, who are behaviorally quiet and compliant with interactions. Passing these compliant students with undiagnosed intellectual disabilities from grade to grade is a serious problem that can carry dire repercussions for life. Without the vocabulary, social understanding, or advocacy skills, students will placidly accept their situation and sadly their aloneness. All students with intellectual disabilities should be registered via their county agency and be given case management services in addition to a school-age transition coordinator by middle school. Students with mild intellectual disabilities can work and graduate, but they need the school program to address their multiple needs in a timely manner to avoid deleterious outcomes for students. Yearly academic and adaptive testing is crucial for identification and referral to appropriate services, positive outcomes, and employment.

CHARACTERISTICS OF ADOLESCENTS WITH MODERATE INTELLECTUAL DISABILITIES

Youth with moderate intellectual disabilities have higher skills than those demonstrated by youth with severe, multiple, and profound intellectual disabilities. Because of their higher functioning, they can benefit from many activities of transition. However, they too must be explicitly taught safety, with multiple lessons and chances to generalize the instruction into other settings. Unlike those with mild intellectual disabilities, they are unable to participate in interactions with peers without disabilities in relationships without supervision. Diverse medical needs and communication constraints are often present. Persons who accompany children or youth with moderate intellectual disabilities need preparation and knowledge of their health status and must read their Individual Health Care Plan (IHP). Adults should be prepared to assist if the youth has a heart condition, food allergies, or diabetes, for example. Adults will need training about the need for emergency procedures if necessary. Depending on where a student functions within a spectrum of moderate intellectual disabilities, he or she may not be able to communicate his or her needs.

Many youths with moderate intellectual disabilities are ambulatory, and, depending on where they function within the range of moderate intellectual disabilities, may wander away at times. Therefore, vigilance is necessary to keep them safe.

Instructional programs that focus on multiple life skills can help teach each young person essential skills. The following skills need continual attention during school years and post-school:

- Communication
- Reading or audiobooks for pleasure and survival
- Social interactions
- Self-care
- Functional academics
- Home management skills
- Food preparation and nutrition
- Community access skills
- CBI for generalization
- Safety instruction
- Social activity
- Work habits
- Vocational skills
- Social issues, such as bullying

Some adolescents with a moderate (i.e., a manifestation of their disability) intellectual disability have, as part of the genetic pattern, disruptive behavior and noncompliance. Functional behavioral assessments, conferencing with the student, and meeting their needs, along with positive behavior support plans may be needed throughout their lifespan.

Each student in the moderate intellectual disability spectrum has unique needs and abilities. To appropriately plan for instruction, students need advocacy training because they may not assert themselves; therefore, the parent gives essential information about what the child has already mastered. This eliminates delays in learning by excluding instruction that is not needed. For example, a young person may already know how to do laundry. If the curriculum includes laundry skills, the student will need to spend time performing the skills he or she has already mastered. When determining the goals of transition, assessing the students requires a complete record of overall functioning at home and in the community. This avoids repeating the same instruction and misusing valuable instructional time.

Impact on Learning and Employment

Students with moderate intellectual disabilities can manage their own self-care needs, prepare food, participate in conversations, interact appropriately with others, use, but not necessarily manage, money correctly, and hold different kinds of jobs in the community (Rosenberg et al., 2011, p. 204).

Students with moderate intellectual disabilities will need support and supervision for employment, such as job coaching and sheltered workshops. However, this requires the persistence of the IEP team along with their supports coordinator because the availability of sheltered workshops has dwindled in favor of more inclusive employment settings. Some large companies have special employment programs for post-school youth with disabilities. These programs have essential duties that may not fit every student with moderate disabilities.

Some colleges have programs for persons with intellectual disabilities. These college-based programs provide campus jobs and some non-credit classes geared to their needs. Types of employment situations may include the following:

- Competitive employment, part-time or full-time with market wages
- Supervised work in private companies
- Publicly funded sheltered workshops
- Supported employment with job coaching services
- Customized employment in jobs specifically suited to the student's skills
- College-based post-school programs
- Employment in a family business
- Day programs with pre-employment skills development

The availability of employment and post-school programs can vary considerably across the country. Often family, governmental agencies, and community members are instrumental in increasing the types of employment available to students with moderate intellectual disabilities.

Communication and Students With Moderate Intellectual Disability

The development of communication skills is paramount for success in the workplace. When there is little to no speech or speech is unintelligible, it will be difficult to find employment except with significant support or well-designed roles. When communication is limited in its complexity, communication devices can fill the gap and provide a means of back-and-forth communication with peers, classmates, and adults. Improving communication can reduce emotional outbursts that result when children or youth cannot be understood by the others in their lives. If there is no history of back-and-forth exchanges, then it will be difficult to participate in the family, in a supported workplace, or in school. Therefore, the early introduction of assistive communication devices and access to more advanced systems of communication within those devices is needed for social inclusion. Many devices offer limited responses and choices, such as a limited array of food choices and communication of hygiene needs. A limited approach to assistive technology also limits the conversational development of students with moderate intellectual disabilities with oral motor problems. Options for communication best prepare adolescents for adult life when implemented during the earliest developmental periods. Implementing the use of assistive devices for the first time during late childhood does not foster social inclusion but rather isolates the child and does not meet the criteria of appropriate practice. The following case report is about a family whose preschooler was denied assistive technology.

Case Report: Jonathan Dean

Mr. and Mrs. Dean's 4-year-old son was diagnosed with Down syndrome at birth. They could not understand their son due to unintelligible speech. They desperately wanted to talk to him. Jonathan would get very frustrated trying to communicate his wants and needs, often falling to the floor crying in desperation. At the early intervention IEP meeting, the parents asked for assistive technology. The mother said, "Is this too much to ask? He is trying to talk to us."

Jonathan was receiving speech therapy three times per week in a pull-out program at his preschool. He lost 30 minutes three times a week from his half-day inclusive preschool. He napped in the afternoon, eliminating the possibility of additional preschool time.

An assistive technology evaluation was completed, and it was determined that Jonathan could not benefit from a device. It was recommended that speech therapy continue. In the state where the family resides, the child's speech therapist has to recommend a device, but his speech therapist had determined that he was making appropriate progress. *Appropriate progress* is a nebulous term used to report some level of improvement. When one thinks about progress, appropriate may seem like enough progress or some amount of progress. However, the definition of appropriate means: suitable for a particular person, condition, occasion, or place. Therefore, Jonathan's progress was deemed acceptable based on Jonathan as a person, given his condition, and the time or place assuming where he utilizes his communication skills. So, the standard used for Jonathan hearkened back to assuming a fixed level of ability. Even with a high level of speech services, Jonathan's oral motor problems, inherent in Down syndrome, continued to render his speech unintelligible.

The Dean family decided to purchase a device independently and, with the assistance of the device provider, taught Jonathan on their own. The device had multiple screens for each topic, such as foods, activities, relatives, and stores. Each page had symbols for verbs, nouns, adjectives, and a method for putting sentences together. As he selected his preferences, the device spoke for him.

His device generated much excitement with his peers in his preschool. Jonathan mastered the device quickly. The parents invited the new early intervention supervisor to the preschool class to see their son. The following was noted:

- The other children were excited to communicate with Jonathan.
- Jonathan taught the other children to use the device.
- Most had learned how to use the device.
- Jonathan had mastered the device.
- Jonathan could program new pictures into the device.
- The parents said that Jonathan taught them about other device options they did not know about.

The special education supervisor recognized her own bias when she realized she was surprised that a child with Down syndrome could develop such a high level of vocabulary and social relationships.

EXERCISE

1. Research the successful use of assistive technology for children or adolescents with Down syndrome

DISCUSSION

Transition begins during preschool. If more children in early intervention were given a means to meaningfully communicate, by the time they reached school age and later middle and secondary school age, they could be a significant part of mainstream life. Sadly, few children with the inability to produce intelligible speech are provided assistive technology. Children within this disability category are social, like their peers, and they crave interaction. They can understand basic communications but cannot be understood.

This is an area of bias toward children with oral motor problems, and even though it is inherent in their disability, supports like assistive technology are not typically provided. Oral motor problems impair the exchange of language and slow the cognitive development of children with intellectual disabilities. Early deprivation of interactive communication also has far-reaching effects on the later inclusion for youth with intellectual disabilities and communication disabilities. Although not all students with moderate intellectual disabilities have communication disorders and disabilities, many do.

Students with moderate intellectual disabilities have many strengths: they are social and engage easily with others; they will participate in activities, travel easily, and manage community settings without becoming overstimulated; and they can display a sense of humor and can tease or joke with others, demonstrating an understanding of the behavioral characteristics of others.

Case Report: Donny

Donny was of transition age and was categorized as having a moderate intellectual disability. He was raised by parents who had moderate intellectual disabilities and who had little support to raise him. Intellectual stimulation at home was limited. By high school, his school district of origin moved him to a special education program in a neighboring school district because he was not making progress. As far as they knew, he could not speak. His parents asserted this was not true.

At his new placement, he was given choices, many self-help training activities, and direct reading instruction. Donny began to speak and learn to read in his new setting. His expressive language skills improved and were at the fourth-grade level and his reading at the third-grade level. Donny participated in an assertiveness training lesson designed to decrease bullying from peers. After the training, he and a classmate reported being pushed and teased in the bathroom. They had not reported it sooner because they did not have the vocabulary to identify it. The boys could not identify their bullies. The option of using the bathroom between classes was considered, as well as an assertive strategy. The strategy was to say, "Stop," look the young men who were bullying them in the eyes, and say, "Do not touch me." Rather than avoid the bathroom or have to go during classes, the boys chose the second option. It did not take long to implement. When the boys began pushing them in the bathroom, Donny and his friend Dean stood up to them and thwarted them using the technique his teacher taught him. This indicated that they could recognize and respond to a situation in the relative safety of a school.

There is some risk to this. When it was revealed to be a group of football players, youth of far greater size than Donny and Dean, the classroom staff debated the effectiveness and wisdom of expecting students with disabilities to defend themselves.

EXERCISE

1. Research the effects of bullying on students with intellectual disabilities. What are the characteristics of those who perpetrate bullying of students with intellectual disabilities, and what is being done to prevent it?

DISCUSSION

Abuse of persons with disabilities and any youth is the school's responsibility because the perpetrators may be significantly more powerful than the students they harass. The positive of the situation is that Donny and Dean could recognize and report such actions. In a more independent workplace setting, they could recognize, respond to, and report danger. Students with intellectual disabilities can be instructed to recognize police and public safety officers and know how to contact help when they need it (Westling & Fox, 2008). To do so, they also need knowledge about who can be of help to them in multiple settings. Students with moderate intellectual disabilities can be taught to seek help and describe situations where they feel uncomfortable. Given the problems with bullying in American schools, children and youth with intellectual disabilities should be prepared. In the next case report, Donny and Dean are prepared for a community-based training program.

Community-Based Instruction and Travel Instruction

During transition, attention must be given to community access as directed under the Individuals with Disabilities Education Act (IDEA, 2004). Therefore, the use of CBI is part of all IEP transition plans. Preparing students with intellectual disabilities to enter the community requires an environmental assessment, selection of a goal, and a task analysis to design how to teach the skills needed to reach the selected goal.

Students with moderate intellectual disabilities benefit from learning via task analysis. According to Browder, Spooner, and Mims (2011), a task analysis breaks a task into multiple sets, and each set becomes a teachable component or steps leading to a goal. The steps of each task can be individualized to the student. The number of steps is dependent upon the abilities of the individual learner. For mastery of specific skills, the steps need to be explicitly stated, and nonessential steps to the task should be excluded. The transition goals inherent in each task can be easily measured using task analysis and assessments, such as a checklist, oral review, and observation. A task analysis can be a direct assessment to measure the progress on the transition goal. The task is used to create a systematic instruction plan for the target goal. For example, the teacher defines a target goal such as using public transportation. Then the teacher designs a systematic method of instruction by analyzing what tasks are part of the scheme to learn to use public transportation. A plan of the essential components is written, and the instructional method is designed, including a number of practice sessions prior to independent use of the selected public transit. Each selected goal should increase the student's ability to complete other goals, such as taking the bus to buy various items, eating in a restaurant, and going out with friends. The following case report is an example of teaching two students how to use public transit as part of their transition plan.

Case Report: Donny and Dean

Donny and Dean were accepted into a work-training program. They needed to use the local bus to get to the job. The following is how Donny and Dean learned to use the public transit system. The task included fading their supports as they developed the skill of using the bus. To make the plan work for the group, the teacher, assistant, and four other class members went with Donny and Dean.

The task analysis was as follows:

1. The group walked to the bus stop, rode to town, exited the bus, and walked to the job site. The group returned to school via the bus. The group did this about three times.

2. Then the teacher rode with the students, and the teaching assistant drove to the destination bus stop, meeting the class in the town. That was done two times. The next step was to walk the students to the bus stop and have them ride alone. The teaching assistant met them at the destination, and the teacher followed via car.

3. The group then rode back alone, and the teacher and teaching assistant met them at the destination.

4. Finally, Donny and Dean walked to the bus stop alone with the teaching assistant, who waited with them at the stop.

5. The teaching assistant then drove to the destination and met them there when they arrived. This was done for about four rides.

6. Then the two students approached the teacher and insisted they could do it alone.

DISCUSSION

Preliminary classroom activities and instruction included reading bus schedules, social skills instruction with role-playing activities, discussing possible unexpected events, the job coaching relationship, and workplace dress and interactions.

Generalization of Transition Skills

Students with moderate intellectual disabilities will need transition goals to address generalization. Generalization skills involve being able to use information across settings. Students with moderate intellectual disabilities may have difficulty taking the information they have learned in school and applying it to their lives outside of school. Therefore, all goals must be supported with opportunities to use the skills in the community or at home.

During Donny and Dean's year in the training program, only one distressing situation arose, when a passenger became out of control on the bus. Although he accosted Donny and Dean, they responded with the assertiveness strategy taught for the bullying that occurred in the high school. The disruptive passenger person stopped disrupting the ride. The boys were able to describe the situation and how they resolved it. They generalized what they had learned but applied it in a completely different scenario outside the more protective walls of the school.

Both young men completed the work training program and worked after graduation. Donny loved cleaning and went to a restaurant, working there for many years. Dean worked in a family business doing multiple tasks.

Students with moderate intellectual disabilities, depending on factors such as medical and physical needs, can work. However, many still may be unable to work due to additional disabilities unrelated to their intellectual disabilities.

Characteristics of Adolescents With Severe Intellectual and Multiple Disabilities

IDEA places students with severe intellectual disabilities under an umbrella term called *multiple disabilities*. Children and youth diagnosed as such perform at different levels noted in the following sections.

> §300.8 Child with a disability.
>
> Multiple disabilities means concomitant impairments (such as intellectual disability-blindness or intellectual disability-orthopedic impairment), the combination of which causes such severe educational needs that they cannot be accommodated in special education programs solely for one of the impairments. Multiple disabilities does not include deaf-blindness.
>
> (§300.8 Child with a disability [71 FR 46753, Aug. 14, 2006, as amended at 72 FR 61306, Oct. 30, 2007; 82 FR 31912, July 11, 2017])

Severe Intellectual Disabilities

The definition of *severe intellectual disability* describes a poor prognosis regarding independent functioning. Students with severe intellectual disabilities and multiple disabilities are described as having an IQ of 20/25 to 35/40. Students with multiple disabilities differ from those with severe intellectual disabilities because they have significant medical, physical, and sensory disabilities as well. The following is a description of the projected adaptive and academic functioning.

These students may or may not learn many academic skills in school, such as reading, but may be able to recognize some words and common signs and enjoy books being read aloud to them or, for example, to access a variety of books with text to speech on the computer. This provides autonomy when a student with limited fine motor skills advances through a story or slides by pressing a switch that does not require small motor movements.

With instruction to support functional and educational activities, a student with severe intellectual disabilities will have learned several useful skills by adulthood, like being able to eat on his or her own, dress and bathe with supervision, use the toilet independently, and wash his or her hands without help but with reminders. These skills will increase independence and decrease dependence on others and the need for physical support. The individual's physical ability may be fair to good, and he or she will be able to move around independently. One of the most significant outcomes of early intervention services is that young people with severe disabilities now receive physical therapy in early intervention, which not only improves motor skills, but also leads to many young children with severe physical disabilities learning to walk. This has enabled them to participate in self-care and be less likely to need others to handle all areas of their care. As adults with this disability, they will also be able to communicate using signs, symbols, or words (Rosenberg et al., 2011, p. 205).

Multiple Disabilities

Children and youth who are diagnosed with multiple disabilities have severe to profound intellectual disabilities. In addition, they have other severe disabilities. The following disabilities are or may be present in any combination; this is not meant to be an exhaustive list. Some students with multiple disabilities have medical conditions. This can be congenital or acquired as a result of anoxia or other accidents that result in a lack of oxygen or injury to the brain, such as loss of blood, carbon monoxide poisoning, asthma, or pneumonia. Because of the number disabilities present, they cannot be educated in a program for students who only have one disability (34 C.F.R., Sec. 300[b][6]):

- Nonverbal
- Nonambulatory
- Contractures
- Brain injury (various parts of the brain)
- Vision impairments
- Hearing impairments
- Seizure disorders
- Respiratory problems, such as asthma and repeated pneumonia
- Poor feeding due to oral motor problems and often choke on food. Many need pureed food if not tube fed.
- Require tube feeding
- Incontinence or undeveloped bowel and bladder control
- Nonfunctional communications

Communication is a major impediment for youth with multiple disabilities. Many of these young people have limited ability to move. If movement is present, fine motor skills are not present. Therefore, only rudimentary sign language communication is used if it can be used at all.

Many children and youth have multiple seizures per day that cannot be controlled. As discussed in Chapter 4, Seizures cause language, intellectual, learning, and physical disabilities, including the failure to develop speech. When skills are learned, sometimes they are lost after repeated seizures. Some of these conditions can result in prolonged hospitalizations, and this is fairly common in children and youth with multiple disabilities.

Impact on Learning and Employment

Young adults with severe and multiple intellectual disabilities do not work because their disabilities preclude them from doing the essential functions of most jobs. The additional medical needs and medical treatments further complicate school participation. They often have seizures that are grand mal, and if they are ambulatory, these seizures can cause falls, which further complicate independence and require the support of staff to ensure safety and avoid injuries. Many who fall or have self-injurious behavior need to wear helmets to prevent injury or use wheelchairs because of balance problems, as was the case with Gracie.

If a youth reaches age 12 and significant progress has not been made and evidence of progressive intellectual decline is present, the team begins the process of preparing for post-school residential or day center placements for people with severe cognitive disabilities. Sheltered workshops are not available, and if they are, they are typically funded by the government and are for students with moderate intellectual disabilities.

The transition planning specialist and the team must consider a range of possible outcomes when the adolescent has a high degree of impairment and medical need. Ongoing attention is given to increasing opportunities to enjoy activities and to continue learning as best practice. Transition plans for students with severe intellectual disabilities and multiple disabilities includes engaging them in the following:

- Preferred activities
- Cognitively stimulating activities
- CBI to habituate them to community activities
- Support plans that increase their communication of wants and needs
- Activities that expand their ability to care for themselves
- Using technology to promote communication and learning
- Engagement in daily activities that are varied and stimulating

CHARACTERISTICS OF STUDENTS WITH PROFOUND INTELLECTUAL DISABILITIES

A student with a profound intellectual disability performs at a developmental level comparable to that of a child younger than 12 months of age. Along with intellectual disability, there are medical conditions and profound physical disabilities as well. Limited interests are evident. For example, if the young person likes music, it may be limited to one song, often to the exclusion of others. If vision and hearing are present, cartoon media may be preferred. However, presenting other types of media at a young age can help develop a broader range of interests later.

The most profoundly impaired children are often blind, deaf, physically impaired, and profoundly intellectually disabled. This can result from total anoxia or partial anoxia. Some young persons at the most profound levels of disability continue to function anatomically but may have only part of the brain intact and have limited sensory awareness. They are often tube fed, and they often can not breathe without suctioning or may require oxygen or respirators.

Severe, Profound, and Multiple Intellectual Disabilities

A degree of variability exists among those students with severe, profound, and multiple disabilities, so there is no single profile that can describe each adolescent. They may be capable, with supervision, of near-independent functioning in everyday self-care activities, such as eating and using the toilet, whereas others may not speak or have limited to profound vision or hearing disabilities and profound physical disabilities.

For students with the most profound intellectual disabilities and physical disabilities, there are minimal ways to determine whether they are learning. According to Spooner and Browder (2015), students with more complex disabilities often lack the communication responses to indicate learning in ways that can be reliably coded for research. When this is present, assistive technology can fill that gap.

Assistive technology has moved to the forefront as a means to help students with the most severe disabilities to communicate and learn. Expanding communication and instructional options are now becoming available for these children and youth. The *Endrew F. v. Douglas County School District* case (2017) has increased attention to providing better educational programs, opportunities, and technology for students with intellectual disabilities. Increasing attention to the type and quality of resources for learning can help teachers better recognize learning for even the most intellectually disabled. IQs and the label intellectual disability are no longer justification for denying instruction. Other educational options are tactile books, adapted stories, and audio and video lessons that can be used to design, for instance, science lessons. There are curricula for students with severe impairments with specialized interventions. As more attention is paid to the education of our children and youth with the most severe disabilities, more options will emerge and research can support improvements. At times, however, as mentioned, there is brain injury that is so severe that the only indication of response is wakefulness and sleep.

Three other educational strategies that improve in-school and post-school life and expand options are the use of sensory rooms, hand-over-hand activities, and hand-over-hand instruction. Young people who do not have the ability to move of their own volition or have sensory disabilities, such as deaf-blindness, can benefit from the use and implementation of these strategies. When all or some sensory and motor function are not present, it is difficult to provide educational programs. To work with this challenge, teachers often employ hand-over-hand techniques to engage each young person in activities as well as give them physical touch. Another intervention is sensory rooms designed to provide a space with multiple sensory activities that engage even the most impaired. These rooms may have water beds, vibrating air mattresses, various color lighting shows, and different seating areas where students can change position in comfort. Music is available and it may be in sync with wall-sized films of animals or other interesting displays that are more accessible to the blind.

Students who are mostly or completely immobile are moved throughout the day to increase mobility. They are moved to different seats and other equipment such as supine, prone, and dynamic standers, which provide the greatest mobility, but most of this equipment is used for physical therapy. The sensory room serves a different purpose; it is both educational and geared toward relaxation and comfort. Each of these practices and strategies can be available in adult programs and residential facilities as well.

When providing activities and educational opportunities, the concept of partial participation is used to describe a student's participation in transition planning, but it also is a concept used to describe academic participation. When a student cannot fully participate in an activity, the teacher develops activities that allow maximum participation, even if it is through the use of technology, such as using a switch to turn on a blender during a cooking activity or the use of sensory rooms for a period of relaxation and accessible educational activities. Making modifications so students can participate in learning experiences should drive their educational and community experiences.

THE FRAMEWORK OF TRANSITION: STUDENTS WITH MODERATE, SEVERE, MULTIPLE, AND PROFOUND INTELLECTUAL DISABILITIES

Individualized Education Plan Development and Conferencing With the Family

Those students with mild intellectual disabilities can participate in transition planning to the greatest extent. Students with moderate intellectual disabilities have a wide variation in the ability to participate with the use of full, supported, or partial participation. Those with the most severe intellectual disabilities and multiple disabilities may only partially participate or be unable to participate because of their severe cognitive, physical, and added sensory disabilities, such as hearing impairments and vision impairments. Depending on the concomitant disabilities, students with moderate intellectual disabilities may be prepared to share their preferences through a PowerPoint presentation or pictures that demonstrate their preferences. Students with moderate intellectual disabilities, at the higher end of the spectrum (e.g., Donny and Dean), may want to attend the meeting as well. Preference should be given to how the student wants to participate. It is worthy to note that if the student does not understand the process or why he or she is at the meeting, most likely the student will not want to be in the room and he or she should not be coerced to do so because unnecessary behavioral challenges may occur.

Although Figure 15-1 has information about supports for students generally in each category, it is important to remember that using tests to indicate a fixed ability when little is known about the cognitive abilities can limit the provision of services and opportunities for inclusion of children and youth with moderate or severe intellectual disabilities, multiple disabilities, and, in some cases, profound intellectual disabilities. Without appropriate communication tools, instructional programs, and regular neurological assessments, cognitive assessment is not possible.

Figure 15-1 gives a basic overview of the differences between intellectual disabilities. The types of activities vary by the skills sets the students will need or the amount they can participate. As the level of impairment increases, there is an increase in support for care.

Employment

Students with multiple, severe, and profound intellectual disabilities differ sharply from students with mild and moderate intellectual disabilities. Due to the severity of their multiple intellectual, physical, communication, and medical disabilities, they are unable to meet the essential functions for work. Also, multiple medical interventions are often required throughout their day.

A significant number of youth with severe disabilities have multiple seizures throughout the day and night. These cause damage to the brain. The medication to treat seizures is sedating, and the drowsiness from medication also causes adolescents with multiple and profound disabilities to sleep on and off throughout the day. When they do awaken, they are perpetually drowsy.

Other considerations for employment are the lack of speech and fine motor and gross motor skills needed for employment. Students with this degree of disability are given assistance in the form of Social Security, medical care, and housing supplements.

Post-School Living and Transition Planning

Adolescent Growth: Planning for Change

As youth with the most severe physical, intellectual, and behavioral disabilities grow older, their physical size increases. Parents who would have wanted to keep their child with a disability with them often begin to realize that they are becoming older too. As they get weaker with age and their children become heavier and harder to assist, parents may reluctantly consider a group home placement. This is a very difficult period for the parents who have loved and cared for their children since birth. However, being knowledgeable and supporting the parents' interagency relationships as they begin to select a community-living setting can help them with this transition.

Parents are essential to the process of selecting a group home for their child. In the next section is a list of considerations when looking at group homes.

Parent Facilitation and Involvement in Community-Living Arrangements

Parents work with their child's case manager, also known as a *supports coordinator* (names may vary by state), to apply for a group home placement. Usually, there is a waiting list, and, as openings occur, parents can visit to see if they can feel confident that their child will be well cared for. If the group home or residential facility is close to the school, the student can transition to the setting and still attend his or her school during the day. The school district where the student lives provides

Mild Intellectual Disabilities	Moderate Intellectual Disabilities	Multiple Disabilities and Severe Intellectual Disabilities	Profound Intellectual Disabilities
Transition Planning	Transition Planning	Transition Planning	Transition Planning
Case management assigned	Case management assigned	Case management assigned	Case management assigned
Parent collaboration	Parent collaboration	Parent collaboration	Parent collaboration
• Cognitive development • Communication instruction • Self-help • Functional academics • Literacy • Leisure activities • Family activities • Community and neighborhood activities • Social activities • School clubs • Sports • Domestic skills • Community access skills • Safety skills • Social skills • Work habits • Vocational skills • Advocacy activities • Safety activities • Chemical safety in the home • Selecting current technology for increased independence • Career explorations • Job preference assessments • Job essential functions • Work-studies • Volunteering • Medical management skills • Plan for change to adult services • Access to Medicaid explored at this time	• Cognitive development • Communication devices • Self-help • Cognitive development • Advocacy activities • Functional academics • Literacy • Domestic skills • Safety skills • Chemical safety in the home • Social activities • School clubs • Community access skills • Social engagement • Regular medical checkups • Person-centered Plans • Job shadowing • Job coaches • Job training programs • School-based jobs • Simulated job environments • School café and school store training • Plan for change to adult services	• Cognitive development • Communication devices • Self-help • Daily activity plans • Literacy • Use of auditory modalities: Adapted stories, tactile stories, and hand-over-hand activities • Self-care supervision • Inclusion • Music • Outdoor activities • Community events • Preferred activities • Physical therapy • Recreational therapy: Sensory rooms • Vision therapist • Hearing therapist • Tube feeding or monitored feeding • Hygiene support • Medication reviews and monitoring • Care of medical devices: Keep wheelchairs in good condition and replace when student outgrows it • Daily physical checks • Weekly medical checkup • Person-centered planning • Ecological inventories • Plan for change to adult services	• Cognitive development • Communication devices • Self-help • Services • Daily activity plans • Literacy • Use of auditory modalities: Adapted stories, tactile stories, and hand-over-hand activities • Access to the community, such as public parks • Care • Inclusion • Music • Outdoor activities healthy • Community events • Preferred activities • Physical therapy • Recreational therapy: Sensory rooms • Tube feeding or hand-over-hand feeding • Hygiene support • Medication reviews and monitoring • Care of medical devices: Keep wheelchairs in good condition and replace when student outgrows it • Weekly medical checkups • Plan for change to adult services

Figure 15-1. Supports and services for students with intellectual disabilities.

transportation or contracts it out to a private company. A district may want to move the student to another location during secondary school, but the IEP team in most situations may not want to agree to the change.

If parents are not comfortable with available settings, they can apply for a waiver to keep their child at home. Keeping the child at home is less costly to the state, and therefore a waiver is given to supply funds for in-home care. However, ultimately, if the parent becomes disabled or unable to care for the child, a group home placement will need to be made, unless another family member takes the parental role. Therefore, going through the process of seeing what is available is a proactive step in planning for unexpected events or when home care is not available or possible.

Group Home and Residential Facility Visitation Checklist

Group home living is an ideological construct that guides the inclusion of persons with disabilities in everyday life. Having youth with disabilities in a group home typically occurs when parents can no longer take care of them. Group homes may or may not have guidelines regarding their access to community activities. In some cases, they are well away from the community in individual homes without access to community environments like parks. This may look more like institutionalization only with smaller groups of people.

Community events, shopping, and other activities should be readily available. If the group home is in a rural or suburban location, transportation must be available, and for those with limited mobility, wheelchair accessible buses are needed. If homes are located far from local communities, visitation is limited when parents have few resources. During the transition IEP meetings, all of these considerations are discussed; however, school districts do not fund community living of home care.

Other Considerations

Employment in a group home is not typically a high-paying job, and turnover is high. Employees do not need advanced training or medical training to work in a group home, so salaries are typically low. For the places with the highest turnover, the young adult may not have a consistent person who knows them. Therefore, when parents research post-school residential placements for their child with severe disabilities, they can select places as close to home as possible or those places with the best reputations and consistent staffing and ensure that someone who knows their child is nearby. Some organizations may have facilities in locations far from the community, and they might have multiple homes with many staff and significant supervision. Other agencies have group homes isolated in more suburban or rural areas with few employees. The transition planning specialist and case manager will be involved in talking about post-school living. Although the transition planning specialist is not the liaison for group home placement, he or she needs to keep abreast of plans because the post-school outcome must be reported in the last report from the transition planning specialist. The case manager or the supports coordinator advises the parents of available placements. Table 15-1 contains some guidelines for evaluating a group home. Parents should feel comfortable about the setting and ensure the following safeguards are present. By using a checklist like the following sample, parents can frame their visits to group homes to inform them about possible choices.

Group Home Placements

Group homes may have different levels of care depending on the residents behavior, or the home will specialize in, for example, individuals with severe medical problems needing the care of a full-time nursing staff. If there are no residents with behavior problems, parents should see the following:

- Residents do not show aggression toward staff or peers.
- Residents demonstrate few noncompliant behaviors.
- When given choices, residents will select from options.
- Residents will transition between activities with little resistance.
- Residents follow a schedule.

TABLE 15-1. GROUP HOME CHECKLIST

- ☐ The group home is not isolated from the community.
- ☐ The group home is not a single home in a rural setting, unless it is a community with many opportunities for outside activities and it provides a lifestyle community.
- ☐ The group home has a proven record of service to people with disabilities.
- ☐ The group home has all fire safety alarms and a flashing alarm system.
- ☐ The group home has food that is nutritional with a well-designed menu, including fresh fruits and vegetables.
- ☐ The group home provides nutritional snacks.
- ☐ The group home has a planned schedule of activities every day.
- ☐ The group home is well staffed. Staff interact positively with the residents.
- ☐ Home has adequate parking and open visitation. The family should be able to come without notice.
- ☐ The home has a work program when appropriate.
- ☐ The group home activities are designed to engage students with multiple disabilities (e.g., sensory rooms, hand-over-hand activities).

- Residents are able to go into the community.
- Residents look engaged in activities and appear content.

Behavior is a significant determiner of placement in group home environments. Children and youth with serious behavioral difficulties and aggressiveness require one-on-one staffing, and they can present risks when accessing the community or when living with others. Therefore, it is essential that positive behavior supports, options for choice making, and engaging programs of instruction and CBI are provided to them to help them develop behavior that will enable them to go into restaurants, stores, and other community locations as a group.

Transition planning for the most aggressive students includes a high level of support. Social behaviors are the critical factor, and when behaviors are aggressive, activities in the community are not possible until behaviors are modified. When behaviors disrupt a school or community to an advanced degree, participation in transition programs that address aggressiveness are needed until they are not a threat to themselves or the community. If these problems continue, placements are in programs or group homes designed for more aggressive youth who have severe disabilities.

Group homes are typically owned and operated by private agencies, who set their criteria for entry. Therefore, students with intellectual disabilities and severe noncompliant behaviors and aggressiveness need early intervention to address these issues to facilitate better adult outcomes. Choice of group home or residential placements should match the needs of the residents. If the behaviors of some residents limit activities of more compliant residents, it is most likely not a good fit for the compliant student, which is the most typical characteristic of students with severe to profound intellectual disabilities. Students who are generally compliant and used to going into the community cannot have satisfactory life experiences in facilities that address problem behaviors. Therefore, parents of adolescents without behavioral problems should select group homes that will provide their child with multiple opportunities and activities in the community.

Case Manager Assignment and Ongoing Involvement

Case managers, also known as *supports coordinators*, typically have a social work or human services degree or a degree in a related field, such as health, nursing, or education. Their role is to help families get the services they need. Case managers work with developmentally disabled adults, children, youth, and their families; individuals with substance abuse problems; school-age children; those with mental health disorders; and the elderly. Students with intellectual disabilities are assigned a case manager to help the family navigate the supports available to children and youth with intellectual disabilities. Case managers assist the family in making plans, accessing respite care, and applying for Social Security and Medicaid.

Case managers are instrumental in making applications for financial support as well. The medical care and treatment of children and youth with severe disabilities are far more than most families can afford. The care of children with multiple disabilities often includes emergency exits from school to the hospital and a complex array of services and care of specialists. The multiple appointments, hospitalizations, and needs tax the ability for many parents to meet employment expectations.

To address all the psychological and life management issues of parenting a child with intellectual disabilities and medical needs, family counseling is typically part of supports to the family. Case managers field calls from their families and guide the families to the supports they want, or they may arrange them directly. As stated previously, if the feasibility of caring for the child at home becomes prohibitive, a case manager helps the family find a group home. Ideally, one case manager would be with a family for many years. However, there can be continual turnover, which degrades intimate knowledge of the family and the child. The transition planning specialist can encourage that the family of a child with intellectual disabilities have a case manager. The case manager must be invited to the annual IEP meeting via phone, conference call, or video conferencing. The case manager's attendance at meetings facilitates a smooth transition and the continuity of services through the transition to adult services when the child turns 18 years old and later when the child turns 21 years old and is no longer eligible for special education. The case manager also helps parents who have chosen to seek guardianship for their child. Parents can seek to obtain legal guardianship of their adult child under conditions when their child cannot care for him- or herself and make decisions about his or her own care due to intellectual disability. The degree and duration of guardianship can change, but, while it is granted, it allows the parents to continue to make decisions on behalf of their children. However, some children become wards of the state, with the state assuming responsibility for their care. During the years of transition planning, although the local education agencies' cannot make the case managers come to meetings, they can encourage them to make contact prior to each IEP meeting to update the school and receive updates about the student. Parents must approve all contact between the school and the agency. When the student ages out, the transition planning specialist will need information about post-school placement.

Goal Setting: Adolescents With Significant Disabilities

Person-Centered Planning

PCP can be used effectively to plan and discuss the needs and wants of students who are unable to communicate on their own. Multiple developmental areas and functional and learning skills are reviewed, as well as the student's history of preferences and interests. In short, PCP is a way of crafting a picture of who the student is, what environments he or she is most comfortable in, what and whom he or she likes and dislikes, and how to meet his or her needs and create goals when a severe disability affects all areas of functioning. PCP is a way to address transition planning, and it facilitates the greatest level of inclusion for the student.

Mazzotti, Kelly, and Coco (2015) describe PCP as a process of developing collaborative, goal-oriented plans for youth to ensure that they live in a community where they can participate in activities and be involved in all aspects of life. The purpose of PCP is to create an effective plan where the student is integral in creating goals for him- or herself as much as possible, with an emphasis on self-determination, making choices, and having increased autonomy (Ratti et al., 2016). For students with the most severe intellectual disabilities and multiple disabilities, observing their performance in multiple settings is paramount for including their preferences in the transition plan.

Although Mazotti et al. (2015) assert that participation is crucial and students with the most severe disabilities must have the tools to share their strengths, needs, goals, disability, and necessary supports, PCP is a method of planning that has been adapted for use with many populations with the most significant disabilities. The goals of PCP are to enable the participant, to the greatest extent possible, along with the parents and the school team, to create a plan.

The use of PCP requires teams to use multiple means of communication so the student can participate by using speech, assistive technology, gestures, or signs, or through the observations of those who live and teach the adolescent in multiple environments. The outcome is the creation of a plan that outlines the current wants and needs of the student along with the family constraints and supports and services available from the school and community services.

Environmental Inventories and Person-Centered Planning

The environmental inventory is used as part of the PCP. This strategy is used to assist multidisciplinary teams in determining appropriate goals for transition. The environmental inventory has been used for many years to systematically identify settings and the functions necessary for success in settings that the student currently encounters or may encounter (Sobsey, 1987). All areas where the student will be or where inclusion is projected go into the inventory. The inventory is a list of skills and subskills needed in each environment. Then the environmental inventory is reviewed, and the content provides a guide for the teacher and the family to plan for in-school instruction and at-home activities to help generalize the tasks learned in various settings. The level of independence that is needed and the actual level of independence possible becomes part of the plan. Some parts of the environmental inventory guide all current and future staff about the student's safety needs. For instance, a student may know how to turn on the water but may not know how to control the degree of hot or cold, an issue with obvious consequences. So, the student may independently turn on the water but with adult supervision would ensure the correct temperature and the student's safety. The PCP and the environmental inventory are communication and planning tools that carry value when planning for students with multiple needs intellectually, physically, and medically. Personal preference indicators are used to effectively plan for students with intellectual disabilities. Moss (2006) recommends seven areas of focus:

1. Identify the person's favorites, such as being outside or inside, being alone or with friends. Can the person project into the future, such as communicating what he or she wants for lunch?
2. Identify emotions that focus on the range of a person's feelings, such as things that elicit emotions, positive or negative or in between.
3. Identify the person's social world, such as how the person communicates and with whom.
4. Focus on areas where the person makes choices, such as activities, music preferences, sports.
5. Establish physical indicators such as the body clock: When does the person get up, eat, go to bed, become most active?
6. Identify health needs by reviewing the IHP and current needs. Can the person communicate pain, and if so, how?
7. Family role indicators: How is the person involved with the family? How does this affect post-secondary adult living, employment and education plans? Who are the caregivers, paid and unpaid support, and how do they relate to employment, post-secondary education, and post-school life (Moss, 2006).

Exercise

1. Visit a classroom for students with multiple disabilities. Some can be seen on YouTube. Pick a focus student and ask yourself the following questions:
   a. Can the student speak or use assistive technology to communicate his or her interests?
   b. Can school peers and adults understand nonverbal cues from the student?
   c. Does the student need an IHP to address his or her needs?
   d. Describe the student's limitations that will prevent or diminish independence and employment.
   e. What can the student accomplish without assistance?
   f. Are there activities the student can accomplish with assistance provided by a job coach or another caregiver?

TRANSITION PLAN FRAMEWORK

This transition framework is aligned with the needs of students who have the most severe disabilities. Students with mild intellectual disabilities are addressed in Chapter 7. This example demonstrates how plans can change to meet diverse needs of students with disabilities:

- Parent involvement and support
  - Parent training about transition for students with severe intellectual disabilities.
  - Become informed about parent's case manager and update the information from the parent section about future supports being developed.
  - Parent meeting with a representative from the OVR.
  - Schedule periodic school nurse meetings to discuss medical updates and to collaborate when changes are needed.
  - Discuss updates for the IHP.
- Agency involvement
  - Secure resources from the appropriate agencies regarding post-school supports.
  - List post-school supports that will be provided.
  - Ensure communication between agencies and their respective roles for transition supports.
  - Share the school-based supports and coordinate the initiation or overlap of services.
- Assessments: Review yearly
  - Communication assessment
  - Picture-based receptive language assessments
  - Progress in the acquisition of communication and language skills via technology (e.g., iPads).
  - Adaptive skills assessments updated and reviewed
  - Assess sensory needs and provide supports such as access to sensory rooms and sensory activities and instruction.
- Instructional goals
  - Picture-based or real-life vocabulary development
  - Communication progress: Receptive language
  - Access to technology throughout the day
  - Reading via multiple modalities: Auditory, visual
  - Consultation and planning for assistive technology for access to instructional materials
  - District provides materials that include multiple means of instruction for students with significant disabilities.

- Goal setting
  - Academic and cognition development activities
  - Behavioral activities: Applied behavior analysis program if necessary
  - Social assessments
  - Student preference assessment: Personal preference indicator
  - Environmental inventory
  - Independence skills
  - Leisure activities
- Habituation to community settings
  - CBI: Ensure that activities in the community habituate the student to diverse settings.
  - Set goals to ensure the student can smoothly transition to and from multiple community settings.
- Developing the transition plan
  - Use a PCP team meeting to ensure all preferences are understood and included in goal construction.
  - Use environmental inventories to address needs in all the environments where the student currently lives.
  - Complete transition plan using state or district forms.
  - Ensure that the student is being instructed in the least restrictive environment by providing multiple instructional settings where the student can make progress on his or her goals.
  - Ensure that all related services, supports to the parent and teacher, current levels of performance, current goals, current medical needs and all components for transition and the IEP are complete.
  - Ensure parental permission is secured for all activities and contacts.

INDIVIDUALIZED EDUCATION PLAN AND TRANSITION PLANNING MEETING

The Meeting

The meeting procedures will follow federal and state regulations, but the content and the discussion will be varied. To ensure that the transition planning specialist provides the needed supports for students with significant disabilities who cannot communicate or lead their meetings, the following meeting structure may be helpful:

- Team preparation
  - Invitations sent to the student, parent, case manager, and the OVR representative when the student is eligible for services.
  - Agenda completed.
  - Transition planning specialist confirms meeting room.
  - Meeting room seating plan.
  - Name cards on the table for student comfort: Student can make seating choices if the student is attending.
- Meeting opening
- Arrival time: Informal greetings
  - Participants sit at assigned seats and sign the attendance sheet.

- ○ Anyone attending via conference call or virtual attendance is brought in.
    - ○ Order of discussion announced.
    - ○ IEP contact information reviewed and confirmed.
- Meeting content
    - ○ Review the eligibility that reviews student needs.
    - ○ IEP discussion: Share student preferences.
    - ○ Discuss how the student will participate: Partial participation or preferences only.
    - ○ Parents review strengths and needs.
    - ○ Team members share current transition goals.
    - ○ Parents share their support to the student currently.
    - ○ Transition planning specialist describes current supports he or she is providing.
    - ○ Team members review current academic progress.
    - ○ Share results of preference assessments.
    - ○ Parents collaborate about the proposed goals and goals and objectives are agreed upon.
    - ○ Review agency supports.
- Discuss IEP goals
    - ○ School experiences
    - ○ Academic
    - ○ Social
    - ○ Communication tools and technology
    - ○ CBI
- Discuss agency involvement
    - ○ Supports: Community-based experiences
    - ○ Community living choices and goals
    - ○ Developing independence skills
    - ○ Developing leisure activities
    - ○ School-based activities
    - ○ Post-school work and living options
    - ○ Using CBI
    - ○ Community access: Paratransit
    - ○ Using public transportation
    - ○ Training in the community
    - ○ Making connections: OVR
- Discuss navigating financial considerations
    - ○ Social Security at 18 years old
    - ○ Waivers
    - ○ Medicaid changes at 18 years old
- Discuss future transition planning goals
    - ○ Review the person-centered plan and environmental inventory.
    - ○ The team develops goals based on the person-centered plan and environmental inventory.
    - ○ Create a long-term plan about post-school life.
    - ○ Agree to new IEP.
- Adjourn meeting

- Special education team discusses post-IEP meeting conference goals to support the student
  - Calendar of planned activities
  - Calendar of planning: Transition planning specialist/parent/team conferences
  - Visits to the community (CBI)
  - Pursue post-school education, independent living, community living, and leisure opportunities
  - Connections to community agencies established

EXERCISES

1. Contact your state's Office of Developmental Disabilities. Describe the supports listed on the website.
2. Research current articles about transition planning for transition-age youth with mild, moderate, severe, multiple, and profound intellectual disabilities. What does the research say about their communication needs?
3. Research the Social Security website and determine their definition of disability and where intellectual disability fits the criteria.
4. Research agencies that support families who have children with intellectual disabilities. What types of guidance do they provide?
5. Interview two students: one with a mild intellectual disability and one with a moderate intellectual disability. Ask them about their future. Compare the two.
6. Using Donny as your hypothetical student, create three goals for his transition plan. Make sure the goals are measurable.

SUMMARY

Originally, IQ was used to determine intellectual functioning related to whether a child was able to be educated; now, IQ and adaptive functioning are used to create goals and design plans of instruction (American Psychiatric Association, 2013, p. 33). It is essential to clarify the impact of the disability when seeking appropriate services. Services are best practice when they are most likely to help the student get to the highest level of independence.

Students with mild and moderate intellectual disabilities can be taught many skills if they are explicitly taught and are given opportunities to generalize the skills. Participation in the workplace will take many forms, and working part-time is a realistic first step for students with mild to moderate intellectual disabilities. Students with mild intellectual disabilities can, in most cases, work full-time post–high school but will most likely stay in their parents' home for some time. Students with moderate intellectual disabilities will most likely work in supported settings, sheltered workshops, or within family businesses. Students with severe, multiple, and profound intellectual disabilities will not be able to perform essential functions of employment situations. Therefore, their plans will focus on increasing their ability to communicate; to participate in learning activities; to increase their self-determination; to participate in community living and quality of life activities.

Parental involvement throughout the transition process is crucial to the support of students with intellectual disabilities. For youth with significant disabilities, the school can be instrumental in working with the parents as they transition their child to the high level of needed post-school supports.

More work and research need to be done to improve educational practices, materials, and assistive technology resources to better reflect the needs and increase learning and self determination of students with intellectual disabilities.

References

American Psychiatric Association. (2013). *Diagnostic and statistical manual of mental disorders* (5th ed.). Washington, DC: American Psychiatric Association Publishing.

Browder, D. M., Spooner, F., & Mims, P. (2011). Evidence-based practices. In D. M. Browder & F. Spooner (Eds.), *Teaching students with moderate and severe disabilities* (pp. 92-124). New York, NY: The Guilford Press.

Child with a disability, 34 C.F.R. § 300.8 (2017).

Endrew F. v. Douglas County School District, 137 S.Ct. 988 (2017).

Individuals with Disabilities Education Act of 2004, Pub. L. No. 108-446, 20 U.S.C. § 1400 *et seq.* (2004).

Mazzotti, V. L., Kelly, K. R., & Coco, C. M. (2015). Effects of self-directed summary of performance on postsecondary education students' participation in person-centered planning meetings. *The Journal of Special Education, 48*(4), 243-244.

Moore v. Texas, 137 S. Ct. 1039 (2017).

Moss, J. (2006). The Personal Preference Indicator. Center for Interdisciplinary Learning and Leadership/UCE, College of Medicine, University of Oklahoma Health Sciences Center, Publication No. CA298.jm. Retrieved from https://www.transitioncoalition.org/wp-content/originalSiteAssets/files/docs/PersonalPreferenceIndicator1253592698.pdf.

Patton, J. R., & Keyes, D. W. (2006). Death penalty issues following Atkins. *Exceptionality, 14*(4), 237-255.

Ratti, V., Hassiotis, A., Crabtree, J., Deb, S., Gallagher, P., & Unwin, G. (2016). The effectiveness of person-centered planning for people with intellectual disabilities: A systematic review. *Research in Developmental Disabilities, 57*, 63-84.

Rosenberg, R. C., Westling, D. L., & McLeskey, J. (2011). *Special education for today's teachers: An introduction.* London, Unite Kingdom: Pearson.

Shurr, J., & Taber-Doughty, T. (2012). Increasing comprehension for middle school students with moderate intellectual disability on age-appropriate texts. *Education and Training in Autism and Developmental Disabilities, 47*(3), 359-372.

Snell, M. E., Luckasson, R., Borthwick-Duffy, S., Bradley, V., Buntinx, W. H. E., Coulter, D. L., ... Yeager, M. H. (2009). Characteristics and needs of people with intellectual disability who have higher IQs. *Intellectual and Developmental Disabilities, 47*(3), 220-233.

Sobsey, D. (1987). *Ecological inventory exemplars.* Edmonton, Canada: University of Alberta, Department of Education.

Spooner, F., & Browder, D. M. (2015). Raising the bar: Significant advances and future needs for promoting learning for students with severe disabilities. *Remedial and Special Education, 36*(1), 28-32.

Westling, D. L., & Fox, L. L. (2008). *Teaching students with severe disabilities* (4th ed.). Upper Saddle River, NJ: Pearson Merrill.

Students With Autism and Accompanying Language and Intellectual Impairment

CHAPTER OBJECTIVES

→ Describe the characteristics of students with autism and substantial needs.

→ Describe the level of supports needed for students with autism and substantial and very substantial support.

→ Describe how a psychologist or psychiatrist used levels of support from the *Diagnostic and Statistical Manual of Mental Disorder, Fifth Edition* (DSM-5) to diagnose autism.

→ Describe why teachers do not diagnose autism and what information teachers supply for the diagnostic process.

→ Describe echolalia and its uses for students with autism.

→ Describe the types of sensory experiences viewed as aversive.

→ Describe essential features of transition plans.

→ Describe how behavior affects post-school outcomes and inclusion in the community for students with autism spectrum disorder (ASD).

Rae, J. M. *A Collaborative Approach to Transition Planning for Students With Disabilities* (pp. 339-356).
© 2020 SLACK Incorporated.

AUTISM

§ 300.8 Child with a disability.

(1)(i) Autism means a developmental disability is significantly affecting verbal and nonverbal communication and social interaction, generally evident before age three, that adversely affects a child's educational performance. Other characteristics often associated with autism are engagement in repetitive activities and stereotyped movements, resistance to environmental change or change in daily routines, and unusual responses to sensory experiences.

(ii) Autism does not apply if a child's educational performance is adversely affected primarily because the child has an emotional disturbance, as defined in paragraph (c)(4) of this section.

(iii) A child who manifests the characteristics of autism after age three could be identified as having autism if the criteria in paragraph (c)(1)(i) of this section are satisfied.

(§ 300.8 Child with a disability [71 FR 46753, Aug. 14, 2006, as amended at 72 FR 61306, Oct. 30, 2007; 82 FR 31912, July 11, 2017])

ASD is a pervasive developmental disorder defined by the presence of atypical development evident before the age of 3 years. The atypical behaviors are evident in three general areas: social interaction, communication, and restricted and repetitive behavior. Students are nonverbal and rely on the support of others to participate in activities that children without autism can perform without support. Typically, they do not progress in academic or adaptive skills without intensive interventions. For the students who require substantial or very substantial supports, they will always need supervision and support to perform life skills. Over 65% of children with ASD have intellectual disabilities, calculated from 14 studies completed since 2000 (Dykens & Lense, 2011). Epilepsy is also present at a higher rate than in the general population (Tuchman, 2011). Therefore, testing for a seizure disorder should be part of all autism diagnoses. There is a high degree of interest in the increasing prevalence of ASD, and although it is not the topic of this text, it is prudent to note that 11 states were used to collect prevalence data, and the increase is not representative of the entire United States (Baio et al., 2018).

As discussed in the previous chapter on intellectual disabilities, there is a range of intellectual disability. This is also true within the group of students generally described as low functioning, but intellectual disability may be better expressed in a way to further define the needs of students within the moderate to severe level of intellectual disability and autism. Intelligence quotients (IQs) of children with ASD are as follows, although testing may result in some mild variations in scores a child may receive, depending upon the measure used. However, children and youth without communication skills have difficulty participating in standardized tests:

- 55% have an intellectual disability (IQ less than 70)
- 16% have a moderate to severe intellectual disability (IQ less than 50)
- 28% have average intelligence (IQ higher than 85, up to a high-average score of 115)
- 3% have above-average intelligence (IQ higher than 115; Charman et al., 2011)

Adolescents with ASDL2-3 may have moderate, severe, or profound intellectual disabilities and require a high level of support depending on their adaptive functioning. For the purposes of this chapter, the identifier *autism spectrum disorder level 2 or level 3* (ASDL2-3) will be used to indicate students with autism who require the most support: a level 3 support (very substantial support) and level 2, support (substantial support; American Psychiatric Association, 2013) There is an overlap in levels because some students with language and without intellectual disabilities can have behavior challenges and need substantial supports.

Neurological Basis of Autism

ASD is described as a neurological disorder. During the first year of life, measures of head size circumference is a part of infant checkups. There is an established average head circumference. By 6 to 14 months, the head circumference of an infant with ASD becomes enlarged from brain and cerebrum overgrowth (Hazlett et al., 2011; Hazlett et al., 2012). The overgrowth declines and stops by 2 years old. Overgrowth occurs in the frontal and temporal lobes and the amygdala, the areas responsible for planning, language, and responses to rewarding interactions, respectively (Courchesne et al., 2011).

The frontal lobe is also involved with flexibility, inhibition, and working memory. Language processing occurs in the temporal lobes, and a study of children who are at risk for ASD revealed deficient responses to speech in the left temporal lobe and temporal cortex (Eyler, Pierce, & Courchesne, 2012). Atypical brain growth and its possible effects on neural pathways continues to be examined, and research is ongoing in this area to determine what other areas are involved and the changes that occur throughout the lifetime (Wegiel et al., 2014). What is known is that ASDL3, which includes both ASD and an intellectual disability in approximately 70% of children and youth with autism, is a permanent and lifelong condition that requires a specialized system of communication and learning that fits the individual's neurological condition and unique personality characteristics. The next section uses the DSM-5 (American Psychiatric Association, 2013) to delineate the levels of support needed by some students on the spectrum.

Levels of Support

As discussed in Chapter 13, the DSM-5 (American Psychiatric Association, 2013) delineates three levels of support for students with ASD. The students described in Chapter 13 would be able to fully participate in transition planning because they can understand the concepts of the process and typically require level 3 support. In Chapter 16, the focus is on students with ASD who require substantial or very substantial supports in all areas of development and who do not have the ability to participate in transition planning as a student with ASDL3. Individual development would determine the transition planning participation, and whether full, supported, or partial participation is possible. The students with autism in this chapter require level 2 or 3 support. They also require alternative strategies for learning that address their learning needs. See Table 16-1 for the DSM-5 (American Psychiatric Association, 2013) descriptions of the severity levels for ASD. These descriptions are used to secure services, and they inform educators about the student's need for communication, supervision, and adaptive skills.

The type of behavior exhibited delineates the student's support needs. Those students needing level 2 and 3 support demonstrate severe deficits in verbal and nonverbal communication skills. The severity of these deficits significantly reduces their adaptive and social functioning. These students often demonstrate severe emotional outbursts to transitions, little initiation of social interactions, and minimal responses to social overtures of others. Their ability to problem solve, plan, and play is well below the skills of their same-age peers; as they age, these skills may not develop.

Adolescents who require level 3 support are typically nonverbal and have *echolalic* speech, meaning they repeat what they have heard, seemingly without communicative intent.

Adolescents who require level 2 support have most likely developed a pattern of behaviors to communicate their needs. They can typically speak and may attempt to communicate with peers. They can also respond to straightforward social and educational practices that use visuals, such as using a picture or an assistive technology picture-based system to ask for something to eat, a preferred book, or an enjoyable activity. However, they may respond with significant behaviors to sensory input and changes in schedule or interference with rituals.

TABLE 16-1. DEGREE OF SUPPORTS OF STUDENTS WITH AUTISM AND INTELLECTUAL DISABILITIES
LEVEL 3: REQUIRING VERY SUBSTANTIAL SUPPORT
Severe deficits in verbal and nonverbal social communication skills cause severe impairments in functioning, very limited initiation of social interactions, and minimal response to social overtures from others. For example, a person with few words of intelligible speech who rarely initiates interaction and, when he or she does, makes unusual approaches to meet needs only and responds to only very direct social approaches.
Inflexibility of behavior, extreme difficulty coping with change, or other restricted/repetitive behaviors markedly interfere with functioning in all spheres. Great distress/difficulty changing focus or action. These children endure gross deficits in verbal and nonverbal communication skills.
LEVEL 2: REQUIRING SUBSTANTIAL SUPPORT
Marked deficits in verbal and nonverbal social communication skills; social impairments apparent even with supports in place; limited initiation of social interactions; and reduced or abnormal responses to social overtures from others. For example, a person who speaks simple sentences, whose interaction is limited to narrow special interests, and who has markedly odd nonverbal communication.
Inflexibility of behavior, difficulty coping with change, or other restricted/repetitive behaviors appear frequently enough to be obvious to the casual observer and interfere with functioning in a variety of contexts. Distress and/or difficulty changing focus or action.
Source: American Psychiatric Association. (2013). *Diagnostic and statistical manual of mental disorders* (5th ed.). Washington, DC: American Psychiatric Association Publishing.

CHARACTERISTICS OF ADOLESCENTS WITH AUTISM NEEDING LEVEL 3 SUPPORT

In this section diagnostic information and levels of support are discussed. Typically, a psychiatrist, clinical psychologist, physician, or other person who is highly qualified and trained to do so may diagnose and be part of a diagnostic team. A school-based diagnostic team will include a special educator who will contribute to data and observations used by the team to determine eligibility for special education and related services. However, a school psychologist or clinical psychologist are most often the people to give the diagnosis.

Level 3 Support

Adolescents who require level 3 support are most likely students who function in the severe to profound range of intellectual disability. Some behavior seen in the classroom and home of with ASDL3 are as follows. They will need ongoing support for all their needs throughout their lifetimes:

- Language
  - Lacks speech and is nonverbal or has echolalic speech
  - Shows no or little response to the attempts of others to interact
  - Gives no evidence of understanding speech and most likely does not understand speech
  - Gives no or little eye contact
  - Watches child-themed movies but with restricted preferences

- Provides little indication or ability to communicate their basic needs and wants to caregivers
    - Responds minimally or never to verbal prompts
    - Responds to music
    - Responds to visual schedules
    - Shows interests in communication devices
    - Requires intensive programming in communication
- Physical behaviors
    - May, during childhood and adolescence, carry a small object at all times and become emotional or anxious when taken away
    - Prefers to bounce, swing, jump, and use objects that can spin
    - Manipulates objects seemingly in a nonfunctional way
    - Has difficulty or is unable to imitate
    - Walks on toes
    - Demonstrated agitated behavior that was difficult to soothe in infancy and continued into adolescence
    - Hits or scratches in childhood and physical aggressiveness may not diminish
    - Walks or may be nonambulatory and need a wheelchair
- Independence
    - Demonstrates severe to profound intellectual disability or moderate intellectual disabilities and severe aggressive behaviors
    - Does not use the toilet independently at the most severe level of disability
    - Wears diapers for an extended period of time but can be toilet trained
    - Eats a limited repertoire of foods
    - Elopes if not supervised
    - Feeds self with or without support
    - Requires supervised meals
- Medical and safety
    - Seizure disorder may be present
    - Vision and hearing impairments may be present
    - Understanding of danger is absent

For professionals who work with young children with ASDL3, their play skills show little self-direction, they do not respond to speech directed toward them, and they do not return smiles in kind. Parents often report that they think their child may be hearing impaired. The list is not part of the DSM-5.

Level 2 Support

As noted previously, students who need very substantial or substantial support have a range of intellectual disability. It can be assumed that if the student participates in the following, he or she may have a higher cognitive ability than adolescents who need level 3 support. Comparing adolescents with ASD to students with intellectual disabilities, adolescents who participate in the following are most likely in the moderate to severe range of intellectual disability, as well as having a higher level of adaptive functioning.

The following list is some behavior seen in home and school:

- Language
    - Uses some speech to communicate about functional activities
    - Enjoys music and movies, selects preferences, and sings or repeats movie phrases

- ○ Participates in activities like being read to or looking at preferred books and magazines, especially with themes about physical objects such as trains, wheels, or idiosyncratic objects of interest
  - ○ Learns receptive vocabulary when built on an area of interest
  - ○ Responds better to verbal information if spoken in a melodic tone
  - ○ Can identify pitch (Stanutz, Wapnick, & Burack, 2012)
  - ○ Can often sing or repeat phrases out of favorite movies
  - ○ Gives some eye contact
- Physical behaviors
  - ○ Enjoys putting objects in a row
  - ○ Watches TV and comprehends when the program is repeatedly watched
  - ○ Can understand some dangers but cannot self-protect
  - ○ Demands access to favorite movies objects and music
  - ○ Can be taught to understand a visual picture schedule
  - ○ Transitions better with the use of a picture prompt
  - ○ Has difficulty imitating in real time but can video-model when repetition is provided
- Independence
  - ○ Eats preferred foods independently
  - ○ Uses toilet by age 5
  - ○ Helps self to food
  - ○ Learns to dress self in preferred clothes
  - ○ Goes into the community with family with some adverse responses to the environment

Some adverse reactions to environmental stimuli seen in childhood are still present in adolescents in a subtler form. The following two sections discuss the challenges of the sensory system. All these behaviors are present early on, and most persist into adulthood. Students who require level 2 support have more behavioral outbursts related to their inflexibility and coping skills when faced with environmental or internal challenges. For example, the inability to accept new information, once an existing schema is imprinted, can result in behavioral outbursts. This aligns with emotional outbursts when a schedule is changed, and the student has a need for a clearly structured schedule. The list is not part of the DSM-5.

Sensory Perception and Sensitivities

Food Selectivity

For young children with ASD, food selectivity is a significant problem. In a narrative review of empirical literature over 25 years, Cermak, Curtin, and Bandini (2010) found that food selectivity occurs frequently along with unusual eating patterns. In addition, that selectivity may be the result of sensory sensitivity (Cermak et al., 2010).

The following are some examples of food-related behaviors in children and youth with ASD:
- May show revulsion to some foods by gagging and vomiting
- May only eat white or light-colored foods, such as cheese and noodles
- May eat other foods but have under 10 foods they will eat
- Rejects some food combinations due to texture
- May be significantly reactive if food items on their plates touch

Sensory sensitivity has been suggested as one possible mechanism to explain these selective food behaviors (Cermak et al., 2010). Sensory over-responsivity (SOR) refers to an exaggerated, intense, or prolonged behavioral response to ordinary sensory stimuli (Conelea, Carter, & Freeman, 2014).

Some of the avoidance of certain foods revolves around smell and texture. SOR to smell and texture significantly predicts severe food selectivity. A study by Chistol et al. (2018) found that more children with ASD presented with atypical sensory processing than children without ASD. Among children with ASD, those with atypical oral sensory sensitivity refused more foods as well and ate fewer vegetables than those with typical oral sensory sensitivity. In a study by Suarez, Nelson, and Curtis (2012), SOR resulted in fewer preferred foods. Food selectivity in children with ASD can be moderate to severe based on the number of foods they eat. Those with the least number of food preferences had the highest SOR scores. There is evidence of food sensitivity continuing into adolescence, mostly related to textures, and these sensitivities can have an effect on social activities (Kuschner et al., 2015).

Interventions and Sensory Perceptions

The concerns of adults about the social impact of a limited food repertoire naturally extend from cultural beliefs and the place of food behaviors. To enable children to participate in eating due to its importance in the culture and the concern for nutrition has led to the creation of an intervention. There have been some interventions to attempt to address this early in the young child's life. One intervention, known as feeding therapy, uses actions by the feeding therapist to acclimate children with ASD to new foods. The therapy includes preparing foods that the child is adverse to, such as textured foods. The nonpreferred food is smeared on the lips of the child. This method of forcing ingestion or tasting of a nonpreferred food type is typically highly aversive to the child, who naturally demonstrates a profoundly negative response.

The evidence to support the use of feeding therapy is limited, including whether a reported increase in food acceptance was maintained over time. Williams, Field, and Seiverling (2010) reported that positive measures alone will not increase food acceptance. Studies on the use of punishment to induce eating require the approval of an institutional review board in a reputable institution in keeping with the barriers created to prevent physical and psychological damage. However, taking away something to induce eating is unlikely to improve eating. In addition, the child would have to make the connection between eating and the reward which is unlikely for ASDL2-3 children and youth.

When new therapies and feeding protocols have been developed without intrusive measures, complete medical checkups, including swallow studies, are required to avoid significant problems such as pneumonia from aspirated foods. Feeding therapy is done by occupational and physical therapists. However, in a school setting, all professions must align with the practices of the special education programs, not the general practices the field may use in hospital-based settings.

By adolescence, children and youth with ASD may or may not have developed a broader repertoire of food. Lifelong food rejections need to be noted in an Individual Health Care Plan (IHP) as part of the Individualized Education Plan (IEP) so that eating does not become a behavioral issue.

Other Sensory Perception Challenges

Sensory issues often result in difficulty coping with being touched by others, maintaining eye contact, or managing noisy environments. Children and youth with ASD perceive sensory information differently than peers without ASD. The following are examples of a phenomenon called *tactile defensiveness*. Tactile defensiveness is a pattern of behavioral and emotional responses akin to pain responses to what most people and children would not view as painful. Children with tactile defensiveness will attempt to escape the feared touch by running away. They will cry and frantically fight even the possibility of touch. In early infancy, they have difficulty being cuddled. They will defend themselves vigorously to avoid touching glue and other sticky substances. As adolescents, preparing food may be difficult. Clothing choices are also important; textures, fabrics, seams of pants, and tags on shirts are distracting, and their reactions to them are as if seams and tags are painful.

If the teaching team suddenly places an adverse substance nearby, a child with tactile defensiveness will panic. This response has been identified for some time and is described as the fright, flight, and fight response, with the child going into high alert; he or she will scream, whine, cling, lash out, and run away (Trott, 1993). Taste and smell aversions may be seen as well, and it would be hard to determine which of these contribute to the fight and flight reaction.

Another sensory difficulty is called *proprioceptive input sensitivities*. When ASD is present, there are difficulties interpreting sensations from muscles, joints, ligaments, and tendons. Children may put too much pressure on a pencil and break it, and there is a tendency to walk or run into things. Vestibular input sensitivities are over- or under-sensitivities to balance and movement sensations.

TRANSITION PLANNING AND LANGUAGE DEVELOPMENT AND COMMUNICATION

Speech and Language

ASD is characterized by persistent impairments in reciprocal-social communication; social interaction; and restricted, repetitive behavior patterns, interests, and activities. Regarding the domain of repetitive behaviors in language, the manifestation can occur as echolalia (Mergl & Azoni, 2015). Repetitive speech is prominent in ASD and can manifest through self-repetition of speech or other environmentally accessed language and song. Young children first use echolalia in response to their mother in identifying objects and people in the environment. In children and youth with ASD, it does not evolve into back-and-forth speech.

There are different views on echolalia in the speech of children with ASD and its meaning. Echolalia can appear to have no meaning, or it may be understood as related to activities in the context in which it occurs. It may also serve no communicative function for speech and represent the repetitious speech seen in students who may repeatedly talk about the same interest or who will tell the same story over many times, seemingly unaware they are repeating themselves.

Echolalia may be considered a means of conversation with others or used for self-stimulation. For example, dialogue from television programs or videos may be used as a means of conversation, and the repetitive use of nonecholalic language routines may serve as initiating or sustaining a conversation. A functional assessment of this type of speech can inform its use. More research needs to be done on the function of echolalia before instituting practices to extinguish it. Nor should assumptions be made about its purpose without research support to justify a position.

Goals for verbal language should focus on receptive vocabulary development. There are picture-based assessments that can monitor the student's progress in receptive language acquisition. Without this focus, social interactions and improved cognitive processing of information will be limited. In-school and post-school goals can focus on developing receptive language skills to continue to develop cognition. Establishing receptive language goals is a primary responsibility when working with students without expressive language. The most important focus is not on what can be said but rather what can be understood and communicated using assistive communication tools. When a student's speech, communication, and understanding of the world and its processes are so limited that he or she are unable to participate in work situations, attention to seeking optimum environments where he or she can participate in activities of interest and activities that are cognitively stimulating is warranted. When parents have children with this level of need, access to post-school services and high quality day programs or residential programs is an area of focus that should begin early. Continued access to activities that advance communication should continue throughout students' lifetimes.

Communication Methods and Tools

Lack of functional communication or alternative communication systems makes it difficult to determine the level of language comprehension. American sign language (ASL) has been promoted as an alternative communication system. However, children with ASDL3 often have poor fine motor skills and most often are unable to sign or relate an abstract symbol to a word. ASL has other constraints that make it unlikely to result in establishing communication.

Some of the challenges are that ASL requires the user pay attention to and imitate the signer. Because children with autism often have difficulty watching the speaker/signer, they cannot learn the signs as effectively. Children with ASD have difficulty imitating during the period when sign language is typically mastered. ASL is taught explicitly, or the student must be in an environment in which ASL is used as the primary mode of communication. Few teachers certified as having ASL fluency are teachers in classrooms for children with ASD, and therefore a consistent level of signing cannot be utilized. However, it is not known if the skill, taught explicitly and intensively, would result in ASL fluency. Reading facial expressions is also a part of ASL and is a well-known difficulty for those with ASD. Teaching students ASL is an example of an unaided strategy, but Rosenberg, Westling, and McLeskey (2011) claim that students with ASD have difficulty learning and using this "through-the-air" language (p. 277).

The lack of practical ways to communicate leads to the need for the use of alternative augmentative communication. Delays in initiating active communication systems in early childhood in favor of speech therapy alone can be avoided. Assistive devices with other means of communication, such as visual schedules, are primary communication tools, and speech therapy with its focus on the significant oral-motor needs supports communication and the ability to manage food when eating. In combination, this approach promotes language and communication development and oral motor development.

Assistive Technology

Technology holds promise for helping students with ASD to learn, communicate, and interact with the people in their world. Students with ASD have had more success with aided strategies, such as picture boards, Picture Exchange Communications System (Pyramid Educational Consultants, Inc.), and voice output communication aids.

The following supports can be included in the transition plans. These are part of the related services that can help students with communicating in post-school life, and they are meant to facilitate more independence. Goals such as learning additional icons on the devices can expand independence and social interactions with other people in the home, the community, and at school. Communication applications can be installed on communication devices. These applications assist with routine communication, educational needs, and behavior regulation.

The iPod Touch (Apple Inc.), a speech-generated device for functional communication, is an example of a useful tool for functional needs. Another category of communication device is voice output communication aid. These are portable devices that allow message access through graphic symbols and words on computerized displays. The output can be printed or spoken text. Some use prerecorded digitized text, and others are synthesized to read what the student creates. These can take the place of scripts for nonverbal students or students without verbal fluency. Students can learn to read, and efforts to teach reading without the use of speech is recommended.

Most of the devices are created with a board of picture symbols and images that students can select to create sentences (Rosenberg et al., 2011). Dyna Vox is one of the more well-known producers of communications aids. The company receives funding from Medicare and Medicaid, and school districts will fund devices.

Multiple technological devices and applications are available. Video modeling and language processing software, customized digital stories, and book creator applications are additional tools to create social experiences and learning opportunities. Multi sensory rooms are also used to engage and calm students with autism. Many technological devices are used to give students a sense of control by a series of activities where they can use switches to change the colors, of light displays, such as LED strips. As mentioned in Chapter 15, the students can control the intensity, speed, and colors of bubble tubes and sensory cocoons. Multisensory environments are also used as break rooms where students engage with other classmates in turn-taking activities by using the devices. However, some students with autism do not like the sensory input. If they do, when the child, regardless of age, is delayed with toilet training, some parents set up sensory bathrooms to encourage toilet training and sensory bedrooms that are turned on only at bedtime to transition children and youth to sleep. Most multisensory rooms have evolved along with technology and now include, for example, virtual bowling and baseball, increasing structured physical activity. Academic activities, such as creating virtual weather experiences, are possible, and there are programs that provide ways to teach core subject matter.

Social Skills Deficits and Communication

Early communicative deficits underlie the numerous difficulties seen in social interactions in youth with ASD. Joint attention and lack of eye contact are the first indicators of possible ASD. These two behaviors emerge during the first years of life and they often persist through adulthood without intervention. The ability to monitor others' gazes to coordinate joint attention between the self and others is the foundation of social interactions. This interaction skill must be explicitly taught if students with ASD are to make eye contact within the accepted social norms.

Generally, early communication is when a child points to something and signals that he or she wants the object. As the parent engages in simple communication, he or she may point to an object, which causes the child to look. In autism, gestures, which are used to respond to and initiate engagement, do not emerge, and joint attention and back and forth engagement do not begin. With early intervention, these basic communications are taught with direct instruction. Without instruction, the child will continue to be noncommunicative and interact less. This process of engaging children and youth with autism should continue throughout school age. If a child is not engaged early, it will be more challenging to develop the social interactions that stem from early communication, also known as *pragmatics*. This is how the back-and-forth conversation begins, and efforts to engage in back-and-forth interactions with adolescents should continue through transition and into post-school life.

The topics just discussed (e.g., sensory sensitivities, speech and language development, assistive technology use, social development) continue through secondary school and into post-school life. When thinking about the characteristics and needs of students with autism, how they learn and the environments they learn best in should be taken into consideration. Autism awareness, includes continuing research on multiple means of teaching, including an understanding about how the disability is effected by external environments and internal environments. In addition, determining each students preferences lays the groundwork for transition planning. Each of these have a place in the design of the transition plan.

BEHAVIORAL AND EMOTIONAL
IMPLICATIONS ON TRANSITION PLANNING

Issues of Severe Self-Injurious and Disruptive Behavior

Individuals with ASD can develop severe self-injurious behaviors (SIBs). SIBs often occur due to deficits in communicative ability and can have undesirable consequences in an individual's environment (Boesch, Taber-Doughty, Wendt, & Smalts, 2015). SIBs can cause permanent brain damage; for example; in early childhood when head-banging begins and is not extinguished. In adolescents, if this behavior has not been remediated, a more restrictive educational environment is the typical course of action. In these more restrictive settings, the staff are trained to stop and redirect behavior, monitor medication using intensive data collection, implement applied behavior analysis

(ABA) strategies, and, at times, use state-approved physical restraint techniques to avoid injury to the student or others. Aggression is also associated with more restrictive school and community-based settings and significantly impairs opportunity for inclusive activities (Dryden-Edwards & Combrinck-Graham, 2010). Although learning theory and operant behavior principles form the basis for current behavioral treatments of aggression in ASD, medication is also used to decrease aggressive behavior (Powers, Palmieri, D'Eramo, & Powers 2011). Medication, including psychotropic medication, is often used, increasing the need for additional medical treatment and intensive supervision (Tsakanikos, Costello, Holt, Sturmey, & Bouras, 2007).

At times, emotional disorders, previous trauma, and mental health disorders may be present. It is believed that comorbid emotional disorders among people with ASD may be more common than previously thought. Comorbid conditions may have consequent impairment in social adjustment, adaptive functioning, and cognitive and global functioning. Learners with ASD can also be homeless, abused, or neglected, and the results of those traumas will also affect behavior.

The presence of mental health disorders necessitates a sophisticated level of planning and IHP, and plans developed during transition form the foundation of post-school activities, which also address these conditions.

Positive and engaging school-based activities, developed based on student medical conditions, preferences, and a communication system, can help adolescents with ASD reduce problem behaviors. Intensive behavior therapy, positive behavior supports (PBSs), ABA, and engaging community-based activities can provide a positive, supervised lifestyle with the possibility of community activities and more independence in daily activities.

Applied Behavior Analysis

ABA is a related service, defined as required to assist a student to benefit from special education. ABA can be implemented as part of transition planning for a variety of aggressive behaviors (Rosenberg et al., 2011). Appropriate social, behavioral, and emotional skills can be taught using ABA as well. ABA uses applied behavior change procedures involving the function of relationships among antecedent events, specific behaviors, and actions that occur after behaviors of interest (Rosenberg et al., 2011).

To develop behavior-planning strategies, students are typically observed in one of two environments to determine a function of the behavior and to develop a strategy for both settings. Students may be observed in a school/center- or home-based environment. Each environment is useful for children with ASD, and both allow professionals to observe students in their natural environment.

The home-based analysis is ideal when families plan to keep their children with them full-time after transition. Developing a plan in the home may be the most effective in the long term to help establish independence and may increase family cohesiveness by enabling the child to exhibit improved behavior.

Many times, when a student needs a high level of behavioral intervention, such as ABA, he or she is already in full-time or even residential school-based programs to change behaviors. However, even students with more mild but persistent behaviors can benefit from both ABA and PBS strategies.

A behavioral issue inherent in ASDL3 is difficulty with transitions between locations and tasks. The following are examples. Although not every learner with ASD has all of these challenges, a statistically significant number may have some or all of them. Students with ASD may have greater difficulty shifting attention from one task to another. Changes in their routine can lead to challenging behaviors during transitions and long periods of disengagement. The most common challenging behaviors exhibited during transitions include aggression, inappropriate vocalizations, off-task behavior, dropping to the floor, and elopement. If this has not changed by middle school, intensive programming is needed. At this point, early transition planning can be started, with more attention given to post-school planning. Significant efforts to help children and youth with ASD transition between activities, home, and school are picture schedules and preparatory signals.

Better transition skills can improve quality of life, including the ability to participate in community activities. Aggressive behavior reflects a level 3 need for support as well as specialized programs. Using either ABA or PBS includes having professionals available to the school and the family. All efforts should be made to change this behavior in all settings so the family and child can have a life that maintains family cohesion.

TRANSITION PLANNING PARTICIPATION

Quality of Life: Learning Goals for Transition Planning

Improving quality of life in school and out can be accomplished by understanding the needs of learners with ASD. Many learners with ASD demonstrate common learning characteristics. Those working with the youth with ASD will need information about the characteristics of ASDL3 and how they affect learning. By working with the positive traits, improved conditions for the learner can result. Individuals with ASD typically process information when presented visually.

The Transition Plan and Parental Supports

Each transition plan should include the use of environmental inventories based on daily environments and future potential environments. Person-centered planning is also used to set current and post-school goals, with all team members sharing what they know about the student when the student has limited mobility, is non-verbal, is unable to participate due to multiple or profound disabilities, and cannot express his or her preferences. Through direct observation and interactions, student preferences are documented in person-centered plans. Parents' knowledge of their child is required in setting goals that will be generalized across environments. Assisting the parents to prepare for the future is an important part of transition planning.

Supports to the parents can include the following conversations:

- Discussion about a future plan with the parents where they share their long-term plan for their child
- Ongoing reviews of their child's IHP
- Discussion about whether they have made contact with supportive governmental agencies, such as Medicaid
- Invitations sent to representatives from the Social Security Administration, Medicaid, and The Office of Developmental Disabilities to meet with parents and special education team
- Discussion about switching their child to adult services
- Discussion about making connections to agencies for Social Security to determine eligibility for support
- Discussion about whether they know about guardianship and whether they plan to apply for it
- Provision of transition support group linkages
- Caseworker/supports coordinator invitations to IEP meeting
- Discussion about residential facilities and evaluation checklist

The Transition Plan

The following transition framework provides an overview of components that should be included in the IEP when transition and transition services are addressed. Included are academic; communication; leisure; behavior; independence; and health goals, activities, and interagency involvement.

This plan can form the foundation for post-school programs available for adults with ASD. Although they are no longer eligible for special education after their 21st birthday, the transition process can provide a framework to guide the parents using future programs and for their own use at home:

- Academic goals
  - Knowledge goals: Receptive vocabulary development.
  - Use assistive technology for communication.
  - Picture schedules or checklists can help ease the anxiety or confusion surrounding unstructured time.
  - Use a curriculum based on the learning style of children and youth with ASD.
  - As much as possible, use activities that are built on prior knowledge; avoid random books or digital media tasks.
- Communication goals
  - Provide the student with multiple means to communicate.
  - Use visual supports and do not remove supports when a task is mastered; if a student needs visual cues to learn a task, he or she will always need visual cues associated with the task.
  - Use assistive technology across settings.
  - Determine if the student uses the location of a picture cue to communicate or picture identification.
  - Never change the location of an icon in a device; devices are not a means to test comprehension.
- Individual leisure plans
  - Create opportunities to participate in activities.
  - Create goals to encourage interactions.
  - Determine student leisure and environmental preferences.
  - Provide opportunities to go into the community; implement community-based instruction.
  - Plan access to preferred leisure activities.
- Behavior plans and goals
  - Create consistent routines.
  - Create responsibilities within those daily routines.
  - Provide situational and environmental analysis to avoid undesirable behaviors.
  - Initiate a functional behavioral assessment if warranted.
  - Initiate intensive interventions for self-injurious behaviors that may emerge during middle and high school.
- Independent living plan and work
  - Develop a living plan.
  - Develop post-school living goals.
  - Plan to live at home.
  - Plan to live in a residential placement.
  - Plan to attend a sheltered workshop.
  - Develop partial independence goals.
- IHP
  - Work with parents and school nurse to create a plan.
  - Participate in training to learn about health issues.
  - Train staff on medication monitoring and emergency care.
  - Ensure the final summary of performance includes all information for the next setting.

- Interagency action plan
  - ○ Collaborate with the parents on sheltered workshop placement.
  - ○ Visit residential placements.
  - ○ Visit sheltered workshops.
  - ○ Agency should ensure completion of paperwork for adult services.

Transition Plan Discussion

Often, behaviors are communications about preferences for the nonverbal student. Positive behavior change strategies can be implemented when the behavior has been analyzed. Daily frustration is present in students who cannot communicate. Therefore, the communicative intent is examined before the institution of a PBS plan.

Transition goal setting for students with autism is challenging, but by getting to know the student through careful observation, a plan can be developed that is optimal based on who the student is as a person. An example of this appears in the following case report about Olivia. Olivia is a student who is nonverbal. Observation of nonverbal students can give insight into activities and preferences that improve their quality of life.

If a student is engaging in challenging behavior, conducting a functional behavior assessment can be the foundation for developing appropriate goals. However, before doing so, teachers can consider the simple most obvious causes for behavior that are occurring in the environment based on the communication abilities of the student. In Olivia's case, the team wanted to stop her disruptive behavior using a PBS plan. Instead, the team decided to observe without deciding it was a disruptive and perseverative behavior.

Case Report: Olivia

Olivia is nonverbal. She repeatedly runs over to smell Mikaela's hair. Mikaela pushes Olivia and disrupts the class as well. Olivia does this cycle again and again. The staff generates some hypotheses to explain the behavior:

- Olivia likes the student.
- Olivia wants to annoy the student.
- Olivia is getting sensory input.

The team decides it may be sensory input, and she may like the scent of Mikaela's shampoo. The team asked Mikaela's parent to tell them the name of the child's shampoo. They asked Olivia's parent to get her the same shampoo. After using the shampoo, Olivia no longer attempted to smell Mikaela's hair. Observation and identifying the behavior is used prior to using more intensive supports.

Trying to stop Olivia by rewarding her for staying in her seat would not have extinguished the behavior nor removed her preference for the scent of the shampoo. In addition, liking the smell of a shampoo is a common conversation, and Olivia, who had no other way to deliver the message, was being a typical teen. It is important to see behaviors, preferences, and needs as indicators first and ensure that transition plans, which include behavior management, do not take away a student's self-advocacy and communication efforts.

RESIDENTIAL SETTINGS

When a family decides their child is ready for a specialized residential setting, choosing one can be challenging. The needs of young people with ASD are more substantial than they are for young people with intellectual disabilities because of communication issues. To help parents, the transition planning specialist and team can give some information on selecting a residential placement.

Supports coordinators and/or the parents go on the visits, but it is good to have knowledge about the process because this is part of the outcomes data. In addition, it is a support for the parents as they go through the process of selecting a setting for their child. Providing a checklist tool to review a setting for students who have autism can provide information about the general quality of a residential treatment setting and, more specifically, the degree to which it is individually adapted to meet the needs of a person with ASD.

The following list is specifically for centers that work with students with ASD, and the criteria reflect the needs of those within the spectrum. This list, except for the professionalism section, is from Van Bourgondien, Reichle, Campbell, and Mesibov's Environmental Rating Scale (1998). This instrument can be a useful tool to structure the selection of a residential setting:

- Communication subscale
  - Caregiver's communications are understood by the resident.
  - Communication is supplemented by visual systems.
  - Training is incorporated into the daily routine.
  - Information is available about communication skills.
  - Directions are communicated clearly to the resident.
- Structure subscale
  - Physical organization of home facilitates independence.
  - Visual systems are used to teach new skills and maintain independence.
  - The daily schedule for client is visible.
  - The daily schedule for home is visible.
  - The daily schedule is full and provides opportunities for leisure pursuits.
  - Systems are in place to facilitate transitions between activities.
- Socialization subscale
  - Socialization training is incorporated into the daily routine.
  - There are clearly stated goals for social and leisure skills.
  - Appropriate leisure activities are planned based on individual interests.
  - Independent skills are developed for free-time use.
  - Social skills training involves skills used in interactions with other people.
  - Social skills are taught in meaningful contexts.
- Developmental assessment and planning
  - Caregivers are aware of cognitive level.
  - Caregivers are aware of social level.
  - Appropriate training activities are selected based on assessment information.
  - Strengths and weaknesses are incorporated into training activities.
  - Emerging skills are incorporated into training activities.
  - Functional needs are incorporated into training activities.
  - Training activities are rethought if the subject is showing too little progress.
  - Efforts are made to generalize skills.
- Behavior management
  - Limits or rules are clear.
  - Consistent strategies maintain behavioral limits.
  - Problem behaviors are analyzed recognizing deficits and reasons behind the behavior.
  - Residents are reinforced for positive behaviors.
  - Behavior management strategies emphasize positive rather than punitive approaches.

- ○ Less intrusive approaches are tried before more intrusive approaches.
- ○ Written data are kept on behavior programs.
- Professionalism and family involvement
  - ○ Staff interacts and dresses appropriately for work.
  - ○ The program has regular training and orientation for new staff.
  - ○ Research-based behavioral and programmatic practices are used.
  - ○ Staff regularly report to the parents about their child.
  - ○ Visiting times are frequent and support family cohesion.
  - ○ Regular family days are on the yearly calendar.
  - ○ Teams work together cohesively.
- Student-centered planning activities
  - ○ Learning and educational program activities are evident.
  - ○ Healthy living activities are available.
  - ○ Community-based activities are available.

Young persons with autism should be afforded opportunities to live an active life. Transition planning is a system of activities that help parents to the next phase of their child's life. Parents need guidance from the school and governmental agencies that support transition to ensure young people with ASD are engaged, cared for, and given many opportunities to live a full life.

EMPLOYMENT: DAY PROGRAMS AND SHELTERED WORKSHOPS

Even with severe communication challenges, Roux et al. (2013) found that among individuals with ASD who had the most impaired conversational abilities, approximately one-fifth did become employed. Strategies for improving engagement in employment activities may include providing in-class work experiences during high school, deliberately matching capabilities to job types during transition planning, and paying attention to the flexibility of institutional supports for adults (Hendricks & Wehman, 2009; McDonough & Revell, 2010; Roux et al., 2013).

Segregated workshops or sheltered employment and day programs can provide the young person with autism entry-level opportunities to be engaged in activity matched to a skill for employment. Parents and special education teams can work together to find options that allow youth with ASD to have multiple opportunities for inclusion. Although that is not always possible, more options have become available over the years.

EXERCISES

1. Describe the three levels of support described in the Student Supplemental Materials and explain how these descriptions would be helpful in designing post-school supports for students with severe disabilities.
2. Read the case studies in the Chapter 18 Student Supplemental Materials. What do these cases tell you about how children with ASD can learn?
3. Contact the Office of Developmental Disabilities for your state and secure a list of sheltered workshops available for young adults with ASD.

SUMMARY

Parents of children on the autism spectrum need significant support and guidance. The need for specialized support continues during the child's transition years and beyond. Addressing the needs of students with ASD requires a willingness to grow and work with the team and the students' parents.

This chapter described the characteristics and needs of learners who are on the spectrum within ASDL3 needs. Like the students with intellectual disabilities discussed in Chapter 13, the transition plan for adolescents will need supports for post-school life that will include social services; an IHP; skills developed for sheltered workshops; ongoing assessments; and a lifespan plan including guardianship, if necessary. Students with ASD will need a communication plan that will continue to be developed into adulthood.

Person-centered plans and the use of environmental inventories can outline what environments the student prefers and those that are conducive to learning and living, where the learner seems the calmest and most independent. In short, the transition plan promotes quality life experiences.

Adolescents within the autism spectrum have a wide range of adaptive functioning and intellectual disabilities. Transition planning varies significantly based on their intellectual, emotional, social, and adaptive skills. Depending upon their individual needs, they will be able to participate partially or with support. However, if the extent of their disability prohibits participation, their parents or guardians will fill their role and share their children's preferences.

Under the umbrella of ASD, the range of intellectual and adaptive performance requires implementation of various evidence-based practices. The type of transition planning, the level of functioning proposed in the DSM-5, learner preferences, and assessment data give structure to the framework for transition to delineate the best fit for the activities, supports, goals, and curriculum. Ultimately, the unique characteristics of each learner with ASD are complex and require instruction and transition planning participation adapted to how they learn and how they can communicate their wants and needs and finding and adapting environments in which they can be their best.

There are many studies on the deficits of children and youth with ASD, and those studies establish characteristics present in ASD. However, studies about how they learn are needed to develop optimum transition plans. ASD was recognized as a separate category of disability in the 1990s, and instructional interventions such as the use of ABA, visual schedules and aids, and music to develop cognition and increase learning have been developing slowly. During transition planning, activities that teach in the way they learn and planning that addresses social, behavioral, and psychological aspects of ASD are crucial to developing plans that can benefit students with ASD.

REFERENCES

American Psychiatric Association. (2013). *Diagnostic and statistical manual of mental disorders* (5th ed.). Washington, DC: American Psychiatric Association Publishing.

Baio, J., Wiggins, L., Christensen, D. L., Maenner, M. J., Daniels, J., Warren, Z., … Dowling, N. F. (2018). Prevalence of autism spectrum disorder among children aged 8 years – Autism and Developmental Disabilities Monitoring Network, 11 sites, United States, 2014. *Morbidity and Mortality Weekly Report: Surveillance Summaries, 67*(6), 1-23.

Boesch, M. C., Taber-Doughty, T., Wendt, O., & Smalts, S. S. (2015). Using a behavioral approach to decrease self-injurious behavior in an adolescent with severe autism: A data-based case study. *Education and Treatment of Children, 38*(3), 305-328.

Cermak, S. A., Curtin, C., & Bandini, L. G. (2010). Food selectively and sensory sensitivity in children with autism spectrum disorders. *Journal of the American Dietetic Association, 110*(2), 238-246.

Charman, T., Pickles, A., Simonoff, E., Chandler, S., Loucas, T., & Baird, G. (2011). IQ in children with autism spectrum disorders: Data from the Special Needs and Autism Project (SNAP). *Psychological Medicine, 41*(3), 619-627.

Child with a disability, 34 C.F.R. § 300.8 (2017).

Chistol, L. T., Bandini, L. G., Must, A., Phillips, S., Cermak, S. A., & Curtin, C. (2018). Sensory sensitivity and food selectivity in children with autism spectrum disorder. *Journal of Autism and Developmental Disorders, 48*(2), 583-591.

Conelea, C. A., Carter, A. C., & Freeman, J. B. (2014). Sensory over-responsivity in a sample of children seeking treatment for anxiety. *Journal of Developmental and Behavioral Pediatrics, 35*(8), 510-521.

Courchesne, E., Mouton, P. R., Calhoun, M. E., Semendeferi, K., Ahrens-Barbeau, C., Hallet, M. J., ... & Pierce, K. (2011). Neuron number and size in prefrontal cortex of children with autism. *Journal of the American Medical Association, 306*(18), 2001-2010.

Dryden-Edwards, R. C., & Combrinck-Graham, L. (2010). *Developmental disabilities from childhood to adulthood: What works for psychiatrists in community and institutional settings.* Baltimore, MD: John Hopkins University Press.

Dykens, E. M., & Lense, M. (2011). Intellectual disabilities and autism spectrum disorder: A cautionary note. In D. Amaral, G. Dawson, & D. Geschwind (Eds.), *Autism spectrum disorders* (pp. 261-269). New York, NY: Oxford University Press.

Eyler, L. T., Pierce, K., & Courchesne, E. (2012). A failure of left temporal cortex to specialize for language is an early emerging and fundamental property of autism. *Brain, 135*(Pt 3), 949-960.

Hazlett, H. C., Gu, H., McKinstry, R. C., Shaw, D. W., Botteron, K. N., Dager, S. R., ... Schultz, R. T. (2012). Brain volume findings in 6-month-old infants at high familial risk for autism. *American Journal of Psychiatry, 169*(6), 601-608.

Hazlett, H. C., Poe, M. D., Gerig, G., Styner, M., Chappell, C., Smith, R. G., ... Piven, J. (2011). Early brain overgrowth in autism associated with an increase in cortical surface area before age 2 years. *Archives of General Psychiatry, 68*(5), 467-476. doi:10.1001/archgenpsychiatry.2011.39

Hendricks, D. R., & Wehman, P. (2009). Transition from school to adulthood for youth with autism spectrum disorders: Review and recommendations. *Focus on Autism and Other Developmental Disabilities, 24*(2), 77-88.

Kuschner, E. S., Eisenberg, I. W., Orionzi, B., Simmons, W. K., Kenworthy, L., Martin, A., & Wallace, G. L. (2015). A preliminary study of self-reported food selectivity in adolescents and young adults with autism spectrum disorder. *Research in Autism Spectrum Disorders, 15-16,* 53-59.

McDonough, J. T., & Revell, G. (2010). Accessing employment supports in the adult system for transitioning youth with autism spectrum disorders. *Journal of Vocational Rehabilitation, 32,* 89-100.

Mergl, M., & Azoni, C. A. S. (2015). Type of echolalia in children with autistic spectrum disorder. *Revista CEFAC, 17*(6), 2072-2080.

Powers, M. D., Palmieri, M. J., D'Eramo, K. S., Powers, K. M. (2011). Evidence-based treatment of behavioral excesses and deficits for individuals with autism spectrum disorders. In B. Reichow, P. Doehring, D. V. Cicchetti, & F. R. Volkmar (Eds.), *Evidence-based practices and treatments for children with autism* (pp. 55–92). New York, NY: Springer.

Rosenberg, R. C., Westling, D. L., & McLeskey, J. (2011). *Special education for today's teachers: An introduction.* London, United Kingdom: Pearson.

Roux, A. M., Shattuck, P. T., Cooper, B. P., Anderson, K. A., Wagner, M., & Narendorf, S. C. (2013). Postsecondary employment experiences among young adults with an autism spectrum disorder. *Journal of the American Academy of Child & Adolescent Psychiatry, 52*(9), 931-939.

Stanutz, S., Wapnick, J., & Burack, J. A. (2012). Pitch discrimination and melodic memory in children with autism spectrum disorders. *Autism, 18*(2), 137-147.

Suarez, M. A., Nelson, N. W., & Curtis, A. B. (2012). Associations of physiological factors, age, and sensory over-responsivity with food selectivity in children with autism spectrum disorders. *Online Journal of Occupational Therapy, 1*(1).

Trott, M. C. (1993). *Sense abilities: Understanding sensory integration.* Tucson, AZ: Therapy Skill Builders.

Tsakanikos, E., Costello, H., Holt, G., Sturmey, P., & Bouras, N. (2007). Behaviour management problems as predictors of psychotropic medication and use of psychiatric services in adults with autism. *Journal of Autism and Developmental Disorders, 37*(6), 1080-1085.

Tuchman, R. (2011). Epilepsy and electroencephalography in autism spectrum disorders. In D. G. Amaral, G. Dawson, & D. H. Geschwind (Eds.), *Autism spectrum disorders* (pp. 381-394). New York, NY: Oxford University Press.

Van Bourgondien, M. E., Reichle, N. C., Campbell, D. G., & Mesibov, G. B. (1998). The Environmental Rating Scale (ERS): A measure of the quality of the residential environment for adults with autism. *Research in Developmental Disabilities, 19*(5), 381-394.

Wegiel, J., Flory, M., Kuchna, I., Nowicki, K., Ma, S. Y., Imaki, H., ... Brown, W. T. (2014). Stereological study of the neuronal number and volume of 38 brain subdivisions of subjects diagnosed with autism reveals significant alterations restricted to the striatum, amygdala and cerebellum. *Acta Neuropathologica Communications, 2,* 141. doi:10.1186/s40478-014-0141-7

Williams, K. E., Field, D. G., & Seiverling, L. (2010). Food refusal in children: A review of the literature. *Research in Developmental Disabilities, 31*(3), 625-633.

Part 7

Evidence-Based
Instruction in
Special Education

Special Education Transitions

The Effectiveness
of Transition Planning
Monitoring the Practices of
the Special Education Team

CHAPTER OBJECTIVES

→ Identify the primary purpose of the teacher–transition planning specialist self-assessment.
→ Identify the purpose of reviewing transition planning practices.
→ Review the student survey and describe how survey items provide program improvement data.
→ Describe principles of successful postsecondary experiences.

ASSESSING SUCCESSFUL STUDENT TRAJECTORIES

Wagner and Davis (2006) discussed six principles from the literature that help students have positive secondary experience and successful trajectories into early adulthood:

1. School-based relationships
2. Challenging curriculum with well-prepared teachers
3. Teaching relevant content and focusing on post-school transition goals that include workplace skills
4. Parent inclusion in the transition planning
5. Attention to the whole child
6. Developing transition frameworks that include the previous five principles and implementing programs that help students with disabilities foster key social competencies can circumvent the

Rae, J. M. *A Collaborative Approach to Transition
Planning for Students With Disabilities* (pp. 359-372).
© 2020 SLACK Incorporated.

poor outcomes facing students with disabilities. In the next section, Table 17-1 defines a matrix of skills and how they relate to an evaluation of transition planning. The contents of the matrix are the areas defined in a study about participation in transition planning.

An Outcome Data Evaluation

Survey Outcomes Matrix: Teacher–Transition Planning Specialist Self-Assessment

Table 17-1 shows the results of student interviews about their perceptions of their transition planning program while they were enrolled in an emotional support program. Three students were asked which transition planning activities they participated in and what strategies they felt were most helpful. An analysis of information was placed in a chart, creating a matrix of strategies the students found useful. Each area, such as social skills, is coded by number. The numbers relate to the strength of the practice. Adding to the authenticity of the information is that none of the participants knew who participated in the self-assessment study.

In column one of the matrices are four areas the three participants selected as crucial to their post-school outcome success: (1) counseling by an experienced adult, (2) social skills within group activities, (3) an age-appropriate academic program and transition planning, and (4) a supportive program climate. Each of these areas is numbered. For instance, item 2.3 is the third of 14 benefits of transition planning and it falls under the area (2) social skills, and the item is *developed empathy*.

Under the area (3), an age-appropriate academic program and transition planning, items 3.7 and 3.8 are *differentiated instruction, curriculum-based instruction, cognitive-level assessment, and instructional materials, respectively, were provided using cognitive and age-appropriate content.*

The items number 1 to 14 are the items that each participant reported as helpful to his or her improved functioning. Interestingly, upon careful review of the matrix, the general mission of transition planning emerges, and these students' perceptions align closely with the research of Wagner and Davis (2006).

This chapter closes with some of their perspectives on the information they provided for the matrix. The participants did not know who else was being interviewed, so these are the individual perspectives of each student.

Differentiating Teacher Self-Assessment and Program Assessment by Disability

One issue with post-school outcomes data collection is that there are youth who do not go on to typical post-school environments due to severe to profound disabilities. The data collection for this group needs further refinement. For students with the most severe disabilities, parent interviews determine if the transition plan helped the parent negotiate the pathways to post-school programs and post-school supports. Question items in the survey are modified and aligned to the needs of the students and are addressed in Chapter 15.

State outcome data collection captures students who will go to work, training, or post-school education, such as college or vocational schools, and who do not have profound intellectual and/or physical disabilities. Therefore, monitoring the outcomes of the most severely impaired can be done at the local school level by the transition team or special education administrator responsible for the transition planning and services of students with the most severe disabilities. It is important that the efficacy of the transition plan be reviewed for all students with disabilities so that they receive the appropriate services, rather than use interview materials unaligned with the student's individual barriers and needs.

TABLE 17-1. MATRIX OF TRANSITION PLANNING SERVICES: EMOTIONAL SUPPORT PROGRAM

EVALUATION MATRIX

Participant Reports of Three Participants From an Emotional Support Program Post-Transition Study

1.0 Counseling by a trained and experienced adult.	1.1 Primary support to the student daily (not the family) Psychoeducation Individual therapy Psychiatric support The counselor was a registered nurse who they felt brought life experience to the program.	1.2 Personal stories Confidential setting One-on-one counseling	Two students mentioned: Problem-solving approach Daily group therapy Psychoeducation	One student mentioned: Evidence-of-solutions approach to problems	Additional community-based services not mentioned that provided support to students.: 24-hour hotline for after-school use Secondary support to the family Individual or family therapy
2.0 Social skills Group activities	2.3 Developed empathy	2.4 Listening	2.5 Practice and guidance	2.6 Modeling	Transportation and funding

(continued)

TABLE 17-1. MATRIX OF TRANSITION PLANNING SERVICES: EMOTIONAL SUPPORT PROGRAM (CONTINUED)

3.0 Age-appropriate academic program Transition planning	**3.7** Differentiated instruction Curriculum-based adaptations Respectful classroom climate One-to-one guidance Structured program	**3.8** Cognitive level assessment Instructional materials at the cognitive level of the participants Career planning for post-school outcomes	**3.9** The academic program flexed to mental health symptoms as needed. Planning for graduation Parent involvement	**3.10** Opportunities for practice at the location and in the community Guidance about credit attainment	Lead agency supports to program personnel
4.0 Supportive program climate	**4.11** Trusted adults Experienced adults who communicated with one another Structured activities	**4.12** Prepared teacher Student feedback Program expectations	**4.13** Social and instructional opportunities in a small group	**4.14** Participation Connectedness	Opportunities for student leadership Ongoing conferencing

The numbers 1 to 14 indicate that each student mentioned these areas of support (Rae, 2011). Unnumbered content in row 1, columns 4 and 5 indicate areas where only 1 or 2 students mentioned those areas.

TEAM REVIEW OF TRANSITION GOALS IN THE INDIVIDUALIZED EDUCATION PLAN

File Reviews for Student Outcome Self-Assessment

Students who follow a full participation model of transition planning are the students who are most at risk for early school leaving without a diploma. As noted in the introduction to Part 6, they are also the most likely to be unemployed or underemployed. Therefore, their file reviews include careful assessment of whether the secondary transition team, including their special education teachers, helped them plan for transition by including the following:

- Appropriate measurable postsecondary goals that cover education or training, employment, and, as appropriate to age and culture, independent living
- Evidence that the postsecondary goals that cover education, training or employment, and, as needed, independent living are updated annually
- The location, frequency, projected beginning dates, anticipated duration, and person(s) and/or agencies responsible for activity/service is listed
- Transition services, including courses of study that will reasonably enable the student to meet his or her postsecondary goals

The transition self-assessment team or individuals completing the self-assessment process document any missing components from the file. This informs the team that the student missed this help. When there is no evidence of support to a student in each area, information about how the shortcoming occurred is noted. An action plan to address the shortcoming is needed for future students. An evaluation of the student's outcomes, his or her satisfaction with the activities of transition, and his or her post-school success are the basis to ensure ongoing successful practices.

Securing Permission to Interview

A formal letter will most likely not inspire student participation in sharing post-school information. Therefore, an example of a letter is provided to give the reader some idea of what may be needed to secure permission.

Permission Form Example

Derry School District   Date: _____
1015 Washington Lane
Derry, New Hampshire 03038

Dear _____,

As you know, I am your transition planning specialist for the Derry School District. Over the past few years, you and I have had planned conferences so that you can plan your life after high school. Now that you are in your 11th-grade year, we would like to know how helpful the transition planning program has been for you. I would like you to participate in three interviews to survey how transition planning has or has not helped you. We want to ensure you are reaching the goals you are planning to reach, and this interview will help us see what the special education team may need to do to better improve transition planning.

Your participation in these interviews is voluntary, and withdrawing is possible at any time.

If you are willing to participate, I will want you to answer questions about your transition plan. The answers you provide can help the transition team learn more about what you think may be helpful to you or others with the same disability.

There will be four interview surveys:

Survey 1: The 11th-grade survey will be at the mid-term.

Survey 2: The 12th-grade survey will be in the mid-term.

Survey 3: Exit Survey 1 will be at the end of the 12th-grade year.

Survey 4: Exit Survey 2 will be at the end of the following year.

The central goal is to get your thoughts about whether and how the transition planning activities are helping or have helped or not helped you reach your goals. If during the interview you think of anything else that is important to you, it will be included as well.

These interviews require your written consent. Your parent should sign the permission form to indicate they are aware of the process. Each interview will take about 20 minutes.

Your survey responses are confidential.

Consent: I, _____, agree to participate in a series of interviews, including a post-graduation follow-up call to share what I am doing. I agree that the information will be kept confidential and that no identifying information will be included in any of the reports unless I give written consent to be identified.

I agree to take part in:

11th-grade interview (approximately 1½ hours): Yes_____ No_____

12th-grade interview: Yes_____ No_____

Exit survey 1: Yes_____ No_____

Exit survey 2 (1-year post-school exit): Yes_____ No_____

Student Signature: _____ Date: _____

Parent Signature: _____ Date: _____

This is just a sample of a personalized request for the data collection used for informed decision making.

THE TRANSITION PLANNING TEAM SELF-ASSESSMENT TOOL

How do teams look at their practices, evaluate them, and adjust them? To do this, they find shortcomings and create target correction goals. Transition goals are already set through legislation so that makes the task easier to quantify for the state requirements. The secondary special education team can collect data that provide an overview of their accomplishments and shortcomings and institute action plans to improve implementation of transition plans and services.

Four samples, three self-assessments, and a program self-assessment are designed to give one example of how secondary transition teams can create a system to self-assess their practice, reflect on those practices, and make adjustments.

The student's perspective is crucial when he or she indicates whether the goals were too complicated or too easy and finally whether transition supports were adequate to facilitate a smooth transition into adult life. The following section gives examples of questions that will inform practice in transition planning.

This document can be used for the first three student interviews. The transition planning specialist and the student can keep data on the student's progression. This document can also provide interrater reliability and prevent divergent views between the transition planning specialist and the student about the services the student received. The secondary team can discuss this survey in their transition meetings.

I. Transition planning specialist self-assessment practices: Ongoing interviews and review of Individualized Education Plan (IEP) documents

Part 1: Student and transition planning specialist document review

This is completed using the student's file. It is a natural part of the conference process.

Do the student's IEP goals include the following?

1. Postsecondary education or training goals and objectives specified.

    Describe:

2. Occupational goals and objectives specified.

    Describe:

3. Community-related and independence goals and objectives specified (e.g., voting registration, selective services, driving).

    Describe:

4. Recreation and leisure goals and objectives specified.

    Describe:

5. Leisure educational program corresponds to specific goals, including elective (e.g., photography classes at a local community college).

    Describe:

6. Pathways to a diploma and a route for earning the needed credits for graduation, such as work studies, summer employment, and independent study.

    Describe:

7. Personal needs are addressed in planning (e.g., financial, medical, guardianship).

    Describe:

II. Student assessment for the transition planning specialist or transition team

Part 2: Student survey

In which of the following did the student participate?

a. Career knowledge and skills

- Career education
- Community-based work instruction
- Community-based life skills instruction
- Unpaid work experience
- Paid work experience
- College preparation
- Planned course of academic instruction
- Planned course of vocational instruction
- Planned course of employment skills

b. Accommodations

While in high school, which of the following accommodations were given?

- Note-taker
- Extra time on tests or assignments
- Books on tape
- Electronic textbooks using read-aloud technology
- Tape recorder to record homework assignments
- Alternate test times
- Personal care assistant
- Extra help with schoolwork
- Sign language interpreter
- Braille
- Mobility trainings
- Assistive technology

- ° Peer tutor
- ° Disability friendly after-school activities
- ° Access to school counselor
- ° Counseling about courses of study

c. Curricular instruction: Activities of transition

Did you have the following in your transition program?

- ° Did you learn how to participate in your IEP meeting? YES/NO
- ° Did you lead your IEP meeting? YES/NO
- ° Did your transition planning specialist discuss career exploration? YES/NO
- ° Was it helpful, and in what way? YES/NO

d. Conferences

- ° Did your conferences with your transition planning specialist help you with your goals? YES/NO
- ° Were there other ways the conferences were helpful? YES/NO
- ° Did you have a dependable conference schedule? YES/NO

e. Internship or job training

- ° Job-coaching YES/NO
- ° College classes during high school YES/NO
- ° After-school transition activities such as community-based instruction YES/NO
- ° What type of instruction?

f. Adaptive skills

Did you learn to take care of adult responsibilities, such as:

- ° Money management YES/NO
- ° Personal appearance for work YES/NO
- ° Goal setting and completion YES/NO
- ° Social skills training YES/NO
- ° Problem solving in school and home settings YES/NO
- ° Avoiding social pitfalls YES/NO

g. Job preparation

Did you learn or participate in the following?

- ° Interview practices YES/NO
- ° Employment vocabulary YES/NO
- ° Essential behaviors for work YES/NO
- ° Self-advocacy skills YES/NO
- ° Attendance and timeliness for work YES/NO
- ° Personal and workspace organization YES/NO
- ° Problem solving at work YES/NO

h. Job placement

- ° Job search YES/NO
- ° Connections to job placement agencies YES/NO
- ° Connections to companies that have special employment programs YES/NO

i. Life success

- ° What did you learn about behaviors that will prevent success in your post-school life?

j. Community agency connections

While in high school, which of the following services were you taught about or did you access?

- ◦ Vocational rehabilitation YES/NO
- ◦ County mental health access YES/NO
- ◦ County services YES/NO
- ◦ Career link YES/NO
- ◦ County Children and Youth services YES/NO
- ◦ Health care clinic/medical consultation YES/NO
- ◦ Medicaid YES/NO
- ◦ Social Security card or Social Security Insurance information YES/NO

III. Teacher self-assessment: 1 to 3 years following graduation

This survey is designed to provide the transition planning specialist with additional information about the success of his or her work.

Part 3: Transition planning specialist–student survey of post-school outcomes

This can be completed 1 to 3 years post-graduation so that a greater time span is reflected.

Outcomes data collection

a. Current situation perspectives

- ◦ Tell me about life after high school.
- ◦ Tell me about what it has been like for you to be a young adult.
- ◦ What challenges do you have now?
- ◦ Did the transition planning program help you in your current situation?
- ◦ Tell me what supports you have in your current situation.
- ◦ Tell me about your current employment.
- ◦ How many positions have you held since graduation?

b. Independent living skills

- ◦ Where are you currently living?
- ◦ Do you participate in the support of your household?
- ◦ Do you participate in doing household maintenance?
- ◦ Do you cook any meals?
- ◦ Do you food shop?
- ◦ Do you take care of your personal needs?

c. Relationships

- ◦ Who do you live with?
- ◦ Are you living independently with a friend or partner?
- ◦ Do you have any children?

d. Medical insurance and treatment

- ◦ How do you get medical treatment?
- ◦ Do you know where and how to get mental health help if you need it?

e. Historical information

- ◦ Do you recall participating in activities to prepare you for life after high school?
- ◦ What were some of those activities?

f. Program questions: Transition education

- ◦ Which activities do you think prepared you for independent living, employment, and social activities?

- o What aspects of your education had the most impact on your life today? Describe:
- o How do you feel about academics? Do you like to learn?
- o What recommendations would you make for improving education for students with disabilities?
- o Do you think your transition planning process helped you to be where you are now?
- o Tell me how you feel in your current situation regarding happiness, connectedness, satisfaction, and success.
- o Are you attending any classes for enjoyment? How many last year?
- o Are you involved in social activities?
- o Are you involved in a special interest club?
- o Do you participate in any community or physical activities?

Demographic information example

Instrument: Review of Transition Planning

Special Educator/Transition Planning Specialist Name: _____

- o Identity Code: _____/Student Initials: _____ Phone: _____
- o Sex: ____
- o High school graduate: _____
- o Age: ____
- o Primary special education disability: _____
- o Date entered high school: _____

Informal data collection

Another way for the transition planning specialist and special education team to review practice is to form a student focus group. One or more years post-graduation, meeting as a group can stimulate conversation on improvements that a group of students, who are now out in the world, would like to see developed for other students with disabilities. Students often enjoy getting together to give their opinions, especially if the opinions are used in something valuable to the program and younger students with disabilities.

IV. Yearly teacher final self-assessment

A simple list of data like this can be a quick way to review program success. If kept over some years, it may help conceptualize long-term success of the work. It also enables the team to target areas needing attention. Use the cohort to define the group.

Cohort: 2014

- o What was the total number of students who entered transition planning in ninth grade?
- o How many students should have graduated in their cohort in 2018?
- o How many of the special education students dropped out from this cohort?
- o What programs were they in?
- o How many graduated on time?
- o How many are in an alternative educational setting such as alternative school or juvenile detention?
- o How many are in entry-level employment?
- o How many are in both work and school?
- o How many are not employed?
- o What are the reasons for unemployment?
- o What linkages do they have to address unemployment?
- o How many are going to sheltered workshops?

- How many are going to be at home without any activities?
- How many are in adult day care?
- How many attended specialized programs for employment or additional schooling for students with autism spectrum disorder, intellectual disabilities, deafness, or deaf-blindness?
- How many are going to college part- or full-time?

Each of these are examples of what the team is interested in knowing that may not be included in state and local data collection. Some of them may be of more importance to the team than others. The surveys, completed while the students are still in school, can be done in a group setting, and due to the comprehensiveness of the questions, this may be a reasonable approach as long as the review of the data is within the conference setting. Districts can convert these using Likert Scales or online surveys made available during the school day.

FUTURE DIRECTIONS ACTION PLANNING

Each year after the transition planning specialist and teachers finish their self-assessment and the state assessment, the following activities can guide improvement or the maintenance of existing practices. The surveys and the post-school outcomes can inform practice. The sample list below can guide the special education team in evaluating their program quantitatively. The process begins by calculating the number of activities each student participated in and the number of IEP goals they developed and attained in each area: independence, educational, training, employment, and leisure.

However, with the help of the school's central administration, a data collection system and analysis can be created with more statistical expertise for these self-assessments.

- Calculate student goals created and accomplished.
  - Calculate the number of goals per area.
  - Calculate the number of independence goals.
  - Calculate the number of employment goals.
  - Calculate the number of social leisure goals.
  - Calculate the number of activities and goals.
  - Divide number of goals and activities completed by the number of goals assigned.
  - Compare to outcome percentages by area and overall.

This is a teacher self-assessment, a review of the teacher and program supports. When students do not complete parts of the plan goals, teachers will want to look for patterns in their practice that may indicate changes need to be made.

Discussion

Teams can review areas of strength and weakness in instructing students on systems of goal setting in the target areas.

- Programmatic data review instrument
  - Did the team:
    - Ensure a range of employment explorations.
    - Define all postsecondary education possibilities.
    - Continue to develop employment training options.
    - Create a school climate that focuses on post-school education, employment, social, and independent living for students with disabilities.

- Track post-school outcomes to drive school-wide attention to the employment needs of students with disabilities.
- Track number of company employment connections.
- Track number of students without post-school placements before graduation.
- Discuss any patterns that emerge from the review of the data.

The team can review if they need to do more to in any of the areas listed above.

After the data collection, the transition planning specialist, special education supervisor, or designated party disseminates the target information. The data is presented to stakeholders in a presentation. This meeting can be a year-end review where team members can make suggestions for the following year.

EFFECTIVENESS OF TRANSITION PLANNING: PERSPECTIVES OF THREE STUDENTS WHO PARTICIPATED IN TRANSITION PLANNING

Assessment of transition planning is not valid without the students' viewpoints. The following case reports are comments from the students who were the participants whose interview questions were the basis of the matrix in Table 17-1. The following case report is about one aspect of the matrix.

Case Report: Perceptions of Students on Transition Planning

The three students, who were educated in a class for students with mental health disorders, reported that learning social skills helped their interactions with peers, but they also reported that they still use these skills as adults. They reported that being with peers and adults who understood them, as well as being able to participate in community-based activities, classroom discussions, and group sessions on structured topics with their peers, helped them learn to socialize. Community-based activities, such as ordering food, learning to shop without assistance, and using community parks and recreational facilities, helped them learn how to socialize and interact in what they described as "normal" settings.

Ms. Gray stated:

> Social skills prepared me the most. It is hard to name the actions because it is not really something you put an object to; it is really something that goes on in the brain. It was more the way communication was taught, expressed, and even modeled by the way that the teachers talked to each other that taught us those skills. It is more important than what you can tell us to do. I noticed with the changes in the other kids; some were really withdrawn. The more we got to know each other and our likes and dislikes and the way that we were, Mary really came out. She might have had her problems at home, but throughout the day, even more toward the middle of the day, she would get happier and express a lot more. I think she felt normal, yeah … normal. Even though at the end of the day, you could see that she was like, 'Oh crap, I got to go home.' And it did not matter so much that we were interconnected and communicating, because she knew what she had to go home to … I think that was the way it was with most of us. For her, it was an extreme example. I think learning the academics without the interpersonal skills would not have worked. It would have been difficult for us to learn academically. I think the more stressed out you are and the more upset you are with your home environment, it [academics] doesn't matter. (Rae, 2011, pp. 54-55)

The participants reported that they learned valuable social and independence skills during community and leisure activities. They reported that they still experience benefits from those skills (Rae, 2011, pp. 54-56).

Ms. Smith and Ms. Gray reported that the activities made them feel "normal" because a lot of "us" did not feel normal (Rae, 2011, p. 57).

Mr. Davis, another participant in this post-school outcomes study, although he did not use the word "normal," described that via his social experiences he developed empathy for others, a significant outcome in social competence (Rae, 2011, p. 58). He also described the positive aspects of the community-based instruction. Mr. Davis stated:

> They, peers [sic], were always pretty fun given the company, and I always learned something, even if it wasn't to a necessarily educational place. Hell, even on trips just to the park when you left us kids to frolic and interact with one another. Someone always introduced me to something, some idea or other, or updated me on how their life was or how it paralleled to mine, establishing a connection with another human, thus creating a stronger empathy center in my head. (Rae, 2011, p. 58)

Ms. Smith stated:

> Beyond social skills, I think it is important to find out what interests them. Continue to stimulate them and show them that there is a future for them somewhere. As long as you can make them feel there is something they can work for and that there is something out there for them, that is the key to it. (Rae, 2011, p. 62)

Discussion

Student responses, post-transition, can inform practice providing information on how the students perceived the help they received. Self-assessment, based on the student's perspectives, can guide the transition planning specialist and special education team to be more introspective about the development of effective transition planning practices and positive outcomes for all students with disabilities. These students, who were on the path to dropping out became students who graduated and went onto work and school.

EXERCISES

1. Use Table 17-1 to define the key parts of the chart and how it relates to what you read in the text. Use citations.
2. Go to the National Technical Assistance Center on Transition (NTACT) website and one other website provided in the following Federal Government Resources section. What strategies are grounded in the research and research support based on the information they have on students with autism spectrum disorder?

Federal Government Resources

To help local educational agencies with collection and reporting of indicator data, the Office of Special Education Programs funds four centers to provide technical assistance for the collection and analysis of data for these indicators:

1. The National Secondary Transition Technical Assistance Center
2. The NTACT is a technical assistance and dissemination project funded by the Office of Special Education Programs and the Rehabilitation Services Administration, Cooperative Agreement Number H326E140004. NTACT is funded from January 1, 2015, until December 31, 2019.
3. The National Dropout Prevention Center for Students with Disabilities
4. The National Post-School Outcomes Center

SUMMARY

An interactive and collaborative approach to transition planning guides the student on a path to adulthood. School environments that focus transition on prosocial behaviors, social skills, teaching students how to learn, and protecting the rights of the most vulnerable students are crucial to improving student outcomes. Practices that are assessed regularly inform future practice and draw administrative attention to the needs of students. Using the data from students is part of the concept of informed decision making that is required for any program hoping to improve practices and student outcomes.

Multiple studies point to parent involvement as a reliable indicator of a student's success. However, schools carry a significant burden when committing to educate students, especially when parents are unable to provide guidance for their children's success in today's marketplace and communities.

In the ever-changing employment environment, retooling for new opportunities is paramount, and learning to learn is more important than ever. Given the new developments in technology, there are many ways to learn new skills and access workplace settings when students cannot learn traditionally. Schools must continuously stay current in what happens outside of the school walls and be able to change practices to meet employment demands.

People with disabilities are at a unique time where, through diverse methods using technological supports, alternative ways to learn are available. Learning is a lifelong activity because it not only leads to immediate positive outcomes but lifelong progress as well.

Many barriers to employment are being addressed in the community at large as more employers address architectural, social, and training roadblocks to inclusive practices in the job market. Hopefully, these efforts and the preparation of students with disabilities will result in a community that can include all persons with disabilities.

This chapter endorsed the practice of team and transition planning specialist self-assessment. Data-based decision making using student outcome data and student input about what worked for students is crucial to developing programs that support them. The transition planning specialist, special education team, and school's administrative team are key players in supporting students to be self-sufficient and autonomous individuals who are engaged in the world.

REFERENCES

Rae, J. M. (2011). Post Transition Planning–Young Adult Stories—Perspectives on School and Life: A Case Study of Employment, Social, Family and Mental Health Management Outcomes of Three Young Adults Who Completed Two or More Years of High School in an Emotional and Behavioral Special Education Program in Partial Hospitalization 1 Setting (Doctoral dissertation). Retrieved from Proquest. (3448164).

Wagner, M., & Davis, M. (2006). How are we preparing students with emotional disturbances for the transition to young adulthood? Findings from the National Longitudinal Transition Study–2. *Journal of Emotional and Behavioral Disorders, 14*(2), 86-98.

18

Special Education Transitions From Birth to Age 21

CHAPTER OBJECTIVES

→ Describe the transitions from infancy to post-school life.

→ Describe eligibility for early intervention in birth to age 3 programs and preschool early intervention programs.

→ Compare birth to age 3 programs and services and preschool early intervention services.

→ Identify the diagnostic areas used for eligibility for early intervention programs.

→ Identify diagnostic areas for school-age special education eligibility.

→ Describe the difference between typical grade-level transitions and the natural transitions in special education.

→ Name the continuum of all transitions and the services provided.

TRANSITIONS IN EARLY INTERVENTION AND SPECIAL EDUCATION

A child's disability or disabilities are discovered at birth; during infancy; preschool age; or elementary, middle, or high school age. During infancy, an attending physician diagnoses based on a series of checks on the baby, and if warranted, will refer the parents for birth to age 3 early intervention services. If not diagnosed in the hospital, once the child is home, the parents, a family physician, or a pediatrician may notice that the child is not meeting developmental milestones, and a referral is made to the birth to age 3 early intervention program.

Rae, J. M. *A Collaborative Approach to Transition Planning for Students With Disabilities* (pp. 373-387).

During preschool the parents and teacher may notice the child is behind when compared to his or her same-age peers and will alert the parents of a possible delay. The Child Find laws also support identifying children with disabilities by requiring that advertisements are posted to alert the community of diagnostic services if parents suspect their child may have a delay or disability.

Once a disability is suspected by the parent or referred through the Child Find process, a screening is administered with the parent's permission. If the screening indicates a possible disability, an evaluation will be used to confirm a disability, again with parental permission. If a disability is present, there are transitions the child will encounter throughout his or her school life.

The Continuum of Early Intervention Transitions

The following transitions occur once a child has been determined to have a disability. Transitions between programs, grades, and schools can be difficult for students with disabilities and their families (Carter, Clark, Cushing, & Kennedy, 2005):

- Transition 1: Transition into early intervention (birth to age 3) services
- Transition 2: Transition from early intervention (birth to age 3) services and into age 3 to 5 preschool early intervention
- Transition 3: Transition out of preschool early intervention (3- to 5-year-old programs) into school-age special education programs

School-Age Special Education Transitions

Some disabilities become apparent during school age. If a child is failing to learn, transition into special education can occur only after interventions using evidence-based practices have been unsuccessful. Then a full evaluation can be initiated.

Transition to middle and high school present difficulties for students with disabilities, and practices are used to help mitigate the effect of location and age-level expectation changes. The last and final transition is the transition to post-school life.

The following section focuses on early intervention transitions. For infants whose disabilities are discovered at birth, parents must transition their children into early intervention services soon after leaving the hospital.

EARLY INTERVENTION TRANSITION SERVICES

Transition during the early intervention years refers to a legal framework of activities meant to provide a smooth transition between two early intervention programs and later to school-age programs and services. Early intervention professionals are familiar with the legal requirements behind transition plans. They guide the parent through the process of change from the birth to age 3 early intervention program to the preschool early intervention (age 3 to 5 programs; Part B) and out of early intervention to school-age programs in special education.

If a child is referred to early intervention prior to age 3, the young child with a disability receives services via an early intervention birth to age 3 program. Prior to the child's third birthday, the family is prepared for the child to transition to receive services through the early intervention preschool program. By the child's 3rd birthday, preschool early intervention services have been determined, and an IEP is written and must be implemented by age 3 or they can begin by 2.6 years old. These services are funded under the Individuals with Disabilities Education Act (IDEA), Part B, whereas the birth to age 3 services are funded under Part C (IDEA, 2004).

When the child becomes eligible for elementary education, also known as *school-age programs*, they transition out of preschool early intervention. They can transition into kindergarten or they can transition later when eligible for first grade or when mandatory schooling begins (Early Childhood Technical Assistance, 2019).

Early Diagnosis and Placements

A primary initiative is to find children with disabilities and refer them for services. The U.S. Department of Health and Human Services (2014) administers the birth to age 3 program. The preschool early intervention program is funded under IDEA and serves students who are 3 to 5 years old or older if they have opted to stay for kindergarten. There are multiple organizations that inform parents of resources when they believe there may be a delay in their child's development. Birth to 3: Watch Me Thrive! helps parents look for developmental signs of progress, identify delays, and tells parents where to have their child screened to ensure the child is developing typically.

Primary health care providers need to be aware of developmental delays and encourage parents to seek a developmental screening to determine if a disability is present. Early diagnosis ensures that infants, toddlers, and preschool-age children who are eligible receive early intervention services. Early intervention services, if appropriately applied, facilitate improved overall functioning. The importance of early screening cannot be overemphasized.

In addition to health care providers, the following agencies are involved in outreach efforts to encourage families to seek early screening for their child:

- Department of Health and Human Services
- Office of Special Education Programs and Rehabilitative Services
- Administration for Children and Families
- Administration for Community Living
- Centers for Disease Control and Prevention
- Centers for Medicaid and Medicare Services
- Health Resources and Services Administration
- Eunice Kennedy Shriver National Institute of Child Health and Human Development
- National Institute of Child Health and Human Development
- Substance Abuse and Mental Health Services Administration
- Local school districts

Hospital Referrals to Early Intervention

Infants from neonatal units; those with congenital disabilities, birth trauma, and childhood abuse and neglect; and those who have parents with drug and alcohol addictions, intellectual disabilities, and mental health disorders are at risk for developmental disabilities. Hospitals staff will introduce families to services and play a role in diagnosing children at risk for disabilities. Follow-up hospital-based evaluations are often recommended to determine if a disability is present.

There are developmental and behavioral screening tools that give an overview of the child's level of functioning. These tools are formal research-based instruments that ask questions about the child's development. The screening will provide a score in each of the five areas assessed. Low scores in any of the areas give guidance about the areas in need of further evaluation. The areas are measured by appropriate diagnostic instruments and procedures. If the child has delays in one or more of the following areas, they will receive developmental intervention and therapy: cognitive development, physical development, fine motor and gross motor skills development, communication development, social or emotional development, and adaptive development.

The screenings for each area determine whether the child is on track developmentally. If not, a full evaluation is administered with parental permission. A formal evaluation is a much more in-depth look at a child's development, usually done by trained specialists, such as an early intervention diagnostic team, developmental pediatrician, child psychologist, or speech-language pathologist.

Typically, evaluations involve parent observations, parental standardized behavioral checklists, child observation by a team of early intervention specialists, parent-child interaction observation, standardized tests, and parent interviews and questionnaires. The results of informal and formal evaluations are used to determine the child's eligibility for early intervention services.

Birth to Age 3 Services and Transition

The purpose of early intervention is ameliorating or decreasing the effect of the child's disability by school age. Each state has a comprehensive plan of early intervention services. The services provided in early intervention birth to age 3 infant/toddler programs are a family service plan, a service coordinator, and services delivered at home or in the community. A child in the birth to age 3 program is considered a child with a developmental disability and is provided with related services, such as occupational therapy, physical therapy, speech therapy, and cognitive development activities in the five developmental areas.

Children who have one disability receive services in multiple areas of disability, without the need for assessment due to potential risks for later global disabilities such as an intellectual disability, which affect all developmental areas. Parents receive support to reinforce therapy practices between services, which include support to the family such as referrals to other agencies and educational materials about the child's disability. Birth to age 3 services are typically provided in natural settings such as the home and the community.

In the birth to age 3 program, the child has an Individual Family Service Plan (IFSP) developed, which includes services provided to the child and the family. The plan is reviewed and revised every 6 months, and the team discusses future program transitions, options, and current planning.

By age 3, the child will need to transition to an early intervention preschool program. Placement proceeds along a timeline that ensures each child is placed by age 3 without delay. The transition regulations follow.

Age of Transition to Preschool Early Intervention

303.209 Transition to preschool and other programs.

(a) Application requirements. Each State must include the following in its application:Agency and appropriate Local Education Agency (LEA).

(1) The State lead agency must ensure that—

(i) Subject to paragraph (b)(2) of this section, not fewer than 90 days before the third birthday of the toddler with a disability if that toddler may be eligible for preschool services under part B of the Act, the lead agency notifies the SEA (state educational agency) and the LEA (local educational agency) for the area in which the toddler resides that the toddler on his or her third birthday will reach the age of eligibility for services under part B of the Act, as determined in accordance with State law

(IDEA 34 C.F.R. §303.209[c] [a] [3] [ii])

Transition Meeting Attendance

Those required to attend the transition meeting is also regulated by law.

A transition meeting that includes, at a minimum, the family, a representative of the Infant/Toddler EI program, and a representative of the Preschool Early Intervention (EI) program shall be scheduled for each toddler. The transition meeting shall be scheduled in accordance with IDEA regulations at 34 C.F.R. §303.209(c) that specifies that the transition meeting for a child who may be eligible for Preschool EI services must be held, with the approval of the family of the toddler, at least 90 days, (and at the discretion of all parties, not more than 9 months) before the child is eligible for Preschool EI services.

(IDEA 34 C.F.R. §303.209[c] [a] [3] [ii] [d] [e])

Documenting the Transition From Birth to Age 3 Early Intervention to Preschool Early Intervention

According to IDEA (2004), steps are taken to ensure that a smooth transition to preschool early intervention occurs. The law requires that transition information is written into a transition plan when exiting a birth through age 3 program. The appropriate transition steps and services that will be taken to support the toddler's transition to the preschool early intervention program shall be documented on the transition page of the IFSP, developed with the family per 34 C.F.R. § 303.209(d) and 34 C.F.R. § 303.344(h) and shall at a minimum include the following records:

- Parent Notification for transition to preschool services
- Begin to talk to the parent by the time the child is 2 years old
- Required transition paperwork completed with parental permissions for the new program
- Formal notification that the birth to age 3 program information has been sent to the preschool early intervention program
- Transition conference initial evaluation for preschool early intervention
- Eligibility determination, planning, and placement
- Invitation to the Individualized Education Plan (IEP) meeting
- IEP meeting and development
- Evidence that the IEP implementation began by the third birthday
- Parent training and future program options
- Location of services: Where the child will be from the third birthday through the end of the school year

Strategies have been developed to help the toddler to adjust to the new settings, such as visits to the preschool and, if busing is provided, visits to the bus garage (particularly children with autism spectrum disorder [ASD], who can be significantly stressed by the change in routine and not understand why they are on a bus and being taken from the home).

TRANSITION TO PRESCHOOL EARLY INTERVENTION

By the third birthday the child with a disability must have transitioned into the preschool-age services. Parents may also elect to continue an IFSP plan and keep the diagnosis of developmental disability. A transition meeting is held with representatives from the preschool programs to discuss whether the child will transition to preschool early intervention. If the birth to age 3 early intervention records indicate a disability, then plans are made and evaluations are scheduled to delineate the areas where a disability is present. If the parent decides to transition to preschool early intervention, the planning process can start at age 2. As mentioned earlier, the child must be evaluated and found eligible and must be a child with a disability, as defined in 34 CFR §300.8.

If the parent wants to transition his or her child to preschool early intervention, a review of the birth to age 3 IFSP records and assessments will indicate the need for additional assessments. The preschool program will, based on assessments, determine if the child continues to be eligible for services. If so, the multidisciplinary team will create an IEP in collaboration with the family.

The following list is the general process for placement in the preschool early intervention program:

- An evaluation by a multidisciplinary team determines eligibility in one or more of the five developmental areas.
- An IEP is developed.
- The IEP and services may be managed by a service coordinator who is certified in special or early childhood education.

- Services are only for diagnosed disabilities based on the results of a multidisciplinary evaluation.
- Children receive services in preschools, center-based programs, and community settings.
- A diagnosis is given, such as ASD or developmental delay.
- Related services, such as occupational therapy, physical therapy, speech therapy, and cognitive development activities, are provided only when the child has a disability in an area of disability established under IDEA.
- Children can receive emotional support programs provided for children with emotional or behavioral needs indicators.
- Parents receive training to reinforce therapy practices between services.
- The IEP is developed one time per year.
- The IEP is governed under Part B of IDEA.

Like the indicators used in secondary school transition planning, early intervention transition to preschool indicators are also used to measure legislative compliance.

- C-8: Percent of all children exiting Part C who received timely transition planning to support the child's transition to preschool and other appropriate community services by their third birthday including:
  - ◦ IFSPs with transition steps and services.
  - ◦ Notification to LEA, if child potentially eligible for Part B.
  - ◦ Transition conference, if child potentially eligible for Part B.
- Referral required 90 days before age 3. State Performance Plan/Annual Performance Report Indicator C-8A.
- Expectations include requiring that by the 3rd birthday, the child will be receiving the preschool services for which they are eligible.

School-Age Placements

Once the child has aged out of preschool early intervention, the child is again evaluated, and if his or her disability has not been given a diagnosis under IDEA eligibility criteria, it happens at this transition. However, parents can opt to keep the developmental disability designation until the child reaches a certain age, determined by each state and the school district when a narrower definition of Child with a disability is required (Developmental delay, 34 CFR § 303.10). A formal diagnosis is difficult for parents who may have hoped that the delay was just that: a delay. At this transition, the family will learn if the delay is a disability. Many children, such as those with autism, sensory disabilities, speech an language impairments, and moderate to profound intellectual disabilities have been diagnosed, but students with the mild intellectual disabilities and cognitive disabilities will receive their eligibility diagnoses.

TRANSITION TO THE SCHOOL-AGE
SPECIAL EDUCATION PROGRAM

Planning for a child's transition to school-age special education will start 1 year before the child is age-eligible to enroll in kindergarten or first grade. To begin the transition process, the preschool early intervention team and the school district or local charter school representatives, such as a school psychologist or special education administrator, begin working together to identify children who are ready to transition to the school-age program. This meeting does not include the parents. It is a records exchange meeting between the preschool and school-age program. Parents need to give permission to transfer the child's records.

Parents can decline to share records with the school district or private school, hoping that the child has gained enough skills to do well without intervention. If the parents do plan to transition their children to school-age special education, they will be invited to a transition meeting.

Transition to School-Age Process

By February 1 of the school year before the fall when the child will start school, a letter is sent from the preschool early intervention program inviting parents to the elementary special education program team meeting. The letter is called *Notice of Your Child's Transition to School-Age Meeting.*

The letter also has additional information about the school-age transition meeting and options for registering the child for school-age programs, school-age evaluations, and contact information. The early intervention preschool team arranges the required meetings and has authority over the process of transition to school-age programs.

Elementary School Registration

There are introductory school-age program meetings and visits to smooth the process for the child and the parents. The parents must register the child at the school administration building and bring all the required identity forms, records of school district residency, and medical and immunization documents. Then the process begins with the parents' completion of the intent to register form. Once registration forms are verified, the final stages of the transition to school-age programs begin. The parents will need to sign permission to evaluate so that the school district psychologist can determine the child's current eligibility for special education programs and services. If the child is eligible for kindergarten, the family can go through the process or decline to send their child until the following year. Once the child is eligible for first grade and has reached the legal age of mandatory attendance, the transition must occur.

After completion of the evaluation, when the areas or area of disability is determined and the student's strengths and needs are defined, an Evaluation Report, which includes the diagnosis report, goes to the parents, and the information about the child is used to develop an IEP. Once the IEP plan is developed, there are meetings with the teachers and tours of the school before beginning school. The family meets the special education teacher, and the teacher provides contact information.

TRANSITION TO MIDDLE SCHOOL

The transition to middle school can be a challenging time for students with and without disabilities. It also represents a critical juncture for students with disabilities (Lane, Parks, Kalberg, & Carter, 2007). Attention to the transition from one school to the next is a concern. As students advance, school environments become larger, increasingly complex, and increasingly teacher centered, and thus may not be responsive to adolescents' developmental needs (Eccles & Roeser, 2011; National Association of Secondary School Principals, 2006). Most students who are transitioning to middle school are entering puberty, a time fraught with bodily and psychological changes. During adolescence, peer status becomes increasingly associated with aggression, and individuals may use the peer system as a point of reference for acquiring and mimicking antisocial, aggressive behaviors (Cillessen & Mayeux, 2004). These challenges contrast sharply with the familiar elementary school environment.

During elementary school, students had one teacher, and they most likely went to specialized teachers for art, music, and gym. They are familiar with the building, the teachers, and the students (Lane, Oaks, Carter, & Messenger, 2015). The practices and procedures are designed for their developmental age. When there are problems, they can go to a school counselor with relative anonymity because in elementary school the scrutiny among students of their peers is not as intense.

In elementary school, the outlet of recess is still available. Typically, elementary schools have far fewer students. In middle school, the intimacy and knowledge of staff and peers decreases because most middle schools have multiple elementary feeder schools whose students all transition into a single middle school. The larger middle schools tend to be impersonal, and teachers see many students per day, decreasing the opportunity for teachers to know any one student well. There is a complete change in how the school day is structured as well.

The middle school day has multiple periods with familiar and unfamiliar students. Even though new relationship possibilities can emerge as peers converge from feeder schools, challenges related to peer acceptance and rejection can also be heightened (Kingery, Erdley, & Marshall, 2011). The shift to larger middle schools may come too soon for less mature students or those with higher physical and social needs. Long hours of sitting and short periods of social interchange may be challenging for some students. Some changes can affect academic success. First, the curriculum is more rapidly paced. Second, content is aligned to state standards, and the expectation is that teachers must present all subject area content during each school year. Third, learning tasks become longer and more complicated. These challenges create obstacles to success when many students with disabilities require adapted content vocabulary, additional reading development, and extended time to complete in-class and out-of-class assignments.

Students who have mild intellectual disabilities, specific learning disabilities, speech and language delays, and emotional and behavioral conditions are already behind in grade-level reading. Therefore, they are at risk of failure because they lack prerequisite skills, and, at this juncture, other deficits are more evident as well. Lectures and note taking requirements make education inaccessible. Although resource rooms are operated to help students keep up in class, it is challenging to complete all the assignments and process the information given in class.

Accessibility is also a problem for students with disabilities. Classroom instructional materials rely almost exclusively on printed text. Students who would perform better with large print due to sensory, physical, emotional, or cognitive disabilities may not be able to advocate for these alternative ways of accessing and processing information. Students with slow reading speed can benefit from audiobooks, although again these are often not provided. All of these accessible materials are required by the Americans with Disabilities Act (1990) legislation, but not every teacher knows about the options available. When students struggle with accessibility, it distracts them from tasks and slows progress. Supporting students by making instruction accessible reduces the risk of behavioral and performance declines. Students with needs related to disability are not going to lose the disability, so more effort into accessibility can produce better outcomes. Thus, it may be more helpful to focus on supporting the transition to and through middle school.

To facilitate a smooth transition, social connectedness should be reestablished during middle school. Some schools offer supportive programs to address the alienation of students. Extended homeroom time and extended teacher planning time were found to foster an intimate setting that supported eighth-grade students' needs for personalization, connectedness, positive peer relations, and community, noted in the literature as outcomes of effective teaching (Arhar, 1990; Ellerbrock & Kiefer, 2013; George & Alexander, 2003; Jackson & Davis, 2000). In a qualitative study by Ellerbrock and Kiefer (2013), students reported that a team approach to their program included two periods and a homeroom with the same students. This structured time developed the students' sense of connectedness. In the same study, unstructured time in middle school was problematic for social interactions and was viewed negatively by the study participants. However, in high school, unstructured time was viewed as having benefits to the more mature high school–age students.

During the final year of elementary school, plans to help students prepare for middle school should begin. The following strategies help students with disabilities to make a smooth transition to middle school and to be successful while there:

- Middle school building orientation
  - Construct the map activities.
  - Give students with disabilities a map of the middle school.

- Use maps to teach them where each part of the building is.
- Play videos of a walk around the building.
- Arrange days to go to the middle school to play "find the room" games, such as during field day when the building will be empty; involve middle schoolers without disabilities in the game.
- Have students go to the middle school and follow a school day schedule.
- Provide opportunities over the summer to visit the middle school to demonstrate accuracy in building navigation.

- Lockers
  - Students with disabilities may avoid using a locker rather than struggle with the locks.
  - Provide instruction about how to open a combination lock.
  - Give the students combination locks and have them practice opening them.
  - Use adapted locks for students with fine motor disabilities or consider push-button locks.
  - Permit students to come to the school in the summer to practice on their lockers.

- Organizing materials
  - Have a locker in the elementary classroom to teach locker organization skills.
  - Teach students a system of organization that promotes the use of lockers.
  - Define the size of the backpacks so they can fit it into the lockers.
  - Simplify the organization of books and materials for easy access and storage.

- Changing classes
  - Teach the middle school bell schedule.
  - Get a recording of the class change bell and acclimate the students by using it to end and begin classes by subject.

- Meet-the-teacher activities
  - Create a digital recording of all the middle school teachers and have them say something to the students.
  - Play picture matching and identify the middle school teachers, administrators, or staff.
  - Show the video and have students practice greetings; use video modeling and real scenarios.
  - Have a meet-the-teachers day; see if the students can identify teachers in person.
  - Have student schedules available at the end of elementary school year so the students know who their teachers will be.
  - Invite future middle school special educators to the incoming students' final IEP meetings; have students attend to meet the new team.

- Teach students to:
  - Learn to be assertive to handle bullying in the bathroom and elsewhere.
  - Learn how to ask for help when bullying does not stop.
  - Learn how to recognize the need for assistance.
  - Learn to use manners with classmates.
  - Learn how to discuss concerns.
  - Role-play scenarios that are expected to be most challenging for the student.
  - Inform students about choices for participation in school clubs and organizations.

Parent Communication

Communicating with parents is essential to ease their concerns. Middle school administrators, educators, and students should visit the feeder elementary schools to build enthusiasm and confidence among elementary students with disabilities and their parents about the upcoming transition to middle school. Parents will benefit from knowing how the school is supporting their children's transition to middle school. Communication tools, such as letters, training, and meetings, acclimate parents to changing expectations during middle school. A well-planned and delivered strategy of communication inspires smooth transitions. Ongoing positive and supportive communication fosters feelings of belonging and connectedness between the parents and the school and the children and the school. As discussed in Chapter 3, feeling connected to schools and the people in them can become a protective factor that can drive a student's success.

The following are introductory materials about the transition to middle school that can be used with parents:

- Send copies of middle school parent newsletters to parents of elementary students.
- Develop and distribute a parent handbook that provides a checklist of transition activities and middle school contacts.
- Provide families with information about courses, rules and regulations, and the school's mission statement for both general and special education.
- Identify an educator, counselor, or administrator who can serve as a primary point of contact for the family.
- Provide the middle school orientation activities described previously to students and parents.
- Have a student information panel.
- Maintain regular contact with family members.
- Provide forums for family members to meet to share strategies, discuss issues, and provide answers to common questions.
- Ensure that parents have met the special education team.

Student Communication and Classroom Success

To ensure that students do not enter their new middle school classrooms unprepared, the following supports should be in place, and students should know the contents of their IEPs:

- Ensure that appropriate modifications and adaptations allow immediate success.
- Arrange peer support systems for students in general education classrooms if the special education student agrees.
- Identify opportunities for students to become actively involved in everyday after-school activities.
- Expect students to need support throughout middle school.
- Special education teachers should have planned recaps of the day with the class and individual students to stay abreast of their needs and challenges.
- For all students with disabilities: Have them create student videos to introduce themselves to the special education team members. Ask the student to tell the team the following:
  - Subjects they find most difficult and why.
  - What situations make it difficult to learn?
  - How do they learn the best?
  - What do they need their peers to do when they are speaking?
  - Identify what other things they may need help with.

Middle School Teacher Preparation

The general and special education team must be prepared for the entry of a new group of students. It is essential that teachers have all the training they will need to work with a new group of students and parents. Thoroughly preparing for the children and the parents enhances trust, collaboration, and the parents' respect for the school and its faculty and staff.

The following are some practices for teachers to prepare for new students:

- Create a child study file for each student.
- Read all Individual Health Care Plans.
- Update Red Cross training.
- View student-created videos.
- Learn every student's name.
- Consider having the general education teachers view the video as well.
- Keep student information confidential.
- Prepare the students for academics.
- Supply the students with accessible textbooks over the summer.
- Enlist the parents to establish times to preread the texts for the following year.
- Purchase e-texts and audio texts for learning through multiple modalities.
- Have all other materials ready at the start of school.
- Provide students with the lesson plan outlines the day before or post it on the classroom website.
- Avoid note taking or using a student scribe. This can create anxiety for the note taker due to accuracy expectations, and it makes students with disabilities appear unable to handle the challenges of disability. Provide an outline of the class instead.
- Develop incentives for attendance.
- Create homework support groups via an online learning platform.

Assessment of the Transition Process

School administrators, teachers, and students assess the transition to middle school process and determine if additions need to be made. Special education programs should consistently monitor and implement transition strategies to ensure fidelity of practice and an accurate strategy assessment. Without fidelity in implementation and documentation of efforts, the process cannot be adequately assessed.

TRANSITION TO HIGH SCHOOL

Special and general education teachers are aware of the multiple ways in which students will handle the transition to high school. It can be with excited, nervous, positive, neutral, defeatist, or negative outlooks. It is the students with the most challenging life courses, such as having a disability, having a family member with a disability, or coming from a family with low economic resources, who can and do benefit from the implementation of activities to support a well-planned transition to high school. Assisting a student to transition smoothly is a protective factor that facilitates improved outcomes. An unplanned transition to high school for students who are struggling can be less than optimum or even destructive to any area of the life trajectory.

For example, a student's increasing loneliness after transitioning to high school may initiate subsequent deterioration in other developmental trajectories, such as declining performance in school (Benner, 2011).

Simple plans, such as signing students up for after-school activities and after-school homework groups, can facilitate social inclusion immediately. Other strategies designed and delivered can reduce problem behaviors related to school failure and immaturity when students are placed in sociocultural situations without the requisite skills.

At the age when students are ready to transition to high school, similar problems exist as those seen during the transition to middle school. Students vary widely in maturity level, academic ability, physical stamina, and size. Many students, often boys, have not fully matured at the same rate as some of their peers. Variations in maturity are evident as one walks into any ninth-grade classroom. Students with disabilities are there as well, many without the language abilities to comprehend on their own the numerous academic and social requirements of high school life.

Because of the similar transition needs, many of the transition strategies developed for the transition to middle school can be used for the transition to high school. Similar activities can be used to help acclimate students with disabilities, connecting them to the new building and staff. Knowing where one is going and how to access building resources can raise confidence in both middle and high school students with disabilities, and even those without disabilities. In both middle and high school, students may become self-conscious, disconcerted, or upset in situations such as getting lost in a school building and forgetting the location of their classrooms; this is a psychological distractor for both general and special education students. By creating an atmosphere of familiarity, special educators can decrease stress inherent in the move to high school. However, physical and psychological comfort will be lost if the student cannot handle the demands of high school classes. By the end of freshman year, the failures have begun, as indicated by the number of students in summer school, which in some school districts can cost hundreds of dollars and additional stress for families as they scramble to help their children pass. Students who do not pass courses in high school will be unable to get enough credits to graduate with their peers.

Just as the plan for middle schoolers plays out over a school year, the middle-to-high-school transition is a process that unfolds over time, rather than as a single event (Hertzog, Morgan, & Borland, 2009).

The transition from middle to high school is often a seminal and challenging transition and is referred to in the literature as "one of the defining parameters of development in the second decade of life" (Barber & Olsen, 2004, p. 3). Indeed, research indicates that for many students, a loss in achievement is associated with the transition from middle school into high school (Alspaugh, 1998).

Juvonen (2006) reported that students derive their sense of belonging to the school from perceptions of the social climate of the school and that social relationships help meet students' belongingness needs. Teachers play critical roles in building a sense of connectedness, and teachers who are considerate and caring are much more likely to ease the transition process. Butts and Cruzeiro (2005) found that supportive, caring teachers with whom students can easily talk are of the utmost importance for ninth graders.

Effective transition programs are necessary as students move from middle school to high school. Educators make a difference when they ensure that student belongingness needs are met. Effective transition to ninth grade has been related to indicators of school success, including achievement, reduced dropout rates, credits earned, attendance, and decreased behavioral problems.

Disability Type and Transition

Being prepared with plans for transition must be disability specific. For example, the special education team can develop a schedule of transition activities for students with more severe disabilities by having them become familiar with their new setting through a gradual transition to their new classroom. Alternatively, a student who is blind will need the assistance of a mobility specialist throughout eighth grade to teach the student how to negotiate the high school. Deaf students will need an interpreter or deaf educator when meeting school staff. Video communications will need transcripts. Therefore, careful consideration to the needs of the individual student must be considered.

TRANSITION TO POST-SCHOOL LIFE

The final transition is the primary focus of this book. Without negotiating smooth transitions, the process of moving through school to life can be fraught with additional problems. The transition from early intervention and the transition to post-school life get the most attention in special education. However, the many transitions throughout the school-age period warrant detailed planning so students with disabilities both visible and invisible receive optimum school programs and do not exit school prematurely.

TRANSITIONING PARENTS: DISCOVERING A DISABILITY

Emotional and Social Implications Over the Child's Lifespan

After experiencing the joy of giving birth to their baby, parents may become slowly aware that their child has a disability. At any time during their infant to school-age years, the revelation that their child has a disability and the fear about how to raise a child with a disability can be overwhelming for every family. Some parents are told at birth by the obstetrician. On the other hand, accidents such as near-drowning and other such tragic events can suddenly bring the realization that the child has become wholly or partially disabled. Parental suspicion of disability may also occur over time when some milestones for language, physical, cognitive, and adaptive development have not been reached. The reaction to disability is an individual response as the parents, their children, their families, and their cultural perspectives underlie and mediate those responses.

Parents must make many psychological transitions. These transitions include perceptions about what their family life would be and how their child will fit into the existing patterns of life and school. The child's transition through the school lifespan continually brings new challenges for the parent, family, and professionals. Each transition is like getting a new child with a disability and again learning how to help this new person through the next stage of life.

Many parents realize that their children may always need some type of support, and this causes fear for the parents of children and youth with the most severe disabilities. Thoughts about where the children will be upon the parents' deaths are prominent. Being knowledgeable about parental fears and needs can help educators provide supports postsecondary school. Transition planning specialists and special educators are in the business of developing robust plans for life's multiple transitions. They may also be part of a discussion of long-term plans, which may include planning for when the parent can no longer care for the child. Parents will eventually transition their child to independent or dependent living settings. This transition is a post-school transition, but by providing support throughout the transition periods and providing connections for post-school supports, special education teams give parents skills they can use as they support their child over his or her lifespan.

EXERCISES

1. Name the areas of delay for eligibility for infant/toddler early intervention.
2. Describe the critical differences between infant/toddler and preschool early intervention services.
3. Describe five strategies to develop feelings of connectedness during the transition to middle and high school.

4. Interview a principal about the strategies that can help students transition to middle school.

5. Interview a high school transition planning specialist about involvement in transition strategies for special education students coming into ninth grade. Analyze those strategies and write a narrative about the evidence supporting improved student success.

SUMMARY

Promoting smooth transitions has been a focus of special education practice for many years. The practices, starting with early intervention and culminating in the transition to post-school life, are positive strategies to promote an understanding of families and students with disabilities who need additional support to manage the multiple lifespan transitions. Depending on the type of disability (e.g., sensory-vision, hearing-motor) and for those who use assistive technology to communicate or who have ASD, the challenges of becoming familiar with and comfortable in a completely different building is especially challenging. To support the success of all students, welcoming them, helping them feel familiar with the setting, knowing who the teachers are, connecting with each of them, and inspiring their success is of the utmost importance. Taking the time to know each student, noticing who they are, and promoting positive relationships can act as a protective factor as they transition to adult life. Transitions are a life process for all of us, and those who do not have disabilities can attest to the challenges of life changes. Therefore, all teachers can be instrumental in promoting student success and inclusion when they support students through the many transitions in special education.

REFERENCES

Alspaugh, J. W. (1998). Achievement loss associated with the transition to middle school and high school. *Journal of Educational Research, 92*, 20-25.

Americans with Disabilities Act of 1990, Pub. L. No. 101-336, 42 U.S.C. § 12101 *et seq.* (1990).

Arhar, J. (1990). Interdisciplinary teaming as a school intervention to increase the social bonding of middle level students. In J. L. Irvin (Ed.), *Research in middle level education: Selected studies 1990* (pp. 1-10). Columbus, OH: National Middle School Association.

Barber, B. K., & Olsen, J. A. (2004). Assessing the transitions to middle and high school. *Journal of Adolescent Research, 19*(1), 330.

Benner, A. D. (2011). Latino adolescents' loneliness, academic performance, and the buffering nature of friendships. *Journal of Youth and Adolescence, 40*(5), 556-567.

Butts, M. J., & Cruzeiro, P. A. (2005). Student perceptions of factors leading to an effective transition from eighth to ninth grade. *American Secondary Education, 34*(1), 70-82.

Carter, E. W., Clark, N. M., Cushing, L. S., & Kennedy, C. H. (2005). Moving from elementary to middle school: Supporting a smooth transition for students with severe disabilities. *TEACHING Exceptional Children, 37*(3), 8-14.

Cillessen, A. H. N., & Mayeux, L. (2004). From censure to reinforcement: Developmental changes in the association between aggression and social status. *Child Development, 75*, 147-163.

Early Childhood Technical Assistance Center. (2019). IDEA statute and regulations relating to early childhood transitions. Retrieved from http://ectacenter.org/topics/transition/reglaw.asp

Eccles, J. S., & Roeser, R. W. (2011). Schools as developmental contexts during adolescence. *Journal of Research on Adolescence, 21*(1), 225-241.

Ellerbrock, C. R., & Kiefer, S. M. (2013). The interplay between adolescent needs and secondary school structures: Fostering developmentally responsive middle and high school environments across the transition. *High School Journal, 96*(3), 170-194.

George, P. S., & Alexander, W. M. (2003). *The exemplary middle school* (3rd ed.). Belmont, CA: Thomson/Wadsworth Learning.

Hertzog, J. C., Morgan, L., & Borland, K. (2009). What research says to the practitioner about middle level to high school transition: Background and practices. Paper presented at the meeting of the National Middle School Association (NMSA), Indianapolis, IN.

Individuals with Disabilities Education Act of 2004, Pub. L. No. 108-446, 20 U.S.C. § 1400 *et seq.* (2004).

Jackson, A. W., & Davis, G. A. (2000). *Turning points 2000: Educating adolescents in the 21st century.* New York, NY: Teachers College Press.

Juvonen, J. (2006). Sense of belonging, social bonds, and school functioning. In P. A. Alexander & P. H. Winne (Eds.), *Handbook of educational psychology* (pp. 655-674). Mahwah, NJ: Lawrence Erlbaum Associates.

Kingery, J. N., Erdley, C. A., & Marshall, K. C. (2011). Peer acceptance and friendships as predictors of early adolescents' adjustment across the middle school transition. *Merrill-Palmer Quarterly, 57,* 215-243.

Lane, K. L., Oakes, W. P., Carter, E. W., & Messenger, M. (2015). Examining behavioral risk moreover, academic performance for students transitioning from elementary to middle school. *Journal of Positive Behavior Interventions, 17*(1), 39-49.

Lane, K. L., Parks, R. J., Kalberg, J. R., & Carter, E. W. (2007). Systematic screening at the middle school level: Score reliability and validity of the Student Risk Screening Scale. *Journal of Emotional and Behavioral Disorders, 15,* 209-222.

National Association of Secondary School Principals. (2006). Activity 4: Transitions. Retrieved from https://www.nassp.org/professional-learning/online-professional-development/leading-success/module-8/activity-4-transitions/

U.S. Department of Health and Human Services. (2014). Birth to 5: Watch Me Thrive! An early care and education provider's guide for developmental and behavioral screening. Retrieved from https://www.acf.hhs.gov/sites/default/files/ecd/ece_providers_guide_march2014.pdf

Transition to preschool and other programs, 34 C.F.R. § 303.209 (2018).

Glossary

A

Ability grouping: Grouping students according to performance so teachers can instruct them at the same level.

Absent seizures: Brief occasions when an individual may stare for a longer period and not respond to environment stimuli or prompts. Time can vary from a few seconds to a minute or more. The person does not remember the event and will return to his or her work. Other behaviors such as unexplained emotional outbursts can also signal absent seizure activity.

Academic achievement: A student's level of academic performance when measured against the general curriculum.

Academic aptitude: The combination of innate and/or acquired skills needed for doing schoolwork.

Accommodations in special education: A student who needs accommodations will require changes in curriculum or instruction. The changes do not substantially alter the requirements of the class, content standards, or class objectives. For example, if a student is blind, he or she can use Braille or an audio recording of the material. Accommodations can include changes in a test format, test setting, or test timing.

Achievement test: A test that measures competency or mastery of a particular area of knowledge or acquisition of a particular skill.

Acuity: Keenness or sharpness of sight, hearing, or touch, including how much a child can see or hear.

ADA: The Americans with Disabilities Act.

Rae, J. M. *A Collaborative Approach to Transition Planning for Students With Disabilities* (pp. 389-410). © 2020 SLACK Incorporated.

Adapted physical education: A diversified program of developmental activities, games, sports, and rhythms suited to the interests, capabilities, and needs of students with disabilities who may not successfully engage in a general physical education program (Parent Information Center of New Hampshire, 2008).

Adaptive behavior: The behavior is measured using scales that identify independence skills within environments. It includes communication, school participation, health and safety, functional academics, leisure, and work.

ADD: Attention-deficit disorder.

ADHD: Attention-deficit hyperactivity disorder.

ADL: Activities of daily living.

Adventitious deafness: Deafness that occurs from illness or injury in an individual who was not born deaf.

Advocate: A special education advocate is an individual who may or may not be an attorney. He or she assists parents to work in collaboration with the school district regarding their children's special education programs and services. Typically, the advocate goes through an advocacy training program.

Affective lability: Emotional instability that will include sudden shifts in emotional expression. Severe forms are seen in mental health disorders such as bipolar disorder.

Age equivalent: Measures a student's performance in relation to students who are the same age.

Agitation: A state of increased physical activity and accompanied by irritability or anxiety.

Alternate achievement standards: Standards that differ from those that are set for other students of the same age or grade.

Alternating Speech Test: A temporal sequencing test that investigates a student's ability to retain information in the correct sequence through auditory means, and it tests a student's attentional and memory strategies.

Alternative assessments: Standardized tests used to provide information about what students know. Also refers to the different type of testing that is done when the abilities of a student with a disability prevent him or her from taking part in the regular statewide or districtwide testing.

Annual goals: Measurable annual goals are written for an individual student to identify what the Individualized Education Plan (IEP) team has determined the student can reasonably be expected to accomplish within a 1-year period of time. Must be written in measurable terms so progress can be monitored.

Anxious depression: An episode of major depression accompanied by high levels of anxiety (American Psychiatric Association, 2000).

Appeal: A procedure in which a parent or group of parents seeks to reverse or modify a judgment or final order of a lower court or administrative agency, usually on the grounds that the lower court misinterpreted or misapplied the law, rather than on the grounds that it made an incorrect finding of fact.

Applied behavior analysis: One research-based method for supporting/teaching children with certain disabilities, most commonly with children with autism spectrum disorder (ASD). Applied behavior analysis does not necessarily help all children with ASD.

Approved program: A program of special education that has been approved by the state board of education and that is maintained by a local school district, collaborative program, private provider of special education, public academy, or state institution for the benefit of children with disabilities. Includes home instruction.

Articulation: The clarity or understandability of a student's speech. Disorders of articulation are shown in omission, substitution, distortion, or addition of sounds that do not belong in the word.

Asperger's Disorder: Asperger's disorder can be defined as a disorder associated with varying degrees of deficits in social and conversational skills, difficulties in the transition from one task to another or changes in situations or environments, and preference for sameness and predictability of events. Obsessive routines and preoccupation with particular subjects of interest may be present, as may difficulty reading body language and maintaining proper social distance. Some people with Asperger's disorder have reported oversensitivity to sounds, tastes, smells, and sights, but the nature of the sensitivity is not well researched. In contrast to autism, language skills develop and there is no clinically significant delay in cognitive or adaptive functioning, and by definition, they have IQ's in the normal to the superior range. As of the *Diagnostic and Statistical Manual of Mental Disorders, Fifth Edition*, publication, Asperger's disorder has been subsumed into ASD and is no longer a distinct diagnosis (VandenBos, 2007).

ASD: Autism spectrum disorder, including autism, Asperger's disorder, and pervasive developmental disorders.

ASL: American Sign Language.

Assessment: Used to identify a student's strengths and weaknesses and to monitor progress. Assessments measure academic performance, basic cognitive functioning, and/or current strengths or weaknesses. They include tests of hearing, vision, mobility, and fine motor skills such as handwriting. Assessments may be observations by a teacher using standardized and criterion-referenced tests or portfolios of student work.

Assessment, educational and cognitive: Used for initial evaluations and reevaluations to determine whether a child has a disability.

Assessment plan: A written description of the assessments used in transition planning that will evaluate a student's current strengths, weaknesses, and progress.

Assessment, progress monitoring: A process of observation and assessment determining what students know and can do in relation to their current IEP goals. Progress monitoring is also used to show teachers and schools where students are not making progress and may therefore need more intensive intervention.

Assistive devices: Devices that support physical movement, such as wheelchairs, walkers, and crutches. Hearing aids, computer software and hardware, screen enlargement devices, grip devices, ramps, and bars fall in this category.

Assistive technology device: Any item, piece of equipment, or product system, whether acquired commercially, modified, or customized, that is used to increase, maintain, or improve functional capabilities of individuals with disabilities (Assistive technology for individuals with disabilities, 2017).

Assistive technology services: The assessment, selection, purchase, leasing, customizing, and coordinating with other therapies and equipment used to maintain or improve the capabilities of a child with a disability.

Attention: The ability to focus (attend) with eyes and/or ears for a period of time without losing the meaning of what is being communicated or spoken.

Audiologist: An individual trained in audiology.

Audiology: The science of testing hearing and diagnosing hearing impairments. It is a related service that includes identification and determination of hearing loss, including referral for medical or other professional attention for the habilitation of hearing; provision of habilitative services; determination of a child's needs for group and individual amplification; selecting and fitting an appropriate aid; and evaluating the effectiveness of amplification.

Auditory discrimination: The ability to discern likenesses or differences in sound. There are many types of auditory discrimination, including individual letter sounds, word prefixes and endings, and sounds in the environment.

Augmentative and alternative communication device (AAC): All forms of communication (other than oral speech) that are used to express thoughts, needs, wants, and ideas.

Autism: A developmental disability significantly affecting verbal and nonverbal communication and social interaction, generally evident before age 3, that adversely affects educational performance. Repetitive activities, stereotyped body movements, resistance to environmental change or change in daily routines, and unusual responses to sensory experiences are present. Behavioral outbursts are related to the disability.

Aversive behavioral interventions: Procedures that subject a child with a disability to physical or psychological harm, such as prolonged or unsupervised confinement, or that deprive the child of necessities.

Awareness: Having knowledge of something through observing or interpreting what one sees, hears, or feels.

B

Behavior intervention plan: A plan to target undesirable or disruptive behaviors with interventions chosen based on observations and student interviews to determine the functions of the behavior. A behavior intervention plan can include prevention strategies and replacement behaviors.

Behavior management: Comprehensive planning in classroom management and/or the use of positive behavior support plans that improve behavior. Management plans should prevent and de-escalate disruptive behavior. Behavior support plans are used with individual students to manage behaviors that impede his or her learning or the learning of peers.

Binaural Fusion Tests: Filters two syllable words presented simultaneously. It can determine neuromaturational levels for auditory closure and phonetic reading readiness. Hemispheric integration can be evaluated.

Bipolar I and II disorder: Disorders that cause significant social and occupational dysfunction. Bipolar I includes manic episodes with a resultant flight of ideas, elevated moods, distractibility, talkativeness, high goal-directed activity, and involvement in activities with a high potential for deleterious outcomes. It results in occupational dysfunction and hospitalization, sometimes with psychosis. Those with bipolar I disorder also have a period of severe depression.

In bipolar II disorder, hypomanic episodes are followed by severe depressive symptoms. There is a significant change in social and occupational functioning without hospitalization or psychosis. Bipolar II disorder is characterized by one or more major depressive episodes and at least one hypomanic episode. Also categorized as bipolar disorder is cyclothymic, which does not meet the criteria but carries the same symptoms of long-term hypomanic and numerous depressive symptoms that do not meet the criteria for major depressive disorder (American Psychiatric Association, 2013).

C

Central Auditory Processing: The act of processing speech is very complex and involves the engagement of auditory, cognitive, and language mechanisms, often simultaneously (Medwetsky, 2011).

CF: Cystic fibrosis.

CFR: Code of Federal Regulations.

Child Find procedures: The procedures by which local school districts locate, count, evaluate, and, if found to be eligible, provide special education services to children with disabilities (Child Find, 2012).

Child Find program: A program mandated by the Individuals with Disabilities Education Act (IDEA, 2004) that continuously searches for and evaluates children who may have a disability. Child Find programs can vary widely from school district to school district (Child Find, 2012).

Child study team: Also called *multidisciplinary evaluation team* (MET), it is composed of the school's psychologist, special education team, and the parents, who meet when a child continues to struggle after attempts have been made to remedy problems without special education services. The child study team decides if the student should be evaluated or if he or she will continue without special education services (Special Education Guide, n.d.).

Closure: The ability to form a whole word from some of its parts.

Cloze: A technique of testing reading comprehension by asking the student to supply missing words.

CMHC: Community mental health center.

Cognitive/cognition: Terms used to refer to reasoning or intellectual capacity, thinking, and understanding.

Cognitive-behavioral therapy: A form of psychotherapy aimed at identifying and modifying the client's maladaptive thought processes and problematic behaviors through cognitive restructuring and behavioral techniques to achieve change. Originally developed by Aaron Beck for depression, it seeks to identify and change distorted cognitions and therefore influence behavior change. The client is an active participant in behavior change activities (Beck, Emery, & Greenberg, 1985).

Committed juvenile student: An individual who is committed to a youth development center, also known as juvenile detention center, pursuant to court.

Community-based instruction: Instruction used to teach students functional skills in the community.

Community-based skills: Skills taught at varied locations in the community rather than in the classroom in order to facilitate generalization and application to multiple locations.

Comorbidity: When two or more mental or physical illnesses, diseases, or disorders occur in the same person. Symptoms assigned to a single disorder may occur in varying degrees in other disorders (American Psychiatric Association, 2013).

Compensating: A means of making up something missing; for example, when a person is born blind, the person uses other learning channels, such as hearing or touch, more effectively.

Compensatory education: Services or education provided to a child to make up for those not provided or for some another deficit found in a child's special education program. Most often awarded to a child as the result of a state administrative complaint, mediation, or due process hearing.

Competing Sentences Test: A test of selective attention when confronted with interesting but irrelevant auditory information along with the focus information.

Competitive integrated employment: According to 29 U.S.C. § 705 (Vocational rehabilitation and other rehabilitation services, 2017), a term that means the following:

[W]ork that is performed on a full-time or part-time basis (including self-employment)—

(A) for which an individual—

(i) is compensated at a rate that—

(II) in the case of an individual who is self-employed, yields an income that is comparable to the income received by other individuals who are not individuals with disabilities, and who are self-employed in similar occupations or on similar tasks and who have similar training, experience, and skills; and

(ii) is eligible for the level of benefits provided to other employees;

(B) that is at a location where the employee interacts with other persons who are not individuals with disabilities (not including supervisory personnel or individuals who are providing

services to such employee) to the same extent that individuals who are not individuals with disabilities and who are in comparable positions interact with other persons; and

(C) that, as appropriate, presents opportunities for advancement that are similar to those for other employees who are not individuals with disabilities and who have similar positions.

Compliance complaint: A formal assertion in writing that agreed-upon services and supports in an IEP have not been delivered or that the school district has violated the IDEA (2004) mandates (Disability Rights Education & Defense Fund, n.d.).

Connors Behavior Rating Scale: A test of a child's behaviors; may be used to identify factors indicating attention-deficit disorder or attention-deficit hyperactivity disorder.

Consent or prior written notice: The requirement that the parent be fully informed (in writing) of all information that relates to any action that the school wants to take about the child, with the parent's agreement documented in writing that the parent understands that consent is voluntary and may be revoked at any time.

Constancy: The ability to know that sounds are the same when heard in different ways.

Content standards: The information, ideas, and facts that students are supposed to learn in a particular grade.

Cooperative learning: An approach through which students learn in small, self-instructing groups and share responsibility for each other's learning.

Coordination: The ability to use one part of the body in combination with one or more other parts to accomplish a single purpose.

Core academic subjects: Under the No Child Left Behind (NCLB, 2001) law, core academic subjects include the following:

- English
- Reading or language arts
- Mathematics
- Science
- Foreign languages
- Civics and government
- Economics
- Arts
- History
- Geography

Correlation: The relationship between two scores or measures. For example, students who score well on mechanical aptitude tests or career assessments may not necessarily show aptitude or interest for fixing cars.

COTA: Certified occupational therapy assistant.

Counseling services: Related services in special education provided by qualified social workers, psychologists, guidance counselors, or other qualified personnel.

CP: Cerebral palsy.

Criterion-referenced tests: Measures of how well a student has learned a specific skill or subject. They are not tests that produce a number quotient but show what a student can or cannot do. These tests compare a child to a set of standards or criteria and not to other children.

Critical thinking: The ability to find information and use it to reach a logical conclusion or solve a problem.

CTONI: Comprehensive Test of Nonverbal Intelligence.

CTOPP: Comprehensive Test of Phonological Processing.

Cumulative file: A general file maintained by the school. The parent has the right to inspect the file and have copies of any information in it.

Curriculum: Planned courses of study in specific subject matter that is to be learned, usually described in terms of a planned scope and sequence; all courses and educational opportunities offered by a school district.

Curriculum-based assessment: Direct assessment of a child's academic skills by measuring and recording the child's progress in the general curriculum at frequent intervals as a basis on which to make instructional decisions.

Curriculum-based measurements: Regularly scheduled evaluations used to determine student learning in various subject areas, such as English or history (Special Education Guide, n.d.).

Curriculum frameworks: The guidelines set by the state departments of education for what children are expected to know in a given subject area by a certain grade level.

D

Data-based decision making: Involves using information collected through the screening process to determine the intensity and duration of the needed intervention.

Deaf-blindness: Simultaneous hearing and visual impairments, the combination of which causes such severe communication and other developmental and educational problems that a child cannot be accommodated in special education programs solely for children with deafness or children with blindness (Disability Rights Education & Defense Fund, n.d.).

Deaf or hard of hearing: A sensory hearing impairment that impairs a child's ability to process sound; there are levels of loss from mild to profound deafness.

Development: Stages of growth from infancy on up, observable in sequential steps. The approximate ages in which development occurs are charted in developmental scales. The scales usually measure fine motor, self-help, gross motor, social-emotional, cognitive, and language skills.

Developmental milestones: A set of functional skills or age-specific tasks that most children can do at a certain age range (Special Education Guide, n.d.).

Diagnostic test: A test that diagnoses areas of strengths and weakness.

Diagnostic testing: A formal diagnostic assessment to determine if a disability is present, usually performed by members of a designated diagnostic team, including a teacher, school psychologist, speech therapist, physical therapist, and occupational therapist, and, when necessary, a behavior specialist. Members of the diagnostic team, also called the *MET*, are certified to perform diagnostic tests.

DIBELS: Dynamic Indicators of Basic Early Literacy (test).

Differentiated instruction: An instructional concept that maximizes learning for all students, regardless of skill level or background. It is based on the fact that in a typical classroom, students vary in their academic abilities, learning styles, personalities, interests, background knowledge and experiences, and levels of motivation for learning. When a teacher differentiates instruction, he or she uses the best teaching practices and strategies to create different pathways that respond to the needs of diverse learners (Danielson, 2007).

Direct instruction: Presents new content and skills in strict order. Students practice the content and skills in class exercises and as homework and are evaluated by tests similar to practice exercises.

Disability: A physical, sensory, cognitive, or affective impairment that causes the student to need special education (Special Education Guide, n.d.).

DS: Down syndrome.

Due process: A legal process to address violations of private rights. Due process is the meaningful opportunity to be heard and have grievances redressed. It consists of legal proceedings according to rules and principles established for enforcement and protection of private rights. It is a legal procedure guaranteed by federal law to resolve disputes relating to the education of children with disabilities. When a parent thinks an educational program is inadequate to meet the needs of a child with a disability, a due process case follows mediation when attempts at compromise fail.

E

Early childhood education: Includes programs for children from birth to age 6.

Early identification and assessment of disabilities in children: A related service that includes implementation of a formal plan for identifying a disability as early as possible in a child's life.

Early intervention: The services provided for at-risk children from birth through age 3, as mandated by IDEA (2004).

Educational goal: The level of educational achievement accepted as reasonable and desirable for a specific child at a specific time and rate of speed.

EH: Emotional handicap (now called *emotional disturbance*).

Emotional disturbance: There are many terms are used to describe emotional, behavioral, or mental disorders. Currently, students with such disorders are categorized as having an emotional disturbance, which is defined under IDEA (2004) as follows:

> *[A] condition exhibiting one or more of the following characteristics over a long period of time and to a marked degree that adversely affects a child's educational performance—*
>
> *(A) An inability to learn that cannot be explained by intellectual, sensory, or health factors.*
>
> *(B) An inability to build or maintain satisfactory interpersonal relationships with peers and teachers.*
>
> *(C) Inappropriate types of behavior or feelings under normal circumstances.*
>
> *(D) A general pervasive mood of unhappiness or depression.*
>
> *(E) A tendency to develop physical symptoms or fears associated with personal or school problems.*
>
> *(ii) The term includes schizophrenia. The term does not apply to children who are socially maladjusted, unless it is determined that they have an emotional disturbance. (Child with a disability, 2017)*

Encode: Express ideas in symbols or words.

Episode: One event or series of events. Mental illness, such as bipolar I disorder, is marked by periodic manic and depressive episodes.

Episodic disorder: Any medical or mental health disorder with symptoms that occur in brief periods or episodes.

ESEA: Elementary and Secondary Education Act of 1965. (Its reauthorization is called NCLB [2001].)

Etiology: The cause or origin of a condition.

Executive functioning: The ability to manage and plan using cognitive processes, including initiating, planning, organizing, and following through on activities.

Expressive language: The ability to communicate by using words, writing, or gestures.

Extended school year: A provision for a special education student to receive instruction during ordinary school vacation periods.

Extracurricular and nonacademic activities: An IDEA (2004) requirement or implementing regulation that includes the requirement that a student's IEP address the special education, related services, supplementary aids and services, program modifications, and supports for school personnel to be provided to enable the student to, among other things, participate in extracurricular and other nonacademic activities (Definition of individualized education program, 2006).

F

Family Educational Rights and Privacy Act: A federal law that regulates the management of student records and disclosure of information from those records, with its own administrative enforcement mechanism (Family educational and privacy rights, 2017).

FAS: Fetal alcohol syndrome.

Figure-ground: The ability to distinguish at will what one wishes to see (figure) from the environment (ground).

Filtered Speech Test: Single syllable words are filtered to reduce intelligibility, and it can identify auditory closure and word discrimination problems.

Fine motor skills: Functions that require tiny muscle movements, such as writing or typing.

Frustration level: The level at which a child is tense, hesitates, makes errors, and lacks confidence.

Functional curriculum: A curriculum focused on practical life skills and usually taught in the community-based setting, with concrete materials that are a regular part of everyday life. The purpose of this type of instruction is to generalize the use of the student's skills into the home and community.

Functional goal: A measurable outcome that is developed for the student by IEP team members, including the student after age 14, to address a need detailed in the analysis of the student's functional performance.

Functional performance: The child's skills and behaviors in cognition, communication, motor, adaptive, social/emotional, and sensory areas.

G

General curriculum: Curriculum adopted by the local education agency or state education agency for all school-age children through high school.

Global Assessment of Functioning scale: Uses scores from 1 to 100 to indicate overall level of functioning. A score of 60 or below indicates more severe difficulty. It is used to indicate other factors that differentiate the effect of the mental illness on the individual (VandenBos, 2007).

Global Burden of Disease Study: A major effort to foster an independent, evidence-based approach to public health policy formulation and to develop internally consistent estimates of the incidence, prevalence, duration, and case fatality for 483 disabling conditions. It also estimates the fraction of mortality and disability attributable to 10 major risk factors and to develop projection scenarios of mortality and disability (World Health Organization, n.d.).

Goal setting and personal behavior plans: A transition plan may target and students' personally selected social or behavior goals. Interventions and self-monitoring plans are developed by the student with the support of the transition team.

Gross motor skills: Functions that require large muscle movements, such as walking and jumping.

Group intelligence tests: Tests, often administered in the general education classroom, that measure a child's academic ability as well as his or her cognitive level. It is through these types of tests that a teacher may first suspect that a student has a learning disability (Special Education Guide, n.d.).

Guardianship: The legal relationship that begins when a person or institution is named in a will or assigned by a court to be responsible for the food, health care, housing, and other necessities for a minor or a person deemed incompetent.

H

Haptic perception: Tactile and kinesthetic perception; the ability to discern likenesses and differences in objects by physical touch, such as identifying a spoon by physically touching the entire object and matching it to a memory of that object.

Hearing impairment: An impairment in hearing, from mild to moderate and may be fluctuating, that adversely affects a child's educational performance but is not included under the definition of deafness.

HEATH: The National Clearinghouse on Postsecondary Education for Individuals with Disabilities.

Helplessness model: A psychological condition in which a human being or an animal has learned to believe that it is helpless in a particular situation, even when it has the power to change its unpleasant or even harmful circumstance (Abramson, Alloy, & Metalsky, 1989; Seligman, 1975).

Home instruction: A home-based special education placement made by a child's IEP team. This is not the same as home schooling.

Hyperactivity: An activity level that disrupts classroom and home routines, is unusual, and includes a large amount of movement in a child when compared to other children in the same setting.

I

Icons: Drawings used for communication for nonverbal students. The icons represent nouns, verbs, and adjectives used in AAC devices.

Inclusion/inclusive education: Every student is entitled to an instructional program that meets his or her individual needs and learning characteristics. It is also a commitment to build and maintain an assured sense of belonging for all students, regardless of strengths or challenges (Parent Information Center of New Hampshire, 2008).

Independent educational evaluation: Testing done by someone who does not work for the school system.

Independent living core services: According to IDEA (2004), these services include:

(A) Information and referral services;

(B) Independent living skills training;

(C) Peer counseling (including cross-disability peer counseling);

(D) Individual and systems advocacy; and

(E) Services that—

(i) Facilitate the transition of individuals with significant disabilities from nursing homes and other institutions to home and community-based residences, with the requisite supports and services;

(ii) Provide assistance to individuals with significant disabilities who are at risk of entering institutions so that the individuals may remain in the community; and

(iii) Facilitate the transition of youth who are individuals with significant disabilities, who were eligible for individualized education programs under section 614(d) of the Individuals with Disabilities Education Act (20 U.S.C. 1414(d)), and who have completed their secondary education or otherwise left school, to postsecondary life. (Vocational rehabilitation and other rehabilitation services, 2017)

Individual intelligence tests: Intelligence tests that are administered to a student one-on-one. These tests are often part of the assessment process. Two common individual intelligence tests are the Wechsler Intelligence Scale for Children and the Stanford Binet Intelligence Scale (Special Education Guide, n.d.).

IEP: A legal document developed at an IEP meeting that describes the child's special education program. It sets up a plan by which special education services are determined appropriate for a child with a disability.

IEP team: The IEP team develops the IEP. By law, the team should include parents, regular teachers, special education teachers, special services providers, school district representatives, people knowledgeable about evaluating the child's disability, others invited by the parent or school district, and, in some cases, the student.

Individualized Family Service Plan: A written treatment plan that outlines the services to be delivered to families of infants and toddlers (from birth to his or her third birthday) receiving early supports and services, as well as how and when these services will be administered. It details a child's current levels of functioning, specific needs, and goals for treatment (referred to as outcomes).

IDEA of 2004: A federal law that entitles students with disabilities to special education services.

Infants and toddlers: Children not yet 3 years old.

Informed consent: The signed consent of a parent that describes what the parent is consenting to; informed consent must be obtained before a district assesses, makes a major revision to, continues, or stops service for a child's disability (Consent, 2018; Prior notice by the public agency, 2018).

In-home interventions: Special education services delivered in a child's own home.

Initial evaluation: Determines whether a student is eligible to receive special education services or needs an IEP.

Input: Any information coming in through the sensory systems.

Instruction: The methods and strategies teachers use to advance student learning.

Instructional level: The level at which a student needs a teacher's assistance. After instruction, the child can continue independently. This level is called the independent level.

Intelligence: The ability to learn from experience and apply it in the future to solve problems and make judgments.

Interest inventory: An assessment in which a person records career and general preferences to assist in planning for secondary transition. The inventory does not indicate ability but only preferences.

Interpreting services: Related services provided by an interpreter for the deaf and hard of hearing who is licensed and that are necessary for a parent, surrogate parent, guardian, or adult student to participate in the special education process. The Americans with Disabilities Act uses the term "auxiliary aids and services" ("aids and services") to refer to the ways to communicate with people who have communication disabilities. According to IDEA (2004), interpreter services include:

> *(i) The following, when used with respect to children who are deaf or hard of hearing: Oral transliteration services, cued language transliteration services, sign language transliteration and interpreting services, and transcription services, such as communication access real-time translation (CART), C-Print, and Type Well; and*

> *(ii) Special interpreting services for children who are deaf-blind. (Related services, 2018)*

Interventions: The sets of teaching procedures to help students who are struggling with a skill or lesson succeed in the classroom.

IOD: Institute on Disabilities.

IQ: Intelligence quotient.

ITP: Individualized Transition Plan.

J

Joint agreement: A voluntary association between school districts and other agencies whose purpose is to provide special education services (e.g., on-site counseling services). Has multiple names, including Memorandum of Understanding.

L

Labile: A persistent instability of mood ranging back and forth from multiple mood states, such as anger, sadness, and joy (American Psychiatric Association, 2013).

Least restrictive environment: A federal mandate that requires the following:

(i) To the maximum extent appropriate, educating children with disabilities, including children in public or private institutions or other care facilities, with children who are nondisabled; and

(ii) Removing children with disabilities to special classes, separate schooling, or other settings apart from the regular educational occurs only if the nature or severity of the disability is such that education in regular classes with the use of supplementary aids and services cannot be achieved satisfactorily. (LRE requirements, 2018)

Also, the child's placement must be as close as possible to the child's home, and the child is educated in the school he or she would attend if not disabled (Placements, 2018).

Local education agency: The local school district.

Localization: Ability to locate the source and direction of sound.

M

Major depressive episode: An episodic disorder with discrete episodes of at least 2 weeks' duration, but most are significantly longer. The individual has either a persistent depressed mood or at least four other symptoms, including poor or increased appetite, excessive sleep, psychomotor agitation, psychomotor retardation, loss of energy with fatigue, feelings of worthlessness or inappropriate guilt, reduced ability to concentrate or make decisions, and recurrent thoughts of death, suicidal ideation, or attempted suicide. All of these symptoms cause significant distress or impair normal functioning in social and occupational functioning. One or more major depressive episodes are a characteristic feature of major depressive disorder and bipolar II disorder, and often occur in bipolar I disorder (American Psychiatric Association, 2013).

MD: Muscular dystrophy.

Memory sequencing: The ability to remember what is heard or read in order for long or short periods of time. Typically, students read stories and must demonstrate knowledge of the plot order.

Mental disorder: A syndrome characterized by a clinically significant disturbance in an individual's cognition, emotion regulation, or behavior that reflects a dysfunction in the psychological, biological, or developmental processes underlying mental functioning. Mental disorders are usually associated with significant distress or disability in social, occupational, or other important activities (American Psychiatric Association, 2013).

Modification: A change in curriculum or instruction that substantially alters the requirements of the class or its content standards or benchmarks.

Monitoring IEP: An IEP that is developed to provide ongoing monitoring but not direct services for a student who is general education but may not be able to succeed in the general education program. This is a proactive strategy to ensure that a student who had received services can achieve success before being removed from special education.

MET: Also called a *multidisciplinary team*. According to IDEA (2004), this is:

> *[T]he involvement of two or more separate disciplines or professions and with respect to—*
>
> *(a) Evaluation of the child in §§303.113 and 303.321(a)(1)(i) and assessments of the child and family in §303.321(a)(1)(ii), may include one individual who is qualified in more than one discipline or profession; and*
>
> *(b) The IFSP Team in §303.340 must include the involvement of the parent and two or more individuals from separate disciplines or professions and one of these individuals must be the service coordinator (consistent with §303.343(a)(1)(iv) (2018). (Multidisciplinary, 2018)*

Multiple disabilities: Simultaneous impairments, including an intellectual disability as the primary disability, the combination of which causes such severe educational needs that they cannot be accommodated in a special education program solely for one of the impairments. The term may include blindness or an orthopedic impairment, but does not include deaf-blindness.

N

NAMI: National Alliance on Mental Illness.

National Instructional Materials Access Center: Center established to assist states in implementing the National Instructional Materials Accessibility Standard.

National Instructional Materials Accessibility Standard: The standards defined in federal law to require states and local education agencies to provide access to instructional materials to persons who are blind or who have print disabilities.

Native language: The language normally spoken by a child's parents, or the first or primary language of an individual. A school district is required to evaluate a student in his or her native language or document proficiency in English before it can identify that student as having a disability and provide special education services. In addition, parents must be offered evaluation plans and IEPs in their native language before giving informed consent.

Natural environment: An educational setting that is comparable to the setting provided to children without disabilities. A term typically used in early intervention. According to IDEA (2004), natural environment means:

> *[S]ettings that are natural or typical for a same-aged infant or toddler without a disability may include the home or community settings and must be consistent with the provisions of §303.126. (Natural environments, 2018)*

NICHCY: National Dissemination Center for Children and Youth With Disabilities.

NCLB: A federal law that requires each state to set higher standards for what children should know and be able to do in third through eighth grades. NCLB includes incentives and consequences for school districts that do or do not show adequate yearly progress toward the standards established in the law.

NPND: National Parent Network on Disabilities.

NVLD: Nonverbal learning disability.

O

Observational records: Information about a child's academic performance provided by school professionals and IEP team members.

Occupational therapist: A professional who treats patients with injuries, illnesses, or disabilities through the therapeutic use of everyday activities. They help these patients develop, recover, and improve the skills needed for daily living and working (Bureau of Labor Statistics, 2018a).

Occupational therapy: A special education related service that is usually focused on the development of a student's fine motor skills.

OCD: Obsessive-compulsive disorder.

ODD: Oppositional defiance disorder.

Office for Civil Rights: An agency of the federal government within the executive branch in the Department of Education. It enforces civil rights statutes, including Section 504. Office of Vocational Rehabilitation definition of youth with a disability:

(A) The term "youth with a disability" means an individual with a disability who—

(i) Is not younger than 14 years of age, and

(ii) Is not older than 24 years of age. (Vocational rehabilitation and other rehabilitation services, 2017)

On-task behavior: Expected behavior at that moment on that task.

Orientation and mobility services: Services provided to blind or visually impaired children by qualified personnel to enable those students to attain systematic orientation to and safe movement within their environments in the school, home, and community. According to IDEA (2004), these services include:

[T]eaching children the following, as appropriate:

(A) Spatial and environmental concepts and use of information received by the senses (such as sound, temperature and vibrations) to establish, maintain, or regain orientation and line of travel (e.g., using sound at a traffic light to cross the street);

(B) To use the long cane or a service animal to supplement visual travel skills or as a tool for safely negotiating the environment for children with no available travel vision;

(C) To understand and use remaining vision and distance low vision aids; and

(D) Other concepts, techniques, and tools. (Related services, 2018)

Orthopedic impairment: According to IDEA (2004):

(8) Orthopedic impairment means a severe orthopedic impairment that adversely affects a child's educational performance. The term includes impairments caused by a congenital anomaly, impairments caused by disease (e.g., poliomyelitis, bone tuberculosis), and impairments from other causes (e.g., cerebral palsy, amputations, and fractures or burns that cause contractures). (Child with a disability, 2017)

Office of Special Education and Rehabilitative Services: An agency of the federal government's executive branch within the Department of Education.

Office of Special Education Programs: An office within the Office of Special Education and Rehabilitative Services charged with ensuring that the various states comply with IDEA (2004).

Other health impairment: According to IDEA (2004):

(9) Other health impairment means having limited strength, vitality, or alertness, including a heightened alertness to environmental stimuli, that results in limited alertness with respect to the educational environment, that—

(i) Is due to chronic or acute health problems such as asthma, attention deficit disorder or attention deficit hyperactivity disorder, diabetes, epilepsy, a heart condition, hemophilia, lead poisoning, leukemia, nephritis, rheumatic fever, sickle cell anemia, and Tourette syndrome; and

(ii) Adversely affects a child's educational performance. (Child with a disability, 2017)

P

Panic disorder: A disorder that begins in adolescence to adulthood and includes unexpected and ongoing episodes of intense fear that become associated with the place where it occurred. These are known as panic attacks. Physical symptoms include shortness of breath, racing heartbeat, and dizziness. People often avoid the places where the attacks occur. Eventually they happen at a number of places, making it difficult for the adolescent or adult to function in the community.

Paraprofessional: An individual who provides direct support to a child, teacher, or other school professional and who works only under the direct supervision of qualified teaching personnel.

Parasuicide: Behavior such as self-harm (e.g., cutting the skin) that injures a person, at times requiring hospitalization but not resulting in suicide.

Parental consent: According to IDEA (2004):

(a) The parent has been fully informed of all information relevant to the activity for which consent is sought, in the parent's native language, as defined in §303.25;

(b) The parent understands and agrees in writing to the carrying out of the activity for which the parent's consent is sought, and the consent form describes that activity and lists the early intervention records (if any) that will be released and to whom they will be released. (Consent, 2018)

Part B of IDEA: The part of IDEA (2004) that applies to school-age children with disabilities (ages 3 to 21).

Part C of IDEA: The part of IDEA (2004) that applies to infants and toddlers with disabilities (birth to age 3).

Partial hospital programs: Short or extended structured programs of psychotherapy and other therapeutic services specifically designed to meet the mental health disorder needs of persons in an acute crisis. Partial hospital programs provide intensive mental health treatment as an alternative to inpatient hospitalization or as an option following inpatient hospitalization. The primary goal of the partial hospital program is to stabilize a person after acute treatment in a more restrictive level of care.

Participant modeling: A procedure for changing behavior in which effective styles of behavior are modeled (e.g., by a therapist) for an individual, and then various aids are introduced to help the individual master the tasks. Live or symbolic models are used. Developed by Albert Bandura (VandenBos, 2007).

Person-centered planning developmental and social history: A narrative assessment formulated by a child's classroom teacher, parents, pediatrician, and school specialists focusing on issues such as the child's health history, developmental milestones, genetic factors, friendships, family relationships, hobbies, behavioral issues, and academic performance. A developmental and social history is a common element of an assessment plan.

Physical therapist: A professional who helps people who have injuries or illnesses improve their movement and manage their pain. Physical therapists are often an essential part of rehabilitation and treatment of patients with chronic conditions or injuries (Bureau of Labor Statistics, 2019).

Picture Exchange Communication System: A type of AAC device initially developed for children with autism. The primary purpose of a Picture Exchange Communication System is to teach individuals with autism to initiate communication. Individuals are taught to initiate by handing a picture to a communication partner in exchange for a desired item (Bondy & Frost, 1994).

PIRC: Parental Information and Resource Center.

PL: Public Law (refers to a federal law).

Placement: The unique combination of facilities, personnel, location, or equipment necessary to provide instructional services to meet the goals as specified in a student's IEP. Placement is a set of services, not a location.

Polarity: The relationship between two opposite tendencies; the shifting of mood states between mania and depression.

Positive behavior support: An approach designed to increase prosocial skills by rewarding on-task and other actions that facilitate an educational environment for learning.

PPVT: Peabody Picture Vocabulary Test.

Present levels: A component of an IEP that defines a student's strengths and weaknesses, current levels of academic achievement, and current levels of functional performance. Before 2004, this part of the IEP was called *present levels of performance;* the current term is *present levels of academic achievement and functional performance.*

Prior written notice: A notice supplied to the other party that includes a description of the action proposed or refused by the school district or by the parent (Prior written notice and procedural safeguards notice, 2018).

Program integrity: The extent to which an intended program is delivered; also called *treatment integrity* or *treatment validity* (VandenBos, 2007).

Psychoeducation: Refers to the education offered to people who live with a psychological disturbance. Those with mental health disorders are taught about their mental health disorders. They are also taught coping skills to avoid a relapse. The theory is, the better knowledge the patient has of his or her illness, the better the person can set goals and plan his or her life.

Psychological services: A related service that includes:

> *(i) Administering psychological and educational tests, and other assessment procedures;*
>
> *(ii) Interpreting assessment results;*
>
> *(iii) Obtaining, integrating, and interpreting information about child behavior and conditions relating to learning;*
>
> *(iv) Consulting with other staff members in planning school programs to meet the special educational needs of children as indicated by psychological tests, interviews, direct observation, and behavioral evaluations;*
>
> *(v) Planning and managing a program of psychological services, including psychological counseling for children and parents; and*
>
> *(vi) Assisting in developing positive behavioral intervention strategies. (Related services, 2018)*

Psychological test: Covers a range of tests used for studying people and how they behave; may include intelligence tests, projective or nonprojective tests to study personality, or other tests to decide if there may be an organic impairment of functioning.

Psychosis: A loss of reality that usually includes delusions and hallucination. Delusions are false beliefs about the person themselves or another despite evidence to the contrary, such as believing that one can be a professional athlete but has never practiced doing so.

Psychotherapy: Methods used to help children and adolescents experiencing difficulties with their emotions or behavior. Psychotherapy may involve an individual child, a group of children, a family, or multiple families. A qualified mental health professional or child and adolescent psychiatrist or psychologist determine the need for psychotherapy. Psychotherapy is best used in combination with other treatments such as medication, behavior management, or work with the school.

Psychotropic: A medication used to change intrusive thoughts and destructive behaviors; affects brain activity, behavior, or perception.

Public stigma and self-stigma: Includes three aspects: Stereotyping: The public negative belief about a group (e.g., dangerousness, incompetence, character weakness); prejudice: Public agreement with a stereotypical belief and having a negative emotional reaction based on that belief (e.g., anger, fear); discrimination: Public responses including a negative behavioral response to prejudice (e.g., avoidance, withhold employment and housing opportunities, withhold help; Corrigan, Larson, & Ruesch, 2009).

Q

Qualified examiner: Typically a teacher or school psychologist who is licensed or certified in the state in which the evaluation is performed. Tests are given levels to provide guidance on who is qualified to administer them.

R

Receptive language: The ability to attach meanings to words and gestures based on experience; understanding what another person is saying. Receptive language is also developed without expressive language when speech is not present.

Rehabilitation technology: The systematic application of technologies, engineering methodologies, or scientific principles to meet the needs of and address the barriers confronted by individuals with disabilities in areas including education, rehabilitation, employment, transportation, independent living, and recreation. The term includes rehabilitation engineering, assistive technology devices, and assistive technology services (Vocational rehabilitation and other rehabilitation services, 2017).

Respite care: This type of care is a service provided to the families of medically fragile children who require relief of 24-hour child care. Families are given respite care personnel who are trained to provide specialized care so that the family can take vacation, handle business affairs, and have some relief from the duties of caring for their child.

S

Section 504: A provision of the Rehabilitation Act of 1973 that prohibits recipients of federal funds from discrimination against persons with disabilities.

Section 504 hearing: An administrative procedure to resolve disputes between parents and school districts about services, accommodations, or modifications to services provided under Section 504.

Self-contained placement: A setting, apart from the general educational environment, where a child with a disability spends more than 60% of his or her school day.

Self-help: The student's ability to care for him- or herself. Self-care includes feeding, toileting, dressing, and personal hygiene.

Self-stigma: also includes three aspects: Stereotype: Having negative belief about the self (e.g., character weakness, incompetence); prejudice: Agreeing with those beliefs, including a negative emotional reaction (e.g., low self-esteem, low self-efficacy); discrimination: Acting on those self-beliefs with negative behavior in response to prejudice (e.g., fails to pursue work and housing opportunities; Corrigan et al., 2009).

Sensory rooms or multi sensory environments: Sensory rooms are designed to help students who find typical leisure and school activities inaccessible due to their disabilities. Sensory/ multisensory environments are created to give an immersive sensory experience specifically for children and youth with disabilities. They can provide academic, physical, and a calming multisensory experience to assist student with autism (and other disorders) to learn, participate in physical activities, and de-escalate.

Sequencing: The ability to understand and remember the order of an event or that certain activities, such as washing your hands, are carried out in a particular order.

Short-term objectives (STOs): A requirement of the IEP that breaks down the measurable annual goals into smaller attainable components. Students with moderate to profound intellectual disabilities must have STOs. (Note: IDEA [2004] only requires STOs for children who take alternate assessments aligned to alternate achievement standards or at times general grade-level standards.)

Social competence: Skills in interpersonal relations, especially the ability to handle a variety of social situations effectively (VandenBos, 2007).

Social-emotional development: The growth in self-concept and social skills that begins in infancy, such as looking into the eyes of the parents, smiling at familiar faces, expressing feelings, and attaching to significant others.

Social promotion: Moving students to the next grade regardless of their academic progress.

Social work services in schools: A related service that includes:

(i) Preparing a social or developmental history on a child with a disability;

(ii) Group and individual counseling with the child and family;

(iii) Working in partnership with parents and others on those problems in a child's living situation (home, school and community) that affect the child's adjustment in school;

(iv) Mobilizing school and community resources to enable the child to learn as effectively as possible in his or her educational program; and

(v) Assisting in developing positive behavioral intervention strategies. (Related services, 2018)

Special education: According to IDEA (2004):

(1) Special education means specially designed instruction, at no cost to the parents, to meet the unique needs of a child with a disability, including—

(i) Instruction conducted in the classroom, in the home, in hospitals and institutions, and in other settings; and

(ii) Instruction in physical education.

(2) Special education includes each of the following, if the services otherwise meet the requirements of paragraph (a)(1) of this section—

(i) Speech-language pathology services, or any other related service, if the service is considered special education rather than a related service under State standards;

(ii) Travel training; and

(iii) Vocational education.

(b) Individual special education terms defined. The terms in this definition are defined as follows:

(1) At no cost means that all specially-designed instruction is provided without charge, but does not preclude incidental fees that are normally charged to nondisabled students or their parents as a part of the regular education program.

(2) Physical education means—

(i) The development of—

(A) Physical and motor fitness;

(B) Fundamental motor skills and patterns; and

(C) Skills in aquatics, dance, and individual and group games and sports (including intramural and lifetime sports); and

(ii) Includes special physical education, adapted physical education, movement education, and motor development.

(3) Specially designed instruction means adapting, as appropriate to the needs of an eligible child under this part, the content, methodology, or delivery of instruction—

(i) To address the unique needs of the child that result from the child's disability; and

(ii) To ensure access of the child to the general curriculum, so that the child can meet the educational standards within the jurisdiction of the public agency that apply to all children.

(4) Travel training means providing instruction, as appropriate, to children with significant cognitive disabilities, and any other children with disabilities who require this instruction, to enable them to—

(i) Develop an awareness of the environment in which they live; and

(ii) Learn the skills necessary to move effectively and safely from place to place within that environment (e.g., in school, in the home, at work, and in the community).

(5) Vocational education means organized educational programs that are directly related to the preparation of individuals for paid or unpaid employment, or for additional preparation for a career not requiring a baccalaureate or advanced degree. (Special education, 2018)

Special education services: Supports school districts must provide to students with IEPs.

Special factors: The factors that the IEP team shall consider when the team develops each child's IEP (Early intervention services, 2018).

Specific learning disability: According to IDEA (2004), a specific learning disability is:

(i) … [A] disorder in one or more of the basic psychological processes involved in understanding or in using language, spoken or written, which may manifest itself in an imperfect ability to listen, think, speak, write, spell or to do math calculations, including conditions such as perceptual disabilities, brain injury, minimal brain dysfunction, dyslexia, and developmental aphasia.

(ii) Specific learning disability does not include learning problems that are primarily the result of visual, hearing, or motor disabilities; of mental retardation; of emotional disturbance; or of environmental, cultural, or economic disadvantage. (Child with a disability, 2017)

Speech-in-Noise Test: A measure that determines the ability to hear in a noisy environment. A student does not need to have a hearing impairment to require this testing.

Sequencing: Perceiving, understanding, or remembering things in a particular order.

Signed English: Manual communication that follows English rules. Like spoken languages, sign language is distinct country to country. Like spoken English, signs for words can vary regionally within the United States.

Sound localization: The ability to locate the source or direction of sound in relation to a person's position.

Speech-language pathologist: Also known as a *speech therapist*, a professional who diagnoses and treats communication and swallowing disorders (Bureau of Labor Statistics, 2018b).

Speech or language impairment: A communication disorder such as stuttering, impaired articulation, language impairment, or voice impairment that adversely affects a child's educational performance (Child with a disability, 2017).

SSDI: Social Security Disability Income.

SSI: Supplemental Security Income.

Staggered Spondaic Word Test: Two different two-syllabic words are presented in each ear in competition and isolation. It tests sequencing, discrimination in noise, and word closure.

Standards-aligned goals: IEP goals developed to align with grade-level content standards. Alternate standards have been developed to align grade-level standards to the goals of the most cognitively impaired students. They are also used to advance the development of age-appropriate curriculum.

State education agency: Oversees local school districts and service units that provide special education services. Also known as *SEA*.

Student baseline: A student's starting point for academic or behavioral achievement or skills determined by data collected through universal screening tools such as observations and academic assessments, including those that determine whether reading is below, at, or above grade level. It is then used to define progress through retesting.

Suicidal ideation: Repetitive periodic thoughts or preoccupation with suicide. Suicidal thoughts signal a major depression. Suicidal ideation often does not progress to a suicide or a suicide attempt (American Psychiatric Association, 2013). Treatment is required to decrease ideation and possible suicide attempts and completions.

T

Tactile: The ability to identify likenesses and differences in objects through feeling.

Tactile defensiveness: Aversions to textures, some forms of touch tactile defensiveness refers to a pattern of observable behavioral and emotional responses, which are aversive, negative and out of proportion, to certain types of tactile stimuli that most people would find to be non-painful (Royeen & Lane, 1991; Mikkelson, Wodka, Mostofsky, & Puts, 2018).

Transition meeting in early intervention: A meeting of the Individual Family Service Plan team prior to a preschool early intervention program or a meeting to transition into a school-age program.

Transition planning: Transition Planning is a process that includes a plan of activities that will result in improved post-school outcomes for students with disabilities.

Transition services: Activities meant to prepare students with disabilities for adult life. This can include developing postsecondary education and career goals; getting work experience while still in school; setting up linkages with adult service providers, such as the vocational rehabilitation agency—whatever is appropriate for the student, given his or her interests, preferences, skills, and needs. Statements about the student's transition needs must be included in the IEP after the student reaches a certain age. IDEA (2004) defines transition services as:

(a) … [A] coordinated set of activities for a child with a disability that—

(1) Is designed to be within a results-oriented process, that is focused on improving the academic and functional achievement of the child with a disability to facilitate the child's movement from school to post-school activities, including postsecondary education, vocational education, integrated employment (including supported employment); continuing and adult education, adult services, independent living, or community participation;

(2) Is based on the individual child's needs, taking into account the child's strengths, preferences, and interests. (Transition services, 2018)

Traumatic brain injury: An acquired injury to the brain caused by an external physical force, resulting in total or partial functional disability and/or psychosocial impairment, that adversely affects a child's educational performance.

TTD/TTY: A teletypewriting device for individuals who are deaf or who have communication impairments.

U

Universal design: A concept or philosophy for designing and delivering products and services that are usable by people with the widest possible range of functional capabilities, which include products and services that are directly accessible (without requiring assistive technologies) and products and services that are interoperable with assistive technologies.

V

Visual discrimination: The ability to discern likenesses and differences in colors, shapes, objects, words, and symbols.

Visual impairment (including blindness): A visual impairment that, even with correction, adversely affects a child's educational performance; includes both partial sight and blindness.

Visual-motor: The ability to coordinate the eyes with the movement of the hands and the process to thinking.

Vocational evaluation: Tests a student's aptitude and interests to provide information to use in designing an appropriate vocational program or transition plan.

VR: Bureau of Vocational Rehabilitation.

W

Waivers: Funding to enable home care for children with severe disabilities. This Medicaid waiver provides needed Medicaid-funded services to children with severe disabilities, without regard to their family's income.

REFERENCES

Abramson, L. Y., Alloy, L. B., & Metalsky, G. I. (1989). Hopelessness depression: A theory-based subtype of depression. *Psychological Review, 96*(2), 358-372.

American Psychiatric Association. (2000). *Diagnostic and statistical manual of mental disorders* (4th ed., text revision). Washington, DC: American Psychiatric Association Publishing.

American Psychiatric Association. (2013). *Diagnostic and statistical manual of mental disorders* (5th ed.). Washington, DC: American Psychiatric Association Publishing.

Assistive technology for individuals with disabilities, 29 U.S.C. § 3002 (2017).

Beck, A. T., Emery, G., & Greenberg, R. L. (1985). *Anxiety disorders and phobias: A cognitive perspective.* New York, NY: HarperCollins Publishers.

Bondy, A. S., & Frost, L. A. (1994). The Picture Exchange Communication System. *Focus on Autism and Other Developmental Disabilities, 9*(3), 1-19.

Bureau of Labor Statistics. (2018a). Occupational therapists. Retrieved from http://www.bls.gov/ooh/healthcare/occupational-therapists.htm

Bureau of Labor Statistics. (2018b). Speech-language pathologists. Retrieved from http://www.bls.gov/ooh/healthcare/speech-language-pathologists.htm

Bureau of Labor Statistics. (2019). Physical therapists. Retrieved from http://www.bls.gov/ooh/healthcare/physical-therapists.htm

Child find, 34 C.F.R. § 300.111 (2012).

Child with a disability, 34 C.F.R. § 300.8 (2017).

Consent, 34 C.F.R. § 300.9 (2018).

Corrigan, P. W., Larson, J. E., & Ruesch, N. (2009). Self-stigma and the "why try" effect: Impact on life goals and evidence-based practices. *World Psychiatry, 8*(2), 75-81.

Danielson, C. (2007). *Enhancing professional practice: A framework for teaching* (2nd ed). Alexandria, VA: ASCD.

Definition of individualized education program, 34 C.F.R. § 300.320 (2006).

Disability Rights Education & Defense Fund. (n.d.). Special education acronyms and glossary. Retrieved from https://dredf.org/special-education/special-education-resources/special-education-acronyms-and-glossary/

Early intervention services, 34 C.F.R. § 303.13 (2018).

Family educational and privacy rights, 20 U.S.C. § 1232g (2017).

Individuals with Disabilities Education Act of 2004, Pub. L. No. 108-446, 20 U.S.C. § 1400 *et seq.* (2004).

LRE requirements, 34 C.F.R § 300.114 (2018).

Medwetsky, L. (2011). Spoken language processing model: Bridging auditory and language processing to guide assessment and intervention. *Language, Speech, and Hearing Services in Schools, 42*(3), 286-296.

Mikkelsen, M., Wodka, E. L., Mostofsky, S. H., & Puts, N. A. (2018). Autism spectrum disorder in the scope of tactile processing. *Developmental Cognitive Neuroscience, 29*, 140-150.

Multidisciplinary, 34 C.F.R. § 303.24 (2018).

Natural environments, 34 C.F.R. § 303.26 (2018).

No Child Left Behind Act of 2001, Pub. L. No. 107–110, 20 U.S.C. § 6319 (2001).

Parent Information Center of New Hampshire. (2008). *Dictionary of common special education terms and acronyms.* Retrieved from http://www.picnh.org/nhpti/documents/Dictionary%20of%20common%20special%20education%20terms%20and%20acronyms.pdf

Placements, 34 C.F.R. § 300.116 (2018).

Prior notice by the public agency; content of notice, 34 C.F.R. § 300.503 (2018).

Prior written notice and procedural safeguards notice, 34 C.F.R. § 303.421 (2018).

Related services, 34 C.F.R. § 300.34 (2018).

Royeen, C. B., & Lane, S. J. (1991). Tactile processing and sensory defensiveness. In A. Fisher, E. Murray, & A. Bundy (Eds.), *Sensory Integration: Theory and Practice.* Philadelphia, PA: F. A. Davis

Seligman, M. E. (1975). Helplessness: On depression, development, and death. A series of books in psychology. New York, NY: WH Freeman/Times Books/Henry Holt & Co.

Special education, 34 C.F.R. § 300.39 (2018).

Special Education Guide. (n.d.). Special education dictionary. Retrieved from https://www.specialeducationguide.com/special-education-dictionary/

Transition services, 34 C.F.R. § 300.43 (2018).

VandenBos, G. R. (Ed.). (2007). *APA dictionary of psychology.* Washington, DC: American Psychological Association.

Vocational rehabilitation and other rehabilitation services, 29 U.S.C. § 705 (2017).

World Health Organization. (n.d.). Global Health Observatory (GHO) data. Retrieved from https://www.who.int/gho/mortality_burden_disease/en/

Index